Environmental Litigation
Law and Strategy

Second Edition

AMERICAN**BAR**ASSOCIATION

**Environment, Energy,
and Resources Section**

Kegan A. Brown
Andrea M. Hogan

Editors

Cover design by Elmarie Jara/ABA Design

Printed in the United States of America.

23 22 21 20 19 5 4 3 2 1

Library of Congress Cataloging-in-Publication Data

Names: Brown, Kegan A., editor. | Hogan, Andrea M., editor. | American Bar Association. Section of Environment, Energy, and Resources, sponsoring body.
Title: Environmental litigation : law and strategy / edited by Kegan A. Brown and Andrea M. Hogan.
Description: Second edition. | Chicago : American Bar Association, [2019] | Includes bibliographical references and index.
Identifiers: LCCN 2019012342 (print) | LCCN 2019013571 (ebook) | ISBN 9781641053662 (ePub) | ISBN 9781641053655 (print : alk. paper)
Subjects: LCSH: Environmental law—United States—Trial practice. | Environmental law—California—Trial practice.
Classification: LCC KF8925.E5 (ebook) | LCC KF8925.E5 E583 2019 (print) | DDC 344.7304/60269—dc23
LC record available at https://lccn.loc.gov/2019012342

Contents

Chapter 2: Environmental Criminal Enforcement   45
Jane F. Barrett, W. Warren Hamel, and Steven P. Solow

Chapter 3: Civil Environmental Enforcement Litigation   97
Joel M. Gross

Chapter 8: Pesticide Litigation 327

Claudia O'Brien, Stacey VanBelleghem, Laura Glickman, and Stijn Van Osch

Preface

Many lawyers—and probably a large majority of those who call themselves "litigators"—believe that that there is nothing "special" about environmental litigation. Litigators are quick studies, and by all appearances mastering the complexities of an environmental case is not inherently more difficult than mastering the complexities of a securities case or a patent infringement case. And, candidly, there is more than a kernel of truth to this view. Most environmental litigation lawsuits are litigated in the same courts as other lawsuits, and they are litigated pursuant to the same rules of civil and/or criminal procedure.

At the same time, however, lawyers who practice environmental litigation with some frequency recognize that the practice is indeed "special." First, the litigation challenges presented by an environmental case frequently are idiosyncratic if not unique. For example, although criminal defense lawyers sometimes defend an accused who has made statements the government introduces to prove guilt, lawyers defending criminal matters in the environmental field routinely defend persons who were *required* to provide the government with all of the facts on which the government's case is built and even were required to certify those incriminating facts as "true and accurate." Similarly, toxic tort lawyers frequently find themselves litigating "science" questions for which our common law jury system is ill-equipped. Cutting-edge epidemiology and toxicology is hard enough for lawyers to understand, without the burden of explaining it to laypersons through an expert and in compliance with the formal rules of evidence.

Second, although the courts have been a forum for social change many times in our nation's history, at this particular time no other litigation discipline presents the same "big social questions" as environmental litigation. For example, in the last couple of decades, environmental issues have filled the Supreme Court's docket. And global climate change issues continue to play themselves out daily on both the front pages of newspapers and in scores of courtrooms throughout the country, including recently in public nuisance litigation.

Third, the scope of what qualifies as "environmental litigation" is huge. There are literally dozens of federal statues, scores of state statutes, hundreds of common law rules, and thousands of pages of regulations to be accounted for. And upon all of these substantive areas is imposed the background litigation framework, which in the environmental arena can be federal or state court, arbitrations, administrative hearings, and more. If "environmental litigation" is a "specialty," it is one that nevertheless encompasses an incredible array of substantive expertise.

This book was conceived as a broad, but not comprehensive, guide for environmental litigators—*we* know how "special" we are. But at the same time, the book extends an open invitation to all lawyers who find themselves litigating environmental matters every now and again or even those lawyers who have a need to evaluate how citizen suits or global warming litigation might affect a client.

The book assumes familiarity with environmental laws generally, as well as familiarity with litigation procedures and techniques. The focus of the book is on how environmental issues are addressed and resolved through litigation. Although statutes and regulatory programs are frequently cited, the book deliberately is organized around environmental *topics*—civil enforcement, criminal enforcement, citizen suits, and so on—not specific statutes or regulations.

Last, it should be apparent to those who read the "About the Authors" section that the background and experience of the authors varies widely. The book deliberately attempted to draw from the ranks of academics, the government (or at least *former* government lawyers), and private practice in order to represent a range of views. Accordingly, even more so than usual in books of this type, the views in the chapters are the views of the authors in their individual capacities. They do not necessarily represent the views of the law firms and universities by whom the authors are employed, nor do they necessarily represent the views of the editors or the American Bar Association.

This book does not provide legal advice and should not be relied upon by any reader to answer particular legal questions for particular clients.

Kegan A. Brown and Andrea M. Hogan, Editors

Acknowledgments

Among members of the Book Publishing Board of the ABA's Section of Environment, Energy, and Resources, this type of book is known as a "multi-author chapter book." On its face, that term discloses that most of the "heavy lifting" for this book was provided by the chapter authors, not the editors who asked them to contribute. We appreciate that each of the authors devoted a significant amount of time to this effort, even when the demands on their time for client work, teaching, and family may have been in conflict. Each of the chapters also received valuable peer review, often by other members of the Book Publishing Board (or their co-workers). We thank the peer reviewers for their valuable contributions.

What is less apparent from the term "multi-author chapter book" is how difficult it is to align approximately 20 authors on approximately the same schedule, to avoid substantive duplication across chapters, and to achieve reasonable consistencies of tone and format. For her invaluable assistance in this task, we wish to thank Margrethe Kearney, a member of the ABA's Book Publishing Board and attorney with the Environmental Law & Policy Center.

Separately, we would like to thank our partners at Latham & Watkins LLP, who offered their encouragement and agreed to write two chapters of the book. Cary Perlman, a partner in Latham's Chicago office and the editor of the first edition of this book, was particularly helpful in teaching us the editing "rules of the road." We are fortunate to have practiced environmental law at a firm where there is so much expertise to draw upon, and where people are so gracious about sharing their time.

On a personal level, Andrea Hogan thanks her mother, Judy (a former English teacher), for teaching her how to write, and more importantly, how to edit. She also thanks her husband, Spencer, and her children, Anderson and Sydney, for their extreme tolerance and understanding of her schedule and commitments, in particular for "fun" work, like editing this book. Kegan Brown thanks his parents, Kathleen and Andrew, for their instillment of a series of life lessons that have proved both true and invaluable over the years. In addition, he thanks his wife, Maryellen, and his three boys, Owen, Everett, and Collin, for their unwavering support in his professional endeavors, even when, to their chagrin, it has resulted in some Sunday mornings without chocolate chip pancakes.

About the Editors

Kegan A. Brown is a partner in the New York office of Latham & Watkins LLP. He represents clients across industry sectors in complex environmental, products liability, and toxic tort litigations. He also advises clients on environmental regulatory and transactional matters, with deep expertise concerning the investigation and remediation of hazardous substances at both the federal and state levels. Mr. Brown earned his J.D. from Rutgers University School of Law–Newark and his B.S. in criminology and justice studies from The College of New Jersey.

Andrea M. Hogan is Senior Counsel at Chevron Corporation, and was formerly a partner in the San Francisco office of Latham & Watkins LLP, where she practiced environmental law. She has represented clients in a range of environmental litigation matters in state and federal court, including under the Comprehensive Environmental Response, Compensation, and Liability Act, Clean Water Act, and Clean Air Act, as well as in tort litigation. Ms. Hogan has expertise in numerous other areas of environmental compliance, enforcement, and regulation, with a focus on issues related to contaminated sites. Ms. Hogan received her J.D. degree from Georgetown University Law Center, and her B.A. in business economics and political science from the University of California Santa Barbara.

About the Authors

Barbara L. Arras is a partner in the New Orleans office of Phelps Dunbar LLP. She represents defendants in toxic tort litigation primarily involving pulmonary diseases allegedly caused by asbestos and other pulmonary irritants and hematopoietic diseases allegedly caused by benzene.

Jane F. Barrett has over 40 years of experience working in the field of environmental criminal law. Her environmental experience began as an attorney with EPA's Office of Water. She also served as an Assistant Attorney General for the State of Maryland, where she was responsible for developing and supervising the prosecution of criminal violations of state environmental laws. Later Professor Barrett was appointed as an Assistant U.S. Attorney for the District of Maryland, where she created and served as Chief of the Environmental Litigation Unit. In both state and federal enforcement roles, Professor Barrett has extensive criminal jury trial experience, including significant environmental criminal cases, and has successfully argued numerous appellate cases. During her career in the Department of Justice, Professor Barrett received numerous recognitions and awards, including U.S. Attorney's Office Barney Skolnik Award for Prosecutorial Excellence in 1997, and the Department of Justice Special Achievement Award for the *Dee* case in 1989 (recognizing the first prosecution of Department of Defense senior managers for environmental crimes). Professor Barrett also has extensive experience in private practice, having chaired the White-Collar, Internal, and Government Investigations Group as a partner with Dyer Ellis & Joseph, PC and later Blank Rome LLP. In addition to litigating complex criminal and civil cases, she also conducted corporate internal investigation and advised clients on the implementation of corporate compliance programs. In 2007, she joined the faculty of the University of Maryland School of Law as an associate professor of law and director of the Environmental Law Clinic, where she taught environmental law and supervised students handling a variety of environmental litigation matters. In 2010, Professor Barrett received the Clinical Legal Education Association Outstanding Advocate Award, and in 2012 the University of Maryland Environmental Law Clinic received the American Bar Association's Award for Distinguished Achievement in Environmental Law and Policy. In 2017, Professor Barrett retired from the faculty of the Maryland Law School, becoming Professor Emeritus, and retired from private practice in 2018.

Joel Beauvais is a partner in the Washington, D.C., office of Latham & Watkins and a member of the firm's Environment, Land & Resources Department. He represents clients on a broad range of environmental matters, including regulatory advocacy, litigation, and transactional advice on issues involving climate and air quality, water quality, waste management, contaminated properties, and project siting and approvals. Mr. Beauvais has held several high-level positions at the U.S. Environmental Protection Agency, including leading the Office of Policy and the Office of Water, as well as leadership positions in the Office of Air and Radiation and the Office of General Counsel. He previously served as Counsel to the House Committee on Energy and Commerce, where he played a key role in the development of energy and climate legislation. He clerked for Justice Sandra Day O'Connor on the Supreme Court of the United States and for Judge Harry T. Edwards on the U.S. Court of Appeals for the D.C. Circuit. Mr. Beauvais earned his J.D. from New York University School of Law and a B.A. in political science from Yale University.

Cynthia Betz is an associate at McCarter & English, LLP. Ms. Betz's practice spans a wide variety of matters, primarily in the areas of environmental law and policy-holder-side insurance coverage. Prior to joining the firm, Ms. Betz was a law clerk to the Honorable Stanley R. Chesler, U.S. District Court Judge for the District of New Jersey. Ms. Betz can be reached at cbetz@mccarter.com.

Karl S. Coplan is a Professor of Law at the Elisabeth Haub School of Law at Pace University, and Co-Director of its Environmental Litigation Clinic. Prior to joining the Pace faculty in 1994, he practiced land use and environmental litigation for eight years with the New York City firm of Berle, Kass & Case. As the principal outside counsel for Riverkeeper, Inc., Professor Coplan and the Pace Environmental Litigation Clinic have brought numerous lawsuits enforcing the Clean Water Act and other environmental laws. These cases include *Catskill Mountains Chapter, Trout Unlimited v. City of New York*, in which the Second Circuit Court of Appeals held that the transfer of polluted, silt-laden water from one watershed to another required a Clean Water Act permit. Professor Coplan also participated in litigation and Clean Water Act permitting proceedings involving several Hudson River power plants, including the proposed Bowline 3 power plant, and the Lovett, Roseton, Danskammer, and Athens plants. Professor Coplan clerked for The Honorable Warren E. Burger, Chief Justice of the U.S. Supreme Court, and The Honorable Leonard I. Garth, Circuit Judge of the U.S. Court of Appeals for the Third Circuit. Professor Coplan received his J.D. degree from Columbia Law School in 1984 and his B.A. degree from Middlebury College in 1980.

Steven P. Croley is a partner in the Washington, D.C., office of Latham & Watkins LLP. His practice focuses on regulation, especially energy and environmental matters, sensitive transactions, and civil litigation and investigations. His clients include private companies, Fortune 500 companies, public bodies, and trade associations. Mr. Croley is also the Harry Hutchins Collegiate Professor of Law at the University of Michigan, where he has taught administrative law, civil procedure, and torts, among other subjects, and currently teaches a seminar on Power Markets. Previously, he served as Deputy White House Counsel to President Obama, and as General Counsel of the U.S. Department of Energy. Earlier in his career, he served as a Special Assistant U.S. Attorney in the Eastern District of Michigan. He is a member of the American Law Institute. Mr. Croley's many publications include *Regulation and Public Interests* (Princeton, 2008) and *Civil Justice Reconsidered* (NYU, 2017). He is a graduate of the University of Michigan (B.A.), the Yale Law School (J.D.), and Princeton University (Ph.D.).

Dr. Rick Dunford is the owner of Environmental Economics Services (EES), a consulting firm in Raleigh, North Carolina, specializing in natural resource damage (NRD) assessment. To date, he has worked on more than 80 NRD assessments on behalf of responsible parties. His specialties include recreation damages, groundwater damages, and a variety of non-market valuation techniques. Dr. Dunford has written expert reports in several NRD cases and has testified in three NRD trials. He also has published extensively on NRD issues. Dr. Dunford received his Ph.D. in Agricultural Economics in 1977 from the University of Wisconsin in Madison.

Laura Glickman is an associate in the Washington, D.C., office of Latham & Watkins, where she practices in the Environment, Land & Resources Department. Ms. Glickman's practice focuses on complex environmental litigation, as well as regulatory and transactional support. She has significant experience in matters involving the Federal Insecticide, Fungicide, and Rodenticide Act, the Endangered Species Act, and the Clean Air Act.

Ira Gottlieb is a partner with McCarter & English, LLP. He is the firm-wide Environment and Energy Practice Group Leader. Mr. Gottlieb's practice involves a wide array of matters concerning environmental law, natural resource damage claims, and insurance coverage negotiation and litigation on behalf of policyholders. He represents and counsels clients concerning several of the nation's largest urban sediment remediation sites. Before joining McCarter & English, Mr. Gottlieb served as an Assistant Regional Counsel for the U.S. Environmental Protection Agency, Region III. He may be reached at igottlieb@mccarter.com.

Joel M. Gross is a partner in the Washington, D.C., office of Arnold & Porter LLP, and a member of the firm's Environmental Practice Group. His practice includes enforcement defense (civil and criminal), litigation, appellate matters, client counseling, and transactional matters, with a special interest in the interplay of environmental issues in bankruptcy. Prior to joining Arnold & Porter in 2000, Mr. Gross worked for 17 years in the Environmental Enforcement Section of the Department of Justice, the last five as Chief of that Section, the largest litigating section in the

Department with over 150 lawyers. While at the Department, he had responsibility for a wide range of civil enforcement matters, and was involved with many policy and legislative issues. Mr. Gross is the co-author of two books, both published by the ABA Section of Environment, Energy, and Resources: *Clean Water Act, Basic Practice Series*, and *Amending CERCLA, The Post-SARA Amendments to the Comprehensive Environmental Response, Compensation, and Liability Act*.

W. Warren Hamel leads the Investigations and White Collar Defense Practice at Venable LLP. Prior to joining Venable, Mr. Hamel served as an Assistant U.S. Attorney in the U.S. Attorney's Office for the District of Maryland from 1990 to 2002, and was chief of the Environmental Crimes and Enforcement Unit from 1997 through 2001. As an Assistant U.S. Attorney, he was responsible for investigation and prosecution of a broad variety of criminal cases and litigation of civil enforcement and defense cases under the Clean Water Act, Clean Air Act, Resource Conservation and Recovery Act, and the full range of other environmental and conservation statutes. Since joining Venable in 2002, Mr. Hamel has conducted internal investigations and represented individual, corporate, and nonprofit clients in a wide variety of white-collar and environmental criminal defense and civil enforcement matters. He has also advised clients on compliance and internal control issues, including environmental compliance and risk assessment, information governance, managing whistleblower issues, and Sarbanes-Oxley-related matters. In addition to his practice, Mr. Hamel has served as an adjunct professor at the University of Maryland School of Law and Georgetown University Law Center, where he taught a seminar on criminal enforcement of environmental laws. He continues to speak as a guest lecturer in environmental crimes for the undergraduate environmental law course at University of Maryland in College Park. Mr. Hamel is a member of the Board of Advisors for the BNA White Collar Crime Reporter, is a member of the board of The Francis D. Murnaghan, Jr. Appellate Advocacy Fellowship, and served as a member of the Board of Trustees of the Chesapeake Bay Trust from 2006 through 2015, including as Chair of the Board of Trustees from 2012 through 2014. During Mr. Hamel's tenure as Chair of Venable's Investigations and White Collar Practice, the firm was named "Law Firm of the Year" in 2013 for Criminal Defense and White Collar Litigation by U.S. News—Best Lawyers.

J. Alan Harrell is a partner in the Baton Rouge, Louisiana, office of Phelps Dunbar LLP. His practice focuses on toxic tort litigation, acting as national and Louisiana counsel for clients. He also handles class actions, commercial litigation, and environmental regulatory compliance.

Nathan Howe is an associate at McCarter & English, LLP and is a member of the Environment and Energy Practice Group. Mr. Howe assists clients in a broad range of litigation, regulatory, and transactional services in both the energy and environmental sectors. Mr. Howe has represented clients in matters before federal and state courts as well as various regulatory agencies. In addition to these core practices, he is actively involved in the development of emerging renewable energy technologies. Mr. Howe may be reached at nhowe@mccarter.com.

Marc S. Mayerson is the principal of The Mayerson Firm PLLC of Washington, D.C., (https://www.mayersonfirm.com). Mr. Mayerson is a lawyer, arbitrator, mediator, and expert witness. Mr. Mayerson's law practice focuses on insurance coverage disputes and advice for policyholders, such as businesses, nonprofits, directors, executives, fiduciaries, and individuals. He has appeared as lead counsel in state and federal trial and appeals courts and in arbitrations concerning a wide range of property-casualty insurance policies and complex losses. For more than three decades, he has spearheaded efforts to recover money for environmental liability, cleanup costs, toxic torts, and natural resources damages under general liability, environmental liability, pollution legal liability, property, and other insurance policies. He also teaches insurance law at both Georgetown University Law Center and George Washington University School of Law, and is the co-editor of *New Appleman Insurance Law Practice Guide*. He graduated from Harvard Law School (J.D. magna cum laude 1986), was a member of the *Harvard Law Review*, and clerked for the Honorable Stephen R. Reinhardt of the U.S. Court of Appeals for the Ninth Circuit.

Elana Nightingale Dawson is an associate in the Washington, D.C., office of Latham & Watkins, LLP, where she is a member of the firm's Supreme Court and Appellate Practice. Ms. Nightingale Dawson has experience practicing before administrative agencies as well as before federal district courts, appellate courts, and the U.S. Supreme Court. Before starting at Latham, Ms. Nightingale Dawson served as a law clerk to Justice Anthony M. Kennedy of the U.S. Supreme Court, Judge Raymond M. Kethledge of the U.S. Court of Appeals for the Sixth Circuit, and Judge Gary Feinerman of the Northern District of Illinois. Ms. Nightingale Dawson also served as a Bristow Fellow in the Office of the Solicitor General of the United States.

Claudia O'Brien is a partner in the Washington, D.C., office of Latham & Watkins LLP. Ms. O'Brien represents clients with respect to a full range of federal environmental statutes on agency petitions, rulemaking proceedings and litigation, and compliance and enforcement. She has specialized technical and business expertise in the pesticide industry, as well as in toxicology and risk assessment. She also has particular expertise in all aspects of the Federal Insecticide, Fungicide, and Rodenticide Act, the Clean Water Act, the Resource Conservation and Recovery Act, and the Endangered Species Act, as well as regulations impacting genetically engineered plants.

Steven P. Solow is a partner at Katten Muchin Rosenman LLP, where he is the head of the White Collar, Investigations and Compliance practice in the firm's Washington, D.C., office. He represents corporate and individual clients in white-collar criminal cases. He is also serving as a court-appointed monitor over the world's largest travel-leisure company, following the company's conviction for several environmental felony violations. His practice focuses on business crimes, internal investigations, corporate compliance programs, and environmental civil and criminal litigation. Mr. Solow is the former Chief of the Environmental Crimes Section at the Department of Justice where he oversaw the investigation and prosecution of environmental criminal cases nationwide. Previous to that he was a prosecutor with the New York State Organized Crime Task Force and a law professor at the University of Maryland and at Pace University. He has been an adjunct professor at Georgetown University and Pace University, and is a Senior Fellow of the Zicklin Center for Business Ethics at Wharton. He is on the Board of Advisors of the BNA White Collar Crime Reporter and was a recipient of the Burton Distinguished Legal Writing Award.

Stacey VanBelleghem is a partner in the Washington, D.C., office of Latham & Watkins and is a member of the Environment, Land & Resources Department. She represents clients in a variety of industry sectors on major project infrastructure and development, administrative petitions and rulemaking, and litigation under federal environmental law. She has particular expertise in the Clean Air Act, Clean Water Act, Endangered Species Act, Federal Insecticide Fungicide, and Rodenticide Act, National Environmental Policy Act, and the National Historic Preservation Act.

Stijn Van Osch is a senior associate in the Washington, D.C., office of Latham & Watkins LLP, where he practices environmental law, focusing on environmental regulatory law, natural resources litigation, and product stewardship matters. Prior to joining Latham, Mr. Van Osch clerked for Judge Stephen H. Glickman of the District of Columbia Court of Appeals. Mr. Van Osch received his J.D. from the University of Michigan Law School, and his bachelor's degree and Master of Laws at Utrecht University in his native country, the Netherlands.

CHAPTER 1

Judicial Challenges to Federal Agency Action

Joel Beauvais, Steven P. Croley, and Elana Nightingale Dawson

I. INTRODUCTION

Federal and state agency regulatory actions, and litigation challenging them, are key drivers of environmental law and policy in the United States. Many of the most important court decisions in environmental law—*Massachusetts v. EPA*, *Chevron U.S.A. v. Natural Resources Defense Council*, *Whitman v. American Trucking Ass'n*, to name a few—are the result of such suits. Decisions such as these set the rules of the road for agency decision-making, with regard both to substantive implementation of environmental statutes and to the procedures agencies must follow. Indeed, most major environmental regulatory decisions at the federal level are challenged in court, and agency decisions accordingly are made with an eye to both past and potential future litigation.

This chapter provides a high-level, practitioner-oriented overview of such litigation, using a mix of landmark and recent court decisions to illustrate some of the central issues. (Given the breadth of the subject matter, our treatment of these issues is necessarily limited. Readers seeking a deeper exploration should refer to appropriate treatises or handbooks on administrative and environmental law.) We refer primarily to the major statutes administered by the U.S. Environmental Protection Agency (EPA), but similar issues arise in connection with agency decisions under conservation, natural resource management, and energy-related statutes administered by other federal agencies. We dedicate the bulk of our analysis to challenges to agency rulemaking, but also touch on issues related to permits, guidance documents, and other agency actions.

Section II provides an overview of the types of agency regulatory actions commonly challenged in court. Section III identifies threshold issues for judicial challenges to agency action. Section IV summarizes the types of claims typically raised in suits challenging regulatory actions—both substantive and procedural—and the standards of judicial review corresponding to those claims. Section V discusses remedies available to successful challengers.

II. TYPES OF AGENCY REGULATORY ACTIONS SUBJECT TO JUDICIAL CHALLENGE

We begin with a brief survey of the relevant procedural landscape. The Administrative Procedure Act (APA) defines a "rule" broadly as "an agency statement of general or particular applicability and future effect designed to implement, interpret, or prescribe law or policy or describing the organization, procedure, or practice requirements of an agency."[1] The term "rule" is typically understood to mean an agency statement that governs a class of entities and situations, but the APA's reference to "particular applicability" contemplates that "rulemaking" can be used to address individual entities or situations, such as the allocation of a license or permit.

The APA and the case law draw a distinction between "legislative rules" and "interpretative rules," as well as policy statements and rules of agency procedure or organization.[2] A legislative rule involves the exercise of congressionally delegated authority to make rules binding upon the agency or third parties, whereas an interpretative rule reflects the agency's reading of a statute but is not an exercise of delegated authority and is not binding.[3]

The APA further distinguishes between "informal" and "formal" rulemaking. Informal rulemaking is typically referred to as "notice and comment" rulemaking because of the APA's requirement that agencies provide public notice and an opportunity to comment on a proposed rule before it is finalized. Formal rulemaking—which is required only in limited circumstances where Congress expressly provides for rulemaking "on the record after opportunity for a hearing"—requires additional trial-type proceedings similar to those required in certain agency adjudication.[4]

Most federal environmental regulations are legislative rules, and virtually all of these are promulgated through informal notice-and-comment rulemaking. The procedures for such rulemaking are governed either by the environmental statute under which the rule is issued, Section 553(b) of the APA (governing informal rulemaking), or some combination thereof. Agencies occasionally issue interpretive rules, but this is comparatively infrequent.

---

1. 5 U.S.C. § 551(4) (2012).

2. *See* 5 U.S.C. § 553(b)(3)(A) (2012) (stating that APA's notice-and-comment requirements do not apply to "interpretative rules, general statements of policy, or rules of agency organization, procedure, or practice").

3. *See, e.g.*, Nat'l Mining Ass'n v. McCarthy, 758 F.3d 243, 251–52 (D.C. Cir. 2014); Nat'l Ass'n of Home Builders v. U.S. Army Corps of Eng'rs, 417 F.3d 1272, 1285 (D.C. Cir. 2005); Am. Mining Cong. v. Mine Safety & Health Admin., 995 F.2d 1106, 1112 (D.C. Cir. 1993).

4. 5 U.S.C. § 553(c) (2012) ("When rules are required by statute to be made on the record after opportunity for an agency hearing, sections 556 and 557 of this title apply instead of this subsection.").

Agencies also frequently issue "guidance" documents, which may be styled as policy statements, policy memoranda, manuals, advisories, Q&A documents, and so forth, as a means of policymaking. Unlike legislative rules, true guidance documents are not legally binding on the agency or other entities. Rather, they are intended to provide stakeholders and the public with information on agency views regarding statutory or regulatory interpretations, policies, or technical or procedural issues, and can play an important role in influencing behavior.[5] Guidance is not subject to the APA's notice-and-comment requirements, but agencies often do take comments on proposed guidance before issuing it in final form. Noting the growing impact of guidance, the White House Office of Management and Budget in 2007 issued a policy memorandum establishing policies and procedures for the development, issuance, and use of "significant" guidance documents by federal agencies—including notice-and-comment procedures for such documents.[6]

Disputes sometimes arise as to whether a purported guidance document constitutes a legislative rule in disguise. In *National Mining Ass'n v. McCarthy*, for example, industry plaintiffs challenged an EPA guidance memorandum addressing Clean Water Act permitting for coal mines, arguing in part that the memorandum was a legislative rule promulgated without notice and comment.[7] After acknowledging that distinguishing legislative rules, interpretive rules, and general statements of policy "turns out to be quite difficult and confused," the D.C. Circuit held that the EPA memorandum was not a legislative rule because it had no binding effect on regulated entities or state permitting authorities and because the memorandum made clear that it did not impose legally binding requirements.[8] In *Appalachian Power Co. v. EPA*, by contrast, the D.C. Circuit held that a Clean Air Act permitting memorandum characterized as "guidance" was a de facto legislative rule, "reflecting a settled agency position which has legal consequences" for state permitting agencies and regulated entities.[9] And in *Iowa League of Cities v. EPA*, the Eighth Circuit held that two letters sent by EPA to a U.S. senator addressing certain Clean Water Act regulatory issues constituted de facto legislative rules issued without notice and comment, on the grounds that the letters had a binding effect on regulated entities.[10]

In addition to rulemaking and guidance, environmental agencies also engage in adjudication, defined by the APA as an "agency process for the formulation of an order," which is "a final disposition . . . of an agency in a matter other than rule making but including licensing."[11] Formal adjudication under the APA involves a

---

5. *See, e.g.*, U.S. Gov't Accountability Office, GAO-15-368, Regulatory Guidance Processes; Selected Departments Could Strengthen Internal Control and Dissemination Practices 7–8 (2015).

6. Final Bulletin for Agency Good Guidance Practices, 72 Fed. Reg. 3432 (Off. of Mgmt. & Budget Jan. 25, 2007).

7. 758 F.3d 243 (D.C. Cir. 2014).

8. 753 F.3d at 251–52.

9. 208 F.3d 1015, 1021–23 (D.C. Cir. 2000).

10. 711 F.3d 844, 863–65 (8th Cir. 2013).

11. 5 U.S.C. § 551(6), (7) (2012).

trial-like hearing before a decision maker not previously involved, and (like formal rulemaking) is required only where the underlying statute requires that the decision be made "on the record after opportunity for an agency hearing."[12] The APA does not prescribe requirements for informal adjudication. The most common types of environmental regulatory actions that can be classified as adjudications involve the issuance of enforcement orders, permits for facilities, and licenses or registrations for products (such as pesticide registrations).

Environmental statutes drive the scope and nature of agency regulatory actions. EPA administers the Clean Air Act (CAA), the Clean Water Act (CWA), the Safe Drinking Water Act (SDWA), the Toxic Substances Control Act (TSCA), the Federal Insecticide, Fungicide, and Rodenticide Act (FIFRA), the Resource Conservation and Recovery Act (RCRA), and the Comprehensive Environmental Response, Compensation, and Liability Act (CERCLA), among others.[13] The scope and pace of action under these laws is driven by their particular characteristics. EPA issues on the order of 500 final rules per year, around 150 of which are typically signed at the level of the EPA administrator—with others signed by regional administrators, assistant administrators, or other officials.[14] The CAA accounts for the majority of EPA rulemaking, owing to that statute's comprehensive and detailed requirements and deadlines. EPA also issues permits under the CAA, CWA, and other statutes for activities in some areas of the country, but in most areas states or tribes have delegated permitting authority.

In addition to EPA, the U.S. Department of the Interior and the U.S. Department of Agriculture (which includes the U.S. Forest Service) manage vast tracts of land, subsurface mineral resources, and offshore resources. These agencies take a broad array of regulatory actions—including rulemakings—under their key statutes of jurisdiction, including the Endangered Species Act, the Federal Land Policy and Management Act, the Mineral Leasing Act, the Coastal Zone Management Act, the Migratory Bird Treaty Act, the Surface Mining Control and Reclamation Act, and the Outer Continental Shelf Lands Act, among others.[15] These and other agencies frequently issue environmental review documentation in connection with federal actions under the National Environmental Policy Act.

Each of these statutes is unique, though many have common elements. Each includes distinct judicial review provisions, typically establishing deadlines and proper venue for judicial challenges to different types of agency actions. Most include "citizen suit" provisions that authorize nongovernmental entities to bring suit to enforce against violations of the statute, or to compel federal agencies to

---

12. 5 U.S.C. § 554 (2011).

13. For a list of statutes administered in whole or in part by EPA, see U.S. Envtl. Prot. Agency, Summaries of Environmental Laws and EOs, https://www.epa.gov/laws-regulations/laws-and-executive -orders (last visited July 16, 2018).

14. *Cf.* Claudia Copeland & James E. McCarthy, Cong. Research Serv., R41561, EPA Regulations: Too Much, Too Little, or On Track? (2016).

15. For a select list of statutes administered in whole or in part by the Department of the Interior, see U.S. Dep't of the Interior, Select Statutory Authorities, https://www.doi.gov/ocl/selStatAuthorities (last visited July 16, 2018).

undertake nondiscretionary duties under the statute. Many define what actions are to be deemed "final" for purposes of judicial review, whether particular types of actions are or are not judicially reviewable, and requirements for administrative remedies that must be exhausted prior to challenging an action in court. Some specify standards of review for some types of actions, which may differ from those under the APA. This variation in key statutory provisions underscores that statute-specific knowledge is critical when challenging agency actions.

While this chapter focuses on judicial challenges to federal regulatory actions, it is important to recognize that state and tribal governments are responsible for a substantial proportion of environmental regulatory decisions in the United States. States, for example, have delegated authority to administer many of the major federal statutes, including the CAA, CWA, SDWA, and RCRA in particular. States do so pursuant to state implementing statutes, and in many cases, they also administer additional state laws covering the same or related issues. Implementation of state environmental laws typically is governed by state administrative procedure. Accordingly, suits challenging state environmental regulatory actions are likely to raise state law issues that are analogous to those addressed here.

III. REQUISITES OF JUDICIAL CHALLENGES TO AGENCY ACTION

Regulated entities, nongovernmental organizations, state and local governments, and others frequently bring court challenges to agency regulations, permits, and other types of agency action outlined in section II. In principle, a party might respond to regulatory action or inaction it considers undesirable by appealing to any of the three branches of government. Such a party might seek some kind of relief from Congress, or seek to appeal to the White House or to senior agency officials, or instead may challenge the legality of the agency's action in court—the focus of this chapter. But whereas a party can pursue political or policy disagreements through the political branches freely, getting a challenge heard by a court in the first place—making it through the proverbial courthouse door—requires first satisfying several conditions that limit the very availability of judicial review.

Those conditions can be usefully organized into four sets, addressing the following questions: (1) Over what kinds of agency action are courts authorized to exercise their review authority at all? (2) Who may bring an authorized challenge? (3) When may such a case be brought? (4) And in what judicial forum? The answers to these questions overlap significantly; many of the relevant legal doctrines address more than one of these questions, and furthermore those doctrines have been characterized by courts in varying ways as well. For example, whether a court has authority to hear a claim at all depends, in part, on who is bringing that claim, and may depend also on when the party does so and where. For another example, whether a party has a legally cognizable claim might depend, among other things, on when the party raises that claim. Even so, these what-who-when-and-where questions provide a practical lens for understanding the essential requirements of judicial review. The following discussion unpacks these questions and notes how they are related, highlighting examples from environmental law.

A. What: Threshold Conditions of Judicial Authority

One set of conditions for judicial review of agency action focuses most centrally on the scope and limits of judicial authority. For starters, challenging federal agency action requires the government's consent through waiver of its sovereign immunity from suit, an immunity from having to answer before courts at all. In addition, judicial review must rest on some grant of jurisdiction by Congress for federal courts to hear a challenge to agency action; courts do not possess that power inherently. Further, courts may entertain judicial challenges to agency action only where Congress has established that certain legal claims are to be recognized. The exercise of judicial authority is also subject to certain inherent constitutional limits as well, which include among others a requirement that a challenge to agency action present a question appropriate for judicial resolution. A failure to satisfy any of these threshold requirements means a would-be challenger will not have its case heard in court.

1. Sovereign Immunity

A claim that a federal official or federal administrative body has acted illegally in some way warranting judicial intervention necessarily subjects the legal propriety of the government's action to judicial scrutiny. But the sovereign United States, embodied by its officials and component agencies, cannot be sued in court, absent its consent.[16] Thus, one preliminary condition of judicial review is a waiver of the sovereign's immunity from suit. As waiving the sovereign's immunity is no small matter, courts have long required that any such waiver be clear and they interpret such waivers narrowly.[17]

Though critical, this condition is easily satisfied in the typical challenge to agency action as the United States has waived its sovereign immunity in the APA itself. APA Section 702 provides that a case stating a claim arising out of the actions of a federal agency or an officer or employee of an agency "shall not be dismissed . . . on the ground that it is against the United States."[18] Thus, whereas sovereign immunity posed a serious obstacle to contesting federal agency action prior

---

16. *See, e.g.*, United States v. Mitchell, 463 U.S. 206, 212 (1983).
17. In the environmental context, see, for example, U.S. Dep't of Energy v. Ohio, 503 U.S. 607, 615 (1992); Hancock v. Train, 426 U.S. 167, 179 (1976); EPA v. California, 426 U.S. 200, 211 (1976).
18. 5 U.S.C. § 702 (2011).

to the APA's passage in 1946,[19] the APA waives the government's immunity from suit unambiguously. Importantly, however, this waiver by its terms extends only to actions "seeking relief other than money damages"—that is, to claims seeking declaratory and injunctive relief against federal agencies. Because parties seeking to enforce environmental statutes or otherwise to contest the actions of environmental regulators do not generally seek monetary damages, this limitation is not important in many environmental contexts.

That said, there are some circumstances in which parties bringing environmental litigation may seek monetary payments from the government. One example is for cases alleging a violation of CERCLA, which imposes monetary liability for the environmental cleanup costs of hazardous waste sites and other contaminants at certain sites. CERCLA expressly waives the government's sovereign immunity even for monetary claims, allowing claims against any agency of the federal government "in the same manner and to the same extent, both procedurally and substantively, as any nongovernmental entity."[20] For another example, and more generally, parties who prevail in cases against a federal agency may be awarded costs and attorneys' fees from the government under the Equal Access to Justice Act, which authorizes the recovery of monetary payments,[21] or under other statutes authorizing fees. Most environmental statutes include provisions specifically authorizing fees.[22] The recovery of costs and fees can be important in particular for some nongovernmental organizations that bring suit to enforce environmental statutes.

2. Federal Jurisdiction

That the government has waived its immunity from suit does not itself mean that the courts can hear a claim alleging the illegality of government action. Rather, the federal courts must be given jurisdiction over such a claim; unlike state courts, they lack jurisdiction except where it is affirmatively conferred.[23] Here again, federal subject-matter jurisdiction does not pose a difficult obstacle to challenging agency action today, though, as with sovereign immunity, matters were not always so simple. Section 1331 of Title 28 (not the APA) provides for federal jurisdiction "of all civil actions arising under the Constitution, laws, or treaties of the United

---

19. Previously, actions challenging federal agency decisions rested, more precariously, on an ultra vires claim according to which a federal officer who acted outside of his or her authority was separate from the government itself. *See* Larson v. Domestic & Foreign Commerce Corp., 337 U.S. 682, 689–90 (1949); United States v. Lee, 106 U.S. 196, 215 (1882). *See generally* Urban A. Lester & Michael F. Noone, Jr., Litigation with the Federal Government 102–07 (3d ed. 1994). Section 702 of the APA was amended to avoid the strictures of *Larson*. Gregory Sisk, Litigation with the Government 608 (2000).

20. CERCLA § 120, 42 U.S.C. § 9620(a)(1) (2011).

21. 28 U.S.C. § 2412 (2012).

22. *See, e.g.*, Toxic Substances Control Act § 19, 15 U.S.C. § 2618(d) (2013) (TSCA); Clean Air Act § 307, 42 U.S.C. § 7607(f) (2015) (CAA); Clean Water Act § 509, 33 U.S.C. § 1369(b)(3) (2011) (CWA).

23. *E.g.*, Mims v. Arrow, 565 U.S. 368, 376 (2012).

States," thus covering in general all actions contesting the validity of agency action or inaction under federal law.[24]

Some regulatory statutes confer jurisdiction—or otherwise condition jurisdiction—over challenges to specified agency actions, however, while explicitly barring review of other agency actions under Section 1331. In other words, while Section 1331 usefully provides a general grant of jurisdiction where there is no other, it does not override more restrictive grants of or limitations on jurisdiction to review agency action. For example, many environmental statutes include "citizen suit" provisions that give district courts jurisdiction over suits to enforce against violations of the statute, but require the plaintiff to have submitted a notice of intent to sue in advance of filing a complaint (typically 60 days beforehand). The Endangered Species Act (ESA), for instance, authorizes "any person" to bring a judicial challenge for violation of the ESA and provides for "jurisdiction" over such suits in the "district courts."[25] The statute requires a potential challenger, before a suit is filed, to provide written notice of the alleged violation to the government and the alleged violator, stating that "no action may be commenced" prior to that notice.[26] A party bringing an ESA challenge must satisfy this additional requirement; Section 1331 does not override the ESA's 60-day notice requirement on which district court jurisdiction expressly depends for challenges under the ESA's citizen-suit provision.

Indeed, wherever Congress confers jurisdiction that is limited to the satisfaction of certain predicate conditions, courts will not allow parties to invoke broader grants of jurisdiction wherever doing so would defeat the purposes of narrower jurisdictional grants. Thus, the D.C. Circuit, among other courts, has long held that parties cannot choose to seek review under a statute granting broad jurisdiction in a manner that would be inconsistent with a more restrictive jurisdictional statute simultaneously, as that would defeat the purposes of the more restrictive statute.[27]

Also important, Section 1331 confers jurisdiction specifically on the "district courts." Often, however, environmental statutes provide for judicial review of agency action in the courts of appeals, conferring jurisdiction there instead.

---

24. For the first few decades following the passage of the APA, Section 1331 conditioned its general federal-question jurisdiction also on a threshold dollar amount in controversy, such that parties could invoke federal-question jurisdiction only when their case raised monetary claims above a minimum amount. But this amount-in-controversy requirement was eliminated in 1976, allowing challenges to agency action to rest on federal jurisdiction granted in Section 1331. State courts, as courts of "general" rather than "limited" jurisdiction, already in some sense "have" federal-question jurisdiction. The federal removal statute, however, allows the government to remove all cases against the United States and its agencies and officers to federal court. 28 U.S.C. § 1442 (2012). Accordingly, litigation against federal agencies outside of the federal courts is rare.

25. Endangered Species Act § 11, 16 U.S.C. § 1540(g)(1)–(2)(A)(i) (2012).

26. *Id.*

27. *See, e.g.*, City of Rochester v. Bond, 603 F.2d 927, 931 (D.C. Cir. 1979) (specialized judicial review procedures apply over generalized, as courts will assume Congress intended the former to be exclusive). *Accord* Am. Bird Conservancy v. FCC, 545 F.3d 1190, 1194 (9th Cir. 2008) (when two jurisdictional statutes provide different routes to the federal courts, the rule for courts is to require parties to follow the more specific route).

Jurisdiction in the courts of appeals is considered appropriate especially where the federal court functions in an appellate capacity by reviewing an already well-developed factual record. Most environmental statutes include provisions giving either the D.C. Circuit specifically, or the courts of appeals generally, jurisdiction over challenges to specified categories of agency actions, and some may direct challenges to other specific categories of agency actions to the district courts. (These provisions are discussed at greater length in section III.D.)

3. Cognizable Legal Claim

A waiver of sovereign immunity and an affirmative grant of jurisdiction are necessary but not sufficient conditions for challenging agency action in court. A party seeking judicial review must also advance a claim that is legally cognizable—that is, must allege a violation of law that the legal system recognizes—a legal harm the courts can consider and for which courts can provide a judicial remedy. Thus, a party cannot contest the abstract fairness of agency action, for example, or base its challenge solely on policy considerations or other extralegal grounds. Rather, the party must state a legal "cause of action," expressed as one or more "counts" in the party's pleading that states the legal theory for why or how the agency acted contrary to law.

Here again, the APA provides one starting point, as it establishes a cause of action for persons "adversely affected or aggrieved" by final agency action, and authorizes courts to "hold unlawful and set aside" agency action that is, among other things, "arbitrary, capricious, an abuse of discretion, or otherwise not in accordance with law."[28] In addition, many environmental statutes also expressly create one or more causes of action for alleged violations of their requirements. These fall into two general categories: "review" provisions creating claims to challenge various specified types of agency actions, and "citizen suit" provisions creating causes of action for claims by private citizens to enforce against specified violations of the statute or to compel the federal agency to undertake a nondiscretionary duty under the statute.[29] The ESA's citizen-suit provision is an example of the latter category, which the Supreme Court has characterized as "an authorization of remarkable breadth."[30] The National Environmental Policy Act (NEPA), by contrast, does not itself create a cause of action. Thus, parties challenging the alleged inadequacy of a federal agency's consideration of the significant environmental consequences of major federal action—a common claim

---

28. 5 U.S.C. § 702 (2011); 5 U.S.C. §§ 704, 706 (2012).
29. Examples include CAA § 304, 42 U.S.C. § 7604(a) (2011); CWA § 505, 33 U.S.C. § 1365(a) (2007); Resources Conservation and Recovery Act § 7002, 42 U.S.C. § 6972 (2016); Safe Drinking Water Act § 1449, 42 U.S.C. § 300j-8 (2011); and Endangered Species Act § 11, 16 U.S.C. § 1540(g) (2012).
30. Bennett v. Spear, 520 U.S. 154, 164 (1997).

brought under NEPA—rely instead on APA Section 702.[31] Substantive claims typically raised in challenges to federal agency action are discussed at greater length in section IV.

4. Preclusion

One way a party may be unable to state a cause of action is where Congress has precluded judicial review. Preclusion is properly understood not as an independent criterion of judicial review, but rather an aspect of the requirement that a party have some cognizable cause of action: having a legally reviewable claim means such a claim is *not* precluded, and where a given claim is precluded, a party by definition has no cause of action for that claim. Preclusion merges with federal jurisdiction too. That is to say, where a claim is precluded, a court simply may not hear it. That said, judicial discussion of preclusion most often focuses on whether the would-be challenger has a claim that courts would recognize and for which a court could provide a judicial remedy. If so, the matter is commonly said to be "reviewable" by the court (as opposed to the court having "jurisdiction" over it).[32]

Accordingly, preclusion and "reviewability" lend themselves to discussion separate from jurisdiction, and there is well-established jurisprudence concerning the preclusion of judicial review of agency action. A central premise of it is the presumed availability of judicial review. That is, the Supreme Court has repeatedly made clear that, as reflected in the APA itself, courts should presume Congress has intended for judicial review of alleged violations of law, and should not be quick to conclude the contrary barring clear evidence of such congressional intent.[33] This presumption in favor of judicial review is overcome, however, in two types of circumstances, set forth in the APA itself.[34]

First, judicial review is precluded where Congress has said so explicitly.[35] Second, an action is precluded from judicial review where Congress implicitly

---

31. *See, e.g.*, Norton v. S. Utah Wilderness All., 542 U.S. 55, 61 (2004); Friends of Tims Ford v. TVA, 585 F.3d 955, 964 (6th Cir. 2009); Biodiversity Conservation All. v. Jiron, 762 F.3d 1036, 1058–59 (10th Cir. 2014).

32. The overlapping relationship between the absence of preclusion and jurisdiction is underscored by the common practice of government attorneys to move to dismiss allegedly precluded claims—as well as claims over which the court lacks jurisdiction or claims against the government where the plaintiff has failed to exhaust—both under Federal Rule of Civil Procedure 12(b)(1) for lack of jurisdiction *and* under 12(b)(6) for failure to state a claim on which relief can be granted. *E.g.*, U.S. Dep't of Justice, Exec. Off. for U.S. Att'ys, Federal Civil Practice Manual § 25.5 (2003) ("[I]f plaintiff fails to allege a waiver of sovereign immunity, the complaint also fails to state a claim. In addition, other defenses such as limitations, failure to exhaust administrative remedies, and exclusive remedy may also warrant dismissal for failure to state a claim."). Moreover, while drawing clear distinctions among the partially overlapping requirements of judicial review aids understanding of them, at times the differences may have little practical significance. At bottom, either a court can hear a claim, because all of the requirement of judicial review are met, or it cannot.

33. *See, e.g.*, Abbott Labs. v. Gardner, 387 U.S. 136, 140–41 (1967); *accord* Ohio Forestry Ass'n v. Sierra Club, 523 U.S. 726, 736–37 (1998); *see also* U.S. Ass'n of Reptile Keepers v. Jewell, 103 F. Supp. 135, 142–43 (D.D.C. 2015).

34. 5 U.S.C. § 701(a)(1)–(2) (2012).

35. *Id.* § 701(a)(1).

intended the matter to be solely a matter of agency discretion.[36] Here, the Supreme Court has held that courts should not review an agency's action where there would be no legal criteria against which to evaluate it—"no law to apply" to the agency action in question.[37] Otherwise, where Congress has not so implicitly (or explicitly) precluded judicial review of a given claim, that claim will be reviewable provided of course that all of the other criteria of judicial review are satisfied.[38]

5. Justiciability: The Political Question Doctrine

Courts are empowered to hear only claims that are "justiciable" as well. Justiciability, considered independent of jurisdiction and other reasons why a court may not be able to hear a claim, focuses on the inherent fitness of the would-be challenge for *judicial* resolution, as opposed to "political questions" best suited to resolution by the political branches. While there is no formulaic jurisprudential test associated with the "political question doctrine," the Supreme Court has identified several key considerations, including whether the issue raised implicates constitutional authority assigned to another branch, whether it is susceptible to judicially manageable standards, and whether it could be resolved by a court consistent with respect for the other branches of government.[39]

The political question doctrine has arisen in environmental cases challenging government action, most notably in the context of litigation relating to contributions to climate change and the adequacy of government action to address climate change. In *Juliana v. United States*, for example, the plaintiffs brought suit against numerous federal agencies for failing to take steps to reduce fossil fuel use, for which the plaintiffs stated numerous constitutional claims.[40] The district court held that the plaintiffs' claims were justiciable, rejecting the government's argument that the case presented nonjusticiable political questions inappropriate for judicial resolution. In the court's view, the case presented core legal questions, despite the fact that, should the plaintiffs prevail, any remedy would have to be framed carefully to avoid judicial interference with the political branches.[41] *Juliana* stands in contrast to cases like *Native Village of Kivalina v. ExxonMobil*, brought by an Alaskan village for damage allegedly caused by the defendants' greenhouse gas emissions.[42] There, in the context of a case brought against a number of oil, energy, and utility companies, the district court concluded that the plaintiff's claims raised

---

36. *Id.* § 701(a)(2).

37. *E.g.*, Heckler v. Chaney, 470 U.S. 821, 830 (1985).

38. An agency's own regulations can provide "law to apply." That is, where a party challenges the agency's compliance with its own regulations, regulatory as opposed to statutory criteria may provide legal standards against which a court can measure the lawfulness of agency action. *See, e.g.*, Ctr. for Auto Safety v. Dole, 846 F.2d 1532, 1534 (D.C. Cir. 1988); *see generally* Harold Krent, *Reviewing Agency Action for Inconsistency with Prior Rules and Regulations*, 72 Chi.-Kent L. Rev. 1187 (1997).

39. *See, e.g.*, Baker v. Carr, 369 U.S. 186, 217 (1962).

40. 217 F. Supp. 3d 1224 (D. Or. 2016). At the time of this writing, an appeal of the district court's decision was pending before the U.S. Court of Appeals for the Ninth Circuit.

41. *Id.* at 1235–42.

42. 663 F. Supp. 2d 863 (N.D. Cal. 2009).

nonjusticiable questions.[43] In particular, the court reasoned that adjudicating the case would require the court to determine the proper level of greenhouse gas emissions and how the costs of global warming are properly allocated, questions not suitable for judicial resolution but instead more properly addressed to the executive and legislative branches.[44]

B. Who: Standing to Bring a Judicial Challenge

Even where the preceding threshold conditions are satisfied, the availability of judicial review depends also on whether the challenging party is one with "standing" to sue. The judicial tests for standing aim to ensure that the party bringing the claim is well positioned to advocate for its position (and thus that a court will have the benefit of able advocacy), that the remedy the court would grant to such a party if successful would address the legal injury alleged, and finally that the courts exercise authority within the bounds prescribed by Article III of the Constitution and congressionally enacted statutes.

Standing doctrine consists of two parallel inquiries: a "constitutional" analysis and a "prudential" one. As famously formulated by the Supreme Court in *Lujan v. Defenders of Wildlife*, the constitutional inquiry asks whether the party challenging agency action is genuinely injured by the agency's alleged illegal action, that is, whether the would-be plaintiff's injury is both "concrete and particularized" and "actual or imminent," not "conjectural" or "hypothetical."[45] The former constitute sufficient "injury in fact" for a court to adjudicate the matter, while the latter do

---

43. *Id.* at 876–77. *See also* Am. Elec. Power v. Conn., 582 F.3d 309, 332 (2d Cir. 2009) (rejecting defendant's argument that the case presented a nonjusticiable political question), *rev'd on other grounds*, 564 U.S. 410 (2011). The discussion in the preceding text is not to suggest, however, that in general courts will tend to conclude that cases concerning climate change are justiciable if brought against federal agencies, and nonjusticiable if brought against private parties. This issue seems likely to be addressed in future cases.

44. As with preclusion, justiciability shares common features both of the requirement that a challenger identify a legally cognizable cause of action, and of the boundaries of federal jurisdiction. Either way, a party seeking to challenge agency action will be unable to advance a claim that is not justiciable, and the court will not exercise its authority over it. A case like *Kivalina*, where again the defendants moved to dismiss under both Federal Rule of Civil Procedure 12(b)(1) and 12(b)(6), supports an understandings of justiciability that is not reducible to federal jurisdiction. *Native Vill. of Kivalina*, 663 F. Supp. 2d 863. There, the district court concluded that the plaintiffs could not state a claim based on federal common law for the defendants' greenhouse gas emissions, given that the regulatory regime created through the CAA displaced common law claims—leaving open the possibility that where the CAA does not reach greenhouse gas emissions, parties like the plaintiffs *would* be able to bring a federal common law action. *Id.* In other words, the court did not conclude simply that it lacked jurisdiction altogether. Federal agency defendants also often move under both Federal Rule of Civil Procedure 12(b)(1) and 12(b)(6) when seeking to dismiss a claim on justiciability grounds.

45. Lujan v. Defenders of Wildlife, 504 U.S. 555, 560–61 (1992) (internal quotations omitted).

not.[46] In addition, the "injury in fact" that the plaintiff suffered must also be "fairly traceable" to the alleged unlawful action by the defendant, and furthermore that injury must be "likely" to be "redressed" by the remedy the court would grant were the plaintiff successful.[47]

Standing doctrine's constitutional requirements overlap with federal jurisdiction. That is, the federal courts' jurisdiction under Article III of the Constitution extends only to "cases" and "controversies," and thus a party not injured sufficiently immediately or distinctly by agency action does not satisfy the case-or-controversy requirement on which the exercise of judicial authority depends.[48] Even where Congress might seek to allow any party to bring a case alleging a violation of an environmental statute, as discussed shortly in the following, there are constitutional limits to Congress's ability to create legal "injury" by bestowing upon a party a right to sue.[49]

That leaves the prudential, judicially imposed leg of standing. Here, courts further ask whether the party bringing the challenge is "arguably within the zone of interests" intended to be protected by the statute (or constitutional provision) the agency is alleged to have violated, or whether instead would-be challengers seek to bring merely a "generalized" or "widely shared" grievances, or to represent the interests only of others and not themselves.[50] In these latter circumstances, or if those challenging agency action are not arguably within the "zone" of interests protected by the law that forms the basis of their claim, courts for prudential reasons will refrain from reviewing a case on standing grounds as well.[51]

With respect to this leg of standing analysis, though, Congress by legislation *can* shape the size of the "zone of interests" protected by statute, toward conferring greater standing so long as constitutional requirements are also met. For example,

---

46. The extent to which a probabilistic risk of harm can satisfy standing's "injury in fact" requirement presents a somewhat complicated question that can be of special relevance in the environmental context. In general, the federal courts of appeals have found that an increased risk of harm can constitute sufficient injury for standing purposes, so long as that risk is not purely speculative but rather reflects substantial probabilities of harm. *See* Nat. Res. Def. Council v. FDA, 710 F.3d 71 (2d Cir. 2013) (exposure to potentially dangerous product sufficient to satisfy standing); Nat. Res. Def. Council v. EPA, 464 F.3d 1, 6 (D.C. Cir. 2006) (substantial probability that some organization members will be injured by EPA action, as opposed to purely speculative injuries, is sufficient to establish standing); Vill. of Elk Grove v. Evans, 997 F.2d 328, 329 (7th Cir. 1993) (alleged increased risk of flood arising out of Army Corps' issuance of a permit in a flood plain sufficient to constitute injury).

47. *Lujan*, 504 U.S. at 560–61 (internal quotations omitted).

48. Sometimes courts link "justiciability" and this aspect of "standing" as well, stating that where the plaintiff lacks standing the case is not justiciable. *See, e.g.*, Steel Co. v. Citizens for a Better Env't, 523 U.S. 83, 102 (1998) ("[S]tanding to sue is part of the common understanding of what it takes to make a justiciable case.").

49. That said, and while Congress cannot legislate away constitutional standing requirements by deeming any violation of law a per se injury, the Supreme Court has held that the "redressability" component of constitutional standing/injury-in-fact, in particular, can be legislatively *satisfied* by a citizen suit to enforce an environmental statute even where the applicable judicial remedy is civil penalties paid to the government (not to the plaintiffs bringing the case). See Friends of the Earth, Inc. v. Laidlaw Envtl. Servs., 528 U.S. 167, 187 (2000).

50. *See generally* Clarke v. Sec. Indus. Ass'n, 479 U.S. 388, 395–97 (1987).

51. *See generally* Elk Grove Unified Sch. Dist. v. Newdow, 542 U.S. 1 (2004).

when Congress adopts citizen-suit provisions in environmental statute that create causes of action to challenge agency action, Congress expands the "zone"[52] and thereby reflects its intent that the laws be enforced through challenges to agency action or inaction, subject of course to the satisfaction of standing's other requirements. Moreover, the "zone" test in application requires not that the challenger be a beneficiary of the statute in question but rather, more loosely, that the challenge be *arguably* within the zone of interests implicated by the statute in question. Economic competitors have been held to have standing when a regulation changes their competitive posture, even where the statute in question does not aim at promoting competition at all.[53]

Standing analysis is well illustrated in the environmental case law. Indeed, much of contemporary standing jurisprudence originates in Supreme Court cases involving claims under the environmental statutes brought by environmental groups and other organizational plaintiffs,[54] as claims by organizational plaintiffs may test the boundaries of both the constitutional and the prudential side of standing doctrine;[55] where regulated parties seek to challenge agency action to contest the application of agency authority over them, in contrast, standing is often rather straightforward in that the challenger's material injury resulting from alleged over-regulation is very likely to satisfy the requirements of standing.

The central lesson from the case law involving organizational plaintiffs is that plaintiffs must allege facts with some specificity, such as through affidavits or other forms of proof, explaining how the federal agency's challenged action has affected their interests beyond or in addition to their purely ideological interests. Environmental organizations must allege that, for example, one or more of their members have used or intend to use certain natural resources allegedly harmed by agency action or inaction, in order to satisfy standing's "injury in fact" requirement.

Massachusetts v. EPA provides an important recent articulation of standing's requirements and illustrates the grounds on which parties seeking to prompt, rather than to limit, federal agency action may have standing to sue, in particular where a litigant seeks to enforce a "procedural right."[56] The case presented

---

52. For this reason, the "zone" test can be understood as a version of the question whether the plaintiff has a cause of action. *See* Lexmark Int'l Inc. v. Static Control Components, Inc., 572 U.S. 118, 128–30 (2014).

53. *See, e.g.*, Honeywell Int'l Inc. v. EPA, 374 F.3d 1363, 1369–70 (D.C. Cir. 2004).

54. *See generally* Lujan v. Defenders of Wildlife, 504 U.S. 555 (1992); Lujan v. Nat'l Wildlife Fed'n, 497 U.S. 871 (1990); Duke Power Co. v. Carolina Envtl. Study Grp., 438 U.S. 59 (1978); United States v. SCRAP, 412 U.S. 669 (1973); Sierra Club v. Morton, 405 U.S. 727 (1972).

55. Environmental organizations can sue on their own behalf, if an organization as such satisfies the requirements of standing. Warth v. Seldin, 422 U.S. 490, 511 (1975); *see generally* NAACP v. Button, 371 U.S. 415 (1963). Or, environmental groups can challenge agency action on behalf of one or more of their members if at least one member satisfies standing's requirements, the interests implicated by the suit are "germane" to the organization's purpose, and the claim asserted and relief requested do not require the individual participation of the organizational member, as opposed to the organization instead. *See* Hunt v. Wash. State Apple Advert. Comm'n, 432 U.S. 333, 343 (1977). *See, e.g.*, Sierra Club v. EPA, 292 F.3d 895, 898 (D.C. Cir. 2002) (applying the criteria).

56. 549 U.S. 497 (2007).

the question whether a coalition of states, local governments, and environmental organizations had standing to challenge a decision by EPA to decline to regulate greenhouse gas emissions from motor vehicles under the CAA. The Supreme Court concluded that Massachusetts had standing to sue based on the state's sovereign interest in protecting its territory against rising sea levels, adverse weather, and other consequences of global warming, which the coalition alleged were exacerbated by greenhouse gas emissions including those from motor vehicles. Although Massachusetts' presence was central to the Court's standing analysis, the Court's decision still illustrates how standing requirements may be met in climate change litigation more generally—even though some lower courts have held that the causal link between private conduct that results in greenhouse gas emissions and weather-related injuries is too attenuated to support standing.[57]

C. When: The Timing of Judicial Review

If a claim satisfies all of the preceding requirements, the next question becomes when such a suit may be brought.

1. Statute of Limitations

One basic timing consideration concerns the applicable statute of limitations. For actions challenging federal agency decisions (indeed, claims against the United States generally), the statute of limitations ordinarily is six years.[58] Thus, challengers have six years from the agency action in question to file suit, though usually parties challenging agency action are motivated for a variety of practical reasons to file suit much sooner than the statute of limitations requires.

Most environmental statutes, though, impose separate deadlines for judicial challenges to specified agency actions—notably in provisions that establish direct appellate review of regulations, permits, or other actions. Challenges to most regulations promulgated under the CAA, for example, are subject to a statutory filing deadline of 60 days after the rule's publication in the *Federal Register*.[59] The CAA further provides that if the challenge is based "solely on grounds arising after such sixtieth day," a petition for review may be filed within 60 days after such grounds arise.[60] Environmental cases often raise questions about whether an agency's legal

---

57. *E.g.*, Comer v. Murphy Oil USA, 585 F.3d 855, 860 (5th Cir. 2009) (connection between plaintiff landowners' alleged injuries following Hurricane Katrina and defendant fossil fuel and chemical companies' conduct not sufficiently traceable to satisfy standing).

58. 28 U.S.C. § 2401(a) (2010).

59. CAA § 307, 42 U.S.C. § 7607(b) (2015); *see also* 40 C.F.R. § 23.3 (providing that for documents not published in the *Federal Register*, the date from which the CAA's 60-day deadline is marked is two weeks after signature). For examples in other statutes, see, among others, CWA § 509, 33 U.S.C. § 1369(b)(1) (2011) (CWA establishes a 120-day deadline for challenges in the court of appeals to seven specified categories of agency actions); TSCA § 19, 15 U.S.C. § 2618 (2013) (TSCA establishes 60-day deadline for suits challenging specified types of rules or orders).

60. 42 U.S.C. § 7607(b)(1) (2015); *see also* 33 U.S.C. § 1369(b)(1) (2011) (providing similar deadline for "arising after" claims).

interpretation was already adopted in an older regulation—such that challenge to that interpretation is now time-barred—or whether an issue has been "reopened" through more recent agency activity.

Where a party challenges a rule at the enforcement stage—that is to say, challenges the rule's application to that party by raising claims about the rule's legality—courts often allow such a challenge after the otherwise applicable statute of limitations. Indeed some even have allowed pre-enforcement challenges to a rule's legal validity (as opposed to challenges to a rule's factual, evidentiary, and discretionary bases) after the default statute has run.[61] Many statutes expressly preclude such review, at least in certain circumstances, however. For example, Section 509(b)(2) of the CWA provides that specified actions for which court of appeals review is available under Section 509(b)(1) "shall not be subject to judicial review in any civil or criminal proceeding for enforcement."[62] The CAA includes similar language.[63]

2. Final Agency Action

The APA imposes another timing requirement for causes of action that are based on it rather than on another statute specifically conferring a private right of action: a challenging party must wait until after the agency action is final. That is because the APA creates a cause of action for persons adversely affected or aggrieved specifically by "*final* agency action" (emphasis added).[64] While the APA's finality condition is commonly characterized as a question of timing,[65] there is overlap here between what will constitute a cognizable claim under the APA—that is, a claim predicated on agency action that is final—and the time at which the challenge to agency action is brought—that is, after the agency has finished its decision making. For claims based on the APA that are not made reviewable by another statute, challenges to agency actions that are not yet final are *for that reason* not cognizable. They become cognizable, however, once an agency has completed its decision-making process. As the Supreme Court has explained, the purpose of requiring parties to give agencies an opportunity to see their decision-making processes through to completion is to ensure that agency actions that are merely tentative or reflect the judgment only of subordinate officials are not challenged prematurely.[66]

---

61. *E.g.*, Am. Rd. & Transp. Builders Ass'n v. EPA, 588 F.3d 1109, 1112 (D.C. Cir. 2009); Dunn-McCampbell Royalty Interest, Inc. v. Nat'l Park Serv., 112 F.3d 1283, 1287 (5th Cir. 1997); Wind River Mining Corp. v. United States, 946 F.2d 710, 715 (9th Cir. 1991).

62. 33 U.S.C. § 1369(b)(2) (2011).

63. 42 U.S.C. § 7607(b)(2) (2015).

64. 5 U.S.C. § 704 (2012).

65. *See, e.g.*, S. Breyer et al., Administrative Law and Regulatory Policy 957 (2011) (presenting finality as a timing doctrine and APA § 704 as codifying ripeness); L. Bressman et al., The Regulatory State 763–64 (2010) (presenting finality as a matter of the timing of judicial review).

66. *See generally* Dalton v. Specter, 511 U.S. 462 (1994); Franklin v. Massachusetts, 505 U.S. 788 (1992).

3. Ripeness and Mootness

Other timing tests find root in the common law, though with a constitutional dimension as well. The "ripeness" doctrine limits judicial challenges to agency action that are brought in some important sense too early, while "mootness" similarly prevents judicial challenges that are brought too late. With respect to ripeness, the Supreme Court has developed a two-part test that considers the fitness of the issue for judicial resolution, on the one hand, and the hardship to the challenging party in the event that judicial review is postponed, on the other.[67] The purpose of the ripeness requirement, as the doctrine's name suggests, is to ensure that the facts or events giving rise to a potential challenge have matured sufficiently so that judicial resolution is not only appropriate but also can be calibrated to address the core controversy fully emerged.

Similarly, but from the other end of the temporal spectrum, the mootness doctrine aims to ensure that courts are called upon to adjudicate controversies that are still relevant and thus can provide meaningful remedies not already overtaken by events. As the Supreme Court has stated, courts must adjudicate disputes that remain "live." As noted, both ripeness and mootness implicate the constitutional case-or-controversy requirement; they seek to extend judicial authority only to disputes that are well developed and thus suitable for judicial relief that is responsive to the dispute. At the same time, courts may, for prudential reasons, determine that a case that would satisfy Article III requirements is nevertheless moot. Where a potentially moot case may repeat itself on the facts such that it would evade review, however, or where a defendant alters its conduct after a case had been filed in a way that might render a case moot, courts have found exceptions to the mootness doctrine.[68]

4. Exhaustion of Administrative Remedies

Another timing requirement that conditions the availability of judicial review and when a claim is brought, one with both common law and statutory variations, is exhaustion of administrative remedies. The doctrine of exhaustion of remedies requires a party that would seek judicial relief to press its claim first before the agency that has taken the action the party wants to challenge. In other words, the

---

67. The classic formulation is found in the companion cases *Abbott Laboratories v. Gardner*, 387 U.S. 136, 149 (1967), and *Toilet Goods Ass'n v. Gardner*, 387 U.S. 158, 162 (1967). Here yet again, while ripeness is frequently understood as a prudential doctrine, courts have sometimes formulated ripeness as an aspect of Article III. For helpful treatment of the status of ripeness in environmental case law, see Nora Coon, *Ripening Green Litigation: The Case for Deconstitutionalizing Ripeness in Environmental Law*, 45 ENVTL. L. 811 (2015). And for the case that mootness should not be understood as a constitutional doctrine, see Evan T. Lee, *Deconstitutionalizing Justiciability: The Example of Mootness*, 105 HARV. L. REV. 605 (1992).

68. Here again, *Friends of the Earth, Inc. v. Laidlaw Environmental Services* is illustrative. 528 U.S. 167, 193 (2000). There, the defendant began to comply with a wastewater discharge permit after an environmental group filed a citizen suit. The Court held the case not to be moot, as it presented a "disputed factual matter" that could affect the defendant's future behavior. *Id.* at 193–94.

party must exercise all options available within the agency in question to contest or appeal the agency's decision. As with the ripeness doctrine and the condition of finality, the exhaustion requirement also seeks to preserve judicial review for instances where judicial review would be meaningful and not wasteful. For parties that have not yet exhausted available administrative remedies, there remains the possibility that they might find relief by appealing their grievance administratively, rendering judicial review unnecessary. When imposing the requirement that parties exhaust available administrative remedies, courts have emphasized other purposes of this requirement as well, including giving agencies a chance to correct their own mistakes, and comity between the judicial and executive branches.

While courts may impose this requirement on their own, many environmental statutes and regulations establish independent exhaustion requirements. In some contexts, parties are required to exhaust statutorily imposed exhaustion, but the government can expressly or impliedly "waive" that requirement either through its actions or by failing to raise exhaustion as an objection to a judicial challenge of an agency's action.[69] In other contexts, however, Congress has conditioned subject-matter jurisdiction on the challenging party having first exhausted administrative remedies.[70] In those settings, jurisdiction and exhaustion overlap, illustrating once again that the requirements of judicial review—presented separately here in the interest of exposition—are often interconnected. And the distinction between jurisdictional and nonjurisdictional statutory exhaustion carries practical significance as well. For where federal courts lack jurisdiction, the agency cannot confer jurisdiction, and thus jurisdictional exhaustion cannot be forgiven by an agency's express or inadvertent waiver of the requirement.[71]

One prominent example of the exhaustion requirement in environmental cases is the requirement under EPA regulations that certain permits under the CAA, CWA, and RCRA be appealed to EPA's Environmental Appeals Board before being challenged in court.[72] In addition, the CAA provides that only an objection that was raised with reasonable specificity during the public comment period can be raised during judicial review of certain regulations.[73] It further provides that if the party can demonstrate that it was impracticable to raise the objection during the comment period or the grounds for the objection arose after the comment period

---

69. *See, e.g.*, Mathews v. Eldridge, 424 U.S. 319, 330 (1976).

70. *E.g.*, Woodford v. Ngo, 548 U.S. 81, 87–88 (2006).

71. Finally, while the exhaustion doctrine focuses in large part on when a party challenging an agency decision may do so—that is, *after* having presented its claim to the agency—there is a procedural dimension to judicially required exhaustion, especially for parties who want to challenge agency rulemakings. For there, courts have at times imposed an "issue exhaustion" requirement, which prevents parties in the context of a rulemaking challenge from pressing objections not raised during notice and comment. *E.g.*, Dep't of Transp. v. Pub. Citizen, 541 U.S. 752, 764–65 (2004) (challenge to adequacy of environmental assessment forfeited by not raising objections during public comment process). For a helpful review of issue exhaustion and its applicability, see Jeffrey Lubbers, *Fail to Comment at Your Own Risk: Does Issue Exhaustion Have a Place in Judicial Review of Rules?*, 70 ADMIN. L. REV. 109 (2018).

72. *See* 40 C.F.R. § 124.19(l)(1) (2012).

73. CAA § 307, 42 U.S.C. § 7607(d)(7)(B) (2015).

(but within the deadline for filing a court challenge), and the objection is of central relevance to the rule, EPA must convene a proceeding to reconsider the rule.[74] The final outcome of such reconsideration proceedings—whether denial of reconsideration or a supplemental rulemaking to amend the underlying rule—are then independently subject to judicial review.

D. Where: The Appropriate Forum for a Judicial Challenge

This leaves the question of where a challenge satisfying all of the preceding requirements is properly brought. Here again, the APA provides a starting point, complemented or altered as the case may be by more specific provisions prescribed by statute. In the absence of a statute-specific provision, APA Section 703 allows for judicial review in any court "of competent jurisdiction," absent a "special statutory review proceeding."[75] The venue statute generally applicable to suits against federal government agencies (in the form of official capacity suits against agency officers) provides for suits in any judicial district where the defendant resides or the claim arises or any relevant real property is situated or, if no real property is involved, where the plaintiff resides.[76]

Where to file a challenge to agency action may present a question not just of venue but—centrally—of jurisdiction. For as noted previously, most of the environmental statutes confer jurisdiction on particular courts to hear challenges to certain agency actions, such as the federal courts of appeals in general or the D.C. Circuit in particular. Unfortunately, sometimes that very issue is not itself clear. One compelling illustration of the potential complexity of forum-specific jurisdictional provisions is the litigation surrounding the 2015 Clean Water Rule promulgated jointly by EPA and the U.S. Army Corps of Engineers, which defined the scope of "waters of the United States" subject to regulation under the CWA.[77] CWA Section 509(b)(1) identifies seven categories of EPA actions, challenges to which are properly brought in the courts of appeals.[78] Other actions must instead be challenged under the APA in federal district court. Many parties challenged the Clean Water Rule in both district courts and courts of appeals, reflecting uncertainty over whether the rule fell within the purview of Section 509(b)(1). The Sixth Circuit requested briefing and heard argument on the question of its jurisdiction, issuing a decision in February 2016.[79] The three-judge panel found that Section 509(b)(1) applied and

---

74. *Id.*

75. 5 U.S.C. § 703.

76. 28 U.S.C. § 1391(e).

77. The Clean Water Rule updated the regulatory definition of "waters of the United States," which determines the scope of waters (including wetlands) subject to regulation under the CWA. *See* Clean Water Rule: Definition of "Waters of the United States," 80 Fed. Reg. 37,054 (June 29, 2015). In July 2017, EPA and the U.S. Army Corps of Engineers proposed to rescind the rule and "recodify" the preexisting definition. Definition of "Waters of the United States"—Recodification of Pre-Existing Rule, 82 Fed. Reg. 34,899 (July 26, 2017).

78. CWA § 509, 33 U.S.C. § 1369 (2011).

79. Murray Energy Corp. v. U.S. Dep't of Def., 817 F.3d 261 (6th Cir. 2016).

it therefore had jurisdiction, but it did so on a fractured 1–1–1 basis.[80] Industry challengers to the rule petitioned the Supreme Court for a writ of certiorari on the jurisdictional issue, and the Court granted review. In January 2018, in *National Ass'n of Manufacturers v. Department of Defense*, the Supreme Court reversed, holding in a unanimous decision that the rule did not fall within the purview of Section 509(b)(1) and, as a result, the district courts had jurisdiction over any challenges to the rule.[81]

FIFRA—which authorizes EPA to regulate the distribution, sale, and use of pesticides, and to issue licenses or "registrations" for pesticides that EPA determines may be sold—provides another useful example. FIFRA provides for district court jurisdiction over challenges to EPA's refusal to cancel or suspend a pesticide registration if EPA's refusal did not follow a "hearing" on the issue.[82] FIFRA further provides, though, for "exclusive jurisdiction" in the courts of appeals over claims challenging a decision by EPA made "following a public hearing."[83] In other words, whether the federal district or the courts of appeals have jurisdiction over certain FIFRA claims depends on the administrative posture of the agency's decision (that is, whether or not the decision followed a hearing). In a recent case against EPA, the D.C. Circuit held that FIFRA's jurisdictional provisions requiring review in the courts of appeals of EPA decisions following a hearing required dismissal of the same challengers' separate district court action under the ESA.[84] In what the court characterized as the "dueling jurisdictional provisions of the ESA and of FIFRA," the more specific provisions of FIFRA trump.[85]

In addition to allocating jurisdiction between the district courts and the courts of appeals, the judicial review provisions of most environmental statutes also establish the appropriate venue for challenges—that is, *which* district court or court of appeals is the appropriate forum in which to file the challenge, often based on the residence of the plaintiff or petitioner and/or the location of activity affected by the challenged action.[86] The CAA, for example, provides for exclusive jurisdiction in the U.S. Court of Appeals for the D.C. Circuit for challenges to specified types of regulations and "any other nationally applicable regulations promulgated" under the CAA—while directing challenges to certain specified actions and actions that are "locally or regionally applicable" to the court of appeals for the "appropriate circuit." To make things more complicated, even actions that would otherwise go to one of the other courts of appeals may be challenged in the D.C. Circuit if EPA's action is "based on a determination of nationwide scope or effect"

---

80. *Id.*
81. 138 S. Ct. 617 (2018).
82. FIFRA § 16, 7 U.S.C. § 136n(a) (2016).
83. *Id.* § 136n(b).
84. Ctr. for Biological Diversity v. EPA, 861 F.3d 174, 188 (D.C. Cir. 2017).
85. *Id.* at 185–88.
86. *See, e.g.*, 33 U.S.C. § 1369(b)(1) (2011) (CWA provision directing review to the courts of appeals for the federal district in which the petitioner "resides or transacts business which is directly affected by" the challenged action).

and EPA, in taking the action, publishes a determination to that effect.[87] Several recent court decisions have held that this provision grants *jurisdiction* generally to the courts of appeals, while allocating *venue* among the D.C. Circuit and the other courts of appeals; and these decisions have addressed which is the appropriate forum in which to challenge particular actions.[88]

IV. CLAIMS AND STANDARDS OF JUDICIAL REVIEW

When preparing substantive challenges to agency environmental actions, two closely related considerations are critical: (1) what types of claims are available, and (2) what are the applicable standards of review. The APA establishes the default standards of review and types of claims applicable to challenges to agency action, but many environmental statutes also address these issues. And here too, when such an organic statute contains judicial review provisions or otherwise disavows the APA's provisions, the organic statute's provisions control. Often, however, the standards and claims set forth in environmental statutes largely mirror the standards in the APA.[89] The APA thus provides a useful starting point when considering a challenge to agency action.

The APA authorizes reviewing courts to "compel agency action unlawfully withheld or unreasonably delayed" and to "hold unlawful and set aside agency action, findings, and conclusions found to be—(A) arbitrary, capricious, an abuse of discretion, or otherwise not in accordance with law; (B) contrary to constitutional right, power, privilege, or immunity; (C) in excess of statutory jurisdiction, authority, or limitations, or short of statutory right; [or] (D) without observance of procedure required by law. . . ."[90] This core provision suggests a framework for the range of different types of claims available to parties challenging agency actions—including challenges to an agency's legal interpretations (both of authorizing statutes and regulations), challenges to policy and factual determinations, constitutional claims, claims of procedural violations, and claims that the agency

---

87. CAA § 307, 42 U.S.C. § 7607(b)(1) (2011).

88. *See, e.g.*, Texas v. EPA, 829 F.3d 405, 418 (5th Cir. 2016) (distinguishing the jurisdictional and venue aspect of the provision and holding that the action challenged in that case was "locally or regionally applicable"); Dalton Trucking, Inc. v. EPA, 808 F.3d 875, 879, 882 (D.C. Cir. 2015) (distinguishing the jurisdictional and venue aspects of the provision and holding that EPA's CAA waiver decision was not properly challenged in the D.C. Circuit because EPA had not published a determination that it was of "nationwide scope or effect").

89. *See, e.g.*, 42 U.S.C. § 7607(d)(9)(A) (2011) ("In the case of review of any action of the Administrator to which this subsection applies, the court may reverse any such action found to be arbitrary, capricious, an abuse of discretion, or otherwise not in accordance with law. . . ."); 42 U.S.C. § 9613(j)(2) (2000) ("In considering objections raised in any judicial action under [CERCLA], the court shall uphold the President's decision in selecting the response action unless the objecting party can demonstrate, on the administrative record, that the decision was arbitrary and capricious or otherwise not in accordance with law.").

90. 5 U.S.C. § 706 (2012).

has failed to undertake a nondiscretionary duty under the law. As set forth in the following, distinct standards of review apply to each of these types of claims.

A. Challenging Agency Legal Interpretations

1. Interpretation of a Statute

Environmental litigation often centers on whether an agency's reading of a statute is permissible. As a result, the degree of deference a court must give to an agency's statutory interpretation plays a critical role in many challenges to agency action. The seminal case addressing the appropriate standard of review is *Chevron U.S.A., Inc. v. Natural Resources Defense Council*,[91] in which the Supreme Court considered "whether EPA's decision to allow States to treat all the pollution-emitting devices within the same industrial grouping as though they were encased within a single bubble" was "based on a reasonable construction of the statutory term 'stationary source'" in the CAA.[92]

To answer that question, the Court had to decide whether, and to what extent, EPA's interpretation of "stationary source" merited deference. The Court concluded that in situations where "Congress has directly spoken to the precise question at issue," no deference is warranted because "the court, as well as the agency, must give effect to the unambiguously expressed intent of Congress."[93] But where "the statute is silent or ambiguous with respect to the specific issue, the question for the court" is not whether the agency's interpretation is right but whether it "is based on a permissible construction of the statute."[94] Following *Chevron*, courts assessing an agency's statutory interpretation engage in a two-step analysis, first determining whether the statutory text is clear and, if it is not, then determining whether the agency's interpretation is reasonable.[95]

Since *Chevron*, the Supreme Court has revised, refined, and narrowed the doctrine's reach. Environmental law, in particular, has provided the Court with numerous opportunities to weigh in on *Chevron*'s application. A walk through the Court's more recent notable decisions highlights the most fertile ground for challenges going forward.

In *Massachusetts v. EPA*, the statutory language at issue was the CAA's requirement that EPA promulgate "standards applicable to the emission of any air pollutant from any class or classes of new motor vehicles or new motor vehicle engines, which in [its] judgment cause, or contribute to, air pollution which may reasonably be anticipated to endanger public health or welfare."[96] A group of states, local

---

91. 467 U.S. 837 (1984).
92. *Id.* at 840.
93. *Id.* at 842–43.
94. *Id.* at 843.
95. *See, e.g.*, Catskill Mountains Chapter of Trout Unlimited v. EPA, 846 F.3d 492, 506–08 (2d Cir. 2017); U.S. Sugar Corp. v. EPA, 830 F.3d 579, 605–06 (D.C. Cir. 2016).
96. 42 U.S.C. § 7521(a)(1); Massachusetts v. EPA, 549 U.S. 497, 528 (2007).

governments, and private organizations challenged EPA's denial of their rulemaking petition, which was based on its conclusion that it did not have authority to regulate greenhouse gas emissions because they are not "air pollutants."[97] When reviewing that challenge, the Supreme Court first noted the "extremely limited" and "highly deferential" review applicable to an agency's refusal to promulgate a rule.[98] Such review is limited, the Court explained, because "an agency has broad discretion to choose how best to marshal its limited resources and personnel to carry out its delegated responsibilities."[99] The Court nevertheless rejected EPA's position, concluding that "[t]he statutory text foreclose[d] EPA's reading."[100] According to the Court, the CAA's "sweeping definition of 'air pollutant' . . . embraces all airborne compounds of whatever stripe."[101] But that was the view of only five justices. The other four justices viewed EPA's interpretation of the statute as both "reasonable" and "the most natural reading of the text," thereby meriting deference.[102]

Less than ten years later, in *Utility Air Regulatory Group v. EPA* (hereafter *UARG*),[103] the Supreme Court again considered EPA's interpretation of "air pollutant" in the CAA, this time reviewing EPA's conclusion that the Act's reference to "any air pollutant" triggered permitting requirements for stationary sources that emit greenhouse gases. With the four *Massachusetts* dissenting justices now in the majority, the Court cautioned that "[e]ven under *Chevron*'s deferential framework, agencies must operate within the bounds of reasonable interpretation."[104] And, the Court went on, "reasonable statutory interpretation must account for both the specific context in which language is used and the broader context of the statute as a whole."[105] "Thus," the Court concluded, "an agency interpretation that is inconsistent with the design and structure of the statute as a whole does not merit deference."[106]

The Court went on to conclude that EPA's interpretation was inconsistent with the design and structure of the CAA and thus did not merit deference. "*Massachusetts*," the Court explained, "does not foreclose the Agency's use of statutory context to infer that certain of the Act's provisions use 'air pollutant' to denote not every conceivable airborne substance, but only those that may sensibly be encompassed within the particular regulatory program."[107] EPA was therefore "mistaken in thinking the Act *compelled* a greenhouse-gas-inclusive interpretation" of the

---

97. *Massachusetts*, 549 U.S. at 505–06, 513.
98. *Id.* at 527–28.
99. *Id.* at 527.
100. *Id.* at 528.
101. *Id.* at 528–29.
102. *Id.* at 552–53 (Scalia, J., dissenting, joined by Roberts, C.J., and Thomas and Alito, JJ.).
103. 134 S. Ct. 2427, 2434 (2014).
104. *Id.* at 2442 (citation omitted).
105. *Id.* (citation omitted).
106. *Id.* (citation omitted).
107. *Id.* at 2441.

permitting requirements.[108] In the Court's view, the Act was unambiguous and EPA was simply wrong. Two factors, in particular, led the Court to conclude that EPA's interpretation was incorrect: (1) EPA's interpretation placed "plainly excessive demands on limited governmental resources"—which was reason enough to reject EPA's interpretation, and (2) EPA's interpretation brought about "an enormous and transformative expansion in EPA's regulatory authority without clear congressional authorization."[109] As in *Massachusetts*, however, this view commanded the votes of only five justices, with four others believing that EPA's interpretation was entitled to deference under *Chevron*.[110]

An important lesson from both *Massachusetts* and *UARG* is that there is almost always value in arguing that the statutory text an agency is interpreting is clear and unambiguous. As both cases show, what is clear to one judge or justice may be ambiguous to another. And since it is much harder to prevail at the second step of *Chevron*, as noted in the following, it is important to try to avoid getting to that step by arguing that the statute is clear. The cases also suggest that if a court is convinced that an agency's interpretation is incorrect, it can likely find a way to conclude that the statutory language is clear, even if that conclusion is open to debate.

The D.C. Circuit's recent decision in *Mexichem Fluor, Inc. v. EPA*[111] is illustrative. The statutory language at issue was the CAA's requirement that manufacturers "replace" ozone-depleting substances with safe substances.[112] EPA interpreted that requirement as imposing a continual replacement obligation, allowing EPA to mandate the replacement of non-ozone-depleting substances if those substances are later deemed problematic.[113] The D.C. Circuit rejected EPA's interpretation, concluding that EPA's interpretation stretched the statute "beyond its ordinary meaning."[114] But here, too, only two of the three judges believed that the statute was clear, with the third believing that *Chevron* deference applied.[115] Perhaps contributing to this disagreement was the majority's concern that EPA's interpretation reflected a change in the agency's long-standing position and would give EPA "indefinite authority to regulate a manufacturer's use" of replacement substances, which the court described as a "boundless interpretation of EPA's authority" under the statute.[116] *Mexichem* reinforces that even when arguing that a statute is unambiguous and the agency's interpretation is wrong in light of the statutory text, it is equally important to show why the agency's interpretation leads to untenable

---

108. *Id.* at 2442.
109. *Id.* at 2444.
110. *Id.* at 2453 (Breyer, J., dissenting, joined by Ginsburg, Sotomayor, and Kagan, JJ.) (observing that EPA was "exercising the legal authority to which it is entitled under *Chevron*").
111. 866 F.3d 451 (D.C. Cir. 2017).
112. *Id.* at 453 (citing 42 U.S.C. § 7671k (2011)).
113. *Id.* at 454.
114. *Id.* at 458.
115. *Id.* at 464–65 (Wilkins, J., dissenting).
116. *Id.* at 459.

results. A court uncomfortable with the implications of an agency's statutory interpretation will often find a way to conclude that the text requires a different result.

When a court proceeds to step two of the *Chevron* analysis, agencies almost always win. From 2003 through 2013, agencies won 93.8 percent of the time in cases where the court concluded that the statute was ambiguous and the only question was whether the agency's interpretation was reasonable (*Chevron*'s step two).[117] In contrast, agencies won only 39 percent of the time in cases where the court concluded that the statutory text was unambiguous (*Chevron*'s step one).[118] These statistics indicate that successfully challenging an agency's statutory interpretation usually requires convincing a court that the statute is clear and clearly shows that the agency is wrong.

In contrast to *Massachusetts*, *UARG*, and *Mexichem*, EPA's statutory interpretation survived judicial scrutiny in *EPA v. EME Homer City Generation, L.P.*[119] There, several states, along with industry and labor groups, petitioned for review of EPA's Transport Rule, which required 27 states to reduce their emissions of nitrogen oxide and sulfur dioxide because those emissions traveled downwind to other states.[120] In particular, they challenged EPA's interpretation of the "Good Neighbor" provision in the CAA. The Court concluded that *Chevron* deference applied: "[T]he Good Neighbor provision delegates authority to EPA at least as certainly as the CAA provisions involved in *Chevron*."[121] In light of that delegation, the only question that remained was whether EPA's interpretation was permissible—and, in the Court's view, it was. In so concluding, however, the Court made two notable observations. First, the Court stated that "EPA must have leeway in fulfilling its statutory mandate."[122] Although the Court made that comment in reference to the agency's need to balance possible undercontrol and overcontrol of emissions, one can imagine arguments for agency leeway reaching far beyond this context. Second, the Court observed: "The possibility that the rule, in uncommon particular applications, might exceed EPA's statutory authority, does not warrant judicial condemnation of the rule in its entirety."[123] Parties challenging agency action would be well advised to keep in mind this seeming invitation to as-applied challenges, especially in situations where the problematic application of an agency rule is discrete and likely atypical.

Though deferential, the second step of the *Chevron* analysis is not toothless. *Michigan v. EPA*[124] provides an example of an agency loss at step two. The question before the Court was whether EPA unreasonably interpreted the CAA when

---

117. Kent H. Barnett & Christopher J. Walker, *Chevron Step Two's Domain*, 93 Notre Dame L. Rev. 1441, 1444 (2017).
118. *Id.*
119. 134 S. Ct. 1584 (2014).
120. *Id.* at 1598.
121. *Id.* at 1603.
122. *Id.* at 1609.
123. *Id.* at 1609.
124. 135 S. Ct. 2699 (2015).

it deemed cost irrelevant to its decision that it was "appropriate and necessary" (CAA Section 112) to regulate power plant mercury emissions.[125] The Court concluded that it did. *Chevron*, the Court explained, "allows agencies to choose among competing reasonable interpretations of a statute; it does not license interpretive gerrymanders under which an agency keeps parts of statutory context it likes while throwing away parts it does not."[126] And, in the Court's view, the Act required EPA to "consider cost . . . before deciding whether regulation is appropriate and necessary."[127] EPA's contrary conclusion was thus "unreasonabl[e]."[128] Although purportedly a step two case, it could easily have been written as a step one decision. The Court seemed to think that the statute was clear and that EPA was clearly wrong.

In his concurring opinion, Justice Thomas used the *Michigan* decision to more broadly call into question the propriety of *Chevron*.[129] In so doing, he joined a growing number of "judges, policymakers, and scholars" who "have advocated for eliminating or narrowing *Chevron* deference."[130] More recently, for example, Judge Janice Rogers Brown of the D.C. Circuit wrote separately in *Waterkeeper Alliance v. EPA*[131] to express her concern that courts' deference under *Chevron* has led to an abdication of the judicial role.[132] Justice Gorsuch, while a judge on the Tenth Circuit, likewise aired his concerns about *Chevron* deference, observing that "[f]or whatever the *agency* may be doing under *Chevron*, the problem remains that *courts* are not fulfilling their duty to interpret the law."[133] And just before he retired, Justice Kennedy penned a concurrence in *Pereira v. Sessions* "to note [his] concern with the way in which the Court's opinion in *Chevron* . . . has come to be understood and applied."[134]

An important constraint on *Chevron*'s application came in the Supreme Court's 2001 *United States v. Mead Corp.* decision.[135] Sometimes referred to as establishing "step zero" in the *Chevron* analysis, *Mead* held that *Chevron* applies only if Congress delegated interpretive authority to the agency with respect to the provision at issue and the agency approached its decision with a "lawmaking pretense."[136] Although *Mead* made clear that *Chevron* applies to agency interpretations beyond

125. *Id.* at 2704; *see also* 42 U.S.C. § 7412 (2009).
126. *Id.* at 2707.
127. *Id.* at 2711.
128. *Id.* at 2712.
129. *See, e.g., id.* at 2713 ("These cases bring into bold relief the scope of the potentially unconstitutional delegations we have come to countenance in the name of *Chevron* deference.").
130. Barnett & Walker, *supra* note 117, at 1441.
131. 853 F.3d 527 (D.C. Cir. 2017).
132. *See, e.g.*, 853 F.3d at 539 ("[I]f *Chevron*'s two-step inquiry can be collapsed into one 'reasonableness' inquiry no different than current Step Two jurisprudence, there is yet another reason to question *Chevron*'s consistency with 'the judicial department['s]' 'emphatic[]' 'province and duty . . . to say what the law is.'") (quoting Marbury v. Madison, 5 U.S. 137, 177 (1803)).
133. Gutierrez-Brizuela v. Lynch, 834 F.3d 1142, 1152–53 (10th Cir. 2016) (Gorsuch, J., concurring).
134. 135 S. Ct. 2105, 2120 (2018).
135. 533 U.S. 218 (2001).
136. *Id.* at 226–27, 233.

those following from a formal adjudication or notice-and-comment rulemaking, the Court did not specify the outer limits of *Chevron*'s reach. Instead, it left it to courts to assess Congress's intent, observing that it can "be apparent from the agency's generally conferred authority and other statutory circumstances that Congress would expect the agency to be able to speak with the force of law when it addresses ambiguity in the statute or fills a space in the enacted law."[137] On the other hand, as the Court has said more recently, "[i]n extraordinary cases, . . . there may be reason to hesitate before concluding that Congress has intended" to implicitly delegate gap-filling authority to the agency.[138] Thus, when an agency's statutory interpretation goes to the heart of a legislative scheme—especially where the interpretation is outside of the agency's area of expertise—parties may wish to consider arguing that *Chevron* has no role to play.

2. Interpretation of a Regulation

Many environmental cases involve an agency's interpretation of its own regulations. The Supreme Court's decisions in *Bowles v. Seminole Rock & Sand Co.*[139] and *Auer v. Robbins*[140] establish that such an interpretation is entitled to significant deference and is controlling unless "plainly erroneous or inconsistent with the regulation."[141] *Auer* also makes clear that, while an agency's post hoc rationalization of an interpretation will not carry the day, an agency's interpretation in a legal brief can warrant deference if it "reflect[s] the agency's fair and considered judgment on the matter in question."[142]

In *Decker v. Northwest Environmental Defense Center*,[143] the Supreme Court had occasion to apply *Auer* to an EPA interpretation. There, the petitioner filed suit under the CWA's citizen-suit provision,[144] alleging that the defendants—firms involved in logging and paper-products operations—did not obtain the permits required under EPA's CWA regulations for the discharge of stormwater runoff.[145] EPA, however, interpreted its permitting regulation to exclude the type of stormwater discharges produced by the defendants.[146] And that interpretation, the Court concluded, was entitled to deference because it was "a permissible one."[147] "[A]n agency's interpretation," the Court observed, "need not be the only possible reading of a regulation—or even the best one—to prevail."[148] Deference under *Auer* was appropriate, the Court concluded, because EPA's interpretation was rational in

---

137. *Id.* at 229.
138. King v. Burwell, 135 S. Ct. 2480, 2488–89 (2015) (citation omitted).
139. 325 U.S. 410 (1945).
140. 519 U.S. 452 (1997).
141. *Id.* at 461 (citation omitted).
142. *Id.* at 462.
143. 568 U.S. 597 (2013).
144. 33 U.S.C. § 1365.
145. 568 U.S. at 606.
146. *Id.* at 601.
147. *Id.* at 613.
148. *Id.*

light of the language used in the regulation, and there was no indication that EPA's current view was a change from prior practice or a post hoc justification adopted in response to litigation.[149]

While an agency's interpretation of its regulation is ordinarily entitled to deference, an agency cannot avoid complying with a regulation based on an untenable interpretation. In *National Environmental Development Ass'n's Clean Air Project v. EPA*,[150] for example, the D.C. Circuit confronted EPA's response to an adverse decision by the Sixth Circuit regarding CAA standards. To account for the adverse decision, EPA issued a directive requiring a different approach to the relevant standards in those areas covered by the Sixth Circuit.[151] The problem for EPA, however, was that separate EPA regulations require regional consistency in the enforcement of the CAA.[152] The court found unconvincing EPA's attempt to argue that the regional consistency regulations did not in fact require consistency across the United States. Deference, the court noted, is required "unless an alternative reading is compelled by the regulation's plain language or by other indications of the [agency's] intent at the time of the regulation's promulgation."[153] And here, the plain language of the regional consistency regulations prohibited EPA from adopting different standards in one region of the country, rendering its decision to do so arbitrary and capricious.[154] The D.C. Circuit therefore vacated EPA's directive.[155]

B. Challenging Agency Policy and Factual Determinations

1. Arbitrary-and-Capricious Review

Agencies make factual findings and policy determinations in a variety of contexts. Unless an agency's factual findings are made during a formal adjudication, those findings—along with the agency's policy determinations and discretionary judgments—are generally subject to review under the APA's arbitrary-and-capricious standard. Under that standard, an agency's action "must be set aside if the action was 'arbitrary, capricious, an abuse of discretion, or otherwise not in accordance

---

149. Some recent opinions have called *Auer*'s vitality into question. In *Decker*, Chief Justice Roberts authored a concurrence, joined by Justice Alito, in which he invited challenges to the doctrine by noting that "it may be appropriate to reconsider th[e] principle [set forth in *Seminole Rock* and *Auer*] in an appropriate case." 568 U.S. at 615. He went on to observe that "[t]he bar is now aware that there is some interest in reconsidering those cases, and has available to it a concise statement of the arguments on one side of the issue." *Id.* at 616. That statement came in the form of Justice Scalia's concurrence and dissent, in which he detailed the reasons why, in his view, *Auer* should be overruled. *See, e.g., id.* at 621 ("In any case, however great may be the efficiency gains derived from *Auer* deference, beneficial effect cannot justify a rule that not only has no principled basis but contravenes one of the great rules of separation of powers: He who writes a law must not adjudge its violation.").

150. 752 F.3d 999 (D.C. Cir. 2014).

151. *Id.* at 1003.

152. *Id.* at 1004 (citing 40 C.F.R. § 56.3(a), (b) (2012)).

153. *Id.* at 1008 (quoting Thomas Jefferson Univ. v. Shalala, 512 U.S. 504, 512 (1994)).

154. *Id.* at 1011.

155. *Id.*

with law.'"[156] As a result, any agency action subject to the APA or a comparable organic statute can be challenged as arbitrary and capricious, and such claims are a standard method of challenging agency rules and policy determinations.

In *Motor Vehicle Manufacturers Ass'n of the United States v. State Farm Mutual Automobile Insurance Co.*,[157] the Supreme Court famously set forth the standard courts use to determine whether an agency action is arbitrary and capricious. "The scope of review under the 'arbitrary and capricious' standard," the Court explained, "is narrow and a court is not to substitute its judgment for that of the agency."[158] Despite that narrowness, agencies must still "examine the relevant data and articulate a satisfactory explanation for its action including a rational connection between the facts found and the choice made."[159] And courts reviewing that explanation "must consider whether the decision was based on a consideration of the relevant factors and whether there has been a clear error of judgment."[160] "Normally, an agency rule would be arbitrary and capricious if the agency has relied on factors which Congress has not intended it to consider, entirely failed to consider an important aspect of the problem, offered an explanation for its decision that runs counter to the evidence before the agency, or is so implausible that it could not be ascribed to a difference in view or the product of agency expertise."[161]

Following *State Farm*, courts reviewing agency actions to determine whether they are arbitrary and capricious tend to consider whether the agency: (1) provided a logical explanation for its decision; (2) considered the potential problems presented by its proposed action; (3) explained any departure from past practice; (4) considered important alternative solutions to the problem being addressed; and (5) considered and addressed relevant and significant comments regarding the proposed action.[162]

Even when undertaking arbitrary-and-capricious review, courts take care not to encroach on areas within an agency's expertise, especially in the environmental arena where scientific evidence abounds.[163] In *Coalition for Responsible Regulation v. EPA*,[164] for example, states and regulated industries filed petitions for review of EPA's greenhouse gas regulations, challenging EPA's determination that greenhouse gases may "reasonably be anticipated to endanger public health or welfare."[165] In response, the court first recounted the exceedingly narrow nature

---

156. Citizens to Pres. Overton Park, Inc. v. Volpe, 401 U.S. 402, 414 (1971) (quoting 5 U.S.C. § 706(2)(A), (B), (C), (D) (2012)).

157. 463 U.S. 29 (1983).

158. *Id.* at 43.

159. *Id.* (citation omitted).

160. *Id.* (citation omitted).

161. *Id.*

162. *See, e.g.*, Del. Riverkeeper Network v. U.S. Army Corps of Eng'rs, 869 F.3d 148, 160–61 (3d Cir. 2017).

163. Balt. Gas & Elec. Co. v. Nat. Res. Def. Council, Inc., 462 U.S. 87, 103 (1983) ("When examining this kind of scientific determination . . . a reviewing court must generally be at its most deferential.").

164. 684 F.3d 102 (D.C. Cir. 2012), *aff'd in part, rev'd in part on other grounds sub nom.* Util. Air Regulatory Grp. v. EPA, 134 S. Ct. 2427 (2014).

165. *See* 42 U.S.C. § 7521(a)(1) (2011).

of its review: "[I]n reviewing the science-based decisions of agencies such as EPA, although we perform a searching and careful inquiry into the facts underlying the agency's decisions, we will presume the validity of agency action as long as a rational basis for it is presented."[166] "In so doing, [the court] give[s] an extreme degree of deference to the agency when it is evaluating scientific data within its technical expertise."[167] Applying that standard, the court refused to "re-weigh the scientific evidence before EPA," asking only whether EPA had taken the "scientific record into account in a rational manner."[168] The court concluded that EPA had.[169]

The deference EPA can often claim, however, does not insulate it from the need to provide a rational explanation for its decisions. In *American Petroleum Institute v. EPA*,[170] for instance, the D.C. Circuit vacated an EPA rule because of EPA's failure to provide a rational explanation. Although it may have been possible for EPA to reach the conclusion it did, the agency's failure to "engage[] in reasoned decision-making" required it to reconsider the issue.[171] *American Petroleum* also provides a good reminder that even if an agency's statutory interpretation is entitled to deference under *Chevron*, actions based on that interpretation must nevertheless be rationally explained in the record.[172]

Although an agency's change in policy is likewise subject to arbitrary-and-capricious review, when an agency changes policy, it often must often provide "a more detailed justification than what would suffice for a new policy created on a blank slate."[173] Such justification is required when a "new policy rests upon factual findings that contradict those which underlay [the agency's] prior policy" as well as "when its prior policy has engendered serious reliance interests that must be taken into account."[174] In such cases, "in order to offer a satisfactory explanation for its action, including a rational connection between the facts found and the choice made," courts require that agencies "give a reasoned explanation for disregarding the facts and circumstances that underlay or were engendered by the prior policy."[175]

2. Substantial Evidence

Whereas challenges to notice-and-comment rulemaking turn largely on arbitrary-and-capricious review, challenges to agency adjudications and formal rulemaking

---

166. 684 F.3d at 120 (citation omitted).

167. *Id.*

168. *Id.* at 122 (citation omitted).

169. *Id.*

170. 216 F.3d 50 (D.C. Cir. 2000).

171. *Id.* at 57.

172. *See id.* ("The second step of *Chevron* analysis and *State Farm* arbitrary-and-capricious review overlap, but are not identical."); *see also* Arent v. Shalala, 70 F.3d 610, 614–17 (D.C. Cir. 1995) (explaining the difference between a *Chevron* and arbitrary-and-capricious review).

173. FCC v. Fox Television Stations, Inc., 556 U.S. 502, 515 (2009).

174. *Id.*

175. Mingo Logan Coal Co. v. EPA, 829 F.3d 710, 719 (D.C. Cir. 2016) (internal quotation marks and citations omitted).

proceedings are subject to substantial-evidence review under the APA.[176] Several environmental statutes also prescribe this standard of review for challenges to specific agency actions. Under FIFRA, for example, a court reviewing EPA's decision to register a new pesticide is directed to uphold the agency's decision "if it is supported by substantial evidence when considered on the record as a whole."[177] And TSCA, as amended in 2016, provides that certain categories of final rules and orders under that statute must be set aside if "not supported by substantial evidence in the record taken as a whole."[178]

"Substantial evidence means more than a mere scintilla but less than a preponderance; it is such relevant evidence as a reasonable mind might accept as adequate to support a conclusion."[179] Under this standard, courts will affirm an agency's findings "where there is such relevant evidence as a reasonable mind might accept as adequate to support a conclusion even if it is possible to draw two inconsistent conclusions from the evidence."[180] The primary difference between substantial-evidence review and arbitrary-and-capricious review is that the former "is limited to evidence developed in formal hearings" or as part of the formal rulemaking process, while the latter "is not so limited, but rather may consider the agency's developed expertise and any evidence referenced by the agency or otherwise placed in the record."[181]

The Ninth Circuit's decision in *Natural Resources Defense Council v. EPA*[182] illustrates the threshold an agency must surpass to survive substantial-evidence review. At issue there was EPA's conditional registration, following public notice and comment, of the pesticide NSP-L30SS (NSPW).[183] To conditionally register a pesticide under FIFRA, EPA must find that "use of the pesticide is in the public interest."[184] The Natural Resources Defense Council (NRDC) challenged three of the factual findings underlying EPA's conclusion that use of NSPW was in the public interest.[185] The Ninth Circuit rejected NRDC's first two challenges, concluding that "EPA need not present evidence to support an outcome with certainty; it only needs to present such relevant evidence as a reasonable mind might accept as

---

176. 5 U.S.C. § 706(2)(E) (2012).

177. FIFRA § 2, 7 U.S.C. § 136n(b) (2016); *see also, e.g.,* Pollinator Stewardship Council v. EPA, 806 F.3d 520, 532–33 (9th Cir. 2015) (vacating and remanding EPA's registration of pesticide based on substantial-evidence review).

178. TSCA § 19, 15 U.S.C. § 2618(c) (2013).

179. Nat. Res. Def. Council v. EPA, 735 F.3d 873, 877 (9th Cir. 2013) (citation omitted).

180. Nat. Res. Def. Council v. EPA, 857 F.3d 1030, 1036 (9th Cir. 2017) (citation omitted); *see also* Epsilon Elecs., Inc. v. U.S. Dep't of Treas., Off. of Foreign Assets Control, 857 F.3d 913, 925 (D.C. Cir. 2017) (If the evidentiary threshold is met, courts "must uphold the agency's judgment regarding the relevant facts, even if [they] think the evidence tends to weigh against the agency's finding." (citation omitted)).

181. Ethyl Corp. v. EPA, 541 F.2d 1, 37 n.79 (D.C. Cir. 1976).

182. 857 F.3d 1030 (9th Cir. 2017).

183. *Id.* at 1034.

184. FIFRA § 3, 7 U.S.C. § 136a(c)(7)(C) (2012).

185. 857 F.3d at 1038–39.

adequate to support a conclusion."[186] The Ninth Circuit agreed with NRDC's third challenge because "EPA cite[d] no evidence in the record to support" the assumption that underlay its decision and instead argued in its brief that its assumption was correct "as a 'logical matter.'"[187] The court refused to "accept appellate counsel's post-hoc rationalizations for agency action,"[188] concluding that "where an essential premise of [an agency's] finding is only supported by bare assumptions, as in the present case, [the court] will find substantial evidence lacking."[189] *Natural Resources Defense Council v. EPA* shows that it takes more than an agency's arguments and claimed justifications to survive substantial-evidence review. Instead, when an agency's action is reviewed for substantial evidence, the agency must be able to point to specific material in the record and explain why that material supports its action.

C. Constitutional Claims

Agencies must of course also comply with the U.S. Constitution. The APA thus specifically provides that agency action will be set aside if it is "contrary to constitutional right, power, privilege, or immunity."[190] As a result, agency action is susceptible to constitutional challenges as well. For example, parties have used the Commerce Clause to challenge various environmental statutes, including CAA,[191] CWA,[192] the Endangered Species Act,[193] and CERCLA.[194] That said, such challenges are often unsuccessful, as the relevant constitutional terrain is by now generally well established. As a result, when pursuing a constitutional challenge, one should consider what other challenges to the agency action can be brought as well.

The Due Process Clause has also provided a basis for constitutional challenges to agency action. In *General Electric Co. v. Jackson*, for example, General Electric argued that the CERCLA provision allowing EPA to issue unilateral administrative orders (UAOs) directing the cleanup of hazardous waste violated the Due Process Clause because EPA issued the orders without a hearing before a neutral decision maker.[195] The D.C. Circuit rejected the challenge, concluding that "[t]o the extent the UAO regime implicates constitutionally protected property interests by imposing compliance costs and threatening fines and punitive damages, it satisfies due process because UAO recipients may obtain a pre-deprivation hearing by refusing to comply and forcing EPA to sue in federal court."[196] Environmental actions that

---

186. *Id.* (citation omitted).
187. *Id.* at 1040.
188. *Id.* (citation omitted).
189. *Id.* at 1042.
190. 5 U.S.C. § 706(2)(B) (2012).
191. *See, e.g.*, Allied Local & Reg'l Mfrs. Caucus v. EPA, 215 F.3d 61, 81 (D.C. Cir. 2000).
192. *See, e.g.*, United States v. Deaton, 332 F.3d 698, 702 (4th Cir. 2003).
193. *See, e.g.*, Rancho Viejo v. Norton, 323 F.3d 1062, 1066 (D.C. Cir. 2003).
194. *See, e.g.*, Freier v. Westinghouse Elec. Corp., 303 F.3d 176, 182 (2d Cir. 2002).
195. 610 F.3d 110, 113 (D.C. Cir. 2010).
196. *Id.*

limit a person's use of property can be subject to due process challenges as unconstitutional takings. In *Lucas v. South Carolina Coastal Council*, for example, the Supreme Court considered a takings challenge to a South Carolina law designed to protect the state's coasts because it prevented the petitioner "from erecting any permanent habitable structures on his" parcels of land.[197] The Court concluded that the challenge was ripe and sent the case back to the South Carolina Supreme Court, which awarded the landowner damages for the temporary taking effected by the law.[198]

D. Procedural Claims: Statutory and APA

The APA as well as many environmental statutes prescribe procedural requirements for agency decision making as well. Under the APA, if an agency fails to comply with such requirements, its action must be set aside. Following is a brief discussion of frequently litigated procedural requirements.

Notice and Comment. As explained previously in section II, when an agency adopts a "legislative" rule the APA requires that notice of the proposed rulemaking be published in the *Federal Register*, that the public be allowed to comment during a specified time period, and that the agency take into account the public's comments when promulgating the final rule.[199] There is, however, an exception to the notice-and-comment requirements for "good cause," which applies when compliance would be "impracticable, unnecessary, or contrary to the public interest."[200] Some environmental statutes, such as the CAA, provide their own requirements for formal rulemaking, but often those requirements largely mirror those in the APA.[201] Unless an organic statute contains a clear expression of congressional intent to depart from the APA's procedures, however, the APA applies.[202] Agencies have run afoul of notice-and-comment requirements by trying to take advantage of the "good cause" exception to the requirements where the exception does not apply,[203] by changing their practices in reliance on another agency's changed practices,[204] and by staying the effective date of an already-promulgated rule.[205]

Logical Outgrowth. When an agency's final regulation differs from the proposed regulation for which it provided notice and requested comment, the final rule

197. 505 U.S. 1003, 1007 (1992).

198. Lucas v. S.C. Coastal Council, 424 S.E.2d 484, 486 (S.C. 1992).

199. 5 U.S.C. § 553 (2012).

200. *Id.* § 553(b)(3)(B).

201. *See, e.g.*, 42 U.S.C. § 7607(d)(4) (2015) (CAA rulemaking requirements).

202. *See* Lake Carriers' Ass'n v. EPA, 652 F.3d 1, 6 (D.C. Cir. 2011); *see, e.g.*, 42 U.S.C. § 7607(d)(1)(V) (2015) ("The provisions of section 553 through 557 and section 706 of Title 5 of the United States Code shall not, except as expressly provided in this subsection, apply to actions to which this subsection applies.").

203. Union of Concerned Scientists v. Nuclear Regulatory Comm'n, 711 F.2d 370, 382–83 (D.C. Cir. 1983).

204. City of Idaho Falls, Idaho v. F.E.R.C., 629 F.3d 222, 230 (D.C. Cir. 2011).

205. Envtl. Def. Fund, Inc. v. Gorsuch, 713 F.2d 802, 804 (D.C. Cir. 1983); *see generally* Clean Air Council v. Pruitt, 862 F.3d 1, 6–7 (D.C. Cir. 2017).

must be a "logical outgrowth" of the proposed rule.[206] Otherwise, "affected parties w[ould] be deprived of notice and an opportunity to respond to the proposal."[207] The "logical outgrowth" test is thus applied to determine "whether a new round of notice and comment would provide the *first* opportunity for interested parties to offer comments that could persuade the agency to modify its rule."[208] If so, a second round of comment is necessary.

A final rule is a logical outgrowth of a proposed rule if commenters "should have anticipated" the final rule based on the provided notice.[209] In *City of Portland, Oregon v. EPA*, for example, EPA proposed a rule that imposed different treatment requirements on potential drinking water.[210] Under the proposed rule, "source water"—the water from a river or lake that becomes drinking water—had to be treated for a microbial contaminant known as *Cryptosporidium*, whereas "finished water"—water that goes directly to consumers—only had to be treated for viruses.[211] In its final rule, EPA required that source water, as well as finished water stored in uncovered reservoirs, be treated for both viruses and *Cryptosporidium*.[212] The cities of Portland and New York, which used uncovered reservoirs, challenged the rule. They argued that EPA did not provide adequate opportunity for notice and comment because the proposed rule did not require treating finished water in uncovered reservoirs for *Cryptosporidium* and, as a result, they did not know they needed to comment on the safety of uncovered reservoirs.[213] The D.C. Circuit disagreed.[214] According to the court, "EPA made clear that it 'continue[d] to be concerned about contamination occurring in uncovered finished water storage facilities,'" including from *Cryptosporidium*, by seeking comments on whether uncovered reservoir water should be treated for *Cryptosporidium*.[215] The court concluded that EPA's notice was sufficient because the cities "should have known . . . that the final rule might require . . . treating [open reservoirs]" for *Cryptosporidium*.[216]

In contrast, the EPA final rule reviewed in *Daimler Trucks North America LLC v. EPA* did not survive the "logical outgrowth" test.[217] There, EPA's notice of proposed rulemaking said that it was considering changes to the rules governing the upper limits of emissions from heavy-duty motor vehicles, and the emission standards for nonconformance penalties, which allow engines to be used even if they

---

206. City of Waukesha v. EPA, 320 F.3d 228, 245 (D.C. Cir. 2003).
207. Small Refiner Lead Phase-Down Task Force v. EPA, 705 F.2d 506, 546–47 (D.C. Cir. 1983).
208. Ariz. Pub. Serv. Co. v. EPA, 211 F.3d 1280, 1299 (D.C. Cir. 2000).
209. *Id.*
210. 507 F.3d 706, 708–10 (D.C. Cir. 2007).
211. *Id.* at 710.
212. *Id.*
213. *Id.* at 715.
214. *Id.*
215. *Id.*
216. *Id.*
217. 737 F.3d 95 (D.C. Cir. 2013); *see also* Fertilizer Inst. v. EPA, 935 F.2d 1303 (D.C. Cir. 1991) (Regulation failed the "logical outgrowth" test because "EPA's notice was not sufficient to advise interested parties that comments directed to the [new regulation] . . . should be made.").

are temporarily unable to meet a new or revised emission standard.[218] In the final rule, however, EPA also changed one of the eligibility criteria for nonconformance penalties, the "substantial work" requirement.[219] When the rule was challenged, the court concluded that those covered by the rule could not have anticipated that change ex ante and, as a result, the new "substantial work" regulation did not satisfy the logical outgrowth test.[220]

Reopener. The reopener doctrine allows courts to review an agency action even if the applicable statute of limitations has otherwise expired. The doctrine is thus "an exception to statutory limits on the time for seeking review of an agency decision."[221] It provides that "[i]f for any reason the agency reopens a matter and, after reconsideration, issues a new and final order, that order is reviewable on its merits, even though the agency merely reaffirms its original decision."[222] "Whether an agency has in fact reopened an issue is dependent upon the entire context of the rulemaking including all relevant proposals and reactions of the agency."[223] An agency's response to a request to revise its existing regulations, for example, is not sufficient to trigger the reopener doctrine so long as the agency "gave no indication that it had undertaken a serious, substantive reconsideration of the rules in question."[224] But where an agency includes the preexisting regulation in a notice of proposed rulemaking and then responds to comments on the provisions later alleged to have been reopened, the reopener doctrine likely does apply.[225]

E. Challenges to Agency Inaction

Challenges to agency *inaction* play a major role in environmental litigation. The APA states that "within a reasonable time, each agency shall proceed to conclude a matter presented to it."[226] The APA also expressly defines the term "agency action" to include "failure to act"[227] and authorizes courts to "compel agency action unlawfully withheld or unreasonably delayed."[228] All of the major federal environmental statutes include directives requiring agency action, many with associated deadlines. Agencies frequently fail to comply with these directives and/or deadlines, however, which often leads to lawsuits intended to force action. Two general types

---

218. *Id.* at 96.

219. *Id.* at 100.

220. *Id.* at 103 ("EPA 'entirely failed' to provide notice of its intention to amend its regulation in the [notice of proposed rulemaking], and offered no persuasive evidence that possible objections to its final rule have been given sufficient consideration, instead treating its revision as a clarification rather than a substantive change.").

221. P & V Enters. v. U.S. Army Corps. of Eng'rs, 466 F. Supp. 2d 134, 144 (D.D.C. 2006), *aff'd*, 516 F.3d 1021 (D.C. Cir. 2008) (citation omitted).

222. 466 F. Supp. 3d at 144 (citation omitted).

223. Bluewater Network v. EPA, 370 F.3d 1, 16–17 (D.C. Cir. 2004) (citation omitted).

224. Am. Rd. & Transp. Builders Ass'n v. EPA, 588 F.3d 1109, 1115 (D.C. Cir. 2009) (citation omitted).

225. *See, e.g.*, Ohio v. EPA, 838 F.2d 1325, 1328 (D.C. Cir. 1988); Montana v. Clark, 749 F.2d 740, 744 (D.C. Cir. 1984).

226. 5 U.S.C. § 555(b) (2011).

227. 5 U.S.C. § 551(13) (2012).

228. 5 U.S.C. § 706(1) (2012).

of suits fall within this overall category of "mandatory duty" litigation: "deadline suits" involving claims that the agency has failed to undertake a nondiscretionary duty by a statutory deadline, and "unreasonable delay" suits, in which a plaintiff or petitioner alleges the agency has unreasonably delayed action that is not subject to a specific statutory deadline.

Several environmental statutes specifically authorize "mandatory duty" suits, and in many cases establish related procedural requirements, such as the filing of a "notice of intent" to sue 60 days prior to filing suit.[229] Virtually all deadline suits and many unreasonable delay suits are filed in the district courts, pursuant to the citizen-suit provisions of the relevant statute and/or the APA. As explained in section III.D., the D.C. Circuit and other courts of appeals have long recognized that "[w]here a statute commits final agency action to review by [the courts of appeals, those courts] also retain exclusive jurisdiction to hear suits seeking relief that might affect [their] future statutory power of review. This includes mandamus actions challenging an agency's unreasonable delay."[230]

Deadline Suits. Deadline suits are common under the CAA and CWA, for example, because of the extensive regime of deadlines and statutory triggers for action. Deadline suits are often resolved through settlement rather than litigation to judgment, because the statute typically clearly defines the agency's obligations and deadline and the agency may view a negotiated timetable for action as preferable to the risks and uncertainty associated with litigating to a court-imposed deadline.

Most of the major environmental statutes include provisions that require the agency periodically to review and, if appropriate, revise existing regulations.[231] Many also require federal agencies to take action within a specific time frame after receiving a specified submission—for example, to approve or disapprove a plan or other action submitted by a state or regulated entity. Parties have brought many suits against EPA over the years challenging failure to meet such deadlines, resulting in court-imposed deadlines for agency action.

Unreasonable Delay Suits. Unreasonable delay suits commonly arise in two scenarios. In one, the statute directs the agency to take a certain action but does not establish a specific deadline. In *In re Idaho Conservation League*, for example, the D.C. Circuit ordered EPA to issue financial assurance rules under CERCLA for the hardrock mining industry, and set deadlines for making final determinations as to

---

229. *See, e.g.*, CAA § 304, 42 U.S.C. § 7604(a), (b) (2011) (CAA citizen-suit provision (1) authorizes suits "against the Administrator where there is alleged a failure of the Administrator to perform any act or duty under [the CAA] which is not discretionary with the Administrator," (2) provides that the district suits shall have jurisdiction, and (3) requires a 60-day notice); CWA § 505, 33 U.S.C. § 1365 (2007) (CWA citizen-suit provision establishing similar requirements).

230. *In re* Bluewater Network, 234 F.3d 1305, 1310–11 (D.C. Cir. 2000) (citation omitted); *see also In re* Aiken Cnty., 645 F.3d 428, 436 (D.C. Cir. 2011); Telecomms. Research & Action Ctr. v. FCC, 750 F.2d 70, 78–79 (D.C. Cir. 1984).

231. The CAA, for example, requires EPA to review and if appropriate revise the National Ambient Air Quality Standards (NAAQS) every five years, 42 U.S.C. § 7409(d)(1) (2012), and to review and, if appropriate, revise New Source Performance Standards every eight years, 42 U.S.C. § 7411(b)(1)(B) (2011).

whether to issue such rules for three other industrial sectors.[232] Leading up to this order, the court noted that it had "been nearly thirty years since Congress charged EPA with issuing such rules" and "[t]here is a limit to how long a court will entertain an agency's excuses for its inaction in the face of a congressional command to act."[233]

A second scenario commonly giving rise to unreasonable delay suits is where an entity has filed a petition for rulemaking requesting a certain agency action and the agency has not yet responded. The APA authorizes "interested persons" to "petition for the issuance, amendment or repeal of a rule,"[234] but does not specify any deadline for a response. Several of the environmental statutes also provide citizens with opportunities to petition EPA for specific rulemaking actions.[235] Whereas the denial of such a petition is generally a final agency action subject to judicial review, an agency's failure to respond generally must be challenged through an unreasonable delay suit.

The D.C. Circuit, in *Telecommunications Research & Action Center v. FCC* (hereafter *TRAC*), identified factors commonly applied by courts in deciding whether an agency has unreasonably delayed, including: whether Congress in the enabling statute provided "a timetable or other indication of the speed with which it expects the agency to proceed"; "delays that might be reasonable in the sphere of economic regulation are less tolerable when human health and welfare are at stake"; "the effect of expediting delayed action on agency activities of a higher or competing priority"; and "the nature and extent of the interests prejudiced by the delay."[236]

The Ninth Circuit recently applied the *TRAC* factors in *In re A Community Voice*, holding that EPA had unreasonably delayed by failing to initiate a rulemaking to address standards applicable to dust-lead hazards in housing, eight years after having granted a nongovernmental organization's petition to do so.[237] The court catalogued the Ninth Circuit and D.C. Circuit case law addressing unreasonable

---

232. No. 14-1149, 2016 WL 374443 (Jan. 29, 2016).

233. *In re* Idaho Conservation League, No. 14-1149 (D.C. Cir. May 19, 2015) (per curiam) (citing *In re* United Mine Workers of Am. Int'l Union, 190 F.3d 545, 554 (D.C. Cir. 1999)).

234. 5 U.S.C. § 553(e) (2012).

235. EPA maintains a website compiling petitions for rulemaking received by the agency. *See* U.S. Envtl. Prot. Agency, Petitions for Rulemaking, https://www.epa.gov/aboutepa/petitions-rulemaking (last visited July 16, 2018).

236. 750 F.2d 70, 80 (D.C. Cir. 1984); *see also, e.g.,* Nat. Res. Def. Council, Inc. v. EPA, 798 F.3d 809, 813–15 (9th Cir. 2015) (applying *TRAC* factors to mandamus petition to require EPA to respond to an administrative petition requesting a ban on a pesticide).

237. *In re* A Cmty. Voice, 878 F.3d 779, 786–88 (9th Cir. 2017).

delay claims, highlighting several decisions in which delays of six years or more were found to constitute an unreasonable delay.[238]

F. A Note on Record Review

As a general matter, challenges to agency action are limited to the record developed before the agency.[239] That said, from time to time, courts do look outside the record in such cases. For example, in *San Luis & Delta-Mendota Water Authority v. Locke*, the Ninth Circuit explained that although "a court reviewing agency action under the APA must limit its review to the administrative record, . . . a reviewing court may consider extra-record evidence where admission of that evidence: (1) is necessary to determine whether the agency has considered all relevant factors and has explained its decision, (2) is necessary to determine whether the agency has relied on documents not in the record, (3) when supplementing the record is necessary to explain technical terms or complex subject matter, or (4) when plaintiffs make a showing of agency bad faith."[240] In this particular case, however, the Ninth Circuit concluded that the district court erred by considering extra-record evidence because it used the evidence—declarations—"as a basis for judging the wisdom of the agency's scientific analysis."[241]

In *Southern Forest Watch, Inc. v. Jewell*, the Sixth Circuit affirmed the district court's denial of a motion for discovery beyond the administrative record.[242] "Supplementation of the administrative record," the court explained, "may be appropriate 'when an agency has deliberately or negligently excluded certain documents from the record, or when a court needs certain "background" information to determine whether the agency considered all the relevant factors.'"[243] But in this case, the court concluded, neither of those circumstances existed.[244]

---

238. *Id.* at 787 (citing *Nat. Res. Def. Council, Inc.*, 798 F.3d 809 (9th Cir. 2015)) (granting mandamus on unreasonable delay grounds where EPA had not responded to an administrative petition for rulemaking for eight years); *In re* Am. Rivers & Idaho Rivers United, 372 F.3d 413, 419 (D.C. Cir. 2004) (six-year delay unreasonable); *In re* Int'l Chem. Workers Union, 958 F.2d 1144, 1150 (D.C. Cir. 1992) (six-year delay unreasonable for rulemaking); *In re* Core Commc'ns Inc., 531 F.3d 849, 857 (D.C. Cir. 2008) (same); *In re* Bluewater Network, 234 F.3d 1305, 1316 (D.C. Cir. 2000) (nine-year delay unreasonable). *Contra* United Steelworkers of Am. v. Rubbers Mfrs. Ass'n, 783 F.2d 1117, 1120 (D.C. Cir. 1986) (14-month delay, without more, not unreasonable).

239. *See* Bos. Redevelopment Auth. v. NPS, 838 F.3d 42, 48 (1st Cir. 2016) ("In a traditional APA case, 'the focal point for judicial review should be the administrative record already in existence, not some new record made initially in the reviewing court.'" (quoting Camp v. Pitts, 411 U.S. 138, 142 (1973)).

240. 776 F.3d 971, 992 (9th Cir. 2014) (citations omitted).

241. *Id.* at 93; *see also* Fence Creek Cattle Co. v. U.S. Forest Serv., 602 F.3d 1125, 1131 (9th Cir. 2010) (rejecting a petitioner's attempt to supplement the record to show bad faith).

242. 817 F.3d 965 (6th Cir. 2016).

243. *Id.* at 977 (citation omitted).

244. *Id.* at 977–78.

V. REMEDIES

Following a successful judicial challenge to agency action, courts generally have authority to grant relief of the type the APA or other relevant statute has authorized. Courts in environmental suits in particular also may award attorneys' fees or other costs to the extent authorized by statute, but most litigation challenging federal agency action focuses on injunctive or declaratory relief—that is, preventing enforcement or implementation of the challenged action in whole or in part, declaring the action to be contrary to law, and/or directing agency action consistent with the requirements of the law. Challenges to environmental regulatory actions raise a host of issues related to remedies, including standards for staying or preliminarily enjoining agency action pending litigation, whether and when an agency action should be vacated or instead left in place pending remand to the agency, and severability, among others.

Preliminary Injunctions/Stays of Agency Actions. It usually takes considerable time to litigate a challenge to agency regulatory action to final judgment, and such actions often impose binding requirements and/or have important effects on third parties long before the case is resolved. Accordingly, it is not uncommon for plaintiffs or petitioners to move a court to preliminarily enjoin or stay the challenged regulatory action, so as to maintain the status quo pending resolution of the suit. Such motions are governed by the familiar four-part test applicable to motions for preliminary injunctive relief: (1) the likelihood that the party seeking the stay will prevail on the merits of the appeal; (2) the likelihood that the moving party will be irreparably harmed absent a stay; (3) the prospect that others will be harmed if the court grants a stay; and (4) the public interest in granting a stay.[245] The moving party bears the burden of demonstrating that a stay is warranted.

Although the bar is generally considered to be high, courts have granted stays in a number of high-profile environmental cases in recent years. In 2015, for example, the U.S. Court of Appeals for the Sixth Circuit issued a nationwide stay of the Clean Water Rule, discussed earlier, which defined the scope of "waters of the United States" subject to regulation under the CWA.[246] And in 2016, the Supreme Court stayed the Clean Power Plan—a CAA regulation addressing greenhouse gas emissions from existing power plants—pending final resolution of challenges to the rule. At the time, challenges to that rule were still pending before the D.C. Circuit, which had denied petitioners' stay motion. The Supreme Court did not issue an opinion supporting its 5–4 decision to stay the rule, but the industry challengers who sought the stay focused on previous litigation challenging EPA's Mercury and Air Toxics Standards (MATS) rule. Just the previous year, the Supreme Court

---

245. *See, e.g.*, Winter v. Nat. Res. Def. Council, Inc., 555 U.S. 7, 20 (2008).

246. *In re* EPA & Dep't of Def. Final Rule, 803 F.3d 804 (6th Cir. 2015). The Sixth Circuit's stay was lifted following the Supreme Court's decision in *National Association of Manufacturers v. Department of Defense*, 138 S. Ct. 617 (2018). Several district courts subsequently entered stays of the same rule, applicable in many but not all states across the country.

in *Michigan v. EPA*[247] overturned a key threshold finding that was a legal predicate for the MATS rule; but by the time the Court handed down the decision, regulated entities had already largely complied with the rule.

In addition to judicial stays, agencies may seek to stay a rule administratively pending resolution of litigation or further agency action. The APA (5 U.S.C. § 705) provides that "[w]hen an agency finds that justice so requires, it may postpone the effective date of action taken by it, pending judicial review." Some environmental statutes also include provisions authorizing such administrative stays.[248] Several recent court decisions have interpreted the scope of these authorities. The district courts in *California v. U.S. Bureau of Land Management*[249] and in *Becerra v. Department of Interior*[250] held that 5 U.S.C. § 705 allows postponement of the *effective date* of a regulation only if that date has not already passed; the courts held that Section 705 does not permit extension of *compliance dates* after a rule has already become effective.

In *Sierra Club v. Jackson*, the D.C. District Court construed the scope of 5 U.S.C. § 705, holding (1) that EPA had authority to stay a CAA regulation under Section 705 notwithstanding its separate, narrower authority to stay a regulation pending reconsideration under CAA Section 307(d)(7)(B); (2) that a stay under Section 705 was not a substantive rule and therefore did not require notice and comment rulemaking; and (3) that EPA must justify a stay under Section 705 pursuant to the four-part preliminary injunction test set forth previously, which the court held EPA had failed to do in the case before it.[251] And in *Clean Air Council v. Pruitt*,[252] the D.C. Circuit vacated EPA's use of CAA Section 307(d)(7)(B) to administratively stay a CAA regulation of methane emissions from oil and gas operations pending reconsideration of that rule. The D.C. Circuit held that this provision did not authorize EPA to stay a rule where, as in that instance, its reconsideration of the rule was not required by the statute.

Vacatur versus Remand without Vacatur. The APA also provides that "[t]he reviewing court shall . . . hold unlawful and set aside" agency action found to be "arbitrary, capricious, an abuse of discretion, or otherwise not in accordance with law," "in excess of statutory jurisdiction, authority, or limitations, or short of statutory right," or "without observance of procedure required by law."[253] Judicial review provisions in some environmental statutes use similar language.[254] "Setting aside" agency action here has often been thought to refer, at least as a default matter, to vacatur of the action—which effectively nullifies the action. That said, there

---

247. 135 S. Ct. 2699 (2015).
248. *See, e.g.*, 42 U.S.C. § 7607(d)(7) (2015) (CAA provision authorizing stay of effectiveness of rule pending reconsideration, for three months or less).
249. 277 F. Supp. 3d 1106 (N.D. Cal. 2017).
250. 276 F. Supp. 3d 953 (N.D. Cal. 2017).
251. 833 F. Supp. 2d 11 (D.D.C. 2012).
252. 862 F.3d 1, 4 (D.C. Cir. 2017).
253. 5 U.S.C. § 706(2).
254. *See, e.g.*, CAA § 307, 42 U.S.C. § 7607(d)(9) (2015) (CAA provision authorizing court to "reverse" defective agency actions).

is a long-standing debate and ample case law in environmental litigation regarding whether and when a reviewing court, in lieu of vacating a regulatory action found to be legally infirm, may instead leave the action in place pending agency proceedings to cure the relevant defect.

The D.C. Circuit and several other courts have found that remand without vacatur is an appropriate remedy in some circumstances. The courts have looked both at the nature of the error in the agency's action and how easily it can be cured, as well as the potential effects of vacatur. For example, the D.C. Circuit in *Allied-Signal, Inc. v. United States Nuclear Regulatory Commission* stated that a court's decision about whether to vacate, in addition to remanding, depends on "the seriousness of the order's deficiencies (and thus the extent of doubt whether the agency chose correctly) and the disruptive consequences of an interim change that may itself be changed."[255] In *Mississippi v. EPA*, the D.C. Circuit remanded without vacatur one of the CAA national ambient air quality standards under review.[256] The court left the standard in place because EPA's failure "to explain itself is in principle a curable defect" and "vacating a standard because it may be insufficiently protective would sacrifice such protection as it now provides, making the best an enemy of the good."[257]

In its 2008 decision in *North Carolina v. EPA*, the D.C. Circuit initially vacated the Clean Air Interstate Rule based on fundamental flaws in EPA's legal interpretation, but on rehearing changed its remedy to a remand without vacatur based on concerns with the impacts of vacatur on public health and state and industry plans with regard to regulatory implementation.[258] Underscoring the controversy this issue can raise, the D.C. Circuit's 2007 decision in *Natural Resources Defense Council v. EPA*—which vacated a CAA rule setting emission standards for boilers and waste incineration units—sparked both a concurring opinion from Judge Randolph and an opinion dissenting in part by Judge Rogers, addressing the circumstances in which vacatur or remand without vacatur are appropriate.[259]

Voluntary Remands and Confession of Error. It is not uncommon for an agency to request a voluntary remand where the agency decides to reconsider a challenged regulatory action. Courts generally have endorsed this approach in environmental cases.[260] Although not an environmental case, the Federal Circuit's decision in *SKF USA, Inc. v. United States* provides an extensive and widely cited judicial discussion

---

255. 988 F.2d 146, 150–51 (D.C. Cir. 1993) (citation omitted); *see also* Idaho Farm Bureau Fed'n v. Babbitt, 58 F.3d 1392, 1405 (9th Cir. 1995) (remanding a Fish and Wildlife Service regulation to the agency with direction to follow required procedures while allowing the rule to remain in effect in the interim).

256. 744 F.3d 1334 (D.C. Cir. 2013).

257. *Id.* at 1362 (quoting Am. Farm Bureau Fed'n v. EPA, 559 F.3d 512, 528 (D.C. Cir. 2009)); *see also* Envtl. Def. Fund, Inc. v. EPA, 898 F.2d 183, 190 (D.C. Cir. 1990).

258. 550 F.3d 1176, 1178 (D.C. Cir. 2008).

259. 489 F.3d 1250, 1261–67 (D.C. Cir. 2007).

260. *See, e.g.*, Ethyl Corp. v. Browner, 989 F.2d 522, 524 n.3 (D.C. Cir. 1993); Anchor Line Ltd. v. Fed. Mar. Comm'n, 299 F.2d 124, 125 (D.C. Cir. 1962) ("[W]hen an agency seeks to reconsider its action, it should move the court to remand or to hold the case in abeyance pending reconsideration by the agency."); Cal. Cmtys. against Toxics v. EPA, 688 F.3d 989, 992 (D.D.C. 2012) ("Generally courts only refuse voluntarily requested remand when the agency's request is frivolous or made in bad faith.").

of the law of voluntary remand.[261] In *SKF*, the court distinguished between three scenarios—cases in which voluntary remand is sought based on intervening events outside the agency's control, those in which the agency seeks to reconsider its position without confessing error, and those in which the agency seeks to correct an acknowledged error—and opined that different standards should govern in each.[262]

The D.C. Circuit in *Limnia Inc. v. Department of Energy* recently clarified that although the agency need not confess error provided it does not seek vacatur of its action, voluntary remand is appropriate only where the agency professes an "intention to reconsider, re-review, or modify the original agency decision that is the subject of the legal challenge."[263] The question whether a court may grant an agency's motion for voluntary remand *with vacatur* of a regulation—notwithstanding the general principle that an agency can only rescind an action by means of the same procedures (e.g., notice-and-comment rulemaking) it used to take the original action[264]—is a source of continuing controversy.[265]

Severability. Where a court finds that an element or provision of a rule or other regulatory action is contrary to law, it may be called on to determine whether this portion can be severed from the broader action of which it is a part. The Supreme Court in *K Mart Corp. v. Cartier* applied to a Customs Service regulation virtually the same test it set forth for statutory severability analysis in *Alaska Airlines v. Brock*:[266] First, would the agency have adopted the regulation but for the inclusion of the portion held to be infirm? And second, would severance of the offending regulatory provision impair the function of the regulation as a whole?[267] In the environmental context, the D.C. Circuit applied this framework in *Davis County Solid Waste Management v. EPA*, amending its initial opinion in the case to hold that the relevant CAA emission standards were severable and accordingly should be vacated only in part.[268]

261. 254 F.3d 1022 (Fed. Cir. 2001). *See generally* Joshua Revesz, *Voluntary Remands: A Critical Reassessment*, 70(2) Admin. L . Rev. 361 (Spring 2018).

262. 254 F.3d at 1027–29.

263. 857 F.3d 379, 386–88 (D.C. Cir. 2017).

264. *See, e.g.*, Clean Air Council v. Pruitt, 862 F.3d 1, 8–9 (D.C. Cir. 2017); Motor Vehicle Mfrs. Ass'n v. State Farm Mut. Auto. Ins. Co., 463 U.S. 29, 44 (1983).

265. *Compare, e.g.*, Nat'l Parks Conservation Ass'n v. Salazar, 660 F. Supp. 2d 3, 5 (D.D.C. 2009) (holding that granting a voluntary remand with vacatur is improper), *with* Ariz. Pub. Serv. Co. v. EPA, 562 F.3d 1116, 1122 (10th Cir. 2009) (granting voluntary remand with vacatur).

266. 480 U.S. 678 (1987).

267. 486 U.S. 281, 286–93 (2012).

268. 108 F.3d 1454, 1455 (D.C. Cir. 1997). *See generally* E. Donald Elliott & Charles W. Tyler, *Administrative Severability Clauses*, Yale Law Sch., Faculty Scholarship Series, Paper 5010 (2015), http://digitalcommons.law.yale.edu/cgi/viewcontent.cgi?article=6018&context=fss_papers.

VI. CONCLUSION

Suits challenging agency action have a uniquely consequential role in environmental law, shaping the interpretation of statutes and setting the parameters for agency decision making. These suits raise the same general types of issues encountered in other administrative law litigation—ranging from threshold jurisdictional and procedural issues to standards of review to remedies. But as the previous discussion makes clear, each statute establishes a unique framework, and environmental cases often raise special concerns—including those related to the standing of citizen groups to challenge agency action, the focus on protection of public health and the environment, and the deeply technical content of much environmental regulation. This chapter gives a 30,000-foot view of the landscape—a starting point for more in-depth inquiry into the myriad issues these important cases raise.

CHAPTER 2

Environmental Criminal Enforcement

Jane F. Barrett, W. Warren Hamel, and Steven P. Solow*

I. INTRODUCTION

A. Issues in Environmental Criminal Cases

Criminal prosecutions of environmental violations continue to constitute a small proportion of both criminal cases and of all environmental enforcement actions in the United States. However, the serious consequences of such cases, which include incarceration, significant fines, multiyear terms of probation, and the loss of government contracting opportunities, compel those involved with any environmental enforcement litigation to understand the unique substantive and procedural issues associated with the prosecution of environmental violations as crimes. Moreover, the decision to pursue an environmental violation as a civil or criminal matter is a choice largely left to the discretion of individual government attorneys; thus, understanding the policies and practices of investigators and prosecutors, and the legal standards at issue, is critical to representing an individual or company that is the subject of an investigation or that becomes an indicted defendant.

Environmental criminal prosecutions feature important differences from the ordinary criminal case that pose substantial challenges to counsel for both the government and the defense: (1) the violations take place in the context of a complex regulatory system in which violation of a regulation or permit requirement can result in a range of enforcement options, including felony charges; (2) rightly or wrongly, some violators may not perceive their violations as criminal behavior; and (3) as stated previously, the government has wide discretion in choosing how to respond to an environmental violation. Counsel in environmental enforcement matters can better assist their clients by becoming familiar with the factors likely

*The authors wish to acknowledge the assistance of Leslie Couvillion, an attorney at Katten Muchin Rosenman LLP, in the preparation of this revised chapter.

to cause a particular environmental violation to be considered a potential *criminal* violation, as opposed to one appropriately addressed in an administrative or civil judicial proceeding.

In that regard, in early 2018 the U.S. Department of Justice (DOJ) issued guidance on the use of civil and criminal enforcement in the form of a guidance memorandum to section chiefs of the Environment and Natural Resources Division (ENRD) outlining ENRD's current enforcement principles and priorities. Key themes from the guidance memorandum include (1) prioritizing enforcement actions that address concrete harms to the environment or human health and safety; (2) encouraging voluntary disclosures and self-audits by regulated parties; and (3) deferring to the enforcement priorities of state and local governments, other federal agencies, and U.S. Attorneys' offices.[1]

The guidance memorandum reiterates ENRD's commitment to recently announced DOJ policies, including the limitation on using guidance documents as the basis for civil enforcement actions[2] and the prohibition on settlement payments to third parties.[3] Notably, the memorandum does not apply to federal prosecutors in U.S. Attorney's offices.

---

1. *See* Memorandum from Jeffrey H. Wood, Acting Assistant Att'y Gen., U.S. Dep't of Justice, to ENRD Section Chiefs & Deputy Section Chiefs, Enforcement Principles and Priorities (Mar. 12, 2018), https://www.justice.gov/enrd/page/file/1043731/download.

2. *See* Memorandum from Rachel Brand, Assoc. Att'y Gen., U.S. Dep't of Justice, to Heads of Civil Litigating Components U.S. Att'ys, Limiting Use of Agency Guidance Documents in Affirmative Civil Enforcement Cases (Jan. 25, 2018), https://www.justice.gov/file/1028756/download.

3. *See* Memorandum from Jeff Sessions, Att'y Gen., U.S. Dep't of Justice, to all Component Heads & U.S. Att'ys, Prohibition on Settlement Payments to Third Parties (June 5, 2017), https://www.justice.gov/opa/press-release/file/971826/download; Memorandum from Jeffrey H. Wood, Acting Assistant Att'y Gen., U.S. Dep't of Justice, to ENRD Deputy Assistant Att'ys Gen. & Section Chiefs, Settlement Payments to Third Parties in ENRD Cases (Jan. 9, 2018), https://www.justice.gov/enrd/page/file/1043726/download.

B. The Initial Development of Environmental Criminal Law[4]

Congress enacted the first criminal law protecting the waters of the United States in 1899 (the Rivers and Harbors Act, also known as the Refuse Act).[5] Until the latter part of the 20th century, environmental regulation was a narrow patchwork of laws, and there was little criminal enforcement. Criminal enforcement began to grow in the 1970s after Congress passed the Clean Air Act Amendments of 1970 (CAA)[6] and expanded the reach of the National Water Pollution Control Act, commonly known as the Clean Water Act (CWA), in 1972,[7] adding criminal misdemeanors to both statutes. Felony provisions were added later (1987 for the CWA, 1990 for the CAA).

In 1976, DOJ and the U.S. Environmental Protection Agency (EPA) undertook the first major environmental criminal prosecution after the enactment of the new statutes. The prosecution grew out of an EPA investigation into contamination of

---

4. Space does not permit a full explication of the history of environmental crime enforcement. Interested readers are directed to Raymond W. Mushal, *Up from the Sewers: A Perspective on the Evolution of the Federal Environmental Crimes Program*, 2009 Utah L. Rev. 1103 (2009). Portions of this revised section draw upon previously published materials by one of the co-authors writing with others. This includes: Steven P. Solow, Anne M. Carpenter & Katherine V. Barajas, *Clean Air Act Criminal Enforcement*, in Am. Bar Ass'n, The Clean Air Handbook 731 (4th ed. 2016); Steven P. Solow, Lily N. Chinn & Anne M. Carpenter, *Criminal Prosecution of Environmental and Workplace Safety Incidents through DOJ's New Worker Endangerment Initiative*, White Collar Crime Comm. Newsl. (Am. Bar Ass'n, Winter/Spring 2017); Steven P. Solow, Anne M. Carpenter & Katherine V. Noble, *The State of Environmental Crime Enforcement: A Survey of Developments in 2014*, Env't Rep. (BNA) (May 8, 2015); Steven P. Solow & Anne M. Carpenter, *The State of Environmental Crime Enforcement: A Survey of Developments in 2013*, Daily Env't Rep. (BNA) (Apr. 11, 2014).

5. The criminal provision in the Rivers and Harbors Act is a strict liability crime, a relative rarity in the universe of federal criminal law. 33 U.S.C. §§ 407, 411 (2012). As discussed further, *infra*, a strict liability criminal statute does not require the government to prove any knowledge or intent whatsoever on the part of the defendant accused of committing the crime, *see, e.g.*, United States v. White Fuel, Inc., 498 F.2d 619, 622 (1st Cir. 1974), a concept that runs counter to the basic thrust of common law and modern criminal theory. Courts have upheld convictions under the Rivers and Harbors Act, noting that (1) the crime is a misdemeanor with a relatively light sentence of incarceration (six months) as penalty, and (2) most cases had been brought against corporations, in which case penalties are limited to fines and orders of restitution. *See, e.g.*, *id.* at 622–24. As federal interest in environmental enforcement grew in the late 1960s and 1970s, the Rivers and Harbors Act was a commonly used criminal provision to reach instances of water pollution.

6. 42 U.S.C. §§ 7401–7671 (2012). The predecessor to the CAA was enacted in 1955. Air Pollution Control Act of 1955, Pub. L. No. 84-159, 69 Stat. 322. As part of the extensive amendments that were enacted in 1970, Congress included misdemeanor criminal penalties for various violations. Clean Air Amendments of 1970, Pub. L. No. 91-604, sec. 4, § 113(c), 84 Stat. 1676, 1687 (codified at 42 U.S.C. § 7413(c) (2012)). It was not until the Clean Air Act Amendments of 1990 that felony penalties were included. Pub. L. No. 101-549, sec. 701, § 113(c), 104 Stat. 2399, 2675–77 (1990) (codified at 42 U.S.C. § 7413(c) (2012)).

7. 33 U.S.C. §§ 1251–1387 (2012). The criminal provisions of the CAA and CWA were originally misdemeanors. Over time, Congress amended the penalty provisions of these statutes to provide felony penalties. For example, the Federal Water Pollution Control Act (FWPCA) was originally enacted in 1948. Pub. L. No. 80-845, 62 Stat. 1155 (1948) (codified as amended at 33 U.S.C. §§ 1251–1387 (2012)). In 1972, Congress passed the extensive amendments that created the CWA. These amendments included misdemeanor-level penalties for first-time willful and negligent violations. Federal Water Pollution Control Act Amendments of 1972, Pub. L. No. 92-500, sec. 2, § 309(c), 86 Stat. 816, 860 (codified at 33 U.S.C. § 1319(c) (2012)). In 1987, the statute was amended to provide felony-level penalties for first-time knowing violations. Pub. L. No. 100-4, § 312, 101 Stat. 7, 43 (1987) (codified at 33 U.S.C. § 1319(c)(2)).

the drinking water drawn from the Ohio and Kanawha rivers. EPA and several manufacturers worked together to study the sources of carbon tetrachloride entering the Kanawha River. However, FMC Corporation declined to participate in the study and refused entry to an EPA inspector. EPA, in turn, brought a civil action seeking a temporary restraining order to close down the facility and allow EPA to conduct its inspection. At the end of February 1977, FMC Corporation disclosed that the company had discharged 6,000 pounds of carbon tetrachloride. Suspecting that FMC Corporation was a primary source for contamination of the rivers and that the company might have failed to fully disclose its releases in its application for a National Pollutant Discharge Elimination System (NPDES) permit, EPA launched a criminal investigation. EPA and DOJ now were confronted with the fact that neither had any environmental criminal investigators, laboratory and analytical capabilities, or specially trained prosecutors. With some creative staffing and resource allocation, however, the agencies were able to carry out an investigation and bring charges, which were resolved by a plea agreement in *United States v. FMC Corp.*[8]

After their experience with FMC Corporation, EPA and DOJ sought congressional support to strengthen and broaden the reach of environmental criminal statutes and to provide the resources for a national criminal enforcement program. Congress responded by increasing enforcement resources and enacting stronger criminal provisions, and the current era of federal criminal enforcement began.[9]

C. Federal Environmental Crime Enforcement

Although the resources available for federal investigation and prosecution now are greater than those available in the 1970s and 1980s, they have remained nearly constant since the early 1990s and are notably modest by comparison to other law enforcement programs. For example, pursuant to the Pollution Prosecution Act of 1990,[10] EPA was authorized to increase the number of criminal investigators to 200. Yet, as of the writing of this chapter, the number of investigators is below 150.[11] By comparison, there are approximately 13,000[12] special agents in the Federal Bureau

---

8. *See* Crim. No. 80-91 (E.D. Pa.).

9. This chapter is focused primarily on federal enforcement. That focus should not be construed as a value judgment as to the value of state and local prosecutions. Indeed, the efforts to hold public officials accountable for lead contamination of drinking water in Flint, Michigan, illuminates the capacity of state and local prosecutors to pursue areas of liability that are seen infrequently in federal enforcement cases. *See* Merrit Kennedy, *2 Former Flint Emergency Managers, 2 Others Face Felony Charges over Water Crisis*, N.P.R., Dec. 20, 2016, https://www.npr.org/sections/thetwo-way/2016/12/20/506314203/2 -former-flint-emergency-managers-face-felony-charges-over-water-crisis.

10. Pollution Prosecution Act of 1990, Pub. L. No. 101-593, sec. 2, §§ 201–05, 104 Stat. 2954, 2962–63 (codified at 42 U.S.C. § 4321 (2012)).

11. *See* Dave Reynolds, *EPA Official Says CWA Jurisdiction Uncertainty Might Deter Enforcement*, Inside EPA (June 12, 2018), https://insideepa.com/daily-news/epa-official-says-cwa-jurisdiction -uncertainty-might-deter-enforcement.

12. A prior version of this chapter referenced a figure of "more than 1,200 agents in the Federal Bureau of Investigation." Jane F. Barrett, W. Warren Hamel, & Steven P. Solow, *Environmental Criminal Enforcement*, in Am. Bar Ass'n, Environmental Litigation: Law and Strategy 71 (2009). This figure should have been 12,000 instead of 1,200.

of Investigation (FBI) (which of course has a far broader enforcement mandate)[13] and approximately 250 U.S. Fish and Wildlife special agents.[14] In that context, whether EPA has 150 or 200 agents is of little consequence in comparison to the long-standing policy question of whether EPA has an appropriately sized and qualified investigative force.

1. Federal Prosecutors

Three main groups of federal attorneys work on environmental criminal cases. EPA provides its criminal investigators with legal support through the work of approximately 20 regional criminal enforcement counsels (RCECs), who are located in EPA's regional counsel offices throughout the country. (The number of RCECs has also fallen, from around 45 or so when the prior edition of this book was published). DOJ created a specialized unit in 1982 to prosecute environmental crimes. This unit grew from four attorneys in 1982 into the Environmental Crimes Section (ECS), which comprises approximately 40 prosecutors who investigate and prosecute environmental criminal cases around the country, including pollution offenses and offenses involving protected species. In addition, as noted previously, U.S. Attorneys' offices have the primary authority to investigate and prosecute environmental crimes occurring in their districts,[15] operating out of the 93 Assistant U.S. Attorneys' offices across the country. Where the case is led by an Assistant U.S. Attorney (AUSA), this means that defense counsel should become familiar with the pattern and practices of that AUSA and U.S. Attorneys' office.

Similar to other complex criminal investigations, when the government pursues an environmental criminal investigation the prosecutor will likely be involved during the investigative stage. Recognizing the risks and benefits to having a prosecutor involved in the investigative stage of a case, the American Bar Association's Criminal Justice Standards Committee developed a new set of criminal justice standards addressing the investigative function of the prosecutor.[16] These standards may be useful to both prosecutors and defense attorneys.

2. Federal Investigators

In the 1990s, the investigation of environmental crimes was undertaken by several federal law enforcement agencies that began assigning agents to investigate environmental crimes in greater numbers, a trend that reached a high point in 2000 and 2001. Following the events of September 11, 2001, EPA reassigned some investigators to antiterrorist investigations and security details for high-ranking agency

---

13. *See* Fed. Bureau of Investigation, FY 2019 Authorization and Budget Request to Congress 1-1 (Feb. 2018).

14. *See* U.S. Fish & Wildlife Serv., Off. of Law Enf't, About Service Special Agents (Sept. 8, 2013), https://www.fws.gov/le/special-agents.html.

15. Memorandum from Janet Reno, Att'y Gen., U.S. Dep't of Justice (Aug. 23, 1994) (Bluesheet Revision of the *United States Attorneys' Manual*, replacing tit. 5, ch. 11).

16. ABA Standards for Criminal Justice: Prosecutorial Investigations 5 (3d ed. 2014).

personnel, a shift that receded and has reemerged in recent years as the former EPA Administrator Scott Pruitt moved a large number of agents into his personal security detail.[17] Environmental criminal investigations, in the broadest sense, are also brought by a number of different federal law enforcement agencies. These include the U.S. Fish and Wildlife Service, U.S. Customs Service, U.S. Coast Guard, elements of the Department of Homeland Security, the Defense Criminal Investigative Service, and criminal investigation agents for the Army, Navy, and Air Force, Occupational Safety and Health Administration (OSHA), the Office of the Inspector General, Department of Transportation, and personnel in the U.S. Park Service, the Bureau of Land Management, and the Office of Mine Safety. In recent years, as discussed later, the Chemical Safety Board (CSB) has played a controversial role in criminal investigations. Like the National Transportation Safety Board (NTSB), the CSB does not have a law enforcement function and when the CSB interviews people, it tells them so. Yet, as described later, DOJ has successfully obtained CSB investigative materials to support criminal investigations. Lastly, following 9/11, the FBI has almost completely withdrawn from involvement in environmental crime investigations.

Some state and local governments have sophisticated environmental crimes programs; the number has varied widely over the years. In some jurisdictions, stereotypical federal-state-local turf battles over cases have been superseded by environmental crimes task forces, allowing law enforcement to leverage their resources. However, state, local, and task force efforts are typically the result of individual leadership, and may come and go depending upon the personalities involved.[18] Where there is no coordination, federal, state, and local law enforcement agencies may compete to be the "first to file" charges against a violator. This lack of cooperation may result in multiple investigations, and may end in prosecutions out of sync with the severity of the violation.[19]

---

17. Juliet Eilperin & Brady Dennis, *At EPA, Guarding the Chief Pulls Agents from Pursuing Environmental Crimes*, Wash. Post (Sept. 20, 2017) http://wapo.st/2fzkWfW.

18. For example, under the leadership of Assistant District Attorney Linda Spahr and investigator Steve Drielak, the Suffolk County, New York, D.A.'s office created a special environmental crimes unit that pioneered many of the investigative and prosecution techniques now used nationwide. Yet today, with Spahr and Drielak gone, the unit is also gone. Such variation in prioritization of environmental crime enforcement also leads to variation of enforcement, with seemingly similar cases being resolved civilly in one jurisdiction and criminally in another.

19. It is important to note that in many instances a federal, state, or local administrative inspector will have had contact with a regulated entity for some time prior to a criminal case, and in some instances will have initiated the criminal investigation. Although such regulators are not criminal investigators, on occasion they will observe conditions or conduct that prompts scrutiny beyond a typical administrative enforcement action. Thus cooperation and communication with inspectors is typically regarded as a direct way to limit the risk of criminal investigation and prosecution. However, the ability of civil investigators to surreptitiously support and cooperate with criminal investigations was supported by a decision of the Circuit Court of Appeals for the Ninth Circuit in 2008, which upheld the secret cooperation of civil enforcers with a criminal investigation in a Securities and Exchange Commission (SEC) case, increasing the wariness of some regulated entities toward their regulators. *See* United States v. Stringer, 535 F.3d 929 (9th Cir. 2008); W. Warren Hamel & Danette R. Edwards, *'Pay No Attention to the Man behind the Curtain':* United States v. Stringer *and the Government's Obligation to Disclose,* 3 White Collar Crime Rep. (BNA) No. 11 (May 23, 2008).

II. STATUTORY OVERVIEW: USING AN ELEMENTS ANALYSIS TO ASSESS A POTENTIAL CASE

Many federal environmental crimes cases have coupled environmental statutes with traditional criminal charges such as conspiracy,[20] false statement,[21] obstruction of justice,[22] and in some cases mail fraud[23] or wire fraud.[24] Indeed, some environmental cases may be brought entirely on the basis of a false statement or fraud prosecution. This chapter is not designed to explore the issues of proof associated with these traditional Title 18 charges under the U.S. Code. Rather, the focus here will be to provide guidance on how to identify the elements of a potential environmental criminal charge. It is a long-standing practice of experienced practitioners in this space to begin this elements analysis at the earliest stage of any possible case. This is because, ultimately, a prosecutor must prove each element of an environmental crime "beyond a reasonable doubt." To assess the strength of a possible criminal case, it is critical to identify the elements of each criminal charge and determine whether there is sufficient admissible evidence to support each element of a potential charge.

In some instances, however, the elements of an environmental crime can be difficult to discern. This is partly because, rather than describing a specific prohibited activity (e.g., larceny, fraud), environmental statutes typically describe a permitting regime for the lawful discharge of a pollutant and then provide criminal sanctions for violation of the permitting regime under certain circumstances. Thus, for environmental crimes cases, it is critical to understand what constitutes permitted conduct, the relevant definitions pertaining to regulated conduct, and the circumstances under which a violation of the regulatory regime becomes subject to criminal sanction. The challenge of this analysis has only increased as the federal government has moved to criminally prosecute statutes that do not use a permitting regime with technical standards for permissible conduct (such as discharge limits contained in a water or air discharge permit). Instead, the government has also sought to prosecute for failing to meet standards that require regulated entities to, for example, meet their obligation to implement procedures designed to make a workplace "safe." Issues associated with proof in such cases is discussed in the CAA section.

---

20. 18 U.S.C. § 371 (2012).
21. 18 U.S.C. § 1001 (2012).
22. 18 U.S.C. § 1512 (tampering with witness); § 1513 (retaliating against witness); § 1503 (more generally obstruction of federal court proceedings) (2012).
23. 18 U.S.C. § 1341 (2012).
24. 18 U.S.C. § 1343 (2012).

A. An Elements Analysis of a Clean Water Act Felony

As noted previously, analysis of the elements of an offense is how many prosecutors approach any criminal case, typically looking at both the elements of the offense and, when available, the jury instructions on those elements. Thus, when evaluating the potential for criminal exposure, an elements analysis allows a subject or target to determine whether the government can meet its burden of proof for the relevant environmental violations that are alleged to have taken place. It must first be established that the government can prove, beyond a reasonable doubt, every element required to establish a *civil* violation, and only then to determine if the requisite mental state was present to make a civil violation a crime.

The CWA is a useful statute to explain the process of an elements analysis, a process that can be used with any environmental statute. Doing so requires a certain amount of statutory (and often regulatory) sleuthing.

To begin, the CWA states:

> Except as in compliance with this section and sections 1312, 1316, 1317, 1328, *1342* and 1344 of this title, the discharge of any pollutant by any person shall be unlawful.[25] [Emphasis added.]

Section 1342 of the CWA is the provision that created the NPDES program, a permitting system that prohibits the discharge of pollutants into the waters of the United States unless the discharger has a NPDES permit. The NPDES permit then sets the amount of pollutant that can be legally discharged, and how that level will be measured and reported. (Reporting is typically undertaken in a monthly discharge monitoring report, or DMR.) For example, a sewage treatment plant will have a NPDES permit that sets limits for the amount of fecal coliform and chlorine that the plant can discharge, and requires a series of sample results that are to be reported in the DMR. Thus, for a pollutant discharge to be lawful under the CWA, it must comply with Section 1342, which first requires that the discharger have an NPDES permit, and second that the discharge be in compliance with the limitations imposed by the permit. Additionally, the sampling must be undertaken using approved methods and the responses accurately and timely recorded and reported in the DMR.

The statute also establishes certain definitions, which, in turn, inform the elements of a criminal prosecution. The CWA defines terms critical to a criminal prosecution for violation of the act as follows:

> (5) The term "person" means an individual, corporation, partnership, association, State, municipality, commission, or political subdivision of a State, or any interstate body.
>
> (6) The term "pollutant" means dredged spoil, solid waste, incinerator residue, sewage, garbage, sewage sludge, munitions, chemical wastes, biological materials, radioactive materials, heat, wrecked or discarded equipment,

---

25. CWA § 301(a), 33 U.S.C. § 1311(a) (2012).

rock, sand, cellar dirt and industrial, municipal, and agricultural waste discharged into water. . . .

(7) The term "navigable waters" means the waters of the United States, including the territorial seas. . . .

(12) The term "discharge of a pollutant" and the term "discharge of pollutants" each means (A) any addition of any pollutant to navigable waters from any point source, (B) any addition of any pollutant to the waters of the contiguous zone or the ocean from any point source other than a vessel or other floating craft. . . .

(14) The term "point source" means any discernible, confined and discrete conveyance, including but not limited to any pipe, ditch, channel, tunnel, conduit, well, discrete fissure, container, rolling stock, concentrated animal feeding operation, or vessel or other floating craft, from which pollutants are or may be discharged. This term does not include agricultural stormwater discharges and return flows from irrigated agriculture.[26]

The statutory language is further defined by case law. As the reader is probably well aware, no single element of the CWA has been as vigorously disputed as the meaning of what waters and wetlands are included in the phrases "navigable waters" and "waters of the United States." A full discussion is beyond the scope of this chapter, but practitioners should review recent Supreme Court cases and EPA and other agency pronouncements and rulemaking for additional insight.[27]

The criminal provisions most frequently used for prosecuting CWA violations are located in CWA Section 309(c)(1) (negligent violations) and Section 309(c)(2) (knowing violations).[28] For knowing violations, the statute provides as follows:

(2) Knowing violations

Any person who—

(A) knowingly violates section 1311, 1312, 1316, 1317, 1318, 1321(b)(3), 1328 or 1345 of this title, or any permit condition or limitation implementing any of such sections in a permit issued under section 1342 of this title by the [EPA] Administrator or by a State, or any requirement imposed in a pretreatment program approved under section 1342(a)(3) or 1342(b)(8) of this title or in a permit issued under section 1344 of this title by the Secretary of the Army or by a State;

. . .

shall be [guilty of a felony].[29]

---

26. CWA § 502, 33 U.S.C. § 1362 (2012).

27. *See, e.g.*, Solid Waste Agency of N. Cook Cnty. v. Army Corps of Eng'rs, 531 U.S. 159 (2001); Rapanos v. United States, 547 U.S. 715 (2006); *see also* News Release, U.S. Envtl. Prot. Agency, EPA, U.S. Army Move to Rescind 2015 "Waters of the U.S." (June 27, 2017), https://www.epa.gov/newsreleases/epa-us-army-move-rescind-2015-waters-us.

28. 33 U.S.C. § 1319(c)(1)–(2).

29. CWA § 309(c)(2)(B), 33 U.S.C. § 1319(c)(2)(B), sets out a separate felony violation for knowing endangerment by discharge into a sewer system or treatment plant of a pollutant that is likely to cause damage to property or personal injury, etc.

Thus, pulling together the necessary elements and the mental state requirements of the CWA reveals that to prove a knowing violation of the CWA, the government must prove that (1) a "person" as defined by the statute (2) knowingly[30] (3) discharged a pollutant (4) from a point source (5) into the waters of the United States (6) without a permit or in violation of a permit.[31] Determining the elements of crimes under other federal environmental statutes presents similar challenges.[32]

The number of CWA criminal cases has declined over the years, but the cases that remain are often a matter of public interest and concern, perhaps because of the often obvious nature of the circumstances when a large discharge to water occurs. The most significant such case in the history of environmental crime followed the explosion, fire, and destruction of the Deepwater Horizon oil rig. The rig was located roughly 40 miles off the coast of Louisiana, and on April 20, 2010, it exploded, killing 11 people and injuring 17.[33] It was the largest marine oil discharge in the nation's history.[34] The 1989 spill from the Exxon Valdez off the coast of Alaska released approximately 11 million gallons of crude oil.[35] The release of oil from the Deepwater Horizon rig ultimately released some 200 million gallons.[36] What both cases illustrate, among other things, is that a significant environmental incident is going to almost always include an inquiry as to whether a crime was committed.[37]

The Deepwater Horizon also illuminates the challenge of criminal prosecution of individuals in the case of significant industrial accidents. In the case of Deepwater Horizon, DOJ elected to have the criminal case handled by a task force of experienced prosecutors, and not by the environmental prosecutors at ECS. Despite obtaining significant corporate guilty pleas, in the end only five individuals were charged with violations stemming from the incident or conduct in

---

30. The question of what the government needs to prove beyond a reasonable doubt about the defendant's knowledge or intent is also a matter of considerable dispute, as discussed *infra*. Suffice it to say here that the government must prove that the defendant had the requisite knowledge and intent with regard to every essential element of the offense; the government need not prove the defendant's knowledge of an element conferring jurisdiction on the federal government to prosecute the crime, *United States v. Feola*, 420 U.S. 671, 676 n.9 (1975), or any element that would give rise to a mistake of law defense, *Staples v. United States*, 511 U.S. 600, 622 n.3 (1994) (Ginsburg, J., concurring).

31. *See, e.g.*, United States v. Dee, 912 F.2d 741 (4th Cir. 1990) (finding defendants guilty of offenses under Resource Conservation and Recovery Act (RCRA)).

32. It should be noted that many of the statutes discussed have multiple criminal provisions, statutory defenses, and permit provisions that will affect the substance of a prosecution. The careful practitioner will thoroughly research each statute and any regulations promulgated pursuant to that statute prior to proceeding.

33. *See* Nat'l Comm'n on the BP Deepwater Horizon Oil Spill and Offshore Drilling, Deepwater: The Gulf Oil Disaster and the Future of Offshore Drilling: Report to the President 1–20, 191 (Jan. 2011), https://www .gpo.gov/fdsys/pkg/GPO-OILCOMMISSION/pdf/GPO-OILCOMMISSION.pdf.

34. *Id.* at 127.

35. *See id.* at 70, 231.

36. *See* Monica Wilson et al., Oil Spill Science: Deepwater Horizon—Where Did the Oil Go? (Mississippi-Alabama Sea Grant Consortium 2017), http://masgc.org/oilscience/oil-spill-science-where-did-oil-go.pdf.

37. *See* Steven P. Solow, Anne M. Carpenter, & Katherine V. Barajas, *The State of Environmental Crime Enforcement: A Survey of Developments in 2015*, Daily Env't Rep. (BNA) (Apr. 8, 2016).

response to the incident. Three plead guilty to a single misdemeanor charge, and none of them was sentenced to serve any prison time. The other two defendants were acquitted at trial.[38]

An area of water-related enforcement that has seen consistent prosecution over time is the discharge of pollutants from vessels. These cases have been an area of intense prosecutorial focus by DOJ and the U.S. Coast Guard since the early 1990s. Well over 150 federal criminal cases have been brought in the past 25 years against companies and individuals under the CWA, the Act to Prevent Pollution from Ships (APPS),[39] the Ports and Waterway Safety Act (PWSA),[40] the Migratory Bird Treaty Act (MBTA),[41] the Refuse Act,[42] and the Oil Pollution Act (OPA 90).[43] Vessel-related prosecutions have taken place not only in cases involving the intentional discharge of oil (e.g., oil-water separator cases), but also whenever there is a significant maritime incident that results in the discharge of oil as a result of a grounding, collision, or allision. In sum, a criminal investigation is likely where there is a major water pollution incident or a failure to properly operate, or truthfully record the operation of, oil-water separation equipment. In such cases, companies and individuals are investigated and may be prosecuted for the underlying substantive environmental violations, as well as postincident conduct involving false statements, conspiracy, obstruction of justice, and aiding and abetting. With respect to individuals, common targets are crew members, mostly engineers, and the master. Shoreside individuals also have been prosecuted, however, generally on the grounds that they knew or should have known of the alleged violations and did nothing to prevent them.[44]

---

38. *Id.*

39. 33 U.S.C. §§ 1901–1915 (2012).

40. In addition to traditional environmental violations, several companies have been criminally prosecuted for failing to report hazardous conditions over the past several years in violation of the Ports and Waterways Safety Act. 33 U.S.C. §§ 1221–1236 (2000 & Supp. 2006). In *United States v. Diaglou*, No. 3:00-CR-00534-WHA-2 (N.D. Cal.) (plea agreement as to defendant Polembros Shipping dated Dec. 19, 2000), the owner, operator, and master of a vessel pled guilty to knowingly and willfully violating the PWSA. This prosecution resulted from a port-state inspection that found inoperative fire pumps and leaking fuel lines, among other hazards. Similarly, a vessel management company, D/S Progress, pled guilty to violations of the PWSA and APPS and conspiracy to violate those statutes based on the concealment of a hazardous leak in the hull of the *Freja Jutlandica*, a Norwegian-flagged oil tanker, and the deliberate failure to notify the Coast Guard of emergency discharges.

41. 16 U.S.C. §§ 703–712 (2012).

42. 33 U.S.C. § 407 (2012).

43. 40 U.S.C. §§ 2701–2720 (2012).

44. United States v. Royal Caribbean Cruise Lines, 11 F. Supp. 2d 1358 (S.D. Fla. 1998); United States v. Evergreen Shipping Lines, No. 2:05-CR-00291 (C.D. Cal. Apr. 4, 2005) (guilty plea); United States v. Overseas Shipping Grp., Inc., Case No. 06-CR-10408-RCL (D. Mass. Dec. 19, 2006) (guilty plea); United States v. Kun Yun Jho, 534 F.3d 398 (5th Cir. 2008).

B. Clean Air Act Section 113(c)[45]

The federal CAA Section 113(c) provides criminal penalties for knowing violations of the act, including making false statements, failure to report, tampering with monitors, failure to pay fees, and negligent and knowing releases of hazardous air pollutants.

There are more than a dozen ways in which the government can criminally prosecute violations of the CAA. These include:

1. Violation of a National Emission Standard for Hazardous Air Pollutants (NESHAP).[46]
2. Violation of the asbestos NESHAP during demolition/renovation.[47]
3. Violation of the general duty clause or risk management program requirements.[48]
4. Violation of stratospheric ozone protection provisions.[49]
5. False statements in CAA documents.[50]
6. Knowing failure to notify or report.[51]
7. Tampering with monitoring device or method.[52]
8. Negligent or knowing endangerment.[53]
9. Violation of a state implementation plan (SIP).[54]
10. Violation of a new source performance standard.[55]
11. Violation of operating permits provisions.[56]
12. Violation of an emergency order.[57]

The second on the list, violation of the asbestos NESHAP during demolition and renovation operations (such as so-called "rip and run" cases) is perhaps the most widely known, utilized in the prosecution of illegal asbestos abatement and removal operations. Asbestos NESHAP cases have been brought for several decades in cases where, at times, young adults, homeless people, or illegal immigrants are enlisted to remove asbestos without training, safe work procedures, or proper personal protective equipment.[58]

---

45. 42 U.S.C. § 7413(c) (2012). Portions of this section were drawn from Solow, Carpenter & Barajas, *Clean Air Act Criminal Enforcement, supra* note 4.
46. 42 U.S.C. §§ 7412, 7413(c)(1); 40 C.F.R. pt. 61 (2012).
47. 42 U.S.C. §§ 7412, 7413(c)(1); 40 C.F.R. § 61.145.
48. 42 U.S.C. §§ 7412(r)(1), 7412(r)(7), 7413(c)(1).
49. 42 U.S.C. §§ 7671, 7413(c)(1).
50. 42 U.S.C. § 7413(c)(2)(A); *see also* 18 U.S.C. § 1001.
51. 42 U.S.C. § 7413(c)(2)(B).
52. 42 U.S.C. § 7413(c)(2)(C).
53. 42 U.S.C. § 7413(c)(4), (5)(A).
54. 42 U.S.C. §§ 7410, 7413(c)(1).
55. 42 U.S.C. §§ 7411, 7413(c)(1); 40 C.F.R. pt. 60.
56. 42 U.S.C. §§ 7661a(a), 7661b(c), 7413(c)(1).
57. 42 U.S.C. §§ 7603, 7413(c)(1).
58. *See, e.g.*, Information at 4, United States v. Califco, LLC, No. 3:13- cr-00131-D (N.D. Tex. Apr. 12, 2013), ECF No. 1 (prosecution for using day laborers without proper personal protective equipment in asbestos abatement).

Third on the list, and what is becoming a trend in environmental criminal cases, is the investigation and prosecution of worker safety violations in tandem with environmental crimes. In May 2005, DOJ, EPA, and OSHA announced an initiative to increase interagency coordination and prosecution of worker safety violations through the use of charges under relevant environmental statutes. The initiative involves, among other things, DOJ-ECS attorneys training OSHA compliance officers to recognize and refer potential environmental violations to EPA and DOJ. DOJ has raised awareness of possible criminal violations among OSHA compliance officers, given regulators a basic grounding in environmental statutes that may be relevant, and informed them that the ECS is interested in pursuing a vigorous enforcement program of Occupational Safety and Health (OSH) Act violations as part of its overall environmental crimes mission.

Violations of the OSH Act and regulations promulgated pursuant to the act are not as simple to pursue as criminal cases, nor do the criminal provisions of OSHA carry a substantial penalty. For example, 29 U.S.C. § 666(e) provides:

> Any employer who willfully violates any standard, rule, or order promulgated pursuant to section 655 of this title [OSHA standards], or of any regulations prescribed pursuant to this chapter, and that violation caused death to any employee, shall, upon conviction, be punished by a fine of not more than $10,000 or by imprisonment for not more than six months, or by both; except that if the conviction is for a violation committed after a first conviction of such person, punishment shall be by a fine of not more than $20,000 or by imprisonment for not more than one year, or by both.

Thus, to bring a criminal case, the government must prove that (1) an employer (2) willfully (3) violated a standard, rule, or order promulgated pursuant to Section 655 of the OSH Act, or any OSHA regulation, and (4) the violation caused the death of an employee.

Significant obstacles to prosecution, especially of individuals, lie in the "willful" standard of knowledge and the definition of "employer," a term with a specific and narrow definition under the statute that severely limits the range of individuals whose status allows them to be prosecuted in a criminal case. Given the comparatively modest penalties associated with a violation, especially one that results in an employee's death, and the obstacles to prosecution embedded in the statute itself,[59] prosecutors may choose not to seek OSH Act criminal charges. Instead, the government will look for charges under related environmental statutes that can be associated with the conduct resulting in the death, or that arise from efforts to cover up the original crime.[60]

---

59. *See* W. Warren Hamel & Tally Parham, *Individual Criminal Liability for Willful OSH Act Violations: A Practice Guide for Navigating Investigation and Prosecution*, 1 WHITE COLLAR CRIME REP. (BNA) No. 12, at 390–94 (July 7, 2006).

60. *See* United States v. Elias, 269 F.3d 1003 (9th Cir. 2001) (conviction for violation of the RCRA knowing endangerment provision and violation of 18 U.S.C. § 1001, the false statement statute).

In December 2015, Deputy Attorney General Sally Yates announced the Worker Endangerment Initiative, which shifts authority for the prosecution of workplace safety violations to ECS and to any of the 93 U.S. Attorneys' offices.[61] Because of the known limits of the OSH Act, which has only a misdemeanor provision applicable to willful violations resulting in fatalities, the memorandum instructs prosecutors to consider the use of environmental criminal statutes and Title 18. The memorandum also references a memorandum of understanding (MOU) between DOJ and the Department of Labor designed to enhance cooperation on criminal prosecutions for workplace safety violations.

The Worker Endangerment Initiative followed Deputy Attorney General Yates's memorandum of September 9, 2015, which reemphasizes the prosecution of individuals in white-collar cases and requires corporations who wish to be considered to have "cooperated" with government investigations to proactively provide information regarding the culpability of individual employees.[62]

The worker safety initiative can be traced back to *United States v. Elias*, the so-called "cyanide canary" case prosecuted in 2000, in which the defendant, Alan Elias, was convicted of knowing endangerment and sentenced to 17 years in prison and ordered to pay $5.9 million in restitution. Elias had ordered an employee to wash the inside of a tank containing phosphoric acid and cyanide. The employee collapsed in the tank and by the time he was rescued had suffered severe and irreversible brain damage. Previously, workplace safety violations were handled civilly, and by a small number of misdemeanor prosecutions.[63]

A year after the *Elias* case, when an explosion and collapse of a highly corroded sulfuric acid tank at a Motiva Enterprises, LLC facility caused a worker fatality, worker injuries, and a discharge into the Delaware River, the government used both the CAA's negligent endangerment provision and the CWA's prohibition against unpermitted discharges to obtain a $10 million criminal fine against Motiva.[64]

Then, in the mid-2000s, the government brought five hybrid environmental-workplace safety prosecutions against the cast-iron-pipe manufacturer McWane, Inc. and several of its divisions, including Atlantic States Cast Iron Pipe Co. In the Atlantic States prosecution, the government alleged that McWane had a history of environmental violations, workplace injuries, and fatalities, as well as activities intended to obstruct justice.[65] Across the five cases, the government relied on a combination of felony charges under the OSH Act, CWA, CAA, Comprehensive Environmental Response, Compensation, and Liability Act (CERCLA), and RCRA,

---

61. Memorandum from Sally Quillian Yates, Deputy Att'y Gen., U.S. Dep't of Justice, Prosecutions of Worker Safety Violations (Dec. 17, 2015), https://www.justice.gov/enrd/file/800431/download.

62. Memorandum from Sally Quillian Yates, Deputy Att'y Gen., U.S. Dep't of Justice, Individual Accountability for Corporate Wrongdoing (Sept. 9, 2015), https://www.justice.gov/archives/dag/file/769036/download.

63. *See* 29 U.S.C. § 666(e), (f), (g) (2012).

64. *See* United States v. Motiva Enters., LLC, No. 1:05-cr-00021 (D. Del. 2005).

65. *See* United States v. Atl. States Cast Iron Pipe Co., No. 3:03-cr-00852 (D.N.J. 2006).

as well as charges of obstruction and false statements, to obtain criminal penalties totaling almost $25 million against the McWane entities and jail time for McWane officials.[66] When there is an accidental release resulting in a fatality, serious injury, or substantial property damages at a chemical plant or a refinery, the CSB investigates the cause. CSB's unique role separates this agency (akin to the NTSB, which investigates transportations accidents) from every other agency that investigates such accidents. Other agencies (e.g., FBI, the U.S. Coast Guard, EPA) investigate to determine whether the accident also involved a violation of law. These differing objectives are profound. When the NTSB and the CSB interview individuals after an accident, they describe their mission as a safety review, and state that they are not a law enforcement agency. Indeed, the CSB MOU with EPA states:

> To ensure that during the conduct of an investigation the CSB is not perceived as an extension of a state or federal enforcement investigation, the CSB will not participate in compliance and enforcement activities conducted by other agencies.[67]

Individuals being so interviewed, typically without counsel present, could reasonably infer that they are being interviewed for the purpose of identifying safety issues, and not as a part of a criminal investigation. But in recent years, DOJ is increasingly seeking to incorporate the work of the NTSB and the CSB into its criminal investigations and to this end has sought to obtain the results of safety agency witness interviews for use in criminal cases.[68]

The CSB has stated that turning over interviews conducted by the CSB for "prosecution purposes" would "likely have a devastating effect" on its work.[69]

In October 2013, the Society of Chemical Manufacturers and Affiliates (SOCMA) presented comments regarding Executive Order 13650 (related to agency coordination on chemical facility safety and security), and cited efforts by DOJ to obtain CSB witness interviews to assist in a criminal investigation. SOCMA cautioned that "witnesses will not be completely forthcoming to CSB if they fear the statements they make may be provided" to criminal investigations, and that pushing to do so would "frustrate CSB's mission."[70]

Similarly, 14 years ago the then chairman of the NTSB, James Hall, publicly raised concerns about the potential for criminal investigations, in and of

---

66. *See id.*; *see also* United States v. Union Foundry Co., No. 2:05-cr-00299 (N.D. Ala. 2005); United States v. Tyler Pipe Co., No. 6:05-cr00029 (E.D. Tex. 2005); United States v. McWane, Inc., No. 2:05-cr-00811 (D. Utah 2006); United States v. McWane, Inc., No. 2:04-cr-00199 (N.D. Ala. 2005).

67. Memorandum of Understanding between the United States Environmental Agency and the United States Chemical Safety and Hazard Investigation Board on Chemical Incidents (1999), https://www.epa.gov/sites/production/files/2013-10/documents/csbepa.pdf.

68. *See* Pete Yost, Associated Press, *Safety vs Enforcement: Agencies at Odds over Probe*, San Diego Union-Tribune (Aug. 27, 2013), http://www.sandiegouniontribune.com/sdut-safety-vs-enforcement-agencies-at-odds-over-probe-2013aug27-story.html. Disclosure: some of the authors have represented clients subject to a safety agency review, where the DOJ has made such a request for the results of witness interviews.

69. *Id.*

70. Letter from Soc'y of Chem. Mfrs. & Affiliates to the Chem. Facility Safety & Sec. Working Grp., Comments on Implementation of Executive Order 13650 (Oct. 17, 2013), http://1.usa.gov/1jwTbQ1.

themselves, to reduce the ability of the NTSB to conduct effective safety investigations.[71] Hall's concern was that the mere presence of a criminal investigation could scare away critical witnesses from the NTSB's efforts.

Hall's concern was about parallel criminal investigations. His concerns did not extend to the possibility that prosecutors would not only run parallel investigations, but would also seek to extract the results of NTSB or CSB safety interviews for use in criminal investigations.

In response to DOJ's effort to use NTSB or CSB interviews in criminal cases, Hall has stated, "Congress knew that it would hamper the fact-finding process to have parallel criminal and safety investigations, and that's why it explicitly addressed this concern in the NTSB's governing statute."[72] Hall pointed to 49 U.S.C. § 1131(a)(2)(B), which requires the NTSB to relinquish control of an investigation to the FBI when circumstances indicate that an accident was caused by a criminal act. "When we found evidence that an accident was caused by criminal wrongdoing, we followed Congress's instructions and turned things over to the FBI. By the same token, when there's no such evidence of criminal wrongdoing, any inquiry into the accident should be handled exclusively by the safety board."[73] As Hall explained, the NTSB fully expects other agencies to conduct their own investigations.

What is DOJ's rationale for seeking the NTSB and CSB work product? One theory that has been raised is that the government will need to do so in order to meet its production obligations under the Federal Rules of Criminal Procedure, *Brady*, and the Jencks Act.[74] These authorities, in addition to guidance by the *United States Attorneys' Manual* (now the *Justice Manual*),[75] require prosecutors to disclose any potential exculpatory and impeachment information to defendants in criminal cases. Such a theory, however, appears to rest on a false premise because the NTSB and CSB are arguably excluded from these criminal disclosure obligations (given what should be their lack of involvement in criminal investigations and prosecutions).

Following concerns raised regarding the failure to disclose evidence in the prosecution of Senator Ted Stevens (R-Alaska) in January 2010, DOJ issued guidance for prosecutors regarding criminal discovery. DOJ's guidance on discovery states that the obligation to produce information to criminal defendants extends only to records of "[m]embers of the prosecution team includ[ing] federal, state, and local law enforcement officers and other government officials participating in

---

71. *See* Matthew L. Wald, *Fear of Prosecution Hinders Crash Inquiries, Some Say*, N.Y. Times, Apr. 17, 2000, http://www.nytimes.com/2000/04/17/us/fear-of-prosecution-hinders-crash-inquiries-some-say.html.

72. *See* Solow & Carpenter, *The State of Environmental Crime Enforcement: A Survey of Developments in 2013*, *supra* note 4, at *4.

73. *Id.*

74. *See* Fed. R. Crim. P. 16, 26.2; Brady v. Maryland, 373 U.S. 83 (1963); 18 U.S.C. § 3500 (1957).

75. *See* U.S. Dep't of Justice, Justice Manual § 9-5.001 (2018).

the investigation and prosecution of the criminal case against the defendant."[76] This appears to plainly exclude the NTSB and the CSB, who by statute are not "members of the prosecution team," and do not "participate" in criminal investigations or prosecutions.

Exclusion of the NTSB and the CSB from the department's production obligations is also supported by a line of cases in which courts have underlined the notion that where a federal agency did not play "any role in the investigative [*sic*] or prosecution" of a case, there is no production obligation on the department.[77] As for the interests of defendants in obtaining such documents to assist in their own defense, the *Upton* court noted that the materials should be available to the defendant via subpoena.[78]

It remains to be seen how this internal conflict between government agencies will develop and how the government will balance its safety and enforcement priorities. As a final note on the CAA, with regard to the 11th potential area of enforcement on the preceding list, because of a "cure opportunity" in the CAA statutory scheme[79] and significant litigation over the meaning of various provisions of the act,[80] CAA criminal prosecutions have not traditionally focused on violations of air emissions permits.

C. Resource Conservation and Recovery Act

RCRA establishes a cradle-to-grave regulatory regime governing the storage, transportation, treatment, and disposal of hazardous waste.[81] The criminal provisions provide criminal penalties for persons who knowingly treat, store, or dispose of hazardous waste without, or in violation of, a permit, or who knowingly omit information or make a false report, or who knowingly transport hazardous material without proper documentation.[82] RCRA also includes a separate violation and penalties for knowing endangerment.[83] In a typical RCRA case, the government

---

76. Memorandum from David W. Ogden, Deputy Att'y Gen., U.S. Dep't of Justice, Guidance for Prosecutors Regarding Criminal Discovery (Jan. 4, 2010), http://www.justice.gov/dag/discovery-guidance.html.

77. United States v. Upton, 856 F. Supp. 727, 750 (E.D.N.Y. 1994).

78. *Id.*

79. A facility violating the terms of its CAA emissions permit issued under a SIP is, under most circumstances, allowed 30 days after notice of violation to cure the violation before a criminal case may be brought. CAA § 113(a)(1), 42 U.S.C. § 7413(a)(1); *see also* United States v. Louisiana-Pacific Corp., 682 F. Supp. 1141, 1155 (D. Colo. 1988).

80. *See, e.g.*, Envtl. Def. v. Duke Energy Corp., 549 U.S. 561 (2007) (resolving the meaning of one regulatory provision that was first promulgated over a quarter of a century ago).

81. The Resource Conservation and Recovery Act, Pub. L. No. 94-580, 90 Stat. 2795 (1976) (codified at 42 U.S.C. §§ 6901–6992k (2012)), has always had felony criminal provisions. *See* Solid Waste Disposal Act Amendments of 1980, Pub. L. No. 96-482, 94 Stat. 2334; Hazardous and Solid Waste Amendments of 1984, Pub. L. No. 98-616, 98 Stat. 3221 (codified as amended at 42 U.S.C. §§ 6901–6992k (2012)). However, there was no program for enforcement until November 19, 1980, when the initial regulations listing and identifying wastes as hazardous wastes subject to regulation became effective. Identification and Listing of Hazardous Waste, 45 Fed. Reg. 33,119 (1980) (codified at 40 C.F.R. § 261 (2017)).

82. RCRA § 3008(1)–(7), 42 U.S.C. § 6928(d)(1)–(7) (2012).

83. RCRA § 3008(e), 42 U.S.C. § 6928(e) (2012).

must prove the following elements: (1) a person[84] (2) knowingly (3) treated, stored, transported, or disposed of[85] (4) a hazardous waste (5) without a permit or in violation of a permit.[86] A waste may be defined as hazardous either because it is listed in 40 C.F.R. §§ 261.30–.33 (2017), or because it has been determined to fall into one of several categories[87] of hazardous waste, typically determined by laboratory testing of samples.

RCRA also has a "knowing endangerment" crime, which provides enhanced criminal penalties for committing a RCRA offense, and in doing so, placing another person in imminent danger of death or serious bodily injury.[88] In a knowing endangerment case, the government must prove all the elements of the underlying RCRA hazardous waste violation described previously, as well as two other elements: (1) the defendant, at the time of the violation, placed another person in imminent danger of death or serious bodily injury, and (2) the defendant knew, at the time of the violation, that his or her acts placed another person in such danger.

D. Wildlife Crimes

Several statutes protecting fish, wildlife, and plants also contain criminal provisions, including the Endangered Species Act (ESA),[89] the Lacey Act,[90] and the MBTA.[91] The ESA criminal provisions prohibit a wide variety of conduct, but a typical case requires proof of the following elements: (1) a person[92] (2) knowingly[93] (3) imports, exports, takes, sells, purchases, receives, or other conduct as listed in Section 1538, (4) a species listed as endangered,[94] or threatened,[95] or listed in an Appendix to the Convention on International Trade in Endangered Species,[96] and (5) that the defendant engaged in the conduct without permit from an authorized government agency.[97]

The Lacey Act prohibits the import, export, transport, sale, receipt, acquisition, or purchase of fish, wildlife, or plants taken, possessed, transported, or sold, and so on, in violation of state, federal, or foreign law,[98] as well as making false records, labels, and markings in relation to fish, wildlife, or plants illegally taken,

---

84. Defined at RCRA § 1004(15), 42 U.S.C. § 6903(15) (2012).
85. Defined at RCRA § 1004(34), (33), (3), 42 U.S.C. § 6903(34), (33), (3) (2012).
86. *See* RCRA § 3008(d)(2), 42 U.S.C. § 6928(d)(2) (2012).
87. The categories include toxicity, ignitability, corrosivity, and reactivity. *See* 40 C.F.R. § 261.3(a)(2) (2017); 40 C.F.R. § 261.30(b) (2017).
88. RCRA § 3008(e)–(f), 42 U.S.C. § 6928(e)–(f) (2012).
89. 16 U.S.C. §§ 1531–1544 (2012).
90. 16 U.S.C. §§ 3371–3378 (2012).
91. 16 U.S.C. §§ 703–712 (2012).
92. Defined at ESA § 3(13), 16 U.S.C. § 1532(13) (2012).
93. *See* ESA § 11(b) 16 U.S.C. § 1540(b) (2012).
94. Defined at ESA § 3(6), 16 U.S.C. § 1532(6) (2012).
95. Defined at ESA § 3(20), 16 U.S.C. § 1532(6) (2012).
96. *See* ESA § 2(a)(4)(F), 16 U.S.C. § 1531(a)(4)(F) (2012); ESA § 3(4), 16 U.S.C. § 1532(4) (2012); ESA § 9(c)(1), 16 U.S.C. § 1538(c)(1) (2012).
97. *See, e.g.*, ESA § 10(g), 16 U.S.C. § 1539(g); United States v. Winnie, 97 F.3d 975 (7th Cir. 1996).
98. *See* 16 U.S.C. § 3372(a) (2012).

transported, possessed, or sold in violation of federal, state, or foreign law.[99] A knowing violation is punishable as a felony, while a violation where the government can prove only that the defendant acted knowingly with regard to the conduct, but in the exercise of due care should have known the status of the species, is a Class A misdemeanor. To prove a typical knowing violation of the Lacey Act, the government must show: (1) a person (2) knowingly (3) imported, exported, transported, sold, received, acquired, or purchased (4) in interstate or foreign commerce (5) fish, wildlife, or plants, where such species were (6) taken, possessed, transported, or sold in violation of state, federal, or foreign law.[100]

E. Other Environmental Crimes

Several other environmental criminal statutes have been used infrequently, but are important to mention. CERCLA[101] requires immediate notification to the appropriate federal agency upon the release of a reportable quantity of a hazardous substance from a facility into the environment.[102] Section 9603(d) of CERCLA requires that certain facilities maintain specific records, and makes it a crime to destroy such records. Failure to report also can be the basis for criminal liability under the Emergency Planning and Community Right-to-Know Act (EPCRA).[103] Under EPCRA, a knowing and willful failure to provide notice of a release of a reportable quantity of a hazardous substance is a felony.[104] Under the Hazardous Materials Transportation Act (HMTA),[105] a person who knowingly alters, removes, destroys, or otherwise tampers with a required hazardous material label or placard or a vehicle used to transport a hazardous material, or who willfully violates any provision of the HMTA or regulations promulgated pursuant to the statute, is guilty of a felony.[106] The Toxic Substances Control Act[107] and the Federal Insecticide, Fungicide, and Rodenticide Act (FIFRA)[108] also carry criminal penalties for violation of the statutes or regulations governing toxic substances and various pesticides.[109]

---

99. *See id.* § 3372(b), (d) (2012).

100. *See id.* §§ 3372(a), 3373(d)(1) (2012).

101. CERCLA, 42 U.S.C. §§ 9601–9675 (2012).

102. CERCLA § 103(a), 42 U.S.C. § 9603(a) (2012). Penalties under CERCLA remained at the misdemeanor level from the time of the statute's initial enactment, Pub. L. No. 96-510, 94 Stat. 2767 (1980), until 1986, when felony sanctions were added. Superfund Amendments and Reauthorization Act of 1986, Pub. L. No. 99-499, 100 Stat. 1613 (codified at 42 U.S.C. § 9601(b) (2012).

103. 42 U.S.C. §§ 11001–11050 (2012).

104. *See* EPCRA § 325(b)94), 42 U.S.C. § 11045(b)(4) (2012).

105. 49 U.S.C. §§ 5101–5127 (2012).

106. *See* 49 U.S.C. § 5124 (2012).

107. 15 U.S.C. 53 §§ 2601–2629 (2012).

108. 7 U.S.C. 6 §§ 121–136y (2012).

109. 15 U.S.C. § 2615(b) (2012) (criminal penalties for HMTA); 7 U.S.C. §§ 136j & l (2012) (criminal penalties for FIFRA). The aforementioned statutes are not a complete list of environmental statutes with criminal provisions, or even a full listing of the criminal provisions available in each of the statutes listed; the facts and circumstances of each case will dictate which regulatory regime will govern the applicable legal requirements.

Following an explosion at a Massey Energy mine that killed 29 workers in 2010, the government prosecuted former Massey CEO Donald Blankenship.[110] In what appears to be the first conviction of a high-level corporate executive under a safety statute, the jury found Blankenship guilty of one misdemeanor count of conspiracy to willfully violate the Mine Safety and Health Act, and the court sentenced him to a year in prison.

F. Title 18 Offenses

A routine part of government investigations, including environmental criminal investigations, is a close examination as to whether there have been attempts to cover up or conceal the underlying environmental violation. In addition, prosecutors look for the emblems of criminality, such as lying, cheating, and stealing, that may convince a jury to punish an environmental violation as a crime. As a result, environmental crimes prosecutions often marry substantive environmental violations with criminal provisions such as conspiracy,[111] aiding and abetting,[112] false statements,[113] and obstruction of justice.[114] Conspiracy—in Judge Learned Hand's famous phrase, the "darling of the modern prosecutor's nursery"[115]—appears as count one in most federal indictments, because it allows the government to state the theory of the case in a narrative format, detailing multiple overt acts (that is, any action taken by any member of the conspiracy to achieve the goals of the conspiracy), and to include prior violations and conduct that may be outside the statute of limitations in the case at issue.[116] The federal conspiracy statute prohibits two or more individuals from combining or agreeing to achieve an unlawful purpose; however, there must be proof of at least one overt act, and one of the overt acts must be within the jurisdiction where the prosecution is being brought.[117] Aiding and abetting punishes an individual who "aids, abets, counsels, commands, induces or procures" the commission of a crime as if he or she were the principal who committed the crime directly.[118] Aiding and abetting is not ordinarily charged as a separate crime; rather, it is an alternate theory of liability that is charged with the underlying substantive count. The false statement statute prohibits, among other things, "[making] any materially false, fictitious, or fraudulent statement or representation," in a matter within the jurisdiction of the executive,

---

110. *See* United States v. Blankenship, No. 5:14-cr-00244 (S.D.W. Va. 2015).
111. 18 U.S.C. § 371 (2012).
112. 18 U.S.C. § 2 (2012).
113. 18 U.S.C. § 1001 (2012).
114. 18 U.S.C. §§ 1501–1518 (2012).
115. Harrison v. United States, 7 F.2d 259, 263 (2d Cir. 1925).
116. *See, e.g.*, Hyde v. United States, 225 U.S. 347, 367–71 (1912) (holding that conspiracy is a continuing violation); Bergschneider v. Denver, 446 F.2d 569 (9th Cir. 1971) (finding that, in conspiracy cases, statute of limitations starts to run on date of last overt act alleged).
117. *See* 18 U.S.C. § 371 (2012), 18 U.S.C. § 3237 (2012) (jurisdiction and venue).
118. 18 U.S.C. § 2(a) (2012).

legislative, or judicial branch of the United States.[119] A false statement may include a false material omission and making or using a false writing or document. Finally, the obstruction of justice statutes[120] make a wide variety of obstructive conduct a crime, ranging from destruction or alteration of documents or other evidence to witness tampering to retaliation against a whistle-blower cooperating with a federal investigation.

III. MENS REA

Mens rea in environmental cases has been the subject of much debate throughout the history of the environmental criminal program. The past 20 years have established clear case law on certain provisions of various statutes, but there continue to be nuances that are the subject of hard-fought battles. Depending upon the particular statute included, criminal environmental violations may be based on strict liability, simple negligence, knowing conduct, or willful conduct.

A. Strict Liability

The oldest environmental criminal statute is the Rivers and Harbors Act of 1899, more commonly known as the Refuse Act.[121] This act provides strict criminal liability for the discharge of any refuse matter into a navigable water of the United States without a permit. Prior to the enactment of the media-specific environmental statutes in the 1970s, DOJ prosecuted a number of dischargers of industrial waste under this statute.[122] The Refuse Act prohibits, among other things, the discharge of any refuse matter of any kind or description including materials that have been thrown aside, rejected, or left behind.[123] For example, oil is considered to be "refuse" and therefore the release of oil into U.S. waters is a violation of the Refuse Act.[124]

The MBTA is another strict liability statute that often comes into play in the case of an oil spill. The MBTA prohibits the killing of a migratory bird "by any means or in any manner."[125] The statute has been applied to circumstances where migratory birds were harmed or killed by oil spills, because no criminal intent to

---

119. 18 U.S.C. § 1001(a)(2) (2012).

120. 18 U.S.C. §§ 1501–1518 (2012).

121. 33 U.S.C. §§ 407, 411 (2012).

122. *See, e.g.*, United States v. Pa. Indus. Chem. Corp., 411 U.S. 655 (1973); United States v. White Fuel Corp., 498 F.2d 619 (1st Cir. 1974); United States v. Consol. Coal Co., 354 F. Supp. 173 (N.D.W. Va. 1973); United States v. Am. Cyanamid Co., 354 F. Supp. 1202 (S.D.N.Y. 1973), *aff'd*, 480 F.2d 1132 (2d Cir. 1973); United States v. U.S. Steel Corp., 328 F. Supp. 354 (N.D. Ind. 1970), *aff'd*, 482 F.2d 439 (7th Cir. 1973), *cert. denied*, 414 U.S. 909 (1973); United States v. Interlake Steel Corp., 297 F. Supp. 912 (N.D. Ill. 1969).

123. For exceptions to the definition of refuse, see 33 U.S.C. § 407 (2012).

124. *See* United States v. Standard Oil Co., 384 U.S. 224, 230 (1966).

125. 16 U.S.C. § 703 (2012).

harm or kill a bird is required for an MBTA violation.[126] Furthermore, because the MBTA is a strict liability statute, the only available defense is that the defendant's conduct did not cause harm to or the death of a migratory bird. Thus, if the court determines that the actions of a "person, association, partnership, or corporation" resulted in the death of or harm to one or more protected birds in violation of the MBTA, then that person is criminally liable for the violation.[127]

The government does not have to prove knowledge, intent, or even negligence in prosecutions involving strict liability crimes. To sustain a conviction under the Refuse Act or the MBTA, the government simply has to prove that refuse went into the waters of the United States, or that a migratory bird was harmed or killed, regardless of whether the defendant intended or knew of the conduct. As a result of the strict liability standard, the Refuse Act and the MBTA frequently are used in oil spill cases, and their use increases the risk of criminal liability for owners, operators, and other persons involved in a spill event.[128]

For example, DOJ used these two strict liability statutes as the sole basis for a prosecution in the IMC Shipping Company (*Selendang Ayu*) case.[129] The *Selendang Ayu* went aground in Alaska in December 2004, spilling a cargo of soybeans, as well as approximately 340,000 gallons of bunker fuel. The spill occurred after the crew shut down an engine upon discovering a crack in it. When the engine could not be restarted, the vessel ran aground after two days of drifting. Hundreds of migratory birds were killed and about 37 miles of coastline were oiled. The government and IMC, the ship operator, disagreed as to whether improper maintenance caused the engine crack, and IMC refused to admit negligence. Despite commending IMC's cooperation in the response and investigation, the government prosecuted IMC, which pled guilty in August 2007 to two counts of violating the Refuse Act for discharging refuse (soybeans and oil) into the water and one count of violating the MBTA, and paid a $10 million fine.

In December 2017, the Department of the Interior, in sharp reversal of decades of prior prosecution positions, issued a solicitor's opinion that stated:

> [C]onsistent with the text, history, and purpose of the MBTA, the statute's prohibitions on pursuing, hunting, taking, capturing, killing, or attempting to do the same apply only to affirmative actions that have as their purpose the taking or killing of migratory birds, their nests, or their eggs.[130]

---

126. Yereth Rosen, *IMC Shipping to Pay Fine for 2004 Alaska Oil Spill*, Reuters (Aug. 14, 2007), https://www.reuters.com/article/us-alaska-spill/imc-shipping-to-pay-fine-for-2004-alaska-oil-spill-idUSN14190660 20070815).

127. 16 U.S.C. § 707 (2012).

128. Recent cases using strict liability statutes include United States v. Empire Transit Mix, Inc., No. 1:05-cr-00319 (E.D.N.Y. 2005); United States v. Hillyer, 457 F.3d 347 (4th Cir. 2006) (defendant pled guilty under Refuse Act); United States v. IMC Shipping Co., No. 3:07-cr-00096 (D. Alaska 2007).

129. *See IMC Shipping Co.*, No. 3:07-CR-00096-RRB (plea agreement); Dan Joling, *Guilty Plea Planned in Ship Breakup*, Wash. Post, Aug. 15, 2007.

130. U.S. Dep't of the Interior, Solicitor's Opinion M-37050 at 2 (Dec. 22, 2017).

Thus, it appears for now that the government will not prosecute so-called "incidental takes" as criminal violations of the MBTA. It remains to be seen whether and to what extent this remains the position of the federal government.

B. Negligence

Only two environmental statutes have negligence provisions: the CWA[131] and the CAA.[132] The CWA has the broader provision of the two, for it criminalizes negligent discharges of pollutants that are either unpermitted or that violate permit conditions.[133] Prosecutions of CWA criminal negligence cases have been consistent over the years and the use of the provision was reinforced by the Ninth Circuit's decision in *United States v. Hanousek,* which held that CWA violations can be based on simple negligence rather than on a higher standard of gross or criminal negligence. The court also accepted the ordinary definition of the term *negligence,* namely, "a failure to use such care as a reasonably prudent and careful person would use under similar circumstances."[134]

The CAA negligence provision is significantly different from the CWA provision. Under the CAA, it is a crime to "negligently release[] into the ambient air any hazardous air pollutant . . . and . . . at the time negligently place[] another person in imminent danger of death or serious bodily injury."[135] There have been relatively few prosecutions using the CAA negligence provision, and the authors are aware of no reported decisions addressing whether this provision also will be viewed as requiring proof only of simple negligence.

C. Knowing

The courts have repeatedly found "knowing" criminal offenses to be general intent crimes[136] under a wide variety of environmental laws. The majority of the case law on this issue has arisen in the context of the felony provisions of both the CWA and RCRA. Under the general intent standard, the government must prove that a defendant had knowledge of the nature of his or her acts and acted intentionally, not as a result of a mistake or accident or other innocent reason. The issues addressed by these cases dealt with whether, and what, the government must

---

131. FWPCA § 309(c)(1), 33 U.S.C. § 1319(c)(1) (2012).
132. CAA § 113(c)(4), 42 U.S.C. § 7413(c)(4) (2012).
133. *See* Steven P. Solow & Ronald A. Sarachan, *Criminal Negligence Prosecutions under the Federal Clean Water Act: A Statistical Analysis and an Evaluation of the Impact of* Hanousek *and* Hong, 32 ENVTL. L. REP. No. 10 at11, 153–61 (Oct. 2002).
134. 176 F.3d 1116, 1120 (9th Cir. 1999).
135. 42 U.S.C. § 7413(c)(4) (1990).
136. *See, e.g.,* United States v. Wagner, 29 F.3d 264, 265–66 (7th Cir. 1994) (RCRA); United States v. Laughlin, 10 F.3d 961, 965–68 (2d Cir. 1993) (RCRA, CERCLA); United States v. Dee, 912 F.2d 741, 745 (4th Cir. 1990) (RCRA); United States v. Reilly, 827 F. Supp. 1076, 1077–78 (D. Del. 1993), *aff'd,* 33 F.3d 1396 (3d Cir. 1994) (Ocean Dumping Act); United States v. Buckley, 934 F.2d 84, 88–89 (6th Cir. 1991) (CERCLA, CAA).

prove a defendant knew about (1) the law and regulations, (2) the party's permit status, and (3) the nature of the pollutant or hazardous waste.

1. "Knowing" under the CWA

Typical of other decisions, the Ninth and the Second Circuits, after considering the statutory language, the legislative history, and the nature of the CWA, have held that under the criminal provisions of the CWA,[137] a defendant need only be aware of his or her acts; he or she need not have knowledge of the statute or regulations or that his or her conduct was unlawful. In *United States v. Weitzenhoff*, the district court ruled that under Section 1319(c)(2)(A), "[t]he government did not need to prove that [defendants] knew that their acts violated the permit or the CWA" and the court of appeals affirmed.[138] Similarly, in *United States v. Hopkins*, the court held that "in a prosecution under § 1319(c)(2)(A), the government was required to prove that [defendant] knew the nature of his acts and performed them intentionally, but was not required to prove that he knew those acts violated the CWA, or any particular provision of that law, or the regulatory permit."[139] The court reasoned that the purpose and legislative history of Section 1319(c)(2)(A) indicate that Congress meant that section would be violated if the defendant's acts were proscribed, even if the defendant was not aware of the proscription.[140]

In *United States v. Ahmad*, the defendant asserted a mistake of fact defense and argued that the government needed to prove not only that he knew that there was an unpermitted discharge, but also that he knew that what he was discharging was a pollutant and not simply water.[141] The Fifth Circuit agreed and held that "[w]ith the exception of purely jurisdictional elements, the *mens rea* of knowledge applies to each element of the crimes."[142]

2. "Knowing" under RCRA

As in cases brought under the CWA, courts addressing mens rea issues under RCRA have held that the government does not need to prove that the defendant knew that the materials were, in fact, hazardous wastes. In *United States v. Dee*, the defendants argued that the government had to prove that they knew the chemical wastes were regulated as hazardous wastes and that violation of RCRA was a crime.[143] In affirming the convictions, the Fourth Circuit found that the government only was required to prove that the defendants knowingly committed the acts charged in the indictment and that they knew the general nature of the wastes involved. This decision is consistent with the majority of circuits that have

---

137. FWPCA § 309(c)(2)(A), 33 U.S.C. § 1319(c)(2)(A) (2012).
138. 35 F.3d 1275, 1286 (9th Cir. 1994), *cert. denied*, 513 U.S. 1128 (1995).
139. 53 F.3d 533, 541 (2d Cir. 1995), *cert. denied*, 516 U.S. 1071 (1996).
140. *Id.* at 539–40.
141. 101 F.3d 386, 390 (5th Cir. 1996).
142. *Id.* at 391.
143. 912 F.2d 741, 745–46 (4th Cir. 1990).

interpreted the knowledge requirement of RCRA as it applies to the nature of the waste.[144] However, there is a split in the circuits as to whether knowledge of the permit status must be proven to convict a defendant of RCRA violations. In an early case, the Third Circuit held that under Section 6928(d)(2)(A), all elements of the violation had to be done "knowingly."[145] The Third Circuit's reasoning has been rejected in subsequent cases. In *United States v. Hoflin*, the Ninth Circuit concluded that as a matter of both statutory construction and public policy, it was illogical to interpret Section 6928(d)(2)(A) as requiring that the government prove that the defendant knew the permit status.[146]

3. Corporate Workplace Safety Prosecutions: Use of the "Collective Knowledge" Doctrine[147]

Identifying a single individual whose mental state and actions can serve as the basis for corporate criminal liability in a hybrid environmental-workplace safety enforcement can be difficult. This challenge may result in an increase in the government's use of novel legal theories, including corporate collective knowledge. This theory aggregates knowledge held by different employees and imputes the totality of that knowledge to the corporation as a basis for imposing criminal liability on the company. Recently, the U.S. District Court for the Northern District of California affirmed the use of this theory in in the government's prosecution of Pacific Gas & Electric (PG&E) for knowing and willful violations of Pipeline Safety Act (PSA) regulations.[148] PG&E was indicted in 2014 for PSA violations and obstruction of an NTSB investigation following a 2010 gas line rupture in San Bruno, California, that led to the death of eight people, injuries to 58 people, and damage to numerous homes. On August 9, 2016, PG&E was convicted of five counts of violating the PSA and one count of obstruction after a lengthy jury trial.

At the outset of the PG&E matter, the prosecution proceeded under a theory that intertwined corporate collective knowledge and collective intent to simultaneously prove the knowing and willful mens rea required for violation of the PSA. In an early order by the court denying PG&E's motion to dismiss the indictment, the court approved the prosecution's theory in the statement that "where a corporation has a legal duty to prevent violations, and the knowledge of that corporation's employees collectively demonstrates a failure to discharge that duty, the

---

144. *See* United States v. Wagner, 29 F.3d 264, 266 n.1 (7th Cir. 1994); United States v. Laughlin, 10 F.3d 961, 965 (2d Cir. 1993); United States v. Hoflin, 880 F.2d 1033, 1036–39 (9th Cir. 1989); United States v. Hayes Int'l Corp., 786 F.2d 1499, 1502–03 (11th Cir. 1986).

145. United States v. Johnson & Towers, Inc., 741 F.2d 662, 667–69 (3d Cir. 1984), *cert. denied*, 469 U.S. 1208 (1985).

146. 880 F.2d 1033, 1036–40 (9th Cir. 1989), *cert. denied*, 493 U.S. 1083 (1990). *See also* United States v. Dean, 969 F.2d 187, 190–93 (6th Cir. 1992); United States v. Laughlin, 768 F. Supp. 957, 961–66 (N.D.N.Y. 1991).

147. Portions of this subsection can also be found at Solow, Chinn & Carpenter, *Criminal Prosecution of Environmental and Workplace Safety Incidents through DOJ's New Worker Endangerment Initiative*, *supra* note 4.

148. United States v. Pac. Gas & Elec. Co., No. 3:14-cr-00175 (N.D. Cal. 2015) (indictment).

corporation can be said to have 'willfully' disregarded that duty."[149] Some months later, however, the court embraced only the theory of corporate collective *knowledge* (not intertwined with collective *intent*) in its instructions to the jury on the PSA violations, backing away from its earlier statement regarding the use of such knowledge to establish corporate willfulness.

The court instructed that "[t]he corporation is . . . considered to have acquired the collective knowledge of its employees" and "[t]he corporation's 'knowledge' is therefore the totality of what its employees know within the scope of their employment."[150] With respect to willfulness, the court instructed that "if a specific employee acted willfully within the scope of his or her employment, then the corporation can be said to have acted willfully."[151]

The court's decision to break the dual knowing and willful mens reas into separate categories of proof, that is, collective versus individual, raises questions for appeal, including how an individual employee could possess the specific intent required for a PSA violation when he or she has only a discrete portion of the necessary knowledge for such a violation. PG&E challenged the verdict through a motion for judgment of acquittal, but the court denied the motion, finding that when viewed "in the light most favorable to the prosecution, any rational trier of fact could have found the essential elements of the crime beyond a reasonable doubt."[152] At the sentencing in January 2017, PG&E was sentenced to a statutory maximum criminal fine of $3 million and required to employ a monitor to oversee a court-imposed compliance program.

The PG&E case is not the first time the government has relied on an aggregate of employee knowledge to show specific intent in a workplace safety enforcement (and will likely not be the last). The government also relied on the theory in the 2009 OSH Act enforcement of Tyson Foods in connection with the death of an employee exposed to hydrogen sulfide gas (H2S) at one of the company's poultry plants.[153] The charges, and subsequent plea agreement, recited that management's collective awareness of the presence of H2S at the plant was sufficient to prove the company's failure to effectively limit exposure of its employees to H2S (in compliance with regulations) was willful. The Tyson Foods matter, however, was not litigated, and OSH Act precedent premises corporate liability on discrete and intentional individual acts of disregard for, or plain indifference to, safety regulations.[154]

---

149. Order Denying Defendant's Motion to Dismiss for Erroneous Legal Instructions at 8:19–22, United States v. Pac. Gas & Elec. Co., No. 3:14-cr-00175 (N.D. Cal. 2015), ECF No. 219.

150. Jury Instructions at 27, United States v. Pac. Gas & Elec. Co., No. 3:14-cr-00175 (N.D. Cal. Aug. 10, 2016), ECF No. 888.

151. *Id.* at 29.

152. Order at 1, United States v. Pac. Gas & Elec. Co., No. 3:14-cr-00175 (N.D. Cal. Nov. 17, 2016), ECF No. 901.

153. United States v. Tyson Foods, Inc., No. 4:09-mj-04001 (W.D. Ark. Jan. 6, 2009).

154. *See* United States v. Ladish Malting Co., 135 F.3d 484 (7th Cir. 1998); United States v. Dye Constr. Co., 510 F.2d 78 (10th Cir. 1975).

D. Willful

A few environmental statutes have criminal provisions that require proof of willful conduct. These include the Safe Drinking Water Act,[155] the HMTA,[156] and the Toxic Substances Control Act.[157] To prove a willful violation, the government must prove that the defendant acted "intentionally and purposely and with the intent to do something the law forbids, that is, with the bad purpose to disobey or to disregard the law,"[158] but need not prove that the defendant knew the specific regulation or statute that the conduct violates. Although there have not been reported decisions interpreting this term in the context of environmental cases, in criminal tax law cases, the word *willfully* is presumptively construed to "connote[] a voluntary, intentional violation of a known legal duty."[159]

E. Responsible Corporate Officer Liability

Another issue central to mens rea in environmental criminal cases is the concept of responsible corporate officer liability. Under the responsible corporate officer (RCO) doctrine, individual liability may be imposed on those with the responsibility or authority to prevent or correct a violation, as well as the individual who actually commits the unlawful act. Although this term was codified in the CWA[160] and CAA,[161] the RCO doctrine actually originated with two Supreme Court decisions, *United States v. Dotterweich*[162] and *United States v. Park*.[163] In these two cases, which involved strict liability misdemeanor violations of the federal Food, Drug, and Cosmetic Act, the Court held that a corporate officer could be convicted if the officer bore a responsible relationship to the violation and was capable of preventing the violation, but failed to do so.

Under the RCO doctrine, (1) actual knowledge of the conditions or actions giving rise to liability may be inferred from an individual's position and authority as a responsible corporate officer; (2) knowledge of the law on the part of corporate officer is not required, even in highly regulated industries; (3) liability cannot be avoided by intentionally avoiding learning the facts; and (4) liability may be found where the officer should have known of the violation.[164]

---

155. Public Health Service Act §§ 1401–1465, 42 U.S.C. §§ 300f–300j-26 (2012). Criminal provision at Public Health Service Act § 1423(b), 42 U.S.C. § 300h-2(b) (2012).
156. 49 U.S.C. §§ 5101–5128 (2012). Criminal provision at 49 U.S.C. § 5124(c) (2012).
157. Toxic Substances Control Act § 2-30, 15 U.S.C. §§ 2601–2629 (2012). Criminal provision at Toxic Substances Control Act § 14, 15 U.S.C. § 2614 (2012).
158. Bryan v. United States, 524 U.S. 184, 190 (1998).
159. United States v. Bishop, 412 U.S. 346, 360 (1973); *see also* United States v. Cheek, 498 U.S. 192, 201 (1991) (willfulness in 26 U.S.C. §§ 7201 and 7203, prohibiting federal tax evasion).
160. FWPCA § 309(c)(6), 33 U.S.C. § 1319(c)(6) (2012).
161. CAA § 113, 42 U.S.C. § 7413(c)(6) (2012).
162. 320 U.S. 277, 284–85 (1943).
163. 421 U.S. 658, 671–73 (1975).
164. *See* United States v. Dotterweich, 320 U.S. 277, 280–81 (1943); United States v. Park, 421 U.S. 658, 671–74 (1975); United States v. MacDonald & Watson Waste Oil Co., 933 F.2d 35, 55 (1st Cir. 1991).

The first environmental case in which the government attempted to use the RCO was *United States v. MacDonald & Watson Waste Oil Co.*[165] The First Circuit reversed the conviction, holding that the trial court erred when it instructed the jury that as an alternative to finding that the defendant had actual knowledge of the violations, it could find that the defendant was guilty if it found that he (1) was an officer of the corporation, (2) had direct responsibility for the illegal activity, and (3) "must have known or believed that the illegal activity of the type alleged occurred."[166]

However, *MacDonald & Watson* was followed by two cases, *United States v. Brittain*[167] and *United States v. Iverson*,[168] in which defendants were convicted under the RCO doctrine. In *Brittain*, the defendant argued that he could not be liable for NPDES permit violations at the facility because he was neither the permittee nor the "responsible corporate officer" of the discharging facility. In rejecting this argument, the Tenth Circuit stated that "[w]e interpret the addition of 'responsible corporate officers' as an expansion of liability under the Act rather than, as defendant would have it, an implicit limitation."[169]

The Ninth Circuit took it a step further, holding:

> Under the CWA, a person is a "responsible corporate officer" if the person has authority to exercise control over the corporation's activity that is causing the discharges. There is no requirement that the officer in fact exercise such authority or that the corporation expressly vest a duty in the officer to oversee the activity.[170]

It is important to note that a defendant need not be an actual corporate officer to fall within the scope of the RCO. In *United States v. Hong*,[171] the defendant was not a corporate officer although he was the owner of the company. The Fourth Circuit reviewed the historical background of the doctrine and concluded that an individual's title was not as important as "whether the defendant bore such a relationship to the corporation that it is appropriate to hold him criminally liable for failing to prevent the charged violations of the CWA."[172]

These enforcement trends put corporate officers and senior managers with authority over employees with operational, environmental, health, and safety duties at risk of the imposition of criminal liability, even in cases where the corporate officer may have taken no affirmative action to cause the violation.

---

165. *MacDonald & Watson*, 933 F.2d at 50.
166. *Id.* at 50–51 (emphasis omitted).
167. 931 F.2d 1413 (10th Cir. 1991).
168. 162 F.3d 1015 (9th Cir. 1998).
169. *Brittain*, 931 F.2d at 1419.
170. *Iverson*, 162 F.3d at 1025.
171. 242 F.3d 528 (4th Cir. 2001).
172. *Hong*, 242 F.3d at 531.

IV. ISSUES OF IMPORTANCE WHEN RESPONDING TO THE ENVIRONMENTAL CRIMINAL INVESTIGATION

While practitioners must deal with myriad issues that are present in every criminal case, the environmental criminal case presents unique challenges that are the result of the inevitable intertwining of administrative and civil regulatory issues in virtually every environmental crime case. This section highlights some of the government policies that are important in environmental criminal investigations.

As is the case with most white-collar criminal cases, the initiation of a criminal investigation typically triggers an internal investigation on the part of the company. On occasion, the client becomes aware of potential criminal conduct before the government does. The latter situation requires swift analysis of the facts and the law in light of the various voluntary disclosure policies, parallel proceeding policies, attorney-client privilege, and work product doctrine issues that can control the resolution of such cases.

A. Voluntary Disclosure—Policies and Practice

Environmental regulatory law is premised on the concept of self-reporting as the basis for establishing compliance. As a result, the practitioner must first evaluate whether there is a specific statutory obligation to disclose information to government agencies. The answer to that question, in conjunction with the various policies on disclosure and voluntary compliance, sets the framework for the appropriate action plan.

EPA began acknowledging the importance of voluntary disclosures in 1986 when it issued its Environmental Auditing Policy Statement,[173] which evolved into EPA's Incentives for Self-Policing: Discovery, Disclosure, Correction and Prevention of Violations.[174] On April 30, 2007, Granta Y. Nakayama, EPA Assistant Administrator for Enforcement and Compliance Assurance, issued a memorandum addressing frequently asked questions about EPA's audit policy and reaffirmed EPA's fiscal year 2001 goal of increasing the number of facilities that use this incentive policy.[175]

Although a company's compliance with these policies will affect the civil resolution of an environmental matter, there is *no guarantee that compliance will insulate a company from criminal investigation*, particularly because U.S. Attorneys' offices and DOJ retain the right to exercise their prosecutorial discretion, even if a civil settlement has been reached.

---

173. Environmental Auditing Policy Statement, 51 Fed. Reg. 25,004 (July 9, 1986).

174. Incentives for Self-Policing: Discovery, Disclosure, Correction and Prevention of Violations, 65 Fed. Reg. 19,618 (Apr. 11, 2000). This policy revised the original issued in 1995 (60 Fed. Reg. 66,706 (Dec. 22, 1995)).

175. Memorandum from Granta Nakayama, Assistant Adm'r for Enf't & Compliance Assurance, U.S. Envtl. Prot. Agency, to Reg'l Adm'rs, Issuance of "Audit Policy: Frequently Asked Questions" (Apr. 30, 2007), https://www.epa.gov/sites/production/files/documents/2007-faqs.pdf.

DOJ issued its first guidance on voluntary disclosure in the context of environmental criminal enforcement on July 1, 1991.[176] The guidance explains DOJ's positions on the nature of the voluntary disclosure, the extent of cooperation with the government, and what preventive and corrective measures have been taken since discovery of the violation. The disclosure must be voluntary, timely, and complete to justify leniency, and the determination of the quality of the disclosure is wholly in the hands of the government. Prosecutors will evaluate the degree and timeliness of the cooperation as well as the willingness of the company to make all relevant information available. In some instances, the government has relied on this guidance to demand lists of potential witnesses, copies of internal investigation reports, and copies of interview reports of witnesses conducted by counsel or company investigators—a possibility that should be taken into account by the company and its counsel when evaluating a potential voluntary disclosure.

The EPA Office of Criminal Enforcement also has issued guidance on how a company's implementation of EPA's audit policy will affect a criminal investigation and prosecution.[177] The memorandum covers the nine criteria set forth in the EPA policy that must be met to avoid a criminal referral to DOJ or other prosecuting agencies.[178]

These policies provide broad guidance in the context of a potential criminal case, but they do not provide guarantees. For example, EPA may recommend prosecution if it believes that the audit has uncovered a violation that is "closely related" to other violations or constitutes part of a "pattern." Exactly what this means is unclear. For example, if the company discovers violations of the same law at different plants but involving different processes, are these "closely related"? How many violations taken together constitute a "pattern"? Similarly, are plant managers, line supervisors, or other supervisors considered "high-level" corporate officials or managers? In sum, voluntary disclosure can be an important means for the government to discover violations that it otherwise might never know about. It also can be an important means for a company to make full disclosure and avoid serious consequences, perhaps including criminal prosecution of the company. In making a voluntary disclosure, however, a company takes the risk that the government will find the disclosure to be untimely or insufficient, and will still bring criminal charges.[179]

---

176. Memorandum from the Dep't of Justice, Env't & Nat. Res. Div., Factors in Decisions on Criminal Prosecutions for Environmental Violations in the Context of Significant Voluntary Compliance or Disclosure Efforts by the Violator (July 1, 1991), https://www.justice.gov/enrd/selected-publications/factors-decisions-criminal-prosecutions.

177. Memorandum from Earl E. Devaney, Dir. of the Office of Criminal Enf't, Forensics & Training, U.S. Envtl. Prot. Agency, to All EPA Emps. Working in or in Support of the Criminal Enforcement Program, Implementation of the Environmental Protection Agency's Self-Policing Policy for Disclosures Involving Potential Criminal Violations (Oct. 1, 1997).

178. 60 Fed. Reg. 66,706, Dec. 22, 1995, at 66,711–12.

179. In some instances, the relationship between counsel representing the company and the government attorney may be the most important factor in determining whether a voluntary disclosure is the appropriate course to pursue.

All of these policies should be read in connection with the most recent pronouncements from EPA and DOJ, which, on the environmental side, have stated a need to "move toward a more collaborative partnership between the EPA and authorized States" on enforcement,[180] and DOJ's commitment when "compliance issues arise . . . to resolve some issues informally through compliance assistance programs and self-audit and self-reporting policies" that EPA administers.[181] Moreover, in May 2018, Deputy Attorney General Rod Rosenstein announced a new DOJ policy to discourage so-called "piling on ... in imposing multiple penalties on a company in relation to investigations of the same misconduct."[182]

B. Parallel Proceedings Policies

In some instances, EPA may seek to bring both a civil enforcement case and a criminal prosecution to address a single set of violations. In 2006, Granta Y. Nakayama, EPA Assistant Administrator for Enforcement and Compliance Assurance, instructed EPA regional enforcement offices to change the way that they handle large civil cases. Historically, EPA or DOJ attorneys working on large civil enforcement matters were unlikely to consider those cases for criminal prosecution and vice versa. While few would disagree that there should be thoughtful coordination between the civil and criminal programs, parallel proceedings raise concerns about possible misuse of various criminal and civil investigative tools.[183]

The specifics of the various parallel proceedings policies are discussed in Chapter 3 of this book, "Civil Environmental Enforcement Litigation." This section highlights the criminal law concerns raised by parallel proceedings.

1. Grand Jury and the Nondisclosure Requirement

Federal Rule of Criminal Procedure 6(e) prohibits the disclosure of grand jury material except in very limited circumstances. Specifically, Rule 6(e) limits the use of grand jury material to enforce criminal law only—information gathered by the grand jury may not be disclosed to the civil enforcement side, and it may not be

---

180. Memorandum from Susan P. Bodine, Assistant Adm'r for Enf't & Compliance Assurance, U.S. Envtl. Prot. Agency, to Reg'l Adm'rs, Interim OECA Guidance on Enhancing Regional-State Planning and Communication on Compliance Assurance Work in Authorized States (Jan. 22, 2018), https://www.epa.gov/sites/production/files/2018-01/documents/guidance-enhancingregionalstatecommunicationon compliance.pdf.

181. *See* Memorandum from Jeffrey H. Wood, Acting Assistant Att'y Gen., to ENRD Section Chiefs & Deputy Section Chiefs, Enforcement Principles and Priorities (Mar. 12, 2018), https://www.justice.gov /enrd/page/file/1043731/download.

182. Rod Rosenstein, Deputy Att'y Gen., Remarks to the New York City Bar White Collar Crime Institute (May 9, 2018), https://www.justice.gov/opa/speech/deputy-attorney-general-rod-rosenstein -delivers-remarks-new-york-city-bar-white-collar (announcing changes to the *United States Attorneys' Manual* (now the *Justice Manual*); *see* U.S. Dep't of Justice, Justice Manual § 1-12.100, Coordination of Corporate Resolution Penalties in Parallel and/or Joint Investigations and Proceedings Arising from the Same Misconduct; and *id.* at § 9-28.1200, Civil or Regulatory Alternatives).

183. *See, e.g.*, Steven P. Solow, *The State of Environmental Crime Enforcement: Survey of Developments in 2006*, 38 Env't Rep. (BNA) No. 9, Mar. 2, 2007, at 1–12.

used to enforce either administrative or civil law, except under very restricted circumstances. Violations of Rule 6(e) can result in contempt or motions to dismiss the indictment. Although grand jury material may be disclosed to "an attorney for the government for use in performing that attorney's duty,"[184] this refers only to government attorneys working on the criminal matter and does not include attorneys working for EPA, agency debarment counsel, or those working for other regulatory agencies.[185]

2. The Role of Civil Investigative Tools

Almost 50 years ago, the Supreme Court established in *Kordel* that government civil enforcement attorneys are free to share civil discovery information with investigators and prosecutors in related criminal actions as long as the civil action was brought in good faith.[186] However, the government may not use the civil information-gathering tools available in the environmental statutes solely for the purpose of supporting a criminal investigation.[187]

However, the *Kordel* rule of what constitutes "good faith" in cooperation between civil and criminal cases has become unclear.[188] The bottom line is that there is "the lack of a clear and unambiguous test for when the government's failure to disclose a parallel criminal matter [while engaging in civil discovery] crosses the line and becomes a bad-faith denial of constitutional rights."[189]

The Supreme Court first set forth principles that address the question of whether administrative warrants can be used to gather evidence for a criminal case in *United States v. LaSalle National Bank*.[190] In that case, the Supreme Court held that the Internal Revenue Service could not use its civil summons power "solely for the purpose of unearthing evidence of criminal conduct."[191] Similarly, prosecutors may not use evidence gathered through the civil provisions of the various environmental laws if the administrative action was taken purely to support the criminal case.[192] Of course, as with *LaSalle*, this is a factual issue that only can be explored once charges have been filed.

---

184. Fed. R. Crim. P. 6(e)(3)(A)(i).
185. *See* United States v. Sells Eng'g, Inc., 463 U.S. 418, 427 (1983).
186. *See* United States v. Kordel, 397 U.S. 1, 5–7 (1970) (holding that, in a case involving alleged violations of the Food, Drug, and Cosmetic Act, the government may use answers to interrogatories from a civil investigation in the related criminal prosecution when no evidence of bad faith was present).
187. *See* Michigan v. Tyler, 436 U.S. 499, 508 (1978) (finding that once the purpose behind the search shifts from administrative compliance to a quest for evidence to be used in a criminal prosecution, the government may constitutionally enter the premises only upon securing a warrant supported by full probable cause).
188. *See* Hamel & Edwards, *supra* note 19.
189. *Id.* at 6.
190. 437 U.S. 298 (1978).
191. *See id.* at 316.
192. *See Tyler*, 436 U.S. at 508.

In *United States v. Lawson*,[193] the misuse of civil investigative tools to support a criminal investigation resulted in the dismissal of the indictment without prejudice. Among several problems that the district court identified with the government's investigation was its improper use of Drug Enforcement Administration administrative warrants. Although the Drug Control Act "expressly authorizes the use of traditional search warrants to aid in the enforcement of its criminal provisions, the government in this case purposefully employed an administrative inspection warrant with its lower standard of probable cause."[194] As a result, the indictment obtained with the results of the administrative inspection warrant was thrown out.

3. Civil Discovery and the Fifth Amendment

Another conundrum presented by parallel proceedings is the interplay between civil discovery and the Fifth Amendment privilege against self-incrimination. This issue comes up when a client is informed that he or she is a subject or target of criminal investigation while there is an ongoing civil matter. The Fifth Amendment privilege against self-incrimination applies both in civil and criminal proceedings.[195] The Supreme Court outlined the extent of the privilege in *Hoffman v. United States*.[196]

Understanding the extent and ramifications of assertions of the Fifth Amendment is critical, because statements made during civil discovery can be used as evidence against a defendant in a parallel criminal case. Similarly, there are consequences when a defendant refuses to testify in a civil case by asserting his or her Fifth Amendment privilege, including the inference (which could be used in the civil case only) that the answers would be adverse to the defendant's interest.[197]

C. Attorney-Client Privilege and Attorney Work Product

The "cooperation" requirements of the various audit and self-policing policies also trigger issues related to the attorney-client privilege and the work product doctrine. The issue of whether prosecutors could request the waiver of the attorney-client privilege or the production of attorney work product was the subject of intense debate. At one point, one of the factors that federal prosecutors could consider in deciding whether to charge a company with a crime included whether the company was willing to waive attorney-client or work product protections. This position was laid out in what was then known as the Thompson Memorandum.[198]

---

193. 502 F. Supp. 158 (D. Md. 1980).

194. *Id.* at 165 (internal citations omitted).

195. *See* Lefkowitz v. Turley, 414 U.S. 70, 77 (1973); Kastigar v. United States, 406 U.S. 441, 444 (1972).

196. 341 U.S. 479 (1951).

197. *See* Baxter v. Palmigiano, 425 U.S. 308, 318 (1976).

198. Memorandum from Larry Thompson, Deputy Att'y Gen., U.S. Dep't of Justice, to Heads of Dep't Components, U.S. Att'ys, Principles of Federal Prosecution of Business Organizations (Jan. 20, 2003), https://www.americanbar.org/content/dam/aba/migrated/poladv/priorities/privilegewaiver/2003jan20_privwaiv_dojthomp.authcheckdam.pdf.

This controversy continued, with revisions to DOJ policies[199] and proposed legislation.[200] The issue was ultimately resolved in favor of protection of privilege and work product protections. This came about in connection with widespread attention to a decision by the Second Circuit,[201] which upheld a lower court's dismissal of criminal fraud charges against 13 employees because of the government's position that payment of attorneys' fees for the employees would undermine the company's ability to receive credit for cooperation with the investigation.[202] Under that threat, the company cut off payment of the attorneys' fees for several of the employees, a result that the court found directly attributable to the government's actions and that was therefore a violation of the employees' Sixth Amendment right to counsel.[203]

As a result, in September 2008, DOJ significantly revised the Principles of Federal Prosecution of Business Organizations. In a departure from the prior memos, the guidelines now prohibit federal prosecutors from routinely requesting that corporations waive the attorney-client privilege in the context of criminal investigations.[204] The revised document also protects the right of corporations to advance or reimburse the attorneys' fees of officers and directors who are the subject of a criminal investigation. The guidelines state that federal prosecutors may not take into account such reimbursement when assessing whether a company has cooperated with a criminal investigation.

---

199. The Thompson Memorandum was revised in December 2006, and again in 2008. *See* Memorandum from Mark Filip, Deputy Att'y Gen., U.S. Dep't of Justice, to Heads of Dep't Components, U.S. Att'ys, Principles of Federal Prosecution of Business Organizations (Aug. 28, 2008), https://www.justice.gov/sites/default/files/dag/legacy/2008/11/03/dag-memo-08282008.pdf. The guidelines were set forth in a revised "Principles of Federal Prosecution of Business Organizations," known as the McNulty Memorandum. Responding to scrutiny from Capitol Hill, DOJ signaled an intent to further revise the guidelines. *See* Letter of Deputy Att'y Gen. Mark Filip, July 9, 2008, to Senators Leahy and Specter (July 9, 2008).

200. *See, e.g.*, The Attorney-Client Protection Act of 2007, H.R. 3013, 110th Cong. (2007). This bill was passed by the House in November 2007 and referred to the Senate Judiciary Committee.

201. United States v. Stein, 541 F.3d 130 (2d Cir. 2008).

202. *See generally* United States v. Stein, 435 F. Supp. 2d 330 (S.D.N.Y. 2006) (*Stein I*) (granting motion to dismiss an indictment on the grounds that government pressure to cease advancement of legal fees interfered with defendants' Fifth and Sixth Amendment rights); United States v. Stein, 440 F. Supp. 2d 315 (S.D.N.Y. 2006) (*Stein II*) (granting motion to suppress statements coerced in violation of Defendants' Fifth Amendment rights). For a comprehensive review of this issue in the context of white-collar crime generally, see Susan Hackett, *Pragmatic Practices for Protecting Privilege*, Ass'n of Corp. Counsel (Oct. 23, 2006), http://www.acc.com/vl/public/Article/loader.cfm?csModule=security/getfile&pageid=15983&recorded=1.

203. *Stein*, 541 F.3d at 156–57.

204. The revised guidelines are incorporated into the *Justice Manual*. *See* U.S. Dep't of Justice, Justice Manual § 9-28.710, Principles of Federal Prosecution of Business Organizations, Attorney-Client and Work Product Protections, https://www.justice.gov/jm/jm-9-28000-principles-federal-prosecution-business-organizations#9-28.710.

V. PRETRIAL CONSIDERATIONS[205]

As is typical of white-collar cases in general, approximately 95 percent of environmental criminal cases that result in convictions do so through pleas of guilty.[206] Cases may, of course, advance to pretrial and even commence trial before resulting in a plea. While for purposes of chronological clarity this discussion of pretrial and trial considerations appears well along in the chapter, those experienced in the litigation of environmental criminal matters will consider the possibility of a trial from the very beginning of an investigation. Like any criminal case, an environmental criminal case ultimately turns on the government's ability to prove every element of the alleged offense beyond a reasonable doubt. Competent prosecutors are mindful of this burden as they work with investigators on a case, and defense counsel should be no different.

A. Pretrial Motions

The evidentiary issues in environmental criminal cases compel an intensive review of records alleged to provide proof of the violation, close analysis of alleged statements of defendants and others and an understanding of the context in which those statements occurred, and evaluation of the particular regulatory violation and the relationship of that regulation to facts likely to be accepted into evidence. For these and other reasons, pretrial motions of interest in environmental criminal cases typically include the following:[207]

- *Discovery motions pursuant to Rule 16(a)(1)(C) of the Federal Rules of Criminal Procedure.* These may include, for example, a demand that the government specify the particular documents it intends to rely upon at trial, rather than a production of thousands of undifferentiated, and potentially irrelevant, records; a demand for the rough notes of statements made by defendant taken by the government; and, for corporate defendants, the statement(s) of any current or former employee(s) who were in a position to legally bind the corporate entity, or were personally involved in the allegedly illegal conduct in a manner that could legally bind the corporate entity. The government, in turn, may file its own motions seeking discovery from the defendant.

---

205. Space considerations alone prevent extensive discussion of federal practice (which is the focus of this chapter), or even a cursory consideration of state practice rules. There are, of course, many practical similarities to the procedure and practices in state and federal criminal proceedings, which the authors hope will make this chapter of use in federal, state, and local jurisdictions.

206. *See* U.S. Sentencing Guidelines Manual § 1A1.4(c) (U.S. Sentencing Comm'n 2016) ("Nearly ninety percent of all federal criminal cases involve guilty pleas").

207. Note that it is critical to learn the manner in which the Rule 16 requirements have been interpreted by the district court in which the case has been indicted. Many district courts have standing orders relating to the timing and extent of discovery in criminal cases that go well beyond the requirements of Rule 16. More important, each district court (and each district court judge) may have unwritten practices or expectations relating to discovery that are every bit as important to understand, and make use of, as Rule 16 or the local rules.

- *Expert testimony.* Rule 16(a)(1)(E) provides for reciprocal disclosure of the intent to rely on expert opinion testimony, including the bases of the testimony, and requires upon demand that a party intending to rely on such testimony provide a written summary of the testimony intended to be used at trial.

- *Bill of particulars.* Given the complex regulatory basis for some environmental criminal charges, use of Rule 7(f) serves two purposes: by providing details of the allegations of the indictment, the defendant can better prepare a defense; in addition, given the lack of familiarity of many judges with environmental matters, it serves to clarify to the court the particular details of proof that may be critical to the success or failure of the government's case in chief.

- *Motions pursuant to* Brady v. Maryland.[208] These are a standard part of pretrial motion practice in criminal cases. It is a widely accepted view that lawyers should avoid filing a boilerplate or cookie-cutter *Brady* motion in any case, but this is particularly so in an environmental case where there may be a wide range of sources of potentially favorable evidence. These include:
  - statements of cooperating or potential witnesses as to the defendant's good-faith efforts to comply with environmental laws;
  - statements of witnesses that, despite being in a position to do so, did not see, smell, or hear any of the alleged acts that constitute the alleged violations;
  - inconsistent statements of witnesses as to the acts, or failure to act, that constitute the alleged violations;
  - evidence, reports, data analysis, or conclusions of the government's hired or otherwise engaged expert or consulting witnesses;
  - information relevant to sentencing considerations, such as evidence of actual harm resulting from the alleged acts, duration of the alleged offense, specific costs of any cleanup or other disruptions alleged to have been caused by the violation.

- *Motions in limine.* The motion in limine is simply a request that the court exclude evidence from the trial when there is a basis to believe that even the mention of the evidence would wrongly prejudice the jury against a party, even if the judge were to instruct the jury to disregard or limit their consideration of the evidence. A simple example would be a motion to exclude a defendant's statement to the police based upon the failure of the police to provide the defendant with his or her *Miranda* rights prior to a statement having been obtained from the defendant. An example from an environmental criminal case could be if the government sought to introduce an analysis of a defendant's emissions of pollutants over time,

---

208. 373 U.S. 83 (1963).

but was basing the analysis on an incomplete set of data that excluded critical variables that could affect the outcome, a defendant may move to exclude the testimony, for even an effective cross-examination might not be a sufficient remedy to the prejudicial impact of the testimony itself.[209]

Another area of frequent motion practice in environmental criminal cases addresses the government's intention to offer into evidence Rule 404(b)[210] evidence, which would include evidence of prior bad acts of the defendant(s). Such testimony can, of course, have a tremendous impact on a jury, yet may not be related to the actions that are the subject of the current prosecution. Note that this issue makes it crucial that, at an early stage, defense counsel learn all that they can about the prior compliance history of the client, whether the client is a corporation or an individual. A request under the Freedom of Information Act (FOIA),[211] or its state counterpart, to various regulators seeking the entire compliance record of the person or entity of concern is often an early and important tool in this regard.

B. Plea Negotiations

If the government believes that the defendant is unwilling or unprepared to litigate every phase of a criminal case, the entire process of the investigation and prosecution sometimes is referred to as a "slow plea." This means that a business or an individual must have a clear understanding of the legal risks faced by both sides in such a case, and take the steps necessary to make clear to the government that if litigation is the only reasonable course of action, the defendant will pursue litigation with vigor.

Moreover, unlike other criminal cases, the interests of the government in a particular environmental case may be better addressed by recourse to civil remedies, and a criminal prosecution (or plea) may not be an appropriate exercise of prosecutorial discretion. Again, the best way to determine this is to examine on the basis of actual experience the potential charges and their potential outcome should a case proceed to trial. As in all cases, there are numerous variables that make such a decision a matter of careful analysis, but uncertain prediction.

---

209. Another motion in limine that is often filed in environmental cases relates to the presence, or absence, of harm to the environment. Where there is harm to the environment caused by the environmental violation, the government may seek to introduce evidence of such damage, and the defense will seek to exclude such evidence as unduly prejudicial. Conversely, where there is no damage to the environment, the government may seek to exclude such evidence, and it is certainly in the interest of the defense to introduce such evidence, if only for purposes of jury nullification. The basis for a motion in limine to exclude such evidence is that the typical environmental statute does not include harm to the environment as an element of proof to show a violation of the statute. *See, e.g.,* U.S. Pub. Interest Research Grp. v. Atl. Salmon of Me., LLC, 215 F. Supp. 2d 239, 246 n.3 (D. Me. 2002).

210. Federal Rule of Evidence 404(b) allows introduction of evidence of other wrongs or bad acts to prove knowledge or intent or that the defendant's actions were not the product of mistake or accident. Such evidence is typically highly prejudicial to the defense, and the prejudice is difficult if not impossible to limit through the use of limiting instructions to the jury.

211. 5 U.S.C. § 552 (2012).

In some instances, however, close analysis of the evidence and the applicable law will lead to the conclusion that a negotiated plea offers the most promising route to a reasonable outcome.

A discussion of the typical components of an environmental crime plea agreement follows.

1. Representative Counts

In many instances, such as when the underlying conduct constitutes repeated violations of the effluent limitations of an NPDES permit, the government may have charged, or may threaten to charge, dozens of counts in an indictment, and could seek to negotiate a plea to all of them. More typically, the parties will agree to a plea that has a limited number of counts, each of which will serve to represent the broader conduct alleged to have taken place.

2. Terms of Imprisonment and Fine Amounts

These issues are discussed more fully in section VII—Sentencing and Collateral Consequences of Conviction.

3. Supplemental Sentencing Measures

Many environmental lawyers are familiar with supplemental environmental projects (SEPs) as a part of civil settlements, as well as EPA's policies on the use of SEPs.[212] Less well known is a guidance developed and promulgated by the Environmental Crimes Section in December 2000, which provides guidelines to federal prosecutors wishing to use measures that go beyond the usual criminal sanctions of fine, imprisonment, and terms of probation. The use of such measures raises important concerns in the criminal context, and prior to negotiating a plea that contains such provisions, it is prudent that both sides be familiar with and abide by these guidelines, though like other such documents they create no enforceable substantive or procedural rights.[213] These policies must be further assessed in light of recent policy positions taken by the attorney general and the acting assistant attorney general of ENRD regarding prohibitions of payments to certain parties during the settlement of federal enforcement actions.[214]

---

212. *See* U.S. Envtl. Prot. Agency, EPA Supplemental Environmental Projects Policy (Mar. 10, 2015), https://www.epa.gov/sites/production/files/2015-04/documents/sepupdatedpolicy15.pdf.

213. *See* U.S. Dep't of Justice, Sentencing Guidance in Environmental Prosecutions, Including the Use of Supplemental Sentencing Measures (Dec. 2000), https://republicans-judiciary.house.gov/wp-content/uploads/2016/04/Uhlmann-Supplemental-Material.pdf.

214. *See* Memorandum from Jeff Sessions, Att'y Gen., U.S. Dep't of Justice, to all Component Heads & U.S. Att'ys, Prohibition on Settlement Payments to Third Parties (June 5, 2017), https://www.justice.gov/opa/press-release/file/971826/download; *see also* Memorandum from Jeffrey H. Wood, Acting Assistant Att'y Gen., U.S. Dep't of Justice, to ENRD Deputy Assistant Att'ys Gen. & Section Chiefs, Settlement Payments to Third Parties in ENRD Cases (Jan. 9, 2018), https://www.justice.gov/enrd/page/file/1043726/download.

4. Global Settlements

When there are parallel civil and criminal proceedings, and in some other circumstances, it may be in the interest of both the government and a defendant to resolve all the potential civil and criminal claims in a single process. It is important to note that civil DOJ attorneys cannot, as a part of their settlement of a case, resolve potential criminal claims, and the reciprocal limitation applies to federal prosecutors. There is, however, a procedure for such global resolutions, described in ENRD Directive 99-20.[215]

The directive is short and to the point, and the main provisions are set forth below:

- *Criminal plea agreements must be handled by criminal attorneys and civil settlements by civil attorneys.* The criminal plea agreements and civil settlements generally should be negotiated separately. Each resolution—criminal and civil—should be negotiated by attorneys who have the appropriate civil or criminal authority, respectively, and who are working within the appropriate ENRD unit or a U.S. attorney's office.
- *Each part of the settlement must separately satisfy the appropriate criminal and civil criteria.* The criminal plea agreement must satisfy the criteria set out in the Principles of Federal Prosecution and in other DOJ policies for consideration of a plea agreement. The civil settlement must satisfy DOJ policies governing civil settlements, and in addition should conform to the policies of affected client agencies, to the same extent as other civil settlements.
- *With respect to a civil settlement, all affected client agencies must approve the settlement.* Other agencies may have their own requirements for approval of civil settlements. For example, an agency may require headquarters approval of a global settlement. If the affected client agencies require concurrence, such concurrence must be obtained from them prior to entering into a global settlement.
- *There should be separate documents memorializing the criminal plea agreement and the civil settlement.* The criminal plea agreement and the civil settlement must be embodied in separate documents. Criminal releases should be made only in the criminal plea agreement documents, and civil releases in the civil documents.
- *A defendant may not trade civil relief in exchange for a reduction in criminal penalty.* As noted previously, the criminal plea agreement must satisfy the appropriate department criteria.

A critical component of this guidance is that, unlike the resolution of many other environmental criminal matters, a global settlement requires the approval of the ENRD assistant attorney general. And once a global criminal and civil

---

215. *See* U.S. Dep't of Justice, Env't & Nat. Res. Div., Policy Directive 99-20, Global Settlement Policy (1999), https://www.justice.gov/enrd/enrd-directive-99-20-global-settlement-policy-april-1999.

settlement is struck, a defendant will have the comfort of peace with the government—at least the federal government.

VI. TRIAL

As noted previously, defense counsel should begin preparation for a possible trial of an environmental crimes case from the outset of a response to a criminal (and sometimes to a civil) government investigation. There are numerous guides to preparation for the trial of a criminal case, and rather than duplicate those materials, this section is intended to highlight issues that are unique to trials of environmental crimes cases.[216]

A. Jury Selection and Voir Dire

Rule 24(a) of the Federal Rules of Criminal Procedure states that the "court may examine prospective jurors or may permit the attorneys for the parties to do so."[217] The rule also provides that if the court examines the jurors, "it must permit the attorneys for the parties to: (A) ask further questions that the court considers proper; or (B) submit further questions that the court may ask if it considers them proper."[218] It is commonplace in federal courts for the court to conduct the voir dire based upon written voir dire requests submitted by counsel, and to give little opportunity for counsel to participate in direct questioning. That said, counsel for the government and defense typically develop written questions designed to determine whether any relationships exist between potential jurors and any of the parties, to ascertain the potential jurors' past experience with law and law enforcement, and to identify jurors' prejudgments as to particular questions that may bear on the specific issues of the case.

Both the government and the defense will seek to probe for hidden biases that are specific to environmental criminal cases. For instance, the government may seek to identify members of property rights organizations to determine whether the potential juror may object to any regulation of activity on private property, or who may believe that environmental violations should not be the subject of criminal prosecution under any circumstances. On the other hand, defense counsel may seek to identify members of environmental activist organizations such as the Sierra Club or the Natural Resources Defense Council, to probe into whether the potential juror harbors such zealous beliefs that he or she would be a sure vote to convict.[219] Other considerations will affect the jury selection strategy of both sides: Is the geographical area from which the jury venire will be drawn one that

---

216. For an excellent summary of all the ways that investigative errors can create reasonable doubt, readers are directed to Steven C. Drieklak, Environmental Crime Trials: The Road to Reasonable Doubt (2017).

217. Fed. R. Crim. P. 24(a)(1).

218. Fed. R. Crim. P. 24(a)(2).

219. One creative suggestion for a voir dire question aimed at teasing out a juror's latent biases is "What bumper stickers do you have on your car?"

has a history of high-profile environmental disasters (such as the Love Canal or Alaska after the *Exxon Valdez* oil spill)? Is the area one with a high percentage of government employment in the workforce, or a high percentage of "independents" who historically disdain government services and regulation? These are but some examples of aspects of jury behavior that the government and defense may seek to explore in voir dire; others will be suggested by the specific allegations in the case to be tried.

B. *Daubert* Issues—Expert Testimony

In all criminal litigation, an expert's opinion on issues such as DNA, blood spatters, accounting techniques, or environmental sampling can be a turning point in the case. Therefore, it is critical that counsel develop a strategy on how to address the credibility and reliability of expert witnesses, as well as the substance of their likely testimony. The Supreme Court's decision in *Daubert v. Merrell Dow Pharmaceuticals, Inc.*,[220] and its progeny,[221] established the test that governs the admissibility of expert testimony. Put simply, the Court has created a two-part test to determine the admissibility of expert testimony: whether the expert will (1) provide testimony regarding "scientific knowledge" and (2) aid the trier of fact to understand or determine an issue of fact. The Supreme Court in *Daubert* identified four factors that inform this inquiry: (1) whether the theory/technique has been tested; (2) whether the theory/technique has been subject to peer review and publication; (3) the known or potential rate of error of a technique; and (4) acceptance of the theory/technique within the relevant scientific community.[222]

Application of this analysis can be difficult and may involve close work with an expert, but the preparation for cross-examination of expert testimony is a process that should begin long before trial. Challenges to potential expert testimony should, at the least, be considered at the following three pretrial stages.

1. The Expert Report

Pursuant to Federal Rule of Criminal Procedure 16(a)(1)(G), the defense must request a copy of a written summary of any expert testimony that the government intends to use in its case in chief at trial. All subsequent arguments by the defense regarding the admissibility of the expert's testimony begins with the information contained in this report. One key matter to consider is the amount of relevant experience the expert has in the area in which he or she is supposed to testify. Mere anecdotal experience in relation to the question at issue in the trial should

---

220. 509 U.S. 579 (1993).

221. *See* Gen. Elec. Co. v. Joiner, 522 U.S. 136 (1997); Kumho Tire Co. v. Carmichael, 526 U.S. 137 (1999); *see also* Gerson Smoger, *From Rule 702 to* Daubert *to* Joiner *to* Kumho Tire: *A Review of the Supreme Court's Analysis of the Admissibility of Expert Testimony*, 14 WHITE COLLAR CRIME REP. (BNA) No. 1 (Jan. 2011).

222. *Daubert*, 509 U.S. at 593–95.

not suffice. Moreover, attention must be paid to those portions of an opinion that are more art than science, reflecting perhaps the bias of a particular witness.

2. Motion to Strike and *Daubert*/Rule 104 Hearings

There are two primary ways to challenge an expert pretrial: first, that the methodology employed by the expert is flawed or inappropriate, and second, that the expert is not qualified to render an expert opinion on the matters. A motion to strike should contain affidavits and any other material upon which the motion relies, and must identify the specific anticipated testimony challenged, state the basis for objection with sufficient particularity to permit a response, and set forth all relief sought. The advantage of this strategy is that it can preclude flawed or misleading testimony and can provide otherwise unavailable discovery for the defense in the prosecution's opposition briefs. The risk is that it can help refine the government's trial presentation and avoid later problems related to proof of required elements of the offense.

In lieu of a motion to strike, a party can request a pretrial *Daubert* hearing to challenge the underlying methodology or have the expert declared unqualified. Such a motion provides an excellent opportunity to educate the court and a free shot at cross-examination of the expert. Courts are not required to hold such hearings, and the Supreme Court in *Kumho Tire* made clear that doing so is at the court's discretion based upon the relative novelty or complexity of the issues.[223]

In environmental criminal cases, a key issue is whether a proffered expert's testimony is primarily being used in an effort to impermissibly bolster the testimony of a fact witness. In making such arguments, it may be useful to consider the Tenth Circuit case of *United States v. Davis*,[224] which noted that expert testimony should not have the effect of impermissibly bolstering the government's key fact witness.

3. Motion in Limine

If an expert survives review through either a *Daubert* hearing or a motion to strike, then the practitioner should consider how to limit the scope of the testimony through the use of in limine motions. Even if a motion is granted, the practitioner must pay close attention to ensure that no testimony is elicited outside the realm of what the court has allowed. Moreover, on cross-examination, counsel must be careful not to go beyond the scope of the direct testimony and thus open the door for redirect that goes into broader territory.

Other issues that will bear on the credibility of an expert include his or her regular employ as an expert for the government, or whether a substantial portion of the expert's income is derived through expert testimony. A surprisingly common

---

223. *See Kumho Tire*, 526 U.S. at 152.
224. 40 F.3d 1069, 1074 n.6 (10th Cir. 1994).

problem for many experts is their lack of firsthand knowledge of the subject matter of their opinion. Another issue is the expert's prior testimony in other matters that contradict the opinion in the case at hand. If a rebuttal expert is to be called by the defense, then the cross-examination of the prosecution expert may be limited to questions that establish agreement by the government's expert on matters that will support the rebuttal expert's testimony.

There is a constant stream of cases considering the application of *Daubert* and its progeny, and it is important to keep abreast of these changes as they may affect the admissibility of expert testimony. A successful motion to strike or a *Daubert* hearing can significantly revise the government's view of the strength of its case, sometimes bringing the parties back to the table and precluding the trial altogether.

VII. SENTENCING AND CONSEQUENCES OF CONVICTION

In January 2005, the U.S. Supreme Court revolutionized federal sentencing with its decision in *United States v. Booker*.[225] In *Booker*, the Supreme Court determined that the mandatory application of the federal sentencing guidelines violated the right to trial by jury under the Sixth Amendment. The Court sought to remedy the Sixth Amendment violation by removing the provisions of the Sentencing Reform Act that made the federal sentencing guidelines mandatory. While the ultimate impact of *Booker* is still unfolding, at base, *Booker* and more recent Supreme Court cases[226] have made it clear that sentencing is no longer a rote application of the sentencing guidelines. The Supreme Court instructed that the sentencing guidelines are *guidelines*—to be calculated and considered in sentencing, along with other factors such as those set out in 18 U.S.C. § 3553(a), and sentencing courts must "consider every convicted person as an individual and every case as a unique study in the human failings that sometimes mitigate, sometimes magnify, the crime and the punishment to ensue."[227] Studies of federal sentencing in the wake of *Booker* show that, on the whole, federal sentences have tended to stay within the guideline ranges provided for by the sentencing commission.[228] In a growing number of instances, however, district judges appear to be less constrained by the guidelines and are taking the opportunity to impose sentences that they believe are reasonable, but

---

225. 543 U.S. 220 (2005).

226. *See* Rita v. United States, 551 U.S. 338 (2007); Kimbrough v. United States, 552 U.S. 85 (2007); Gall v. United States, 552 U.S. 38 (2007).

227. *Gall*, 552 U.S. at 52.

228. *See* U.S. Sentencing Comm'n, Final Report on the Impact of United States v. Booker on Fed. Sentencing (Mar. 2006), https://www.ussc.gov/sites/default/files/pdf/news/congressional-testimony-and-reports/submissions/200603-booker/Booker_Report.pdf; U.S. Sentencing Comm'n, Post-Kimbrough/Gall Data Report (2008), https://www.ussc.gov/sites/default/files/pdf/data-and-statistics/federal-sentencing-statistics/kimbrough-gall/USSC_Kimbrough_Gall_Report_Final_FY2008.pdf.

that depart from or vary substantially from what the guidelines establish as the appropriate sentencing range.

A. How the Guidelines Work for Organizations and Individuals

1. Organizations

An organization convicted of a felony or misdemeanor in a criminal prosecution that does not involve an environmental violation receives a sentence guided by Chapter Eight of the sentencing guidelines.[229] Environmental offenses, however, are *not* covered by Chapter Eight for fine purposes. The commission long ago considered creating a Chapter Nine, which would specifically address the sentencing of organizations for environmental crimes, but thus far the proposed guidelines have not been adopted.

Instead, organizations convicted of environmental violations are sentenced pursuant to 18 U.S.C. § 3553 and 18 U.S.C. § 3572, two statutory provisions that predate the organizational guidelines. Under Section 3572, the court must consider several factors in assessing a fine against an organization: (1) size, income, earning capacity, and financial resources; (2) the "burden imposed" by the fine on the organization and others; (3) pecuniary loss on others by the violation; (4) the need to deprive the organization of "illegally obtained gains"; (5) the ability of the organization to "pass the fine to consumers or other persons"; and (6) measures taken by the organization to discipline those responsible and prevent recurrence of the offense.

In addition, the Alternative Fines Act, 18 U.S.C. § 3571, provides for an alternative fine of twice the gross gain or gross loss caused by the offense. Notably, in *Southern Union Co. v. United States*,[230] the Supreme Court, following the rule it applied in *Apprendi v. New Jersey*,[231] held that courts could no longer find facts to support criminal fines above the statutory maximum under the Alternative Fines Act based on a preponderance of the evidence. Instead, the government will have to present facts supporting the enhanced fine amounts to a jury and the jury must be convinced beyond a reasonable doubt before any enhanced fines can be imposed by a court. As a result, this may create obstacles to the threat of enhanced fines if the proof requirements in an environmental case are difficult to

---

229. These provisions seek to advance four principles: (1) remedy of any harm caused by the offense; (2) if the organization is primarily criminal in purpose or operated primarily by criminal means, the fine should divest the organization of all its assets; (3) the fine range should be based upon the seriousness of the offense and the culpability of the organization; and (4) probation is appropriate when needed to ensure that steps will be taken to reduce the likelihood of future criminal conduct by the organization. U.S. Sentencing Guidelines Manual § 8, Introductory Commentary (U.S. Sentencing Comm'n 2016).
230. 567 U.S. 343, 352 (2012).
231. 530 U.S. 466 (2000).

achieve, and may also result in the use of the use of special verdict forms that will require juries to make specific findings of fact to support an enhanced fine.[232]

When organizations are convicted of nonenvironmental counts in addition to (or instead of) environmental counts, Chapter Eight applies. Under the Chapter Eight guidelines, the organization's "base fine" is determined in relation to its offense level. The offense level then is multiplied by a number based on a "culpability score." The culpability score is the product of a determination related to the size of the organization; whether or not high-level personnel participated, condoned, or tolerated illegal conduct; whether there was prior history of punishment for similar offenses (either administrative, civil, or criminal); whether the violation was also in violation of a judicial order or injunction; whether there was obstruction of justice involved; and whether the organization had an effective program to prevent and detect violation of law (discussed further later). Once a fine range is determined, the court considers several factors to determine where the fine will be set, such as the seriousness of the offense, the organization's role in the offense, and collateral consequences of the fine. The guidelines also state that the court should impose a fine that causes the organization to disgorge financial gain from the offense.[233]

2. The Impact of the Organizational Guidelines beyond Sentencing

The Chapter Eight guidelines have had a powerful effect on corporate management practices since the commission issued the organizational guidelines in 1991, even in corporate environmental matters. The guidelines have led to massive increases in the development and implementation of internal programs to prevent, detect, and report violations by organizations. Moreover, the structure of these programs has unquestionably been shaped by the language of the organizational guidelines.

Notably, Section 8B2.1 of the Chapter Eight guidelines sets forth the minimum requirements for a program that "is generally effective in preventing and detecting criminal conduct." There is a strong connection between the guidance in Chapter Eight and the exercise of discretion by prosecutors in determining whether to prosecute organizational defendants. Far from being a matter only for consideration at the sentencing phase, prosecutors scrutinize the Chapter Eight guidelines early in a case to determine whether the behavior of the organization falls within the more severe sanctions the law affords (making a prosecution more appealing) or stands closer to the line between civil or criminal enforcement that may cause a prosecutor to decline a case.

---

232. *See* Bruce Pasfield & Elise Paeffgen, *Supreme Court's* Southern Union *Decision Helps Level the Playing Field for Corporations Subject to Criminal Fines*, LEXISNEXIS, July 13, 2012, https://www.lexisnexis.com/legalnewsroom/environmental/b/environmentalregulation/archive/2012/07/13/environmental-law-apprendi-sotomayor-supreme-court-southern-union-decision-level-playing-field-corporation-subject-criminal-fine.aspx.

233. *See generally* U.S. SENTENCING GUIDELINES MANUAL §§ 8A–8C (U.S. Sentencing Comm'n 2016).

Moreover, effective November 2004, the sentencing commission issued amendments to the sentencing guidelines that revised the definition of an "effective program to prevent and detect violations of law" and clarified the role of the waiver of the attorney-client privilege and work product protections in receiving mitigating credit. The compliance program provisions now exist in a stand-alone guideline that specifically identifies the purposes of an effective compliance program, describes the minimum steps for such a program, and provides guidance for implementation.

The organizational guidelines also have profoundly influenced bargaining between prosecutors and defendant corporations. They have become central to the resolution of the vast majority of investigations involving alleged corporate crime and play a central but largely hidden role in the fact and charge bargains struck between prosecutors and defendants. These impacts far outweigh the effect of the organizational guidelines on criminal sentences, a result that was in large part the commission's goal.[234] The commission sought to use the organizational guidelines to enroll organizations in the effort to prevent crime, by rewarding such efforts with meaningful reductions in liability when violations occur despite good-faith efforts to comply.

3. Individuals

The U.S. sentencing guidelines *do* apply to sentencing of individuals convicted of environmental crimes. The guidelines work by assigning each crime a base offense level, which serves as the starting point for determining the seriousness of a particular crime. More serious crimes have higher-base offense levels. The base offense level then is increased or decreased based on two sets of factors: specific offense characteristics, which apply to particular crimes, and adjustments that can apply to any offense. Individuals convicted of environmental crimes will be sentenced under Chapter Two, Part Q of the guidelines, "Offenses Involving the Environment." Most environmental offenses are sentenced under Sections 2Q1.2 and 2Q1.3. Section 2Q1.2 involves offenses involving "hazardous or toxic" substances and has a base level of eight, while Section 2Q1.3 involves all other pollutants and has a base level of six. Section 2Q1.1 involves knowing endangerment under RCRA and has a base offense level of 24. If death or serious injury results, an upward adjustment may be warranted.

a. Adjustments

Certain offense characteristics that are specific to environmental crimes are reflected in a set of adjustments to the applicable base offense level:

---

234. As recognized by Commissioner Richard S. Gruner, who noted that the guidelines' "biggest influence may be behind the scenes, in plea negotiations," quoted in David E. Rovella, *Sentencing Reformers*, 24 NAT'L L.J. A15 (2002).

- *"Without or in violation of a permit."* This adjustment allows for an increase of four levels for offenses involving transportation, treatment, storage, or disposal of hazardous or toxic pollutants or pesticides "without or in violation of a permit."[235] This may be an element of the underlying offense.

- *"Discharge, release, or emission"* permits an increase of six levels for "ongoing, continuous, and repetitive releases," and four levels for other releases.[236]

- *"Disruption, evacuation, or cleanup"* permits a four-level adjustment for offenses that result in "disruption of a public utility," "evacuation of a community," or "substantial" cleanup costs.[237]

- *"Substantial likelihood of injury/death"* allows a nine-level adjustment under Section 2Q1.2 and 11 under Section 2Q1.3. The reason for the difference is to eliminate the base level difference for cases involving hazardous versus nonhazardous pollutants where mishandling of either creates a "substantial likelihood" of death or serious bodily harm.

- *Record-keeping and reporting:* An offense that reflects an "effort to conceal a substantive environmental offense," such as failure to file or maintain records, filing false records, or failing to report releases or discharges when required to do so, is to be sentenced as though it were a violation of the substantive offense itself—thus, if a defendant knew a plant was discharging in violation of permit limits and knowingly filed a false DMR, the government need not present test data showing that the relevant discharges actually exceeded the permit limits.

- *Simple record-keeping violations:* In Section 2Q1.2 offenses involving hazardous pollutants, there is a two-level *reduction* if the offense did not involve a discharge. This brings the base offense level in line with Section 2Q1.3.

- *Upward departure for related misconduct:* Similar offenses handled in administrative or civil actions are not typically evaluated as part of the "criminal history" calculations. However, if prior misconduct can be shown through past civil adjudication or failure to comply with an administrative order, an upward departure may be warranted.[238]

The guidelines also include adjustments that are factors that apply to any offense. They include categories such as victim-related adjustments, offender's role in the crime, and obstruction of justice.[239] In addition, when a defendant is sentenced for two or more separate counts that "involve substantially the same harm," the counts may be grouped for sentencing purposes and sentenced as a

---

235. U.S. Sentencing Guidelines Manual § 2Q1.2(b)(4) (U.S. Sentencing Comm'n 2016).
236. *Id.* § 2Q1.2(b)(1).
237. *Id.* § 2Q1.2(b)(3).
238. *Id.* § 2Q1.2 Application Note 9(A).
239. *See id.* § 3.

single offense.[240] Thus, three counts of discharge of toxic materials from a single facility will likely be "grouped" as a single offense, and this grouping rule creates a perverse law of diminishing sentencing sanctions for continued environmental offenses. After a defendant commits a single repeat violation (prompting application of the repetitive discharge enhancement), each additional violation results in no greater offense level under the guidelines.

Fines are imposed in all cases except where the court finds that a defendant is unable to pay and is unlikely to become able to pay.[241] Courts may award fines based on the environmental statutes' per diem formula[242] or, under the Alternative Fines Act,[243] they may impose a fine equal to twice the gross pecuniary gain from an offense or twice the gross pecuniary loss to victims caused by the offense. Restitution generally is ordered in environmental cases as a term of probation. In instances where there often are no identifiable victims, restitution may not be applicable.

b. Criminal History and Determining the Guideline Range

Once a final offense level number is reached, the court consults a chart that matches the offense level number with the defendant's criminal history to determine the sentencing guideline range. There are six criminal history categories, with Category I covering those with the least serious criminal record and most first-time offenders. As would be expected, Category VI covers those with the most lengthy criminal records. A sample portion of the sentencing table follows:

Sentencing Table (in months of imprisonment)

Offense Level	Criminal History Category					
	I	II	III	IV	V	VI
19	30–37	33–41	37–46	46–57	57–71	63–78
20	33–41	37–46	41–51	51–63	63–78	70–87
21	37–46	41–51	46–57	57–71	70–87	77–96

Thus, an offender with a criminal history category of I and a final offense level of 20 would be subject to a guideline range of 33 to 41 months. At the low end of the guidelines are sentences of zero to six months and defendants in that category are eligible for a guidelines sentence of probation.

---

240. *Id.* § 3D1.2.
241. *Id.* § 5E1.2(a).
242. For example, the CWA, RCRA, and Toxic Substances Control Act each authorize a specific fine for each day of violation. *See* CWA § 309(c), 33 U.S.C. § 1319(c) (2012); RCRA § 3008(d), 42 U.S.C. § 6928(d) (2012); Toxic Substances Control Act § 16(b), 15 U.S.C. § 2615(b) (2012).
243. 18 U.S.C. § 3571 (2012).

c. Departures

Next, courts may "depart" from the guidelines, going either above or below the range suggested by the guideline calculation. The guidelines and relevant case law have recognized that a departure may be appropriate when the guidelines themselves fail to take into account a factor or characteristic of the defendant that the defendant raises at sentencing, or for cases that lie outside the "heartland" of guidelines cases. The most common and significant downward departure is when a defendant provides "substantial assistance" in the investigation or prosecution of another offender, pursuant to Section 5K1.1 of the guidelines. While the prosecution must make a motion for such a departure, it is the judge who decides whether to grant the motion and, if so, to what extent.

When departing from the applicable guidelines range, the sentencing judge must state the reasons for departure on the record, and both upward and downward departures are subject to appeal—the government may appeal a downward departure, and the defendant may appeal an upward departure.

d. Variance Sentencing under Booker and Gall

Determination of the applicable sentencing guideline range after application of all relevant adjustments and departures, however, is merely the first step in determining the appropriate sentence.[244] As the Supreme Court has made clear, both sides are free to argue for whatever sentence they deem proper, and the court should consider not only the guidelines but all the sentencing factors under Section 3553(a).[245] At the trial court level, there is no presumption that the guidelines range is reasonable, and the court must make an individual assessment based on all the facts presented. A sentence that varies from the guideline range based on an evaluation of Section 3553(a) factors typically is referred to as a "variance" to the sentence (as opposed to an adjustment or a departure). A major variance from the guideline range ordinarily should be supported by a more significant justification than a minor departure; and the sentencing court must provide an adequate explanation for the basis of the sentence imposed.[246]

After *Booker* and *Gall*, district courts have far more leeway to impose a sentence that the sentencing judge considers to be "reasonable" and just, regardless of the guideline range. In effect, the Supreme Court has reestablished the primacy

---

244. *See* Gall v. United States, 552 U.S. 38, 49 (2007).

245. *Id.* at 49–50. The seven factors are (1) the nature and circumstances of the offense and the history and characteristics of the defendant; (2) (an omnibus factor) the need for the sentence imposed to reflect the seriousness of the offense, promote respect for the law, and provide just punishment, to afford deterrence to criminal conduct, to protect the public from further crimes, and to provide the defendant with needed educational or vocational training, medical care, or other correctional treatment; (3) consideration of the kinds of sentences available; (4) reference to the sentencing guidelines; (5) reference to any relevant policy statement issued by the Sentencing Commission; (6) the need to avoid unwarranted sentencing disparities; and (7) to provide restitution to any victim of the crime. 18 U.S.C. § 3553(a)(1)–(7) (2012).

246. *See Gall*, 552 U.S. at 50 (citing Rita v. United States, 551 U.S. 338, 356–58 (2007)).

of judicial discretion in sentencing. A 2012 report from the U.S. Sentencing Commission found that post-*Booker*, "the identity of the judge has played an increasingly important role in sentencing outcomes in many districts."[247] The report concluded that "[i]n the aggregate, federal sentences have shown general stability, as seen in the Commission's analysis of sentence lengths and their relation to the minimum of the guideline range over time. Nonetheless, unwarranted disparities in federal sentencing appear to be increasing. Judges are following the dictates of the Supreme Court in *Booker* and subsequent decisions in different ways, with some judges weighing factors such as the characteristics of the offense and the offender differently than other judges in similar cases. Indeed, the role of the guidelines has become less pronounced[.]"[248] Counsel for the government and for the defense, therefore, must be prepared to litigate both the guideline calculations and Section 3553(a) factors to achieve the sentence that each seeks from the court.

B. Collateral Consequences: Suspension and Debarment

Often referred to as the "sleeping tiger" of an environmental criminal case, for persons or businesses who rely for a significant part of their work on government contracts, debarment can be a corporate "death penalty." Too often, defendants are not made aware of the impacts of the debarment provisions until late in a case, sometimes even on the eve of or after a plea or conviction. This is unfortunate, for early planning and analysis can help to mitigate or avoid the impacts of suspension and/or debarment.

Suspension is an immediate, temporary disqualification from contracting with a government entity, typically employed where the government believes that there is cause for debarment, but there is an immediate need to protect the public interest and the public fisc from supporting an alleged bad actor. Debarment is a long-term disqualification from government contracting, either for a specified period of time, or until such time as the condition that gave rise to the violation has been (in the opinion of the office of suspension and debarment) corrected, remedied, or removed. The federal government has a highly developed suspension and debarment regime, and many states have provisions that parallel those of the federal government.

Debarment can be either discretionary or statutory. Discretionary debarment is for a set period of time. Statutory debarment goes into effect automatically upon sentencing and stays in place until the conditions giving rise to the conviction have been corrected. Correcting the condition giving rise to the violation may require different actions depending on the circumstances. For instance, in some circumstances the required implementation of an ethics and compliance program

---

247. U.S. Sentencing Comm'n, Report on the Continuing Impact of United States v. Booker on Federal Sentencing, pt. A 3 (Dec. 2012), https://www.ussc.gov/sites/default/files/pdf/news/congressional-testimony-and-reports/booker-reports/2012-booker/Part_A.pdf#page=5.

248. *Id.*

that may go well beyond that sought by either a civil or criminal resolution will be necessary; the government may insist on actual remediation of the effects of a violation; it also may require that certain officers or employees no longer exercise management of business processes that gave rise to the original violation. The regulations in this area are critical to navigating the process, and reference to them early in a case is essential to a positive outcome.[249] Equally important, defense counsel should engage debarment counsel from the relevant government agency early on once plea negotiations commence to determine what debarment counsel will want the defendant to have in place for the defendant to limit suspension or debarment, or to avoid it altogether.

C. Appeals

On appeal, standards of review for issues presented at trial are generally the same as those applicable to any criminal case—"clearly erroneous" review for findings of fact, abuse of discretion for discretionary issues such as admissibility of evidence, and rulings of law are considered de novo. As to sentencing, the line of cases stretching from *Booker* through *Gall* has substantially changed the nature of appellate review. As the Supreme Court noted in *Gall*, appellate courts must apply a "deferential abuse-of-discretion standard" of review to appeals of sentences.[250] Although a reviewing court may adopt a presumption of reasonableness for a sentence within the guideline range, such a presumption is not required, and a reviewing court may not presume that a sentence *outside* of the guideline range is *unreasonable*.[251] A court of appeals may not substitute its judgment for that of the district court and may not decide de novo whether the justification for a variance is justified or not. The fact that a court of appeals may disagree with the conclusion reached by the district court is not, of itself, sufficient justification to overturn the trial court's sentence.[252] In short, a court of appeals must give "due deference" to the district court's "reasoned and reasonable decision that the § 3553(a) factors, on the whole justif[y] the sentence."[253]

---

249. *See, e.g.*, 2 C.F.R. § 180(H) (2018) (debarment regulations for federal agencies).
250. *Gall*, 552 U.S. at 40.
251. *See Rita*, 551 U.S. at 354–55 (2007).
252. *Gall*, 552 U.S. at 59–60.
253. *Id.*

CHAPTER 3

Civil Environmental Enforcement Litigation

Joel M. Gross

I. INTRODUCTION

Civil enforcement of the environmental laws is one of the principal methods by which the government seeks to ensure environmental compliance by those subject to environmental regulation. The major federal environmental statutes provide broad civil enforcement authorities, and those authorities have been widely used and have resulted in some of the most complex pieces of environmental litigation. This chapter discusses that litigation, including what the government can seek, what it typically does seek, how it approaches these cases, how the cases can best be defended, and how they can be resolved.

At the outset, it is important to define what it is this chapter will be discussing. The term *civil enforcement* most often is used to distinguish this type of enforcement from criminal enforcement. The modern environmental statutes reflect a recognition that criminal enforcement may be too difficult, cumbersome, or severe for many cases of environmental noncompliance, and so have provided for civil enforcement options that can be pursued by the government without the need for criminal procedures and protections.

Within this noncriminal realm, the government typically is given two "civil" enforcement options—through judicial action or through administrative proceedings. The term *civil environmental enforcement* sometimes is used to include both judicial and administrative enforcement. In fact, the Environmental Protection Agency (EPA) uses the term in this way. The focus of this chapter, however, will be on judicial enforcement.

It is important to keep in mind that the largest volume of civil enforcement by the federal government is undertaken administratively. For example, in fiscal year 2017, which ended on September 30, 2017, EPA issued 1,220 complaints seeking administrative penalties and issued 600 administrative compliance orders.[1] In contrast, EPA referred 110 cases to the Department of Justice (DOJ) for civil judicial enforcement, and DOJ filed 80 civil complaints in federal court.[2]

Whether EPA will pursue a particular enforcement case judicially or administratively is sometimes a function of the specific enforcement authority granted in the applicable statute, sometimes a function of EPA discretion, and sometimes a function of both. For example, under the Clean Water Act (CWA), EPA may pursue only administratively those cases where the penalty sought is under $125,000.[3] Cases seeking larger penalties must be pursued judicially. Similarly, under the Clean Air Act (CAA), EPA may pursue cases administratively where the penalty sought is under $200,000 and where the violations took place within one year prior to the commencement of the proceeding.[4] Older or larger cases can be pursued administratively only with the concurrence of DOJ.[5] In contrast, it is in EPA's discretion to choose whether to pursue any particular enforcement case administratively or judicially under the Resource Conservation and Recovery Act (RCRA).[6] For this reason, EPA has tended to pursue relatively more cases under the CWA in court and relatively more RCRA cases administratively.

When EPA has the discretion to choose between pursuing enforcement administratively or judicially, a number of factors will enter in the decision. For example, smaller and less-significant cases tend to fall on the administrative side of the ledger. Cases viewed as needing long-term injunctive relief generally will be pursued judicially. That DOJ is involved only in judicial enforcement cases also may play a role in EPA's decision. Sometimes, EPA chooses administrative enforcement to maintain its control over the enforcement process. Other times, it prefers to take advantage of DOJ's resources or expertise and pursue matters judicially. Another factor weighing into EPA's decision may include the perceived enforcement receptivity of the district court where the action would be brought. On occasion, bureaucratic considerations (meeting internal EPA enforcement targets) may enter into EPA's decision.

---

1. U.S. Envtl. Prot. Agency, Enforcement and Compliance Annual Results: Numbers at a Glance for Fiscal Year 2017, https://www.epa.gov/enforcement/enforcement-annual-results-numbers-glance -fiscal-year-2017 (last visited May 24, 2018).

2. *Id.* The number of civil enforcement cases initiated by EPA decreased over the ten years ending in fiscal year 2017. *See* U.S. Envtl. Prot. Agency, Fiscal Year 2017: EPA Enforcement and Compliance Annual Results 12 (Feb. 8, 2018), https://www.epa.gov/sites/production/files/2018-01/documents/fy17-enforce ment-annual-results-data-graphs.pdf (graph showing total civil enforcement case initiations and conclusions from fiscal year 2007 to fiscal year 2017). In fiscal year 2007, EPA issued 2,237 complaints seeking administrative penalties, issued 1,247 administrative compliance orders, and referred 278 cases to DOJ for civil judicial enforcement, and DOJ filed 127 civil complaints in federal court. U.S. Envtl. Prot. Agency, Enforcement and Compliance Annual Results: Numbers at a Glance Fiscal Year 2007, at 1–2 (Nov. 13, 2007), https://archive.epa.gov/enforcement/annual-results/web/pdf/eoy2007.pdf (PDF at 47–48).

3. CWA § 309(g), 33 U.S.C. § 1319(g) (2012). These statutory penalty maximums are adjusted for inflation. *See* 40 C.F.R. § 19.1–19.4 (2017) (setting forth inflation-adjusted penalties for violations of federal environmental statutes).

4. CAA § 113(d), 42 U.S.C. § 7413(d) (2012).

5. *Id.*

6. RCRA § 3008(a)(1), 42 U.S.C. § 6928(a)(1) (2012).

It bears emphasis that EPA's judicial enforcement statistics include two discrete types of enforcement—regulatory enforcement and enforcement under the Comprehensive Environmental Response, Compensation, and Liability Act (CERCLA).[7] These two types of cases are fundamentally different. While regulatory enforcement generally seeks to address noncompliance with environmental requirements, CERCLA enforcement focuses on the liability that accrues because of status or conduct, independent of past compliance. This chapter is focused on regulatory enforcement.

It also bears emphasis that most government environmental enforcement is conducted by states and, in some cases, by local governments.[8] For a state to be given delegations or primacy to run programs under federal environmental laws, such as to be granted National Pollutant Discharge Elimination System (NPDES) authority under the CWA, EPA must find that the state has adequate authority to enforce the programs.[9] States, on their own, have created an array of enforcement mechanisms to be employed at the state level. Although the focus of this chapter is on federal enforcement litigation, many of the matters discussed apply to state enforcement as well. Further, both EPA and DOJ have stressed the importance of joint enforcement, and coordinating efforts between DOJ and states' attorneys general.[10]

II. THE LOGISTICS OF FEDERAL CIVIL ENFORCEMENT

Before turning to the legal and factual issues that typically arise in federal civil environmental enforcement litigation, it is useful to consider who the players are in the process and the roles that they play. The starting point for this discussion is the fact that EPA generally does not have its own "litigating authority." It may not commence litigation itself or represent itself in litigation in federal courts, but rather it must be represented by DOJ in such litigation. That is one side of the equation—EPA cannot act alone. The other side of the equation is that neither can DOJ, which is required to work closely with EPA and to allow EPA to actively participate in the litigation process. The terms of engagement between the two offices were spelled out 40 years ago in a memorandum of understanding (MOU) between EPA and DOJ.[11] This MOU provides that DOJ will commence action on all matters referred by EPA within 60 days of the referral or will report to EPA why action has not been commenced, and that EPA attorneys will be permitted to participate fully

---

7. CERCLA § 101, 42 U.S.C. §§ 9601 *et seq.* (2012).

8. *See* CWA § 402(b), 33 U.S.C. § 1342(b) (2012).

9. *Id.*

10. U.S. Dep't of Justice, Env't & Nat. Res. Div. & Nat'l Atty's Gen. Training & Res. Inst., Guidelines for Joint State/Federal Civil Environmental Enforcement Litigation (2017), https://www.justice.gov/file/928531/download.

11. Memorandum of Understanding between Department of Justice and Environmental Protection Agency, 42 Fed. Reg. 48,942 (Sept. 26, 1977).

in the process. In practice, few cases are filed within 60 days after referral, and DOJ fulfills its MOU commitment by reporting to EPA each month on a long list of cases not filed.

This MOU is incorporated into the CAA, which specifically addresses the relationship between EPA and DOJ. Section 305 of the CAA provides:

> (a) The Administrator shall request the Attorney General to appear and represent him in any civil action instituted under this Act to which the Administrator is a party. Unless the Attorney General notifies the Administrator that he will appear in such action, within a reasonable time, attorneys appointed by the Administrator shall appear and represent him.
>
> (b) In the event the Attorney General agrees to appear and represent the Administrator in any such action, such representation shall be conducted in accordance with, and shall include participation by, attorneys appointed by the Administrator to the extent authorized by, the memorandum of understanding between the Department of Justice and the Environmental Protection Agency, dated June 13, 1977, respecting representation of the agency by the department in civil litigation.[12]

In practice, EPA never has exercised the right to appear through its own attorneys in cases where DOJ has not agreed to act. DOJ has always represented EPA in court.

Within EPA, civil enforcement authority is divided between the Office of Civil Enforcement at EPA headquarters, which is part of the Office of Enforcement and Compliance Assurance (OECA), and the ten EPA regional offices.[13] Most referrals for civil enforcement are developed in one of the ten regional offices and then forwarded directly to DOJ. The referrals are accompanied by a "litigation report" (a detailed description of the factual and legal bases for the enforcement case, and a discussion of potential defenses), the relief EPA seeks, and EPA's settlement position. The government views this report as exempt from disclosure under the Freedom of Information Act, and exempt from discovery under attorney-client privilege and attorney work product.[14]

Certain referrals of national significance are developed and managed by EPA's Office of Civil Enforcement. This office also is responsible for exercising oversight over regional activities, developing national enforcement priorities, and approving settlements in certain categories of cases. The office is composed of three enforcement divisions and administrative offices for Cross Cutting Policy Staff and Resource Management Staff.[15] The enforcement divisions are the Air Enforcement

---

12. CAA § 305(a)–(b), 42 U.S.C. § 7605(a)–(b) (2012).

13. U.S. Envtl. Prot. Agency, About EPA: About the Office of Enforcement and Compliance Assurance (OECA), https://www.epa.gov/aboutepa/about-office-enforcement-and-compliance-assurance-oeca (last visited July 17, 2018).

14. *Cf.* Envtl. Prot. Servs. v. EPA, 364 F. Supp. 2d 575, 587–88 (N.D. W. Va. 2005) (holding documents prepared in advance of civil enforcement are not subject to freedom of information request).

15. U.S. Envtl. Prot. Agency, About EPA: Organization Chart for the Office of Enforcement and Compliance Assurance (OECA), https://www.epa.gov/aboutepa/organization-chart-office-enforcement-and-compliance-assurance-oeca (last visited May 5, 2018).

Division, the Waste and Chemical Enforcement Division, and the Water Enforcement Division.[16]

On the DOJ end, responsibility for civil enforcement is divided between the Environment and Natural Resources Division (ENRD) and the 93 U.S. Attorneys' offices around the country. Most of the work in this area, however, tends to be performed by the ENRD. In fact, the initiation of civil enforcement actions, with limited exceptions, has to be approved by the ENRD.[17] While some of the larger U.S. Attorneys' offices often play active or lead roles in civil enforcement cases, many offices act only as local counsel to the lawyers at the ENRD. Overall, U.S. Attorneys' offices have been substantially less involved in civil enforcement cases than in criminal enforcement cases.

Within the ENRD, most enforcement cases are handled by the Environmental Enforcement Section (EES), which is an office of about 150 attorneys, divided into six litigating groups corresponding to the ten EPA regions.[18] Some litigating groups work with two regions. Each group is headed by an assistant chief who reports to one of the three deputy section chiefs and to a section chief. There is also an assistant chief for special litigation, who manages, among other things, certain multi-regional cases, such as cases "involving violations of the Clean Air Act's mobile source requirements and lead paint cases."[19]

The only civil enforcement cases not handled by the EES are those cases that are brought under Sections 10 and 13 of the Rivers and Harbor Act of 1899,[20] and under Sections 301 and 404 of the CWA.[21] These cases are enforced by the Environmental Defense Section (EDS) rather than the EES. For the most part, these cases involve allegations that wetlands have been illegally filled. That wetlands cases are enforced by the EDS and not the EES is a vestige from when the two sections were created in 1980.

What all this means is that on a typical federal civil enforcement case, the government team may include the following: (1) an engineer and a lawyer from the EPA regional office, (2) possibly a legal and technical representative of EPA's Office of Civil Enforcement, (3) one or more lawyers from DOJ's Environmental Enforcement Section, unless the case involves the wetlands, in which case the lawyers will be from the Environmental Defense Section, and (4) possibly one or more Assistant U.S. Attorneys. The number of offices potentially involved in the process is certainly a reflection of the importance the government places on civil

---

16. *Id.*

17. U.S. Dep't of Justice, United States Attorneys' Manual § 5-1.310, Authority of United States Attorneys to Initiate Civil Actions without Prior Authorization, i.e., Direct Referral Cases, https://www.justice.gov/jm/jm-5-1000-policy#5-1.300 (setting forth the exceptions to the ENRD approval requirement).

18. U.S. Dep't of Justice, The Organization of EES, https://www.justice.gov/enrd/organization-ees (last updated Oct. 14, 2015).

19. *Id.*

20. Rivers and Harbors Appropriation Act of 1899 §§ 10, 13, 33 U.S.C. §§ 403, 407 (2012).

21. CWA §§ 301, 404, 33 U.S.C. §§ 1311, 1344 (2012).

environmental enforcement. But it often can come at the cost of bureaucratic cumbersomeness that can make decision making and settlement both difficult and time-consuming.

Understanding the bureaucratic aspects of the federal civil enforcement process is important not only as a means of knowing the players, but also as a tool for ascertaining where potentially helpful information may be found. For example, the ENRD not only has responsibility for enforcing the environmental laws, but also represents federal agencies when they are sued by states or citizens for alleged violations of the environmental laws. In defending these cases, the EDS may be asked to take positions that are at odds with the enforcement positions that EPA and the EES have taken or wish to take in cases where the United States is the enforcer. Generally, the management at the EES, the EDS, and the ENRD work hard to ensure consistency in this area, but the dockets on both sides are large and complex, and it is simply not possible to achieve complete consistency. It is therefore a fruitful avenue of inquiry when defending a federal enforcement case to ascertain what positions have been taken on similar issues by the United States wearing its defensive hat in cases where federal agencies have been sued for similar violations or where similar types of relief were sought against them. Finding examples of such inconsistencies, while not always simple, is easier than it used to be, for the pleadings the government has filed now are increasingly available and often searchable online in resources such as Pacer, Westlaw, and LexisNexis.

III. THE GOVERNMENT'S CLAIMS

In bringing civil enforcement cases, the government can assert a range of claims as broad as the environmental laws and regulations that it enforces. These claims can be as simple as an allegation that an advance notice of an asbestos renovation was not sent in a timely manner or as complex as claims that power plants and other industrial facilities were modified in the past without necessary new source review construction permits and now need to be retrofitted with extremely expensive controls or that auto companies manufactured and sold cars with illegal "defeat devices" designed to circumvent emissions control systems.

While the subject matter of the government's claims can vary widely, all enforcement claims can be placed into one of four categories. It is useful to consider, for each category, what the government needs to prove to establish its case, and the type of issues likely to arise. In bringing an enforcement case, the government will assert that a defendant's action or inaction: (1) violates a requirement or prohibition set forth directly in the statute; (2) violates a requirement or prohibition set forth in a federal regulation or federally enforceable state regulation; (3) violates a requirement or prohibition in a state or federally issued permit that is federally enforceable; or (4) does not necessarily violate any legal requirement, but nonetheless endangers public health or the environment. Sometimes, the various claims in a complaint will fall into multiple categories. Each category will be addressed in subsequent sections of this chapter.

One important and common element of each of these claims is that proof of scienter is not required. It is not necessary that the defendant intended to violate the law or even intended to perform the action at issue. Because all the federal environmental laws create strict liability, the government must show only that the defendant's actions are inconsistent with the applicable standard.[22] The strict liability element, however, does not mean that intent is irrelevant to civil enforcement cases. Intent can be relevant to a number of commonly occurring issues, discussed later, ranging from whether a defendant had fair notice of what a regulation meant to the degree of penalty to be imposed. But courts have consistently held that the government need not show intent to prove a prima facie case.[23]

Another aspect of civil enforcement cases is who is named as the defendant by the government. Typically, in cases involving a company, it is usually the company and not its individual owners/officers/employees who are sued. This remains the case even in light of the so-called Yates Memorandum. The September 9, 2015, memorandum from then Deputy Attorney General Sally Yates, titled "Individual Accountability for Corporate Wrongdoing,"[24] encouraged the naming of individual defendants even in civil enforcement cases. The memorandum states:

> Pursuit of civil actions against culpable individuals should not be governed solely by those individuals' ability to pay. In other words, the fact that an individual may not have sufficient resources to satisfy a significant judgment should not control the decision on whether to bring suit. Rather, in deciding whether to file a civil action against an individual, Department attorneys should consider factors such as whether the person's misconduct was serious, whether it is actionable, whether the admissible evidence will probably be sufficient to obtain and sustain a judgment, and whether pursuing the action reflects an important federal interest.[25]

There are three reasons why individuals, even with the Yates Memorandum, are not usually named in civil environmental enforcement cases. First, pursuing an individual could require a potentially greater level of evidence than pursuing the business, which typically will hold the relevant permits and own and operate the facility. Second, as opposed to criminal cases where an individual found to have committed an offense can be incarcerated, in civil cases the government can

---

22. *See, e.g.*, United States v. BP Expl. & Prod., Inc. (*In re* Deepwater Horizon), 753 F.3d 570, 575 (5th Cir. 2014) ("Courts . . . now acknowledge that civil-penalty liability under [Section 311 of the CWA] arises irrespective of knowledge, intent, or fault."); United States v. Dell'Aquilla, 150 F.3d 329, 332 (3d Cir. 1998) ("The [CAA] imposes strict liability upon owners and operators [of a facility that contains asbestos] who violate the Act."); United States v. Smithfield Foods, Inc., 965 F. Supp. 769, 782 (E.D. Va. 1997) ("[T]he Clean Water Act is a strict liability statute.").

23. *See id.*

24. Memorandum from Sally Yates, Deputy Att'y Gen., U.S. Dep't of Justice, to All Component Heads & U.S. Att'ys, Individual Accountability for Corporate Wrongdoing (Sept. 9, 2015), https://www.justice.gov/archives/dag/file/769036/download.

25. *Id.* at 6–7.

generally obtain all the relief it seeks from the business entity. And third, in those situations where an individual's conduct was sufficiently egregious to consider naming that person as a civil defendant, DOJ is likely to be more interested in pursuing that individual criminally.

A. Direct Statutory Claims

The federal environmental laws contain a number of core requirements and prohibitions, and also authorize EPA to promulgate regulations to further implement the statutory program. Certain enforcement claims are premised on direct violations of core statutory requirements.

A good example of this type of claim is one to enforce the simple prohibition in Section 301 of the CWA, which holds that except as otherwise permitted under the Act, "the discharge of any pollutant by any person shall be unlawful."[26] The term *discharge of any pollutant* is defined to include "any addition of any pollutant to navigable waters from any point source."[27] Thus, a Section 301 violation is premised on five statutory terms: *person*, *addition*, *pollutant*, *navigable waters*, and *point source*.[28] All these terms, except *addition*, are separately defined in the statute, and in all cases, they are defined broadly.[29] Yet the courts have not always interpreted these terms as broadly. Most notably, the Supreme Court unleashed a torrent of litigation over the definition of *navigable waters* with its 2004 decision in *Rapanos v. United States*, which narrowed the scope of the term.[30] Thus, if the government alleges that a defendant's conduct violated Section 301, the issues that will be raised go to each of the five critical elements of the claim (although denying that the defendant is a person is not usually a fruitful defense strategy) and whether the government can prove that the statutory terms are met.

Often in these cases, there will be litigable issues as to at least one of the statutory terms. In considering why this is so, it is important to bear in mind two important aspects of the government's case selection process. On the one hand, the government would not typically bring a case unless it had analyzed the statutory requirements and believed it had a strong case that each element was met. And that analysis is subject to multiple levels of review at EPA and DOJ. One might think, therefore, that when the government selects a case for civil enforcement, the government would make sure not to leave itself hard issues to litigate. And in some cases that is true. But there is a countervailing dynamic. If the case were a "slam dunk," if a company were knowingly discharging nasty stuff (clearly a

---

26. CWA § 301(a), 33 U.S.C. § 1311(a) (2012).
27. *Id.* § 502(12), 33 U.S.C. § 1362(12) (2012).
28. *See id.* § 502(5)–(7), (14), 33 U.S.C. § 1362(5)–(7), (14).
29. *Id.*
30. Rapanos v. United States, 547 U.S. 715 (2006). The *Rapanos* decision resulted in an effort during the Obama administration to define "Waters of the United States" by a rule, which was then challenged by numerous states and industry groups, and later withdrawn by the Trump administration. For a discussion of the background of these rules, see the Supreme Court's January 22, 2018, decision in *National Association of Manufacturers v. Department of Defense*, 138 S. Ct. 617 (2018).

pollutant) from a pipe (clearly a point source) into the Mississippi River (clearly a navigable water, even under *Rapanos*),[31] that case would very likely have been brought criminally. A case generally is brought civilly because elements of the case are unattractive in a criminal context, which often means that there are significant issues that can be raised by the defense against the government's civil claims. Conversely, a statutory element that is not clearly met could undermine the higher scienter requirement that would apply if the case were pursued criminally.

Therefore, in defending direct statutory violation claims, it is important to focus on the key statutory terms and how these terms are defined in the statute and, sometimes, the applicable regulations. It also is important to consider any relevant legislative history and how the courts have interpreted the statutory terms. Usually, there will be many prior cases on these issues, and litigation should focus on how the facts of the case fit into the framework developed by these previous cases. In addition to looking at prior judicial cases, it also is important to examine closely how EPA has interpreted these terms when it has taken administrative enforcement, to consider how administrative law judges or EPA's Environmental Appeals Board have interpreted the statutory terms, and to look for positions taken on the key terms by the United States when it has been in a defensive posture.

B. Regulatory Claims

A large percentage of enforcement cases are premised on violations of regulations. These regulations can be ones promulgated by EPA or they can be regulations promulgated by states that are federally enforceable. An example of the latter category would be a claim that a defendant was violating the provisions of a state implementation plan (SIP) under the CAA. The following are the three issues raised in these cases: "What is the regulation?" "What does it mean?" and "Is the defendant violating it?"

One might think that the first question, "What is the regulation?" would be as straightforward as opening the Code of Federal Regulations—and often it is this simple. But if, for example, the federal government is seeking to enforce a SIP, determining what the relevant SIP is can be a complicated process. It has become simpler as EPA has tried to include the text of SIPs on its website,[32] but the history of SIP promulgation is sufficiently complicated that it is generally a good idea in SIP enforcement cases to review the actual regulatory docket.

The key issue in these types of cases will be the meaning of the regulation. Despite government-wide efforts to write regulations in "plain English," environmental regulations often deal with highly technical subjects and reflect more the work product of engineers than of lawyers—although it has been a longtime

---

31. *Id.* at 734 ("[T]he Act's use of the traditional phrase 'navigable waters' (the defined term) further confirms that [the CWA] confers jurisdiction only over relatively *permanent* bodies of water.").

32. U.S. Envtl. Prot. Agency, Approved Air Quality Implementation Plans, https://www.epa.gov/air-quality-implementation-plans/approved-air-quality-implementation-plans (last visited July 18, 2018).

priority of EPA's Office of General Counsel to ensure that regulations are clear and enforceable. But that is a tall order, given the magnitude of regulations being promulgated and their increasing complexity.

If there is a good-faith dispute about what a regulation means, and a defendant's conduct would be lawful under one interpretation but not under the one taken by EPA, then this may become the central issue in the case. Thus, it will be crucial to expansively examine all relevant materials. These relevant materials will include those generated as part of the rulemaking process and those generated subsequently. The most authoritative interpretations will be those set forth in the regulatory preamble that accompanied the proposed and final rule, as set forth in the *Federal Register*. The remainder of the regulatory docket, including comments submitted by interested parties, also could be relevant to this analysis, and would be found on EPA's regulatory docket, not in the *Federal Register*.

The relevance of interpretations of the regulation issued through guidance subsequent to its promulgation has been the subject of considerable controversy. Until recently, DOJ and EPA often relied on such guidance, and courts generally gave substantial deference to EPA's interpretation of its own regulations,[33] although they also required that the interpretation be issued prior to the litigation.[34] Recently, during the Trump administration, DOJ's leadership has declared that the government should *not* rely on EPA guidance documents that did not go through notice and comment when establishing regulatory violations. The associate attorney general stated that "the Department may not use its enforcement authority to effectively convert agency guidance documents into binding rules. Likewise, DOJ litigators may not use noncompliance with guidance documents as a basis for proving violations of applicable law" in enforcement cases.[35] Of course, the new DOJ policy would not preclude a defendant in an enforcement case from relying on EPA guidance documents defensively to assert that its conduct was consistent with the regulation as interpreted in the guidance.

While a defendant certainly may challenge EPA's interpretation of the regulations, the law is clear that the defendant may not challenge the regulation itself in an enforcement case. Regulations may be challenged only in the context of the issuance of the regulation. Thus, for example, the CAA provides that "Action of the Administrator with respect to which review could have been obtained under paragraph (1) [which provides for judicial review of regulations] shall not be subject

---

33. *See, e.g.,* Marine Shale Processors, Inc. v. EPA, 81 F.3d 1371, 1384 (5th Cir. 1996).

34. *See* Bowen v. Georgetown Univ. Hosp., 488 U.S. 204, 213 (1988); S. Utah Wilderness All. v. Dabney, 222 F.3d 819, 828 (10th Cir. 2000); *see also In re* Acevedo, 497 B.R. 112, 119 n.19 (D.N.M. Bankr. Ct. 2013).

35. Memorandum from the Assoc. Att'y Gen., U.S. Dep't of Justice, to Heads of Civil Litigating Components & U.S. Att'ys, Limiting Use of Agency Guidance Documents in Affirmative Civil Enforcement Cases (Jan. 25, 2018), https://www.justice.gov/file/1028756/download.

to judicial review in civil or criminal proceedings for enforcement."[36] Similar provisions are found in other environmental statutes.[37]

C. Permit Enforcement

Over the years there has been an increased focus on facility-specific environmental permits. The CWA has long used the tool of the NPDES permit, which established specific discharge limits and reporting requirements for permitted discharges to navigable waters.[38] RCRA has long required facility-specific permits for hazardous waste treatment, storage, and disposal facilities.[39] Furthermore, this permit concept is also central to the CAA through the Title V permitting process.[40]

Permits lend themselves to more efficient enforcement because the standards are established for the specific facility and because the reporting requirements under the permit generally are closely tied to the emission or discharge limitations. A classic enforcement scenario has been for EPA to compare the effluent, as measured in the discharge monitoring reports required under a NPDES permit, to the effluent limits in the permit, and if the first exceeds the second, to allege a violation. The defendant is essentially put in a position where it establishes its own violations.

In these situations, the government has long argued that the defendant's own reports are conclusive proof of violation. In other words, the defendant could not argue that its reports were in error. And a defendant would be hesitant to allege such error in any event, because it essentially would be admitting to a new series of reporting violations. However, in those cases where the best evidence is that the reports submitted were not accurate, and that the effluent limits were not violated, at least two appellate courts have suggested that a defendant can indeed allege "lab error" and assert that the reports it submitted were not conclusive, though such defendants will face a heavy burden in impeaching their own reports.[41]

Several issues relevant to permit enforcement bear mention. First, sometimes the permits sought to be enforced may have expired, and a permit renewal application is pending or is under appeal. In such cases, it is vital to establish which requirements are in effect while the permitting process goes forward. It typically is the case that the terms of the old permit remain in effect until a new permit is issued, if a timely application was filed.

Second, even when permits are facility-specific, there can be issues as to what certain terms mean. In that regard, it is crucial to examine the permit file,

---

36. CAA § 307(b)(2), 42 U.S.C. § 7607(b)(2) (2012).

37. *See, e.g.*, CWA § 509(b)(2), 33 U.S.C. § 1369(b)(2) (2012); RCRA § 7006(a)(1), 42 U.S.C. § 6976(a)(1) (2012).

38. CWA § 402, 33 U.S.C. § 1342 (2012).

39. RCRA § 3005, 42 U.S.C. § 6925 (2012).

40. CAA §§ 501–502, 42 U.S.C. §§ 7661–7661a (2012).

41. United States v. STABL, Inc., 800 F.3d 476, 485–86 (8th Cir. 2015); United States v. Allegheny Ludlum Corp., 366 F.3d 164, 171–76 (3d Cir. 2004).

including the application, to see what light that sheds on the permit interpretation issue. Because most permits use boilerplate provisions found in numerous other permits, it also is important to see whether the provision at issue is indeed found in other permits, and, if so, how it has been interpreted there. If the permit provision comes out of a regulatory process, one would, of course, want to examine the regulatory record, as discussed previously.

Third, issues can arise as to who exactly is subject to the provisions of the permit, especially if the government enforces it against a person not listed as the permit holder, such as an individual facility operator. The predicament that person faces is that he or she may need to rely on the permit to authorize his or her actions, and that will make it difficult to dispute the applicability of permit terms. For example, an individual who discharges pollutants to a river can hardly claim not to be subject to a permit issued to a related corporation, because if that were the case, then the discharge would not be permitted or legal.

Finally, in permit enforcement cases, EPA also may seek to allege violations of related regulations. In that context, the "permit as a shield" provisions of the CWA and CAA, discussed in section V, Defenses to Enforcement, will come into play, and will protect permit holders who comply with their permits from enforcement for matters within the scope of the permit.

D. Use of Endangerment Authorities

The final category of enforcement is one based not on violations of the law but on assertions that a defendant's conduct is creating a public health or environmental risk. An example of a statutory provision creating such an enforcement remedy is Section 303 of the CAA. It provides:

> Notwithstanding any other provision of this Act, the Administrator, upon receipt of evidence that a pollution source or combination of sources (including moving sources) is presenting an imminent and substantial endangerment to public health or welfare, or the environment, may bring suit on behalf of the United States in the appropriate United States district court to immediately restrain any person causing or contributing to the alleged pollution to stop the emission of air pollutants causing or contributing to such pollution or to take such other action as may be necessary. If it is not practicable to assure prompt protection of public health or welfare or the environment by commencement of such a civil action, the Administrator may issue such orders as may be necessary to protect public health or welfare or the environment.[42]

Thus, under the CAA, EPA may act through issuing an order or commencing a lawsuit whenever it receives evidence that an air-pollution source "is presenting

---

42. CAA § 303, 42 U.S.C. § 7603 (2012).

an imminent and substantial endangerment to public health or welfare, or the environment."[43]

The CWA and RCRA also have endangerment authorities, with the CWA's being narrower and RCRA's being somewhat broader. The "Emergency powers" provision in Section 504 of the CWA contains no administrative order authority,[44] and EPA cannot sue for all endangerments to "public health or welfare, or the environment." It must allege, to meet the rather peculiar statutory language, that a water pollution source is "presenting an imminent and substantial endangerment to the health of persons or to the welfare of persons where such endangerment is to the livelihood of such persons, such as inability to market shellfish."[45]

Section 7003 of RCRA creates very broad authority. It allows EPA to issue orders or to sue whenever it receives "evidence that the past or present handling, storage, treatment, transportation or disposal of any solid waste or hazardous waste may present an imminent and substantial endangerment to health or the environment."[46] There are two key aspects of this provision. First, it does not require that the endangerment relate to hazardous waste—it can relate to non-hazardous "solid waste." Second, unlike the CAA and CWA, there does not have to be evidence that there "is" an endangerment—there only has to be evidence that there "may" be one.

EPA interprets the phrase *imminent and substantial endangerment* quite broadly. For example, EPA has stated that "courts have repeatedly recognized that the endangerment standard of RCRA § 7003 is quite broad."[47] EPA goes on to explain:

> [N]either certainty nor proof of actual harm is required, only a *risk* of harm. . . .
> An endangerment is "imminent" if the present conditions indicate that there may be a future risk to health or the environment even though the harm may not be realized for years. It is not necessary for the endangerment to be immediate or tantamount to an emergency.
> An endangerment is "substantial" if there is reasonable cause for concern that health or the environment may be seriously harmed. It is not necessary that the risk be quantified.[48]

Notwithstanding EPA's broad endangerment authorities, and its broad interpretation of those authorities, it has not brought suits based on these authorities nearly as often as one might have predicted. There are a number of explanations for this. First, in situations involving risks from wastes, EPA has tended to use its

---

43. *Id.*
44. CWA § 504, 33 U.S.C. § 1364 (2012).
45. *Id.*
46. RCRA § 7003, 42 U.S.C. § 6973(a) (2012).
47. Memorandum from the Office of Enf't & Compliance Assurance, U.S. Envtl. Prot. Agency, Guidance on the Use of Section 7003 of RCRA 10 (Oct. 20, 1997), https://www.epa.gov/sites/production/files/2013-10/documents/use-sec7003-mem.pdf.
48. *Id.* at 10–11 (citing a number of cases for these assertions, including *Dague v. City of Burlington*, 935 F.2d 1343 (2d Cir. 1991), and *United States v. Valentine*, 856 F. Supp. 621, 626 (D. Wyo. 1994)).

even broader CERCLA authorities to address any perceived emergencies. Second, in cases where it has authority to issue orders administratively, EPA has tended to use that authority more frequently than commencing litigation. Third, in endangerment authority cases, EPA does not have the leverage of seeking penalties for past noncompliance (unless other claims are asserted as well). Fourth, these cases present higher burdens of proof and can be more resource-intensive than cases premised on merely showing that a regulatory requirement was not met.

Furthermore, it can take EPA such a long time to develop certain of its civil enforcement cases that it becomes very difficult to allege an emergency. (Although EPA asserts that its enforcement authorities do not necessitate showing an emergency, its enforcement case certainly is much more compelling when there is a true emergency.) In other words, it can be difficult for EPA to allege after a two-year investigation that the conditions at issue are an emergency, especially if such conditions have not changed since the investigation began. If there were an emergency, why didn't EPA act two years ago? It is for similar reasons that the government rarely seeks preliminary injunctions in civil enforcement cases. And a fruitful avenue of defense in endangerment authority cases or in defending a request for a preliminary injunction can be to establish that the government knew about the conditions at issue for a long time and did not think immediate action needed to be taken.

Finally, endangerment authority cases present challenges to EPA because they are premised on the idea that there can be gaps in the existing regulatory framework. Sometimes, asserting that there is such a gap can put EPA in a position at odds with its regulatory promulgation. In other words, if EPA asserts that an air endangerment exists in a situation where the National Ambient Air Quality Standard is not exceeded, a defendant will want to try to show that EPA considered the relevant health risk in setting the applicable standard, and determined that a certain level of air pollution would not present an unacceptable health risk.

While endangerment authority cases are relatively uncommon, they do present a significantly greater risk of adverse collateral consequences. A judicial finding that a defendant's conduct has endangered public health is an open invitation to the plaintiff tort bar to bring follow-on cases in which the adverse public health effects already will have been established by the government. Thus, these cases can be difficult for the government to prove, but also can be very risky for the defendant to litigate and risk losing.

IV. THE RELIEF THE GOVERNMENT SEEKS

A. Injunctions

If the violations alleged by the government are continuing, the government generally will seek injunctive relief. In cases where achieving compliance will require significant capital expenditure—such as upgrades to a sewage system or retrofitting air-pollution controls on an operating plant—the relief sought usually will be to impose a compliance schedule on the defendant, requiring that the defendant install necessary improvements on a predetermined schedule. Where there have been long-standing compliance problems, especially by municipalities, the government in the past has sought and obtained more extensive injunctive relief aimed at facilitating compliance. These forms of injunctive relief have ranged from a ban on new sewer connections until compliance is achieved[49] to the appointment by the court of a special administrator to run the sewer system.[50]

One fundamental issue raised by the government's requests for injunctive relief is whether the government can obtain an injunction based merely on demonstrating that there are continuing violations, or whether the government must prove that harm to public health or the environment will result if an injunction is not obtained.

This is an issue on which the federal government has tended to take inconsistent positions, depending on whether it is seeking an injunction or opposing one sought against it. The central case in this debate is the Supreme Court's 1982 decision in *Weinberger v. Romero-Barcelo*.[51] In that case, the Navy was engaged in training operations by which it was discharging ordnance into water of the United States without a permit. There was no dispute that there were violations of the CWA. The question was whether an injunction should be issued simply because there was a violation. The United States argued that it should not, and the Supreme Court agreed. The Court stated that Congress had not intended the CWA "to deny courts their traditional equitable discretion" with regard to injunctions.[52] It held that the CWA does not require a "court to issue an injunction for any and all statutory violations"[53] and noted that the Navy's discharge "had not polluted the waters . . . nor undercut the purpose and function of the permit system."[54] A number of

---

49. United States v. Metro. Dist. Comm'n, 930 F.2d 132, 134 (1st Cir. 1991); *see also* Nat'l Wildlife Fed'n v. Nat'l Marine Fisheries Serv., 839 F. Supp. 2d 1117, 1130 (D. Or. 2011) (noting that in these situations, the "court has discretion to retain jurisdiction to ensure compliance with a court order").

50. United States v. City of Detroit, 476 F. Supp. 512, 515 (E.D. Mich. 1979), *modified*, 2013 U.S. Dist. LEXIS 42869 (E.D. Mich. Mar. 27, 2013) (terminating and closing the case after the Detroit Water and Sewage Department "achieved substantial compliance with its NPDES permit and the Clean Water Act").

51. Weinberger v. Romero-Barcelo, 456 U.S. 305 (1982).

52. *Id.* at 316.

53. *Id.* at 320.

54. *Id.* at 315.

post-*Romero-Barcelo* cases support the proposition that irreparable harm is a precondition to the issuance of an injunction.[55]

Notwithstanding *Romero-Barcelo*, the government still will routinely take the position when bringing enforcement cases that the mere fact of a continuing violation necessitates an injunction, without any showing of irreparable harm. The government will point to the legislative findings in the underlying statutes that highlight the harm to public health and the environment that the statute was intended to remediate. In many cases, the harm to the environment from the alleged violations will be clear enough and large enough that arguing against the issuance of an injunction if a violation is found will not be productive. But there will be other cases where the violations the government alleges do not readily translate into proof of environmental harm, and in those cases it may be quite productive to dispute the appropriateness of injunctive relief.

An example of a case where this approach was successful is *United States v. Massachusetts Water Resources Authority*.[56] In that case, the government alleged that the drinking water system for the Boston area was in violation of the Safe Drinking Water Act because it was not complying with regulations requiring water filtration.[57] The defendant argued that it had equally good measures in place to protect its water supply.[58] The court of appeals upheld a denial of injunctive relief even though the defendant was found to be in violation of regulatory requirements.[59] The district court had found that the measures taken by the defendant were as good as, or better than, those required by the regulations.[60] According to the court of appeals, under such circumstances the district court had the authority to deny injunctive relief.[61]

One way to undermine the government's request for injunctive relief is for the defendant to take measures to bring itself into compliance even while the enforcement case is pending. This approach may not make sense if the defendant truly does not believe it is in violation. But in those cases where it is reasonably likely

---

55. *See, e.g.*, Town of Huntington v. Marsh, 884 F.2d 648 (2d Cir. 1989) (finding that violations of the Ocean Dumping Act and the National Environmental Policy Act by the Army Corps of Engineers did not necessitate an injunction without a showing of irreparable injury); Nat. Res. Def. Council v. Texaco Ref. & Mktg., Inc., 2 F.3d 493 (3d Cir. 1993) ("Not every violation of the Clean Water Act justifies the issuance of an injunction. . . . Although the district court exercises considerable discretion in making this determination, proof of irreparable injury and the inadequacy of legal remedies are prerequisites to the granting of injunctive relief in a Clean Water Act case."); Idaho Conservation League v. Atlanta Gold Corp., 879 F. Supp. 2d 1148, 1158 (D. Idaho 2012) (considering how "to ensure timely compliance with the terms of the NPDES Permit" and listing irreparable injury and inadequate legal remedies among requirements for an injunction).

56. United States v. Mass. Water Res. Auth., 256 F.3d 36 (1st Cir. 2001); *see also* Total Petroleum P.R. Corp. v. Colon, 819 F. Supp. 2d 55, 70 (D.P.R. 2011) (including "that the public interest would not be adversely affected by an injunction" in its decision whether to issue a permanent injunction (quoting 256 F.3d at 51 n.15)).

57. *Mass. Water Res. Auth.*, 256 F.3d at 44.

58. *Id.* at 45.

59. *Id.* at 58.

60. *Id.*

61. *Id.*

that a violation will be found, early compliance will reduce the chance of an injunction. Avoiding an injunction is beneficial, even when such avoidance requires the defendant to do that which the injunction would compel. That is because an injunction can keep the defendant under the court's supervision for an extended period of time and can be enforced through the court's contempt powers.

Moreover, if the defendant is able to take injunctive relief off the table, the case then will be a penalties-only case, and those cases—which are solely about past problems that now are fixed—are likely to be less compelling to the courts and receive lower priority.

The foregoing discussion deals with the classic type of injunctive relief that the government typically seeks—to restrain ongoing violations. The government also has sought injunctive relief that goes beyond prospective compliance. For example, in a number of cases the government has sought to require defendants to remove contaminants in receiving waters that allegedly resulted from prior discharges, through dredging of contaminated sediments. The government claimed that this is justified as "appropriate relief" authorized under Section 309(b) of the CWA. A few district courts addressing the issue found that contaminant removal could be sought under the act.[62]

In a number of cases, the government has gone beyond seeking removal of the specific contaminants that were unlawfully discharged and has sought injunctive relief to mitigate the impact of past violations. For example, in one of the most significant and most publicized enforcement cases ever brought, DOJ filed a complaint on January 4, 2016, against Volkswagen AG and affiliates alleging that nearly 600,000 diesel engine vehicles had illegal defeat devices that impair emission control systems, resulting in excess emission of nitrogen oxides (NOx) and other pollutants.[63] In its prayer for relief in the complaint, DOJ asked the court, in addition to seeking injunctive relief to restrain the violation and civil penalties, to "[o]rder VW to take appropriate steps, including, but not limited to, mitigation of excess NOx emissions, to remedy the violations . . . alleged above."[64] In settlement of that

---

62. U.S. Pub. Interest Research Grp. v. Atl. Salmon of Me., LLC, 339 F.3d 23 (1st Cir. 2003) (in a citizen-suit action, a First Circuit panel upheld an injunction aimed at remedying harm from past violations, even though it required measures that went beyond the terms of the defendant's general NPDES permit); United States v. Alcoa, Inc., 98 F. Supp. 2d 1031, 1038–39 (N.D. Ind. 2000) (holding that a "court's authority to grant an injunction 'to require compliance' in Section 309(b) is broad enough to include the mandated clean up of contaminated sediments where the sediments are contaminated as a direct result of NPDES Permit violations"); *see also* United States v. Cinergy Corp., 582 F. Supp. 2d 1055, 1062 (S.D. Ind. 2008) (holding 'that its equitable authority granted by § 113(b) [of the CAA] includes the authority to order relief aimed at redressing the harms caused by Defendants'. . . violations").

63. Press Release, U.S. Dep't of Justice, United States Files Complaint against Volkswagen, Audi and Porsche for Alleged Clean Air Act Violations (Jan. 4, 2016), https://www.justice.gov/opa/pr/united-states-files-complaint-against-volkswagen-audi-and-porsche-alleged-clean-air-act.

64. Complaint at 27, United States v. Volkswagen AG, No. 2:16-cv-10006 (E.D. Mich. 2016), https://www.justice.gov/opa/file/809826/download; *see also* Memorandum from the U.S. Envtl. Prot. Agency, Securing Mitigation as Injunctive Relief in Certain Civil Enforcement Settlements (2d ed.) (Nov. 14, 2012), https://www.epa.gov/sites/production/files/2016-08/documents/2ndeditionsecuringmitigationemo.pdf.

demand, Volkswagen later agreed to spend $14.7 billion "to mitigate the pollution from these cars and invest in green vehicle technology."[65] Although it is unclear whether there is a legal basis for seeking such relief, and also unclear whether such relief will be sought by DOJ during the Trump administration,[66] this type of demand, if successfully sought, could lead to the imposition of very large additional requirements on defendants.

B. Penalties

In addition to seeking injunctive relief, the government almost always seeks penalties for past violations. The principal environmental statutes all set maximum daily penalties (usually $25,000 per day, which have been adjusted periodically for inflation[67]) and allow the court to assess a penalty up to the maximum. Moreover, in some situations, the statutes allow for penalties on a per-unit basis—per barrel of oil spilled under the CWA,[68] or per car or truck unlawfully sold under the CAA[69]— that can result in much higher penalties.

The statute of limitation for penalties is five years,[70] meaning the government can seek penalties for violations during the five-year prefiling period, as well as for postfiling violations. Given this, and the fact that violations often continue for long periods of time, the maximum penalty can amount to millions or tens of millions of dollars, and billions of dollars in the case of per-unit penalties. EPA and DOJ over time have sought ever greater penalties in civil enforcement cases to deter, they assert, violations and incentivize compliance. Thus, the government obtained, in settlement, a civil penalty of $5.5 billion from BP arising from the *Deepwater Horizon* oil spill,[71] and of $1.45 billion from Volkswagen arising from the diesel car defeat device violations.[72]

The various statutes provide a number of factors for the court to consider in determining the precise amount of a civil penalty. For example, the CWA refers to "the seriousness of the violation or violations, the economic benefit (if any) resulting from the violation, any history of such violations, any good-faith efforts to comply with the applicable requirements, the economic impact of the penalty

---

65. Press Release, Fed. Trade Comm'n, Volkswagen to Spend up to $14.7 Billion to Settle Allegations of Cheating Emissions Tests and Deceiving Customers on 2.0 Liter Diesel Vehicles (June 28, 2016), https://www.ftc.gov/news-events/press-releases/2016/06/volkswagen-spend-147-billion-settle-allegations-cheating.

66. *See infra* section VII.C.

67. *See* sources cited *supra* note 3.

68. 33 U.S.C. § 1321(b)(7)(A) (2012).

69. 42 U.S.C. § 7524(a) (2012).

70. 28 U.S.C. § 2462 (2012).

71. U.S. Dep't of Justice, Env't & Nat. Res. Div., Proposed Consent Decrees, https://www.justice.gov/enrd/deepwater-horizon (last visited June 28, 2018).

72. Press Release, U.S. Dep't of Justice, Volkswagen AG Agrees to Plead Guilty and Pay $4.3 Billion in Criminal and Civil Penalties; Six Volkswagen Executives and Employees are Indicated in Connection with Conspiracy to Cheat U.S. Emissions Tests (Jan. 11, 2017), https://www.justice.gov/opa/pr/volkswagen-ag-agrees-plead-guilty-and-pay-43-billion-criminal-and-civil-penalties-six.

on the violator, and such other matters as justice may require."[73] Although courts will consider all these factors, the economic benefit factor is one that the government usually emphasizes as critical to create a level playing field. The government argues that a court cannot assess a penalty that is less than economic benefit, because that would reward the defendants for their violations.

The courts generally have not adopted per se rules that economic benefit must be awarded but have emphasized the importance of this factor. As one court put it, "the goal of the economic benefit analysis is to prevent a violator from profiting from its wrongdoing."[74] One Fifth Circuit panel, in a case involving an oil spill at a facility owned by Citgo Petroleum, found that a district court's failure to quantify the economic benefit to the defendant of deferring environmental compliance warranted vacating the civil penalty the district court had imposed and remanding the case to the district court.[75] The court called the economic benefit factor "a nearly indispensable reference point."[76] However, in a subsequent appeal in the same case, another Fifth Circuit panel affirmed the district court's $81 million penalty assessment and, in an unpublished opinion, rejected DOJ's argument that the penalty was too low because the economic benefit had been found to be $91.7 million, emphasizing the district court's large amount of discretion in making such assessments.[77] The panel upheld the district court's reduction below economic benefit in light of the fact that the defendant had spent $65 million to clean up the spill.[78]

In calculating the economic benefit, the government typically has focused on the deferred and avoided costs from delayed compliance. For example, if a facility has delayed installing necessary pollution controls, both the interest saved in not borrowing money to finance the equipment and the costs saved in not operating the equipment during the period of noncompliance would be components of the government's economic benefit calculation.

EPA has a computer model (called BEN) that it uses in the settlement context for determining economic benefit.[79] It is important to remember, however, that the model is not the result of rulemaking and typically is not utilized by EPA and DOJ in court proceedings. Rather, EPA and DOJ usually retain financial experts to

---

73. CWA § 309(d), 33 U.S.C. § 1319(d) (2012).

74. United States v. Mun. Auth. of Union Twp., 150 F.3d 259, 263 (3d Cir. 1998); *see also* Friends of the Earth, Inc. v. Laidlaw Envtl. Servs., Inc., 528 U.S. 167, 186 (2000); *see also* United States v. BP Expl. & Prod. (*In re* Oil Spill by the Oil Rig "Deepwater Horizon" in the Gulf of Mexico, on April 20, 2010), 148 F. Supp. 3d 563, 570 (E.D. La. 2015) (describing the purpose of the economic benefit factor as "to ensure that the violator does not wrongfully profit from its misconduct").

75. *See* United States v. CITGO Petrol. Corp., 723 F.3d 547, 551–54 (5th Cir. 2013); *see also In re Oil Spill by the Oil Rig "Deepwater Horizon" in the Gulf of Mexico, on April 20, 2010*, 148 F. Supp. at 570 ("The Fifth Circuit requires that this Court make a 'reasonable approximation' of economic benefit.").

76. *CITGO Petrol. Corp.*, 723 F.3d at 554.

77. United States v. CITGO Petrol. Corp., 711 F. App'x 237, 239–40 (5th Cir. 2018) (unpublished).

78. *Id.*

79. The BEN model, as well as other models for analyzing economic and financial aspects of environmental enforcement actions, can be downloaded from EPA's website, https://www.epa.gov/enforcement/penalty-and-financial-models.

analyze and calculate the economic benefit in particular cases, and defendants are well advised to hire such experts as well.

One key issue in calculating economic benefit will be the correct interest rate to use in translating past delayed and avoided costs into present dollars. EPA has historically sought to use a very high interest rate, which would result in a high economic benefit. It argues that environmental upgrades are traditionally financed with capital funds, and, therefore, one should look at the company's weighted average cost of capital, or WACC, rate. Defendants, not surprisingly, argue for lower rates, and typically point to such things as the statutory interest rate or the company's costs of debt.

In one CWA enforcement case, the district court found after trial that the economic benefit of noncompliance was $4.12 million and then doubled that to assess a penalty of $8.24 million.[80] In calculating the economic benefit, the district court had utilized the government's proposed WACC rate of 12.73 percent and had rejected much lower rates proposed by the defendant in the 5.2 percent to 6 percent range. The court of appeals reversed for a number of reasons, including the district court's use of the WACC rate. It stated that it was "unconvinced that the use of the 12.73 percent interest rate achieves the stated purpose of 'leveling the economic playing field,' nor are we sure that it bears much connection to a meaningful measure" of the defendant's "cost of capital (much less its return on capital)."[81] The court remanded the case, and the parties then settled for a much reduced penalty ($2.37 million). This highlights the importance of the discount rate issue in penalty calculation. One consideration defendants should keep in mind is that EPA may well look at how the company actually finances its compliance expenditures when it does come into compliance. If the company has a record of financing those expenditures with low-cost debt, that could assist the defense of the penalty case.

Another issue that arises with respect to economic benefit is accounting for remedial costs that would not have occurred but for the violation. For example, in the *Citgo Petroleum* case discussed previously, the defendant was found to have saved $91.6 million by not taking steps to avoid oil spills, but then spent $65 million to clean up the spill. EPA's policy does not allow for reducing the economic benefit by such remedial costs, and the courts typically have not done so either, but one could reasonably argue that if the goal is to ensure that the defendant does not profit from its violation, all costs flowing from the violation should be counted.

As an alternative to looking at delayed and avoided costs, the government has pursued other methods of calculating economic benefit, including what it alleges are "wrongful profits" or "illegal competitive advantage" obtained by the defendant during periods of operation in violation of the act. Accepting this approach, the Third Circuit found that the economic benefit of noncompliance could be

---

80. United States v. Allegheny Ludlum Corp., 366 F.3d 164, 177 (3d Cir. 2004); *see also* United States v. Righter, 2010 U.S. Dist. LEXIS 127721, at *3 (M.D. Pa. 2010) (noting that district courts have "wide discretion in setting the amount of the penalty within the statutorily prescribed maximum").

81. *Allegheny Ludlum Corp.*, 366 F.3d at 184.

measured by the profit realized from the increased production that the defendant had pursued, which resulted in the CWA violations alleged by the government.[82]

This entire subject of alternate methods of calculating economic benefit has been the focus of much debate. EPA commissioned a study by its Science Advisory Board, which issued a report on September 7, 2005, recommending changes in how EPA looks at this issue.[83] EPA addressed these recommendations and implemented at least one change.[84] It no longer uses the term *illegal competitive advantage*, but instead refers to this alternate type of economic gain as *beyond BEN benefit.*[85]

Because these alternate methods of calculating economic benefit can lead to much higher calculations—and that is the principal reason EPA has been pursuing them—it will be important for defense counsel to anticipate the possibility that this issue may be raised, and to be prepared to address it with expert economic testimony. It also is important to keep in mind that it is for the court to determine what the economic benefit is. EPA's reports and issued guidance are relevant for settlement purposes, but are not binding on the courts, nor even necessarily admissible.

It also is important to remember that economic benefit, although it receives a lot of attention, is only one statutory factor. How do courts then, once they have calculated economic benefit, arrive at the final penalty number? Two approaches have been used.

Some courts have utilized a "top down" method, in which the statutory maximum penalty is determined and then reduced as appropriate based on mitigating factors, but not below economic benefit.[86] One issue that arises in determining the statutory maximum is how to count violations of standards that are not measured on a daily basis. For example, various permits and regulations are based on monthly averages. Is a violation of a monthly average a single violation, or one for every day of the month, or one for every day of the month that the facility operated? Not surprisingly, courts have taken different approaches to this issue,

---

82. United States v. Mun. Auth. of Union Twp., 150 F.3d 259, 267 (3d Cir. 1998).

83. U.S. Envtl. Prot. Agency, Sci. Advisory Bd., EPA-SAB-ADV-05-003, Letter on an Advisory of the Illegal Competitive Advantage (ICA) Economic Benefit (EB) Advisory Panel of the EPA Science Advisory Board (Sept. 7, 2005), https://perma.cc/E4DQ-Z7D9.

84. *See* Letter from Granta Y. Nakayama, Ass't Adm'r, Off. of Enf't & Compliance Assurance, Envtl. Prot. Agency, to M. Granger Morgan, Chair, Sci. Advisory Bd., Envtl. Prot. Agency (July 19, 2006), https://perma.cc/AJ6P-C263.

85. *See* U.S. Envtl. Prot. Agency, Sci. Advisory Bd., EPA-SAB-ADV-05-003, Letter on an Advisory of the Illegal Competitive Advantage (ICA) Economic Benefit (EB) Advisory Panel of the EPA Science Advisory Board, *supra* note 83.

86. L.A. Waterkeeper v. A & A Metal Recycling, Inc., 2015 U.S. Dist. LEXIS 156792, at *18 (C.D. Cal. Nov. 18, 2015) (holding top-down approach was more reliable and less speculative method for calculating penalty); Catskill Mountains Chapter of Trout Unlimited, Inc. v. City of N.Y., 244 F. Supp. 2d 41, 48 (N.D.N.Y. 2003) (holding "the 'top down' approach provides the appropriate manner in which to determine the amount of civil penalties that should be awarded against Defendants.").

although most seem to find that a monthly violation is a violation for each day the facility operated.[87]

Because the statutory maximum penalty often is orders of magnitude larger than the highest plausible penalty the court might assess, one might think that arguing over statutory maximums is not important. But it is important, both because some courts utilize a top-down approach and because the government will argue for such an approach along the following lines: "Your honor, we have established over 122,000 separate violations and so the statutory maximum penalty is over $4 billion. We are not seeking that full amount, but even if the Court assessed penalties of only 1 percent of the maximum, that would be $40 million." It is important to be able to refute that, although if the refutation were that there were only 83,000 violations, another line of argument is probably in order.

Other courts utilize a "bottom up" method, which begins with the economic benefit for noncompliance and then adjusts that number up or down based on the other statutory criteria.[88] The latter method was utilized in the *Smithfield Foods* case, where the district court found a $4.2 million economic benefit and tripled that amount to reach a total penalty of $12.6 million.[89]

Whichever method is used, it is important for defense counsel to pay attention to the other statutory factors. So much attention often is paid to economic benefit that the other statutory factors may be glossed over. They should not be, for the government will be prepared to offer proof on each factor, and the defendant needs to be as well. It is especially important that the defense counsel be able to establish, if possible, the lack of environmental harm from the violations and the good-faith efforts the defendant had taken to comply. In the CWA civil enforcement action after the *Deepwater Horizon* incident, the district court found that while the seriousness of the spill weighed in favor of a maximum penalty, the lack of culpability of a nonoperating, minority owner of the well weighed in favor of a minimum penalty. The court imposed a $159.5 million penalty on the minority owner, which while "high when viewed out of context," was "only 4.5% of the maximum penalty, and therefore on the low end of the spectrum."[90]

If defense counsel cannot make a compelling case on at least one of the statutory factors (because, for example, they are not true), he or she is well advised to carefully reexamine with the client whether this is a case it can afford to litigate, as opposed to settle.

---

87. *See Allegheny Ludlum Corp.*, 366 F.3d at 169; Nat. Res. Def. Council v. Texaco Ref. & Mktg., Inc., 2 F.3d 493, 508 (3d Cir. 1993); Friends of the Earth v. Chevron Chem. Co., 2006 U.S. Dist. LEXIS 21864, at *6 (E.D. Tex. Mar. 29, 2006); *but see* Atl. States Legal Found., Inc. v. Tyson Foods, Inc., 897 F.2d 1128, 1139 (11th Cir. 1990); Chesapeake Bay Found., Inc. v. Gwaltney of Smithfield, Ltd., 791 F.2d 304, 314 (4th Cir. 1986), *vacated on other grounds*, 484 U.S. 49 (1987).

88. United States v. CITGO Petrol. Corp., 711 F. App'x 237, 239–40 (5th Cir. 2018) (unpublished) (using bottom-up approach to adjust penalty downward from the economic benefit to account for Citgo's efforts to clean up the spill).

89. United States v. Smithfield Foods, Inc., 191 F.3d 516, 528 (4th Cir. 1999).

90. United States v. BP Expl. & Prod. (*In re* Oil Spill by the Oil Rig "Deepwater Horizon" in the Gulf of Mexico, on April 20, 2010), 148 F. Supp. 3d 563, 583 (E.D. La. 2015).

V. DEFENSES TO ENFORCEMENT

Environmental enforcement provisions tend to be very broad and preclude many possible defenses. In the civil context, the statutes impose strict liability independent of any intent.[91] There are, however, a number of potential defenses that can be asserted. Following are some of those defenses.

A. Fair Notice

A defendant can assert that it did not receive fair notice of the legal requirement that it allegedly violated. Courts have ruled that a person cannot be penalized if he or she did not have fair notice of the applicable requirement, such as if the regulatory language was ambiguous or confusing.[92] As discussed previously, to establish this, a defendant will need to undertake a comprehensive review of all EPA pronouncements on the applicable legal requirement.[93] The ability to establish such a defense will benefit significantly if the defendant had received an interpretation from EPA (or possibly a state) on what the requirement meant and had documented that interpretation.

It also will bear consideration how the new DOJ policy, discussed previously, against relying on EPA guidance to prove violations will affect fair notice defenses. The DOJ policy states that "the Department may use evidence that a party read such a guidance document to help prove that the party had the requisite knowledge of the mandate."[94] It is unclear whether this would allow reliance on guidance to show that the regulated community had a fair understanding of what the regulation meant.

B. Permit as a Shield

Important defensive provisions of the CWA and the CAA are the so-called "permit as a shield" provisions that provide that anyone in compliance with an NPDES permit or CAA Title V permit is deemed in compliance with specified provisions of the

---

91. *See* Kelly v. EPA, 203 F.3d 519, 522 (7th Cir. 2000); United States v. Winchester Mun. Util., 944 F.2d 301, 304 (6th Cir. 1991); United States v. Jones, 267 F. Supp. 2d 1349, 1361 (M.D. Ga. 2003) ("Civil liability under the CWA is strict.").

92. Wis. Res. Prot. Council v. Flambeau Mining Co., 727 F.3d 700, 708 (7th Cir. 2013); United States v. Hoechst-Celanese Corp., 128 F.3d 216, 224 (4th Cir. 1997).

93. EPA has made progress in implementing its commitment to put all of its regulatory interpretations on its website. One early manifestation of this effort was "RCRA Online," which EPA describes as "an electronic database that indexes thousands of letters, memoranda, publications, and questions and answers issued by EPA's Office of Resource Conservation and Recovery (ORCR). These documents represent past EPA headquarters' interpretations of the RCRA regulations governing the management of solid, hazardous, and medical waste." RCRA Online, https://rcrapublic.epa.gov/rcraonline/. It is important to keep in mind, though, that EPA headquarters is not the only place where pronouncements relevant to fair notice may have originated. Other sources will be EPA regional offices and, in the case of delegated programs, the state environmental agency as well.

94. Memorandum from the Assoc. Att'y Gen., U.S. Dep't of Justice, to Heads of Civil Litigating Components & U.S. Att'ys, Limiting Use of Agency Guidance Documents in Affirmative Civil Enforcement Cases (Jan. 25, 2018), https://www.justice.gov/file/1028756/download.

statute, including, in the case of the CWA, the central provision of Section 301.[95] NPDES permittees can argue that if their discharge contained pollutants that were disclosed in the permit application, the discharge of those pollutants is allowed even if there is not a discharge limitation for that pollutant in the permit itself.[96] The Fourth Circuit has articulated a two-part test for determining whether the permit shield defense applies: the permit holder must be in compliance with the permit's express terms and "with the Clean Water Act's disclosure requirements," and the permit holder must not "make a discharge of pollutants that was not within the reasonable contemplation of the permitting authority."[97]

The CAA "permit shield" provision provides that compliance with a Title V permit is compliance with the Title V program (which is somewhat redundant). It also can constitute "compliance with other applicable provisions" of the CAA if either "the permit includes the applicable requirements of such provisions" or if the permitting authority finds such other provisions not applicable.[98]

C. "Upset" and "Bypass"

A defendant accused of violating its CWA permit sometimes can allege, if the violations were caused by some unintended and unavoidable events, that the violation was caused by "upset" or was an allowed "bypass."

Most permits contain a provision addressing upset, which is defined as "an exceptional incident in which there is unintentional and temporary noncompliance with technology based permit effluent limitations because of factors beyond the reasonable control of the permittee."[99] The regulations greatly limit the use of the upset defense through a series of substantive and procedural requirements. To successfully invoke an upset defense, the permit holder must carefully document the cause of the upset and demonstrate that the facility was being properly operated at the time, that proper notice was given to the appropriate permitting authorities within 24 hours, and that required remedial measures were taken.[100] If permits issued pursuant to state law do not contain an upset provision, the defense cannot be invoked.[101]

---

95. CWA § 402(k), 33 U.S.C. § 1342(k) (2012); CAA § 504(f), 42 U.S.C. § 7661c(f) (2012).

96. *See* E. I. du Pont de Nemours & Co. v. Train, 430 U.S. 112, 138 n.28 (1977); *see also* Atl. States Legal Found., Inc. v. Eastman Kodak Co., 12 F.3d 353, 357 (2d Cir. 1993); Sierra Club v. ICG Hazard, LLC, 2012 U.S. Dist. LEXIS 146140, at *26–27 (E.D. Ky. Sept. 28, 2012).

97. S. Appalachian Mountain Stewards v. A & G Coal Corp., 758 F.3d 560, 565 (4th Cir. 2014) (citing Piney Run Pres. Ass'n v. Cnty. Comm'rs, 268 F.3d 255, 259 (4th Cir. 2001)) (holding that the permit shield defense did not apply because defendants had not complied with disclosure requirements in permit application); *see also* Ohio Valley Envtl. Coal. v. Fola Coal Co., 845 F.3d 133, 142 (4th Cir. 2017).

98. CAA § 504(f), 42 U.S.C. § 7661c(f) (2012).

99. 40 C.F.R. § 122.41(n)(1) (2017).

100. *See id.* § 122.41(n)(3).

101. *See* Sierra Club v. Union Oil of Cal., 813 U.S. 1480, 1487–88 (9th Cir. 1987), *vacated on other grounds*, 485 U.S. 931 (1988).

A bypass is an "intentional diversion of waste streams from any portion of a treatment facility."[102] It is primarily this intentional or preplanned nature that makes a diversion a bypass, as opposed to an upset, which is an unintentional exceedance. Under most circumstances, bypass is prohibited under the act, and EPA may take enforcement action against a permit holder for engaging in a bypass.[103] Bypass is allowed, however, when it is "unavoidable to prevent loss of life, personal injury, or severe property damage" and there is no "feasible alternative" available.[104] Whenever possible, the permit holder must provide advance notice of any bypass to the appropriate authority.[105] In the case of unanticipated bypass, such as that resulting from a severe storm event, notification is required within 24 hours following the event.[106] This exception is intended to be very limited, and courts have consequently rejected attempts to expand its scope to include events such as routine maintenance.[107]

D. Statute of Limitations

Statute of limitations issues come up frequently in enforcement cases, and can give rise to important approaches for defending such cases.

As a starting point, there is no generally applicable statute of limitations to claims for injunctive relief. In cases where the violation is continuing—and therefore there is a request for injunctive relief—that makes good sense. On the other hand, there is a five-year statute of limitations for governmental claims for penalties.[108] This period begins to run from the time of violation (although if the violation is of a continuing nature, such as where an unpermitted discharge has been going on for ten years and is continuing, it will run separately for each day of violation). Although the government has argued that the time should run from its discovery of the violation, this "discovery rule" has been rejected by the courts.[109]

That part is relatively simple. The harder issue is how this all works when events happened in the past and those events are not continuing, but their effects are. Examples would include a situation in which a company modified a facility without a new source review construction permit required by the CAA, and the

---

102. 40 C.F.R. § 122.41(m)(1)(i) (2017).

103. *See id.* § 122.41(m)(4)(i).

104. *See id.* § 122.41(m)(4)(i)(A)–(B); *see also* United States v. City of Toledo, 63 F. Supp. 2d 834 (N.D. Ohio 1999).

105. *See* 40 C.F.R. § 122.41(m)(3)(i) (2017).

106. *See id.* § 122.41(m)(3)(ii).

107. *See, e.g.,* United States v. Weitzenhoff, 35 F.3d 1275, 1288–89 (9th Cir. 1994); *see also* Iowa League of Cities v. EPA, 711 F.3d 844, 859 (8th Cir. 2013) (emphasizing that "[b]ypass is generally prohibited unless there are 'no feasible alternatives'" (quoting 40 C.F.R. § 122.41(m)(4) (2017)).

108. 28 U.S.C. § 2462 (2012); *see* U.S. SEC v. Collyard, 861 F.3d 760, 763–64 (8th Cir. 2017); United States v. Telluride Co., 146 F.3d 1241, 1245 (10th Cir. 1998); United States v. Banks, 115 F.3d 916, 918–19 (11th Cir. 1997).

109. Minn. Mining & Mfg. v. Browner, 17 F.3d 1453, 1460 (D.C. Cir. 1994); *see also* Gabelli v. SEC, 568 U.S. 442, 450–52 (2013) (noting "the fraud discovery rule has not been extended to Government enforcement actions for civil penalties" and declining to apply it to a civil enforcement action brought by the SEC).

construction was completed far more than five years ago, but the plant still operates. Or there can be cases where a wetlands was illegally filled ten years ago, and the filling process is not continuing but the fill is still there, and EPA wants it removed. How does the statute of limitations apply in these cases?

This issue has come up several times in prevention of significant deterioration (PSD) cases. At issue in those cases generally is whether the alleged violation is "continuing" or occurred only at the time of the alleged modification to the plant. Some courts have held that violations of the CAA's PSD preconstruction permit requirements occur only at the time of construction or modification of the emitting facility and, therefore, do not constitute continuing violations during the entire period of a facility's operation for statute of limitations purposes.[110] For example, the Court of Appeals for the 11th Circuit concluded that the applicable regulatory language "cannot reasonably be construed to mean that building or altering a machine without a permit is a violation that continues as long as the machine exists or is operated."[111]

In contrast, the Court of Appeals for the Sixth Circuit concluded that the operator of a source modified without a required permit had an ongoing obligation to apply required controls, and that the obligation to obtain the construction permit also is ongoing. Accordingly, the court of appeals concluded that the statute of limitations had not run.[112]

E. Laboratory Error

The courts are divided about whether a permit holder who has reported in its discharge monitoring reports that it has discharged in excess of allowable levels can assert, when enforcement commences, that there were not, in fact, exceedances, and that the discharge monitoring report was based on laboratory error. The

---

110. *See, e.g.*, United States v. EME Homer City Generation L.P., 823 F. Supp. 2d 274, 286 (W.D. Pa. 2011) ("The majority rule is that a failure to obtain a PSD permit is a one-time violation and is not a continuing violation."); United States v. Ill. Power Co., 245 F. Supp. 2d 951, 957 (S.D. Ill. 2003) (finding that "[a]lthough the Court recognizes that the underlying intent behind the Act, the EPA regulations, and the Illinois SIP is to assure continuing air quality, these provisions cannot reasonably be construed to mean that building or altering a machine without a permit is a violation that continues as long as the machine exists or is operated."); New York v. Niagara Mohawk Power Corp., 263 F. Supp. 2d 650, 661 (W.D.N.Y. 2003) (holding that the "requirement to secure a preconstruction permit applies *prior* to construction or modification. Once the construction or modification is complete, the window in which to apply for and obtain a preconstruction permit is gone. Thus, a violation of the Clean Air Act's preconstruction permit requirement is singular in nature, and does not constitute an ongoing violation."); *see also* United States v. Westvaco Corp., 144 F. Supp. 2d 439, 444 (D. Md. 2001); United States v. Brotech Corp., No. 00-2428, 2000 WL 1368023, at *11–12 (E.D. Pa. Sept. 19, 2000).
111. Nat'l Parks & Conservation Ass'n, Inc. v. Tenn. Valley Auth., 502 F.3d 1316, 1323 (11th Cir. 2007) (quoting *Ill. Power Co.*, 245 F. Supp. 2d at 957); *see also* United States v. EME Homer City Generation LP, 727 F.3d 274, 291 (3d Cir. 2013) (rejecting the EPA argument that failure to obtain preconstruction permit constitutes a continuing violation); United States v. Mid-west Generation, LLC, 720 F.3d 644, 647 (7th Cir. 2013) (agreeing with other appellate courts that operating a new or modified plant despite failure to obtain a construction permit is not a new violation); Sierra Club v. Otter Tail Power Co., 615 F.3d 1008, 1014 (8th Cir. 2010) (holding that claims for civil penalties for PSD violations were time-barred).
112. Nat'l Parks Conservation Ass'n, Inc. v. Tenn. Valley Auth., 480 F.3d 410 (6th Cir. 2007).

United States has argued that a permittee should not be allowed to impeach its own reports, and this position was upheld in *Sierra Club v. Union Oil Co.*, where a Ninth Circuit panel held that to allow permitees to defend enforcement by alleging laboratory error would "undermine the efficacy of the self-monitoring program."[113] But a Third Circuit panel, in *United States v. Allegheny Ludlum Corp.*, reached a contrary result, and found that laboratory error, if proven, would be a defense to permit violations.[114] The court held that while the government could rely on the discharge monitoring reports to prove its case, the "trier of fact must still be convinced that the permit was in fact violated," and evidence should be admitted showing that it was not violated because the reports overreported the level of discharge.[115] Defendants attempting to impeach their own reports face a heavy evidentiary burden.[116]

F. State Involvement

There are a range of defenses or defense strategies that are premised on the actions of the applicable state regulator. As a threshold matter, it is always important to focus on the role the state will play in a federal enforcement case. In some cases, the state may be a co-plaintiff, working in tandem with the United States. From a defense perspective, that usually is unfortunate (although it can, in certain cases, facilitate a comprehensive settlement agreeable to both regulators).

In other cases, the state may not be a party to the case, and may even be opposed to the federal government bringing the case.[117] States sometimes feel that such an action reflects adversely on the state's own enforcement program. In such a situation, it is important to establish contact with the state early, and to analyze whether the state's action can be helpful to the defendant.

In certain situations where the state has taken enforcement action for the same alleged violations that the United States is alleging, the state action may preclude federal enforcement. For example, Section 309(g)(6) of the CWA provides that

> any violation— . . . (ii) with respect to which a State has commenced and is diligently prosecuting an action under a State law comparable to this subsection, or (iii) for which the Administrator, the Secretary, or the State has issued a final order not subject to further judicial review and the violator has paid a penalty assessed under this subsection, or such comparable State law, as the case may be, shall not

---

113. Sierra Club v. Union Oil of Cal., 813 F.2d 1480, 1491–92 (9th Cir. 1987).

114. United States v. Allegheny Ludlum Corp., 366 F.3d 164, 174 (3d Cir. 2004); *see* United States v. STABL, Inc., 800 F.3d 476, 485–86 (8th Cir. 2015) (agreeing with the Third Circuit and finding "that a defendant who wishes to assert laboratory error as a defense has a heavy burden" but may do so).

115. *Allegheny Ludlum Corp.*, 366 F.3d at 174.

116. *See STABL, Inc.*, 800 F.3d at 485–86.

117. In one category of enforcement cases, the state must be joined as a party whether it wants to be or not. Section 309(e) of the CWA, 33 U.S.C. § 1319(e) (2012), requires the state to be joined as a party in enforcement actions against municipalities. If the state does not want to join as a plaintiff, the United States must join it as a defendant.

be the subject of a civil penalty action under subsection (d) of this section or section 311(b) or section 505 of this Act [33 U.S.C.S. § 1321(b) or 1365].[118]

There has been a long history of cases construing when that preclusion applies. In general, the courts have interpreted the preclusion narrowly, and most often have allowed federal enforcement to proceed. For example, in one case the court refused to dismiss a federal enforcement action, finding that the state law was not comparable to the federal enforcement provision.[119] Still, it will be important to analyze whether there is a basis for preclusion based on prior or current state enforcement.

But even if federal enforcement is allowed to proceed, the state's role still can be a positive one for the defendant. If the defendant can document that the state (1) sanctioned the defendant's conduct or (2) believes the federal interpretation of the applicable regulations is in error, then the defense can benefit because, among other things, it supports the defendant's argument that it acted in good faith.

G. Technological or Economic Infeasibility

Defendants sometimes have tried to argue that it simply was not possible to comply with the regulation at issue, claiming that either the technology did not exist or was too expensive to install. The courts generally have rejected these defenses, finding that the regulations were technology-forcing—to continue to operate, regulated sources needed to develop the technology.[120] Furthermore, projected costs were taken into account in the development of the regulation and cannot be revisited in an enforcement case.

That said, this type of argument often can be persuasive to a judge concerned about the burdens of complying with regulations that are too difficult or costly with which to comply. Additionally, these types of arguments certainly are relevant to the penalty factor of "good-faith efforts to comply."

But these type of arguments—especially economic infeasibility—can be a double-edged sword. In essence, a defendant is arguing: "It was so expensive to comply, I simply could not afford it." EPA then may seize on this argument and respond that what the defendant really is saying is that its economic benefit of noncompliance was so great, it elected not to expend the required funds. Therefore, EPA would say, the court needs to impose a very substantial penalty to recoup that economic benefit.

---

118. CWA § 309, 33 U.S.C. § 1319(g)(6) (2012).

119. *See* United States v. Smithfield Foods, Inc., 191 F.3d 516, 526 (4th Cir. 1999).

120. Whether technological or economic infeasibility is a defense to an enforcement action was left open by the Supreme Court in *Union Electric Co. v. EPA*, 427 U.S. 246, 268 n.18 (1976). Subsequent cases have rejected the defense. *See, e.g.*, United States v. Ford Motor Co., 814 F.2d 1099, 1103–04 (6th Cir. 1987) ("Clean Air Act [] envisions situations where standards currently economically or technologically infeasible will nonetheless be enforced."); *see also* Nat. Res. Def. Council v. EPA, 804 F.3d 149, 168 (2d Cir. 2015) (explaining that the CWA "is technology-forcing.").

VI. PROCEDURAL AND EVIDENTIARY ISSUES

Although the bulk of the procedural issues that will arise in connection with civil enforcement litigation will be case-specific, a number of procedural issues that occur with some frequency in this context bear special mention. What follows is a description of some of these issues and some strategies for dealing with them.

A. Prefiling Discovery

The federal environmental laws give EPA very broad authority to obtain information from potential defendants prior to filing a civil action, and EPA uses this authority extensively. An example of the breadth of the authority EPA has is Section 114(a) of the CAA, which, among other things, allows EPA, "[f]or the purpose . . . of determining whether any person is in violation" of various standards or requirements, to "require any person who owns or operates any [air] emission source" to establish, maintain, and submit records and reports and "provide such other information as the Administrator may reasonably require."[121] If a recipient of an information request fails to comply, EPA has the authority to seek daily penalties for such noncompliance under the general enforcement provisions of the respective statutes.[122]

This broad authority means that much of the pivotal discovery relating to the enforcement case will take place prior to its filing. The government certainly will seek additional discovery once the case actually is filed, especially because there are no provisions for administrative depositions to be taken prefiling, but much of the "written discovery" may have taken place prefiling. From the government's perspective, obtaining discovery in this manner has many advantages. First, because there is no judge yet involved, there are no readily available mechanisms for an information-request recipient who thinks the requests are either overbroad or seeks irrelevant information to utilize. Second, the administrative requests are backed up by potentially enormous penalty sanctions, far in excess of what typically may be sought for failure to comply with discovery requests in litigation. Third, those administrative requests that resemble interrogatories are not subject to the 25-interrogatory limitation in Rule 33 of the Federal Rules of Civil Procedure that would apply once litigation is commenced. Finally, administrative information requests often are responded to before defense counsel has been retained for the enforcement case, and may not receive the same level of care as when responding to discovery during litigation.

From the recipient's perspective, it is crucial to treat administrative information requests with the same seriousness and care that would be given to discovery requests during litigation. First, a company's legal department certainly should

---

121. CAA § 114, 42 U.S.C. § 7414(a)(1) (2012). Similar provisions are included in Section 3007(a) of the RCRA, 42 U.S.C. § 6927(a) (2012), and Section 308 of the CWA, 33 U.S.C. § 1318 (2012).

122. *See* CAA § 113(b)(2), 42 U.S.C. § 7413(b)(2) (2012); RCRA § 3008(a), 42 U.S.C. § 6928(a) (2012); CWA § 309(d), 33 U.S.C. § 1319(d) (2012).

be involved in crafting responses, and in many cases the recipient will benefit from the input of outside counsel experienced in enforcement matters. Second, the recipient should be prepared to engage the assigned EPA representatives to raise any concerns about the clarity or breadth of the requests, to seek to clarify or narrow the requests, and, if necessary, to elevate the matter within EPA. Finally, the recipient does not need to stand idly by and respond to the government's requests. During the prefiling period, the recipient can, and in many cases should, begin its own discovery process by utilizing the Freedom of Information Act (FOIA).[123]

Such FOIA requests are not nearly as effective a tool as the government's administrative information-gathering authorities. They are not backed up by penalties. The government often will not respond timely and will assert broad defenses, and enforcing the requests necessitates filing a lawsuit. Still, important information can be obtained through the FOIA earlier than if one waited for litigation to ensue. Moreover, just like the dynamics of discovery during litigation, in which having both sides seeking and providing information at the same time can on occasion curb each side's aggressiveness in pursing information, the potential defendant's judicious use of the FOIA can temper EPA's use of its own information-gathering authorities.

To the extent a potential defendant is concerned that proactively using the FOIA may irritate the government, it should not be. The government does not hesitate to use its own information-gathering facilities, and potential defendants should not hesitate to use the more limited FOIA tool available to them, so long as it is not done for harassment purposes but rather to obtain needed information.

B. Litigation Hold

Although this may be obvious, it is worth mentioning that among the very first things a defense counsel should do when becoming involved with a potential enforcement case is ensure that the defendant or potential defendant has an adequate procedure in place to maintain all documents relevant to the alleged violations, especially electronic documents, notwithstanding anything to the contrary in the defendant's usual document-retention policy. Even if a lawsuit has not been commenced, the government will view any notice of violation it may have issued as triggering the responsibility to maintain relevant documents.

C. Preemptory Changes to Potential Enforcement[124]

On occasion, parties facing potential enforcement by EPA have filed preemptory lawsuits, typically challenging EPA's notice of violation (NOV). An NOV is generally a prerequisite for the commencement of an enforcement action. If this type

---

123. *See* 5 U.S.C. § 552 (2012).
124. For further discussion of litigating agency action, see Chapter 1 of this book.

of challenge were an available tool, there could be many advantages. Specifically, it would let the defendant control the timing of the litigation, select the venue, and have an earlier opportunity to challenge such things as EPA's information requests and NOVs. However, the courts generally have dismissed such lawsuits seeking "pre-enforcement review" of EPA's actions.[125] These courts have ruled that they lack jurisdiction to hear such challenges, and that an NOV is not a final agency action.

That is because the NOV imposes no legal consequences by itself. In cases where EPA has issued an administrative order, and is threatening to enforce that order, there could be a basis for challenging it prior to EPA's commencing an enforcement action. In *Tennessee Valley Authority v. Whitman*, EPA had issued a CAA compliance order to the TVA.[126] The TVA challenged the order in federal court, and in 2003, the court of appeals held that (1) it could not consider a pre-enforcement review challenge to the order, but (2) because it could not consider such a challenge, the underlying statutory provision allowing for such an order was an unconstitutional deprivation of due process.[127] The order, therefore, was invalid and did not need to be complied with. EPA sought certiorari, which was denied.

In 2012, the Supreme Court held in *Sackett v. EPA* that an administrative compliance order issued pursuant to Section 309 of the CWA was a final agency action subject to judicial review.[128] The Court said that the order imposed legal obligations on the defendants to take action to rectify the alleged violation under an EPA-approved plan and to allow EPA access to their site as well as to site records, and that legal consequences flowed from issuance of the order.[129] The Court further found that issuance of the order "marked the 'consummation' of the [EPA's] decisionmaking process."[130] In addition, the Court concluded that the CWA did not preclude judicial review.[131]

Given these decisions, there could be grounds to challenge other types of administrative orders imposing compliance obligations and possible penalties. EPA then is placed in a difficult situation. On one hand, if it does not object to such review, it is undermining its position against pre-enforcement review. On the

---

125. Luminant Generation Co., L.L.C. v. EPA, 757 F.3d 439, 444 (5th Cir. 2014) ("Issuing a notice of violation does not create any legal obligation, alter any rights, or result in any legal consequences and does not mark the end of the EPA's decisionmaking process."); Royster-Clark Agribusiness, Inc. v. Johnson, 391 F. Supp. 2d 21 (D.D.C. 2005) (noting that "a NOV is merely a first step in a potential enforcement process"); Pacificorp v. Thomas, 883 F.2d 661 (9th Cir. 1988); Lloyd A. Fry Roofing Co. v. EPA, 554 F.2d 885, 890–91 (8th Cir. 1977) (pre-enforcement review of NOV is "wholly inconsistent with the enforcement mechanism established by Congress"); W. Penn Power Co. v. Train, 522 F.2d 302, 310–11 (3d Cir. 1975) (notice of violation does not impose any legal consequences, and it is not final agency action).

126. Tenn. Valley Auth. v. Whitman, 336 F.3d 1236 (11th Cir. 2003), *cert. denied*, 541 U.S. 1030 (2004).

127. *Id.* at 1258–59.

128. Sackett v. EPA, 566 U.S. 120, 131 (2012).

129. *Id.* at 126.

130. *Id.* at 127.

131. *Id.* at 128–31.

other hand, if it objects to such review, then the order recipient can argue that the order is unconstitutional because no review is provided before penalties may attach. One also might challenge the EPA administrative information requests on this basis, although one court that considered such an argument rejected it.[132]

D. Demanding a Jury

One early decision that a defendant needs to make in a civil enforcement action is whether or not to demand a jury. In many cases, it will make good sense to ask for a jury.

In *Tull v. United States*, a CWA civil enforcement case, the Supreme Court ruled that the defendant had a right to a jury trial to determine his liability under the statute, although the size of any penalty would be determined by the trial court.[133] The Court concluded "that the Seventh Amendment required that petitioner's demand for a jury trial be granted to determine his liability, but that the trial court and not the jury should determine the amount of penalty, if any."[134]

The United States as a matter of practice usually will not ask for a jury trial in the civil enforcement cases it files. Thus, a defendant who wants a jury trial on liability issues must ask for one within 14 days after service of the last pleading directed at the issue to be tried,[135] which often will be the answer to the complaint.

A defendant should seriously consider including in its answer to the complaint a demand for a jury trial for a number of reasons. First, as discussed previously, civil enforcement cases often have aspects that keep them from being pursued criminally, such as uncertainty as to what the law means, conflicting state/federal interpretations, or violations that arose notwithstanding good-faith efforts to comply. These are the type of arguments that could be attractive to a jury.

Second, if a jury is asked for, the trial court may be less inclined to grant summary judgment, and thus take the fact-finding away from the jury. Third, asking for a jury introduces an element of uncertainty into the case that the government will have to weigh in settlement negotiations. Fourth, there is not the risk of a runaway jury imposing massive damages that defendants worry about in other types of cases. In civil enforcement cases, the jury will determine only liability. Penalties (the damages in these cases) will be decided by the court, as will any request for injunctive relief. Finally, if at a later point the defendant decides it prefers a bench trial, the government, given its preference for bench trials, probably will consent

---

132. United States v. Gurley, 384 F.3d 316, 326 (6th Cir. 2004); *see also Luminant Generation Co.*, 757 F.3d at 443–44 (dismissing challenges to notices of violation under the CAA because notices were not final agency actions).

133. Tull v. United States, 481 U.S. 412, 427 (1987); SEC v. Badian, 822 F. Supp. 2d 352, 265 (S.D.N.Y. 2011) (citing *Tull* when explaining "[t]he SEC's argument . . . improperly conflates the determination of whether the . . . defendants can be subjected to a civil penalty, which is a question for the jury, with the determination of the severity of the civil penalty to be imposed, which is a question for the Court, once liability is established.").

134. *Tull*, 481 U.S. at 427.

135. Fed. R. Civ. P. 38(b).

to a withdrawal of the jury demand under Rule 38(d) of the Federal Rules of Civil Procedure.

Factors that could weigh against asking for a jury might include that the violations at issue are alleged to have resulted in serious environmental harm in the area where the jury will be drawn from or that the defendant has shut down its facility in the area resulting in loss of local employment.

An example of what happens when a jury is involved is a high-profile enforcement case involving alleged CAA violations at a number of coal-fired power plants owned by Cinergy Corporation. In May 2008, an Indianapolis jury found in the defendants' favor on ten of the government's alleged 14 counts, and found violations at only one of the power plants.[136]

E. Seeking Sanctions against Government Counsel

On occasion, defense counsel may take strong issue with certain actions of government counsel and be inclined to seek sanctions from the court. In most cases, that will not be a good idea, and even if the client is pushing hard for such a step, defense counsel would be well advised to dissuade his or her client from taking it.

In this regard, it is important to keep in mind that government counsel have a great deal of influence over the eventual resolution of the case and over the amount that the case will settle for, because most cases settle. While one might think that a sanctions motion would influence the government to settle for less, most often the opposite is true. Filing a sanctions motion raises the profile of the case, helps ensure that the case will receive the resources it needs to be adequately litigated, and makes it harder for the government to settle, lest it appear that it settled for less because of the pendency of the sanctions motion. In fact, the government typically will not discuss settlement while a sanctions motion is pending for exactly that reason.

Rather than seeking sanctions from the court, in most cases of questionable conduct by government counsel, the better course of action would be to raise the issue directly with the government counsel, and if a satisfactory response is not received, to elevate the issue within DOJ. Of course, if the actions at issue were to threaten the defendant's ability to defend itself, there might be no choice but to seek relief from the court. But as a tactical maneuver, sanction motions backfire more than they succeed.

F. Retaining Experts

An early priority of defense counsel will be to consider the need for possible expert testimony, and to identify and retain possible experts. In doing so, it is important to keep in mind that expert testimony may be necessary not only with respect to

---

136. Howard Greninger, *Vigo County Power Station's Future in Question*, Tribune-Star (May 23, 2008), http://www.tribstar.com/news/local_news/vigo-county-power-station-s-future-in-question/article_4fd0ad8d-707f-5b42-914c-6ac4335f6e27.html.

liability but also with respect to the relief the government is seeking (the need for and type of injunctive relief and the amount of penalties). Furthermore, litigation over penalties will implicate the various penalty criteria, such as economic benefit of noncompliance, environmental harm, the effect of penalties on the defendant's financial position, and so on.

In considering possible experts, it may make sense to consider people who have testified as experts for EPA and DOJ in the past. Such prior work will enhance the experts' credibility and make it harder for the government to challenge the experts' opinions and methodology. If such persons were contacted about possible retention and responded that they would only testify for the government, that would undermine such persons' credibility were they, in fact, to be retained by the government in that case.

G. Offers of Judgment

One option rarely utilized by defendants in civil enforcement cases, and that could profitably be used more, is to make an offer of judgment under Rule 68 of the Federal Rules of Civil Procedure. One difficulty of utilizing Rule 68 in this context is that the government usually seeks nonmonetary relief as well as monetary relief. However, Rule 68 allows an offer of a judgment of not just money or property but also "on specified terms."[137] A defendant, therefore, might try to include injunctive relief in the offer.

The benefit of making an offer of judgment is that if it is not accepted, and the plaintiff does less well after trial than the offer, the defendant is entitled to its costs from the point of the offer forward. "Costs," for these purposes, do not include attorneys' fees and therefore may not be that substantial. But while the benefit of an offer of judgment may not be great, there is little downside to conveying under Rule 68 an offer already made by the defendant in settlement negotiations and rejected by the government.

Even in situations where Rule 68 would appear to allow a defendant to recover its costs, the government still may argue that it is protected by sovereign immunity from having to pay those costs. There is little law on this subject,[138] but again there is little downside in making an offer of judgment when a settlement proposal has been rejected, and later arguing that costs can be obtained from the government.

H. Audit Privilege

A number of states have adopted laws that provide certain privileges for information uncovered through self-audits.[139] EPA and DOJ have strongly opposed such

---

137. Fed. R. Civ. P. 68.

138. *See* United States v. Fla. Cities Water Co., No. 93-281-CIV-FTM-21-D, 1997 WL 373746 (M.D. Fla. Feb. 3, 1997) (defendant not entitled to recover costs from government under Rule 68).

139. U.S. Envtl. Prot. Agency, State Audit Privilege and Immunity Laws & Self-Disclosure Laws and Policies, https://www.epa.gov/compliance/state-audit-privilege-and-immunity-laws-self-disclosure-laws -and-policies (last visited July 19, 2018).

laws. As EPA has stated in its audit policy: "The Agency remains firmly opposed to statutory and regulatory audit privileges. . . . Privilege laws shield evidence of wrongdoing and prevent States from investigating even the most serious environmental violations."[140] In light of this position, EPA and DOJ also take the position that state audit laws are not applicable under Rule 501 of the Federal Rules of Evidence to federal enforcement proceedings.

Thus, if a defendant in a civil enforcement action is seeking to withhold from production the results of self-audits, it will be necessary to have utilized the attorney-client privilege for the audit and to cite attorney-client privilege, and not a state-audit privilege, as the basis for its position.

I. Credible Evidence

An important evidentiary issue relates to how the government can prove in an enforcement action that violations of its regulations actually have occurred. Under the CAA, EPA's air-pollution standards had historically specified not only the maximum permissible level of emissions, but also the reference test that should be used as a means of sampling and analyzing to see if the particular standard was exceeded. In 1997, because of the challenges presented in being limited to specific test methods, EPA engaged in rulemaking to ensure that non-test methods also could be used to show noncompliance. EPA added language to five sections of its regulations, providing that nothing in them "shall preclude the use, including the exclusive use, of any credible evidence or information, relevant to whether a source would have been in compliance with applicable requirements if the appropriate performance or compliance test or procedure had been performed."[141]

This so-called "any credible evidence rule" was challenged in the D.C. Circuit, which ruled that the challenge was not ripe, but rather could be raised in specific enforcement cases.[142] As the court stated, "the effect of the credible evidence rule on compliance obligations is difficult to assess without any information or experience showing how the rule operates in particular settings."[143]

Thus, the "any credible evidence rule" remains in force, although a defendant could seek to challenge it as part of a particular enforcement action. Beyond that, if EPA seeks to rely on the rule, it will be important for the defendant, if possible, to develop evidence that the particular test method EPA is seeking to rely on, which method is different from the reference test method in the regulations, is so different that it does not credibly indicate whether the regulation is, in fact, being complied with.

---

140. Incentives for Self-Policing: Discovery, Disclosure, Correction and Prevention of Violations; Notice, 65 Fed. Reg. 19,618, 19,623 (EPA Apr. 11, 2000), https://www.gpo.gov/fdsys/pkg/FR-2000-04-11/pdf/00-8954.pdf.
141. 40 C.F.R. § 60.11(g) (2017); see also id. §§ 51.212(c), 52.12(c), 52.33(a), 61.12(e).
142. Clean Air Implementation Project v. EPA, 150 F.3d 1200, 1205-06 (D.C. Cir. 1998).
143. Id. at 1206.

VII. SETTLEMENT

A. Advantages of Settlement

Most proposed civil enforcement cases are resolved through settlement. This is a good thing. The government avoids having to expend resources to litigate the case, and the defendant avoids the risks and burdens of litigation.

For defendants, in most cases, settlement is the strategy of choice. While the government talks a lot about level playing fields, civil enforcement litigation is by no means a level playing field, but an uphill ordeal for defendants for a variety of reasons:

- The government gets to pick the case, the defendants, the court, and the timing of the litigation.
- The government does not have to prove fault and often can prove its case from the defendant's own records.
- The courts often give deference to EPA's and DOJ's positions in enforcement cases.
- The penalties the government can seek are often enormous.
- Defending enforcement cases is expensive.
- Defending enforcement cases can be a major burden for the defendant's managers and divert their time from their already full-time jobs.
- Environmental regulation is pervasive and 100 percent compliance is very hard to achieve.
- If the government is allowed to pursue intense discovery of a company's operations, it is likely to find more violations, which means that the case is likely to get worse, not better, for the defendant during discovery.
- Discovery will be much more focused on the defendant than on the government.
- The government can afford to lose. The defendant often cannot.

For these reasons, litigation should happen only when the settlement process falls apart and a settlement cannot be reached. The government almost always provides an opportunity to settle prior to commencing litigation,[144] and the defendant should take full advantage of that opportunity. None of this is to suggest that the goal is settlement at all costs. In fact, like with all litigation, preparing a strong

---

144. Exec. Order No. 12,988 on Civil Justice Reform, 61 Fed. Reg. 4729 (Feb. 7, 1996), mandates such an opportunity to settle before the federal government commences litigation. It provides that

> [n]o litigation counsel shall file a complaint initiating civil litigation without first making a reasonable effort to notify all disputants about the nature of the dispute and to attempt to achieve a settlement, or confirming that the referring agency that previously handled the dispute has made a reasonable effort to notify the disputants and to achieve a settlement or has used its conciliation processes.

Even if EPA has had settlement discussions with a defendant prior to referral of an enforcement action to DOJ, DOJ will typically insist on making its own offer of settlement discussions to the defendant before suit is filed.

defense, and being able to communicate it to the government, will provide the best context in which to negotiate a favorable settlement.

B. Settlement Process

If a settlement is reached, it will be embodied in a judicial consent decree and, if injunctive relief was sought in the complaint, lodged with the court for a 30-day public comment period.[145] Following the public comment period, the United States may withdraw its consent based on the comments received, although that rarely happens. Otherwise, the United States will seek court approval and entry of the settlement.

EPA negotiates settlements in accordance with its civil penalty policy, and particular penalty policies apply to specific kinds of cases.[146] The policy requires the computation of two components: the economic benefit that EPA believes the defendant realized from the violation and the "gravity" component, reflecting the seriousness of the violation and other factors. The various penalty policies have formulas or matrixes for calculating the gravity factor. For example, the CWA policy provides that the gravity component is calculated for each month of violation and incorporates factors and schedules to measure the "significance of violation," including: (1) the percentage exceedance of permit limits, (2) the "health and environmental harm" (including the impact on human health and aquatic environments), (3) the "number of effluent limit violations," and (4) the "significance of non-effluent limit violations."[147] (The factors are derived from the statutory penalty factors discussed previously.) The policy allows for a number of adjustment factors, including an upward adjustment if the violator is viewed as recalcitrant and a downward adjustment for a quick settlement.[148] The penalty also may be adjusted for certain litigation considerations, such as issues with the quality of the government's evidence.[149]

C. Supplemental Environmental Projects and Mitigation Projects

One important component that can be utilized in settlements with EPA is a supplemental environmental project (SEP). SEPs are defined by EPA "as environmentally beneficial projects which a defendant agrees to undertake in settlement of

---

145. 28 C.F.R. § 50.7 (2017). DOJ posts the proposed consent decree on its website during the public comment period and then takes it down once the period ends. *See* U.S. Dep't of Justice, Proposed Consent Decrees, http://www.usdoj.gov/enrd/Consent_Decrees.html.

146. The EPA penalty policies can be found at U.S. Envtl. Prot. Agency, Enforcement Policy, Guidance & Publications, https://www.epa.gov/enforcement/enforcement-policy-guidance-publications (last visited June 29, 2018).

147. U.S. Envtl. Prot. Agency, Interim Clean Water Act Settlement Penalty Policy 6–9 (1995), https://www.epa.gov/sites/production/files/documents/cwapol.pdf.

148. *Id.* at 12–13.

149. *Id.*

an enforcement action, but which the defendant, or any other third party, is not otherwise legally required to perform."[150] The use of SEPs is covered generally by EPA's SEP policy.[151] In essence, the SEP policy allows a violator to perform certain types of environmentally beneficial projects—such as pollution reduction, pollution prevention, and environmental restoration—which it would not otherwise be required to do and, in essence, get a credit against its penalty. The SEP policy says that "SEPs are not penalties, nor are they accepted in lieu of a penalty," but that "a violator's commitment to perform a SEP is a relevant factor for EPA to consider in establishing an appropriate settlement penalty."[152] Defendants often prefer to perform a SEP because public perception of a defendant that is performing a SEP may be less stigmatizing than the payment of a penalty. Furthermore, because SEPs are available only as settlement options and cannot be ordered by the court if the case goes to trial, they are yet another incentive for a defendant to settle rather than to litigate.

There are a number of disadvantages that should be considered before agreeing to perform a SEP as part of a settlement. First, the government will not give "dollar for dollar" credit for most SEPs (there are narrow exceptions where 100 percent credit is allowed), so agreeing to perform a SEP will cost the defendant more money. Second, because implementing a SEP often can take longer than just paying a penalty, the SEP can prolong a relationship with DOJ and EPA that the defendant might well prefer to end sooner. Third, there is more potential for complications with SEPs, which may not always work out as planned, than with simply paying a penalty. Fourth, the public relations benefit of a SEP is undermined by the government's standard "Scarlet Letter" consent decree requirement that any publicity the defendant does with respect to the project must confess that the project arises from an enforcement action for violating the law.[153] Finally, it is important to keep in mind that the costs of SEPs, like penalties, are not deductible for federal income tax purposes.[154]

---

150. U.S. Envtl. Prot. Agency, Supplemental Environmental Projects Policy: 2015 Update 6 (Mar. 10, 2015), https://www.epa.gov/sites/production/files/2015-04/documents/sepupdatedpolicy15.pdf.

151. Id.

152. Id. at 21.

153. Id. at 26. The government specifies the standard language to be included in a SEP agreement:

> Any public statement, oral or written, in print, film, or other media, made by Defendant making reference to the SEP under this Agreement/Decree from the date of its execution of this Agreement/Decree shall include the following language: "This project was undertaken in connection with the settlement of an enforcement action United States v. Defendant, taken on behalf of the U.S. Environmental Protection Agency to enforce federal laws."

> Id.

154. This had been the position of the federal government for some time and was made explicit in the 2017 Tax Cuts and Jobs Act, Pub L. No. 115-97, § 13306(a)(1)(f)(1), which amended Section 162(f) of the Internal Revenue Code to provide that no deduction will be allowed "for any amount paid or incurred . . . to, or at the direction of, a government or governmental entity in relation to the violation of any law." There are exceptions for certain restitution expenses and expenses to come into compliance, but neither of those would apply to SEPs.

EPA encourages using SEPs because of EPA's ability to, in essence, direct funds toward environmentally beneficial purposes, as opposed to a payment of penalties that is directed to the U.S. Treasury. In general, SEPs may be used to reduce the gravity component, but not the economic benefit component, of a penalty.

One recent development that has engendered confusion on the use of SEPs was the June 5, 2017, directive from Attorney General Sessions titled "Prohibition on Settlement Payments to Third Parties." It provided: "It has come to [the attorney general's] attention that certain previous settlement agreements involving the Department included payments to various non-governmental, third-party organizations as a condition of settlement with the United States. These third-party organizations were neither victims nor parties to the lawsuits. . . . The Department will no longer engage in this practice."[155] This directive was read by some as limiting the ability to utilize SEPs, even though the SEP policy requires that the project be implemented by the defendants and not be merely a third-party payment. The Sessions directive was followed by a January 9, 2018, memorandum from the acting assistant attorney general for ENRD, titled "Settlement Payments to Third Parties in ENRD Cases."[156] That memorandum states the following about SEPs: "This policy does not prohibit, as part of a settlement, a defendant from agreeing to undertake a supplemental environmental project related to the violation, so long as it is consistent with EPA's [SEP] Policy, which already expressly prohibits all third-party payments."[157]

While the Sessions directive should not affect the use of SEPs, it has already affected the use of so-called "mitigation projects," which, as discussed above, are injunctive remedies the government sometimes has sought to redress the impact of the violations on the environment, and have often involved payments to third parties. For example, one component of the Volkswagen settlements discussed previously was the payment by Volkswagen of $2.925 billion to fund two environmental mitigation trusts for the benefit of the states and Indian tribes.[158] However, in light of the Sessions directive, DOJ modified a settlement that had been reached with Harley-Davidson, Inc. relating to devices that increased emissions from motorcycles. When the settlement was initially announced on August 18, 2016, it provided for, in addition to a $12 million civil penalty, a requirement for the defendant to spend $3 million on a mitigation project to replace conventional woodstoves

---

155. Memorandum from Jeff Sessions, Att'y Gen., U.S. Dep't of Justice, to All Component Heads & U.S. Att'ys, Prohibition on Settlement Payments to Third Parties (June 5, 2017), https://www.justice.gov/opa/press-release/file/971826/download.

156. Memorandum from Jeffrey H. Wood, Acting Assistant Att'y Gen., U.S. Dep't of Justice, to ENRD Deputy Assistant Att'ys Gen. & Section Chiefs, Settlement Payments to Third Parties in ENRD Cases (Jan. 9, 2018), https://www.justice.gov/enrd/page/file/1043726/download.

157. *Id.* at 8.

158. U.S. Envtl. Prot. Agency, Frequently Asked Questions (FAQ) for Beneficiaries to the Volkswagen Mitigation Trust Agreements (Oct. 2017), https://www.epa.gov/sites/production/files/2017-10/documents/faq-ben.pdf.

with cleaner-burning stoves in local communities.[159] On July 20, 2017, DOJ filed a notice with the district court with a proposed substitute consent decree that eliminated the clean stoves mitigation project.[160] DOJ stated that "[q]uestions exist as to whether this mitigation project is consistent with the new policy" and so the project was eliminated.[161]

D. The Consent Decree Document

If the principal terms of a settlement can be reached, it can take some time to negotiate the language of the consent decree. In that regard, it will be very important to review similar decrees that the government has entered into. The government will say that it is not bound by prior decrees and curiously does not maintain a comprehensive database of all prior decrees, presumably to make it harder for defendants to cite earlier provisions in other cases.[162] Still, the government negotiating team will try to hold fast to the government's boilerplate language, and if it can be shown that a deviation was approved in another case, it will be easier to get it approved in the case being negotiated.

E. Early Settlement

One issue that has engendered much debate is whether when EPA pursues an industry-wide initiative, early settlers are treated better than later ones are. Both sides have credible arguments here. On the one hand, EPA wants to encourage early settlements. EPA typically will represent that the first settlers will get the best deal, and it can point to examples where later settlers paid significantly higher penalties than earlier ones. On the other hand, early settlers often have felt that their proactivity was, in the end, not rewarded, that the early settlements become a benchmark that later settlers try to negotiate down from, and that in hindsight they would have been better off to have waited to settle.

A defendant considering whether to become an early settler would be well advised to study the recent history of early settlements, particularly in the EPA program at issue. But in doing so, it also should consider that enforcement is never a

---

159. Press Release, U.S. Dep't of Justice, Harley-Davidson to Stop Sales of Illegal Devices that Increased Air Pollution from the Company's Motorcycles (Aug. 18, 2016), https://www.justice.gov/opa/pr/harley-davidson-stop-sales-illegal-devices-increased-air-pollution-company-s-motorcycles.

160. Consent Decree, United States v. Harley-Davidson, Inc., No. 1:16-cv-1687, Docket No. 6 (D.D.C.), https://www.epa.gov/sites/production/files/2017-12/documents/harleydavidson-cd.pdf.

161. Notice of Lodging of Proposed Consent Decree under the Clean Air Act, 82 Fed. Reg. 34,977, 34,978 (U.S. Dep't of Justice, July 27, 2017). As of August 8, 2018, DOJ's motion to approve the revised consent decree was still pending and had been opposed by Illinois, Iowa, Maine, Maryland, Massachusetts, New York, Oregon, Rhode Island, Vermont, Washington, the District of Columbia and the Puget Sound (WA) Clean Air Agency, and a number of environmental organizations, which preferred the original settlement with the mitigation project.

162. A comprehensive searchable file of DOJ and EPA consent decrees going back to 1970 is available on LEXIS in its "EPA Consent Decrees" database.

pleasant thing, and there is certainly an advantage, as with other unpleasant things, in simply bearing the pain and getting it over with sooner rather than later.

VIII. PARALLEL PROCEEDINGS

This book contains a chapter on criminal enforcement litigation and also this chapter on civil enforcement litigation—separate chapters for separate proceedings. The problem is that criminal enforcement and civil enforcement are not always so separate. Rather, at the federal level, there is an increasing push to pursue "parallel proceedings"—civil enforcement and criminal enforcement both proceeding at the same time for the same alleged violations and on parallel tracks. The 2015 Yates Memorandum, discussed earlier, directs that "[c]riminal and civil attorneys handling corporate investigations should be in routine communication with one another."[163] This dynamic can substantially increase the pressure on a defendant and can create very difficult challenges and choices for the target of so much enforcement.

It was not always this way. It used to be that the government would make an "either/or" choice about whether a case should go criminal or civil. Generally, if the criminal prosecutors thought the case merited a criminal investigation or prosecution, that would go first, and the civil matter would wait until the criminal matter was resolved. The one exception, and it was rare, was if there was a need for preliminary injunctive relief to protect health or the environment, the civil case could go forward until such relief was obtained, and then would be stayed pending the resolution of the criminal case.

The strong presumption that existed against parallel proceedings minimized the many pitfalls that loom in this area, as well as the potential for unfairness. Thus, if civil and criminal matters are proceeding simultaneously, the criminal prosecutors need to be scrupulously careful not to share grand jury information with their civil counterparts, which would violate Rule 6(e) of the Federal Rules of Criminal Procedure. Also, the civil enforcers need to ensure that they are not seeking civil discovery to advance the criminal case, nor holding out the possibility of tougher criminal enforcement to leverage a civil settlement. All these things would be very wrong.

The strong presumption against parallel proceedings was eliminated in 1999 when the ENRD issued its integrated enforcement policy, which stated as its goal "to assure that the Division's exercise of civil and criminal enforcement authority will address the effects of violations, deter future violations by the violator and by others, and impose appropriate penalties for violations of the law."[164] The intent of this directive was to create a lower bar to the pursuit of parallel proceedings.

---

163. Memorandum from Sally Yates, Deputy Att'y Gen., U.S. Dep't of Justice, to All Component Heads & U.S. Att'ys, Individual Accountability for Corporate Wrongdoing 2 (Sept. 9, 2015), https://www.justice.gov/archives/dag/file/769036/download.

164. U.S. Dep't of Justice, Env't & Nat. Res. Div., Directive 99-21, Integrated Enforcement Policy (1999).

The policy encourages civil enforcement attorneys to consider referring their cases for review on the criminal side:

> Civil attorneys should consider the possibility that their civil case may include criminal conduct and should remain alert for information indicating criminality. For example, a civil case yielding evidence of falsification of data, concealment of evidence, or repeated violations despite prior enforcement efforts should alert the trial attorney to potential criminal liability. If a referral package received from an agency includes evidence of potential criminal violations, or if such evidence emerges at any time during the course of a civil proceeding, the attorney handling the matter should consult with Section management and the matter should be brought to the attention of [the Environmental Crimes Section], regardless of the status of the civil case.[165]

Similarly, criminal prosecutors are encouraged to consider whether civil enforcement may be appropriate, such as "where it appears that an injunction to halt ongoing unlawful activity or remedial action is necessary (or desirable) or when an investigation establishes a violation of law, but there is insufficient evidence of criminal mental state."[166]

Although the policy still provides that civil enforcement "generally" will wait for the criminal enforcement to end, this decision will be made on a case-by-case basis, and there are a number of circumstances where the civil action may proceed:

> When proceeding with both criminal and civil enforcement, the Division generally will delay the civil case until criminal proceedings are resolved. However, the Division will assess the circumstances of each matter to determine whether to delay the civil case. Factors that may weigh in favor of allowing the civil case to proceed before the resolution of the criminal matter include:
> (1) the violations present a threat to public health or the environment such that injunctive relief should not be delayed;
> (2) the defendant's assets are in danger of dissipation;
> (3) there is a timing concern in light of a statute of limitations or bankruptcy deadline for the civil claim, or other potential statutory bar;
> (4) there is only a marginal relationship between the civil and criminal violations; and
> (5) civil case development is in an advanced stage when the potential criminal liability is brought to light.[167]

The first of these circumstances is broad enough to cover a wide range of situations. DOJ seeks an injunction to protect public health or the environment in the majority of its civil cases. So, in most cases the first test, which is not limited

---

165. U.S. Dep't of Justice, Env't & Nat. Res. Div., Directive 2016-12, Integrated Enforcement Policy, at 4 (Dec. 20, 2016), https://www.justice.gov/file/953081/download.

166. *Id.*

167. *Id.* at 8.

to those rare cases in which a preliminary injunction would be sought in the civil case, will be met. The other criteria also will cover a wide range of situations.

The policy, as updated, contains requirements to ensure that each side complies with the legal and ethical restrictions applicable to it. So, for example, once the grand jury process begins, information flow needs to be tracked to ensure that only non-grand-jury information is shared with the civil team.[168] Prior to the 2016 update to the policy, the commencement of the grand jury process created a presumption against sharing of information. Information flow became one way—civil to criminal only.[169] The 2016 update requires that the prosecutors "keep careful track" of their sources of information so that grand jury information is identifiable and other information can be shared.[170] Even with these safeguards, parallel proceedings can put a defendant into a difficult, if not untenable, situation. Here are some of the challenges that the defendant will face and some thoughts for addressing them, or at least containing them.

First, the reality of facing two proceedings, from aggressive enforcers on both the civil and criminal side, can overwhelm a defendant and sap the energy of its key personnel. It becomes imperative for defense counsel to help maintain order and calm in the face of all this activity. In that regard, clients often retain separate counsel to handle the civil and the criminal proceedings, and that is one reasonable approach. But there can be advantages in having one lawyer, or firm, leading the defense effort on both sides of the house to ensure consistency in the positions taken and messages conveyed (to employees, customers, regulators, prosecutors, etc.).

A second challenge will be that key employees, or officials, of the defendant may refuse to cooperate with the defendant because of the possibility that they could become targets of the investigation and related Fifth Amendment concerns. It can be very difficult for a civil defense counsel to represent his or her client in such a situation. If the civil action is already commenced, or is filed after the criminal investigation is commenced, defense counsel should seriously consider seeking an immediate stay of the civil case until the criminal investigation is resolved.

A third challenge arises if the criminal investigation is taking place while efforts are being made to resolve the civil case. In that context, the defendant will be heavily motivated to show cooperation and responsiveness to EPA and DOJ on the civil side because such cooperativeness is a factor that could influence the prosecutorial decision on whether to pursue a criminal charge against the company. DOJ's Principles of Federal Prosecution of Business Organizations lists, as a factor in the department's decision of whether to charge a corporation, the company's efforts

---

168. *Id.* at 1.
169. *Id.*
170. *Id.* at 3.

to "cooperat[e] with the relevant government agencies."[171] Whether intended or not, this gives the government's civil negotiator greatly increased leverage.

Two approaches to consider in this situation are polar opposites of each other. On the one hand, the defendant can push to slow down the civil negotiation until the criminal issue has been clarified to remove the government's leverage. It often takes DOJ or EPA a lot of time to begin the settlement process, and slowing down that process may not be that hard to accomplish.

Alternatively, a defendant may want to speed up the civil negotiation process so that an agreement, at least in principle, can be reached before the criminal-charging decision is made. Then the defendant can use that agreement as a basis to argue against criminal prosecution. DOJ lists "the adequacy of remedies such as civil or regulatory enforcement actions" as a factor weighing against prosecution of a company.[172]

Finally, whether facing civil enforcement, criminal enforcement, or both, the experience will not be a pleasant one for the defendant, and a crucial part of the defense attorney's responsibility should be to help the client understand what it needs to do to avoid future enforcement actions. In that regard, DOJ or EPA, in settling civil enforcement cases, often will seek the defendant's commitment to undertake an independent audit of its environmental management systems (EMS). Such an evaluation, however, need not wait until a settlement is concluded, and an early evaluation of the company's EMS, even while the enforcement process is ongoing and performed at the request of counsel, can be very valuable in the defense of the ongoing enforcement action and in the prevention of future enforcement.[173]

---

171. U.S. Dep't of Justice, United States Attorneys' Manual § 9-28.300, Principles of Federal Prosecution of Business Organizations (2018), https://www.justice.gov/jm/jm-9-28000-principles-federal-prosecution-business-organizations#9-28.300.

172. *Id.*

173. For an excellent discussion of environmental management systems, see Frank Friedman, Practical Guide to Environmental Management (11th ed. 2011).

CHAPTER 4

Insurance Recovery for Environmental Liabilities

Marc S. Mayerson

I. INTRODUCTION

Insurance is an important potential source of recovery for companies facing environmental or toxic tort liabilities or legal proceedings by municipal, state, or federal regulatory agencies. There may be coverage under older general liability policies for pollution that is alleged to have taken place before the inception of the pollution exclusion, or with respect to "polluting events" to which such exclusions do not apply. Additionally, many companies today purchase specialty environmental insurance policies specifically tailored to their operations, or to fund the remediation of a particular environmental site. Transactional lawyers need to be aware of the possibility of absorbing the risk of liability depending on whether assets are being acquired, stock is being transferred, or some form of corporate reorganization is taking place. At all points, the possibility that investigative, defense, and remediation costs might be covered in whole or in part always should be considered. This chapter provides an overview of several coverage issues arising in connection with each type of coverage that can potentially respond to environmental claims and related costs.

II. NOTICE

Insurance companies need to be informed as soon as practicable that their help and money are requested, and policyholders promise to notify the insurer of incidents and claims.

Lawyers who lack insurance expertise have been sued for legal malpractice when insurance issues are overlooked, resulting in the pertinent insurance company being notified late or in a manner that forfeits or curbs insurance recovery.[1] Thus, in any situation in which environmental liabilities, cleanup costs, or regulatory compliance arises, counsel should consider insurance implications. It is not enough to review whatever current insurance policies might be in effect; counsel should determine whether there are entities with which the client might have contracted that might have added the client to the contracting party's insurance. Counsel should create a record of his or her investigation into applicable insurance policies in the event that it is later discovered that a policy exists and notice later is provided; such documentation will help show that the search for policies was conducted reasonably diligently, and that the policyholder (or the lawyer) acted with appropriate attention to the potential for insurance recovery.

III. GENERAL LIABILITY POLICIES

Private and public entities typically purchase comprehensive or commercial general liability policies that cover a wide range of third-party liabilities. These policies typically include, among other things, coverage for property damage to third-party property arising out of the policyholder's business operations. Property damage encompasses traditional environmental liability arising from waste disposal operations, leaks and spills at manufacturing facilities (to the extent that third-party property is affected), and the like. Subject to their terms, general liability policies will cover the cost of judgments, orders, and settlements under the indemnity portion of the coverage, as well as the costs of lawyers and experts under the defense portion.

Most general liability insurance policies sold to corporate policyholders are standard-form, preprinted policies drafted by insurance carriers in participation with other insurance industry members. Even where policy forms are customized or manuscripted, the actual language is largely lifted from standard-form policies. Although most policies contain language that is similar or identical to that found in policies sold to numerous policyholders, the terms of individual policies may differ from the standard-form language that has evolved over the years.

Speaking broadly, there are two distinct populations of general liability policies: those written on an occurrence basis and those written on a claims-made basis. In general terms, occurrence-based policies respond when the occurrence (the unintentional injury or accident) or the damage for which the insured seeks coverage happened during the policy period, regardless of whether the suit is brought long after the policy period has ended. By contrast, claim-based policies, which have become more commonplace since the mid-1980s, respond to claims made against an insured during the policy period even if the basis for the

---

1. *See, e.g.*, Jordache Enters., Inc. v. Brobeck, Phleger & Harrison, 958 P.2d 1062 (Cal. 1998).

claimed liability results from harm caused years before.[2] Because the widespread adoption of claims-made general liability policies postdates the introduction of the absolute pollution exclusion,[3] it is usually only the older occurrence-based policies (and even earlier-in-the-20th-century "accident"-based policies) that might respond to environmental liabilities. Accordingly, this section addresses common and important issues pertaining to occurrence-based general liability policies with respect to environmental liabilities.

A. Determining the Coverage Program

A typical corporation's coverage program involves the purchase of:

- Comprehensive general liability policies that respond on a first-dollar basis, perhaps subject to a deductible or retention;
- First-layer excess or "umbrella" policies, providing limits of liability to supplement the first-dollar layer or "primary" coverage; and
- Upper-layer excess policies that often "follow form," meaning that they adopt the terms of an underlying policy.[4]

Excess policies supplement the limits of the underlying coverage, while umbrella policies both supplement the limits and provide gap-filling coverage that is broader in scope than that of the underlying primary policies. Within the gap, umbrella policies effectively function as primary coverage, providing first-dollar indemnity and defense coverage, subject to a retained limit. Excess policies often are written in layers. Sometimes a layer will be split among more than one insurer, with each assuming a specified proportion of the risk within the single layer of coverage. These are referred to as "quota share" policies. The following model coverage chart represents the structure of a typical American corporate coverage program:

---

2. The presence of both occurrence- and claim-based policies in an insured's program can have some unexpected results on recovery. *See generally* Marc S. Mayerson et al., *Allocation of Insured Loss between Claims-Made and Occurrence Coverage*, Ins. Allocation (Mealey's 2003).

3. *See* discussion *infra* section II.E.2.

4. A "follow form" policy incorporates the terms of the underlying policies. Upper-layer excess policies generally "follow form" to an underlying policy or policies, though identifying which underlying policy is the governing form may be difficult. *See, e.g.*, World Trade Ctr. Props. v. Hartford Ins. Co., 345 F.3d 154, 169–82 (2d Cir. 2003).

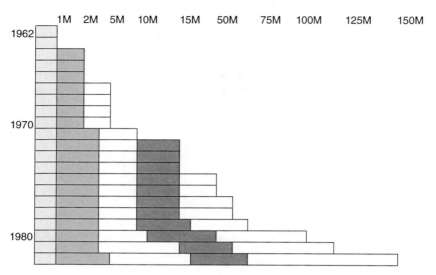

Figure 4-1

A corporate policyholder facing environmental liabilities should attempt to gather records of all policies that were in force at any time during the course of any activities that led to the underlying claims or litigation, including the policies of any corporate predecessors, and throughout the entire period of alleged injury or damage. Policy record-keeping is important, because insurers have no financial incentive to maintain older insurance policies. Policyholders should search the files at their headquarters, field offices, and document-storage facilities; the files of past or present insurance agents and insurance brokers; and, potentially, government-contract archives. For missing policies, the policyholder may be able to use secondary evidence of its insurance, such as binders or cover notes, to satisfy its burden of proving the existence of the policy and the terms of the coverage.[5] Special consultants, known as "insurance archaeologists," can assist in the search for, or reconstruction of, older policies that are incomplete or missing from a variety of third-party sources.

---

5. *See, e.g.*, Burt Rigid Box, Inc. v. Travelers Prop. Cas. Corp., 302 F.3d 83 (2d Cir. 2002) (presentation of plethora of secondary evidence, and carrier's concession that, if issued, the policy was a standard form, were sufficient to prove the terms of lost policy); Century Indem. Co. v. Aero-Motive Co., 254 F. Supp. 2d 670, 676–80 (W.D. Mich. 2003) (insurance ledgers and other secondary evidence were admitted as evidence of policies; expert on insurance policy reconstruction allowed to testify regarding lost policies); ACMAT Corp. v. Greater N.Y. Mut. Ins. Co., 869 A.2d 1254, 1260 (Conn. App. Ct. 2005) (certificate of insurance and other secondary evidence proved existence of policies).

B. The Basic Elements of Coverage under Occurrence-Based Policies

Occurrence-based general liability policies cover the policyholder's liability to third parties arising from a wide variety of its business activities. Such policies typically include coverage for business operations, premises liability, product liability, advertising injury, and sometimes even automobile liability. They generally cover both bodily injury and property damage caused by most of these activities.

As related to environmental liabilities, the typical insuring agreement in such policies is substantially like the following:

> The company will pay on behalf of the insured all sums which the insured shall become legally obligated to pay as damages because of
> A. bodily injury, or
> B. property damage
> to which this insurance applies, caused by an occurrence, and the company shall have the right and duty to defend any suit against the insured seeking damages on account of such bodily injury or property damage, even if any of the allegations of the suit are groundless, false or fraudulent. . . .[6]

Thus, pollution coverage under occurrence-based general liability policies includes the following elements:

1. Property damage;
2. Caused by an occurrence;
3. Resulting in damages for which the insured is alleged to be liable;
4. Thus triggering the insurer's separate obligations to
   a. pay "all [such] sums" (known as the duty to indemnify), and
   b. defend against "suits" on account of such property damage (known as the duty to defend).

Each of these elements is examined next, adopting the perspective of a generalist. Counsel needs to consult the current law in the applicable jurisdiction because case law in this field is dynamic and state statutes, such as one in Oregon,[7] may powerfully supplant common law rulemaking.

---

6. Susan J. Miller & Philip Lefebvre, MILLER'S STANDARD INSURANCE POLICIES ANNOTATED (Legal Res. Systems 5th ed. 2007), form GL 00 02 01 73 at 421.5.

7. *See* 2017 OR. REV. STAT. § 465.480 (insurance for environmental claims); for state authority to adopt such legislation, see *Watson v. Employers Liability Corp.*, 348 U.S. 66 (1954) (applying Louisiana insurance statute to Louisiana victims of an insured Illinois subsidiary of Massachusetts company with policies issued and delivered in either or both Massachusetts and Illinois).

1. Property Damage: Environmental Contamination

General liability policies typically define property damage as "physical injury to or destruction of tangible property which occurs during the policy period."[8] Most courts have little difficulty concluding that environmental contamination of soil or groundwater falls within this broad definition. Indeed, environmental contamination plainly affects "tangible property"—surface and subsurface soil and water—and plainly causes "physical injury" to such property—the degradation and sullying of the soil and water by the introduction of foreign contaminants. Under the definition's expansive terms, both active releases and passive migration of contaminants cause property damage.[9]

Courts generally hold that costs incurred to mitigate actual past contamination and prevent it from migrating to cause further property damage are incurred "because of" property damage and thus fall within coverage.[10] Certain cleanup costs incurred by a potentially responsible party (PRP), however, might be characterized as preventive or prophylactic when they are intended solely to avoid future contamination rather than redress past contamination. Most courts hold that such anticipatory preventive costs are incurred not because of extant property damage, as required under the typical general liability policy's insuring agreement, but rather because of *potential* property damage.

In addition, the standard-form general liability policy requires that the damaged property belong to a third party, as the nature of such a policy is one of third-party liability insurance rather than first-party property insurance. The policies effectuate this requirement through a standard "owned property" exclusion that bars coverage for damage to the policyholder's own property.[11] However, the policyholder may be able to recover the costs of remedial activities at its own site if

---

8. MILLER'S STANDARD INSURANCE POLICIES ANNOTATED, form GL 00 00 01 73 at 421.3.

9. *See* Olin Corp. v. Certain Underwriters, 468 F.3d 120, 131 (2d Cir. 2006) ("We . . . hold that property damage occurs as long as contamination continues to increase or spread, whether or not the contamination is based on active pollution or the passive migration of contamination into the soil and groundwater."); Unimax Corp. v. Lumbermens Mut. Cas. Co., 908 F. Supp. 148, 155 (S.D.N.Y. 1995) (finding that "contamination is deemed to be physical injury" under both New York and North Carolina law). *See also* Olin Corp. v. Am. Home Assur. Co., 704 F.3d 89, 100 (2d Cir. 2012) (holding "that the spread of earlier contamination met the definition of property damage").

10. *See, e.g.,* AIU Ins. Co. v. Superior Ct., 799 P.2d 1253, 1272 (Cal. 1990) (finding that "purely prophylactic" measures are not covered, but response costs "incurred largely to prevent damage previously confined to the insured's property from spreading to government or third-party property" are covered); Watts Indus. v. Zurich Am. Ins. Co., 18 Cal. Rptr. 3d 61 (Cal. Ct. App. 2004); A.Y. McDonald Indus. v. Ins. Co. of N. Am., 475 N.W.2d 607, 624 (Iowa 1991) (finding that "response costs for preventive measures employed after pollution has taken place are incurred 'because of property damage' under the CGL policies. However, costs incurred to pay for preventive measures taken in advance of pollution are not incurred 'because of property damage.'").

11. The standard-form owned-property exclusion provides, "This insurance does not apply . . . to property damage to (1) property owned or occupied by or rented to the insured, (2) property used by the insured, or (3) property in the care, custody or control of the insured or as to which the insured is for any purpose exercising physical control." MILLER'S STANDARD INSURANCE POLICIES ANNOTATED, form GL 00 02 01 73 at 421.5.

the remediation is directed, at least in part, toward an effort to mitigate or redress damage to third-party property or to groundwater.[12]

In certain states, policyholders may argue that the owned-property exclusion does not apply to contaminated groundwater beneath their own land because the subjacent water is owned by the state rather than the landowner above.[13] The viability of this argument usually turns on the property and riparian laws of the state in which the site is located. Moreover, some courts have concluded that the owned-property exclusion does not apply because any viable liability claim necessarily involves third-party property interests.[14]

2. Trigger: Property Damage during the Policy Period

The property damage, or occurrence, generally must take place during the policy period for a general liability policy to be "triggered," that is, for the policy potentially to respond. Pollution typically is a long-term process, which encompasses a number of stages that may be spread over many years, starting with the initial release and the resulting passive migration, and ending with the remediation after the problem has been discovered. This extended, multistage process presents the question of precisely what constitutes property damage during the policy period to trigger a policy. A number of trigger theories have emerged, including:

---

12. *Compare, e.g.*, Chem. Leaman Tank Lines, Inc. v. Aetna Cas. & Sur. Co., 788 F Supp. 846, 852–53 (D. N.J. 1992) (holding that the owned-property exclusion did not bar coverage for remedial measures taken to correct injury or prevent further damage to neighboring properties), *aff'd*, 89 F.3d 976 (3d Cir. 1996), *with* Spartan Petrol. Co v. Federated Mut. Ins. Co., 162 F.3d 805, 807–08, (4th Cir. 1998) (predicting South Carolina law, holding that policies are not triggered by injury in fact until migrating pollution actually reaches off-site property).

13. *See, e.g.*, Intel Corp. v. Hartford Accident & Indem. Co., 952 F.2d 1551, 1565 (9th Cir. 1991) ("Damage to groundwater is not damage to property owned or occupied by or rented to [the insured]. Release of hazardous waste into groundwater and surface water constitutes actual harm to property in which the state and federal governments have an ownership interest.") (applying California law) (internal quotation marks omitted); Claussen v. Aetna Cas. & Sur. Co., 754 F. Supp. 1576, 1580 (S.D. Ga. 1990) ("The right of the owner to ground water underlying his land is to the usufruct of the water and not to the water itself. The ownership of the land does not carry with it any ownership of vested rights to underlying ground water. . . .") (applying Florida law). *But see* Am. States Ins. Co. v. Hanson Indus., 873 F. Supp. 17, 24 (S.D. Tex. 1995) (owned-property exclusion applies to groundwater because surface owner has property interest in underground water "percolating, oozing, or filtrating through the earth"); Allstate Ins. Co. v. Dana Corp., 759 N.E.2d 1049, 1054–55 (Ind. 2001) (same).

14. *See, e.g.*, Patz v. St. Paul Fire & Marine Ins. Co., 15 F.3d 699, 704 (7th Cir. 1994) (owned-property exclusion does not apply to remediation costs because insured is not seeking recovery for damage to owned property, but for costs of liability imposed by the Department of Natural Resources). *See also* Anderson Dev. Co. v. Travelers Indem. Co., 49 F.3d 1128, 1133–34 (6th Cir. 1995) (holding that the owned-property exclusion does not apply to environmental cleanup costs imposed by EPA).

- *Continuous trigger,* which holds that any insurer on the risk from initial exposure until manifestation of the environmental problem or initial remedial action potentially is liable;[15]
- *Injury-in-fact trigger,* which requires a factual inquiry into whether the injury more likely than not took place during a particular policy period (even if the injury cannot be precisely quantified).[16] In a case where the injury is continuous or ongoing, such as a continuous leak of contaminants into groundwater, this trigger theory is practically indistinguishable from the continuous trigger theory;[17]
- *Exposure trigger,* which holds that those policies in effect when the injured property is exposed to the harmful agent are triggered. In the environmental context, the triggering event is the date of the leak or spill, that is, each date on which the releases into the environment took place (focusing though on their initial impact). Unlike the continuous trigger theory, policies in effect when already-released contamination is migrating through the soil or groundwater would not be triggered;[18] and
- *Manifestation trigger,* which holds that the only policies triggered are those in effect at the time when property damage from environmental

---

15. *See, e.g.,* Montrose Chem. Corp. v. Admiral Ins. Co., 913 P.2d 878, 901–02 (Cal. 1995) (applying continuous trigger to progressive pollution at landfill); Benoy Motor Sales, Inc. v. Universal Underwriters Ins., 679 N.E.2d 414, 418 (Ill. App. Ct. 1997) (applying a continuous trigger because "[e]nvironmental pollution does not stop and start in discrete time periods. When pollutants are released or discharged the damage is immediate. There is a continuing process. If we were to pour black ink into white milk we could not find a time when the coloring process did not occur."); Outboard Marine Corp. v. Liberty Mut. Ins. Co., 670 N.E.2d 740, 748 (Ill. App. Ct. 1996) (continuous trigger applies to property damage claims arising from release of PCBs into lake); Century Indem. Co. v. Golden Hills Builders, Inc., 561 S.E.2d 355, 357 (S.C. 2002) (applying continuous trigger in context of defective building material).

16. *See, e.g.,* Stonewall Ins. Co. v. Asbestos Claims Mgmt. Corp., 73 F.3d 1178 (2d Cir. 1995) (asbestos bodily injury and property damage), *op. modified,* 85 F.3d 49 (2d Cir. 1996); Am. Home Prods. Corp. v. Liberty Mut. Ins. Co., 748 F.2d 760 (2d Cir. 1984) (DES bodily injury claims); *In re* Wallace & Gale Co., 275 B.R. 223 (D. Md. 2002) (asbestos bodily injury), *vacated in part on other grounds,* 284 B.R. 557 (D. Md. 2002), *aff'd,* 385 F.3d 820 (4th Cir. 2004); *Montrose Chem. Corp.,* 913 P.2d at 893 (environmental contamination); Mayor & City Council of Balt. v. Utica Mut. Ins. Co., 802 A.2d 1070, 1098 (Md. Ct. Spec. App. 2002); *In re* Silicone Implant Ins. Coverage Litig., 667 N.W.2d 405, 415–16, 421–22 (Minn. 2003) (only insurers on the risk at time of breast implantation, the actual injury, are liable for losses, as opposed to allocating losses pro rata to insurers based on the time they had insured against the particular injury); Kief Farmers Coop. Elevator Co. v. Farmland Mut. Ins. Co., 534 N.W.2d 28, 36 (N.D. 1995) (latent product defect).

17. *See Utica Mut. Ins. Co.,* 802 A.2d at 1098 ("The 'injury-in-fact' and 'continuous' trigger theories are not mutually exclusive, but instead may in an appropriate circumstance be complimentary," such as where the insured can show that injury was the initial triggering event and the insured has shown that the damage was continuing in nature).

18. *See, e.g.,* Gelman Scis., Inc. v. Fid. & Cas. Co., 572 N.W.2d 617, 621 (Mich. 1998) ("The exposure trigger places the 'occurrence' at the earliest time, i.e., when the exposure to injury-causing conditions occurs. In the environmental pollution context, this is the date on which the pollution began."), *overruled on other grounds* by Wilkie v. Auto Owners Ins. Co., 469 Mich. 41, 63 (Mich. 2003). *See also* Norfolk S. Corp. v. Cal. Union Ins. Co., 859 So. 2d 167, 192 (La. Ct. App. 2003) (under exposure theory, trigger limited to years of active wood-preserving operations).

contamination is discovered.[19] The manifestation trigger is a distinct minority position, for it is difficult to reconcile with the policy language requiring property damage during the policy period. The manifestation trigger generally limits the number of policies triggered, though some courts applying the trigger stretch their jurisprudence to favor coverage.[20]

Although the continuous trigger theory allows each policy on the risk from first exposure through manifestation of injury or damage to be called upon to provide coverage, policyholders should not favor it reflexively. Instead, they must consider the implications of the trigger theory on their ultimate recovery.[21] For instance, if multiple policies across time are triggered, the policyholder may be required to satisfy a separate deductible, retention, or retrospective premium adjustment under each triggered policy.[22] Depending upon the size of the liability and the amount of coverage in any one year, policyholders whose coverage contains restrictions of this type may benefit from a trigger-of-coverage theory under which the injury or damage is confined to a narrower, rather than broader, period.

In the environmental context, joint and several liability under the Comprehensive Environmental Response, Compensation, and Liability Act[23] (CERCLA) raises an additional trigger question: whether pollution caused by a third party for which the policyholder is liable can trigger the policyholder's own coverage in place at the time the pollution occurred. For example, if a policyholder purchased a site in 1990, and is jointly and severally liable under CERCLA for the pollution activities of the prior site owner in 1980, can the policyholder recover under its own 1980 occurrence-based general liability policy? The terms of the standard-form insuring agreement seem to be met in such circumstances: there is property damage during the policy period resulting in damages for which the policyholder is legally obligated to pay. The insuring agreement does not, by its terms, require that the property damage be caused by the policyholder himself or herself, only that he or she be liable for

---

19. *See* Hughes Aircraft Co. v. Century Indem. Co., 1998 WL 166534, at *5 (9th Cir. Mar. 31, 1998) ("Applying the manifestation trigger to this case compels entry of summary judgment in favor of defendant INA. To wit, the Court has previously found that the TCE contamination at issue manifested itself upon removal of the clarifier in 1986 and thus outside of the period of coverage afforded by INA's policies, which ran from January 1, 1965 to December 31, 1969."); *Gelman Scis., Inc.*, 572 N.W.2d at 621 ("The manifestation theory places the 'occurrence' at the latest possible time, i.e., when the property damage is ultimately discovered.").

20. *See, e.g.*, Travelers Cas. & Sur. Co. v. Providence Wash. Ins. Co., 685 F.3d 22, 30–31 (1st Cir. 2012) (holding that the underlying complaint gave rise to an inference that the property damage was discoverable in the exercise of reasonable diligence during the policy period); Textron, Inc. v. Aetna Cas. & Sur. Co., 754 A.2d 742, 745–47 (R.I. 2000) (triggering policy for all policy periods where manifestation of property damage could have been discovered by policyholder exercising "reasonable diligence" even if actual discovery not made until years later); Textron, Inc. v. Aetna Cas. & Sur. Co., 723 A.2d 1138, 1142–43 (R.I. 1999).

21. *See, e.g.*, Olin Corp. v. OneBeacon Am. Ins. Co., 864 F.3d 130 (2d Cir. 2017). *See also* Keyspan Gas E. Corp. v. Munich Reinsurance Am., Inc., 2018 WL 1472635 (N.Y. Mar. 27, 2018).

22. *See, e.g.*, Benjamin Moore & Co. v. Aetna Cas. & Sur. Co., 843 A.2d 1094 (N.J. 2004) (all deductibles across multiple triggered policies must be satisfied before any coverage is available).

23. CERCLA §§ 101–405, 42 U.S.C. §§ 9600–9675 (2000).

it. However, insurers contend that they did not underwrite the policy to cover such a risk, nor would it have been possible to do so because they could not have anticipated at the time the policy was issued what sites the policyholder might acquire, and thus the liability for which it may become jointly and severally liable in the future.[24] However, at least after CERCLA's enactment in 1980, insurers should have anticipated *some* future joint and several liability for their corporate policyholders.

3. Occurrence

Standard-form general liability policies also require that the property damage be caused by an occurrence, which typically is defined as "an accident, including continuous or repeated exposure to conditions, which results in bodily injury or property damage neither expected nor intended from the standpoint of the insured."[25] The basic purpose of the occurrence requirement is to prevent coverage for injuries that were not accidental, because the policyholder either intended to cause the injury or acted with knowledge and disregard of the practically certain consequence that damage would result. Such nonaccidental injuries generally are outside the scope of liability policies.

a. Expected/Intended

The fundamental element of an occurrence is that the damage for which coverage is sought must not have been expected or intended by the policyholder. The proper standard for determining this question has been the subject of litigation. Policyholders generally advocate a subjective or "in fact" standard that focuses on a particular policyholder's actual knowledge and understanding, under which the insurer must show that the policyholder, in fact, subjectively expected or intended its actions to cause the resulting harm.[26] In *City of Johnstown v. Bankers Standard Insurance Co.*, for example, the defendant insurers denied coverage to a landfill operator on expected/intended grounds based on the fact that the operator had

---

24. *Compare* Weyerhaeuser Co. v. Commercial Union Ins. Co., 15 P.3d 115, 129 (Wash. 2000) ("[T]he plain language of the policy requires coverage as the definition of 'occurrence' is not limited to actions taken by *Weyerhaeuser* but includes *any* event which unexpectedly causes injury during the policy period. . . . Because the property damage occurred during the policy period and Weyerhaeuser has become obligated by reason of law, the plain language of the contract requires coverage."), *with* Crucible Materials Corp. v. Aetna Cas. & Sur. Co., 228 F. Supp. 2d 182, 191 (N.D.N.Y. 2001) ("Crucible's joint and several liability under CERCLA and the fact that third parties damaged the CCCI site during the coverage period does not actuate the Travelers Policies; such a trigger requires Crucible's direct involvement. . . . Since Crucible had no legal or factual connection with the CCCI site during the coverage period, Travelers is not required to indemnify plaintiff for its abatement costs.").

25. Miller's Standard Insurance Policies Annotated, form GL 00 00 01 73 at 421.3.

26. As with other policy exclusions, the insurance company generally has the burden to prove that "expected" or "intended" exclusionary language in its policy precludes coverage for a particular claim. *See, e.g.,* B.B. v. Cont'l Ins. Co., 8 F.3d 1288, 1291 (8th Cir. 1993) (applying Missouri law; inferring intent from the act itself); Colonial Gas Co. v. Aetna Cas. & Sur. Co., 823 F. Supp. 975, 979 (D. Mass. 1993) (applying Massachusetts law); Aydin Corp. v. First State Ins. Co., 959 P.2d 1213, 1215 (Cal. 1998); Am. Star Ins. Co. v. Grice, 854 P.2d 622, 625 (Wash. 1993), *op. supplemented,* 865 P.2d 507 (Wash. 1994) (applying Washington law). *But see* FMC Corp. v. Plaisted & Cos., 72 Cal. Rptr. 2d 467, 481 (Cal. Ct. App. 1998) (insured has burden of proving damage is "unexpected").

received notice that the landfill was believed to be leaking contaminants into the groundwater.[27] The Second Circuit rejected that argument, holding that recovery would be barred "only if the insured intended the damages . . . or if it [could] be said that the damages were, in a broader sense, 'intended' by the insured because the insured knew that the damages would flow directly and immediately from its intentional act."[28] The court determined that warnings of possible damage alone were not sufficient to show that the policyholder had expected or intended the damage in question.[29]

By contrast, insurance companies typically urge courts to adopt an objective standard that turns on whether the policyholder reasonably should have expected the resulting injury or damage.[30] Thus, some courts applying an objective approach have barred coverage where the harm was "reasonably anticipated."[31] This is not the majority rule.

Because there rarely will be direct evidence of a corporate insured's subjective "state of mind," some courts tend to blur the rhetoric of the subjective and objective approaches, relying on objective indicia of subjective intent. In *Carter-Wallace Inc. v. Admiral Insurance Co.*, for example, the New Jersey Supreme Court laid out the following subjective and objective criteria that should be used to determine the policyholder's subjective mindset:

- Duration of discharge;
- Whether the discharges occurred intentionally, negligently, or innocently;
- Quality of the insured's knowledge concerning the propensities of the pollutants;
- Whether regulatory authorities attempted to discourage or prevent the insured's conduct; and
- The existence of subjective knowledge as to the possibility of harm.[32]

---

27. Johnstown v. Bankers Standard Ins. Co., 877 F.2d 1146, 1147 (2d Cir. 1989).

28. *Id.* at 1150 (citations omitted).

29. *Id.* at 1152. *See also, e.g.*, Chem. Leaman Tank Lines, Inc. v. Aetna Cas. & Sur. Co., 89 F.3d 976, 989 (3d Cir. 1996) (requiring subjective knowledge of the insured's intent to cause harm before exclusion will apply); Armstrong World Indus. Inc. v. Aetna Cas. & Sur. Co., 52 Cal. Rptr. 2d 690, 719–21 (Ct. App. 1996) (same); Travelers Indem. Co. v. PCR Inc., 889 So. 2d 779, 797–98 (Fla. 2004) (same).

30. Some carriers have tried to take matters a step further by changing the focus from the insured's intent to cause *damage* to the insured's intent to engage in the act in question—for example, the deliberate act of disposing of waste in a landfill—but this position ignores the fact that liability insurance routinely covers the unintended results of intentional acts. *See, e.g.*, Lyons v. State Farm Fire & Cas. Co., 811 N.E.2d 718 (Ill. App. Ct. 2004) (finding coverage for insured who mistakenly constructed retaining pond on wrong person's property).

31. *See, e.g.*, Calvert Ins. Co. v. W. Ins. Co., 874 F.2d 396, 399 (7th Cir. 1989); City of Carter Lake v. Aetna Cas. & Sur. Co., 604 F.2d 1052, 1059 n.4 (8th Cir. 1979) (discussing the difference between "reasonably foreseeable" and "substantial probability" tests).

32. Carter-Wallace, Inc. v. Admiral Ins. Co., 712 A.2d 1116, 1126–27 (N.J. 1998). *See also* Northbrook Prop. & Cas. Ins. Co. v. Kenosha Auto Transp. Corp., No. C-92-3329TEH, slip op. at 14–15 (N.D. Cal. July 19, 1993), *reprinted in* 7-39 Mealey's Litig. Rep. Ins. 6 (1993) (carrier can establish "expected or intended" through either subjective intent or reasonable, substantial certainty); New Castle Cnty. v. Hartford Accident & Indem. Co., 778 F. Supp. 812, 820 (D. Del. 1991) (utilizing the "substantial probability" test), *rev'd on other grounds*, 970 F.2d 1267 (3d Cir. 1992). For examples of the factual nature of the inquiry, see Shell Oil Co. v. Winterthur Swiss Ins. Co., 15 Cal. Rptr. 2d 815 (Ct. App. 1993), and Diamond Shamrock Chems. Co. v. Aetna Cas. & Sur. Co., 609 A.2d 440 (N.J. Super. Ct. App. Div. 1992).

The expected/intended battle often turns on the question of the quantum of expected or intended damage necessary to defeat coverage. For example, is there coverage for unexpected contamination of groundwater resulting from expected soil contamination because of regular industrial operations? Insureds have won victories in states such as New Jersey, where the courts recognize that coverage for a significant unintended problem should not be forfeited merely because the insured understood there would be some impact on the environment.[33] Insurers, not surprisingly, have taken a minimalist position, arguing that an insured's expectation or intention of *any* property damage or bodily injury, no matter how slight, defeats coverage, even if the resulting harm is of a different order of magnitude or different kind.

b. Number of Occurrences

Because deductibles and policy limits generally include a per-occurrence limitation, the number of occurrences presented by an underlying claim or claims can have a significant impact on insurance recovery. If each claim in a series of related claims against the policyholder constitutes a separate occurrence, then a low-layer policy with either a per-occurrence limit or a per-claim or per-occurrence deductible "mathematically" might limit the insured's effective recovery.[34] In contrast, if multiple claims are deemed to arise from a single occurrence, then claims can be aggregated for purposes of satisfying the deductible.[35] Thus, whether the amount of the deductible is significant in relation to the potential liability for a particular claim generally will determine whether it is in the policyholder's or the insurer's interests to obtain a single-occurrence or multiple-occurrence result.

The parties' positions also may be affected by the presence or absence of aggregate limits. In many circumstances, there may not be an overall aggregate or total limit on how much the policy pays for environmental claims. For instance, in many occurrence-based general liability policies, especially those issued prior to 1986, it is common for there to be no aggregate limits on coverage of a company's

---

33. *See, e.g., Chem. Leaman Tank Lines*, 89 F.3d at 988; Pittston Co. v. Allianz Ins. Co., 905 F. Supp. 1279, 1302 (D.N.J. 1995) (expected damage must be "qualitatively comparable" to actual damage before coverage is forfeited), *rev'd in part on other grounds*, 124 F.3d 508 (3d Cir. 1997).

34. *See, e.g.*, Secura Ins. v. Lyme St. Croix Forest Co., LLC, 2018 WI 103 (Oct. 30, 2018) (a fire that ended up burning multiple properties counts as a single occurrence, and not multiple occurrences even though no tort claim takes place to the particular victim until its property is actually affected); Stonewall Ins. Co. v. Asbestos Claims Mgmt. Corp., 73 F.3d 1178, 1214 (2d Cir. 1995) (finding each asbestos claimant's alleged injury to constitute a separate occurrence to which a new per-occurrence limit applies), *op. modified*, 85 F.3d 49 (2d Cir. 1996); Am. Red Cross v. Travelers Indem. Co., 816 F. Supp. 755, 759 (D.D.C. 1993) (each act of distribution of HIV-contaminated blood constitutes a separate occurrence); Commercial Union Ins. Co. v. Porter Hayden Co., 698 A.2d 1167, 1210–11 (Md. Ct. Spec. App. 1997) (each asbestos injury constitutes a separate occurrence to which a new per-occurrence limit applies); Sec. Ins. Co. of Hartford v. Lubrizol Corp., 2009 WL 10676776, at *9–10 (E.D. Tex. Aug. 27, 2009) (finding a single occurrence in the case of hazardous waste disposal practices).

35. *See, e.g.*, EOTT Energy Corp. v. Storebrand Int'l Ins. Co., 52 Cal. Rptr. 2d 894, 901–02 (Ct. App. 1996) (aggregating multiple thefts of fuel caused by a single conspiracy as a single occurrence subject to a single deductible).

ongoing business operations, which is the hazard set forth in the policy under which environmental contamination often falls (as opposed, for example, to the products hazard covering liability associated with a company's products). The application of the aggregates may turn on the hazard generating the claim and the manner in which the insurance policy premium had been calculated.

The number of occurrences also may be important for determining the availability of excess insurance coverage, which can be important when there are large losses. If multiple claims are treated as multiple occurrences, excess coverage may not apply until a single claim exceeds the primary per-occurrence limits or until multiple claims combine to exhaust the aggregate limit. By contrast, if the underlying circumstance giving rise to multiple claims is deemed a single overarching occurrence, the claims can be aggregated for purposes of exhausting primary policies to access the excess coverage immediately.

The general test for the number of occurrences is whether multiple claims were the result of one or multiple causes.[36] Many courts applying this test appear to have reached whatever result maximized the policyholder's insurance recovery. For example, in serial litigation where each individual claim was small and the policyholder's deductible was large, courts often have found that multiple injuries and claims were proximately caused by a single, uninterrupted, and continuing cause, such as the policyholder's decision to manufacture and sell its product, thus warranting a single-occurrence result. Otherwise, the courts reasoned, the policyholder effectively would be deprived of the benefit of the coverage it purchased.[37] However, the courts' coverage-maximizing tendency has been less certain as of late.[38]

In the environmental context, all contamination at a single site generally is considered a single occurrence regardless of the number of leaks and spills over the years, unless there are spill incidents that are particularly significant and

---

36. *See, e.g.*, Appalachian Ins. Co. v. Liberty Mut. Ins. Co., 676 F.2d 56, 61 (3d Cir. 1982) ("The general rule is that an occurrence is determined by the cause or causes of the resulting injury."); Champion Int'l Corp. v. Cont'l Cas. Co., 546 F.2d 502, 506 (2d Cir. 1976) ("policy not intended to gauge coverage on the basis of individual accidents giving rise to claims, but rather on the underlying circumstances which resulted in the claim"); *Diamond Shamrock Chems. Co.*, 609 A.2d at 470 (the cause of the injury or damage determines the number of occurrences). Though there is some case law that adopts the rhetoric of number of effects as the determinative element of the number of occurrences, virtually all policies have added language that makes such an argument difficult and the point is rarely accepted. *E.g.*, *Lyme St. Croix Forest*, 2018 WI 103.

37. *See, e.g.*, *Champion Int'l Corp.*, 546 F.2d at 505–06 (sale of defective paneling installed on 1,400 separate vehicles constituted a single occurrence); Atchison, Topeka & Santa Fe Ry. v. Stonewall Ins. Co., 71 P.3d 1097, 1121, 1125 (Kan. 2003) (failure to implement a hearing conservation program was one occurrence in action involving multiple claims for noise-induced hearing loss).

38. *See* World Trade Ctr. Props. v. Hartford Ins. Co., 345 F.3d 154, 190 (2d Cir. 2003) (a fact finder could determine that the September 11 attacks on the twin towers constitute either one or two occurrences); Metro. Life Ins. Co. v. Aetna Cas. & Sur. Co., 765 A.2d 891, 897 (Conn. 2001) (finding each asbestos claimant's exposure to asbestos to be a separate occurrence, rejecting policyholder's argument that "occurrence" is ambiguous); *see also* Marc Mayerson, *E Pluribus Plures: More on Number of Occurrences*, INS. SCRAWL, Dec. 1, 2005, https://perma.cc/492W-VEPB.

independent; but claims involving pollution at multiple sites likely will be considered as multiple occurrences.[39]

4. "As Damages"

The standard general liability policy requires the insurance company to pay "all sums which the insured shall become legally obligated to pay as damages."[40] Insurance carriers have argued that environmental remediation and response costs incurred pursuant to a government mandate are injunctive, restitutionary, or other equitable relief and, consequently, are not money damages in the traditional legal sense (i.e., damages at law, as opposed to at equity).

Policyholders counter that the term *damages* must be given its common, ordinary meaning, and encompass any monies paid on account of third-party property damage, as opposed to drawing upon technical distinctions between legal and equitable relief. The issue has been heavily litigated, and most courts have held that environmental response costs are covered damages.[41]

In some instances, insurers have resisted paying by pursing the circumstances and precise bases on which the insured (purportedly) was required by law to pay. For example, in *Certain Underwriters at Lloyd's of London v. Superior Court*,[42] the California Supreme Court ruled that under the policy wording at issue, the insurer had no duty to indemnify the insured for an award following an administrative proceeding before an environmental agency, not because response costs are not susceptible of being characterized as "damages" (i.e., the type of liability costs the policy otherwise it is meant to cover); but because, the court reasoned, the term

---

39. *See, e.g.*, Endicott Johnson Corp. v. Liberty Mut. Ins. Co., 928 F. Supp. 176, 181 (N.D.N.Y. 1996) ("[W]hile many instances of 'property damage' resulted at each site that triggered plaintiff's insurance policies, which cover liability for property damage, they all derived from one 'occurrence' at each site."); Norfolk S. Corp. v. Cal. Union Ins. Co., 859 So. 2d 167, 192 (La. Ct. App. 2003) ("To the extent that the releases, drips, and spills were due to the wood-preserving operations in one policy period they are to be considered as one occurrence. Therefore, a single occurrence took place in each policy period from 1969 to 1972 at the Bayou Bonfouca site, and a single occurrence took place in each policy period from 1963 to 1971 at the Pearl River site."). *But see* Centennial Ins. Co. v. Lumbermens Mut. Cas. Co., 677 F. Supp. 342, 346 (E.D. Pa. 1987) (each act of disposing waste at a landfill is a separate occurrence).

40. Miller's Standard Insurance Policies Annotated, form GL 00 02 01 73 at 421.5.

41. *See, e.g.*, Lindsay Mfg. Co. v. Hartford Accident & Indem. Co., 118 F.3d 1263, 1270–71 (8th Cir. 1997) (CERCLA response costs are damages); Bituminous Cas. Corp. v. Vacuum Tanks, Inc., 75 F.3d 1048, 1053 (5th Cir. 1996) (under Texas law, CERCLA response costs are damages); New Castle Cnty. v. Hartford Accident & Indem. Co., 933 F.2d 1162, 1190 (3d Cir. 1991) (under Delaware law, the ordinary meaning of the term "damages" does not distinguish between legal and equitable remedies); Aetna Cas. & Sur. Co. v. Pintlar Corp., 948 F.2d 1507, 1513 (9th Cir. 1991) (under Idaho law, the term "damages" encompasses CERCLA response costs); Outboard Marine Corp. v. Liberty Mut. Ins. Co., 607 N.E.2d 1204, 1216 (Ill. 1992) (under Illinois law, CERCLA response costs are damages); Morton Int'l, Inc. v. Gen. Accident Ins. Co. of Am., 629 A.2d 831, 846–47 (N.J. 1993) (under New Jersey law, environmental response costs and remediation expenses are sums the policyholder must pay "as damages"); Boeing Co. v. Aetna Cas. & Sur. Co., 784 P.2d 507, 516 (Wash. 1990) (under Washington law, CERCLA costs are damages).

42. Certain Underwriters at Lloyd's of London v. Superior Court, 16 P.3d 94, 104 (Cal. 2001) (known as the "*Powerine* decision," after the underlying plaintiff, Powerine Oil Co.).

damages "is limited to money ordered by a court."[43] Thus, the court held, "the duty to indemnify does not extend to any expenses required by an administrative agency pursuant to an environmental statute."[44] Such expenses, though perhaps not covered under primary policies, may be covered by umbrella policies. Courts also have disagreed about whether costs incurred to prevent or mitigate further pollution are included within the term *damages*.[45] In general, a policyholder is well served by documenting what environmental-liability-related costs are incurred, and putting processes in place to ensure their reasonableness.

C. The Duty to Defend: Important Coverage for Litigation Costs

Most comprehensive general liability policies provide a form of insurance in the event of litigation, offering coverage for the policyholder's costs of defending against underlying claims. This coverage aids the policyholder even if the allegations of the underlying action are "groundless, false or fraudulent."[46] For example, the standard-form language in use for half-a-century provides that the insurer shall have the "right" and the "duty" to

> defend any suit against the insured seeking damages . . . even if any of the allegations of the suit are groundless, false or fraudulent . . . but the company shall not be obligated to pay any claim or judgment or to defend any suit after the applicable limit of the company's liability has been exhausted by payment of judgments or settlements.[47]

Subsequent standardized policies share language that is largely similar in substance even if somewhat different in wording.

---

43. *Id.* at 105.

44. *Id.* at 107. What other successes carriers have had in the past rest on a shaky foundation. The carrier arguments have been built on two federal appellate decisions predicting that state law would hold response costs outside the term "damages," both of which were subsequently rejected by the relevant state supreme court. *See* Cont'l Ins. Cos. v. N.E. Pharm. & Chem. Co. (NEPACCO), 842 F.2d 977, 985 (8th Cir. 1988) (predicting Missouri law), *cert. denied*, 488 U.S. 821 (1988), *rejected by* Farmland Ind., Inc. v. Republic Ins. Co., 941 S.W.2d 505 (Mo. 1997); Md. Cas. Co. v. Armco, Inc., 822 F.2d 1348, 1350 (4th Cir. 1987) (predicting Maryland law), *cert. denied*, 484 U.S. 1008 (1988), *rejected by* Bausch & Lomb, Inc. v. Utica Mut. Ins. Co., 625 A.2d 1021, 1032–33 (Md. 1993). Based on *NEPACCO* and *Armco*, carriers initially achieved some success at the trial court level and before the Wisconsin Supreme Court. *See, e.g.,* City of Edgerton v. Gen. Cas. Co., 517 N.W.2d 463 (Wis. 1994), *overruled by* Johnson Controls v. Emp'rs Ins. of Wausau, 665 N.W.2d 257 (Wis. 2003); Cent. Me. Power Co. v. Moore, 1995 WL 18022853 (Me. Super. Ct. Dec. 13, 1995) (applying Maine law). Following the rulings by the Missouri and Maryland Supreme Courts (and the subsequent reversal by the Wisconsin Supreme Court), however, such successes are unlikely to be repeated.

45. *Compare* A.Y. McDonald Indus. v. Ins. Co. of N. Am., 475 N.W.2d 607, 624 (Iowa 1991) (response costs for preventive measures are covered if incurred after pollution has taken place, but not before), *with* Braswell v. Faircloth, 387 S.E.2d 707, 710 (S.C. Ct. App. 1989) (costs of purely preventive measures not covered).

46. Miller's Standard Insurance Policies Annotated, form GL 00 01 01 73 at 421.7.

47. *Id.*

The duty to defend generally is held to be a separate and (largely) independent obligation from the insurer's duty to indemnify, namely, its duty to pay claims against the policyholder. An insurer's obligation to provide a defense often, though not always, is outside of the policy's limits, which means that the costs of the defense do not erode the policy limits, and are not otherwise capped at any dollar amount. Where the duty to defend is outside of policy limits in this manner, it can be an extremely valuable element of the coverage provided, in many cases dwarfing the financial value of the duty to indemnify the liability claims themselves. For example, a primary policy may provide coverage up to only $100,000 per occurrence but also feature an unlimited duty to defend under its "supplementary payments" provisions. As a result, the policyholder can collect all its defense costs regardless of their total, in addition to $100,000 against an adverse judgment or settlement. Whether defense is a separate obligation outside of the policy's limits is specifically stated in the policy and should be reviewed carefully.

1. Trigger: Based on the Underlying Allegations

Case law generally holds that the duty to defend is broader than the duty to indemnify. It applies based upon the allegations of the underlying complaint rather than the actual facts, which cannot be determined until the underlying case is tried.[48] The duty to defend is construed liberally: it is activated whenever the underlying complaint alleges facts that, if proven at trial, potentially would bring the claim within the indemnity coverage of the policy.[49]

An insurer's obligation to defend under a policy usually is expressed in terms of defending "the suit," which has at least two important ramifications. First, vis-à-vis its own policyholder with privity of contract, a primary insurer's obligation to defend the suit is not reduced by the presence of other insurers with separate obligations to defend the same suit; insurers usually are held obligated to defend the suit, and not simply to contribute their pro rata share of the costs of defense.[50] Second, many courts hold that where only some of the claims alleged against the policyholder fall within the policy's coverage, the insurer must defend the entire

---

48. *See, e.g.*, Montrose Chem. Corp. v. Super. Ct., 861 P.2d 1153, 1157, 1160 (Cal. 1993). *See also* Hartford Accident & Indem. Co. v. Beaver, 466 F.3d 1289, 1294 (11th Cir. 2006).

49. *See, e.g.*, Emp'rs Ins. of Wausau v. Duplan Corp., 899 F. Supp. 1112, 1115 (S.D.N.Y. 1995) (under New York law, reasonable possibility of covered risk obligates insurers to provide a defense); Am. Bumper & Mfg. Co. v. Hartford Fire Ins. Co., 523 N.W.2d 841, 845 (Mich. Ct. App. 1994) (a duty to defend is owed until the insurer can establish that allegations against its insured are outside the scope of the policy), *aff'd*, 550 N.W.2d 475 (Mich. 1996).

50. *See* TPLC, Inc. v. United Nat'l Ins. Co., 44 F.3d 1484, 1493–94 (10th Cir. 1995); Aerojet-Gen. Corp. v. Transp. Indem. Co., 70 Cal. Rptr. 2d 118, 129–30 (Cal. 1997); Cont'l Cas. Co. v. Rapid-American Corp., 609 N.E.2d 506, 513–14 (N.Y. 1993).

suit even though its duty to indemnify will be limited to only the covered liabilities.[51] Some states, such as California, permit insurers in certain circumstances to seek to recoup the defense costs it paid that it later can prove relate solely to claims that never triggered a duty to defend and are unrelated to potentially covered claims or aspect of loss.[52]

2. The "Suit" Issue: What Is a Suit?

There has been considerable litigation in the environmental context about what, precisely, constitutes a "suit" against which the insurer must provide a defense. For instance, insurance carriers have asserted that state or federal administrative agency proceedings, such as those initiated by the issuance of a PRP letter by the Environmental Protection Agency (EPA), are not the type of "suit" they are contractually obligated to defend. When faced with something other than a lawsuit pending in a court of law, policyholders contend that the term *suit*, at the very least, is ambiguous and reasonably can be understood to include any attempt to impose liability or gain an end through the legal process. A significant majority of cases has found in favor of coverage for a variety of legal processes in a variety of fora, including the Wisconsin Supreme Court's 2003 decision in the case *Johnson Controls, Inc. v. Employers Insurance of Wausau*, which overturned its earlier decision in *City of Edgerton v. General Casualty Co.*[53] Because *City of Edgerton* was one of the leading cases that restrictively interpreted "suit" as limited to proceedings in a court of law and frequently was cited by insurers seeking to deny a duty to

---

51. *See, e.g.*, Blackhawk-Cent. City Sanitation Dist. v. Am. Guar. & Liab. Ins. Co., 214 F.3d 1183, 1189 (10th Cir. 2000) (applying Colorado law); Titan Holdings Syndicate v. City of Keene, 898 F.2d 265, 269 (1st Cir. 1990) (applying New Hampshire law); Gen. Agents Ins. Co. v. Midwest Sporting Goods Co., 828 N.E.2d 1092, 1098 (Ill. 2005); Schultze v. Cont'l Ins. Co., 619 N.W.2d 510, 515 (N.D. 2000); Abrams v. Gen. Star Indem. Co., 67 P.3d 931, 935 (Or. 2003).

52. *See* Buss v. Superior Court, 939 P.2d 766, 776 (Cal. 1997). *But see* Shoshone First Bank v. Pac. Emp'rs Ins. Co., 2 P.3d 510, 517 (Wyo. 2000) (rejecting *Buss*). That an insurance company may be allowed to seek recoupment does not mean that its recoupment efforts will bear fruit. The California Supreme Court's *Buss* decision contains restrictions that are likely to prevent many successful recoupment efforts. *See* Donald R. McMinn, *The Duty to Defend Following* Buss *and* Domtar: *Restrictions on Insurance Carriers' Ability to Avoid Defense Costs through Allocation*, 11-47 MEALEY'S LITIG. REP. INS. 7, at 15–22 (1997); Marc Mayerson, *Recoupment of Defense Costs*, INS. SCRAWL, June 9, 2005, https://perma.cc/7UEE-WRNY.

53. *See* Johnson Controls v. Emp'rs Ins. of Wausau, 665 N.W.2d 257. 263–64 (Wis. 2003), *overruling* City of Edgerton v. Gen. Cas. Co., 517 N.W.2d 463 (Wis. 1994). *See also, e.g.*, Spada v. Unigard Ins. Co., 80 F. App'x 27, 29 (9th Cir. 2003) (directive to stabilize slope on property is a "claim" for "property damage"); Town of Windsor v. Hartford Accident & Indem. Co., 885 F. Supp. 666, 669–70 (D. Vt. 1995) (applying Vermont law to hold communications between a state agency and an insured were sufficiently adversarial to constitute "suit"); Compass Ins. Co. v. City of Littleton, 984 P.2d 606, 615 (Colo. 1999) (PRP letter constituted a suit); R.T. Vanderbilt Co. v. Cont'l Cas. Co., 870 A.2d 1048, 1055 (Conn. 2005) (same); Pac. Emp'rs Ins. Co. v. Servco Pac., Inc., 273 F. Supp. 2d 1149, 1156 (D. Haw. 2003) (state administrative regulatory proceeding seeking environmental remediation constituted a suit); Aetna Cas. & Sur. Co. v. Commonwealth, 179 S.W.3d 830, 837 (Ky. 2005) (EPA administrative process constituted a suit); Preferred Mut. Ins. Co. v. Gordon, 2003 WL 21077026, at *8 (Mass. Super. Ct. May 13, 2003) (notice of responsibility from agency is a suit); Westling Mfg. Co. v. W. Nat'l Mut. Ins. Co., 581 N.W.2d 39, 47 (Minn. Ct. App. 1998) (finding order of Minnesota Pollution Control Agency to be a suit); Carpentier v. Hanover Ins. Co., 670 N.Y.S.2d 540, 542 (App. Div. 1998) (finding state PRP letter to be a suit).

defend, its overruling calls into question other opinions that have relied on that (now-overruled) decision.

Insurers have prominently prevailed, however, in the California and Illinois Supreme Courts in construing *suit* as restricted to court proceedings.[54] In these jurisdictions, the other shoe has dropped (or may drop), because some courts have held that without a suit there can be no duty to indemnify.[55] Specific policy language may be able to overcome this result, however, as in the case of excess policies that often feature a broad definition of *ultimate net loss*.[56]

3. Control of Defense

Policies obligating the insurer to defend its policyholder against suits usually grant the insurer the right to control the defense if the insurer performs. This generally vests in the insurer the power to select defense counsel, experts, and strategy. Ceding control of its own defense to the insurer may not cause the environmental policyholder concern where the insurer is performing fully, has waived objections to its indemnification obligation, and has provided policy limits adequate to resolve any eventual indemnification obligation. In such instances, the financial impact of an inadequate or ineffective defense should fall solely upon the insurer.

Even in such circumstances, however, defense counsel principally owes ethical duties to the policyholder he or she is representing, not the insurer that has selected him or her for retention and is paying his or her fees.[57] That said, the policyholder's role in directing the defense may be significantly constrained by contract.

In some cases, an insurer may decline to acknowledge an unfettered duty to defend and indemnify the insured, typically by issuing a letter purporting to reserve the insurer's right to deny coverage for any number of reasons. In that circumstance, states have taken a variety of approaches to safeguard the interests of an insured who might be disadvantaged by the control exercised by the insurer. Most examine the basis of the underlying allegations and the insurer's reservation

---

54. *See* Foster-Gardner, Inc. v. Nat'l Union Fire Ins. Co., 959 P.2d 265, 267, 274–75 (Cal. 1998) (where insurance policies use both "suit" and "claim," the two cannot be synonymous); Lapham-Hickey Steel Corp. v. Prot. Mut. Ins. Co., 655 N.E.2d 842, 847 (Ill. 1995) ("suit" refers to a proceeding in a court of law; San Diego Unified Port Dist. v. Nat'l Union Fire Ins. Co. of Pittsburgh, 2018 WL 1629742, at *5 (S.D. Cal. Mar. 29, 2018) (differentiating between "suits" and "claims").

55. Certain Underwriters at Lloyd's of London v. Superior Court, 16 P.3d 94, 102 (Cal. 2001); Cnty. of San Diego v. Ace Prop. & Cas. Ins. Co., 131 Cal. Rptr. 2d 100, 105–06 (Ct. App. 2003), *aff'd*, 118 P.3d 607, 609 (Cal. 2005).

56. Powerine Oil Co. v. Superior Court, 128 Cal. Rptr. 2d 827, 843 (Ct. App. 2002) (umbrella policy in Powerine insurance program provided coverage for administrative claims—definition of ultimate net loss was ambiguous as to whether coverage was limited to actions seeking legal damages), *superseded by* 67 P.3d 644 (Cal. 2003), *aff'd*, 118 P.3d 589 (Cal. 2005). *See also* Marc Mayerson, *Grab Your Umbrella— and Magnifying Glass*, INS. SCRAWL (Aug. 30, 2005), https://perma.cc/2TZB-4W8V.

57. While the insured *always* is a client of defense counsel, states disagree as to whether the relationship between the insurer and defense counsel also is one of client and counsel. For a further discussion of this issue, see Charles Silver, *Does Insurance Defense Counsel Represent the Company or the Insured?*, 72 TEX. L. REV. 1583 (1994).

to determine whether a divergence of interest exists between the insurer and the insured with regard to the insured's defense. They examine whether the manner in which the insurer defends the underlying claim could affect its ultimate obligation to provide coverage to the insured. For example, the insurer might be able to avoid its indemnification obligation by strategically choosing to lose the case through its control of the defense on a basis falling outside of coverage. The paradigmatic example is where an insured is alleged to have injured a third party either negligently or intentionally, and negligent conduct is covered, but intentional conduct is not. In such circumstances, a divergence or "conflict" of interest arises because while the insured's interest is to be exonerated of both alternative allegations, the insurer is indifferent if the insured instead is found to have caused the injury intentionally—in either case, the insurer will pay no indemnity.[58]

In such cases, the insurer is said to have a conflict of interest, and most jurisdictions hold that the terms of the insurance contract vesting control of the defense with the insurer cannot be enforced and must yield to the public policy concern of ensuring litigants' counsel has undivided loyalties.[59] Some jurisdictions even go so far as to require insurer-provided defense counsel to alert insureds to their rights in the event of a conflict.[60] A minority of jurisdictions, however, take a minimalist approach that relies on the professionalism of counsel (and the possibility of a legal malpractice suit) and warns the insurer that there is an enhanced

---

58. *See, e.g.*, Thornton v. Paul, 384 N.E.2d 335, 343–44 (Ill. 1978) ("If Illinois Founders would have assumed the defense, it would have had the right to control the defense of the case. Its interest would not necessarily lie in a finding of not guilty, but would have been just as well served by a finding that the defendant was guilty by virtue of having committed a battery upon the plaintiff. In Maryland Cas. Co. v. Peppers (1976), 64 Ill.2d 187, 355 N.E.2d 24, this court noted the serious ethical problem involved in such a situation. . . . [W]hen there is a conflict of interests, as in the present case, the insurer should not be obligated or permitted to participate in the defense of the case. Its obligation to provide a defense should be satisfied by reimbursing the insured for the costs of the defense."), *overruled in part on other grounds,* Am. Fam. Mut. Ins. Co. v. Savickas, 739 N.E.2d 445 (Ill. 2000); Moeller v. Am. Guar. & Liab. Ins. Co., 707 So. 2d 1062, 1070 (Miss. 1996) ("When an attorney is offered employment by an insurance carrier, he should first ascertain if there is any reason there might be a conflict in representing the carrier and the insured. Is the carrier defending under a reservation of rights? Is the amount sued for in excess of the policy limits? Is it possible that a portion of the claim may be covered, and another not, or that the policy covers one theory of liability, but not another one? If so, he should undertake to represent only the interest of the insurance carrier for the part covered, and the insurance carrier should afford the insured ample opportunity to select his own independent counsel to look after his interest.").

59. *See* State Farm Mut. Auto. Ins. Co. v. Hansen, 357 P.3d 338 (Nev. 2015); N. Cnty. Mut. Ins. Co. v. Davalos, 140 S.W.3d 685, 689 (Tex. 2004); CHI of Alaska, Inc. v. Emp'rs Reins. Corp., 844 P.2d 1113, 1117 n.8 (Alaska 1993) (stating "prevailing view" and collecting cases). *See also, e.g.,* Howard v. Russell Stover Candies, Inc., 649 F.2d 620, 625 (8th Cir. 1981) (insurer may provide independent attorney or pay costs of insured's chosen counsel); San Diego Navy Fed. Credit Union v. Cumis Ins. Soc'y, Inc., 162 Cal. App. 3d 358, 371–72 (Ct. App. 1984), *superseded by* Cal. Civ. Code § 2860; *Thornton*, 384 N.E.2d at 348 (insurer facing conflict must reimburse insured's defense costs rather than control the defense).

60. *See, e.g.,* Fla. Bar Rules of Prof'l Conduct R. 4-1.8(j), available at 2002 WL 716773; *see also In re Rules of Prof'l Conduct & Insurer Imposed Billing Rules and Procedures,* 2 P.3d 806, 822 (Mt. 2000).

duty of good faith requiring the insurer not to interfere in defense counsel's strategic and tactical decisions.[61]

Significantly, where the insurer and insured disagree as to defense strategy but there are no coverage implications inherent in the disagreement, there is no "conflict" for counsel, and the insurer generally retains the power to control the defense subject only to general contractual doctrines requiring it to act in good faith and not frustrate the insured's reasonable expectations from the benefit of its bargain. Similarly, a disagreement over coverage that has no relevance to facts or issues involved in the defense of the action at issue does not necessarily divest the insurer of control.[62]

4. Investigative and Oversight Costs: Loss (Indemnity) or Expense (Defense)?

Liability insurance policies typically do not define *defense cost*, and this lack of a definition leads to numerous opportunities for disagreement over which amounts are covered. The only words used in the policy are *duty to defend*, *investigation*, and *expense*, all of which are to be contrasted with third-party *damages* for which the insured is liable, which are covered under the duty to indemnify.

The question whether a cost falls within a policy's defense or indemnity coverage is particularly trenchant in the environmental context. When the government initiates remedial activity at a site, a PRP may face both an administrative action focusing on cleanup efforts and a court action seeking recovery of response costs and the establishment of legal liability. Complex sites often are resolved only after years of studies and reports generated by consultants for the government and the PRP. In such complex environmental cases, the efforts by experts, consultants, and environmental engineers may be every bit as essential to the policyholder's defense against the environmental claim as the work of its defense lawyers. When the costs of the environmental consultants and experts are substantial, and the defense obligation unlimited, insurers may dispute that some or all of those costs are "expenses" covered by their duty to defend and investigate. They may contend that such costs are "damages" payable, if at all, under the duty to indemnify. Sorting out which efforts in an environmental case are defensive in nature may be somewhat more complicated than in an ordinary case, but the applicable principles are the same.

---

61. *See, e.g.,* L & S Roofing Supply, Inc. v. St. Paul Fire, 521 So. 2d 1298, 1303–04 (Ala. 1987); Finley v. Home Ins. Co., 975 P.2d 1145, 1156 (Haw. 1998); Ferguson v. Birmingham Fire Ins. Co., 460 P.2d 342, 349 (Or. 1969); St. Paul Fire & Marine Ins. Co. v. Engelmann, 639 N.W.2d 192, 201 (S.D. 2002); Tank v. State Farm Fire & Cas. Co., 715 P.2d 1133, 1137–38 (Wash. 1986).

62. *See, e.g.,* Twin City Fire Ins. Co. v. Ben-Arnold Sunbelt Beverage Co. of S.C., 433 F.3d 365, 374 (4th Cir. 2005) (reservation of rights alone is not sufficient to create a conflict of interest entitling policyholder to choose counsel); Armstrong Cleaners Inc. v. Erie Ins. Grp., 364 F. Supp. 2d 797, 807 (S.D. Ind. 2005) (same).

Investigation is the first thing any defense counsel does in formulating the defense strategy and planning for the presentation of evidence to support the insured's case. Under their plain language, standard-form general liability policies expressly include, within the duty to defend, amounts incurred pursuing "investigation" that is "expedient."[63] Courts, as a matter of course, find that costs of investigation are recoverable defense expenses. As a Michigan appellate court explained, "The duty to defend necessarily includes any investigation necessary and proper in preparing a defense, for absent such investigation the defense of [the suit] . . . will be seriously impaired."[64]

In environmental cases, the insured's consultants may perform studies showing that the conditions at a site have not produced injury (e.g., if the level of contaminants is found to be below regulatory thresholds), or are not so serious as to warrant remedial action or the degree of remedial action contemplated by the government. A consultant's work also may support the insured's argument for a different and cheaper remedy than what the government proposes. The cost of these types of studies should be payable as a covered defense expense.[65]

In the environmental context, courts generally have tried to draw a line between the costs of investigation and the costs of developing or implementing the remedy actually adopted.[66] Some courts have found that investigative studies in connection with performing the selected remedy fall under the duty to indemnify, not defend, while other courts have held that all costs of investigation are defensive in nature regardless of their precise purpose.[67] To maximize the likelihood of recovery, policyholders should, where feasible, emphasize a study's investigative nature, and its potential to reduce the policyholder's potential liability or costs, even if the study also serves the dual purpose of assisting the implementation of

---

63. MILLER'S STANDARD INSURANCE POLICIES ANNOTATED, form GL 00 02 01 73 at 421.5.

64. Cooley v. Mid-Century Ins. Co., 218 N.W.2d 103, 105 (Mich. Ct. App. 1974). *See also* Ballard v. Citizen's Cas. Co., 196 F.2d 96, 102 (7th Cir. 1952); Ins. Co. of N. Am. v. Am. Home Assurance Co., 391 F. Supp. 1097, 1100 (D. Colo. 1975); Hertzka & Knowles v. Salter, 6 Cal. App. 3d 325, 336 (Ct. App. 1970).

65. As explained in one environmental treatise:

> While not strictly a defense to liability, a defendant may seek to avoid its exposure to injunctive relief under section 106 by demonstrating that the government's proposed remedy is unnecessary or unjustified to abate the risk presented by a particular site. The variations on this argument include showing that the relief is not "necessary to abate (the) damage or threat" at the site, that the remedy is improper because of inconsistency with the section 121 clean-up standards or the [National Oil and Hazardous Substances Pollution Contingency Plan (NCP)] or that the proposed remedy will be ineffective, unfeasible, or impractical (*e.g.*, due to technical, economic, or logistical reasons).

Christopher P. Davis, *Liability under CERCLA for Cleanup of Hazardous Waste, in* THE LAW OF HAZARDOUS WASTE MANAGEMENT, CLEANUP, LIABILITY, AND LITIGATION § 14.02[6][k], at 14-254 (S. Cooke ed. 1990). *Cf.* United States v. Hardage, 663 F. Supp. 1280 (W.D. Okla. 1987); Lone Pine Steering Comm. v. EPA, 600 F. Supp. 1487, 1498–99 (D.N.J. 1985), *aff'd*, 777 F.2d 882 (3d Cir. 1985); United States v. Vertac Chem. Corp., 588 F. Supp. 1294, 1297 (E.D. Ark. 1984).

66. An example of a comprehensive judicial treatment of this question is found in Fireman's Fund Ins. Cos. v. Ex-Cell-O Corp., 790 F. Supp. 1322, 1333–39 (E.D. Mich. 1992). *See also* New York v. Blank, 745 F. Supp. 841, 852 (N.D.N.Y. 1990); Gen. Accident Ins. Co. of Am. v. State Dep't of Envtl. Prot., 672 A.2d 1154, 1162 (N.J. 1996).

67. *See, e.g.*, Aerojet-General Corp., 17 Cal. 4th at 62–66.

a remedy. Regardless, a policyholder's claim for defense costs in environmental cases should presumptively include the costs of the consultants and engineers who conduct the site investigation.[68]

5. The Reasonableness Limitation on the Defense Obligation

An insurer's duty to defend generally is limited to incurring or paying only those defense costs that are "reasonable." Where the insurer is not in control of the defense, but rather is funding the defense directed by the policyholder—or where the insurer has denied coverage, but has been ordered to pay damages for breach of the duty to defend—the insurer typically will engage in thorough oversight, and even formal audits, of defense invoices, in an effort to weed out those expenses it deems unnecessary or unreasonable. However, some courts have cast a questioning eye toward insurer efforts to reduce their defense obligations through aggressive audits.[69]

Insurers in disputes over the reasonableness of the insured's defense costs also sometimes question whether the insured has selected appropriate counsel. The insurer might argue, for example, that "big firm" counsel is not required. If the nature of the case reasonably requires such counsel, courts ordinarily defer to the insured's selection of its defense team and find that the associated costs are recoverable.[70] The complex nature of environmental claims and the sophisticated scientific evidence involved in litigating such claims provides fertile opportunity to contend that experienced counsel is required.

---

68. Defense and supplementary payments coverage may apply to government-imposed costs in the context of CERCLA actions. For example, under CERCLA section 104, 42 U.S.C. § 9604(b)(1) (2000 & Supp. 2005), EPA is authorized to assess "planning, legal, fiscal, economic, engineering, architectural and other studies or investigations . . . to plan and direct response actions." Costs imposed on an insured under this taxation-of-costs statute should be recoverable supplementary payments. *See* Argento v. Vill. of Melrose Park, 838 F.2d 1483, 1489 (7th Cir. 1988).

69. Note that most policies contain a contractual limitation on the right of the insurer to audit the insured's records. The "Inspection and Audit" provision of the standard CGL policy states: "The [insurance] company may examine and audit the named insured's books and records at any time during the policy period and extensions thereof and within three years after the final termination of this policy, as far as they relate to the subject matter of this insurance." Miller's Standard Insurance Policies Annotated, form GL 00 02 01 73 at 421.3. The contractual limitation, and the attendant risk the insurer has assumed concerning the quality of the insured's records that may exist after the expiration of the policy's document retention, arguably lessens the insured's burden of production of evidence establishing its contract damages for coverage claims pursued years after the policy's expiration.

70. One decision rebuffing a carrier's efforts to reduce counsel rates is Continental Corp. v. Aetna Cas. & Sur. Co., No. 85-C-1165, 1987 U.S. Dist. LEXIS 16133 (E.D. Wis. Oct. 30, 1987). In that case, Aetna refused to pay the full rates charged by the defense attorneys because they "were higher than the usual and customary rates for insurance defense work in the Milwaukee area." *Id.* at *17. The court dismissed the objection because the underlying litigation was a complex fraud case, including a RICO claim, alleging millions of dollars of liability. *Id.* at 20. *See also* Oscar W. Larson Co. v. United Capitol Ins. Co., 845 F. Supp. 458, 462–63 (W.D. Mich. 1993). Some unique questions arise on this issue concerning the application of California law, particularly the so-called *Cumis* statute, which requires an insurer to pay only "the rates which are actually paid by the insurer to attorneys retained by it in the ordinary course of business in the defense of similar actions in the community where the claim arose or is being defended." Cal. Civ. Code Ann. § 2860(c) (Deering 2008). *See also* Nat'l Union Fire Ins. Co. v. Hilton Hotels Corp., 1991 WL 405182, at *3 (N.D. Cal. May 6, 1991).

Courts ordinarily defer to counsel's and the insured's determination of the scope of the defense effort required in a given case; courts are highly reluctant to second-guess a decision to pursue a line of inquiry that was thought to hold promise in the defense of the action.[71] For the same reasons, if the complexity and size of a litigation reasonably warrant it, for example in the case of a mass tort, the insurer generally will be obligated to pay for local as well as national coordinating defense counsel, and, where appropriate, "generic" defense efforts applicable to a number of claims.[72] Courts are especially deferential when a case presents unusual factual or scientific complexities or a substantial amount of potential damages, particularly with "bet the company" stakes.[73] In the appropriate case, all these costs may be recoverable as reasonably foreseeable damages flowing from an insurer's breach of its duty to defend.

6. Coverage for In-House "in Lieu of" Defense Costs

When an insured has in-house counsel participate in a case, or draws upon its own resources in developing evidence for the defense of the case, at least some of the associated costs to the company may be recoverable under liability insurance policies. The question for coverage purposes is what portion of in-house counsel's efforts reflect ordinary business oversight of the matter (which generally is not recoverable), as opposed to defense work that otherwise would be performed by outside consultants or counsels (which is recoverable).

The courts have recognized that "where an insured . . . assigns an already hired employee to defend, it has incurred an expense just as surely as if it had hired outside counsel."[74] As the Third Circuit explained:

> If [the insured's in-house] attorneys had refrained from activity, the workload and consequently the fee of [outside counsel] would have been increased. There is

---

71. *See, e.g., Ex-Cell-O Corp.*, 790 F. Supp. at 1345–46.

72. *See* Jostens, Inc. v. Cont'l Cas. Co., 403 N.W.2d 625, 631 (Minn. 1987), *overruled on other grounds by* N. States Power Co. v. Fid. & Cas. Co., 523 N.W.2d 657, 664 (Minn. 1994). As to the appropriateness of the fees charged by someone whose work would otherwise be a reasonable part of the defense, the courts generally defer to the rates actually charged, but, as part of a determination of the appropriateness of the fee, may inquire into (1) the education and professional experience of the provider; (2) the skill, time, and labor required; (3) the amount at issue in the litigation; (4) the difficulty and complexity of the case; (5) the nature and length of the professional relationship with the client-insured; and (6) whether the fees charged by the provider were similar to those charged in similar professional relationships with its clients in similar matters. *See also Oscar W. Larson Co.*, 845 F. Supp. at 458; *Cont'l Corp.*, 1987 U.S. Dist. LEXIS 16133; Aetna Cas. & Sur. Co. v. Pitrolo, 342 S.E.2d 156 (W. Va. 1986).

73. As one court put it, "[t]here are wide parameters of reasonableness within which lawyers can exercise professional judgment about which tactics, strategies, and efforts are needed to defend a client. If, after refusing to provid[e] a defense, an insurance carrier wishes to second-guess the judgment of the defense counsel that was retained by the insured, it is the insurer's burden to demonstrate that the service provided was outside the parameters of this wide range of reasonable professional assistance." *Ex-Cell-O Corp.*, 790 F. Supp. at 1346.

74. Travelers Ins. Co. v. State Ins. Fund, 588 N.Y.S.2d 973, 975 (Ct. Cl. 1992).

no reason in law or in equity why the insurer should benefit from [the insured's] choice to proceed with some of the work through its own legal department.[75]

Courts have permitted insureds to recover this type of "in lieu of" expense even under policies containing a definition of covered *costs* that expressly carves out salaries of the insured's employees.[76]

While such in-house costs are recoverable, it may be difficult to prove which costs are recoverable "in lieu of" litigation costs, and which are nonrecoverable general oversight or other business expenses. To aid in establishing the amount of recoverable in-house defense costs, it is helpful to document that in-house counsel's ordinary responsibilities are being expanded or that resources are being diverted by the litigation. The actual time or other measure of effort devoted to defense by in-house personnel also should be documented.

7. Coverage of the Costs Associated with Affirmative Claims

Insurers sometimes contend that a policyholder's so-called "offense" costs are not covered by the duty to defend. Thus, an insurer may argue that the policyholder's costs of pursuing counterclaims, cross-claims, third-party claims, or independent actions are outside of coverage. No exclusion creates this gap in the insured's coverage; rather, insurers rest entirely on the policy's use of the word *defend* in the insuring agreement, which, as the Washington Supreme Court observed, is an "odd place to look for exclusions of coverage."[77]

An insured should be able to seek the costs of affirmative claims that are "part of the same dispute and were advanced to defeat or offset liability."[78] Such claims should be covered if the insured would later be barred under principles of res judicata from seeking setoff or contribution, thus potentially impairing the insurer's subrogation claims against that party. Similarly, coverage should be afforded if the insured initiates an independent action against other parties in an effort to reduce the amount of its ultimate liability. Nevertheless, the courts are not uniform in their treatment of this issue.[79] For example, the Massachusetts Supreme Judicial Court ruled that a counterclaim was not within the insurer's obligations to pay defense costs.[80]

---

75. Pittsburgh Plate Glass Co. v. Fid. & Cas. Co., 281 F.2d 538, 542 (3d Cir. 1960).

76. *See, e.g.*, V. Van Dyke Trucking, Inc. v. Seven Provinces Ins., Ltd., 406 P.2d 584, 589 (Wash. 1965). *See also* Cont'l Cas. Co. v. Pittsburgh Corning Corp., 917 F.2d 297, 299–301 (7th Cir. 1990).

77. Boeing Co. v. Aetna Cas. & Sur. Co., 784 P.2d 507, 511 (Wash. 1990).

78. Safeguard Scis., Inc. v. Liberty Mut. Ins. Co., 766 F. Supp. 324, 333–34 (E.D. Pa. 1991), *aff'd in part, rev'd in part without opinion*, 961 F.2d 209 (3d Cir. 1992); *see also* Great W. Cas. Co. v. Marathon Oil Co., 315 F. Supp. 2d 879, 882 (N.D. Ill. 2003); *Oscar W. Larson Co.*, 845 F. Supp. at 461, *aff'd*, 64 F.3d 1010 (6th Cir. 1995); Citadel Holding Corp. v. Roven, 603 A.2d 818, 824 (Del. 1992).

79. Decisions expressing a less expansive view of the recoverability of the cost of prosecuting affirmative claims include Scottsdale Ins. Co. v. Homestead Land Dev. Corp., 1992 WL 453356, at *7 (N.D. Cal. Dec. 3, 1992), and Silva & Hill Constr. Co. v. Emp'rs Mut. Liab. Ins. Co., 97 Cal. Rptr. 498, 506 (Ct. App. 1971).

80. Mount Vernon Fire Ins. Co. v. VisionAid, Inc., 477 Mass. 343 (2017).

This issue is particularly important in the environmental context, given the statutory scheme established by CERCLA of imposing joint and several liability and providing for an apportionment among the PRPs through Sections 107(a)(4) and 113(f) contribution and private cost recovery actions.[81] At least one court has expressly held that the costs of contribution claims under Section 113(f) are defensive in nature, and thus included within an insurer's duty to defend.[82] Insurance also may be the only source from which to recover legal fees incurred in pursuing contribution from other PRPs, as the Supreme Court has held that such litigation expenses may not be recovered from the other PRPs in a Section 113(f) action because such costs are not "necessary costs of response" under CERCLA.[83]

D. Additional Issues Raised by Occurrence-Based General Liability Policies

1. Notice: Involving the Insurer

Standard-form general liability policies include in the "Conditions" section an obligation to provide notice to the insurer of an occurrence or a claim.[84] Until the insurer has notice of a triggering event, it cannot come to the assistance of its insured. Moreover, it is prudent for policyholders to have procedures in place to provide prompt notice under any and all policies that even arguably may respond to the event. When the policyholder did not notify the insurer seasonably, the insurer might argue that coverage has been forfeited in whole or in part.

a. Notice and Occurrence-Based Policies

Most occurrence-based general liability policies require the policyholder to satisfy two separate notice obligations: notice of occurrence and notice of claim.[85] Providing notice of an occurrence means informing the insurer of events that are likely to give rise to claims under the policy. Notice of occurrence typically is to be given "as soon as practicable,"[86] or some other variant of "a reasonable time."[87] The notice-of-claim provision applies when actual claims or suits are asserted against

---

81. CERCLA §§ 107(a)(4), 113(f), 42 U.S.C. §§ 9607(a)(4), 9613(f) (2000 & Supp. 2002).

82. Emhart Indus. v. Home Ins. Co., 2006 WL 2460908, at *2 (D. R.I. Aug. 2, 2006) ("In view of CERCLA's statutory liability/contribution scheme, this Court concludes that Emhart's pursuit of other PRPs is defensive in nature and the costs of such pursuit are recoverable if a duty to defend is established.").

83. Key Tronic Corp. v. United States, 114 S. Ct. 1960, 1967–68 (1994).

84. MILLER'S STANDARD INSURANCE POLICIES ANNOTATED, form GL 00 02 01 73 at 421.3–4.

85. *See generally* Marc S. Mayerson, *Perfecting and Pursuing Liability Insurance Coverage*, 32 TORT & INS. L.J. 1003 (1997).

86. *See* MILLER'S STANDARD INSURANCE POLICIES ANNOTATED, form GL 00 00 01 73 at 421.4. *See also, e.g.*, CPC Int'l, Inc. v. Aerojet-General Corp., 825 F. Supp. 795 (W.D. Mich. 1993).

87. *See, e.g.*, Am. Motorists Ins. Co. v. Gen. Host Corp., 919 F. Supp. 1506, 1510 (D. Kan. 1996) (applying New York law); Am. States Ins. Co. v. Hanson Indus., 873 F. Supp. 17, 27 (S.D. Tex. 1995) (applying Texas law).

and known by the policyholder, in which case policyholders generally are required by the policies to forward the claim or suit papers to the insurer "immediately."[88]

Insurance companies deny coverage on the grounds that the policyholder failed to provide timely notice of occurrence, claim, or suit. State laws vary on whether forfeiture of coverage automatically follows. Most courts consider factual issues in determining whether notice was timely or reasonable in the circumstances, including the reason for any delay in giving notice, the length of the delay, and the stage of the proceedings at which notice finally is given.[89]

Once the insurer has established that the insured's notice was contractually deficient, the majority of states hold that a policyholder's failure to give prompt notice does not automatically result in a forfeiture of policy benefits unless the insurer also can demonstrate actual and substantial prejudice resulting from the lack of prompt notice.[90] Policyholders often point to an insurer's denial of coverage on substantive grounds other than notice to contend that the insurer was not prejudiced by the late notice, arguing that the insurer would have denied coverage even if the notice had been timely.[91] The insured should be aware of the differences between primary and excess coverage; because excess insurers typically do not have the defense obligation of primary insurers, they "are not as likely as primary insurers to suffer harm from late notice and more typically call for notification only once it appears a particular claim will likely involve monies sufficient to implicate its coverage."[92]

Some states, like Arkansas, have held that a primary insurer is not required to demonstrate prejudice in order to prevail on a late-notice claim, but a recent Texas Supreme Court decision shows that this is the minority view.[93] Courts in these states find the notice requirement to be a contractual condition precedent for coverage rather than a contractual covenant. Consequently, they hold that the

---

88. *See* MILLER'S STANDARD INSURANCE POLICIES ANNOTATED, form GL 00 00 01 73 at 421.4. Policyholders should consult their policies for applicable notice provisions. Insurance policies sometimes specify, for example, that the obligation to give notice arises when an occurrence or a claim comes to the attention of a corporate office or a member of the risk management department. Other policies may contain definite notice periods, such as a specific number of days. *See* Matador Petrol. Corp. v. St. Paul Surplus Lines Ins. Co., No. 396-CV-1697, 1998 WL 59493 (N.D. Tex. Feb. 6, 1998) (denying coverage where insured failed to abide by 30-day notice provision), *aff'd*, 174 F.3d 653, 657–58 (5th Cir. 1999).

89. *Compare* Emp'rs Ins. of Wausau v. Tektronix, Inc., 156 P.3d 105, 111–15 (Or. Ct. App. 2007) (12-year delay not per se unreasonable), *with* Fireman's Fund Ins. Co. v. Care Mgmt., Inc., 361 S.W.3d 800 (Ark. 2010).

90. *See, e.g.*, Arrowood Indem. Co. v. King, 39 A.3d 712, 726–27 (Conn. 2012) ("[T]he insurer bears the burden of proving, by a preponderance of evidence, that it has been prejudiced by the insured's failure to comply with a notice provision."); Invensys Sys., Inc. v. Centennial Ins. Co., 473 F. Supp. 2d 211, 217–18 (D. Mass. 2007) (no presumption of prejudice even where delayed notice is "extreme"); Aetna Cas. & Sur. Co. v. Dow Chem. Co., 10 F. Supp. 2d 800, 808, 810 (E.D. Mich. 1998) (same).

91. Helman v. Hartford Fire Ins. Co., 664 N.E.2d 991, 995–96 (Ohio Ct. App. 1995).

92. *Invensys Sys., Inc.*, 473 F. Supp. 2d at 219–20; Harbor Ins. Co. v. Trammel Crow Co., 854 F.2d 94 (5th Cir. 1998).

93. *See* PAJ, Inc. v. Hanover Ins. Co., 243 S.W.3d 630, 634 (Tex. 2008).

mere fact that the policyholder has failed to give prompt notice is sufficient to bar recovery, even without the insurer being harmed from the late notice in any way.[94]

b. Coverage of Prenotice Defense Costs

Even if a policyholder gives timely notice of an occurrence or claim, insurers often refuse to pay any of the defense costs that were incurred prior to notice. The arguments against coverage have been: (1) that an insurance carrier's duty to defend does not arise until it receives notice such that prenotice defense costs are outside the scope of the policy's defense provision; and (2) that prenotice defense costs are voluntarily undertaken by policyholders, and thus are barred by the standard-form policy's "voluntary payments" provision.[95] While some courts accept these arguments, others find that prenotice defense costs are recoverable, unless the insurer can show it actually was substantially prejudiced by the incurrence of such costs prior to notice.[96] At all events, the risk of forfeiting those expenses incurred before the insurer was notified illustrates the importance of considering potential insurance recovery any time an environmental matter targets or potentially implicates a particular policyholder.

2. Scope/Allocation

Where an occurrence triggers multiple policies, such as continuous, long-term pollution over a period of years, the question arises as to how much of the attendant loss each triggered policy must pay (e.g., what is the scope of the

---

94. *See* Country Mut. Ins. Co. v. Livorsi Marine, Inc., 856 N.E.2d 338, 346 (Ill. 2006); Sec. Mut. Ins. Co. v. Acker-Fitzsimons Corp., 293 N.E.2d 76, 78 (N.Y. 1972).

95. *See* discussion *infra* section II.D.3. *Compare* Rent-A-Roofer, Inc. v. Farm Bureau Prop. & Cas. Ins. Co., 869 N.W.2d 99 (Neb. 2015), *with* Domtar, Inc. v. Niagara Fire Ins. Co., 563 N.W.2d 724, 739 (Minn. 1997) (finding no coverage for prenotice defense costs even where policyholder's delay was caused by its diligent investigation of its coverage program and it provided notice at the earliest practical date). Some carriers have argued that no defense obligation is owed until the defense is "tendered" to the carrier, that is, until the insured specifically requests the carrier to provide a defense, suggesting some formal action that the insured must take, beyond simple notice, before the defense obligation attaches. Several courts have held that the provision of notice is sufficient to "tender" the duty to defend; no magic words are required. *See, e.g.*, Cincinnati Cos. v. W. Am. Ins. Co., 701 N.E.2d 499, 504 (Ill. 1998) (notice sufficient unless insured has knowingly forgone insurer's involvement; if unclear, burden on insurer to clarify whether noticing insured desires defense); Home Ins. Co. v. Nat'l Union Fire Ins., 658 N.W.2d 522, 532–33 (Minn. 2003). *But see* Ingalls Shipbuilding v. Fed. Ins. Co., 410 F.3d 214, 227 (5th Cir. 2005) (finding it "absurd to require an insurance company to force itself on such a sophisticated party [as a corporate insured] if its services have not been requested"); Unigard Ins. Co. v. Leven, 983 P.2d 1155, 1160 (Wash. Ct. App. 1999) ("insured must affirmatively inform the insurer that its participation is desired"); Towne Realty, Inc. v. Zurich Ins. Co., 548 N.W.2d 64, 68 (Wis. 1996) (finding tender of defense was condition precedent to a duty to defend).

96. *See, e.g.*, TPLC, Inc. v. United Nat'l Ins. Co., 44 F.3d 1484, 1488 (10th Cir. 1995) (finding prenotice defense costs covered where carrier failed to prove substantial prejudice); Sherwood Brands, Inc. v. Hartford Accident & Indem. Co., 698 A.2d 1078, 1083–84 (Md. 1997) (duty to defend arises when policyholder is sued, not when it gives notice); Roberts Oil Co. v. Transamerica Ins. Co., 833 P.2d 222, 230–31 (N.M. 1992) (voluntary payments provision bars coverage only upon a showing of substantial prejudice); Griffin v. Allstate Ins. Co., 29 P.3d 777, 779–81 (Wash. Ct. App. 2001) (unless the insurer is prejudiced by the absence of notice, it "is liable for fees and costs incurred before the insured tenders defense of a covered claim"), *op. modified*, 36 P.3d 552 (2001).

coverage provided). Scope of coverage often is referred to as a question of allocation because the loss may be said to be allocated across the block of triggered policies. Allocation principles are in flux, with approaches differing considerably from state to state.[97] The financial consequences to policyholders from the adoption of one rule or another can be quite dramatic.

There are two primary positions regarding allocation. One position holds that each triggered policy must pay the entire loss up to policy limits, even when part of the injury or property damage occurred in years outside of that policy's coverage. Another position holds that each triggered policy only pays its "fair share" of the loss (an aliquot share measured by time or quantum of damage), leaving the remainder of the loss to be covered by other triggered policies or even by the policyholder itself in years for which no other policy applies (because existing insurance was exhausted, the insurer for the period became insolvent, or the insured either chose not to or was unable to secure coverage during the period). Assigning the entire loss to a single policy or year is known as a vertical or "all sums" allocation, while spreading the loss across multiple policies and years is called horizontal or "pro rata" allocation.

The diversity of approaches all grows from the policy language in the standard-form insuring agreement requiring the insurer to pay "all sums" caused by an occurrence: "[T]he company will pay on behalf of the insured *all sums* which the insured shall become legally obligated to pay as damages because of . . . bodily injury or property damage . . . caused by an occurrence."[98] Policyholders generally contend that the "all sums" language requires insurers to pay all the policyholder's liability, even if some or most of the liability relates to pollution in other policy years, because the extent of the policyholder's liability for damage during any one year equals the entirety of the (indivisible) loss.[99] Insurers generally posit that the "all sums" language must be read in conjunction with the policy's "occurrence" requirement of property damage or injury taking place during the policy period, and argue that only a fraction of the total liability is attributable to the policy year.

The all sums or vertical allocation approach contemplates a two-step allocation process in which: (1) a single insurer (or single year), which is severally and independently liable to the insured, pays the insured's full loss subject to policy limits; and (2) the paying insurer(s) then may seek equitable contribution from

---

97. *See, e.g.*, Bos. Gas Co. v. Century Indem. Co., 910 N.E.2d 290 (Mass. 2009); Olin Corp. v. OneBeacon Am. Ins. Co., 864 F.3d 130 (2d Cir. 2017).

98. Miller's Standard Insurance Policies Annotated, form GL 00 02 01 73 at 421.5.

99. The seminal case first advocating an "all sums" approach was Keene Corp. v. Ins. Co. of N. Am., 667 F.2d 1034, 1048 (D.C. Cir. 1981) ("There is nothing in the policies that provides for a reduction of the insurer's liability if an injury occurs only in part during a policy period."). *See also* Nooter Corp. v. Allianz Underwriters Ins. Co., 536 S.W.3d 251 (Mo. Ct. App. 2017); ACandS, Inc. v. Aetna Cas. & Sur. Co., 764 F.2d 968, 974 (3d Cir. 1985); Hercules, Inc. v. AIU Ins. Co., 784 A.2d 481, 491 (Del. 2001); Zurich Ins. Co. v. Raymark Indus., 514 N.E.2d 150, 165 (Ill. 1987); Allstate Ins. Co. v. Dana Corp., 759 N.E.2d 1049, 1057–58 (Ind. 2001); Goodyear Tire & Rubber Co. v. Aetna Cas. & Sur. Co., 769 N.E.2d 835, 840 (Ohio 2002); J.H. France Refractories v. Allstate Ins. Co., 626 A.2d 502 (Pa. 1993); Century Indem. Co. v. Golden Hills Builders, Inc., 561 S.E.2d 355, 357 (S.C. 2002).

any other insurers that also have several and independent liability to the insured. Thus, the difference between vertical and horizontal allocation may be thought of as whether the allocation among the triggered policies takes place before or after the policyholder is paid, and secures the full measure of protection from the designated insurers. The difference is anything but academic for policyholders, as horizontal or pro rata allocation creates a significant risk that the policyholder may not be able to recover substantial portions of its loss because of insurer insolvency, insurer recalcitrance, or the lack of insurance in certain years within the pro rata allocation block.

Some states, such as New Jersey, apply complicated formulas that allocate the indemnified loss to particular years based on the amount of each triggered year's coverage limits in proportion to the overall amount of coverage available in the coverage period.[100] Other states spread the amounts across time on a straight pro rata basis.[101] Where the trigger period stretches further than the available coverage, some jurisdictions require the policyholder to accept an allocation as if it were the insurer for those uninsured years.[102]

Other jurisdictions look to the reason for the lack of insurance. Loss will not be allocated to the policyholder for years in which insurance was not reasonably available in the marketplace, such as after the advent of the asbestos exclusion in the case of asbestos liability. On the other hand, loss will be allocated to the insured for years in which there is existing coverage that has been exhausted by earlier liabilities or in which the policyholder simply elected to "go bare" by purposefully not purchasing available insurance.[103]

In the environmental context, this approach generally would preclude allocation to the policyholder in triggered years after 1973, when the "qualified" pollution exclusion was added to the standard-form liability policy, or 1986, the advent of the "absolute" pollution exclusion.[104] However, specialty environmental liability policies have since become available, which could affect the allocation calculus

---

100. Carter-Wallace, Inc. v. Admiral Ins. Co., 712 A.2d 1116, 1123–24 (N.J. 1998); OneBeacon Ins. Co. v. Pa. Mfrs.' Ass'n Ins. Co., 73 A.3d 465, 424–25 (N.J. 2013) (applying *Carter-Wallace* to equitable allocation of defense costs).

101. *See, e.g.*, Pub. Serv. Co. of Colo. v. Wallis & Cos., 986 P.2d 924, 929 (Colo. 1999).

102. *See, e.g.*, Ins. Co. of N. Am. v. Forty-Eight Insulations, Inc., 633 F.2d 1212, 1225 (6th Cir. 1980), *clarified*, 657 F.2d 814 (6th Cir. 1981); Maremont Corp. v. Cont'l Cas. Corp., 760 N.E.2d 550, 554 (Ill. App. Ct. 2001); Mayor & City Council of Balt. v. Utica Mut. Ins. Co., 802 A.2d 1070, 1101–02 (Md. Ct. Spec. App. 2002).

103. This is generally known as the "Stonewall" approach after the Second Circuit decision announcing it. *See* Stonewall Ins. Co. v. Asbestos Claims Mgmt. Corp., 73 F.3d 1178, 1203 (2d Cir. 1995) (allocating to insured for years when coverage was exhausted but not years when coverage was unavailable in the insurance market), *op. modified*, 85 F.3d 49 (2d Cir. 1996); Keyspan Gas E. Corp. v. Munich Reinsurance Am., Inc., 2018 WL 1472635 (N.Y. Mar. 27, 2018).

104. *See* discussion *infra* section II.E.2.

under this approach.[105] The issue in the environmental context is likely to be litigated in each state until eventually resolved by the state supreme court.

Where policyholders have prevailed on a vertical allocation approach, the next issue becomes what to do in the event that the insured's liability consumes all the available policy limits for any one year. Insureds tend to argue in favor of "stacking," meaning that after a single year's limits are exhausted, the remaining liability will be paid out of another triggered year's limits. Not surprisingly, insurers oppose arguments for stacking liability limits of successive policy years. Insurers generally have prevailed in precluding policyholders from stacking limits in this manner,[106] although the supreme courts of Louisiana and Pennsylvania expressly have rejected the rationale that finds stacking impermissible.[107]

3. Voluntary Payments

General liability policies typically include language requiring the insurer's consent and approval of any settlements of liability for which coverage will be sought, which allows the insurer to enforce its right to control the defense for which it is paying. The standard-form policy directs that "[t]he insured shall not, except at his own costs, voluntarily make any payment, assume any obligation or incur any expense other than for first aid to others at the time of accident. No costs will be incurred by the [insured] without the written consent of the [insurer]."[108] The purpose of this requirement is "'to ensure that *responsible* insurers that *promptly* accept a defense tendered by their insureds thereby gain control over the defense and settlement of the claim.'"[109] Thus, where the insurer fails to provide a defense, it cannot successfully avoid coverage by arguing that the insured, in its absence, made voluntary payments to defend or settle the underlying claim.[110]

---

105. *See* Olin Corp. v. Ins. Co. of N. Am., 221 F.3d 307, 326 (2d Cir. 2000) (allocating to the policyholder for uninsured years where "EIL [environmental impairment liability] insurance was available to companies like Olin in the marketplace beginning at least in 1980 and . . . Olin did not obtain such insurance.") (internal quotation marks omitted); Champion Dyeing & Finishing Co. v. Centennial Ins. Co., 810 A.2d 68, 72 (N.J. Super. Ct. App. Div. 2002) (carriers must prove availability of EIL coverage for bare periods before allocating to insured; in absence of such proof, liability allocated only to insurers until policies exhausted).

106. *See, e.g., Keene Corp.*, 667 F.2d at 1046–47 (holding that only single policy's limits would apply to each asbestos-related bodily injury claim); *Forty-Eight Insulations, Inc.*, 633 F.2d at 1212 n.28 (same).

107. *See* Cole v. Celotex Corp., 599 So. 2d 1058, 1080 (La. 1992); *J.H. France Refractories*, 626 A.2d at 508–09. California courts of appeals have split on the issue. *Compare* FMC Corp. v. Plaisted & Cos., 72 Cal. Rptr. 2d 467, 501–03 (Cal. Ct. App. 1998) (rejecting stacking of limits), *with* Stonewall Ins. Co. v. City of Palos Verdes Estates, 54 Cal. Rptr. 2d 176, 199 (Ct. App. 1996) (permitting stacking of limits) *and* Emp'rs Ins. of Wausau v. Granite State Ins. Co., 330 F.3d 1214, 1221 (9th Cir. 2003) (reversing antistacking ruling).

108. MILLER'S STANDARD INSURANCE POLICIES ANNOTATED, form GL 00 00 01 73 at 421.4. *See generally* Aerojet-General Corp. v. Commercial Union Ins. Co., 155 Cal. App. 4th 132, 137 (2007).

109. Superpoweraffiliates.com, Inc. v. Transp. Ins. Co., 186 F. App'x 723, 725 (9th Cir. 2006) (quoting Jamestown Builders, Inc. v. Gen. Star Indem. Co., 77 Cal. App. 4th 341, 346 (Ct. App. 1999)).

110. Ingalls Shipbuilding v. Fed. Ins. Co., 410 F.3d 214, 234 n.61 (5th Cir. 2005) (insurer's nonperformance excuses insured from further compliance with policy provisions).

Similarly, where the insured's payment was made as a matter of duress or economic necessity, it will not be deemed to have been voluntarily made.[111] Some recent authority supports requiring the insurer to prove breach and prejudice before denying coverage on voluntary payment grounds.[112] Just as a disagreement over the direction of the defense does not transform defense costs into uncovered voluntary payment,[113] the insurer cannot unreasonably withhold approval of a proposed settlement offer. The insurer, as always, is bound by an implied contractual duty to act in good faith.[114]

The foregoing principles sometimes have not been applied to excess insurance coverage, which in some environmental cases have litigated the contours of their liability for amounts incurred without their consent.

4. Corporate Successorship

Given the long-tail nature of many environmental claims and the fact that CERCLA imposes liability on current site owners and operators regardless of whether they participated in polluting activities, it is often the case that the corporation sued by the government or by other PRPs for environmental contamination is not the entity whose conduct caused the contamination.[115] The liable entity generally will have difficulty recovering under its own policies for the conduct of a predecessor for which it now is responsible, but, as successor, it may be able to access the policies covering its predecessor at the time of the offending conduct. This issue turns on analysis of the corporate transactions through which the current defendant became the successor to the polluter.

Virtually all courts recognize that in the case of a merger, even a de facto merger or a corporate reorganization and asset transfer, the surviving entity may access coverage under the merged corporation's insurance program.[116] Courts also generally recognize a successor's right to access its predecessor's insurance coverage where there has been an actual or implied assignment to the successor of the right to recover under the predecessor's policy for a loss that already occurred prior to the assignment. This assignment often will be part of the corporate acquisition

---

111. Bausch & Lomb, Inc. v. Utica Mut. Ins. Co., 625 A.2d 1021, 1031–32 (Md. 1993) (costs incurred under threat of administrative order or injunction are not voluntary); *Superpoweraffiliates.com*, 186 F. App'x at 724 (reversing summary judgment for trial on factual issue as to whether settlement was "voluntary").

112. Belz v. Clarendon Am. Ins. Co., 158 Cal. App. 4th 615, 625 (Ct. App. 2007); Roberts Oil Co. v. Transamerica Ins. Co., 833 P.2d 222, 229 (N.M. 1992).

113. *See* Universal Underwriters Ins. Co. v. M.F. Salta Co., 215 F. App'x 573, 574 (9th Cir. 2006).

114. *See, e.g.*, N. River Ins. Co. v. Cigna Reins. Co., 52 F.3d 1194, 1210, 1210 n.21 (3d Cir. 1995) (collecting cases interpreting Ohio law); Coastal Iron Works, Inc. v. Petty Ray Geophysical, 783 F.2d 577, 585 (5th Cir. 1986) (where policy requires carrier consent for expenditures, such consent not to be unreasonably withheld); Smart Style Indus. v. Penn. Gen. Ins. Co., 930 F. Supp. 159, 164 (S.D.N.Y. 1996); Bellville v. Farm Mut. Ins. Co., 702 N.W. 2d 468, 483–84 (Iowa 2005).

115. *See* CERCLA § 107(a)(1), 42 U.S.C. § 9607(a)(1) (2000).

116. *See, e.g.*, Westoil Terminals Co. v. Harbor Ins. Co., 86 Cal. Rptr. 2d 636, 640 (Ct. App. 1999) ("a *de facto* merger passes the benefits of the insurance policies of the predecessor entity to the successor entity").

or reorganization itself. The assignment of a preexisting right to recover, unlike an assignment of the policy itself, does not alter the risk borne by the insurer, and courts therefore generally have declined to apply anti-assignment clauses requiring the insurer's consent before such assignments will be upheld.[117]

In the absence of an actual or implied assignment, some corporate successors still seek to recover under their predecessor's policies by asserting that the insurance follows the liability; that is, if the successor is liable for the preacquisition conduct of its predecessor, then the insurance rights transfer to the successor by operation of law. The treatment of this theory in the courts is mixed. Some courts accept this argument, including in the case of environmental liabilities;[118] others reject it outright;[119] and others hold, or at least imply, that the argument may succeed where the successor does not voluntarily assume the predecessor's liability by contract, but rather has it imposed by law or statute, including environmental statutes such as CERCLA.[120] As with other policy provisions, courts should analyze: (1) whether the no-assignment provision applies by its terms; (2) if breached, whether the provision is a covenant or a condition; and thus (3) whether materiality or prejudice needs to be shown.[121]

E. The Pollution Exclusion

In the early 1970s, members of the insurance industry began to include the so-called "sudden and accidental" or "qualified" standard-form pollution exclusion in their general liability policies. This exclusion bars coverage for pollution,

---

117. *See, e.g.*, Cooper Indus. LLC v. Columbia Cas. Co., (N.J. App, Div. Apr. 13, 2018); Gen. Accident Ins. Co. v. Superior Court, 64 Cal. Rptr. 2d 781, 788 (Ct. App. 1997) (remanded for determination of whether rights under policy had been assigned); Greco v. Or. Mut. Fire Ins. Co., 12 Cal. Rptr. 802 (Ct. App. 1961) (choses in action freely assignable without consent of insurer); Ardon Constr. Corp. v. Fireman's Ins. Co., 185 N.Y.S.2d 723, 729 (N.Y. Sup. Ct. 1959) (rights under policy may be assigned postloss). *See also* Straz v. Kan. Bankers Sur. Co., 986 F. Supp. 563, 569 (E.D. Wis. 1997); McLaren v. Imperial Cas. & Indem. Co., 767 F. Supp. 1364, 1377 (N.D. Tex. 1991); Int'l Rediscount Corp. v. Hartford Accident & Indem. Co., 425 F. Supp. 669, 673 (D. Del. 1977); Conrad Bros. v. John Deere Ins. Co., 640 N.W.2d 231, 238 (Iowa 2001); Bolz v. State Farm Mut. Auto. Ins. Co., 52 P.3d 898, 901 (Kan. 2002).

118. *See, e.g.*, B.S.B. Diversified Co. v. Am. Motorists Ins. Co., 947 F. Supp. 1476, 1479 (W.D. Wash. 1996) (predecessor's coverage for pretransaction CERCLA liabilities transfers to successor by operation of law); Total Waste Mgmt. Corp. v. Commercial Union Ins. Co., 857 F. Supp. 140, 151 (D. N.H.1994) (same); Century Indem. Co. v. Marine Grp., LLC, 848 F. Supp. 2d 1238, 1259 (D. Or. 2012) (finding that "benefits of the insurance policies" will flow to corporate successors if the underlying liability flows to successors).

119. *See, e.g.*, *Gen. Accident Ins. Co.*, 64 Cal. Rptr. 2d at 788 ("[A] transfer [of insurance rights] by operation of law is a violation of the basic principles of contract and is also bad public policy"); Red Arrow Prods. Co. v. Emp'rs Ins. of Wausau, 607 N.W.2d 294, 301 (Wis. Ct. App. 2000) (rejecting argument that imposing tort liability by operation of law equates to imposing contract liability by operation of law).

120. *See* Henkel Corp. v. Hartford Accident & Indem. Co., 29 Cal. 4th 934, 942 (2003) (noting that "some statutes, notably [CERCLA], impose liability upon successor corporations without regard to contract."), *overruled and limited on other grounds*, Flour Corp. v. Superior Ct., 61 Cal. 4th 1175 (2015). *See also* Glidden Co. v. Lumbermens Mut. Cas. Co., 861 N.E.2d 109, 115 (Ohio 2006) (denying transfer of predecessor's insurance by operation of law where successor assumed liability by contract).

121. Marc Mayerson, *'Round and 'Round the Tort Liability Goes—When It Stops, Whither the Insurance Chose?*, Ins. Scrawl, Dec. 26, 2006, https://perma.cc/4HW5-8SZZ.

broadly defined, but carves out an exception for releases of pollution that were "sudden and accidental." This provision spawned decades of litigation, which ultimately resulted in little change in the coverage of pollution claims in some jurisdictions and a drastic reduction in such coverage in many others. The industry instituted the so-called "absolute" pollution exclusion in the mid-1980s, which is drafted in broad terms and does not provide any exception for "sudden and accidental" releases.

When an environmental liability matter involves actions or contamination, occurring in part before the mid-1980s, general liability policies containing a qualified pollution exclusion may provide coverage. However, this largely depends on the law of the jurisdiction deemed to govern the exclusion. Policies containing an absolute pollution exclusion almost certainly will not cover such claims and might even be construed to preclude coverage of claims not traditionally considered pollution claims.

I. The "Sudden and Accidental" Pollution Exclusion

The standard-form "sudden and accidental" pollution exclusion that was introduced in the early 1970s provides that coverage does not apply

> to bodily injury or property damage arising out of the discharge, dispersal, release, or escape of smoke, vapors, soot, fumes, acids, alkalis, toxic chemicals, liquids or gases, waste materials or other irritants, contaminants or pollutants into or upon land, the atmosphere or any water course or body of water, but this exclusion does not apply if such discharge, dispersal, release, or escape is sudden and accidental.[122]

A large body of case law interpreting the standard-form "sudden and accidental" pollution exclusion clause has developed.[123] The focus of the litigation has been the exception to the exclusion, which reinstates coverage if the "discharge, dispersal, release, or escape" of pollutants is "sudden and accidental."

Courts disagree over whether the term *sudden* in the exception to the exclusion necessarily has a temporal component, or whether it can be interpreted to mean unexpected and unintended. With a temporal construction, only a release of pollution that occurs quickly and abruptly, such as a catastrophic failure of a storage tank because of an explosion, would remain covered (that is, within the exception to conclusion). Policyholders have been able to demonstrate ambiguity

---

122. MILLER'S STANDARD INSURANCE POLICIES ANNOTATED, form GL 00 02 01 73 at 421.5.

123. In July 1991, the Third Circuit compiled a list of cases holding that the pollution exclusion bars coverage and a list holding the opposite. Although the court did not purport to have compiled an exhaustive list, the two footnotes filled nearly an entire page of the *Federal Reporter*. *See* New Castle Cnty. v. Hartford Accident & Indem. Co., 933 F.2d 1162, 1196 nn.60–61 (3d Cir. 1991) (applying Delaware law and holding that the term "sudden" was ambiguous).

in the term *sudden* based on its polysemy, buttressed through the use of drafting history and other extrinsic evidence.[124]

Courts in a number of jurisdictions have held that *sudden* either in context means unexpected or else does not plainly mean only quick. The effect of these holdings is that the "sudden and accidental" pollution exclusion does not result in a significant decrease in the coverage for unexpected damage afforded under the 1966 standard-form general liability policy.[125] Other jurisdictions, however, hold that *sudden* does plainly include a temporal element and, therefore, that the exclusion bars coverage for pollution taking place over a period of time.[126]

The "sudden and accidental" pollution exclusion arguably should not be given an expansive construction for a different reason: in seeking state regulatory approval of the exclusion, the insurance industry represented to state regulators, and suggested in contemporaneous public statements, that the "sudden and accidental" exclusion barred coverage only in the case of intentional polluters. The Supreme Court of New Jersey applied the doctrine of regulatory estoppel or estoppel in pais to preclude insurers from now contending that the exclusion

---

124. The drafting history of the "sudden and accidental" pollution exclusion, which policyholders have obtained in discovery, supports the policyholder position that the addition of the "sudden and accidental" language in the pollution exclusion was intended as a mere clarification of the "expected or intended" language in the standard-form definition of an "occurrence." *See, e.g., New Castle Cnty.*, 933 F.2d at 1197; Stonewall Ins. Co. v. Nat'l Gypsum Co., No. 86 Civ. 9671, 1992 U.S. Dist. LEXIS 7607, at *65 (S.D.N.Y. May 27, 1992), *aff'd in part, rev'd in part*, 73 F.3d 1178 (2d Cir. 1995), *op. modified*, 85 F.3d 49 (2d Cir. 1996); Ala. Plating Co. v. U.S. Fid. & Guar. Co., 690 So. 2d 331 (Ala. 1996). This conclusion is consistent with the insurance industry's representations to state regulatory agencies when the industry sought approval of the proposed "sudden and accidental" pollution exclusion language in the late 1960s. *See, e.g.,* Queen City Farms, Inc. v. Cent. Nat'l Ins. Co., 882 P.2d 703, 721–23 (Wash. 1994). *See* Marc S. Mayerson, *Affording Coverage for Gradual Property Damage Claims under Standard Liability Insurance Policies: A History*, 8 COVERAGE 3 (Sept./Oct. 1998).

125. *See, e.g.,* CPC Int'l, Inc. v. Northbrook Excess & Surplus Ins. Co., 962 F.2d 77, 97 (1st Cir. 1992); Aetna Cas. & Sur. Co. v. Gen. Dynamics Corp., 968 F.2d 707 (8th Cir. 1992); Harleysville Mut. Ins. Co. v. Sussex Cnty., 831 F. Supp. 1111, 1120 (D. Del. 1993), *aff'd*, 46 F.3d 1116 (3d Cir. 1994); MAPCO Alaska Petrol., Inc. v. Cent. Nat'l Ins. Co., 795 F. Supp. 941 (D. Alaska 1991); *Ala. Plating*, 690 So. 2d at 334; Hecla Mining Co. v. N.H. Ins. Co., 811 P.2d 1083, 1088 (Colo. 1991); Claussen v. Aetna Cas. & Sur. Co., 380 S.E.2d 686, 688 (Ga. 1989); Outboard Marine Corp. v. Liberty Mut. Ins. Co., 607 N.E.2d 1204, 1218 (Ill. 1992); Am. States Ins. Co. v. Kiger, 662 N.E.2d 945, 948 (Ind. 1996); Federated Mut. Ins. Co. v. Auto-Owners Ins. Co., 1995 WL 855426 (Mich. Ct. App. Sept. 8, 1995); St. Paul Fire & Marine Ins. Co. v. McCormick & Baxter Creosoting Co., 923 P.2d 1200, 1218 (Or. 1996); Greenville Cnty. v. Ins. Reserve Fund, 443 S.E.2d 552, 553 (S.C. 1994).

126. *See, e.g.,* Dutton–Lainson Co. v. Cont'l Ins. Co., 716 N.W.2d 87, 97 (Neb. 2006); Demaray v. De Smet Farm Mut. Ins. Co., 801 N.W.2d 284, 289 (S.D. 2011); E. I. du Pont de Nemours & Co. v. Allstate Ins. Co., 693 A.2d 1059, 1061 (Del. 1997) ("sudden" in context has only one meaning—abrupt; the exclusion applies to the initial discharge of pollutants). *See also* Buell Indus., Inc. v. Greater N.Y. Mut. Ins. Co., 791 A.2d 489, 498 (Conn. 2002); Dimmitt Chevrolet, Inc. v. Se. Fid. Ins. Corp., 636 So. 2d 700, 704 (Fla. 1993); Iowa Comprehensive Petrol. Underground Storage Tank Fund Bd. v. Farmland Mut. Ins. Co., 568 N.W.2d 815, 816 (Iowa 1997); Am. Motorists Ins. Co. v. ARTRA Grp., Inc., 659 A.2d 1295, 1306 (Md. 1995); Lumbermens Mut. Cas. Co. v. Belleville Indus., 555 N.E.2d 568, 572 n.4 (Mass. 1990); Bd. of Regents v. Royal Ins. Co., 517 N.W.2d 888, 892 (Minn. 1994); Northville Indus. v. Nat'l Union Fire Ins. Co., 679 N.E.2d 1044, 1048 (N.Y. 1997); Hybud Equip. Corp. v. Sphere Drake Ins. Co., 597 N.E.2d 1096, 1100 (Ohio 1992); Kerr-McGee Corp. v. Admiral Ins. Co., 905 P.2d 760, 764 (Okla. 1995); Sharon Steel Corp. v. Aetna Cas. & Sur. Co., 931 P.2d 127, 134–35 (Utah 1997); Sinclair Oil Corp. v. Republic Ins. Co., 929 P.2d 535, 541 (Wyo. 1996).

has broader application.[127] Other states peg nonenforcement of such exclusions on the ground that they did not comply with or were not approved by the applicable insurance regulations.[128]

For policies containing the "sudden and accidental" pollution exclusion, then, choice of law becomes the single most important issue in determining whether the policies will provide coverage for environmental claims. Policyholders should consider whether to initiate litigation in a strategically selected forum before the insurer does to maximize the likelihood of a favorable choice-of-law outcome.[129]

Similarly, several cases that have addressed the "sudden and accidental" pollution exclusion have focused not only on whether the discharge, dispersal, release, or escape was sudden, but also on whether it was accidental. These courts have stressed that the exception to the pollution exclusion addresses the policyholder's intention with respect to the discharge of hazardous materials, as opposed to the "unintended and unexpected" element in the occurrence definition, which focuses on the policyholder's state of mind with respect to the resulting injury or damage.

This distinction is important in the context of environmental liability, because it is far easier for an insurer to show that the policyholder intended to dispose of waste than to show that the policyholder intended or expected the escape of pollutants into the environment. Thus, even if a policyholder can surmount the "sudden" obstacle to coverage by arguing, for example, that the policy language is ambiguous, the policyholder still may not prevail if the insurer can convince the court that the discharge of pollutants was not accidental.[130]

The Illinois Supreme Court held in favor of policyholders on this issue, ruling that the proper focus was whether the policyholders had intended the pollutants to be released into nearby waters, not whether they had intended to discharge pollutants into a ditch on their own property.[131] Applying the same logic, a number of jurisdictions have held that the pollution exclusion does not apply to property

---

127. *See* Morton Int'l, Inc. v. Gen. Accident Ins. Co. of Am., 629 A.2d 831, 876 (N.J. 1993); Sunbeam Corp. v. Liberty Mut. Ins. Co., 781 A.2d 1189, 1193 (Pa. 2001); *cf.* Festo Corp. v. Shoketsu Kinzoku Kogyo Kabushiki Co, 535 US. 722, 733–36 (2002) (discussing patent-prosecution estoppel or "file wrapper" estoppel).

128. *E.g.*, Cincinnati Specialty Underwriters Ins. Co. v. Energy Wise Homes, Inc., 120 A.3d 1160 (Vt. 2015) (ruling that nonadmitted insurers were not subject to mandatory pollution coverage rules and thus an exclusion could be enforced in a Vermont court).

129. *See* Marc S. Mayerson, *Conflicts of Law and Insurance Disputes: Choice of Law or Choice of Outcomes?*, 5 Ins. Cov. L. Bull. 1 (Oct. 2006).

130. *See* S.C. Ins. Reserve Fund v. E. Richland Cnty. Pub. Serv., 789 S.E.2d 63 (S.C. Ct. App. 2016); Transamerica Ins. Co. v. Duro Bag Mfg. Co., 50 F.3d 370, 373 (6th Cir. 1995) (because the insured deliberately discharged waste over a period of years, it was not entitled to the protection of the "sudden and accidental" exception under Kentucky law); *New Castle Cnty.*, 933 F.2d at 1202–03 (no coverage under Delaware law where evidence showed insured expected landfill to discharge leachate, even if no damage to off-site property was expected); Lumbermens Mut. Cas. Co. v. Belleville Indus., Inc., 938 F.2d 1423, 1430 (1st Cir. 1991) (secondary dispersal of pollutants by natural forces, after initial discharge into environment, cannot be "sudden and accidental"); Standun Inc. v. Fireman's Fund Ins. Co., 73 Cal. Rptr. 2d 116, 121–22 (Ct. App. 1998) (finding that because a landfill is not a containment vessel but is itself land, the disposal of waste into a landfill is the relevant "discharge" under the pollution exclusion).

131. *Outboard Marine Corp.*, 607 N.E.2d at 1222.

damage caused by the release or leaching of pollutants from a landfill into the environment, even though the discharge of pollutants into the landfill was intentional. According to these decisions, the exclusion does not apply to the initial delivery of pollutants to a landfill or other places of expected containment. Thus, when the secondary discharge is sudden and accidental, there is coverage.[132]

This has been referred to, pejoratively by insurers, as the "secondary discharge" analysis and has restricted the application of the pollution exclusion clause. According to these courts, the other words in the exclusion support this conclusion. The terms *discharge*, *dispersal*, *release*, and *escape* are commonly defined, and commonly used, to suggest an escape or release from confinement or a dispersal from a fixed place.[133]

2. The So-Called "Absolute" Pollution Exclusion

In 1985 and 1986, members of the insurance industry modified the standard pollution exclusion language they had adopted in the early 1970s to eliminate the "sudden and accidental" exception (that is, the exception that preserved coverage for certain claims otherwise excluded). Policies containing the "absolute" version of the exclusion effectively provide no coverage for traditional pollution claims involving waste disposal or releases of contaminants during industrial operations.[134]

However, because the exclusion still includes a broad—or, as policyholders contend, overbroad—definition of *pollution* or *pollutant*, an issue remains about how far the absolute pollution exclusion extends. The standard-form absolute pollution exclusion defines pollutants as "any solid, liquid, gaseous or thermal irritant or contaminant, including smoke, vapor, soot, fumes, acids, alkalis, chemicals and

---

132. *See* Bell Lumber & Pole Co. v. U.S. Fire Ins. Co., 60 F.3d 437, 444 (8th Cir. 1995) (the "sudden and accidental" exception did not apply because, under Minnesota law, the "release" refers to the entry of contaminants into the groundwater, not the spillage or disposal of waste); Patz v. St. Paul Fire & Marine Ins. Co., 15 F.3d 699, 704 (7th Cir. 1994) ("The initial placement, although intentional, is not the discharge. The leakage . . . is the discharge. . . ."); Compass Ins. Co. v. City of Littleton, 984 P.2d 606, 610 (Colo. 1999) ("we construe the words 'discharge, dispersal, release or escape' contained in the pollution exclusion clause to refer to the release of pollution from the Lowry Landfill and not the initial disposal of sewage sludge into the landfill"); Sylvester Bros. Dev. Co. v. Great Cent. Ins. Co., 480 N.W.2d 368, 373–74 (Minn. Ct. App. 1992) ("[T]he deposit of pollutants into a landfill cannot be the triggering event; rather, the 'escape' is the critical inquiry for purposes of determining the applicability of the pollution exclusion."). *But see* Quincy Mut. Fire Ins. Co. v. Borough of Bellmawr, 799 A.2d 499, 514 (N.J. 2002) (critical triggering event was dumping of waste into unlined landfill—in contrast to lined landfill—not discharge of contaminants into the environment).

133. *See, e.g.*, Queen City Farms, Inc. v. Cent. Nat'l Ins. Co., 882 P.2d 703, 719 (Wash. 1994) ("We therefore hold that the relevant polluting event is the discharge, dispersal, release, or escape of toxic material into the environment, and where material has been deposited in a place which was believed would contain or safely filter the material, such as a waste disposal pit or sanitary landfill, the polluting event is the discharge, dispersal, release, or escape from that place of containment into or upon the land, the air or water, including groundwater.").

134. Whittier Props., Inc. v. Ala. Nat'l Ins. Co., 185 P.3d 84, 89–92 (Alaska 2008); Schilberg Integrated Metals Corp. v. Cont'l Cas. Co., 819 A.2d 773, 785 (Conn. 2003); Doe Run Res. Corp. v. Am. Guar. & Liab. Ins., 531 S.W.3d 508 (Mo. 2017).

waste. Waste includes materials to be recycled, reconditioned or reclaimed."[135] Insurers have attempted to rely on this definition to bar claims not traditionally considered pollution claims, primarily involving injury caused by a policyholder's products or involving releases of fumes or chemicals in an indoor setting. Court decisions are mixed on this question, and it remains a subject of substantial litigation.

Policyholders possess good arguments that the absolute pollution exclusion never was meant to bar coverage for products liability or other nontraditional pollution activities.[136] Policyholders can contend, and many courts agree, that the term *pollutant* does not encompass useful products that also happen to be toxic. For example, the Massachusetts Supreme Judicial Court has held that the exclusion does not bar coverage for bodily injury claims resulting from lead poisoning because lead-based paint, a useful product, is not a "pollutant."[137] A policyholder also can argue that an escape or release of a hazardous substance inside a building or other enclosed area does not come within the purview of the absolute pollution exclusion because the policy language—in some of its forms

---

135. MILLER'S STANDARD INSURANCE POLICIES ANNOTATED, form CG 00 39 12 04, at 408.0. *See generally* Whitney v. Mut. Ins. Co., 135 A.3d 272 (Vt. 2015); Mont. Petroleum Tank Release Comp. Bd. v. Crumleys, Inc., 174 P.3d 948, 959 (Mont. 2008).

136. *See* Am. States Ins. Co. v. Koloms, 687 N.E.2d 72, 81–82 (Ill. 1997); Country Mut. Ins. Co. v. Bible Pork, Inc., 42 N.E.3d 958 (Ill. App. Ct. 2015) (pollution exclusion does not preclude coverage for alleged nuisance by hog farmers).

137. Atl. Mut. Ins. Co. v. McFadden, 595 N.E.2d 762, 764 (Mass. 1992). *See also* Nautilus Ins. Co. v. Jabar, 188 F.3d 27, 31 (1st Cir. 1999) (exclusion does not apply to claims for injuries from inhalation of roofing material fumes); Bituminous Cas. Corp. v. Advanced Adhesive Tech., Inc., 73 F.3d 335 (11th Cir. 1996) (exclusion ambiguous under Georgia law with respect to drying adhesive vapors); Stoney Run Co. v. Prudential-LMI Commercial Ins. Co., 47 F.3d 34, 38 (2d Cir. 1995) (exclusion does not apply to claim for carbon monoxide poisoning); Westchester Fire Ins. Co. v. City of Pittsburgh, 791 F. Supp. 836, 837 (D. Kan. 1992) (pesticide made from mixture of malathion and diesel fuel not a "pollutant"); Porterfield v. Audubon Indem. Co., 856 So. 2d 789, 806 (Ala. 2002) (exclusion ambiguous when applied to lead-based paint bodily injury claims); Anderson Gas & Propane Inc. v. Westport Ins. Corp., 140 S.W.3d 504, 508–09 (Ark. Ct. App. 2004) (finding ambiguity whether gasoline is a pollutant since the exclusion does not specifically incorporate the substance); MacKinnon v. Truck Ins. Exch., 3 Cal. Rptr. 3d 228, 243–44 (Cal. 2003) (exclusion does not apply to claims of injuries from sprayed pesticide in an apartment building); Sullins v. Allstate Ins. Co., 667 A.2d 617, 624 (Md. 1995) (exclusion inapplicable to lead claims); W. Alliance Ins. Co. v. Gill, 686 N.E.2d 997, 1000–01 (Mass. 1997) (exclusion inapplicable to carbon monoxide poisoning emitted from a malfunctioning restaurant oven); Minn. Mining & Mfg. Co. v. Walbrook Ins. Co., 1996 WL 5787, at *3 (Minn. Ct. App. Jan. 9, 1996) (isotope polonium-216 not a pollutant); Weaver v. Royal Ins. Co. of Am., 674 A.2d 975, 977–78 (N.H. 1996) (exclusion ambiguous as to lead-poisoning action); E. Mut. Ins. Co. v. Kleinke, 739 N.Y.S.2d 657 (App. Div. 2002) (exclusion applies only to traditional environmental contamination; ambiguous when applied to *E. coli* contamination of food), *leave to appeal dismissed*, 775 N.E.2d 1289 (N.Y. 2002) (tbl.); Lititz Mut. Ins. Co. v. Steeley, 785 A.2d 975, 982 (Pa. 2001) (exclusion does not apply to bodily injury arising from ingestion of lead-based paint); Kent Farms v. Zurich Ins. Co., 998 P.2d 292, 295–96 (Wash. 2000) (diesel fuel not a pollutant when it engulfed and choked tank truck worker); Donaldson v. Urban Land Interests, Inc., 564 N.W.2d 728, 733 (Wis. 1997) (exclusion inapplicable to personal injury arising from the inadequate ventilation of exhaled carbon dioxide).

expressly—contemplates a discharge or release into the "atmosphere."[138] Finally, as with the original pollution exclusion, a policyholder can point to the statements of the insurance industry at the time it sought state approval of the absolute pollution exclusion. The New Jersey Supreme Court relied in part on such statements in its ruling that an absolute pollution exclusion cannot apply outside the context of a traditional pollution claim as a result of regulatory estoppel.[139]

Despite the arguments that the absolute pollution exclusion was not intended to, and does not plainly, extend beyond traditional environmental pollution claims, a number of courts have applied a broad definition of pollutant to bar coverage even in such nontraditional contexts.[140] Again, choice of law becomes the crucial determinant of coverage and should be the prime focus in any coverage strategy for claims involving contaminants or toxic products outside of traditional pollution claims.

---

138. *See, e.g.*, Essex Ins. Co. v. Avondale Mills, Inc., 639 So. 2d 1339, 1342 (Ala. 1994) ("atmosphere" does not include internal environs); *Koloms*, 687 N.E.2d at 493–94 ("discharge," "dispersal," "release" and "escape" are environmental terms of art necessarily connoting a release into the atmosphere or environment); U.S. Fid. & Guar. Co. v. Wilkin Insulation Co., 578 N.E.2d 926, 933 (Ill. 1991) ("[t]he ordinary, popular meaning of the phrase 'the atmosphere' connotes the external atmosphere which surrounds the earth"); Bd. of Regents v. Royal Ins. Co., 517 N.W.2d 888, 892 (Minn. 1994) ("atmosphere" does not merely mean "air," but outdoor air); Cont'l Cas. Co., 609 N.E.2d at 512, 513 (term "atmosphere" is ambiguous, and pollution exclusion clause must therefore be construed in favor of policyholder); Belt Painting Corp. v. TIG Ins. Co., 742 N.Y.S.2d 332, 335–36 (App. Div. 2002) (exclusion inapplicable to indoor discharge of paint and paint solvent fumes), *aff'd*, 795 N.E.2d 15 (N.Y. 2003); Gamble Farm Inn, Inc. v. Selective Ins. Co., 656 A.2d 142, 146–47 (Pa. Super. Ct. 1995) ("atmosphere" clearly refers to air outside of buildings).

139. *See* Nav-Its, Inc. v. Selective Ins. Co. of Am., 869 A.2d 929, 936 (N.J. 2005).

140. *See, e.g.*, Hiland Partners GP Holdings, LLC v. Nat'l Union Fire Ins. Co., 847 F.3d 594 (8th Cir. 2017); Sulphuric Acid Trading Co., v. Greenwich Ins. Co., 211 S.W.3d 243 254 (Tenn. Ct. App. 2006); Assicurazioni Generali, S.p.A. v. Neil, 160 F.3d 997, 1006 (4th Cir. 1998) (exclusion applies to indoor release of carbon monoxide); Technical Coating Applicators, Inc. v. U.S. Fid. & Guar. Co., 157 F.3d 843, 845–46 (11th Cir. 1998) (exclusion applies to vapors emitted during roof repair); Am. States Ins. Co. v. Nethery, 79 F.3d 473, 475–76 (5th Cir. 1996) (paint and glue fumes are chemicals and gaseous irritants within meaning of pollution exclusion); Allen v. Scottsdale Ins. Co., 307 F. Supp. 2d 1170, 1177 (D. Haw. 2004) ("fugitive dust" from concrete recycling plant's operations constitutes pollutant); Vander Hamm v. Allstate Ins. Co., 286 F. Supp. 2d 790, 795 (N.D. Tex. 2003) (exclusion applies to claims against office building owners for injuries due to exposure of chemical fumes); Hartford Underwriters Ins. Co. v. Estate of Turks, 206 F. Supp. 2d 968, 975 (E.D. Mo. 2002) (exclusion applies to ingestion of lead-based paint); Whiteville Oil Co. v. Federated Mut. Ins. Co., 889 F. Supp. 241, 246 (E.D.N.C. 1995) (exclusion applies to gasoline fumes), *aff'd*, 87 F.3d 1310 (4th Cir. 1996); Great N. Ins. Co. v. Benjamin Franklin Fed. S&L Ass'n, 793 F. Supp. 259, 263 (D. Or. 1990) (asbestos is a pollutant), *aff'd*, 953 F.2d 1387 (9th Cir. 1992); Carpet Workroom v. Auto Owners Ins. Co., 2002 WL 1747884 (Mich. Ct. App. July 23, 2002) (exclusion applies to carpet adhesive fumes); Ferrell v. State Farm Ins. Co., 2003 WL 21058165 (Neb. Ct. App. May 13, 2003) (exclusion applies to claim for presence of mercury in an apartment); Matcon Diamond, Inc. v. Penn. Nat'l Ins. Co., 815 A.2d 1109, 1113 (Pa. Super. Ct. 2003) (carbon monoxide is a "pollutant"); Zaiontz v. Trinity Universal Ins. Co., 87 S.W.3d 565, 573 (Tex. App. 2002) (exclusion applies to spraying of deodorant inside airplane); Quadrant Corp. v. Am. States Ins. Co., 76 P.3d 773, 777 (Wash. Ct. App. 2003) (exclusion applies to fumes from waterproofing sealant put to intended use), *aff'd*, 110 P.3d 733 (Wash. 2005); Peace v. Nw. Nat'l Ins. Co., 596 N.W.2d 429, 437–38 (Wis. 1999) (exclusion applies to lead paint chips); Landshire Fast Foods of Milwaukee, Inc. v. Emp'r's Mut. Cas. Co., 676 N.W.2d 528, 532 (Wis. Ct. App. 2004) (foodborne bacteria is a contaminant within the pollution exclusion).

IV. SPECIALTY POLLUTION POLICIES

This section focuses on the two primary types of specialty pollution insurance available on the market beginning in the 1980s: environmental impairment liability (EIL) policies and remediation cost-cap/pollution legal liability (cost-cap/PLL) policies, a product that has been inconsistent in its uptake. These policies are not especially standardized, so close examination of wordings and facts drives outcomes. Moreover, many policies contain arbitration provisions, which generally are enforceable, unless a particular state's insurance regulation precludes arbitration.[141] In contrast to standard-form general liability policies that incidentally cover environmental liability (i.e., that do not contain an absolute pollution exclusion), these specialty pollution policies generally are issued on a claims-made basis instead of on an occurrence basis. Accordingly, we begin by examining the general issues raised by the claims-made nature of this coverage.

A. General Issues regarding Claims-Based Policies

1. Trigger and Claims-Based Policies

In contrast to occurrence-based policies, which are triggered by injury during the policy period, claims-based policies respond to the assertion of a claim of liability within the policy period or a specified time thereafter. Such policies typically are written on either a "claims made" or "claims made and reported" basis, which means that the policies respond, respectively, when an insured receives a claim during the policy period or when an insured receives a claim *and reports it* to its insurer, *both* of which must occur during the policy period.[142] Either way, for an insured to have coverage, the insured must be the subject of a claim made during the policy period. Because there are many variants of claim-based triggers, it is important to consider the exact policy language involved before concluding that a particular liability either does or does not trigger a policy.

a. Meaning of "Claim"

Even though the existence of a claim is central to claim-based policies, many, surprisingly, do not define that term, thus leaving the definition open to judicial interpretation. Typically, courts define a "claim" as being one party's assertion of its

---

141. Mut. Reinsurance Bureau v. Great Plains. Mut. Ins. Co., 969 F.2d 931 (10th Cir. 1992).

142. Most policies permit a brief grace period to address the problem of unreportable claims. *See, e.g.*, Graman v. Cont'l Cas. Co., 409 N.E.2d 387, 388 (Ill. App. Ct. 1980) (claim-reporting period extends 60 days past policy expiration). This is different from an optional "discovery period" or "extended reporting period," which some insurers offer under certain conditions (including the cancellation or nonrenewal of the policy). If there is a "discovery period" or "extended reporting period," an insurer will allow the insured to report claims made during a defined period after policy expiration provided those claims arise out of an act or omission that occurred prior to the end of the policy period. *See generally* Marc Mayerson, *Late Reporting in Claims-Made Policies: Getting to the Root of the Issue*, Ins. Scrawl, July 14, 2005, https://perma.cc/A6JZ-W68B.

entitlement to receive something from another party "as a right or as due."[143] While the plain-meaning definition of the term encompasses more than just a formally filed suit in a court of law, courts differ about the vigor required for a matter to rise to the level of a claim. For instance, one court has held that correspondence complaining of unsatisfactory service and requesting additional services can constitute a claim.[144]

In the case of environmental liability, at least one court took a more stringent view, determining that even when an insured receives correspondence about a specific property from EPA, the governmental agency charged with enforcing environmental laws, "mere correspondence between the EPA and an insured concerning hazardous waste disposal would not necessarily develop into a claim."[145] Because the definition of *claim* is uncertain, at least at the margins, the language should be interpreted broadly or narrowly, as the case may be, to favor coverage.

b. Trigger in the Context of Multiple or Repeated Claims

Because the definition of "claim" can be subject to a variety of interpretations, insureds and insurers may dispute the coverage implications when the claimant takes various steps to assert its claim over a period of time or when it appears that a related claim may have been asserted either before or after the policy period. For instance, where the insured has been subject to progressively more assertive correspondence from a government agency concerning an environmental issue and that correspondence began prior to the inception of the current policy, the insurer might argue that the earliest correspondence evidences a claim and that all subsequent claims merely "relate back" to the first. Thus, if the first "claim" occurred prior to the policy period, the insurer may argue that coverage is not triggered under its policy.

With the variability in claim-based policy language, not all policies contain a "relation back" clause providing that only the first in a series of related claims triggers the policy. Because some policies do contain such provisions,[146] those without them should not be judicially modified to imply such provisions when the

---

143. *See* Abifadel v. Cigna Ins. Co., 9 Cal. Rptr. 2d 910, 920 (Ct. App. 1992). *See also* Dico, Inc. v. Emp'rs Ins. of Wausau, 581 N.W.2d 607, 613 (Iowa 1998) (in occurrence-based policy, turning to *Webster's Collegiate Dictionary* "definition of 'claim' as 'a demand for something due or believed to be due.'").

144. Phx. Ins. Co. v. Sukut Constr. Co., 186 Cal. Rptr. 513, 515 (Ct. App. 1982). *See also* Presidio Wealth Mgmt., LLC v. Columbia Cas. Co., 2014 WL 1341696, at *6 (N.D. Cal. Apr. 03, 2014) (e-mails making demands for money can be claims).

145. *See Dico*, 581 N.W.2d at 614. *But see* Cent. Ill. Light Co. v. Home Ins. Co., 821 N.E.2d 206, 225 (Ill. 2004) (claim does not have to involve a lawsuit or administrative action).

146. For instance, Insurance Company of North America offered a policy stating that related claims "shall be deemed to have been made at the time the first of the claims is made." Other policies contain language that arguably would impose a prior-claim exclusion through the requirement that coverage is provided only for "claims first made" during the policy period where "claim first made" is subject to a clear definition providing the insured with adequate notice of the policy's limitation.

insurer did not choose to include such language.[147] Many courts have rejected the notion that a "prior claim" exclusion inheres in claim-first-made coverage to preclude coverage in the event of a prior or pending claim.[148]

The case of *Homestead Insurance Co. v. American Empire Surplus Lines Insurance Co.*[149] is instructive. In that case, an insured faced two suits, one brought during one insurer's policy period and the other brought during a second insurer's policy period. Because the two suits were related, the insured asked the first insurer to defend both. The insured pointed to the definition of *claim*, which provided that "claims arising out of the same act or out of a series of interrelated acts shall be . . . treated as a single claim." The first insurer denied coverage for the second suit, arguing that it was a claim made after the policy period. The court agreed, finding that the definition of *claim* and the treatment of "related claims" should apply only to claims advanced within the first insurer's policy period. As the court noted, the definition of claims in the successive claims-made policies does not "make it possible for claims submitted during different policy periods to merge into a single claim."[150] It further noted that the definition of claim "remains subordinate to, and does not vary, the . . . insuring agreements," which referred to events happening within the policy period.[151] Questions thus arise as to which of a series of policies apply either to a series of claims or to related claims. In the absence of clear policy language (and assuming adequate underwriting disclosures by the insured), nothing as a matter of insurance law precludes the application of more than one insurance policy.

c. Notice of Circumstances

While a "claim" is necessary to trigger the insuring agreement, some policies include supplemental provisions extending coverage should the insured, during the policy period, have knowledge of circumstances that could reasonably be expected to result in a future claim that might arise after the policy period

---

147. The canons of insurance law dictate that the absence of an exclusion is purposeful and that the language actually used cannot be read to import the omitted exclusion. *See* Pan Am. World Airways, Inc. v. Aetna Cas. & Sur. Co., 505 F.2d 989, 999–1001 (2d Cir. 1974); Tahoe Nat'l Bank v. Phillips, 480 P.2d 320, 325–28 (Cal. 1971).

148. *See, e.g.*, Attorneys Ins. Mut. of Ala., Inc. v. Smith, Blocker & Lowther, 703 So. 2d 866, 869 (Ala. 1996); Homestead Ins. Co. v. Am. Empire Surplus Lines Ins. Co., 52 Cal. Rptr. 2d 268, 273 (Ct. App. 1996); Edward J. Beder, *Triggering Coverage for Related Claims under Claims-Made Coverage*, 9 COVERAGE 19 (Jan./Feb. 1999).

149. *Homestead Ins. Co.*, 52 Cal. Rptr. 2d at 268.

150. *Id.* at 273. Significantly, the insured had already been indemnified by its insurers, and the question was of allocation between the two insurers. The court held that the definition of claim does not "shift liability from one insurer to another."

151. *Id.*

terminates.[152] To avail itself of this option, the insured must provide the insurer with written notice prior to the expiration of the policy. That notice generally must include specific details regarding the potential claim.[153] As a result, some insureds provide their insurers with extensive written notices, nicknamed "laundry lists," as policy periods draw to a close in an effort to secure the broadest possible coverage under an existing policy for claims asserted in the future.[154] However, should subsequent out-of-period claims eventually arise, the insurer who had received the laundry list might argue against coverage on the ground that the insured's notice was speculative, and did not describe with sufficient specificity the circumstances that "could reasonably be expected to result in or lead to a 'Claim.'"[155]

d. Retroactive Dates

Because claim-based policies reach back to provide coverage for conduct or injury preceding the triggering claims, some insurers shorten that reach by limiting coverage to claims arising out of conduct prior to a "retroactive date."[156] These provisions preclude coverage for claims arising out of acts or omissions that took place prior to a date certain, whether that date is the policy's inception or some earlier date. Insureds should consider the impact of a proposed policy's "retroactive date" (sometimes called a "continuity date") at the time coverage is arranged.

---

152. For example, a policy might state: "If during the policy period the Insured shall first become aware of any circumstances which may subsequently give rise to a claim against the Insured . . . and if the Insured shall during the policy period herein give written notice to the Company of such circumstances, any claim which may subsequently be made against the Insured . . . shall be deemed for the purpose of this policy to have been made during the policy period. . . ." Knowledge of circumstances that may give rise to a claim differs from a claim itself because a claim requires a demand on the insured by a third party seeking recovery as a matter of right. *See, e.g.*, City of Marion v. Nat'l Cas. Co., 431 N.W.2d 370, 373–74 (Iowa 1988) (defining "claim").

153. *See* Cont'l Cas. Co. v. Coregis Ins. Co., 738 N.E.2d 509, 521 (Ill. App. Ct. 2000) (potential claim provision satisfied where insured identified issues that became the subject of a claim). *See also* Edward J. Beder Jr. & Rebecca E. Kuehn, *It Is a Mistake to View Insurance Policies as Self-Executing*, NAT'L L.J., Nov. 4, 1996, at B5.

154. *See, e.g.*, Cont'l Ins. Co. v. Metro-Goldwyn Mayer, Inc., 107 F.3d 1344, 1345 (9th Cir. 1997). Insureds have a particular incentive to provide broad notice if, as one policy comes to an end, they are considering purchasing coverage from a different insurer—and therefore facing inquiry into these matters by the underwriters—because the new insurer likely will exclude coverage for potential claims identified during underwriting.

155. *Compare* FDIC v. Alexander, 78 F.3d 1103, 1108 (6th Cir. 1996) (notice of occurrence was not sufficiently detailed), *and* McCullough v. Fid. & Deposit Co., 2 F.3d 110, 113 (5th Cir. 1993) (notice of financial institution's worsening condition not sufficient notice of wrongful act leading to claim), *with* Metro-Goldwyn Mayer, 107 F.3d at 1347–48 (insured's notice sufficiently detailed; included documents indicating dates and nature of wrongful acts); Slaughter v. Am. Cas. Co., 842 F. Supp. 376 (E.D. Ark. 1993) (notice generally referring to certain losses without more detail sufficient because policy did not require more detail), *rev'd on other grounds*, 37 F.3d 385 (8th Cir. 1994); Cont'l Ins. Co. v. Superior Court, 43 Cal. Rptr. 2d 374, 380 (Ct. App. 1995) (notice sufficient).

156. For example, the insuring agreement of a policy might provide that "[t]his insurance applies . . . only if . . . [t]he 'bodily injury' or 'property damage' did not occur before the Retroactive Date, if any, shown in the Declarations." MILLER'S STANDARD INSURANCE POLICIES ANNOTATED, form CG 00 02 12 04 at 402.8. In claims-made pollution liability policies, there may be a retroactive date restricting coverage to releases commencing after a particular date. *See, e.g.*, Invensys Sys., Inc. v. Centennial Ins. Co., 473 F. Supp. 2d 211, 215 (D. Mass. 2007).

Retroactive dates generally are negotiable, and some insurers will agree to use the "retroactive" date of expiring coverage written by a different insurance company so that the insured is not faced with a gap in coverage.

2. Notice of Claim under Claim-Based Policies

Where claim-based policies require that the claim be reported to the insurer during the policy period as a requirement for trigger, courts have tended to enforce such requirements strictly—even in states that otherwise would require a showing of prejudice before they would enforce a late-notice defense to coverage under an occurrence-based policy.[157] The reason for this is plain, as "'[o]ne of the purposes of a claims-made policy is to allow the insurance company to easily identify its risk, allowing it to know in advance the extent of its claims exposure and thus compute its premiums with greater certainty.'"[158] In the claims-made context, notice may be an explicit element of the insuring agreement rather than merely a policy "condition," indicating materiality of the reporting requirements.

B. Environmental Impairment Liability Insurance

The insurance industry has consistently recognized that insureds should be able to purchase coverage against the risk of environmental and pollution liabilities as long as the risks are adequately disclosed and the policyholder's environmental practices managed.[159] While the introduction of the standard qualified pollution exclusion in the early 1970s increased the opportunity for dispute about the availability of coverage under comprehensive General Liability policies, some underwriters seized the opportunity to develop specialty pollution-only liability insurance policies marketed to corporate America. This was especially true following the passage of the federal Superfund law in late 1980. While there was no formal standardization of these policies, they typically were referred to as environmental impairment liability (EIL) policies.

EIL policies often covered all of a policyholder's known and unknown environmental sites and hazards associated with its past and present operations, with the exception of whatever sites or hazards may have been specifically excluded at the time of underwriting. The EIL market flourished in the early to mid-1980s in the United States. However, the general EIL market largely collapsed following the presentment of losses[160] and the general withdrawal of the market's appetite

---

157. *See* Medmarc Cas. Ins. Co. v. Craytor, 2007 WL 1585142, at *10 (E.D. Tex. Apr 30, 2007). *See generally* Mayerson, *Late Reporting in Claims-Made Policies, supra* note 142; Marc Mayerson, *Better by Fax? Perfecting Coverage under Notice-of-Circumstances Provisions of Claims-Made Policies*, INS. SCRAWL, Apr. 9, 2005, https://perma.cc/C4ND-4L7R.

158. *Coregis Ins. Co.*, 738 N.E.2d at 518 (quoting Gen. Ins. Co. of Am. v. Robert B. McManus, Inc., 650 N.E.2d 1080 (Ill. App. Ct. 1995)).

159. Marc Mayerson, *Affording Coverage for Gradual Property Damage under Standard Liability Insurance Policies: A History*, 8 COVERAGE 3 (Sept./Oct. 1998).

160. *See, e.g.*, Wolf Bros. Oil Co. v. Int'l Surplus Lines Ins. Co., 718 F. Supp. 839 (W.D. Wash. 1989).

for pollution risks in the mid-1980s (as evidenced by the forces leading to the introduction of the "absolute" pollution exclusion). This began to change in the early 1990s, when some specialty insurers started to write coverage for the risk of excessive cleanup costs at known sites.

Litigation often centers on (1) whether a site or hazard was properly disclosed during underwriting, (2) when a claim was "first made," and (3) when a claim was first reported (i.e., whether notice was adequate). Insureds are advised to be aware of any EIL coverage in their program and to have a process in place for prompt reporting of claims.

Cleanup liability coverage may be required in marine businesses, and specialized groups known as protection and indemnity clubs (P&I clubs) will underwrite marine-based risks of oil and other types of pollution under marine, hull, or cargo policies. P&I club insurance is a specialty form, and it usually is governed either by maritime law if there is jurisdiction in the United States, or otherwise by English law (because England is the seat of most P&I clubs).

Over time, various types of limited-scope or targeted-sector forms of specialized EIL or pollution insurance have become available. For example, recent years have seen the introduction (and withdrawal) of these types of coverage in the following sectors: abatement and environmental remediation contractors, agrichemical and pesticide users and sprayers, brownfields developers, coal mines, dry cleaners, power suppliers, construction contractors, truckers and haulers, laboratories, real estate developers and lenders, recyclers and scrap companies, and owners of underground storage tanks.[161] Coverage for remediation contractors and engineers can be thought of as a form of errors and omissions (E&O) insurance with respect to operational negligence. Other forms are more akin to premises liability insurance.

C. Cost-Cap/PLL Policies

Cost-cap policies insure against the risk that remediation costs will exceed expectations at a particular site with known environmental problems that is subject to an existing administrative remediation order. Cost-cap policies quantify and cap the upside financial risk of remediating a property, and are commonly, though not exclusively, purchased by developers of brownfield sites. Such policies may be an integral element of the financial transactions relating to the purchase and development of such sites and often are required by a developer's lenders.

Before issuing a cost-cap policy, insurers engage in a thorough and intensive review of the environmental conditions at the site and the proposed remedies. The policyholder is required to disclose its (nonprivileged) files relating to the

---

161. Typical nuclear exposures are excluded, as is typical since the Prince-Anderson Act of 1957, but some forms of radiation and related loss may be covered under CGL or specialty policies. *See* Aetna Cas. & Sur. Co. v. Commonwealth, 179 S.W.3d 830, 838–39 (Ky. 2005). For underground storage tank losses, state "insurance"-type funds are available in some states.

remediation, and the insurers usually employ their own in-house environmental engineers and other experts to assess (and in some cases help develop) the policyholder's approved remedial plan. The insurer then estimates the cost of implementing the remedial plan and agrees to pay any costs incurred by the policyholder pursuant to the remedial plan during an agreed time period that exceeds the projected costs plus a multiplier (typically 10 percent). In essence, the insurer is betting on its ability to accurately gauge the future costs of implementing a remedial plan (and charging what it believes to be a commensurate premium). The insurer's interest is to secure governmental approval of the remediation as quickly and efficiently as possible, and in this regard its interests are aligned with the policyholder's.

Cost-cap policies sometimes may be combined with pollution liability coverage that insures against liability at the site beyond the costs of implementing the approved remedial plan—including both remedial costs for unknown pollutants not covered within the remedial plan and third-party tort liability relating to the site. PLL coverage is site-specific and limited to sites with known environmental issues. It does not provide general pollution coverage for all of a company's operations across multiple sites. Insurers feel comfortable issuing PLL coverage in tandem with cost-cap coverage where they have a reasonable degree of confidence that the approved remedial plan will be effective.

Cost-cap policies generally contain the following key elements:

- An expressly defined "Insured Property," which may be limited to certain subdivisions of the site if part of the property is not subject to the remediation order or is deemed by the insurer to be too risky or uncertain;
- An explicitly defined "Remedial Plan," often by reference to particular documents constituting the plan;
- A "Self-Insured Retention" (SIR) equal to the projected costs of implementing the Remedial Plan plus a multiplier;
- A "Termination Date," typically defined as the earlier of the date on which the applicable regulatory authority certifies that the remediation has been completed pursuant to the Remedial Plan (often in the form of a "no further action" letter) or a future date certain (often in two or three years);
- Explicitly defined "Cleanup Costs," typically requiring work pursuant to the Remedial Plan to be performed by approved vendors; and
- A reporting requirement by which the policyholder must keep the insurer well apprised of the status and progress of the remediation.

Such policies usually contain an exclusion for cleanup costs resulting from a modification in the preapproved remedial plan unless the modification is required by the regulatory authority. Costs resulting from an "unreasonable delay" by a scheduled contractor also are typically excluded.

PLL policies generally feature a variety of coverages that may insure against first-party costs (incurred by the policyholder to clean up his or her own site) and third-party liabilities for property damage or bodily injury. The first-party coverage may include both preexisting conditions that were unknown when the remedial plan was prepared and are first discovered during the policy period, as well as new conditions that first arise during the policy period. However, combined cost-cap/PLL policies will contain a policy exclusion that channels remediation costs incurred pursuant to the remedial plan to the cost-cap coverage and not the PLL coverage, which generally has a deductible far smaller than the cost-cap's SIR.[162]

Insurers issuing cost-cap/PLL policies truly become financial partners with their policyholders in the effort to remediate the subject site and obtain regulatory sign-off. Friction may develop between the "partners" that will necessitate arbitration (most such policies contain an arbitration clause) or litigation over any of the following issues: (1) whether the remediation is proceeding in reasonable accordance with the preapproved remedial plan; (2) what is the appropriate response to a regulatory order requiring that the approved remedy be modified or altered; (3) whether an altered remedy takes the cleanup costs outside of the cost-cap coverage; (4) whether cleanup costs are approved costs that are counted toward exhausting the SIR; or (5) whether certain remedial work is done pursuant to the approved remedial plan, and thus covered by the cost-cap policy (unless performed after the cost-cap coverage has terminated), or is in response to new conditions or a new "claim" by the regulatory authority, which might be covered under the PLL coverage.[163] If policyholders are vigilant about keeping the insurer apprised of progress and developments at the site and commit to working with the insurer and allowing the insurer some input into the remediation, these types of policies generally can prove to be valuable tools for hedging against the unforeseen costs of cleaning up a site.

V. CONCLUSION

When faced with potential environmental liabilities, a company's first priority is to defend against the claims and, where appropriate, ensure that the remediation is accomplished as efficiently and effectively as possible. But an important secondary concern should be whether the costs of defense, remediation, or both can be defrayed through insurance recovery. Companies should consider whether they may be entitled to coverage under their older, preabsolute pollution exclusion

---

162. *See, e.g.*, Denihan Ownership Co. v. Commerce & Indus. Ins. Co., 37 A.D.3d 314, 315 (1st Dep't 2007) ("[T]he exclusion was clearly intended to ensure no overlap between the underlying CCC [cleanup cost-cap coverage] policy, which provided coverage for petroleum contamination on the site, and any new and different pollution conditions covered by the PLLS [pollution legal liability select] policy.").

163. *See* Frazer Exton Dev., L.P. v. Kemper Envtl., Ltd., 153 F. App'x 31, 33 (2d Cir. 2005) (policy covers changes to remedial plan resulting from newly discovered pollution or changed environmental standards).

general liability policies or those of their corporate predecessors. They also may have coverage under more recent specialty policies specifically intended to cover pollution liabilities. Companies are well advised to gather and maintain all such policies in advance and to put in place a process for prompt notice under all potentially responsive policies so that they can act quickly when environmental claims arise.

CHAPTER 5

CERCLA Cost Recovery and Contribution and a Primer on Natural Resource Damages Law: Regulation, Litigation, and Basic Economic Principles

Ira Gottlieb, Nathan Howe, Rick Dunford, and Cynthia Betz

I. INTRODUCTION

Comprehensive Environmental Response, Compensation, and Liability Act (CERCLA): The main goal of this part of the chapter is to provide a discussion of statutory and case law core concepts that arise most frequently and pervade practice. In doing so we give the reader a narrative explanation of how these concepts are practically woven together in practice areas that we often confront in daily practice, focusing on recovery actions between private parties, but without trying to be too wide-ranging or delve into the many topics and nuances that can arise (e.g., National Priority List listing, definitions, National Contingency Plan consistency, defenses). We also address some key policy (guidance) changes that have occurred in the last several years, particularly with the rise of urban sediment sites.

Natural Resource Damages (NRD): In this part of the chapter we address key concepts related to natural resource damage claims. After providing basic background, an explanation of key concepts concerning statutes/common law claims, and the assessment process (including damage determination and valuation), we briefly address allocation, the restoration process itself, and some of the innovations and issues that have arisen post-*Deepwater Horizon*. We also briefly address climate change and some of the suits and citizen efforts that have arisen in the last ten years.

II. CERCLA'S LIABILITY SCHEME

The engine powering CERCLA's liability scheme is the central policy premise that those who are responsible for contamination will be held strictly accountable for the costs of remediation.[1] Courts have invoked this purpose as the basis for many decisions interpreting CERCLA's liability provisions throughout its history. For instance, CERCLA is construed to impose strict liability on potentially responsible parties (PRPs), and as a result, there is no knowledge requirement, or even the need to prove that a PRP was negligent in its handling or discharge of hazardous substances.[2] Moreover, CERCLA exposes PRPs to joint and several liability at the receiving end of cost recovery actions, placing the burden on PRPs to recoup costs from other PRPs when they have paid more than an equitable share.[3] Additionally, liability under CERCLA is generally retroactive, and therefore PRPs are subject to liability for contamination that occurred before its enactment in 1980.[4]

Regardless of the positive remedial policy goals underlying CERCLA, the practical realities and complex nature of environmental contamination can lead to severely inequitable outcomes among those grappling with liability and damages issues. This is particularly true when parsing the responsibility of PRPs for multi-party sites. The difficulty of this task, and the resultant potential for disagreements and inequity, is aggravated by the sometimes substantial and even enormous costs that need to be borne upfront, and for many years, before questions of apportionment and allocation of responsibility for those costs are addressed and resolved. This situation can be even more complicated when one or more PRPs will be insolvent, or are otherwise unavailable, thus resulting in further inequitable results. Complicating matters further, the design and language of CERCLA does not afford great clarity into issues that inevitably arise in such complex situations, and leave in its wake a convoluted series of court interpretations that are occasionally inconsistent, at least among some federal circuits.

Although many questions arise regarding the administration of the Superfund program of the Environmental Protection Agency (EPA), and the implementation of removal and remedial activities, because of the high costs of environmental

---

1. *See* the Comprehensive Environmental Response, Compensation, and Liability Act of 1980, Pub. L. No. 96-510, 94 Stat. 2767 (1980) (CERCLA, also commonly known as Superfund) and the Superfund Amendments and Reauthorization Act of 1986, Pub. L. No. 99-499, 100 Stat. 1613 (1986) (SARA).

2. *See, e.g.*, Pakootas v. Teck Cominco Metals, Ltd., 452 F.3d 1066, 1078 n.18 (9th Cir. 2006); *In re* Bell Petrol. Servs., 3 F.3d 889, 897 (5th Cir. 1993); United States v. Aceto Agric. Chems. Corp., 872 F.2d 1373, 1377 (8th Cir. 1989).

3. Like strict liability, CERCLA is also not explicit in this regard, but courts have construed Section 107(a) to include joint and several liability under common law tort principles, except in limited circumstances when the harm is divisible. Burlington N. & Santa Fe Ry. Co. v. United States, 556 U.S. 599, 613–14 (2009) (discussing and reaffirming the approach to joint and several liability initially recognized in United States v. Chem-Dyne Corp., 572 F. Supp. 802, 810–11 (S.D. Ohio 1983)).

4. *See* Gould, Inc. v. A & M Battery & Tire Serv., 933 F. Supp. 431, 438 (M.D. Pa. 1996) (noting federal district courts have uniformly determined CERCLA to have retroactive effect, with but a single exception). This comports with one of the primary reasons CERCLA was created, which was to remediate abandoned hazardous waste sites and historic contamination.

remediation, the one issue that spawns intense litigation is cost recovery and contribution. CERCLA provides distinct rights and remedies depending on whether a plaintiff is a government agency, or a private party. CERCLA presently provides two avenues of recoveries for response costs. The first is referred to as cost recovery, provided under Section 107(a), and is available to government, private parties, and most recently PRPs. The second avenue, provided under Section 113(f), empowers PRPs to seek contribution from other PRPs for their proportionate share of costs.

The interplay between 107(a) and 113(f) in circumstances where PRPs seek to recoup costs from other PRPs has been the source of much confusion over recent years. While these two avenues are described as "complementary yet distinct" remedies,[5] the relationship between them remains murky, and determining where the boundary of one ends and the other begins is no simple task. This confusion is largely the product of the U.S. Supreme Court's closely related decisions in *Aviall* and *Atlantic Research*, which severely disrupted established norms in this area. These decisions and their impact are discussed later in this chapter.

Even more recently, the change of administrations at the White House in 2017 brought renewed attention to the Superfund program, though it is unclear to what extent these changes may alter the liability scheme applicable to private parties. In May 2017, the newly minted and now former EPA Administrator, E. Scott Pruitt, announced his commitment as head of the agency to restore Superfund and related cleanup efforts "to their rightful place at the center of the agency's core mission."[6] Then-Administrator Pruitt commissioned a Superfund Task Force "to provide recommendations on an expedited time frame on how the agency [could] restructure the cleanup process," among other things.[7]

Two months later, in July of 2017, that Superfund Task Force released its report, which included "42 specific and detailed recommendations to streamline and improve the Superfund program,"[8] which were noted to be possible "without legislative change."[9] Among the proposals included "high attention" to long-standing NPL sites; third-party investment in NPL cleanups; acceleration of

---

5. *See* Cooper Indus. v. Aviall Servs., Inc., 543 U.S. 157 (2004); United States v. Atl. Research Corp., 551 U.S. 128, 138 (2007).

6. *See* Memorandum from E. Scott Pruitt, EPA Adm'r, Prioritizing the Superfund Program (May 22, 2017), https://www.epa.gov/sites/production/files/2017-05/documents/prioritizing_the_superfund _program_memo_5-22-2017.pdf.

7. *Id.*

8. *See* News Release, U.S. Envtl. Protection Agency, EPA Announces Superfund Task Force Recommendations (July 25, 2017), https://www.epa.gov/newsreleases/epa-announces-superfund-task-force-recommendations (last visited Feb. 14, 2019).

9. *See* U.S. Envtl. Protection Agency, EPA Superfund Task Force Recommendations (July 25, 2017), https://www.epa.gov/sites/production/files/2017-07/documents/superfund_task_force_report.pdf. However, former administrator Pruitt's response to the recommendations did note that "[s]ome of the task force's recommendations will require future administrative actions, such as rulemakings or the issuance of guidance, by the agency for them to come to fruition." *See* Memorandum from E. Scott Pruitt, EPA Adm'r, Receipt of Superfund Task Force Report and Next Steps for Revitalizing the Superfund Program (July 25, 2017), https://www.epa.gov/sites/production/files/2017-07/documents/receipt_of _superfund_task_force_report_and_next_steps_for_revitalizing_the_superfund_program_memo.pdf.

cleanups at NPL sites where a remedy has already been selected; the application of new technologies and approaches for NPL sites still in assessment and investigation stages; incentives to secure early PRP commitments; and the "development of strong stakeholder relationships."[10] At this juncture, it is too early to measure the impact of the task force's recommendations, or whether these recommendations will alter the ability of PRPs to seek or recoup costs, but early signs suggest that EPA intends to work diligently toward the lofty goals set by the task force.[11]

III. KEY DEFINITIONS

Because CERCLA is a highly technical statutory framework, there are innumerable definitions and terms, with nuances, that one must recognize and be able to apply fluently in this practice area. To delineate the full range of these definitions and terms would be a large task in and of itself. The following list includes some of the most basic, yet essential, definitions and terms that one must be familiar with in order to build a foundational understanding of CERCLA and related litigation. This is a simplified list that attempts to reduce the definitions and terms to their core meaning. A practitioner should always refer to the precise definitions set out in the statute or in relevant case law.

- *Release*—"spilling, leaking, pumping, pouring, emitting, emptying, discharging, injecting, escaping, leaching, dumping, or disposing into the environment (including the abandonment or discarding of barrels, containers, and other closed receptacles containing any hazardous substance or pollutant or contaminant)."[12] Specifically excluded are releases in the workplace subject to workers' compensation claims, as well as releases from vehicle emissions, nuclear energy facilities, and normal fertilizer use.[13]

- *Hazardous substances*—includes a large array of chemical substances designated pursuant to various statutes and regulations, including the Federal Water Pollution Control Act, the Solid Waste Disposal Act, the Clean Air Act, and the Toxic Substances Control Act. Specifically excluded from this definition is petroleum or any form of natural gas.[14]

---

10. *See* EPA Superfund Task Force Recommendations, *supra* note 9, at iv–v.

11. *See, e.g.*, U.S. Envtl. Protection Agency, Superfund Sites Targeted for Immediate, Intense Action, https://www.epa.gov/superfund/superfund-sites-targeted-immediate-intense-action (last visited Feb. 14, 2019).

12. CERCLA § 101(22), 42 U.S.C. § 9601(22).

13. *Id.*

14. CERCLA § 101(14), 42 U.S.C. § 9601(14). The petroleum exclusion has been the subject of EPA guidance, commentary, and case law. *See, e.g.*, Memorandum from Francis S. Blake, EPA Gen. Counsel, to J. Winston, Assistant Adm'r for Solid Waste & Emergency Response, Scope of the CERCLA Petroleum Exclusion under Sections 101(14) and 104(a)(2) Mem. EC-G-1999-012 (Jul. 31, 1987), https://www.epa .gov/sites/production/files/2013-09/documents/petro-exclu-mem.pdf; Westwood Assoc. v. Atl. Richfield Corp., 881 F.2d 801(9th Cir. 1989) (discussing the scope of the exclusion as well as its legislative history and holding that it applies to both unrefined and refined gasoline under the statute's plain meaning).

- *Removal action*—short-term cleanup efforts that include "removal of released hazardous substances from the environment, such actions as may be necessary taken in the event of the threat of release of hazardous substances into the environment, such actions as may be necessary to monitor, assess, and evaluate the release or threat of release of hazardous substances" and necessary to address immediate threats to the public health or environment.[15]
- *Remedial action*—actions consistent with a long-term and permanent remedy.[16] Such actions can be done "instead of or in addition to removal actions in the event of a release or threatened release of a hazardous substance into the environment, to prevent or minimize the release of hazardous substances so that they do not migrate to cause substantial danger to present or future public health or welfare or the environment."[17]
- *PRP*—potential responsible parties can include any of four categories of persons, including business entities or individuals, that are or were (1) current owners and operators of vessels or facilities, (2) former owners and operators of facilities "who at the time of disposal of any hazardous substance owned or operated any facility at which such hazardous substances were disposed," (3) "any person who by contract, agreement, or otherwise arranged for disposal or treatment, or arranged with a transporter for transport for disposal or treatment, of hazardous substances owned or possessed by such person," or (4) transporters of hazardous substances.[18]
- *Facility*—an intentionally broad term, it encompasses "(A) any building, structure, installation, equipment, pipe or pipeline (including any pipe into a sewer or publicly owned treatment works), well, pit, pond, lagoon, impoundment, ditch, landfill, storage container, motor vehicle, rolling stock, or aircraft, or (B) any site or area where a hazardous substance has been deposited, stored, disposed of, or placed, or otherwise come to be located."[19]

IV. ELEMENTS OF COST RECOVERY AND CONTRIBUTION CLAIMS

Presently, there are two avenues by which a private party may recover costs under CERCLA: either through cost recovery under Section 107(a) or contribution through Section 113(f). The distinctions between these two avenues are described

---

15. CERCLA § 101(23), 42 U.S.C. § 9601(23).
16. CERCLA § 101(24), 42 U.S.C. § 9601(24).
17. *Id.*
18. CERCLA § 107(a), 42 U.S.C. § 9607(a).
19. CERCLA § 101(9)(B), 42 U.S.C. § 9601(9)(B).

in more detail in the following sections of this chapter, but regardless of which avenue is pursued, there are four essential elements for any action by a private party to recover costs under CERCLA: (1) the site in question qualifies as a "facility," (2) there exists a "release" or "threatened release" of a (3) "hazardous substance," and (4) the defendant falls within one of the four categories of PRPs.[20] Also, for Section 107(a) cost recovery actions, the plaintiff must have incurred "necessary costs of response," and for nongovernmental plaintiffs, these costs must have been "consistent" with the NCP.[21]

Of particular significance is the omission of any requirement to prove traditional causation with respect to liability for removal, remedial, or other response action costs. Instead, consistent with the strict liability scheme of the statute, typically a plaintiff need only demonstrate the statutory elements and the incurrence of response costs, with respect to specific defendant PRPs. Of particular importance is that there is no need to prove that the particular substances that are the subject of a cleanup are those that were specifically discharged by a particular defendant.[22]

However, in some instances there is still a requirement that a plaintiff prove a defendant's causal "nexus" to the facility or alleged source. This requirement is far removed from what would be required under a traditional tort "but-for" causation or "proximate" causation test, and it is often met by a defendant's status as an owner/operator, or where a defendant has directly discharged a substance at the facility, but may become problematic when a defendant's connection to the site is attenuated, or mixed with other hazardous substances, such as when a defendant is alleged to be an arranger.[23] But once a nexus has been demonstrated, all PRPs

---

20. CERCLA § 107(a), 42 U.S.C. § 9607(a).

21. The National Contingency Plan (NCP) is located at 40 C.F.R. 300 (1995) and sets forth the regulations and criteria for cleanup procedures for incidents involving the discharge of hazardous substances. An understanding of the NCP is vital to CERCLA practice, as this necessary element of recovery—that costs are "consistent with" the NCP—is sometimes the subject of dispute. *See, e.g.*, Young v. United States, 394 F.3d 858 (10th Cir. 2005), Goodrich Corp. v. Town of Middlebury, 311 F.3d 154 (2d Cir. 2002). For plaintiff governmental agencies, the defendant bears the burden of demonstrating that the costs are "not inconsistent" with the NCP. Wash. State Dep't of Transp. v. Wash. Nat'l Gas Co., 59 F.3d 793, 799–800 (9th Cir. 1995); United States v. Hardage, 982 F.2d 1436, 1441–42 (10th Cir. 1992); United States v. Simon Wrecking, Inc., 481 F. Supp. 2d 363, 367 (E.D. Pa. 2007).

22. United States v. Wade, 577 F. Supp. 1326, 1332 (E.D. Pa. 1983) ("[T]o require a plaintiff under CERCLA to 'fingerprint' wastes is to eviscerate the statute."); *see also* Dedham Water Co. v. Cumberland Farms Dairy Inc., 889 F.2d 1146, 1154 (1st Cir. 1989) (the question is not whether the release "caused the contamination," but whether the release caused the plaintiff "to incur response costs"); Castaic Lake Water Agency v. Whittaker Corp., 272 F. Supp. 2d 1053, 1066 (C.D. Cal. 2003) (In a "two-site CERCLA case, the plaintiff meets its burden on summary judgment if it (a) identifies contaminant at its site, (b) identifies the same (or perhaps a chemically similar) contaminant at the defendant's site, and (c) provides evidence of a plausible migration pathway by which the contaminant could have traveled from the defendant's facility to the plaintiff's site.").

23. *See* N.J. Tpk. Auth. v. PPG Indus., 197 F.3d 96, 105 (3d Cir. 1999) (where the New Jersey Turnpike Authority, a PRP plaintiff, argued that the defendant should be held liable as an arranger due to its disposal of chromate ore processing residue, but the court determined that the Turnpike Authority had not met is burden of demonstrating a causal "nexus" due to the absence of proof that the defendant had deposited the substance at each of seven individual sites, as opposed to the broad geographical region of the Turnpike "eastern spur").

who meet statutorily defined terms and definitions are liable for the hazardous substances at the site.

Once this liability has been established in multiparty sites, a defendant may seek to limit its responsibility through a clear showing that the harm is divisible, or that costs should be allocated between multiple PRPs. As explained later in this chapter, the concept of apportionment has been a subject of great debate in the realm of CERCLA litigation following the Supreme Court's decision in *Burlington Northern & Santa Fe Railway Co. v. United States*.

V. THE LANDMARK *AVIALL* AND *ATLANTIC RESEARCH* DECISIONS

Originally, Section 107(a) of CERCLA was the only statutory and textual avenue for recovery of response costs in CERCLA's pre-SARA regime.[24] This section is commonly known as the "cost recovery" section of CERCLA.[25] While Section 107(a)(4)(A) explicitly provides that the U.S. government, states, and Indian tribes are entitled to "all costs of removal or remedial action" that are not "inconsistent with the national contingency plan," private entities, by comparison, were not originally afforded this explicit statutory right, due to the absence of a "civil suit" provision.[26] Even though private parties were soon permitted to bring cost recovery actions through judicial interpretation,[27] such actions were limited to so-called "innocent" (non-PRP) private parties.[28]

CERCLA's original formulation further omitted the remedy of contribution from its text. In spite of this notable absence, courts determined that the right to contribution was implied under Section 107(a)(4)(B).[29] Through SARA, Congress formally incorporated the remedy of contribution into CERCLA's text, now located at Section 113(f).[30] Section 113(f)(1) created two triggers that permit a PRP to seek contribution: (1) a PRP has been subject to a CERCLA civil action (under Section

---

24. "SARA" refers to the Superfund Amendments and Reauthorization Act of 1986, Pub. L. No. 99-499, 100 Stat. 1613 (1986).

25. Cooper Indus. v. Aviall Servs., Inc., 543 U.S. 157, 161 (2004).

26. Rather than providing a civil suit provision, Section 107(a)(4)(B) instead states that a PRP is liable for "any other necessary costs of response incurred by any other person consistent with the national contingency plan."

27. Walls v. Waste Res. Corp., 761 F.2d 311, 318 (6th Cir. 1985) (at the time, "District Court decisions [were] virtually unanimous in holding that section 9607(a)(4)(B) creates a private right of action against section 9607(a) responsible parties").

28. New Castle Cnty. v. Halliburton NUS Corp., 111 F.3d 1116, 1120 (3d Cir. 1997) ("Every court of appeals that has examined this issue has come to the same conclusion: a section 107 action brought for recovery of costs may be brought only by *innocent parties* that have undertaken clean-ups. An action brought by a potentially responsible person is by necessity a section 113 action for contribution.") (citations omitted).

29. *See* Agere Sys. v. Advanced Envtl. Tech. Corp., 602 F.3d 204, 217 (3d Cir. 2010).

30. "Any person may seek contribution from any other person who is liable or potentially liable under section 107(a), during or following any civil action under section 106 or under section 107(a)." CERCLA § 113(f)(1), 42 U.S.C. § 9613(f)(1).

106 (actions for relief to abate contamination or to enforce unilateral administrative orders by EPA) or Section 107 (a cost recovery claim)), whether ongoing or concluded, or (2) a PRP has resolved its liability to the government through an "administratively or judicially approved settlement."[31] For PRPs who enter into such settlements, this section provides a limited benefit of immunity against certain contribution claims brought by nonsettling PRPs.[32]

For several decades, contribution was the predominant method or recovery for PRPs against other PRPs, whereas cost recovery was available only to non-PRP plaintiffs. In two landmark decisions, however, the Supreme Court rejected this distinction, remarkably altering the cost recovery/contribution distinction.

In *Cooper Industries, Inc. v. Aviall Services, Inc.*, the Supreme Court focused on when a contribution claim arises under Section 113(f) of CERCLA. The Court held that Section 113(f) requires contribution actions to be brought "during or following" a Section 106 or Section 107(a) civil action.[33] While *Aviall* limited the circumstances by which Section 113(f) contribution actions are available to PRPs, *Atlantic Research* did the opposite for cost recovery actions under 107(a), expanding this form of relief in certain narrow circumstances, primarily when a 113(f) claim is unavailable. The Court's reasoning in *Atlantic Research* further suggests that the door of Section 107(a) has been opened to PRPs more as a safety net than a place of first resort.

In *Aviall Services, Inc.*, the Supreme Court upended the status quo of PRPs seeking contribution as the exclusive means of obtaining recoupment for cleanup costs from other PRPs.[34] The *Aviall* case was instituted by a landowner, Aviall, who had purchased four sites, and conducted operations at the sites for several years before discovering contamination attributable to both its own operations and the previous owner, Cooper Industries.[35] Under threat of enforcement by a state authority, Aviall undertook cleanup efforts.[36] However, no outward administrative efforts (orders or civil actions) by governmental authorities compelled Aviall to take action.[37]

Prior to *Aviall*, it was widely understood that a PRP who undertook remedial activities could seek contribution at any time within the applicable statute of limitations. But in *Aviall*, the Court determined that the phrase "[a]ny person *may*

---

31. CERCLA § 113(f)(1), (f)(3)(B), 42 U.S.C. § 9613(f)(1), (f)(3)(B); United States v. Atl. Research Corp., 551 U.S. 128, 131 n.5 (2007).

32. Because EPA wields significant enforcement authority in administering response activities, and good cause frequently exists to undertake removal actions or pursue remedial investigations without administrative orders or civil litigation, settlements often provide the most beneficial and sensible course for PRPs. As an additional incentive, CERCLA § 113(f)(2), 42 U.S.C. § 9613(f)(2), states: "a person who has resolved its liability to the United States or a State in an administrative or judicially approved settlement shall not be liable for claims for contribution regarding matters addressed in the settlement."

33. Cooper Indus. v. Aviall Servs., Inc., 543 U.S. 157, 165–66 (2004).

34. *Id.* at 169 (providing a list of decisions that have so held).

35. *Aviall Servs.*, 543 U.S. at 163–64.

36. *Id.* at 164.

37. *Id.*

seek contribution . . . *during or following* any civil action under [Section 106] or [Section 107]" rendered contribution unavailable to a PRP who was not yet subject to suit.[38] And even though the Court imposed this limitation for claims arising under Section 113(f), it purposely did not address whether PRPs could present cost recovery claims under Section 107(a), or whether an implied right of contribution under 107(a)(4)(B) had survived the SARA adoption of 113(f), paving the way for the Court to revisit CERCLA's liability scheme in *Atlantic Research*.[39]

Atlantic Research was an action brought by a manufacturer of rocket motors against the federal government, seeking partial recovery of costs under 107(a).[40] The plaintiff had performed cleanup at its own expense, and only afterward sought to recover a portion of these expenses from the federal government.[41] In the intervening period between *Aviall* and *Atlantic Research*, the issue of whether PRPs could bring cost recovery claims under Section 107(a) had resulted in inconsistent responses by the circuit courts of appeal.[42] The *Aviall* Court put to rest any notion that PRPs are excluded from bringing such claims, and definitively concluded that PRPs do, in fact, fall within the category of potential plaintiffs described as "any other person" in the text.[43]

In reaching this decision, the Court reasoned that Section 107(a)(4)(B) must be read in conjunction with Section 107(a)(4)(A), and as a result, the plain meaning of "any other person" includes any person or entity other than federal/state governments, and Indian tribes.[44] Excluding PRPs from this category would also, by the Court's logic, "reduce the number of potential plaintiffs to almost zero."[45] Consequently, Section 107(a) cost recovery claims are not available only to "innocent" private parties, but also to PRPs generally, under limited circumstances, such as when a PRP has voluntarily incurred the costs of cleanup.[46] However, the full contours defining the scope of this statutory right were, at best, vague, given the Court's limited discussion and holding.

The two things that are clear based upon the Supreme Court's decisions can be summarized as follows: (1) a PRP who is subject to a lawsuit, whether under Section 106 or 107, is limited to a contribution claim pursuant to Section 113(f); and (2) a PRP who has voluntarily incurred response costs independent of a civil

---

38. *Id.* at 166.

39. *Id.* at 168–71.

40. *Atl. Research Corp.*, 551 U.S. at 133.

41. *Id.* at 133.

42. *Compare* Consol. Edison Co. of N.Y. v. UGI Utils., Inc., 423 F.3d 90 (2d Cir. 2005) (determining PRPs did possess such a right), *and* Metro. Water Reclamation Dist. of Greater Chi. v. N. Am. Galvanizing & Coatings, Inc., 473 F.3d 824 (7th Cir. 2007) (same), *with* E.I. du Pont de Nemours & Co. v. United States, 460 F.3d 515 (3d Cir. 2006) (limiting PRPs to actions pursuant to CERCLA § 113(f)).

43. *Atl. Research Corp.*, 551 U.S. at 128–29.

44. *Id.* at 134–41.

45. *Id.* at 137.

46. The Court disposed of this distinction, noting that several categories of PRPs could also be considered "innocent." *Id.* at 136.

action or settlement may seek cost recovery under Section 107(a).[47] The Court has provided only vague guidance for the range of scenarios that fall between these two holdings, leaving it to lower courts to flesh out this framework.

VI. THE CERCLA WORLD AFTER *AVIALL* AND *ATLANTIC RESEARCH*

Aviall and *Atlantic Research* have propagated questions that are perhaps more numerous and ubiquitous than those it has answered, and these two groundbreaking decisions created an atmosphere of unpredictability clouding CERCLA's private-party-liability scheme. Countless are the situations that do not fall neatly into the parameters identified by the Supreme Court for sorting claims into Section 107(a) or 113(f), most notably when a PRP has performed remediation pursuant to a consent order or other circumstances that may squarely be defined.[48]

In light of the above, it is important to discuss and understand some of the advantages of bringing a cost recovery action under Section 107(a) as opposed to a contribution action, whether pursuant to common law or Section 113(f). First and foremost, cost recovery actions provide for joint and several liability. As a result, if a Section 107(a) cost recovery action is available to a party, even a PRP may seek to impose joint and several liability on other PRPs. Because contribution actions place the burden of proof upon the plaintiff to demonstrate the proportionate share of liability for which a defendant is responsible, for obvious reasons, joint and several liability is not available in such an action.

Another difference that should be borne in mind is the statute of limitations period applicable to each category of claims. As discussed later in this chapter, contribution actions are subject to a three-year statute of limitations, while cost recovery actions can survive up to six years for remedial actions, providing a much longer window to bring suit.

Yet another concern that has arisen in the aftermath of *Aviall* and *Atlantic Research* is whether a PRP cost recovery action would overcome the contribution protection afforded to PRPs who settle with EPA, an outcome that would substantially reduce the value of settlement. Hypothetically, the *Atlantic Research* Court

---

47. The Supreme Court's opinions, by implication, pose an interesting question: Did the Court limit this to 113(f)(3)(B) settlements? There is no explicit limitation; however, the question could very well fall along the same lines as the issue over whether certain non-CERCLA settlements serve to trigger a contribution claim based on the Court's following statement: "And § 107(a) permits cost recovery (as distinct from contribution) by a private party that has itself incurred cleanup costs. Hence, a PRP that pays money to satisfy a settlement agreement or a court judgment may pursue § 113(f) contribution." *Atl. Research Corp.*, 551 U.S. at 139.

48. Agere Sys. v. Advanced Envtl. Tech. Corp., 602 F.3d 204, 218 (3d Cir. 2010) ("[N]avigating the interplay between [CERCLA] § 107(a) and § 113(f) remains a deeply difficult task."). Notably, PRPs and government agencies have taken strides to ensure settlements and other arrangements do not create impediments to cost recovery and contribution or run afoul of the Court's *Aviall* and *Atlantic Research* opinions (*see, e.g.*, EPA's employment of Model Administrative Settlement Agreements and Orders on Consent).

had provided a solution to this dilemma, positing that a defendant would undoubtedly counterclaim for contribution to combat the possible inequity created by joint and several liability.[49] However, as has been demonstrated, such a counterclaim may not always be available to a defendant.

Regarding the proper avenue for PRPs who have entered consent orders, the court in *Niagara Mohawk Power Corporation v. Chevron U.S.A., Inc.* determined that while these PRPs may not qualify to pursue contribution under Section 113(f)(1), due to the absence of a 106 or 107 action, they did qualify under Section 113(f)(3)(B), as they have entered into an "administratively or judicially approved settlement that resolved their liability for some or all response costs."[50] Specifically, the court stated that to do otherwise, and permit a cost recovery action under 107, "would in effect nullify the SARA amendment and abrogate the requirements Congress placed on contribution claims under [Section 113]."[51]

In *Agere Systems, Inc. v. Advanced Environmental Technology Corp.*,[52] the Third Circuit Court of Appeals went one step further than *Niagara Mohawk*, reaching the same conclusion that contribution is the proper avenue following a consent decree, but when contribution was not available, Section 107(a) would provide an alternative remedy.

Agere involved the Boarhead Farms Superfund Site in Pennsylvania, where a chemical waste disposal company had illegally dumped its customers' hazardous wastes over a period of four years.[53] Five PRP plaintiffs commenced litigation to recover costs funded through either consent orders with EPA or private settlements for reimbursement of costs.[54] The plaintiffs sought contribution and cost recovery from 23 defendants, but by the time of the appeal, only one such defendant remained, and all other defendants had either been dismissed or reached settlement.[55] This lone defendant had previously been one of the customers of the defunct waste disposal company.[56]

In *Agere*, the court first determined that contribution was not available to the plaintiffs because the statute of limitations had expired for the government to institute a Section 106 or 107 action.[57] Because a contribution action was unavailable, the *Agere* court looked to the *Atlantic Research* Court's characterization of

---

49. Notably, the *Atlantic Research* Court has pointed out that the potential of an inequitable result due to joint and several liability between PRPs may be "blunt[ed]" by the defendant PRP bringing a counterclaim for contribution, which would force an equitable apportionment of costs among liable parties. *Atl. Research Corp.*, 551 U.S. at 140.

50. Niagara Mohawk Power Corp. v. Chevron U.S.A., Inc., 596 F.3d 112 (2d Cir. 2010).

51. *Id.* at 128.

52. *Agere*, 602 F.3d at 204.

53. *Id.* at 210.

54. *Id.* at 212–14.

55. *Id.* at 214.

56. *Id.* at 213. To make matters worse, this customer was already aware the waste company's founder had a proclivity to pollute illegally, having already suffered the loss of two companies for such practices, yet still hired his new company due to it being the cheapest bid. *Id.* at 215.

57. *Id.* at 225–27. For a PRP to seek contribution under 113(f)(3)(b), there must also remain at least a "potential" CERCLA lawsuit. This is because a lawsuit against both parties must be available to satisfy

Sections 107(a) and 113(f) as "overlapping," and determined that a remedy would have to be available under 107(a) when 113(f) did not apply.[58] Due to this overlapping nature, Section 107(a) provides a backstop, supplying a remedy to PRPs who otherwise have no recourse under Section 113(f).

Next, the *Agere* court recognized the inequitable and "perverse" outcome of granting PRPs the ability to assert joint and several liability under Section 107(a) when a defendant lacks the means to counterclaim for contribution and force an allocation.[59] To prevent this injustice, the *Agere* court disallowed PRPs who have received the benefit of contribution protection from bringing actions under Section 107(a) with respect to those costs that are subject to protection.[60]

Having concluded that Section 107(a) was available for those plaintiffs who had only entered private settlements rather than consent orders, the *Agere* court was left to decide whether costs that first travel through an intermediary before going to response activities could still meet the definition of "response costs," and thus, merit recovery pursuant to Section 107(a).

In its *Atlantic Research* decision, the Supreme Court had seemingly imposed this somewhat arbitrary distinction to preclude recovery of such costs under Section 107(a).[61] The defendant in *Agere* tested the merits of this distinction, arguing that because two of the plaintiffs had paid costs pursuant to private settlements rather than consent decrees, those costs should not have been recoverable under Section 107(a).[62] The *Agere* court disagreed and departed from this distinction. It was irrelevant that the funding provided via private settlements went through intermediary group trust accounts, rather than directly to cleanup; either way, the plaintiffs were still entitled to recovery.[63]

In addition to *Niagara Mohawk* and *Agere*, several other courts have determined that Section 113(f)(3)(B) contribution is the exclusive avenue of recoupment available to PRPs who have entered consent decrees.[64] However, simply because a

---

the "common liability" requirement; otherwise there would be no basis for the PRPs to ever be subject to joint and several liability.

58. *Id.* at 226 (quoting *Atl. Research Corp.*, 551 U.S. at 139 n.6).

59. *Id.* at 228.

60. *Id.* at 229.

61. *Atl. Research Corp.*, 551 U.S. at 139 ("[A] PRP that pays money to satisfy a settlement agreement or a court judgment may pursue § 113(f) contribution. But by reimbursing response costs paid by other parties, the PRP has not incurred its own costs of response and therefore cannot recover under § 107(a).").

62. *Agere*, 602 F.3d at 225.

63. *Id.* Specifically, the court did not believe that the Supreme Court had intended to "deprive the word 'incurred' of its ordinary meaning," and the funding had all gone to the same "pot." *Id.*

64. *See, e.g.*, Hobart Corp. v. Waste Mgmt. of Ohio, Inc., 758 F.3d 757, 767 (6th Cir. 2014) ("[A] PRP, which has entered into an administrative settlement with the government, thereby having met a statutory trigger for filing a contribution action, can bring only a [CERCLA] § 113(f)(3)(B) action for contribution—not a § 107(a)(4)(B) cost-recovery action."); NCR Corp. v. George A. Whiting Paper Co., 768 F.3d 682 (7th Cir. 2014) (rejecting PRP's argument that it could bring claims under 107(a) for costs incurred pursuant to consent orders entered into in 2004 and 2007, and prior to the government's 2010 lawsuit); Solutia, Inc. v. McWane, Inc., 672 F.3d 1230, 1235–37 (11th Cir. 2012) (noting the issues that would arise if claims under both 107(a) and 113(f) were permitted for PRPs who have entered consent decrees); Morrison Enter., LLC v. Dravo Corp., 638 F.3d 594, 603 (8th Cir. 2011).

PRP has entered a consent decree does not mean that contribution is immediately available. In *Asarco LLC v. Atlantic Richfield Co.*,[65] the Ninth Circuit addressed two issues that may affect a PRP's ability to recover contribution after entering into a consent decree. The circuits are split on both issues.

First, the language of Section 113(f) is unspecific as to whether settlements must be entered pursuant to CERCLA, or whether settlements under other environmental laws such as the Resource Conservation and Recovery Act (RCRA) or state environmental statutes qualify. In *Asarco*, the court joined with the Third Circuit and ruled in the affirmative,[66] but noted that the Second Circuit has previously held to the contrary, specifically requiring a CERCLA-based settlement. This split, however, may already have softened, as the Second Circuit has expressed a shifted view of this issue in light of EPA's position to the contrary, and if not already, will likely soon join the ranks of the Ninth Circuit and Third Circuit in accepting accept other types of settlements.[67]

Second, the court in *Asarco* investigated the issue of when a PRP has satisfactorily "resolved" its liability, which is not necessarily accomplished by the mere entrance into a settlement agreement. Previously, the Seventh Circuit determined that liability had not been resolved by entry into a settlement when the agreement included a PRP's disclaimer of liability, or when the government had reserved some rights to pursue future litigation, which created only a conditional promise of release.[68] Thus, in the details of consent decrees or other arrangements there may be pitfalls that hinder cost recovery and contribution claims.

The Ninth Circuit disagreed with this approach, pointing out that CERCLA itself "prevents a covenant not to sue from 'tak[ing] effect until the President certifies that remedial action has been completed.'"[69] Instead, the court in *Asarco* opined that preventing PRPs from seeking contribution due to liability disclaimers would discourage settlements with EPA because PRPs would be forced to concede liability and potentially incur additional liability.[70] With a strong likelihood of joint and several liability at stake, conceding any amount of liability is a dangerous

---

65. Asarco LLC v. Atl. Richfield Co., 866 F.3d 1108 (9th Cir. 2017).

66. *Id.* at 1118–21 (determining that a RCRA decree could serve as a predicate agreement for purposes of 113(f)), Trinity Indus., Inc. v. Chi. Bridge & Iron Co., 735 F.3d 131 (3d Cir. 2013) (involving a settlement entered under state law).

67. *See* Consol. Edison Co. of N.Y. v. UGI Utils., Inc., 423 F.3d 90 (2d Cir. 2005) (rejecting a state law settlement agreement as sufficient for purposes of 113(b)). However, as noted by the *Asarco* court, the Second Circuit may no longer abide by this rule, referring to a more recent Second Circuit decision that had agreed with EPA's position that an agreement need not be CERCLA-specific. *Asarco*, 866 F.3d at 1120; *see also* Niagara Mohawk Power Corp. v. Chevron U.S.A., Inc., 596 F.3d 112, 124–27 (2d Cir. 2010).

68. *See Asarco*, 866 F.3d at 1123 (discussing Bernstein v. Bankert, 733 F.3d 190, 212–13 (7th Cir. 2013); Fla. Power Corp. v. FirstEnergy Corp., 810 F.3d 996, 1004 (6th Cir. 2015)). One year later, the Seventh Circuit again encountered this issue, and distinguished the language of an administrative settlement with the agreement at issue in *Bernstein*, and determined the agreement to effectively resolve liability, and therefore provided relief exclusively under 113(f), rather than 107(a). *NCR Corp.*, 768 F.3d at 691–92 (where the mutual covenants against suit took effect upon the effective date of the agreement, and notwithstanding the inclusion of a disclaimer).

69. *See Asarco*, 866 F.3d at 1124 (quoting CERCLA § 122(f)(3), 42 U.S.C. § 9622(f)(3)).

70. *Id.* at 1125.

proposition for PRPs. In light of this concern, *Asarco* set forth a fact-specific test, requiring that an administrative settlement agreement must "decide with certainty and finality a PRP's obligations for at least some of its response actions or costs," and would require "a case-by-case analysis of a particular agreement's terms."[71] While this approach is more flexible than the Seventh Circuit's strict rejection for provisions that are quite prevalent in administrative settlement agreements, it may not provide an effectively predictable blueprint for PRPs to identify whether, or at what point, their settlement agreement has resolved liability sufficiently to make contribution available.

As a result of these decisions, it is evident that the fallout of *Aviall* and *Atlantic Research* is by no means completed. There is also no guarantee that if a contribution claim fails, a cost recovery claim will rescue the case. Nevertheless, prudent pleading practice by PRPs—particularly those who have entered consent decrees and other forms of administrative settlements—necessitates filing both contribution and cost recovery claims, to ensure that if contribution is unavailable, there remains at least a possibility that cost recovery will bridge the gap.

VII. *BURLINGTON NORTHERN & SANTA FE RAILWAY CO. V. UNITED STATES*

In 2007 the U.S. Supreme Court decided *Burlington Northern & Santa Fe Railway Company v. United States* (*BNSF*), another landmark decision that has caused some disarray in lower courts that continued to cope with CERCLA's then-changing liability scheme.[72] *BNSF* notably altered the landscape of arranger liability, ratcheting up the threshold by adopting a requirement of intent. Also, the manner in which the Court upheld the district court's apportionment of costs has caused lower courts (and private parties) to question whether the standard is now lower than the one that existed pre-*BNSF*. The effects of *BNSF* continue to be felt as lower courts across the country grapple with the interpretation of arranger status and struggle to discern the quantum of proof that may permit apportionment in lieu of joint and several liability. The *BNSF* opinion has similarly caused some ripples of new thought across the waters of private-party allocation proceedings where there may be additional equitable allocation considerations.[73]

In *BNSF*, Shell Oil Company was alleged to be responsible for selling hazardous substances to an operator of two adjacent parcels, B&B, who would then store and distribute the chemicals to agricultural businesses.[74] Initially, Shell delivered the useful chemicals in drums, but later required B&B to install bulk storage facilities on the property so that Shell could convert its delivery service to more

---

71. *Id.*
72. Burlington N. & Santa Fe Ry. Co. v. United States, 556 U.S. 599 (2009).
73. *See* discussion *infra* at 28–30.
74. *Burlington N. & Santa Fe Ry. Co.*, 556 U.S. at 602–03.

cost-effective tanker trucks.[75] Over the course of many years, transfers to and from the storage facilities resulted in numerous incidental and occasional leaks and spills.[76] In general, Shell attempted to mitigate the problem of downstream spills and leaks by incentivizing purchasers to install upgrades to storage equipment and requiring inspections of storage facilities.[77] Notwithstanding these efforts, EPA and state agencies discovered significant contamination in the soil and groundwater of the site, including a plume that threatened a local drinking water supply.[78] The cleanup efforts rendered B&B insolvent, and the governmental agencies redirected their cost recovery focus to Shell as an arranger, as well as two railroad companies who jointly owned one of the parcels.[79]

Initially, the federal district court determined Shell was liable as an arranger, and despite the fact that neither of the defendants presented a case requesting apportionment, the court acted sua sponte and apportioned liability between Shell (91 percent) and the railroad companies (9 percent).[80] The Ninth Circuit affirmed Shell's liability as an arranger, utilizing a "foreseeable byproduct" standard of its own design,[81] and reversed the district court's apportionment. The Ninth Circuit ruled that by acting sua sponte, the district court improperly alleviated the burden that rested with a defendant to prove an adequate basis for apportionment, and therefore did not overcome the presumption of joint and several liability.

In a remarkable opinion on the subject, the Supreme Court disagreed with the Ninth Circuit's "foreseeable byproduct" standard, and while acknowledging that any inquiry into arranger status is often "fact intensive and case specific,"[82] the Court looked to the common meaning and understanding of "arranger" and concluded that "the word 'arrange' implies action directed to a specific purpose."[83] As a result, to be considered an arranger, an entity must take "intentional steps to dispose of a hazardous substance."[84] The Court clarified that "knowledge alone" that a hazardous chemical will be leaked or spilled by a purchaser is insufficient to prove that an entity "intended" disposal, particularly when the disposal is "peripheral" to a sale of an "unused, useful product."[85]

Applying these principles to Shell, the Court highlighted Shell's mitigation attempts as evidence that Shell did not intend the disposal, even though Shell may have held knowledge of their occurrence and was unsuccessful in its preventative

---

75. *Id.* at 603, 621.

76. *Id.* at 604.

77. *Id.*

78. *Id.*

79. *Id.* at 605.

80. *See id.* at 615 (The district court criticized the "scorched earth" position of both Shell and the railroad defendants, who refused to accept any responsibility for the contamination.).

81. United States v. Burlington N. & Santa Fe Ry. Co., 520 F.3d 918, 949 (9th Cir. 2008). The Ninth Circuit offered a rationale that arranger status was appropriate when disposal is a "foreseeable byproduct" of the transaction, even if not the underlying purpose. *Id.*

82. *Burlington N. & Santa Fe Ry. Co.*, 556 U.S. at 610.

83. *Id.* at 611.

84. *Id.* at 611.

85. *Id.* at 612.

efforts. Without the requisite intent, Shell did not "arrange" for disposal, and thus, could not be held liable pursuant to Section 107(a)(3).[86]

The Court then evaluated whether to uphold the apportionment analysis performed by the district court.[87] There was no dispute between the lower courts regarding whether the harm was theoretically capable of apportionment, only whether there was a reasonable basis.[88] Interestingly, at the district court level, the railroad companies had taken an "all-or-nothing approach," while the government had held firm in its belief that the harm was not divisible at all, and therefore no parties had provided any basis to apportion the costs. Regardless, the district court undertook this task itself, and used a simple formula that considered three factors: (1) the percentage of land owned by the railroad defendants (19 percent of the site), multiplied by (2) the length of time the land was leased to the polluting company (45 percent), and then multiplied by (3) 66 percent, representing the court's finding that only two-thirds of the contamination requiring remediation had been caused by the chemicals released on the railroad parcel.[89] This led to liability of 6 percent total.[90] The court then adjusted for a 50 percent margin of error, and determined the railroad defendants were responsible for 9 percent of the costs.[91]

The Ninth Circuit criticized this approach on the basis that there had been no facts sufficient to establish the volume of contamination that occurred on the railroad portion relative to the nonrailroad portion, nor the amount that occurred during the lease period relative to the nonlease period, and that the district court's three factors "relied on estimates rather than specific and detailed records."[92]

The Supreme Court disagreed with the Ninth Circuit and reinstated the apportionment of liability against the railroad defendants. The Court approved the district court's methodology with the exception of the third factor. However, the Court determined that the 50 percent margin of error compensated for this shortcoming, and still arrived at 9 percent liability for the railroad defendants.[93]

VIII. THE AFTERMATH OF *BNSF*

A. Divisibility of Response Costs

Commonly, courts engaging in CERCLA multiparty liability analysis have relied on common law principles, specifically the *Restatement (Second) of Torts*, to determine whether to apportion damages or impose joint and several liability.[94] In the

---

86. *Id.* at 613.
87. *Id.* at 613–19.
88. *Id.* at 615.
89. *Id.* at 615.
90. *Id.* at 616.
91. *Id.*
92. *Id.* at 617.
93. *Id.* at 616–19.
94. *See, e.g.*, New York v. Next Millennium Realty, LLC, 160 F. Supp. 3d 485 (E.D.N.Y. 2016) ("'[T]he universal starting point for divisibility of harm analyses in CERCLA cases is § 433A of the Restatement

context of CERCLA this test involves two essential steps: (1) whether the harm is "capable of apportionment," and if so, (2) whether there is proof that a "reasonable basis" for apportionment exists.[95] Notably, *BNSF* also begins its analysis with this fundamental standard,[96] and while the elements of this two-step test remain unchanged, the functional application of this test before and after *BNSF* has instigated extensive debate.[97] This debate has centered on whether the Supreme Court interpreted this standard differently in *BNSF* from those courts preceding it, imposing a lower threshold, and moreover, to what extent. This question has perplexed some lower courts and PRP defendants alike, and continues to do so.

The practical reality, however, has shed much more light on the subject. As demonstrated in recent cases, regardless of a court's view regarding a lower standard, there has been no significant change in outcome, with courts almost unanimously finding apportionment inappropriate.[98] As a result, the sea change anticipated by *BNSF* has been perhaps exaggerated, and for PRPs, the substantial financial advantages that would accompany successful apportionment defenses have yet failed to materialize.[99]

(Second) of Torts[,]' which provides, '(1) Damages for harm are to be apportioned among two or more causes where (a) there are distinct harms, or (b) there is a reasonable basis for determining the contribution of each cause to a single harm. (2) Damages for any other harm cannot be apportioned among two or more causes.'") (quoting RESTATEMENT (SECOND) OF TORTS § 433A (1965) and *Burlington N. & Santa Fe Ry. Co.*, 556 U.S. at 614).

95. *See, e.g.*, APL Co. Pte. Ltd. v. Kemira Water Sols., Inc., 999 F. Supp. 2d 590, 624 (S.D.N.Y. 2014); United States v. Chem-Dyne Corp., 572 F. Supp. 802, 810 (S.D. Ohio 1983).

96. *Burlington N. & Santa Fe Ry. Co.*, 556 U.S. at 614.

97. *See generally* Ryan Brady, *CERCLA Apportionment Following Burlington Northern: How Joint and Several Liability Still Thrives—To the Surprise of Many*, 4 WASH. J. ENVTL. L. & POL'Y 141 (2014).

98. Before *BNSF*, only four cases out of 160 had deemed apportionment to be appropriate. *Id.* at 144 (citing Martha Judy, *Coming Full CERCLA: Why* Burlington Northern *Is Not the Sword of Damocles for Joint and Several Liability*, 44 NEW ENG. L. REV. 249, 283 (2010)); *See also In re* Bell Petrol. Servs., 3 F.3d 889, 903 (5th Cir. 1993) ("[M]ost CERCLA cost-recovery actions involve numerous, commingled hazardous substances with synergistic effects and unknown toxicity. In contrast, this case involves only one hazardous substance—chromium—and no synergistic effects."). To date, there appears to be only a single instance where apportionment was deemed appropriate after *BNSF*. *See* Reichold, Inc. v. U.S. Metals Ref. Co., 655 F. Supp. 2d 400, 448–49 (D.N.J. 2009) (finding that each of two PRPs had contributed sufficient contamination to require a cap, and therefore the costs could be reasonably apportioned between them, with each responsible for one-half). Curiously, the *Reichold* court felt it would be inappropriate to consider "the exact amount of metals contamination for which each was responsible," only that either PRP's contributions were sufficient to cause the remedial action. *Id.*

99. Apportionment in the first instance may offer substantial benefits as compared to allocation in litigation or in the context of private-party proceedings. When successful in an apportionment defense, a PRP is responsible only for its divisible share and avoids the burden of joint and several liability entirely. Allocation, on the other hand, is implicated when a defendant collaterally seeks contribution from other defendants, and that defendant may have already been held accountable for the entire sum of response costs due to joint and several liability. When seeking contribution, a defendant is further restrained to collecting only those costs for which the contributing defendant is responsible, and may have no recourse when there are financially unavailable PRPs, such as those attributed to orphan shares. If a PRP prevails in apportioning costs, there is no subsequent allocation phase unless one or more apportioned shares involve multiple PRPs who are jointly and severally liable. Allocation will be discussed in greater length later in this chapter, but it is important to note that by achieving apportionment in the first instance, a PRP can avoid significant expense and effort, as well as the possibility of being held responsible for the shares of unavailable PRPs. *See Burlington N. & Santa Fe Ry. Co.*, 556 U.S. at 615 ("[A]pportionment . . . looks to whether defendants may avoid joint and several liability by

Perhaps one of the most closely watched series of decisions on this topic has been in the Lower Fox River litigation, which has had several twists and turns, and serves as a prime example of the uphill climb PRPs face in establishing an apportionment defense.

United States v. NCR Corp. involved several PRP paper manufacturers who had contaminated the Lower Fox River with polychlorinated biphenyls (PCBs).[100] As part of EPA's remediation plan, the site was divided into five operable units (OU1 through OU5), and remediation activities were designed to proceed in several stages.[101] One of the defendants, NCR Corporation, operated along and discharged waste into the second OU; however, the contaminants had flowed downstream to other operable units.[102] Pursuant to a unilateral administrative order issued by EPA, NCR led the remediation efforts in operable units two and three, and part of four, before halting its participation and claiming that it had already contributed more than its fair share.[103] In response, the district court issued a preliminary injunction requiring NCR to continue the remediation work.

In its first decision in the matter, the Seventh Circuit upheld the injunction, finding that NCR had failed to demonstrate that the harm in OU4 was capable of apportionment. The Seventh Circuit based its decision on the premise that NCR's discharges alone, even if only a small percentage of the contaminants present in OU4, would still be independently sufficient to cause the remediation activity due to the low threshold for required remedial action.[104]

The case then returned to the district court, which held a bench trial that included the issue of divisibility, and at the conclusion of the trial the district court once again reached the conclusion that the harm was incapable of apportionment.[105] NCR then joined with three other PRP defendants and brought a second appeal. With the benefit of a more complete record now before it, the Seventh Circuit disagreed with the district court's approach, and determined that the harm was not "binary in nature" (i.e., concentrations of PCBs above 1.0 ppm were harmful, but below 1.0 ppm were not), and the district court's adherence to this notion as the record developed was an "oversimplification" because it later became clear during the trial that levels below these thresholds "still pose a threat to human health and the environment."[106] The record also included the availability of alternative

---

establishing a fixed amount of damage for which they are liable, while contribution actions allow jointly and severally liable PRPs to recover from each other on the basis of equitable considerations.").

100. United States v. NCR Corp., 688 F.3d 833, 835–36 (7th Cir. 2012).

101. *Id.* at 836.

102. *Id.*

103. *Id.* at 837.

104. As the court described, "because EPA has set a maximum safety threshold of 1.0 ppm of PCB . . . a cubic yard of sediment would need to be dredged whether it contained 10 ppm or 100 ppm. . . . Put another way, the need for cleanup triggered by the presence of a harmful level of PCBs in the River is not linearly correlated to the amount of PCBs that each paper mill discharged. Instead, once the PCBs rise above a threshold level, their presence is harmful and the River must be cleaned." *Id.* at 839–40.

105. United States v. P.H. Glatfelter Co., 768 F.3d 662 (7th Cir. 2014).

106. *Id.* at 676–77. This change in view is attributable to the recognition of EPA's remedial goal, which was not to reduce all concentrations below 1.0 ppm, but rather to achieve surface-weighted

lower-cost remedies, such as sand covering or capping, when the levels of contamination are lower.[107] In this way, remediation costs were "positively correlated with the level of contamination" and were "continuous" rather than binary.[108] Based on this new understanding, the court determined that the harm was, in fact, capable of apportionment so long as NCR could demonstrate "the extent to which it contributed to PCB concentrations in OU4," and again, remanded to the district court.[109]

On remand, the district court considered the expert testimony presented during the bench trial, which provided a volumetric analysis estimating the percentage of PCBs NCR had contributed to OU4.[110] The court accepted that testimony as credible, and with the threshold question already decided by the Seventh Circuit, the court considered whether NCR had demonstrated a reasonable basis for apportionment. The court first noted its view that *BNSF* has "lowered the bar" and emphasized that the test demands only "reasonableness" and not "scientific precision."[111] The court provided a range for NCR's responsibility of "somewhere between twenty and forty percent of the PCBs remaining in OU4," and accepted NCR's proposal of 28 percent, because it "falls solidly in the center of the range of reasonableness."[112]

That decision, however, would not be the end of discussion on this topic, as the government requested that the district court reconsider its decision. The court indulged this request, and agreed with the government's position, determining for a third time that the harm was not divisible.[113] Motivating this reconsideration was the absence of discharge estimates attributable to two PRPs who could not be accounted for and rendered the entire stand-alone scheme to be mere "guesswork."[114]

One lesson that can be gleaned from these decisions is that it is unclear to what extent *BNSF* has truly modified the standard for apportioning liability. On the other hand, courts do now reference the *BNSF* decision, and the Seventh Circuit has even determined that in some cases, apportionment would be available in actions involving sites as complex as the Lower Fox River sediment site. While it

---

average concentration (SWAC) of 0.25 ppm, which it believed could be reached by remediating all areas that were above 1.0 ppm. *Id.*

107. *Id.* at 677–78.

108. *Id.* at 677.

109. *Id.*

110. United States v. NCR Corp., 107 F. Supp. 3d 950 (E.D. Wis. 2015). NCR had actually relied on expert witness testimony presented by an adversary for these estimates. *Id.* at 955.

111. *Id.* at 959 ("This court has already noted that *Burlington Northern* seemed to lower the bar for what kind of evidence would be acceptable for a PRP to establish apportionment. In that case, it was clear to all concerned that the size of the leased parcel and the amount of time the PRP had controlled it were not *necessarily* linked to the amount of harm or damages. Instead, those metrics were just rough proxies the district court used in the absence of actual knowledge, an absence of information caused by the fact that the railroads did not even *argue* divisibility.").

112. *Id.* at 960.

113. United States v. NCR Corp., No. 10-C-910, 2015 WL 6142993 (E.D. Wis. Oct. 19, 2015).

114. *Id.* at *2.

remains to be seen to what extent courts will actually permit apportionment, there at least appears to be a basis for such a change in the wake of *BNSF*.

B. Arranger Liability

While *BNSF* does not appear to have lowered the burden for a defendant asserting an apportionment defense, or at least not practically speaking, the Court's inclusion of an explicit intent element has had an immediate impact on arranger liability jurisprudence. Post-*BNSF* cases stand in stark contrast to many of the decisions that preceded it. Prior to *BNSF*, defendants could be held liable as an arranger when a defendant maintained ownership of hazardous materials,[115] control over the process that resulted in the waste or discharges,[116] or directed disposal,[117] even when the hazardous materials were commercially useful.[118] It did not matter whether a defendant's purpose for engaging in the activities was to dispose of the materials, either directly or indirectly. Instead, so long as the entity held some degree of authority over the materials, ultimate discharge or disposal was sufficient for arranger status to attach. *BNSF* has refocused this analysis, and by prioritizing the intent of the transferring party, has perhaps realigned the arranger liability doctrine with the conceptual framework under which it was originally contemplated.[119]

In *Vine Street LLC v. Borg Warner Corp.*, a seller of dry cleaning machines had sold a hazardous substance, PERC, as well as water separators to a cleaner.[120] The defendant further designed and installed the separators, so that they would dispose of wastewater into the sewer as well as recycle PERC for future use. Defendant was aware that some amount of PERC would inevitably escape from the

---

115. *See* United States v. Aceto Agric. Chems. Corp., 872 F.2d 1373, 1373 (8th Cir. 1989) (where pesticide manufacturer was considered an arranger by having contractor process its products, and this process inherently caused waste to be generated and disposed, noting that the contractor operated for defendant's benefit and under its direction, and defendant owned the product throughout the formulation procedure); *but see* United States v. Shell Oil Co., 294 F.3d 1045 (9th Cir. 2002) and United States v. Vertac Chem. Corp., 46 F.3d 803 (8th Cir. 1995) (determining that the government was not liable as an arranger even though it was aware of by-product waste in the manufacturing process of products it had required to be produced, including Agent Orange and avgas, but had not directed disposal).

116. *See* United States v. Ne. Pharm. & Chem. Co., 810 F.2d 726 (8th Cir. 1986) (where defendant neither owned or possessed the hazardous substance but held the authority to control the disposal).

117. *See* Cal. Dep't of Toxic Substances Control v. Payless Cleaners, 368 F. Supp. 2d 1069 (E.D. Cal. 2005) (defendant was a manufacturer of dry cleaning equipment and directed locations of dry cleaner's drains so that PERC waste would be discharged into the sewer).

118. Generally, arranger liability does not apply to the transfer of useful products that are sold for a commercial purpose, whereas transfers of materials classified as scrap or requiring processing before they could be reused are much more susceptible to findings of arranger status. Cal. Dep't of Toxic Substances Control v. Alco Pac., Inc., 508 F.3d 930, 934 (9th Cir. 2007) ("A person may be held liable as an 'arranger' under § 9607(a)(3) only if the material in question constitutes waste rather than a useful product.") (internal quotation marks omitted).

119. United States v. Gen. Elec. Co., 670 F.3d 377, 382 (1st Cir. 2012) ("Within the CERCLA scheme, arranger liability was intended to deter and, if necessary, to sanction parties seeking to evade liability by "contracting away" responsibility.") (internal citation omitted).

120. Vine St. LLC v. Borg Warner Corp., 776 F.3d 312 (5th Cir. 2015).

recycler component and discharge into the sewer. Eventually these accumulated discharges required remediation.

In its decision, the Fifth Circuit concluded that the defendant had not intended to arrange for disposal since the system was designed to recycle the hazardous substance, and it had undertaken additional measures to reduce the discharges after learning the PERC had escaped. The court further looked to the nature of the relationship between the defendant and the cleaner as "centered around the successful operation of a dry cleaning business—not around the disposal of waste," and remarked that PERC was a "useful product that was necessary" to the cleaner's operations.[121] Another factor in the court's decision was the absence of any indication of subterfuge or attempt to disguise a disposal transaction as one having commercial significance. The court also took into consideration, much like the Court in *BNSF*, the remedial measures defendants undertook to mitigate further discharges.[122] Unlike in decisions predating *BNSF*, it was irrelevant that the defendant had installed the machines, connecting them to the drain and sewer.[123]

Another example of a decision that likely would have resulted in arranger liability before *BNSF* is *Consolidated Coal Co. v. Georgia Power Co.*[124] In that case, the utility defendant sold used transformers at auction. Before auctioning the transformers, the utility would test to determine whether the oil inside contained PCBs exceeding 50 ppm, and if so, the utility would drain them. These drained transformers, however, still contained residual PCB oil. One of the purchasers at these auctions, Ward Transformer Company, a reconditioner, purchased a total of 101 used transformers from the utility, some of them undrained, others containing residual oil. All of the transformers were repaired or rebuilt and then resold to third parties. However, during the reconditioning process, PCB oil was discharged at the Ward Transformer site.

The court determined that the utility was not an arranger under these circumstances. First, the utility had sold the transformers in order to generate revenue, even though it referred to these transactions as "scrapping" and "disposals" internally.[125] Because the products were sold at a competitive auction, the court further noted the transformers were sold at values greater than scrap value, and the purchaser exclusively intended to resell the equipment for future use, rather than disposal.[126] Another fact weighing against any intent to dispose was that the utility had no indication any of the transformers were leaking at the time of sale, and those that were drained had been capped. Nor was there an arrangement between

---

121. *Id.* at 318–19.

122. *Id.* at 319.

123. *See also* Team Enters., LLC v. W. Inv. Real Estate Tr., 647 F.3d 901, 911 (9th Cir. 2011) (also involving a dry cleaner equipment manufacturer and where the equipment directed wastewater into a bucket, where the PERC would separate and could be recycled, but the remainder of PERC would remain with the wastewater for disposal).

124. Consol. Coal Co. v. Ga. Power Co., 781 F.3d 129 (4th Cir. 2015).

125. *Id.* at 158.

126. *Id.* at 151–53.

the utility and purchaser to dispose of the PCB oil, and the understanding was entirely that the transformers would be resold and reused. Instead, any spills or leaks were attributable solely to the purchaser's subsequent "business judgment" in reconditioning the transformers to particular customers' specifications. The opinion in *Consolidated Coal* seems to stretch the bounds of arranger liability and the lines between useful products and disposal activities.

As can be seen in the preceding and other recent decisions, *BNSF* has affected the role of arranger liability in CERCLA practice.[127] Nevertheless, it remains an active avenue for holding entities responsible for cleanup costs even when they are not directly involved in the release of hazardous substances into the environment.[128] With the element of intent now established as an important part of arranger status, in order to avoid this basis for liability, it is of vital importance that any transfers involving useful hazardous substances hold legitimate ongoing commercial purposes for the materials in question. This is especially true when used materials are being resold. Comparatively, transfers where the substance is treated as mere scrap or refuse are far more likely to result in a finding of intentional disposal by courts, rendering the disposing entity liable as an arranger for any subsequent mismanagement of the hazardous waste by the purchaser.

IX. STATUTE OF LIMITATIONS

Under CERCLA's statute of limitations provisions, cost recovery actions differ based on whether recovery is sought for a removal or a remedial action, and there are many nuances presented by particular cases and circumstances.[129] Inasmuch as the understanding and application of statute of limitations may be a critical and case-sensitive question, practitioners should be careful to conservatively mind the rules. The following discussion therefore is, by necessity, general in its nature.

For removal actions, the period is three years after removal has completed.[130] Remedial actions can be brought up to six years after physical on-site construction

---

127. *See* NCR Corp. v. George A. Whiting Paper Co., 768 F.3d 682, 703–05 (7th Cir. 2014) (NCR's predecessor had sold scraps of carbonless paper to recyclers who would then rinse the PCBs and recycle the pulp, discharging the PCBs into the Lower Fox River, but no finding of arranger status because the sale was intended "to place it on a competitive market and recoup some of its costs of production"; also important were the efforts undertaken to recapture the scrap for sale to the paper recyclers).

128. *See* Gen. *Elec. Co.*, 670 F.3d at 377 (determining defendant was an arranger after selling "scrap Pyranol" to a paint manufacturer at bargain prices for use as a paint additive, reasoning that defendant had intentionally disposed of the hazardous substance by pursuing other arrangements to dispose of the overstock, lack of marketing as a usable product, and defendant's specific actions toward the purchaser, which included continued and increasing sales despite paint manufacturer's complaints the scrap Pyranol was often unusable and repeated failures to remit payment); *see also* Litgo N.J., Inc. v. N.J. Dep't of Envtl. Prot., 725 F.3d 369 (3d Cir. 2013) (United States government was held liable as an arranger for transporting hazardous wastes to a facility for ultimate disposition, regardless of claim that waste was transported for purpose of storage rather than disposal).

129. CERCLA § 113(g)(2), 42 U.S.C. § 9613(g)(2).

130. CERCLA § 113(g)(2)(A), 42 U.S.C. § 9613(g)(2)(A).

began.[131] If a remedial action begins within three years of the removal action's completion, recovery of removal costs may attach to a later lawsuit brought within the six-year period of remedial actions, notwithstanding the shorter three-year period applicable to removal actions.[132] Therefore, distinguishing between removal actions and remedial actions is essential to any determination of the appropriate statute of limitations period.[133]

One issue that has arisen in recent years involves sites with multiple operational units or phases, where response activities proceed in linear fashion but are divided and addressed at different times or locations. The majority of jurisdictions have reached the conclusion that there can be only one removal or remedial action at any given site for purposes of determining the applicable statute of limitations.[134] In the case of remedial actions, this means that only one six-year period applies, and an action must commence within this period, even if additional contamination is discovered at a later date and additional response activity becomes necessary. However, as an exception to this rule, "subsequent actions" still receive the benefit of an additional three-year period of limitations from the date of completion, so long as the initial recovery litigation has commenced within the original six-year period.[135]

CERCLA provides additional statutes of limitations for claims other than cost recovery. Contribution actions are subject to a three-year commencement period from the date of judgment for which contribution is sought.[136] Similarly, subrogation and indemnification claims must also commence within three years

---

131. CERCLA § 113(g)(2)(B), 42 U.S.C. § 9613(g)(2)(B); *see* United States v. Navistar Int'l Transp. Corp., 152 F.3d 702 (7th Cir. 1998) (determining statute of limitations to be triggered at the first placement of clay upon a landfill for the purpose of constructing a clay cap).

132. *See Navistar Int'l Transp. Corp.*, 152 F.3d at 710. *See also* United States v. Bos. & Me. Corp., 2016 WL 5339573, at *7 (D. Mass. Sept. 22, 2016) ("[I]f . . . [a] remedial action was initiated within 3 years after the completion of the removal action, costs incurred in the removal action may be recovered in the cost recovery action for the remedial action.") (internal quotation marks omitted); Asarco LLC v. Atl. Richfield Co., 866 F.3d 1117 (9th Cir. 2017) (action for recovery of removal costs can be initiated within the six-year remedial action statute of limitations period if brought "within 3 years after the completion of the removal action.") (citation omitted).

133. New York v. Next Millennium Realty, LLC, 732 F.3d 117, 124–25 (2d Cir. 2013) ("Removal actions are clean-up or removal measures taken to respond to immediate threats to public health and safety. . . . Remedial actions are generally actions designed to permanently remediate hazardous waste.") (citations omitted); Cal. *ex rel.* Cal. Dep't of Toxic Substances Control v. Hyampom Lumber Co., 903 F. Supp. 1389, 1391–94 (E.D. Cal. 1995) (concluding that the installation of fences was a removal action, but installation of utilities was a remedial action, lending to the fact that the utilities "played a critical role in the implementation of the permanent remedy").

134. N.Y. State Elec. & Gas Corp. v. FirstEnergy Corp., 766 F.3d 212, 235–36 (2d Cir. 2014) (upholding district court's dismissal of actions for remediation of coal tar contamination by determining that only one remedial period applied even though the response activities involved two different operational units, where OU-1 involved removal of contaminated soil from a manufactured gas plant, and OU-2 was created only after it was later discovered that a pipe had contributed to contamination in the nearby Susquehanna River prompting further removal of contaminated sediment and the pipe). *First Energy Corp.* further provides a recitation of authorities that have similarly applied the one-removal/one-remediation per-site rule, and the minority who have held otherwise. *Id.* at 236.

135. *Id.* at 236 (referring to CERCLA § 113(g); 42 U.S.C. § 9613(g)).

136. CERCLA § 113, 42 U.S.C. § 9613(g)(3).

of payment.[137] Carve-outs apply to minors and incompetents, which toll the commencement date.[138]

Natural resource damages (NRD) must also commence within three years, with a starting point of either the later of (1) the time it is discovered that a harm is connected to a hazardous substance, or (2) the applicable Department of Interior (DOI) regulations are promulgated.[139] As is discussed later in this chapter, in the context of NRD the connection of a harm to a hazardous substance is often difficult to prove, rendering the trigger date under the first option difficult to estimate. A separate provision permits an NRD action to be filed within three years after "completion of the remedial action" for a facility that has been designated on the NPL.[140] Less clear is to what extent this provision applies to facilities that are added to the NPL list long after the contamination was discovered. One district court has recently commented that the designation as an NPL "restarts" the statute of limitations, and provides a "virtually unlimited duration," because EPA must first complete its remediation to trigger the limitations period.[141]

SARA also included language that extends state statute of limitations with regard to tort claims caused by hazardous substances. The amendment, located at Section 158, imposes a federal "discovery rule" that commences the statute of limitations only once a plaintiff knows or reasonably should know of the injury caused by the hazardous substance.[142] Any state law that would cause an earlier commencement has been preempted.[143] By contrast, in its most recent CERCLA-related decision, the Supreme Court has determined that statutes of repose have not been superseded through preemption.[144]

Therefore, it is important to comprehend the distinction between the two. While statutes of limitations accrue at the time of a plaintiff's discovery of harm, statutes of repose accrue when a defendant's conduct has ceased. Practitioners initiating or defending against tort claims must be mindful of any such statutes within their local jurisdiction, such as North Carolina, which could bar suits

---

137. CERCLA § 113(g)(4)–(5), 42 U.S.C. § 9613(g)(4)–(5).

138. CERCLA § 113(g)(6), 42 U.S.C. § 9613(g)(6).

139. CERCLA § 113(g)(1), 42 U.S.C. § 9613(g)(1). It should also be noted that CERCLA § 126(d), 42 U.S.C. § 9626(d), further provides a separate limitation period for tribal NRD claims. In general a tribe has until the later of the expiration of the applicable period of limitations or "2 years after the United States, in its capacity as trustee for the tribe, gives written notice to the governing body of the tribe that it will not present a claim or commence an action on behalf of the tribe or fails to present a claim or commence an action within the time limitations specified in this chapter." *Id.*

140. *Id.*

141. New York v. Next Millennium Realty, LLC, 160 F. Supp. 3d 485 (E.D.N.Y. 2016); *see also* United States v. Asarco Inc., 214 F.3d 1104 (9th Cir. 2000) (where the longer statute of limitations applied even when the NPL site boundary was later extended to include the PRP's property).

142. CERCLA § 158(a)(4)(A), 42 U.S.C. § 9658(a)(4)(A).

143. CERCLA § 158(a)(1), 42 U.S.C. § 9658(a)(1).

144. *See* CTS Corp. v. Waldburger, 134 S. Ct. 2175 (2014). The Court concluded that Congress had not intended to preempt statutes of repose, because preemption is a specific limited exception, and despite being aware of both the statutes of repose and statutes of limitations decided only to expressly preempt state statutes of limitations. The Court further invoked a presumption against preemption in favor of state policies regarding health and safety.

brought against defendants whose conduct ended long ago. Because statutes of repose limit the window of liability for defendants after their conduct has terminated, these statutes typically do not allow equitable tolling, and can lead to harsh results for plaintiffs who were unaware of contamination or its negative health effects for long periods of time.

X. EQUITABLE ALLOCATION

Under CERCLA Section 113(f), a court is authorized to allocate response costs "using such equitable factors as [it] determines are appropriate," which provides courts with significant flexibility to fashion an equitable allocation of shares.[145] Under this flexible approach, courts possess authority to select "which equitable factors will inform [their] decision," and the court can exercise considerable discretion in this procedure, as any given court "may consider several factors, a few factors, or only one determining factor depending on the totality of the circumstances."[146] Similarly, those who engage in private mediated allocations can and often do, follow a flexible approach tailored to the needs of the site and contaminants in question.

When engaged in an allocation analysis, courts have predominantly relied on the "Gore factors" to divide liability among multiple PRPs. These factors include:

- The ability of the parties to demonstrate that their contribution to a discharge, release, or disposal of a hazardous substance can be distinguished;
- The amount of hazardous substances involved;
- The degree of toxicity of the substances;
- The degree of involvement by parties in the generation, transportation, treatment, storage, or disposal of the substances;
- The degree of care exercised by the parties with respect to the substances; and
- The degree of cooperation of the parties with government officials to prevent any harm to public health or the environment.[147]

A second list of factors that the courts have looked to for guidance include the "Torres factors," which include:

- The extent to which cleanup costs are attributable to wastes for which a party is responsible;

---

145. CERCLA § 113(f)(1), 42 U.S.C. § 9613(f)(1).

146. NCR Corp. v. George A. Whiting Paper Co., 768 F.3d 682, 695–96 (7th Cir. 2014) (citation omitted).

147. These Gore factors are named for then Representative Al Gore, who sought to add them through amendment to CERCLA. The bill passed the house, but was not adopted in the final version. *See* United States v. A&F Materials Co., 578 F. Supp. 1256 (S.D. Ill. 1984); 126 Cong. Rec. 26,781 (1980). For additional cases applying these factors, see Litgo N.J. Inc. v. N.J. Dep't of Envtl. Prot., 725 F.3d 369, 387–90 (3d Cir. 2013), United States v. Consol. Coal Co., 345 F.3d 409 (6th Cir. 2003), Boeing Co. v. Cascade Corp., 207 F.3d 1177, 1187–92 (9th Cir. 2000), Envtl. Transp. Servs. v. Ensco, Inc., 969 F.2d 503, 508 (7th Cir. 1992).

- The party's level of culpability;
- The degree to which the party benefited from disposal of the waste; and
- The party's ability to pay its share of the cost.[148]

But even these two separate lists are not exhaustive of the full panoply of circumstances a court or private allocator may consider when conducting an equitable allocation, which are otherwise limitless in scope given the broad flexibility afforded to this endeavor. However, there are some circumstances that are particularly likely to receive attention, such as when there is an indemnification agreement that evidences the parties' intent to allocate costs regardless of the agreement's enforceability,[149] or when the contamination is the product of war mobilization efforts.[150]

In any event, allocation will always be treated on a fact-rich, sometimes science-driven case-by-case basis, where facts and data unique to the case will be determinative to the outcome. Therefore, it is critical for practitioners to use the full resources at their disposal, and engage qualified experts who can competently perform various methods of analysis such as volumetric quantification, geographical and morphological studies, time-based calculations, and relative toxicity and risk-based assessments. Parties should also be willing to conduct a thorough investigation into the circumstances surrounding the contamination to discover facts that will assist in evaluating not only their own culpability, but the relative culpability of other PRPs as well, including investigation into the knowledge and conduct of all parties. This evidence may not assist in defending against liability, but it could be highly relevant toward an allocation analysis.

XI. ORPHAN SHARES

The inevitable existence of orphan shares has long plagued contributing PRPs, who almost always shoulder the burden of these absent parties' shares. Orphan shares can arise under a variety of circumstances, most often when a PRP has become financially unavailable through bankruptcy or dissolution, or its identity is unknown. Other circumstances may include when a PRP has been acquired and

---

148. United States v. Davis, 31 F. Supp. 2d 45 (D.R.I. 1998) (in setting forth these factors, the *Davis* court rejected a proposal by the defendant to apply a *per capita* approach, accepting that though there may be cases where such an allocation is appropriate, the great inequities that would ordinarily result from this method render it inappropriate in most situations). The Torres factors take their name from District Court Judge Ernest Torres, who wrote the *Davis* opinion.

149. Halliburton Energy Servs., Inc. v. NL Indus., 648 F. Supp. 2d 840, 878–84 (S.D. Tex. 2009) (where indemnification agreements were examined to determine that a zero percent allocation was not contemplated with regard to a specific PRP); Kerr-McGee Chem. Corp. v. Lefton Iron & Metal Co., 14 F.3d 321 (7th Cir. 1994) ("Although contractual agreements between parties are not necessarily determinative of statutory liability, [a party's] intent to indemnify [another party] should be considered in the allocation of cleanup costs.").

150. United States v. Shell Oil Co., 294 F.3d 1045, 1059–61 (9th Cir. 2002) (affirming district court's allocation of 100 percent of costs to the federal government due to its unfettered demand as part of war efforts for the products that caused the hazardous waste).

the purchaser cannot be held liable as a successor entity, or the PRP is protected by immunity of some kind (e.g., contribution protection). The defining characteristic of an orphan share is that it belongs to a party who is unavailable, and should not be confused with a recalcitrant party who chooses not to cooperate with remediation efforts.[151] The issue commonly posed by orphan shares is who should shoulder these costs, and how the costs should be allocated.

Most often, this burden has fallen on the remaining, financially solvent PRPs through a reallocation of the missing share, spreading the cost among these parties. But this is not always the case, particularly with regard to contribution claims, where courts have occasionally limited recovery to several liability, and only the costs for which that defendant is responsible.[152] This harsh application of the rule can lead to inequitable results for PRPs who have already been subject to joint and several liability through a cost recovery claim, and are then unable to recover any amounts for which unavailable PRPs are responsible. Fortunately for most PRPs faced with this possibility, such decisions are relatively rare. Instead, the vast majority of courts have recognized these unjust consequences, exercised the flexibility referenced in Section 113(f)(1) that permits courts to consider any appropriate equitable factor when assigning liability shares, and included orphan shares in their calculations.[153] Outside of court, in a private allocation process or settlement discussion, parties may have even greater flexibility to mold solutions to this vexing problem.

There is another avenue for limited relief from the burden imposed by orphan shares. EPA is authorized, in certain circumstances, to provide supplementary funding for orphan shares up to a maximum of 25 percent.[154] This relief is only available to PRPs who enter into negotiated settlements, and is intended as an incentive for remedial activities. This relief, however, is not an apportionment of mixed funding, but, rather, EPA is permitted to offer only "forgiveness of past costs and reduction of liability for future oversight costs."[155] As such, while EPA's orphan share policy may provide some relief, it may still prove inadequate for large shares of costs left behind.

---

151. *Davis*, 31 F. Supp. 2d at 68 ("The mere fact that a party bearing responsibility is not before the Court does not make its share of liability an orphan share.") (internal quotation marks omitted).

152. Gould Inc. v. A & M Battery & Tire Serv., 901 F. Supp. 906, 913 (M.D. Pa. 1995) ("Defendants are only liable for their share of the harm caused.").

153. *Litgo N.J.*, 725 F.3d at 379 n.4 ("A court may equitably allocate orphan shares among liable parties at its discretion.") (citation omitted); Pinal Creek Grp. v. Newmont Mining Corp., 118 F.3d 1298, 1303 (9th Cir. 1997) ("Under [CERCLA] § 113(f)(1), the cost of orphan shares is distributed equitably among all PRPs, just as cleanup costs are."); United States v. Kramer, 953 F. Supp. 592 (D.N.J. 1997).

154. Memorandum from Steven A. Herman, EPA Assistant Adm'r, Office of Enf't & Compliance Assurance, to Regional Adm'rs, Interim Guidance on Orphan Share Compensation for Settlors of Remedial Design/Remedial Action and Non-Time-Critical Removals 1–3 (1996), https://www.epa.gov/sites/production/files/2013-10/documents/orphan-share-rpt.pdf.

155. *Id.*

XII. THE RISING TIDE OF SEDIMENT SITES

In recent years, and certainly since the beginning of the 21st century, contaminated sediment sites (e.g., rivers, creeks, and tidal estuaries) have gained prominence.[156] From an administrative standpoint, the extraordinary difficulties posed by Superfund sediment sites are explained, in part, in three EPA separate guidance documents, as well as an audit by the Government Accountability Office (GAO) regarding EPA's consistency in applying procedures at these sites.[157] There is good reason for prioritization of some of these sites, as they constitute many of the most complex and expensive Superfund cleanups, largely due to the wide distribution of contaminants discharged to surface waters, which can spread throughout a local ecosystem, as well as the long-term persistence of contaminants in sediment media.

Similar challenges are evident in the difficulties PRPs face in working together to investigate and address sediment site conditions (that can span many acres or river or creek miles). Surface water sediment sites often present complex issues related to the parties' nexus to the contamination, which sometimes involve multiple parties (both successor and predecessor owners and operators, as well as multiparty upland sites). The duration, extent, and magnitude of varying alleged discharges to a waterway, as well as other complicating factors (e.g., orphan shares) can cause substantial proof issues in contribution actions as well as in calculating equitable shares. Some of the technical and related legal issues that often need to be addressed, that are either unique to waterway sediment sites or of special significance, include (1) determining the extent of fate and transport of contaminants between upstream and downstream sources, which can be complicated by tidal exchanges, storm events, and historical changes in stream morphology; (2) the fact that investigation and assessment costs can be substantial, but do not correlate with volume or toxicity of contaminants of potential concern; (3) contaminant fate may be difficult to model between the different times, inputs, and sedimentation conditions; (4) the impact of human (anthropogenic) discharges; and (5) the difficulties in determining appropriate reference areas for establishing baseline conditions for risk to receptors and other reference points.

---

156. Those generally familiar with so-called Superfund megasites will readily recognize some of these sites by name. For example, some sediment sites to garner special attention or to be the subject of litigation include the Lower Passaic River Study Area, Portland Harbor, and the Lower Fox River, to name just a few. While these and other sites have been around for many years, during the last decade they have commanded extra attention as EPA and natural resource trustees turn their focus on them.

157. U.S. Envtl. Protection Agency, Principles of Managing Contaminated Sediment Risks at Hazardous Waste Sites (2002); U.S. Envtl. Protection Agency, Contaminated Sediment Remediation Guidance for Hazardous Waste Sites, EPA-540-R-05-012, OSWER 9355.0-85 (Dec. 2005); Mathy Stanislaus, EPA, Remediating Contaminated Sediment Sites—Clarification of Several Key Remedial Investigation/Feasibility Study and Risk Management Recommendations, and Updated Contaminated Sediment Technical Advisory Group Operating Procedures, OLEM Directive 9200.1-130 (Jan. 9, 2017) [hereinafter *2017 EPA Sediment Site Guidance*]; U.S. Gov't Accountability Office, Report to Congressional Requesters, Superfund Sediment Sites, EPA Considers Risk Management Principles but Could Clarify Certain Procedures, GAO-16-777 (Sept. 2016) [hereinafter *GAO Report*].

Ultimately, many of these issues present even higher hurdles when parties cannot resolve their differences and must seek contribution through litigation. The factual and scientific proofs in such cases can be daunting.

With respect to allocation of damages, in a recent decision involving PCB contamination at the Kalamazoo River in western Michigan, a federal district court rejected the parties' attempts to provide allocation methods based primarily on volume and geography as "too legalistic and mathematically precise than an allocation" in the case could actually be.[158] In rendering its decision, the court noted there was a "lack of reliable data from the production period," and determined that overall allocation figures for each party were appropriate.[159] The parties' relative culpability weighed heavily in the court's decision, particularly NCR Corporation's continued encouragement of the use of its product after obtaining knowledge of the environmental hazards posed, and Georgia-Pacific's friction with regulators, both justifying a greater share of costs.[160] At least in this decision, the court emphasized intangible allocation factors to arrive at higher allocation factors for these two parties, even where objective data was lacking in many important respects.

As part of its prioritization of these sites, EPA has designated particularly large sites into two upper tiers, with Tier 1 sites requiring cleanups of 10,000 cubic yards or more of contaminated sediment, and Tier 2 composed of sites EPA characterizes as "large, complex, or controversial."[161] Some sediment megasites are estimated to incur costs of several billion dollars. Sediment sites further represent a category of growing concern given the human health consequences due to the consumption of contaminated fish or shellfish, a problem that is particularly troublesome when sediment contaminants exhibit bioaccumulative qualities that enter marine ecosystems.

EPA has identified two primary challenges for administering sediment sites: technical complexities and stakeholder involvement.[162] As the prior discussion of these issues suggests, straightforward solutions to sediment sites are rare, largely because of the size and complexity of these sites, most often due to their aquatic nature when compared to land-based contamination. Understandably, the decision-making process of how best to administer cleanup at these sites inherently stokes conflict due to the tension that lies between the need to effectuate a relatively rapid, cost-effective response, while simultaneously conducting a thorough, science-based investigation of site conditions to effectively analyze the full scope of risks and feasible remediation methods. Governmental agencies and stakeholders sometimes hold different views and competing interests when engaging in

---

158. Georgia-Pacific Consumer Prods. LP v. NCR Corp., No. 1:11-CV-483, 2018 WL 1556418, at *24 (W.D. Mich. Mar. 29, 2018).

159. *Id.*

160. *See id.* at *24–26 (imposing 40 percent allocations to each of NCR Corp. and Georgia-Pacific).

161. *GAO Report, supra* note 157, at 1.

162. *Id.*

these planning activities, which can lead to disagreements.[163] The result can often include stalled response activities and the expenditure of massive resources, without significant progress.

In an effort to address these issues, EPA first issued guidance in 2002 that provides 11 recommendations that seek to streamline the administration of sediment sites. These recommendations have evolved through the two updates EPA issued in 2005, and most recently 2017, which draw on EPA's experience in handling the challenges posed by sediment sites. Even though these recommendations are nonbinding, they serve as a helpful resource when engaged in the difficult process of fashioning a cost-effective remediation action plan.

EPA's recommendations state a preference for early intervention at sediment sites, but also emphasize the need to consider risk reduction and to gather sufficient information to create an informed plan.[164] As for remediation planning, the updated guidance emphasizes effective monitoring, preferring the use of concrete endpoints by monitoring specific indicators such as levels in sediment and fish tissue.[165] Adaptive management processes are also recommended to effectively modify action plans as unanticipated issues arise during the course of cleanup, or when the remedial activities prove less effective than expected.[166]

For Tier 2 sites, EPA has further established the Contaminated Sediments Technical Advisory Group (CSTAG), for consultation purposes.[167] During its audit, the GAO commented on the assistance provided by CSTAG in both monitoring and providing advice related to remedial activities. However, the GAO recommended changes to EPA's procedural directives, suggesting that it provide more clarity to the materials that should be provided in advance of CSTAG update meetings so that CSTAG would be more adequately informed of progress at the site.[168] EPA has incorporated these recommendations into its most recent guidance, opening the door for CSTAG to play a more integral role in the future.[169]

---

163. Stakeholders frequently disagree with who should bear responsibility for cleanup, the extent of cleanup that is truly necessary, the timing and scope of remedial action, preferences for more or less expensive remedies, and concerns about the effects of the cleanup and recontamination. These disagreements can be further frustrated by stakeholders' varying levels of knowledge regarding the Superfund process. *See id.* at 33–35.

164. *2017 EPA Sediment Site Guidance, supra* note 157, at 2–5.

165. *Id.* at 5–10.

166. *Id.* at 8–9.

167. CSTAG includes one representative from each of EPA's ten regions, two representatives from the EPA Office of Research and Development and OSRTI, and two representatives from the U.S. Army Corps of Engineers. *GAO Report, supra* note 157, at 19.

168. *Id.* at 36.

169. *2017 EPA Sediment Site Guidance, supra* note 157, at 13–16.

XIII. NATURAL RESOURCE DAMAGES

A. What Are Natural Resources?

Natural resources share one preeminent characteristic—they are inherently public and are not owned as personal property. Aside from this distinction, natural resources are defined broadly to include "land, fish, wildlife, biota, air, water, ground water, drinking water supplies, and other such resources."[170] Natural resources further extend to the "supporting ecosystems," upon which they rely.[171] Together and individually, these resources provide many benefits to the public in the form of natural resources services, which are described more fully below. Thus, as resources available to the commons but not owned by any private individual, in order for legal protections to accrue, natural resources are further defined as "belonging to, managed by, held in trust by, appertaining to, or otherwise controlled by" a sovereign entity, such as the federal or state governments who have been entrusted with their protection as trustees.[172] There are several laws, both federal and state, that provide civil remedies for when these resources have been harmed either by contamination or other causes.[173]

B. What Are Natural Resource Services?

Natural resource services are defined in DOI's regulations as

> the physical and biological functions performed by the resource including the human uses of those functions. These services are the result of the physical, chemical, or biological quality of the resource.[174]

Services are often categorized as either ecological services (e.g., benthic organisms in a river provide food for fish) or human-use services (e.g., sport fishing in a river).[175] Services play a key role in assessing NRD, because the public values

---

170. CERCLA § 101(16), 42 U.S.C. 9601(16); Robinson Twp. v. Commonwealth, 623 Pa. 564, 652 (2013) ("At present, the concept of public natural resources includes not only state-owned lands, waterways, and mineral reserves, but also resources that implicate the public interest, such as ambient air, surface and groundwater, wild flora, and fauna. . . .").

171. 40 C.F.R. § 300.600(b).

172. CERCLA § 101(16), 42 U.S.C. § 9601(16).

173. These include, among others, CERCLA § 101, 42 U.S.C. §§ 9601 *et seq.*; Oil Pollution Act of 1990 (OPA) §§ 1001–7001, 33 U.S.C. §§ 2701–2761 (2000 & Supp. V 2005); Park System Resource Protection Act (PSRPA) §§ 1–5, 54 U.S.C. §§ 100701–100725; Marine Protection, Research and Sanctuaries Act (Sanctuaries Act) §§ 302–313, 16 U.S.C. §§ 1431 to 45c-1 (2000 & Supp. V 2005), and similar state statutes. *See, e.g.*, New Jersey's Spill Compensation and Control Act, N.J. Stat. Ann. § 58:10-23.11 to -23.24; Cal. Gov't. Code § 8670.56.5(a), (h), & (i); Washington's Model Toxics Control Act, Wash. Rev. Code. Ann. §§ 70.105D.010 *et seq. See generally* Brian Israel, State-by-State Guide to NRD Programs in All 50 States and Puerto Rico (2018), https://www.arnoldporter.com/~/media/files/perspectives/publications/2018/03/state-by-state-nrd-guide.pdf.

174. 43 C.F.R. § 11.14(nn).

175. NOAA Damage Assessment and Restoration Program, Scaling Compensatory Restoration Actions: Guidance Document for Natural Resource Damage Assessment under the Oil Pollution Act of 1990, at 2-1 (1997) [hereinafter *NOAA 1997*].

natural resources for the services they provide.[176] Some of the services directly benefit the public, such as providing outdoor recreation activities, while other services indirectly benefit the public by supporting wildlife.

When an injury to a natural resource reduces the services provided by that resource, then the public will experience a loss in welfare.[177] The goal of the NRD process is to compensate the public for that welfare loss (i.e., make the public whole).[178] Specifically, "compensable values" in the DOI process[179] focus exclusively on the loss of natural resource services. If there is no loss of services from a natural resource injury, then there is no loss of compensable values.

In some instances, ecological and/or human-use service losses may continue after the completion of cleanup/remediation activities. For example, the oiling and subsequent cleanup of wetlands may reduce the amount of food available for resident wildlife. If the full recovery of food sources in the oiled wetlands takes two years, then the reduction in food-web services of the wetlands over the two years will be compensable. Similarly, if a recreation area is closed during the cleanup from an oil spill, then the use of the area by the public may not return to typical use levels immediately upon the reopening of the site. In that situation the site is not injured in the postclosure period, but recreation use is below typical levels for some days or weeks after the site reopens. In general, the reduction in public use during the recovery period is compensable, even though the site is not injured during that period. Alternatively, some sites may experience an increase in postclosure use above the typical use as a result of temporal substitution from the closure period to the postclosure period. Temporal substitution mitigates some, but not all, of the recreation losses from an oil spill.

XIV. TRUSTEESHIP

A. The Public Trust Doctrine

The public trust doctrine is the product of long-standing common law, originating in ancient Rome.[180] The first case addressing the public trust doctrine in the United States dates as far back as 1821, where it was recognized as a form of natural law.[181] In its nascent years, the public trust doctrine was most often invoked to

---

176. Freeman, A. Myrick III, The Measurement of Environmental and Resource Values: Theory and Methods 5 (Joseph A. Herriges ed., 2d ed. 2003).

177. Raymond J. Kopp & V. Kerry Smith, Valuing Natural Assets: The Economics of Natural Resource Damage Assessment 11 (1993).

178. 51 Fed. Reg. 27,688 (Aug. 1, 1986).

179. 43 C.F.R. § 11.83(c)(1).

180. *In re* Water Use Permit Applications, 9 P.3d 409, 445 (Haw. 2000) ("In its ancient Roman form, the public trust included the air, running water, the sea, and consequently the shores of the sea.") (internal quotation marks omitted).

181. *See* Arnold v. Mundy, 6 N.J.L. 1, 11 (N.J. 1821) (recognizing the public trust doctrine to be "the law of nature, which is the only true foundation of all the social rights" and noting peoples' natural rights to common liberties such as fisheries preserved since *Magna Carta*, which restored the

protect water resources vital to the economy and providing food, but it has since branched out to many other forms of natural resources identified here previously.[182] But there is no text in the U.S. Constitution that explicitly provides this sovereign duty. Instead, this responsibility has been implied as part of the "reserved powers doctrine," which prohibits any current legislature from infringing upon future legislatures' decision-making ability, and in the case of natural resources, the government may not "abdicate its trust over property in which the whole people are interested."[183] Several states have since included explicit public trustee provisions in their constitutions related to natural resources.[184]

B. Who Are the Trustees?

The foundational principle for the public trust doctrine rests on the premise that the government serves as the steward for the land and natural resources of our nation, acting as a trustee for the benefit of the public. As a result, it is the trustees who serve as the agents who take action to protect natural resources and restore them as necessary. By virtue of their appointed stewardship, trustees are empowered to pursue legal actions requesting damages or injunctive relief against polluting parties responsible for harming natural resources or impairing their value.

Under CERCLA, trustees include the U.S. government, state governments, or any Indian tribe, for the respective natural resources held in trust by the sovereign trustee.[185] The Oil Pollution Act of 1990 (OPA) also includes foreign sovereignties as trustees.[186] Both CERCLA and OPA vest authority in the U.S. president to designate federal officials who may take action as trustees on behalf of the federal government, and the governor of each state to likewise designate state officials who may exercise this authority.[187] Pursuant to this directive, the president has designated the secretaries of the Interior, Agriculture, Defense, Commerce, and Energy departments as trustees.[188] Under the Park System Resource Protection

---

principles of the ancient law, and that the sovereign's interest in the ports, the bays, the coasts of the sea, including both the water and the land under the water, is for the sake of order and protection, and not for the sovereign's own use, but for the use of the citizen); see also Roath v. Driscoll, 20 Conn. 533 (1850) (water, whether moving or motionless in the earth, is not, in the eye of the law, distinct from the earth and is capable of common protection); Georgia v. Tenn. Copper Co., 206 U.S. 230, 237 (1907) (in its parens patriae capacity, "the State has an interest independent of and behind the titles of its citizens, in all the earth and air within its domain. It has the last word as to whether its mountains shall be stripped of their forests and its inhabitants shall breathe pure air.").

182. Martin v. Waddell's Lessee, 41 U.S. 367 (1842).

183. Ill. Cent. R.R. Co. v. Illinois, 146 U.S. 387, 453, 459–60 (1892).

184. These states include Pennsylvania, Louisiana, Montana, Hawaii, Rhode Island, and Illinois. Pa. Const. art. I, § 27 ("Wherever occurring in their natural state, fish, wildlife, and waters are reserved to the people for common use."), La. Const. art. IX, § 1; Mont. Const. art. IX, § 1; Haw. Const. art. IX, § 1; R.I. Const. art. I, § 17; Ill. Const. art XI, § 1.

185. CERCLA § 107(f)(1), 42 U.S.C. § 9607(f)(1).

186. Pub. L. No. 101-380, 104 Stat. 484 (1990); OPA § 1006(a)(4), 33 U.S.C. § 2706(a)(4).

187. CERCLA § 107(f)(2)(A)–(B), 42 U.S.C. 9607(f)(2)(A)–(B); 40 C.F.R. § 300.600(a).

188. Exec. Order No. 12,580, 52 Fed. Reg. 2923 (Jan. 23, 1987); 40 C.F.R. § 300.600(b).

Act (PSRPA) and the Sanctuaries Act, it is the secretary of the Interior who holds exclusive trustee status.[189]

Notably, EPA is not designated as an authorized trustee, as it is instead responsible for the investigation of and response to hazardous substance spills that cause injury to natural resources, and further, to notify and coordinate with trustees when such events occur.[190] CERCLA and OPA also do not provide for municipalities or other local authorities to act as trustees but courts have in some instances permitted them to bring such actions, while denying standing in others.[191]

C. The Concept of Trusteeship

At its core, the public trust doctrine recognizes that there exist certain types of public property that are inherently owned or managed by the government in order to safeguard these resources for the public. Because the public trust doctrine relies on the fundamental concepts of property held in trust for the benefit of others, trustees owe fiduciary responsibilities to the public beneficiaries, such as duties of good faith and loyalty, as well as duties to avoid waste and maximize value.[192] Under these concepts of fiduciary duty, trustees are not only obligated to react to contaminating events, they may also be obligated to take affirmative action when necessary to protect natural resources for the benefit of future generations.

Trustees are responsible for not only the assessment of natural resource injuries, but also their restoration, should it become necessary. Also due to their role as fiduciaries, any damages recovered pursuant to an NRD claim is not recovered for use by the sovereign, they are recovered solely for the benefit of the public and to restore or replace the natural resources that have suffered injury.[193]

---

189. PSRPA § 3, 54 U.S.C. § 100723; Sanctuaries Act § 312(c)(1), 16 U.S.C. § 1443(c)(1) (2000 & Supp. V 2005).

190. CERCLA § 104(b)(2), 42 U.S.C. § 9604(b)(2). The same holds true for OPA. OPA § 4201(a), 33 U.S.C. § 1321(c).

191. Decisions allowing municipalities to proceed with NRD claims include Mayor & Bd. of Aldermen of Town of Boonton v. Drew Chem. Corp., 621 F. Supp. 663 (D.N.J. 1985), and City of New York v. Exxon Corp., 633 F. Supp. 609 (S.D.N.Y. 1986). Examples of cases where this right has been denied include Rockaway v. Klockner & Klockner, 811 F. Supp. 1039, 1049 (D.N.J. 1993) ("[O]nly a 'state official,' specifically appointed by the governor of the state, may be an 'authorized representative' for purposes of bringing an action to recover for natural resource damages."); Town of Bedford v. Raytheon Co., 755 F. Supp. 469, 473 (D. Mass. 1991) ("The Congressional determination to require the Chief Executive of the sovereign to designate the trustee to pursue such a claim represents an understandable preference that litigation strategy and settlement decisions be centralized in this developing area to avoid a proliferation of inconsistent approaches by a range of different plaintiffs with counsel of variable quality and experience."); Werlein v. United States, 746 F. Supp. 887 (D. Minn. 1990).

192. *In re* Water Use Permit Applications, 9 P.3d 409, 451–52 (Haw. 2000) ("[T]he water resources trust also encompasses a duty to promote the reasonable and beneficial use of water resources in order to maximize their social and economic benefits to the people of this state. . . . In short, the object is not maximum consumptive use, but rather the most equitable, reasonable, and beneficial allocation of state water resources, with full recognition that resource protection also constitutes use.") (internal quotation marks omitted).

193. United States v. Asarco Inc., 471 F. Supp. 2d 1063, 1068 (D. Idaho 2005) ("Under CERCLA the recovery, if any, is not for the benefit of a given party, but goes to the trustee as the fiduciary to accomplish the stated goals.").

D. Thorny Issues of Co-Trusteeship

Problems can arise when natural resources are held jointly by trustees, requiring coordination between the co-trustees for both assessment and restoration. This is primarily owing to CERCLA's explicit bar against double recovery, which disallows multiple recoveries for a single natural resource injury, a well-established principle of damages in any civil action and the common law.[194] This bar against double recovery can apply in many contexts, such as when multiple trustees pursue NRD regarding the same resources or services, or when remedial actions minimize the impact on such resources or services, which would similarly reduce any amount of NRD awards.

However, when multiple trustees do become involved as co-trustees, they are encouraged to "coordinate and cooperate in carrying out [their collective] responsibilities."[195] OPA's regulations similarly state that "If there is a reasonable basis for dividing the natural resource damage assessment, trustees may act independently . . . so long as there is no double recovery of damages."[196] However, it is unclear which trustee has priority to initiate legal action, but equally if not more problematic is when certain trustees are disinterested in pursuing legal action, either due to a lack of funding, political pressure, or economic impacts, which can cause trustees to be at odds with each other. When the latter occurs, such conflicts can frustrate the ability to appropriately recoup NRD, as well as impair the ability to reach a comprehensive settlement with PRPs. This can frustrate and delay timely restoration action.

Another issue that has arisen over the years is to what extent an individual trustee may recover damages when there are other co-trustees who are not parties to the action. The case of *Coeur d'Alene Tribe v. Asarco, Inc.* provides insight into the difficulty presented by this issue.[197] In *Coeur d'Alene Tribe*, federal, state, and Indian tribe trustees sought NRD for contamination to the Coeur d'Alene Basin due to mining activities. The state trustee settled its claims early in the litigation; however, the federal and tribal trustees pursued the case through a bench trial. The court determined that a trustee could only recover an allocated share of NRD based upon the proportion of its stewardship over that resource. In order to make this allocation, the court first investigated the relative responsibility each trustee possessed over the resources by statutory right.[198] However, because responsibility for some of the natural resources overlapped between the three trustees, the court resorted to analyzing the proportional management exercised by each

---

194. CERCLA § 107(f)(1), 42 U.S.C. § 9607(f)(1) ("There shall be no double recovery under this chapter for natural resource damages, including the costs of damage assessment or restoration, rehabilitation, or acquisition for the same release and natural resource.").
195. 40 C.F.R. § 300.615(a).
196. 15 C.F.R. § 990.14(a)(2).
197. Coeur d'Alene Tribe v. Asarco, Inc., 280 F. Supp. 2d 1094 (D. Idaho 2003).
198. *Id.* at 1116.

trustee over the resources, and requested that they present evidence so that it could conduct an allocation on this basis.[199]

Two years later, the court reversed course and determined that individual trustees were not limited to an allocated share.[200] Instead, relying on the policy notion of making-whole restitution for underlying NRD actions, the court determined that any individual co-trustee was entitled to pursue the full amount of NRD.[201] The ability to pursue this full amount would not be hindered by a previous settlement because one co-trustee may not bind the others.[202] However, consistent with the law of damages, the award was reduced by the amounts already recovered via settlement.[203]

Another example of the problems that may arise when a co-trustee does not participate in litigation is the case of *Oklahoma v. Tyson Foods, Inc.*[204] In *Tyson Foods*, the Cherokee Nation trustee did not participate in litigation brought by a state trustee and others. The court dismissed the action entirely on the basis that the Cherokee Nation was an indispensable party, and proceeding without it would impair or impede its ability to protect its interests. Without explanation, the court relied on the first *Coeur d'Alene Tribe* decision to reach this determination, focusing on the state trustee's lack of any attempt to allocate stewardship of the natural resources between the state and the tribal nation. Based on this lack of allocation, the court concluded that "the State—is therefore likely to be unjustly enriched at the expense of the Nation."[205] The court appeared unaware that the *Coeur d'Alene Tribe* decision had been later overruled, even though the successive opinion predated *Tyson Foods* by four years.[206] Indeed, there is support for the idea that tribal nation trustees may consent to the federal government representing its NRD interests, a concept that may avoid this basis for dismissal.[207]

Following the preceding decisions, it remains unclear to what extent the defense of double recovery is viable when there are multiple co-trustees. These decisions are instructive that no recovery beyond 100 percent of the compensable NRD will be awarded, precluding straightforward double recovery cases where

---

199. *Id.* at 1116–17.

200. *Asarco*, 471 F. Supp. 2d at 1063.

201. *Id.* at 1068.

202. *Id.*

203. *Id.* However, PRPs should exercise caution when allocating settlement funds between NRD and response costs, as the NRD portion will only reduce future awards by the dollar amounts and the allocation itself is not subject to relitigation if a party feels the amount is disproportionate. United States v. NCR Corp., No. 10-C-910, 2017 WL 25467 (E.D. Wis. Jan. 3, 2017).

204. Oklahoma v. Tyson Foods, Inc., 258 F.R.D. 472 (N.D. Okla. 2009).

205. *Id.* at 480.

206. This reliance was later questioned by a dissenting judge in a later Tenth Circuit decision that addressed unrelated issues. *See* Oklahoma *ex rel.* Edmondson v. Tyson Foods, Inc., 619 F.3d 1223, 1241 (10th Cir. 2010) (Tacha, D., dissenting) ("For this point, the district court relied on *Coeur d'Alene Tribe*, 280 F. Supp. at 1094. That decision, however, had been subsequently reconsidered and reversed by the judge who issued it.") (citing *Asarco*, 471 F. Supp. 2d at 1068).

207. Century Indem. Co. v. Marine Grp., LLC, 131 F. Supp. 3d 1018, 1035 (D. Or. 2015) ("[A] Tribe may consent to the United States acting on their behalf with regard to NRD claims.") (citing *Asarco*, 471 F. Supp. 2d at 1068).

multiple trustees pursue litigation, each seeking full recovery for the same natural resource harms. The issue is further complicated when one or more trustees pursue a settlement, or have entered into a settlement, while one or more others proceed to litigation. In these instances, PRPs must be cautious with how the settlement is structured, because a future NRD award at trial will only be reduced by the finite dollar amount attributed to NRD via settlement. But PRPs can at least take solace in the comment found within the second *Coeur d'Alene Tribe* court's decision that "if there is a later disagreement between the co-trustees, that disagreement would have to be resolved by successive litigation between the trustees, but it could in no way affect the liability of the responsible party or parties."[208] This comment, however, does not address other co-trustee parties who are neither party to the settlement or the trial.

XV. KEY STATUTORY REGIMES

There are four main sources of statutory authority respecting natural resource damages, and these include (1) CERCLA, (2) OPA, (3) PSRPA, and (4) corollary state statutes that create their own NRD causes of action. Each of these regimes works within its own framework though these regimes can and often do overlap. CERCLA and OPA are the most frequent authority for trustees bringing NRD actions in federal court, but PSRPA and the Sanctuaries Act occasionally serve niche roles in this larger scheme. States vary greatly in their approach and volume of NRD claims, with New Jersey recently serving as the most active jurisdiction.

A. CERCLA and OPA

Under CERCLA, a responsible party "shall be liable for . . . damages for injury to, destruction of, or loss of natural resources, including the reasonable costs of assessing such injury, destruction, or loss resulting from such a release."[209] In order to establish a prima facie NRD case under CERCLA, a trustee must meet its burden on four elements: (1) injury to, destruction, or loss of (2) natural resources, (3) resulting from the release (4) of hazardous substances.[210] These elements are discussed in more depth later in the chapter, including how the element of causation is (perhaps) a distinguishing and complicating feature in an NRD action under CERCLA.

Recoveries for damages under CERCLA are earmarked "for use only to restore, replace, or acquire the equivalent of such natural resources."[211] Like its response cost provisions for removal and remedial actions, NRD liability under CERCLA is also ostensibly strict, joint, and several, though a defendant may be able to

---

208. *Asarco*, 471 F. Supp. 2d at 1068.
209. CERCLA § 107(a)(4)(C), 42 U.S.C. § 9607(a)(4)(C).
210. *Id.*
211. CERCLA § 107(f)(1), 42 U.S.C. § 9607(f)(1).

overcome this presumption if it is able to demonstrate apportionment is appropriate.[212] However, there is no retroactive liability for NRD for releases of hazardous substances occurring prior to 1980 when CERCLA was first enacted.[213] Importantly, before bringing suit, a trustee must first provide notice to the president and all PRPs 60 days before filing the action.[214] As a separate prerequisite to this notice requirement, an NRD action will be deemed premature if brought before a remedial action has been selected, so long as the "President [through EPA] is diligently proceeding with a remedial investigation and feasibility study."[215]

The OPA framework is similar in many respects to CERCLA. OPA was created to deal specifically with hazards presented by oil spills and discharges.[216] Much like CERCLA, OPA provides for the assessment and restoration of natural resources, but applies to resources harmed by oil contamination, filling the gap intentionally left in CERCLA that excludes petroleum from its definitions of hazardous substances.[217] Due to the complementary nature of this framework, OPA shares many of the same definitions governing NRD claims with CERCLA.[218] There are some differences, however, such as that foreign governments are eligible to act as trustees under OPA, which is not provided for by CERCLA.[219] Due to its nature and focus, OPA does not subscribe to the same definitions of PRPs as CERCLA, and instead, responsible parties may include owners or operators of vessels, onshore/offshore facilities, pipelines, deepwater ports, or those who have abandoned any of the above.[220] Moreover, OPA provides other avenues for lawsuits by entities other than trustees that are loosely related to natural resources in the form of economic losses caused by harm to real or personal property.[221]

B. PSRPA and Sanctuaries Act

Natural resources within the national park system are provided extra protection pursuant to the PSRPA and marine sanctuaries under the Sanctuaries Act at

---

212. Idaho v. Bunker Hill Co., 635 F. Supp. 665, 674–75 (D. Idaho 1986).

213. CERCLA § 107(f)(1), 42 U.S.C. § 9607(f)(1) ("There shall be no recovery under the authority . . . of this section where such damages and the release of a hazardous substance from which such damages resulted have occurred wholly before December 11, 1980."). In practice, however, this distinction may present difficulties with respect to the distinction between and division of damages that have continued to occur over a long period of time. See, e.g., Aetna Cas. & Sur. Co. v. Pintlar Corp., 948 F.2d 1507, 1515–16 (9th Cir. 1991).

214. CERCLA § 113(g)(1), 42 U.S.C. § 9613(g)(1).

215. *Id. See generally* Quapaw Tribe of Okla. v. Blue Tee Corp., No. 03-CV-0846-CVE-PJC, 2008 WL 2704482, at *13–21 (N.D. Okla. Jul. 7, 2008) (finding EPA to be "diligently proceeding" at the time the trustee brought suit, and in reaching this decision the court placed little weight on EPA's past conduct, concluding that EPA had not "ignored" evidence of health risks, but, rather, it had "assessed" this risk differently from the trustee).

216. OPA §§ 1001 *et seq.,* 33 U.S.C. §§ 2701 *et seq.*

217. CERCLA § 101(14), 42 U.S.C. § 9601(14).

218. *Compare* CERCLA § 101(16), 42 U.S.C. § 9601(16), *with* OPA § 1001(20), 33 U.S.C. § 2701(20). *Compare* CERCLA §§ 101(6), 107(a)(4)(C), 42 U.S.C. §§ 9601(6), 9607(a)(4)(C), *with* OPA §§ 1001(5), 1002(b)(2), 33 U.S.C. §§ 2701(5), 2702(b)(2).

219. OPA § 1006(a)(4), 33 U.S.C. § 2706(a)(4).

220. OPA § 1001(32), 33 U.S.C. § 2701(32).

221. OPA § 1002(b)(2)(B)–(F), 33 U.S.C. § 2702(b)(2)(B)–(F).

Title 16.[222] These statutes were created in recognition of "the ever increasing societal pressures being placed upon America's unique natural and cultural resources contained in the [National Park] System."[223] Resources protected by PSRPA and the Sanctuaries Act are even more broad than CERCLA and OPA, defined as "any living or non-living resource" within either a "[National Park] System unit," (PSRPA) or a "national marine sanctuary" (Sanctuaries Act).[224] The only exclusion under PSRPA is for resources "owned by a non-Federal entity," with no similar exclusion under the Sanctuaries Act.[225] This definition includes cultural resources, which are not protected under CERCLA or OPA. Recoverable damages are also not limited and include costs for assessment, as well as costs to replace, restore, or acquire equivalent resources; the value of any loss of use of resources, as well as the value of any resources that cannot be restored or replaced.[226]

C. State Statutes

States have increasingly taken an active role in both NRD assessments and litigation to pursue restoration costs. While New Jersey spearheaded this effort, several states now contribute substantial resources toward their local NRD programs, and at this time, nearly every state participates in some form of NRD activity.[227] This proliferation of state action should serve as a testament to the rapid development and growing interest in NRD.

As trustees in their own right, states may participate jointly with the federal government or other trustees, or pursue claims independently under either federal or state laws. A recent prominent example where state trustees worked in tandem with federal authorities in a massive, complex litigation resulting in expansive NRD recovery was the *Deepwater Horizon* oil spill. This combined effort has culminated in an agreement by BP to contribute up to 8.8 billion dollars toward restoration projects, shared between five Gulf states and the federal government.[228]

As further evidence of states' rising interest in NRD activities, many have now employed dedicated personnel in either NRD-focused departments or other state

---

222. 54 U.S.C. §§ 100701–100725. Sanctuaries Act §§ 302–313, 16 U.S.C. §§ 1431 to 45c-1 (2000 & Supp. V 2005). Previously, the Park System Resource Protection Act was codified in Title 16, but that statute was repealed in 2014 and replaced with the new statutes located at Title 54. 16 U.S.C. § 19jj (repealed by Pub. L. No. 113-287, 128 Stat. 3272, § 7 (Dec. 19, 2014)).

223. 54 U.S.C. § 100701.

224. 54 U.S.C. § 100721(3); Sanctuaries Act § 302(6), 16 U.S.C. § 1432(6). The Sanctuaries Act further elaborates in its definition, specifying that resources must "contribute[] to the conservation, recreational, ecological, historical, educational, cultural, archeological, scientific, or aesthetic value of the sanctuary." Sanctuaries Act § 302(8), 16 U.S.C. § 1432(6).

225. *Id.*

226. 54 U.S.C. § 100721(1); Sanctuaries Act § 302(8), 16 U.S.C. § 1432(8).

227. *See* Brian Israel, State-by-State Guide to NRD Programs in All 50 States and Puerto Rico (2018), https://www.arnoldporter.com/~/media/files/perspectives/publications/2018/03/state-by-state-nrd-guide .pdf.

228. *See generally* Nat'l Oceanic & Atmospheric Admin., Deepwater Horizon Oil Spill: Final Programmatic Damage Assessment and Restoration Plan and Final Programmatic Environmental Impact Statement (2016), http://www.gulfspillrestoration.noaa.gov/restoration-planning/gulf-plan.

environmental and land use agencies who work exclusively on NRD matters. Some of these departments and agencies possess their own general counsel who pursue NRD claims, such as New York, but most rely on their attorney generals to pursue litigation. Several states will even employ private attorneys to this end, a method that has greatly assisted New Jersey's progress in this area.[229]

Many states have enacted state statutes specifically addressing NRD claims, with provisions similar, if not identical, to federal statutes and standards. Most often, liability is explicitly strict, joint, and several for these states, and include expansive damages provisions much like their federal counterparts.[230] With a sturdy foundation now established, states may continue to bolster their NRD practices.

XVI. COMMON LAW CAUSES OF ACTION

There are several common law claims that can bolster NRD actions, including actions brought under the public trust doctrine, trespass, and nuisance. Indeed, in states that have not adopted statutes that provide for NRD actions, common law actions will serve as the state court claims of first resort.[231] Of course, these common law actions will vary from state to state, and will be subject to varying statutes of limitations that may be inconsistent with those provided by NRD statutes.

Because common law actions are not statutory in nature, they may not be confined to trustees and thus may be brought by private parties. So far, these claims have met little success due to courts finding these claims preempted by CERCLA. However, these cases have typically claimed that defendants' remediation activities conducted pursuant to CERCLA consent orders were inadequate.[232] It remains to be seen if common law claims may survive when a defendant has negligently failed to conduct remediation activities in conformity with a consent order. But there is reason to anticipate courts will apply preemption broadly, as there is a palpable concern that such actions will lead to a form of double recovery, and by extension, deplete funds that would otherwise be used to effectuate the restoration or replacement of the natural resources at issue.[233]

---

229. These states include California, New Jersey, Indiana, and Hawaii. Israel, *supra* note 227, at 9, 25.

230. New Jersey's Spill Compensation and Control Act provides damages in the form of "removal or attempted removal of hazardous substances" as well as "taking of reasonable measures to prevent or mitigate damage to the public health, safety, or welfare, including, but not limited to, public and private property, shorelines, beaches, surface waters, water columns and bottom sediments, soils and other affected property, including wildlife and other natural resources." N.J. Stat. Ann. § 58:10-23.11(b).

231. N.J. Dep't of Envtl. Prot. v. Ventron Corp., 94 N.J. 473, 499 (1983) (stating that "the Spill Act [did] not so much change substantive liability as it establishe[d] new remedies for activities recognized as tortious both under prior statutes and the common law.").

232. *See generally* Bartlett v. Honeywell Int'l, Inc., 260 F. Supp. 3d 231 (N.D.N.Y. 2017), *aff'd*, 2018 WL 2383534 (2d Cir. May 25, 2018) (providing a history of cases where CERCLA preempted state law actions when remediation activities are conducted pursuant to a consent decree, and determining that state law claims were preempted by actions the contested consent decree sanctioned).

233. New Mexico v. Gen. Elec. Co., 467 F.3d 1223, 1247–48 (10th Cir. 2006) ("CERCLA's comprehensive NRD scheme preempts any state remedy designed to achieve something other than the restoration, replacement, or acquisition of the equivalent of a contaminated natural resource. . . . PRPs

XVII. THE NATURAL RESOURCES DAMAGES ASSESSMENT (NRDA) PROCESS

A. Phases in the NRDA Process

Figure 5.1 shows the four phases in DOI's NRD assessment process. The first phase is the preassessment phase. The primary task in this phase is to conduct a pre-assessment screen, in which the trustees determine whether to proceed with an assessment. Before making that decision, the trustees must determine that the following criteria are met:

- A release of a hazardous substance has occurred;
- Natural resources for which the federal or state agency or Indian tribe may assert trusteeship under CERCLA have been or are likely to have been adversely affected by the release;
- The quantity and concentration of the released hazardous substance is sufficient to potentially cause injury to those natural resources;
- Data sufficient to pursue an assessment are readily available or likely to be obtained at reasonable cost; and
- Response actions, if any, carried out or planned do not or will not sufficiently remedy the injury to natural resources without further action.[234]

If the trustees determine that a release meets the criteria above, then they must develop a written document, known as a preassessment screen determination, to support a decision to proceed with an assessment.

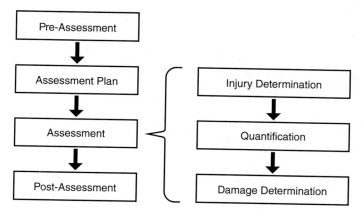

FIGURE 5.1
Phases in DOI's NRD Process

---

conceivably might be liable for double recovery where a state's successful state law claim for money damages precedes an EPA-ordered cleanup.").

234. 43 C.F.R. § 11.23(e).

The trustees develop an assessment plan in the second phase of DOI's NRD process. One of the trustees' first tasks in this phase is to decide whether to use the Type A or Type B procedures in the assessment. Sections 11.34 through 11.36 of DOI's regulations contain guidance on making this choice. The Type A procedures are confined to two types of environments for incidents that are expected to have damages of $100,000 or less.[235] Consequently, the Type A procedures are rarely used. Therefore, we focus on the Type B procedures in the remainder of this chapter.

The DOI regulations provide specific requirements for the content of an assessment plan using the Type B procedures, such as:

- Describe the natural resources and areas involved;
- Explain the basis for asserting trusteeship;
- Confirm exposure to hazardous substances of at least one natural resource identified as possibly injured in the preassessment screen determination;
- Outline objectives for sampling;
- Identify sampling locations, types of samples to be collected, and analyses to be performed;
- Contain procedures and schedules for data collection and data sharing with PRPs and trustees; and
- Present a quality assurance plan with quality assurance and quality control procedures.[236]

The trustees must make their assessment plan available for review by the PRPs and the public. The trustees also must include comments received and the trustees' response to the comments in the final assessment plan.

As part of developing the assessment plan, the trustees are required to develop a preliminary estimate of damages (PED).[237] The purpose of the PED is to ensure that "the anticipated cost of the assessment is expected to be less than the anticipated damage amount determined in the [assessment]."[238] The trustees are not required to disclose their PED with the PRPs or the public. If the available information is insufficient for developing the PED during the assessment plan phase, then the trustees can postpone this step until after the injury determination phase of the assessment.[239]

The third phase of DOI's NRD process is the assessment phase, which we describe in detail in the next subsection. Once the assessment is finished, the postassessment phase is the last phase of DOI's NRD process. In this last phase the trustees create a report of assessment, including supporting documentation for

---

235. Valerie Ann Lee et al., Natural Resources Damage Assessment Deskbook 116 (Envtl. Law Inst., 2d ed. 2014).

236. *Id.* at 115–16.

237. 43 C.F.R. § 11.38.

238. 43 C.F.R. § 11.14(ee).

239. 43 C.F.R. § 11.38(d)(2).

the results of the assessment, the PED, and a restoration and compensation determination plan (RCDP) that the trustees developed in the assessment phase.[240] The trustees are supposed to submit the report of assessment to the PRPs, along with a damages demand including reasonable assessment costs.[241]

The report of assessment is often the basis for settlement negotiations between the trustees and PRPs. If those negotiations are unsuccessful, then the trustees may file a lawsuit to recover the damages and their assessment costs. If the trustees follow the DOI process as promulgated, then the results of their assessment are presumed to be accurate in judicial proceedings, which is commonly known as the rebuttable presumption.[242]

The trustees place the amount that they recover from the PRPs, through settlement negotiations or litigation, in a dedicated account to be used to restore or replace the injured natural resources and their services.[243] Then, the trustees must develop a restoration plan, based on the RCDP from the assessment phase.[244]

B. Injury Determination

The assessment phase of DOI's NRD process is divided into three steps, which DOI confusingly refers to as phases (see Figure 5.1). For the injury determination step, Section 11.62 of the DOI regulations provides definitions for injuries to five categories of natural resources: surface water, groundwater, air, geologic resources, and biologic resources.

Section 11.63 of DOI's regulations focus on exposure pathways for each of the five categories of natural resources. Section 11.64 identifies acceptable testing and sampling methodologies for each of the potentially injured natural resources.

C. Quantification

The quantification phase of the Type B procedures plays a crucial role in linking injuries and damages. In particular, the purpose of this phase is to "quantify the effects of the discharge or release on the injured natural resources for use in determining the appropriate amount of compensation."[245] Every step in the quantification phase focuses on the services provided by the injured natural resources. The baseline level of services provided by the injured natural resources in the absence of the injuries is estimated in the quantification phase. Then, the level of services provided by the injured natural resources in their injured condition is determined, taking into account the recovery of services following the remediation and/or restoration of the injured natural resources. The difference in the baseline level of

---

240. 43 C.F.R. § 11.90.
241. 43 C.F.R. § 11.91(a).
242. 43 C.F.R. § 11.91(c).
243. 43 C.F.R. § 11.92(a).
244. 43 C.F.R. § 11.93(a).
245. 43 C.F.R. § 11.70(b).

services and the with-injury services over time is the loss in services as a result of the injury, which is the basis for damages.

As discussed in the next subsection, the components of natural resource damages in the DOI process are based on service losses. So, if there are no service losses, then there are no damages. This raises the possibility of a situation where natural resources may be injured, but there are no damages because the injuries did not result in a loss of natural resource services. In rare instances a reduction in recreation services may occur after a release of hazardous substances in the absence of natural resource injuries. For example, if the public is misinformed about injuries to a recreation area or if the public expects injuries to a recreation area even though they do not occur, then recreation services may decrease at the uninjured area. A PRP's liability for such service losses seems to be an unresolved legal issue.

D. Damage Determination

As shown in Figure 5.2, damages in the DOI process are the sum of restoration costs and compensable values. Restoration costs are defined as the cost of:

- Restoration or rehabilitation of the injured natural resources to a condition where they can provide the level of services available at baseline, or
- The replacement and/or acquisition of equivalent natural resources capable of providing such services.[246]

In general, restoration costs include direct costs (such as the cost of labor, materials, energy, and equipment for implementing a restoration project) and indirect costs (i.e., traditional overhead costs that cannot practically be directly associated with implementing a restoration project). Compensable value is the "amount of money required to compensate the public for the loss in services provided by the injured resources between the time of the discharge or release and the time the resources are fully returned to their baseline conditions, or until the resources are replaced and/or equivalent natural resources are acquired."[247] The compensable value can be either the:

- Economic value of lost services provided by the injured resources, including both use and nonuse values; or
- Cost of implementing a project or projects that restore, replace, or acquire the equivalent of natural resource services lost pending restoration to baseline.[248]

---

246. 43 C.F.R. § 11.83(b).
247. 43 C.F.R. § 11.83(c)(1).
248. *Id.*

Use values refer to "the economic value of the resources to the public attributable to the direct use of the services provided by the natural resources"[249] (e.g., values derived from recreational uses of natural resources), while nonuse values are economic values that are "independent of any direct use of the services provided"[250] (e.g., existence and bequest values). Economic value can be measured by changes in consumer surplus, economic rent, and any fees or other payments collectible by a federal or state agency or an Indian tribe for a private party's use of the natural resources.[251] Consumer surplus is "the money required to restore an individual's well-being to what it was at the level of the baseline (or pre-injury) situation."[252] It is usually approximated as the difference between a person's maximum willingness to pay for a service and the amount he or she actually pays for it.[253]

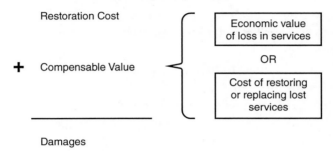

FIGURE 5.2
Measure of Damages in DOI's NRD Process Using Type B Procedures

E. Baseline

The baseline condition of natural resources and their services plays a crucial role in NRD assessments. Specifically, natural resource service losses are measured as the difference between the services provided by injured natural resources following a spill/release and the services of the natural resource in its baseline condition, which is the condition "that would have existed at the assessment area had the discharge of oil or release of the hazardous substance under investigation not occurred."[254] The baseline condition is sometimes referred to as the "but-for" condition, because it reflects the condition in the absence of the injury under investigation.

By definition, the baseline condition of an injured natural resource is not observable—it is a hypothetical condition. In general, there are two ways to estimate the baseline condition:

249. 43 C.F.R. § 11.83(c)(1)(i).
250. 43 C.F.R. § 11.83(c)(1)(ii).
251. 43 C.F.R. § 11.83(c)(1).
252. KOPP & SMITH, *supra* note 177, at 8.
253. FREEMAN, *supra* note 176, at 49.
254. 43 C.F.R. § 11.14(e).

- Use the condition of similar natural resources in a nearby area (i.e., a reference area) that have not been exposed to the spilled oil or released hazardous substances; or
- Model the baseline condition of the injured natural resources in the absence of the injury.

Both alternatives have their challenges. For example, it can be very difficult to find similar natural resources near an assessment area that have not been exposed to the oil or hazardous substance, or have not been affected by other stressors. On the other hand, modeling the baseline condition of an injured natural resource often involves assumptions and/or professional judgments to fill data gaps or to address uncertainties in the available information. Different assumptions and/or differences in professional judgments by trustees and PRPs can lead to substantial differences in estimates of the baseline condition of injured natural resources.

Often, it is more difficult to estimate baseline conditions for hazardous substance releases than oil spills for several reasons. First, hazardous substance releases may require estimates of baseline conditions going farther back in time than oil spills. In general, baseline conditions going back farther in time are more difficult to estimate accurately than baseline conditions in recent years. Second, at many legacy CERCLA-types of sites there are multiple PRPs who may have released different amounts of hazardous substances at different points in time, which leads to much more complicated baseline issues than a pipeline or a barge spilling oil at one point in time. On a related point, the service losses from small and moderate oil spills can be short-lived, in which case a good proxy for the baseline condition might be the condition of the injured natural resources one or two years *after* the spill. This is not an option for releases of more persistent hazardous substances or for larger oil spills with a high probability of multiyear impacts.

Those less accustomed to NRD claims sometimes equate "baseline condition" with "pristine condition." Those two conditions are almost never the same. Consider a river as an example. Over time some of the river's shoreline may have been bulk-headed for commercial or residential development. As cities grew along the shoreline over time, the river probably received some urban runoff. The river might have been used for commercial ship traffic, and maybe the river was dredged several times to support continued shipping. All of these events would cause a divergence in the "pristine condition" and the "baseline condition" of the river, as depicted in Figure 5.3. If a spill occurs in the river, then the difference between the with-spill condition and the baseline condition is the focus of the NRD assessment. The difference between the baseline condition and the pristine condition is not compensable in the NRD process.

Even experienced NRD practitioners sometimes equate "baseline condition" with "before-the-spill condition." This, too, is often inaccurate, because the

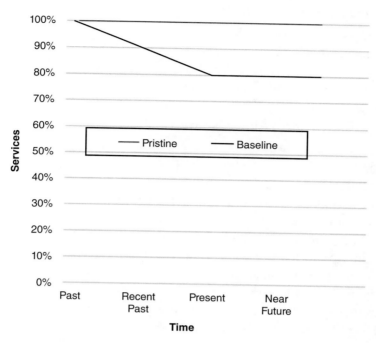

FIGURE 5.3
Pristine versus Baseline Natural Resource Services

baseline condition needs to take into account changes in the injury period that would have affected the services provided by the natural resources in their uninjured condition. For example, suppose that an average of 2,000 people per week were visiting a coastal beach before a spill, which closed the beach for one week while oil was cleaned up. It is well known that weather conditions affect coastal beach use.[255] Specifically, beach use is higher when it is warm and sunny, while beach use is lower when it is cold and rainy, other things being equal. So, the before-the-spill average of 2,000 visits per week is not a good proxy for the baseline visits during the injury period unless the weather conditions were comparable in the two time periods. If the closure period was colder and/or rainier than the pre-spill period, then the baseline visits would be less than 2,000. However, if the closure period was in warmer and/or sunnier weather than the pre-spill period, then baseline visits would be greater than 2,000. Both conclusions assume that other things potentially influencing coast beach visits were equal.

---

255. *See* Alvaro Moreno, Bas Amelung & Lorana Santamarta, *Linking Beach Recreation to Weather Conditions: A Case Study in Zandvoort, Netherlands*, 5 Tourism in Marine Env'ts 111 (2008).

F. Valuation Methodologies

Section 11.83(c)(2) in DOI's regulations identifies acceptable valuation methodologies for estimating compensable values, which are shown in Table 5.1. Some of the methodologies in Table 5.1 are not used in most NRD cases. Below we summarize the commonly used methodologies.

1. Habitat Equivalency Analysis and Resource Equivalency Analysis

Habitat equivalency analysis (HEA) is a technique that is commonly used in NRD assessments to scale restoration projects focusing on the ecological services provided by habitat. Estimates of annual losses of habitat services from a spill or release are converted into their present-value equivalent using the economic process of discounting, and those annual present-value estimates are summed, producing the "debit" in a HEA. Then, estimates of annual gains per acre of habitat services from a restoration project are converted into their present-value equivalent, and those present-value estimates are summed, producing the "credit per acre" for the project. The size (scale) of the restoration project that is needed to produce credits equal to or greater than the debit is determined by dividing the debit by the credit per acre. The cost of the scaled restoration project is the measure of damages.[256] Resource equivalency analysis (REA) is a similar technique that focuses on scaling restoration projects for injuries to wildlife, such as birds, turtles, or fish.[257] However, REA sometimes includes reproductive effects in both the debit and credit estimates. That adds a level of complexity to REA that is not found in HEA.

A key HEA requirement is that the restoration project must provide services of the same type, the same quality, and of comparable value to services that were lost—allowing an apples-to-apples comparison between the debit and credit per acre.[258] When the lost and the replacement services are not equivalent in type and quality, HEA can produce biased results. For example, it can lead to a situation where the restoration project provides gains in services that are more valuable than the services that were lost from the incident. In the absence of a factor to equate the value difference, HEA will not result in an appropriate scale for the restoration project. Similarly, a single service or an index of multiple services (known as the service "metric") must be selected for the HEA.[259] It is crucial that this metric reflects the overall impacts of a spill/release on ecological services, not focusing on the service most adversely or least adversely affected. Finally, the underlying conceptual foundation of HEA is that the public is fully compensated for natural resource injuries when the economic value of service gains from a restoration

---

256. NOAA Damage Assessment and Restoration Program, Habitat Equivalency Analysis: An Overview, at 14 (2006) [hereinafter NOAA 2006].

257. See Matthew Zafonte & Steve Hampton, *Exploring Welfare Implications of Resource Equivalency Analysis in Natural Resource Damage Assessments*, 61 Ecological Econ. 134 (2007).

258. See *NOAA 1997, supra* note 175.

259. See *NOAA 2006, supra* note 256.

Table 5.1: Acceptable Valuation Methodologies in DOI's Regulations

Type of Methodology	Description
Market price	The authorized official may determine the compensable value of the injured resources using the diminution in the market price of the injured resources or the lost services. May be used only if: 1. The natural resources are traded in the market; and 2. The authorized official determines that the market for the resources, or the services provided by the resources, is reasonably competitive.
Appraisal	The measure of compensable value is the difference between the with- and without-injury appraisal value determined by the comparable sales approach as described in the Uniform Appraisal Standards. Must measure compensable value, to the extent possible, in accordance with the Uniform Appraisal Standards for Federal Land Acquisition, Interagency Land Acquisition Conference, Washington, D.C., 1973.
Factor income (sometimes referred to as the "reverse value added" methodology)	May be used only if the injured resources are inputs to a production process, which has as an output a product with a well-defined market price. May be used to determine: 1. The economic rent associated with the use of resources in the production process; and 2. The in-place value of the resources.
Travel cost	May be used to determine a value for the use of a specific area. Uses an individual's incremental travel costs to an area to model the economic value of the services of that area. Compensable value of the area to the traveler is the difference between the value of the area with and without a discharge or release. Regional travel cost models may be used, if appropriate.
Hedonic pricing	May be used to determine the value of nonmarketed resources by an analysis of private market choices. The demand for nonmarketed natural resources is thereby estimated indirectly by an analysis of commodities that are traded in a market.
Unit value/benefits transfer	Unit values are preassigned dollar values for various types of nonmarketed recreational or other experiences by the public. Where feasible, unit values in the region of the affected resources and unit values that closely resemble the recreational or other experience lost with the affected resources may be used.
Contingent valuation	Includes all techniques that set up hypothetical markets to directly elicit an individual's economic valuation of a natural resource. Can determine: 1. Use values and explicitly determine option and existence values; and 2. Lost use values of injured natural resources.
Conjoint analysis	Like contingent valuation, conjoint analysis is a stated preference method. However, instead of seeking to value natural resource service losses in strictly economic terms, conjoint analysis compares natural resource service losses that arise from injury to natural resource service gains produced by restoration projects.
Habitat equivalency analysis	May be used to compare the natural resource services produced by habitat or resource-based restoration actions to natural resource service losses.
Resource equivalency analysis	Similar to habitat equivalency analysis. This methodology may be used to compare the effects of restoration actions on specifically identified resources that are injured or destroyed.
Random utility model	Can be used to: 1. Compare restoration actions on the basis of equivalent resource services provided; and 2. Calculate the monetary value of lost recreational services to the public.

project equals the economic value of the service losses resulting from the injuries.[260] If several simplifying assumptions are met, then equating service gains with service losses will fully compensate the public. Alternatively, if HEA's underlying assumptions are not met, then the HEA result will not accurately reflect the amount of restoration needed to compensate the public for the natural resource injury.

In the 1990s HEA was upheld by the courts in two cases for determining the appropriate compensation for physical injuries to seagrass habitat in coastal areas of Florida.[261] However, no courts have ruled on the validity of HEA for spills/releases involving complex ecological services, complex baseline issues, and long injury/restoration time periods where HEA's underlying assumptions are unlikely to be met. Furthermore, in 2010 a state court rejected an application of REA to groundwater injuries at a site in New Jersey.[262] While HEA is routinely used to settle ecological damages from spills/releases, its usefulness in litigation is uncertain.

2. Revealed Preference Methodologies

The travel cost and random utility maximization models in Table 5.1 are both revealed preference methodologies, which rely upon the actual recreation choices made by the public.[263] In particular, both models use estimates of the out-of-pocket and time costs of travel incurred by the public for their recreation site choices to infer the economic value of recreation trips. If a spill/release closes a recreation area for some period of time, then the average value of trips to the closed site times the number of forgone trips would be the measure of damages, including any forgone trips after the reopening of the closed area. If a spill/release adversely affects a recreation site, but does not result in its closure, then the measure of damages is the sum of the reduction in the value of any diminished-quality trips that still occur to the site and the loss in value associated with any forgone trips.

Revealed preference methodologies have a long history in economics.[264] The conceptual foundation of those methodologies is strong, but economists have not yet reached a consensus on estimating the value of the time associated with

---

260. *See* Richard W. Dunford, Thomas C. Ginn & William H. Desvousges, *The Use of Habitat Equivalency Analysis in Natural Resource Damage Assessments*, 48 Ecological Econ. 49 (2004).

261. See United States v. Fisher, 977 F. Supp. 1193 (S.D. Fla. 1997); United States v. Fisher, 174 F.3d 201 (11th Cir. 1999); Fisher v. United States, 528 U.S. 1022 (1999); United States v. Great Lakes Dredge & Dock Co., Nos. 97-2510-CIV and 97-10075-CIV, 1999 WL 1293469 (S.D. Fla. July 27, 1999); United States v. Great Lakes Dredge & Dock Co., 259 F.3d 1300 (11th Cir. 2001).

262. N.J. Dep't of Envtl. Prot. v. Essex Chem. Corp., No. A-0367-10T4, 2012 WL 913042, at *1, *8–9 (N.J. App. Div. Mar. 20, 2012) (affirming trial court's determination that the use of REA analysis was "flawed and unconvincing" for purposes of determining compensatory restoration damages due to groundwater contamination, because the testimony did not demonstrate that damages would "reflect or be equivalent to the loss.").

263. Kevin J. Boyle, *Introduction to Revealed Preference Methods*, ch. 8 *in* A Primer on Nonmarket Valuation (Patricia A. Champ, Kevin J. Boyle & Thomas C. Brown, eds., Kluwer Academic Publishers 2003).

264. *See* Marion Clawson & Jack L. Knetsch, The Economics of Outdoor Recreation (Johns Hopkins Press 1966) (for an analysis of results of the first travel cost study published in 1966).

traveling to recreation sites.[265] Additionally, information on the recreation choices of the public and their travel costs for revealed preference methodologies typically come from surveys administered to the public. The quality of the information from such surveys, and the reliability of the results, depend on the survey mode (e.g., in-person or telephone survey), the sampling methodology for the survey, the structure and wording of the survey questions, and the quality of the survey administration. Additionally, the value-per-trip estimates are usually sensitive to the statistical analysis applied to the survey data. Consequently, all of these survey and statistical elements should be examined thoroughly in litigating an NRD case with alleged use-value losses.

3. Stated Preference Methodologies

The contingent valuation and conjoint analysis (also known as choice modeling) methodologies in Table 5.1 are both stated preference methodologies. Instead of inferring values from the public's recreation site choices, stated preference methodologies ask the public in a survey for their economic value for natural resource services.[266] For example, a contingent valuation survey might ask the public for their value for a fishing trip to a particular site.[267] A conjoint analysis survey might ask survey respondents to choose among two scenarios involving different site attributes, different fishing attributes, and different costs. Then, this process might be repeated six to ten times in the survey with systematic changes in the two scenarios from which the respondents would choose. A statistical analysis of the scenario choices would produce an estimate of fishing value for a site with specific attributes.[268]

Stated preference surveys are sensitive to the same survey characteristics as revealed preference surveys, namely the survey mode, sampling methodology, structure and wording of survey questions, and quality of the survey administration. Additionally, the responses to questions in stated preference surveys are hypothetical—they do not involve actual behavior or an actual payment of money. Thus, stated responses to survey questions may not accurately reflect the respondent's actual behavior, which is referred to as hypothetical bias. Several studies have shown that hypothetical bias is relatively low for contingent valuation surveys that focus on natural resource services for which the respondents

---

265. *See* FREEMAN, *supra* note 176, at 442; Douglas J. MacNair & William H. Desvousges, *The Economics of Fish Consumption Advisories: Insights from Revealed and State Preference Data*, 83 LAND ECON. 600 (2007).

266. Thomas C. Brown, *Introduction to Stated Preference Methods*, ch. 4 *in* A PRIMER ON NONMARKET VALUATION, *supra* note 263.

267. *See generally* Kevin J. Boyle, *Contingent Valuation in Practice*, ch. 5 *in* A PRIMER ON NONMARKET VALUATION, *supra* note 263 (for more details on the contingent valuation method).

268. *See generally* Thomas P. Holmes & Wiktor L. Adamowicz, *Attribute-Based Methods*, ch. 6 *in* A PRIMER ON NONMARKET VALUATION, *supra* note 263 (for more details on the conjoint analysis method).

have experience spending money, such as recreation activities.[269] However, hypothetical bias can be substantial for unfamiliar or obscure natural resource services (e.g., for nonuse services).[270]

The debate among economists over the reliability of nonuse value estimates from contingent valuation surveys intensified with the 2010 *Deepwater Horizon* oil spill. The trustees sponsored a nationwide contingent valuation survey on the nonuse damages from the spill, concluding that a lower-bound estimate of those damages were $15.3 billion or $17.2 billion for two alternative estimates of per-household losses.[271] The economists who conducted that survey later published best-practices guidelines for such surveys.[272] In contrast, Nobel-laureate Daniel McFadden has concluded that "to this point no one has been able to develop and demonstrate stated preference methods that are reliable for valuation of non-use claims."[273] McFadden and Train recently edited a book critiquing the use of contingent valuation for environmental goods and services.[274] The McFadden & Train book follows an older book critiquing contingent valuation,[275] and other noteworthy critiques by prominent economists.[276] Israel and others[277] summarize the legal obstacles for contingent valuation in NRD litigation, including the fact that courts have not accepted the methodology.

4. Benefits Transfer Methodology

Conducting a valuation survey for one of the revealed preference or stated preference methodologies is expensive and time consuming. In most NRD assessments the trustees transfer the results of an existing valuation study to the NRD site in an effort to reduce assessment costs and expedite settlement. In the economics

---

269. *See, e.g.*, Richard C. Bishop & Thomas A. Heberlein, *Measuring Values of Extramarket Goods: Are Indirect Measures Biased?*, 61 Am. J. Agric. Econ. 926, 929 (1979) (finding that the average value for cash transactions for goose hunting permits equaled the average of two contingent valuation estimates for the permits).

270. Patricia A. Champ et al., *Using Donation Mechanisms to Value Nonuse Benefits from Public Goods*, 33 J. Envtl. Econ. & Mgmt. 151 (1997).

271. *See* Memorandum from NOAA Total Value Team to Katherine Pease, NOAA, Technical Memo TM-11: Aggregate Estimate of Total Lost Value (rev draft, Jan. 25, 2016), https://www.fws.gov/doiddata/dwh-ar-documents/980/DWH-AR0302133.pdf (The estimates were lower bounds because they excluded households in Alaska & Hawaii, households containing no adults who spoke English, and households on American Indian reservations.).

272. Robert J. Johnston et al., *Contemporary Guidance for Stated Preference Studies*, 4 J. Ass'n Envtl. & Res. Econ. 319 (2017).

273. Daniel McFadden, *Stated Preference Methods and Their Applicability to Environmental Use and Non-Use Valuations, in* Contingent Valuation of Environmental Goods: A Comprehensive Critique 180 (Daniel McFadden & Kenneth Train eds., Edward Elgar Publ'g 2017).

274. Contingent Valuation of Environmental Goods: A Comprehensive Critique (Daniel McFadden & Kenneth Train eds., Edward Elgar Publ'g 2017).

275. *See* Contingent Valuation: A Critical Assessment (Jerry A. Hausman ed., North-Holland 1995).

276. Peter A. Diamond & Jerry A. Hausman, *Contingent Valuation Measurement of Nonuse Values, in* Natural Resource Damages: A Legal, Economic, and Policy Analysis (Richard B. Stewart ed., Nat'l Legal Ctr. for the Pub. Interest 1995).

277. Brian D. Israel et al., *Legal Obstacles for Contingent Valuation Methods in Environmental Litigation, in* Continent Valuation of Environmental Goods: A Comprehensive Critique (Daniel McFadden & Kenneth Train eds., Edward Elgar Publ'g 2017).

literature this is known as the benefits transfer approach, which may involve transferring a value estimate or a value function from an earlier study.[278] The study that is transferred should focus on sites that are similar to the NRD site with respect to site characteristics, recreation activities, and user characteristics. Such similarities increase the likelihood that the transferred value accurately reflects the value of recreation at the NRD site. Additionally, the reliability of the benefits transfer approach is enhanced by selecting studies that used high-quality surveys and sound statistical analyses. Finally, transferred values are adjusted for inflation between the date of the original study and the assessment year for the NRD site.[279]

While the benefits transfer approach is often used for settling NRD cases out of court, its use in litigation may be more problematic. In particular, the professional judgments involved in evaluating the similarity of study sites to the NRD site, the quality of the surveys, and the statistical soundness of the analysis may undermine the efficacy of the benefits transfer approach in litigation. However, if the NRD site was the subject of a sound, original study in an earlier year, then the benefits transfer approach may be more likely to be appropriate in litigation.

XVIII. DEFENDING AGAINST NRD CLAIMS

Defending against NRD claims requires a broad approach that gives way to a thorough and detailed strategy. These considerations include, but are not limited to:

- A comprehensive understanding of the jurisprudential, statutory, and regulatory schema governing NRD actions, including recent developments, and how that framework relates or does not relate to the facts and circumstances of the instant case.
- Gaining insight into the entirety of the facts that will be determinative in the case. This includes all facts regarding a site's history and contamination, such as baseline conditions and past uses of the site.
- This investigation of the facts should extend beyond the site in question to include all relevant facts associated with any other facilities or PRPs that may have contributed to the discharges that caused the contamination. These facts should, at the least, include substantial knowledge of all hazardous substances present on or used at these facilities or by PRPs, points of potential discharges, environmental pathways, and their effect on natural resources and services.
- Determining any and all natural resources and services (ecological and human) that may have been affected at the site, as well as the surrounding ecosystems, and determining how and to what extent contaminants may have caused or contributed to harms.

---

278. Randall S. Rosenberger & John B. Loomis, *Benefit Transfer*, ch. 12 *in* A PRIMER ON NONMARKET VALUATION, *supra* note 263.

279. *See* FREEMAN, *supra* note 176, at 453–56.

Once an inventory of these facts and circumstances has been collected, litigants will have a much better idea of what experts will be required to substantiate their case, and where fracture points may lie in the opposition's case. These considerations will further inform the strategy and approach to litigation, and whether settlement may be an appropriate resolution.

A. Assessment

As described earlier, assessment is the first phase of an NRD trustee response, and the stage at which point the trustee conducts an investigation into the possible damages incurred by natural resources as the result of hazardous substance exposures. In some cases, it may prove beneficial for PRPs to be involved in this early stage via a cooperative assessment with the trustees. A cooperative assessment is an integrative process whereby PRPs and trustees work together to assess the scope of resource damages, ranging from merely sharing information to jointly constructing studies and program activities.

Benefits to such an arrangement may include:

- Cost savings;
- Regulatory guidance and input;
- Shared data and data-quality objectives;
- Reduced potential for litigation;
- Public involvement; and
- Shortened time to reach restoration of resources.

There are also potential burdens to engaging in a cooperative assessment. These include:

- Potential high transaction costs (i.e., costs for independent in addition to shared consultants, as well as attorneys);
- Reduced incentive to complete the assessment quickly and continued need to conduct additional studies (i.e., leading to "assessment creep," by which the scope of the assessment expands, new approaches are introduced, and deadlines for deliverables are delayed);
- Trustee unwillingness to accept technical input on the assessment from the PRPs or their consultants;
- Potential impact on cleanup standards in the cases where assessments are conducted in parallel with ongoing remedial investigations; and
- Potential inability to agree on an approach to determining an alleged injury, quantifying an alleged service loss, or determining an alleged damage.

In connection with NRD litigation, parties should consider the implications of the cooperative assessment process with respect to ongoing or potential subsequent litigation. The cooperative assessment process may present litigation complications (such as use of experts, evidentiary issues, and the importance of the cooperative assessment record) if it does not lead to a settlement.

B. Causation

Because CERCLA's NRD provisions state that responsible parties are liable only for damages "resulting from" a release, a plaintiff trustee must meet a burden of proof regarding causation to merit recovery.[280] Aside from this basic acknowledgement, however, the meager and inconsistent jurisprudence on this subject provides little guidance in the way of applicable standards or the requisite proofs to adequately meet this element. Indeed, the D.C. Circuit has held that CERCLA is ambiguous as to what standard applies, and accepted DOI's interpretation that "traditional" causation standards apply, without resolving exactly what those standards are.[281] As a result, it is difficult to place any great weight upon the analysis conducted by the courts to date with regard to this element.

The first decision to address this causation standard was *United States v. Montrose Chemical Corp.*, an unpublished ruling on a motion to dismiss, and which spans just over one page.[282] In support of its decision to dismiss the NRD claims, the court summarily applied the "sole or substantially contributing factor" standard of causation, the standard contemplated in the *Restatement (Second) of Torts* for indivisible injury.[283] Based on this standard, the court stated a plaintiff would have to allege (1) what natural resources have been injured, (2) the locations where each injury and the releases occurred, (3) when each injury and the releases occurred, (4) which defendant released the culprit hazardous substance, and (5) by what pathway exposure occurred.[284] Significantly, the *Montrose* court would be not only the first court to weigh in on the applicable causation standard, it would also be the last court to date that has applied this stringent standard with respect to a CERCLA NRD claim.

Other courts have adopted a more relaxed standard than the substantial factor test, but given that these courts number two total, it would be a stretch to say that the issue is at all settled. In *Acushnet VI*, without referencing the *Montrose* decision,

---

280. CERCLA § 107(a)(4)(C), 42 U.S.C. § 9607 (a)(4)(C) ("damages for injury to, destruction of, or loss of natural resources, including the reasonable costs of assessing such injury, destruction, or loss resulting from such a release").

281. Ohio v. U.S. Dep't of Interior, 880 F.2d 432, 468–72 (D.C. Cir. 1989) ("[W]hile we agree with petitioners that Congress expressed dissatisfaction with the common law as a norm in several areas of damage assessment, we conclude that CERCLA is at best ambiguous on the question of whether the causation-of-injury standard under § 107(a)(C) must be less demanding than that of the common law.").

282. United States v. Montrose Chem. Corp., No. CV 90-3122 AAH (JRX), 1991 WL 183147 (C.D. Cal. Mar. 29, 1991).

283. *Id.* at *1; *see also In re* Nat'l Gypsum, No. 390-37213-SAF-11, 1992 WL 426464, at *5 (Bankr. N.D. Tex. Jun. 24, 1992) ("The Court in *Montrose Chemical Corporation* cited no authority for that proposition. The statute does not state resulting solely or substantially from the release. In the absence of authority, this Court will not impose a restrictive element on the statute's liability provision when the Congress has not done so. The Court accepts the statute as written.").

284. *Id.*

the court determined that a plaintiff need only demonstrate a defendant's releases were a "contributing factor" to an injury.[285] Notably, the court acknowledged in a footnote that in its "original draft," it had, in fact, applied the "substantial contributing factor" standard, but changed course upon the issuance of a First Circuit decision, *O'Neil v. Picillo*.[286] That decision, however, dealt only with traditional cost recovery[287] and not NRD, and as discussed previously in the chapter, there is no textual causation requirement for traditional cost recovery actions, which is not the case for the NRD section.[288] Without delving deeper into this standard, or the import of its decision to eliminate the term "substantial," the court determined that material issues of fact existed regarding the issue of federally permitted and non-federally permitted releases, and denied summary judgment.[289] Also in its decision, the court did acknowledge a de minimis defense to liability, and yet it remains a mystery how that defense may actually be proven.[290]

Fourteen years after *Acushnet VI*, the court in *Coeur d'Alene Tribe v. Asarco Inc.*[291] would be the next court to confront the issue of causation. As discussed earlier, *Coeur d'Alene* involved the Coeur d'Alene Basin in Idaho, which had been the depository for over 100 years' worth of mining refuse before the mining companies installed tailings impoundments in 1968.[292] The accumulation of these tailings in the waterways of the basin caused a variety of injuries to flora, fauna, and the environment.[293] A lengthy bench trial took place before the court rendered its decision with respect to two defendants, Asarco and Hecla, the primary contributors of the mining waste, responsible for "at least" 22 percent and 31 percent of the historical total of all tailings, respectively.[294] Significantly, it was agreed by all parties that the waste included a mixture of lead, cadmium, and/or zinc, but

---

285. *See In re* Acushnet River & New Bedford Harbor: Proceedings re Alleged PCB Pollution (Acushnet VI), 722 F. Supp. 893, 897 n.8 (D. Mass. 1989) (where the court followed the First Circuit in rejecting the plain language of the *Restatement (Second) of Torts* § 433B, which requires proof by the plaintiff that a defendant's conduct was a "substantial" cause of the injury, finding that requirement to have "no role" under CERCLA joint and several liability). The *Acushnet* litigation generated a total of six published decisions, and the remaining five decisions are referred to as follows: *Acushnet I*, 675 F. Supp. 22 (D. Mass. 1987) (addressing jurisdictional issues); *Acushnet II*, 712 F. Supp. 994 (D. Mass. 1989) (right to a jury trial); *Acushnet III*, 712 F. Supp. 1010 (D. Mass. 1989) (successor liability); *Acushnet IV*, 712 F. Supp. 1019 (D. Mass. 1989) (intervenor status and adequacy of consent decree); *Acushnet V*, 716 F. Supp. 676 (D. Mass 1989) (divisibility of pre- and post-CERCLA damages).

286. *Acushnet VI*, 722 F. Supp. at 897 n.8 (citing O'Neil v. Picillo, 883 F.2d 176, 179 n.4 (1st Cir. 1989)).

287. For purposes of these NRD sections of the chapter, the term "traditional cost recovery" refers to both cost recovery actions pursuant to Section 107(a) and contribution actions pursuant to Section 113. As discussed previously, these two actions can have profound differences in application and results; however, they are referred to together for purposes of distinguishing from the CERCLA provisions applicable to NRD claims.

288. *See supra* at Section IV.

289. *Acushnet VI*, 722 F. Supp. at 897–98.

290. *Id.* at 897 n.11.

291. Coeur d'Alene Tribe v. Asarco, Inc., 280 F. Supp. 2d 1094 (D. Idaho 2003).

292. *Id.* at 1101, 1105.

293. *Id.* at 1106–07.

294. *Id.* at 1105.

concentrations of these materials varied, and collectively were a commingled source of contamination.[295]

In its initial pretrial decision regarding causation, the court in *Coeur d'Alene* rejected the defendants' request to apply the *Montrose* "substantial contributing factor" standard, declaring it to be "too restrictive," and furthermore, that due to the opinion's brevity, failure to include "any reasoning," and a conclusion "clearly at odds with the purpose of CERCLA," the decision possessed "very limited value in establishing precedent."[296] The court then set forth two separate causation standards, depending upon whether releases have been commingled. In cases that involve commingling, the burden is on the plaintiff to prove that "a release that results in commingled hazardous substances is a 'contributing factor.'"[297] In cases where commingling is not at issue, the plaintiff must instead demonstrate the release to be the "sole or proximate cause" of injury.[298] The court defined the "contributing factor" standard to be "more than a *de minimis* amount—to an extent that at least some of the injury would have occurred if only the Defendant's amount of release had occurred." Interestingly, the court described this causation standard to be "less restrictive than traditional federal common law," in an apparent abrogation of the earlier court's finding in *Ohio v. Department of Interior*, though without referring to that earlier decision.[299]

Posttrial, the *Coeur d'Alene* court reaffirmed its pretrial findings, and in applying the "contributing factor" test to Asarco and Hecla's commingled releases, determined that each of the two defendants' quantities "was large enough to be considered a contributing factor" due to the sizable percentages for which they were responsible on a volumetric basis.[300] Therefore, the causation requirement was met.

A review of these decisions, therefore, does not provide much assistance in informing the practical mechanics of the prevailing causation standard with respect to NRD actions. Aside from the rejection of the modifier "substantially," the *Acushnet VI* and *Coeur d'Alene* courts, which have explicitly rejected the standard put forth in *Montrose Chemical Corp.*, have provided little to nothing in the way of insight distinguishing the "contributing factor" standard from the "significant contributing factor" standard that they so clearly rejected. The problem is made worse by the fact that the substantial factor test itself has been criticized as amorphous, and can be a very low bar depending upon the court applying it.[301] At

---

295. *Id.* at 1106.

296. Coeur d'Alene Tribe v. Asarco Inc., Nos. CV91-0341NEJL and CV96-0122NEJL, 2001 WL 34139603, at *5 and n.4, 6 (D. Idaho Mar. 30, 2001).

297. *Id.* at *5.

298. *Id.*

299. *Id.* at *5. *See also* Ohio v. U.S. Dep't of Interior, 880 F.2d 432 (D.C. Cir. 1989).

300. *Coeur d'Alene*, 280 F. Supp. 2d at 1124.

301. Ford Motor Co. v. Boomer, 736 S.E.2d 724, 730–31 (Va. 2013) (removing the term "substantial contributing factor" from Virginia's jury instruction lexicon, believing that the term lacks a "single, common-sense meaning," and noting its "explicit rejection" from the *Restatement (Third) of Torts* in favor of the but-for and necessary-condition causation standards).

least in these instances, it is not nearly as demanding as the standard suggested in *Montrose*.[302] Indeed, the practical difference between these standards may very well amount to much ado about nothing, though at least implicitly in *Acushnet VI*, and explicitly in *Coeur d'Alene*, the courts held a view that the "contributing factor" standard is less restrictive than the "substantial contributing factor" standard.

Equally vague is the reference to de minimis amounts, as it would appear that anything that does not arise to a contributing factor would be considered de minimis. Following this logic, the de minimis defense merely serves as another way of stating that the prima facie causation element has not been met, and would not be properly considered to be an affirmative defense.

While teasing out the significance of these standards may be futile, that does not render these decisions worthless to practitioners. Even though the survival of the *Montrose* standard appears doubtful (assuming it has not already met its demise), the criteria it has espoused is instructive in preparing to defend an NRD action. *Montrose* offers a blueprint for investigation, as all of the facts elicited by this criteria will be probative to the issue of causation, regardless of the applicable standard.

C. Divisibility of Harm

The regime of apportionment and allocation for NRD claims in many respects may be similar to traditional CERCLA cost recovery actions, originating in the *Restatement (Second) of Torts*. Under this framework, the "burden of production" lies first with the plaintiff to demonstrate that a harm is indivisible, and only then does it shift to the defendant to prove through a "burden of persuasion" that: "(a) there are distinct harms, or (b) there is a reasonable basis for determining the contribution of each cause to a single harm."[303] Initially, divisibility is a "question of law" and then a "question of fact."[304] It is further "guided by principles of causation alone" and in the event "causation is unclear," courts are not to "'split the difference' in an attempt to achieve equity."[305]

Depending on the causation standard that ultimately gains prominence in NRD cases, the issue of divisibility presents a different landscape than the cost

---

302. Bockrath v. Aldrich Chem. Co., 980 P.2d 398, 403–04 (Cal. 1999) ("The substantial factor standard is a relatively broad one, requiring only that the contribution of the individual cause be more than negligible or theoretical. Thus, a force which plays only an infinitesimal or theoretical part in bringing about injury, damage, or loss is not a substantial factor, but a very minor force that does cause harm is a substantial factor.") (internal quotation marks omitted).

303. Restatement (Second) of Torts § 433A(1) (1965). *See also Acushnet VI*, 722 F. Supp. 893, 897 n.9 (D. Mass. 1989) ("With respect to divisibility of the injury, then, the sovereigns must first meet a burden of production—introducing evidence sufficient to warrant a fact finder's conclusion that the injury was indivisible. That accomplished, the defendant bears the burden of persuasion that the injury and its attendant damages can be apportioned."); *id.* at 901 n.21 ("proving divisibility of harm is, both traditionally and in the CERCLA context, a burden of the defendant where the question is one of dividing harm among tortfeasors"); *Coeur d'Alene*, 280 F. Supp. at 1119–20.

304. *Coeur d'Alene*, 280 F. Supp. 2d at 1120.

305. *Id.*

recovery provisions of CERCLA, as there must be some causal link between a party's releases and the resulting damages, providing fertile ground for argument. This is particularly true for multiparty sites where there are noncontiguous areas of concern, independent discharge points, or only partially overlapping plumes, or when a portion of the releases can be limited or sequestered under the federally permitted release or preenactment exceptions. At this point, it is unclear to what extent such factors will hold sway in a court's divisibility analysis, as there has not been any case law distinguishing the causation element applicable to NRD claims from the lack of such an element in traditional cost recovery actions in the context of divisibility, but there is certainly opportunity within this pivotal distinction.

In conducting its divisibility analysis, the court in *Coeur d'Alene* precluded any need for the defendants to "fingerprint" the wastes to their points of origin, rationalizing that such an approach would be "grossly unfair and unjust" when the plaintiffs are not required to perform such a task in tracing the releases to their respective harms.[306] The court also highlighted the difficulties presented by the fact that the releases occurred over "multiple decades," and involved "changes [in] processing method, and changes in ownership."[307] Moreover, even though the "exact percentages of lead, cadmium and zinc in the tailings" was unknown, and the concentrations were indeterminate between individual mills, "all of the tailings" contained these three metals, and the "milling methodologies" between mills did not "differ significantly."[308] The court then relied on a purely volumetric analysis, and apportioned liability to hold Asarco responsible for 22 percent of the tailings and Hecla for 31 percent.

Interestingly, *Coeur d'Alene* issued its decision to address both plaintiffs' NRD and traditional cost recovery claims. This is made clear in the court's assurance that the defendants maintained the ability to "also seek equitable relief in the form of a contribution action under [Section 113(f)]."[309] Remarkably, *Coeur d'Alene* is not only the sole decision applying the divisibility analysis to NRD claims, it is one of the few decisions to apportion damages with respect to traditional cost recovery claims.[310] This is particularly noteworthy given the presence of multiple commingling hazardous substances at issue in *Coeur d'Alene*, and when considering that the concentrations of which could not be attributed to individual defendants or time frames, factors that often thwart apportionment defenses.

In this case the experts were able to investigate 97–98 percent of the mills responsible for mining production in the Coeur d'Alene Basin, leaving only 2–3 percent unaccounted for.[311] Subsequent courts distinguishing *Coeur d'Alene* have viewed the relatively uniform distribution of hazardous substances present within

---

306. *Id.*
307. *Id.* at 1120.
308. *Id.* at 1120–21.
309. *Id.* at 1102, 1121.
310. *See supra* at Sections VII and VIII.
311. *Coeur d'Alene*, 280 F. Supp. 2d at 1105.

the tailings to be the critical factor warranting a purely volumetric apportionment.[312] And while the *Coeur d'Alene* court accepted the comment of an expert that volumetric calculations were not a "perfect" method, as one court has noted, the *Coeur d'Alene* court had "the good fortune of having experts on both sides of the case agreeing that a volumetric analysis alone is a 'reasonable basis' for apportionment.'"[313]

As a result of the dual nature of this analysis, however, it provides little guidance as to issues that might distinguish the divisibility analysis with respect to NRD claims as compared to traditional cost recovery claims, and how the differing causation standard could play a role.[314] Any such differences remain to be seen, but they have also not been precluded.

D. Defenses

There are several affirmative statutory defenses provided under CERCLA, but they are generally unavailing to NRD defendants. These defenses include (1) an act of God; (2) an act of war; (3) an act or omission of a third party; and (4) any combination of these three defenses.[315] As with any affirmative defense, the burden is on the defendant to prove by a preponderance of the evidence. These defenses further will not protect against liability unless a defendant can demonstrate that releases and discharges "were caused solely by" one or more of these acts.

Given the high burden imposed by these defenses coupled with the fact that they only apply in rare and unconventional circumstances, they have not proven useful in NRD litigation. The preferred course for a party defending against an NRD claim is to attack the elements a plaintiff must prove to establish the claim, such as lack of causation, baseline conditions that were already degraded to the point that there was no negative impact by the discharges, or absence of injury. There are, however, other defenses in the form of statutory exclusions that reduce or defeat liability altogether. These defenses include (1) the bar against double recovery, (2) retroactive liability for discharges and harms that occurred before CERCLA's enactment in 1980, and (3) federally permitted releases.

---

312. *See* United States v. Fed. Res. Corp., 30 F. Supp. 3d 979, 993 (D. Idaho 2014) ("Central to [the *Coeur d'Alene*] holding, however, was that the environmental harm stemmed from the same waste material—tailings—and that the metals composition of the various tailing sources differed only slightly.") (citation omitted); Pakootas v. Teck Cominco Metals, Ltd., 868 F. Supp. 2d 1106, 1119 (E.D. Wash. 2012) (referring to *Coeur d'Alene* as involving "tailings containing three metals generated by similar milling methodologies used by two generators.").

313. *Coeur d'Alene*, 280 F. Supp. 2d at 1120; *Pakootas*, 868 F. Supp. at 1119.

314. New York v. Next Millennium Realty, LLC, 160 F. Supp. 3d 485, 511–18, 525 (E.D.N.Y. 2016) (a case that also involved NRD and traditional cost recovery claims, where contamination was alleged to have occurred due to three plumes of various hazardous chemicals; however, this decision involved a summary judgment motion and due to disputed issues of fact regarding whether one of the plumes had commingled, the issue was permitted to proceed to trial, and the court did not differentiate between the causal standards for purposes of divisibility).

315. CERCLA § 107(b), 42 U.S.C. § 9607(b).

I. Double Recovery

The bar against double recovery, discussed earlier with respect to issues between co-trustees, does not operate in reducing or negating liability of a PRP in the first instance. Nevertheless, it is an important defense that requires awareness when a defendant is subject to an NRD claim regarding resources held by multiple co-trustees. Because co-trustees may not always work in harmony in pursuing NRD claims, trustees may seek to bring multiple actions for recovery of the same harm, whether in the same or different courts and jurisdictions.

These issues can quickly become convoluted when one or more trustees enter settlement, but others do not, and decide to pursue litigation further. Moreover, looking to *Tyson Foods*, the court dismissed the entire action due to the absence of one trustee, considering the trustee to be an indispensable party.[316] It remains to be seen whether other courts will adopt the reasoning employed by *Tyson Foods*, which relied on the first *Coeur d'Alene Tribe* case, without reference to the second decision. After all, the difference in opinions of the court in the two *Coeur d'Alene Tribe* cases was the result of a shifting emphasis by the court from traditional tort concepts of allocation on the one hand to CERCLA's public policy on the other. Other courts may view this policy emphasis differently, particularly when considering that the Supreme Court has favored a textual, rather than a policy-based, interpretation of CERCLA in each of its recent decisions.[317]

2. Retroactive Liability

CERCLA explicitly excludes NRD liability regarding harms and releases previous to CERCLA's date of enactment, and therefore applies liability prospectively. This is one area where CERCLA diverges in its treatment of NRD actions from traditional cost recovery actions. But as will be seen, to characterize its application only as "prospective" would be inaccurate to the extent that it suggests that a PRP who has ceased releasing any hazardous substances prior to the enactment date cannot be subject to liability. Quite the contrary, the focus is instead upon when the "injury" can be said to have occurred (or alternatively is assessed and recognized) as the result of such releases, which may not occur for many years afterward.[318]

Specifically, Section 107(f)(1) states:

> There shall be no recovery under the authority of subparagraph (c) of subsection
> (a) of this section where such [natural resource] damages and the release of a

---

316. Oklahoma v. Tyson Foods, Inc., 258 F.R.D. 472, 480 (N.D. Okla. 2009).

317. *See, e.g.*, Cooper Indus. v. Aviall Servs., Inc., 543 U.S. 157, 161 (2004); United States v. Atl. Research Corp., 551 U.S. 128, 138 (2007); Burlington N. & Santa Fe Ry. Co. v. United States, 556 U.S. 599 (2009).

318. *See, e.g.*, Aetna Cas. & Sur. Co. v. Pintlar Corp., 948 F.2d 1507, 1515–16 (9th Cir. 1991) (examining the differences in the timing of an "occurrence" for insurance purposes and the distinctions between "releases," "injuries" and "damages" that "occur" in the context of a CERCLA statutory liability defense as opposed to how those terms may apply with respect to an insurers' separate contractual obligation to provide coverage for property damage (i.e., NRD)).

hazardous substance from which such damages resulted occurred wholly before December 11, 1980.

Succeeding on this defense is often untenable, even where a substantial portion of a defendant's releases have occurred prior to the cutoff date. A trustee plaintiff may need only to demonstrate that a defendant's discharges are a "contributing factor."[319] Due to this standard, it may prove irrelevant whether a majority of a defendant's discharges are excluded based on the CERCLA enactment date, if there are sufficient remaining discharges that would meet this low threshold. In such a case, the defendant will be subject to liability for the entirety of the harm. Ultimately a defendant will need to demonstrate that all, or at least an overwhelming majority, of its releases occurred prior to December 11, 1980, to receive any benefit from this defense.

In *Coeur d'Alene Tribe*, the court investigated to what extent releases had occurred postenactment with respect to mining tailings that were discharged into the Coeur d'Alene Basin waterways. However, the mining companies constructed impoundment facilities in 1968, halting the vast majority of discharges.[320] Even though this conduct had ceased, the court assessed whether "there were re-releases of hazardous substances via the passive form of seepage, leaching and migration due to flowing water" for the tailings that remained in the waterways from preenactment discharges.[321] The court surmised in the affirmative, noting that the term "leaching" is explicitly within the term of "release" under CERCLA, and there was no requirement of human activity to be associated with the release postenactment.[322]

This analysis is tempered, however, by the court's initial hedge that such passive activities only "[a]rguably" would be considered re-releases, and this portion of the analysis was relegated to mere dicta, as the court further determined that defendants would have been liable even if no postenactment releases had occurred.[323] This is because—as will be discussed in the remainder of this section—the court determined that the damages did not occur until postenactment, and therefore the timing of the release was immaterial.

With this outcome in mind, the timing of release is only the first issue faced by a defendant seeking to assert this defense, as a defendant may still be liable even if all of its releases have occurred prior to December 11, 1980, depending on when the injury is determined to have occurred.[324] The few courts that have encountered

---

319. *See supra* at Section XVIII.B.
320. *Coeur d'Alene*, 280 F. Supp. 2d at 1111.
321. *Id.* at 1112–13.
322. *Id.* at 1113.
323. *Id.* at 1112–14.
324. *See* Idaho v. Bunker Hill Co., 635 F. Supp. 665, 675 (D. Idaho 1986) ("In sum, to the extent that both the release and the resultant damage occurred prior to enactment, Section 107(f) bars recovery. To the extent that both the release and the resultant damage occurred post-enactment, there is no bar to recovery. To the extent the release occurred prior to enactment, but the resultant damage occurred post-enactment, Section 107(f) does not bar recovery."); United States v. Reilly Tar & Chem. Corp., 546

this issue have reached disparate conclusions interpreting the phrase "occurred wholly before." As a result, there is little guidance for litigants who intend to assert this defense, and a future court may go in either direction.

In the first case, *Acushnet V*, the court determined that damages had not "wholly occurred" until monetary expense was incurred relating to the natural resource injuries.[325] The court rejected the view that damage occurs at the earlier time of release and contamination, and referred to the broad policy purpose underlying CERCLA in support of this view, which seeks to place the burden of contamination on those responsible for causing it.[326] As an additional matter, the *Acushnet V* court concluded that the burden of proof lies with the defendant to demonstrate that damages have occurred preenactment for them to be excluded.[327] As a result, the court concluded that postenactment costs were recoverable, but that preenactment costs, to the extent they related to injuries that were divisible, were not.[328] The court did recognize, however, that if a plaintiff has proven that both pre- and postenactment costs are associated with indivisible injuries, and the "damages or the releases that caused the damages continue post-enactment," then the preenactment costs are then recoverable as well as postenactment, with aesthetic injuries serving as an example of the kinds of damages that would fall into this category.[329]

Then, in *Montana v. Atlantic Richfield Co.*, the court reached an opposite conclusion, applying a textual analysis that emphasized the term "occurred."[330] According to this court, the date when injuries or destruction of natural resources has "occurred" is unrelated to the date when expenses related to those harms have been incurred. The court appears to pivot from the previous court's stance that harm has only occurred once there has been a financial harm to the plaintiff to a view that harm occurs the instant physical harm is visited upon the natural resources themselves. Without proof that harms "occurred" after December 11, 1980, the trustee could not meet its burden of proof on the element of causation, and as a result, the court dismissed the action entirely.

Only a few months later, the *Coeur d'Alene* court issued its decision, and reiterated the interpretation of "occurred" set forth in *Acushnet V*, without any regard for or reference to the *Atlantic Richfield Co.* decision.[331] Therefore, once again, damages

---

F. Supp. 1100, 1120 (D. Minn. 1982) (denying motions to dismiss where plaintiff asserted the defendant was responsible for "continuing releases and damages").

325. *See Acushnet V*, 716 F. Supp. 676, 683 (D. Mass 1989) (determining that damages had only "been felt . . . when [a property] owner incurred additional expenses during the building of a wharf due to the expense of disposing of contaminated dredge spoils").

326. *Id.*

327. *Id.* at 687–88.

328. *Id.* at 685–87.

329. *Id.* at 686.

330. Montana v. Atl. Richfield Co., 266 F. Supp. 2d 1238, 1243 (D. Mont. 2003).

331. *Coeur d'Alene*, 280 F. Supp. 2d at 1114.

were deemed by the court to occur only at the point in time when expenses are incurred, and not when the harm is visited upon the natural resources.[332]

As can be seen, even putting aside the slim probability of success on this defense, the measuring stick applied by a court in determining when the injury to natural resources occurred is unclear. The issue of burden of proof is equally convoluted.[333] Yet another issue with this defense is that even if successful, state NRD laws or common law claims may still provide liability, regardless of the CERCLA enactment date, if they permit more expansive retroactive liability.[334]

These dueling interpretations elucidate the unpredictable nature of NRD claims and the interpretation by various courts. There is no guarantee that a subsequent court will take the view of a prior court, particularly when the previous decision is nonbinding on that court. This also highlights the conflicting views that often arise when courts apply differing textual or policy-driven analyses, recognizing that either form of analysis may lead to outcome-driven methodologies.

3. Federally Permitted Releases

CERCLA does not provide liability when releases have been explicitly permitted pursuant to a federally issued permit. Section 107(j) of CERCLA states:

> Recovery by any person (including the United States or any State or Indian tribe) for response costs or damages resulting from a federally permitted release shall be pursuant to existing law in lieu of this section.

The types of permitted releases that are subject to this exemption are defined by CERCLA, and cover several categories.[335] Simply because a permit exists, however, will not shield a defendant against liability. It is the defendant's burden to demonstrate not only that a permit was validly issued, but also that its releases

---

332. *See also* Alabama v. Ala. Wood Treating Corp., Inc., No. 85-0642-CG-C, 2006 WL 8431771, at *7 (S.D. Ala. June 6, 2006) (favoring the analysis of *Acushnet V* over *Atlantic Richfield Co.*, reiterating the view that "damages" are not the same as "injury").

333. One possible way to reconcile these two decisions on the issue of burden of proof would be due to the shifting burden from a plaintiff's need to first demonstrate the release was a contributing factor to injury, and if successful, the defendant may then demonstrate divisibility. In *Acushnet V*, harms were deemed to have occurred both pre- and postenactment, whereas in *Atlantic Richfield Co.*, based on the court's finding, the plaintiff did not meet the initial burden of proving any harm to have occurred postenactment. However, the *Acushnet V* court's analysis rejected the defendant's argument that "proof that the damages occurred post-enactment is an element of a natural resource damages claim and thus must be proved as part of the sovereigns' case." *Acushnet V*, 716 F. Supp. at 687. This is made even more difficult by the court's subsequent reasoning in *Acushnet VI*, where the court distinguished its divisibility analysis regarding the federally permitted releases exception from the retroactivity exception by stating that, with respect to the latter, the plaintiffs had already "established that the defendants [were] liable." *Acushnet VI*, 722 F. Supp. at 897 n.9.

334. *See* Quapaw Tribe of Okla. v. Blue Tee Corp., No. 03-CV-0846-CVE-PJC, 2009 WL 455260 (N.D. Okla. Feb. 23, 2009) (determining that state laws may "provide remedies unavailable under CERCLA, because these types of state laws do not conflict with CERCLA's remedial scheme.").

335. CERCLA § 101(10), 42 U.S.C. § 9601(10). These permits include those issued pursuant to the Federal Water Pollution Control Act; the Solid Waste Disposal Act; the Safe Drinking Water Act; the Clean Air Act; state laws governing injection of fluids to recover crude oil, natural gas, and water (such as hydraulic fracturing); and the Atomic Energy Act.

were expressly permitted, did not exceed the scope of the permit, and did not occur at times other than when the permit was in place.[336] Even where the defense fails to wholly protect against liability, a defendant may attempt to demonstrate that the harm is divisible between permitted and nonpermitted releases.[337]

As is the case with defenses against environmental response cost claims, a party's time may be better spent addressing damages—either by way of apportionment, allocation, or other reductions and offsets—as opposed to combating liability.

XIX. SPECIAL TOPICS

A. Early Restoration Actions

In April of 2011, BP committed $1 billion for implementation of an early restoration program as an initial step toward providing compensation for natural resource damages resulting from the 2010 *Deepwater Horizon* oil spill.[338] The five states affected by the spill, the National Oceanic and Atmospheric Administration, and DOI each received $100 million of the early restoration funds, and the remaining $300 million was allocated for state-proposed projects selected by the federal trustees.[339] The main objective of the program was "to secure tangible recovery of natural resources and natural resource services for the public's benefit while the longer-term process of fully assessing injury and damages is still under way."[340]

The framework agreement for the early restoration program[341] stated that the trustees would select projects that met all of the following criteria:

- Contribute to making the environment and the public whole by restoring, rehabilitating, replacing or acquiring the equivalent of natural resources or services injured as a result of the *Deepwater Horizon* oil spill or response, or compensating for interim losses resulting from the incident;

---

336. *See* United States v. Iron Mountain Mines, Inc., 812 F. Supp. 1528, 1541 (E.D. Cal. 1992); United States v. Wash. State Dep't of Transp., 716 F. Supp. 2d 1009, 1016 (W.D. Wash. 2010) (denying summary judgment where existence of permits was undisputed but determined there remained issues of fact over whether releases complied and were within the scope of the permits); Dep't of Envtl. Prot. v. Lockheed Martin Corp., 684 F. Supp. 2d 564, 583 (M.D. Pa. 2010) (to determine compliance with a permit, "the court must examine both the license itself and the extent of the release.").

337. *See Iron Mountain Mines*, 812 F. Supp. at 1540–41; *Acushnet VI*, 722 F. Supp. at 897 (determining that where a PRP was responsible for both permitted and nonpermitted releases, joint and several liability would attach unless the PRP could prove divisibility between the damages caused by the permitted and nonpermitted releases, respectively).

338. Deepwater Horizon Natural Resources Damage Assessment Early Restoration, http://www.gulf spillrestoration.noaa.gov/sites/default/files/wp-content/uploads/Spring2012_TCToolkit_EarlyCriteria_Large Format_FINAL.pdf (last visited Feb. 14, 2019).

339. *Id.* at 1.

340. *Id.* at 2.

341. Deepwater Horizon Trs., Framework for Early Restoration Addressing Injuries Resulting from the Deepwater Horizon Oil Spill, https://www.restorethegulf.gov/sites/default/files/documents/pdf /framework-for-early-restoration-04212011.pdf [hereinafter Deepwater Horizon Trustees].

- Address one or more specific injuries to natural resources or services associated with the incident;
- Seek to restore natural resources, habitats, or natural resource services of the same type, quality and of comparable ecological and/or human-use value to compensate for identified resource and service losses resulting from the incident;
- Are not inconsistent with the anticipated long-term restoration needs and anticipated final restoration plan; and
- Are feasible and cost-effective.[342]

The trustees also took into account several practical considerations in order to expedite the screening of a large number of potentially qualifying projects. For example, the trustees:

- Took into account how quickly a given project was likely to begin producing environmental benefits;
- Sought a diverse set of projects providing benefits to a broad array of potentially injured resources;
- Focused on types of projects with which they have significant experience, allowing them to predict costs and likely success with a relatively high degree of confidence and making it easier to reach agreement with BP on the offsets attributed to each project; and
- Gave preference to projects that were closer to being ready to implement.[343]

For each early restoration project selected for implementation, the trustees and BP worked cooperatively to agree on the restoration benefits provided by the projects (referred to as NRD offsets). Then, a project stipulation agreement was implemented for each project with mutually agreeable NRD offsets. The framework agreement specified that no project was to be funded unless the trustees and BP agreed upon the NRD offsets and executed a project stipulation agreement.[344]

The trustees and BP settled the NRD claim for the 2010 *Deepwater Horizon* oil spill in 2016 for up to $8.8 billion, including the $1 billion for the early restoration program.[345] If the case had not settled, then it is likely that NRD offsets for the early restoration projects would have been binding in the subsequent NRD litigation, since all trustees and BP signed the project stipulation agreements. However, the legal status of early restoration projects would be uncertain in the absence of a formal agreement between the trustees and PRP on NRD offsets.

---

342. DEEPWATER HORIZON NATURAL RESOURCES DAMAGE ASSESSMENT EARLY RESTORATION, http://www.gulfspill restoration.noaa.gov/sites/default/files/wp-content/uploads/Spring2012_TCToolkit_EarlyCriteria_Large Format_FINAL.pdf (last visited Feb. 14, 2019).

343. *Id.* at 2.

344. *See* Deepwater Horizon Trustees, *supra* note 341, at 4–5.

345. U.S. Dep't of Interior, The Deepwater Horizon Oil Spill and Restoration, https://www.doi.gov /deepwaterhorizon (last visited Feb. 14, 2019).

B. Climate Change

As reported by many sources, the world's climate has changed in several ways, including:

- Increase in average air temperature;
- Lengthening of the growing season;
- Increase in average precipitation;
- Increase in frequency and intensity of extreme precipitation events;
- More frequent and intense heat waves, and less frequent and intense cold waves;
- Increase in sea levels; and
- Increase in acidification of the ocean.[346]

Those climate changes have caused or contributed to several effects on ecosystems, including:

- Adverse impacts on water quality and the regulation of water flows;
- Reduced ability to buffer impacts from extreme events like fires, floods, and storms;
- Change in the mix of plant and animal life, including the disappearance of some species in regions where they have been prevalent; and
- Change in the timing of critical biological events, such as spring bud burst, emergences from overwintering, and the start of migrations.[347]

Most scientists expect the climate changes to continue in the remainder of this century.[348] As a consequence, trustees increasingly want the effects of expected climate change incorporated into NRD assessments.[349]

Presumably, hazardous substance releases and oil spills at specific sites alone will not significantly affect climate changes in the future. Therefore, if climate changes occur in the future, then they will affect the baseline condition of relevant natural resources, which would likely affect service losses from any injuries continuing into the future and service gains from restoration actions. However, several difficulties arise in assessing the potential impacts of future climate change, including:

- The timing and magnitude of impacts from future climate change are uncertain, especially in the more distant future;

---

346. CLIMATE CHANGE IMPACTS IN THE UNITED STATES: THE THIRD NATIONAL CLIMATE ASSESSMENT 20–21 (Jerry M. Melillo, Terese Richmond & Gary W. Yohe eds., U.S. Global Change Research Program 2014).

347. P.M. Groffman et al., *Chapter 8 Ecosystems, Biodiversity, and Ecosystem Services, in* CLIMATE CHANGE IMPACTS IN THE UNITED STATES: THE THIRD NATIONAL CLIMATE ASSESSMENT, *supra* note 346, at 195, 196–220.

348. NASA, Global Climate Change, Effects, https://climate.nasa.gov/effects/ (last visited Feb. 14, 2019).

349. For example, Section 6.14 in Chapter 6 of the Damage Assessment and Restoration Plan for the *Deepwater Horizon* oil spill addressed the effects of climate change on restoration planning. See DEEPWATER HORIZON NAT. RES. DAMAGE ASSESSMENT TRS., ENVIRONMENTAL CONSEQUENCES AND COMPLIANCE WITH OTHER LAWS, http://www.gulfspillrestoration.noaa.gov/sites/default/files/wp-content/uploads/Chapter-6_Environmental-Consequences_508.pdf.

- Some of the impacts from future climate change may be beneficial (e.g., warmer temperatures and increased precipitation may shorten the recovery of injured resources and/or increase the services provided by restoration actions);
- The net effect of changes in the mix of plant and animal species in the future caused by climate change may not be apparent; and
- Any adverse effects of future climate change will be diminished by the discounting process (e.g., a $1,000 loss that occurs 75 years into the future as a result of climate change would have a present value of just $109 using a 3 percent discount rate).

These difficulties support an argument that incorporating the potential effects of climate change in an NRD assessment would be speculative, and speculative damages are prohibited by the DOI regulations and are generally disfavored by the courts.[350] To our knowledge, no court has rendered an opinion on the merits of incorporating climate change into NRD assessment.[351]

---

350. 43 C.F.R. § 11.84(b)(2).

351. Regardless of whether climate change has yet been incorporated into an NRD assessment, social and public interest groups are forging forward with litigation against the United States to hold it accountable for not taking action to safeguard against the impact on the planet's climate, which affects almost all natural resource services. *See* Juliana v. United States, 217 F. Supp. 3d 1224 (D. Or. 2016). While past efforts have failed, this civil action survived an initial motion to dismiss and several subsequent motions and writs of mandamus to the Ninth Circuit. For more information, *see generally* Our Children's Trust, *Juliana v. United States* Youth Climate Lawsuit, https://www.ourchildrenstrust .org/us/federal-lawsuit/ (last visited Feb. 14, 2019); Melissa Scanlan, *Does the US Constitution Ensure a Future Livable Planet?*, Law360 (Jan. 10, 2017 12:26 PM), https://www.law360.com/articles/878065; Mary Christina Wood & Daniel Galpern, *Atmospheric Recovery Litigation: Making the Fossil Fuel Industry Pay to Restore a Viable Climate System*, 45 Envtl. L. 259 (2015) ("At its core, the public trust principle encompasses the reserved and inalienable rights of citizens to a healthy environment. The principle imposes a sovereign duty on government to protect crucial natural resources for the benefit of present and future generations of citizens. The climate system and atmosphere support all life on Earth, yet governments worldwide continue to allow carbon dioxide pollution that propels climate disruption. Scientists have made clear that such pollution imperils the habitability of Earth and jeopardizes the stability of human civilization, yet governments do vanishingly little to force major carbon polluters to change their ways. Irreversible tipping points loom dangerously ahead. The public trust commands governments to protect a viable climate system and authorizes citizens to turn to the courts when government fails."). *See also* Mary Christina Wood, Nature's Trust, Environmental Law for a New Ecological Age (Cambridge Univ. Press 2014) (advancing the notion of an "atmospheric trust" doctrine); Ira Gottlieb et al., *Natural Resource Damages for Climate Change—An Idea Whose Time Is Not Yet Come, Part I: NRD Claims Are Not Currently Viable under CERCLA*, 20 Envtl. Claims J. 256 (2008); Ira Gottlieb et al., *Natural Resource Damages for Climate Change—An Idea Whose Time Is Not Yet Come, Part II: Climate Change NRD Claims—Get Coverage*, 21 Envtl. Claims J. 2 (2009).

CHAPTER 6

Toxic Tort Litigation

J. Alan Harrell and Barbara L. Arras

I. INTRODUCTION

Toxic tort litigation involves single or repeated exposure to a toxic agent. Many cases arise from long-term exposure, such as a worker's use of particular products over the course of a career. Other claims relate to one-time events, such as a release from a chemical manufacturing facility. Common issues in both types of cases include whether the substance to which the plaintiff was exposed is capable of causing the claimed ailment and, if so, whether the exposure duration is sufficient for causation purposes. Accordingly, both sides regularly engage toxicologists, epidemiologists, industrial hygienists, and other experts. Working with experts who are well credentialed, follow methodologies that pass muster under *Daubert*, and have a knack for relaying complex concepts to juries in a persuasive and understandable manner, all become paramount considerations.

In long-latency cases, the availability of historical documents and records retention issues can play a role. In cases involving a more recent fact pattern, the same electronic discovery principles that permeate virtually all modern litigation can move to the forefront. In many scenarios, defendants tend to work cooperatively, whether through a formal joint defense group or more informal means, often without the co-defendant finger-pointing that sometimes exists in other types of litigation. Companies that routinely find themselves as defendants in certain types of litigation may also consider it helpful to use a national coordinating counsel model to help ensure consistency of their approach to discovery, expert, and overall strategic issues, simultaneously relieving some of the burden on in-house counsel. Although certain types of toxic tort cases can follow similar patterns, practitioners should also remain mindful of how individual cases invariably generate unique issues that require creativity and not a one-size-fits-all approach.

The authors wish to thank Gregory J. Reda and Lillian M. Grappe for their valuable research assistance.

The discussion that follows addresses a number of issues that can arise at various stages of toxic tort litigation. After first touching on key theories of liability and defenses, this chapter covers common discovery issues; the emergence of personal jurisdiction as an early battleground; the role of expert witnesses and the related importance of causation assessment; and finally practical considerations pertaining to settlement and trial.

II. THEORIES OF LIABILITY AND DEFENSES

An overview of all possible theories of recovery and corresponding defenses in toxic tort litigation is beyond the scope of this chapter. However, the discussion that follows covers the highlights of several causes of action, as well as corresponding defenses and trends.

Routine standard bearers such as negligence and strict liability are prevalent theories of recovery, including in chemical products liability cases. Causation questions are critical under these theories, of course. In the personal injury and exposure context (and as further discussed in section V of this chapter, "Science"), for example, much energy is devoted to working with toxicologists and other experts dueling over whether a particular contaminant and the extent of the plaintiff's exposure to it can and did cause the plaintiff's injuries. Selection of a well-qualified expert who can convey opinions to the trier of fact in layman's terms therefore becomes crucial. This is made all the more difficult by long-latency cases in which symptoms may not manifest themselves until years after exposure.

Counsel and their experts may also seek to rely on regulatory risk assessment to bolster their causation theories. A plaintiff may point to exposure above Agency for Toxic Substance and Disease Registry (ATSDR) minimal risk levels (MRLs) for a particular substance, for example, while defendants may counter that risk estimates and corresponding agency exposure guidelines are built upon conservative assumptions and likely overstate the actual risk. Indeed, according to ATSDR, "[e]xposure to a level above the MRL does not mean that adverse health effects will occur."[1] Putting similar arguments into practice, the court in *Molden v. Georgia Gulf. Corp.* granted the defendant's motion for summary judgment on lack of physical injury, commenting that according to plaintiffs' experts "the level of phenol released into the atmosphere was not considered harmful based on prophylactic standards set forth by various governmental and regulatory agencies."[2] The U.S. Fifth Circuit Court of Appeal has observed that regulatory and advisory bodies like the International Agency for Research on Cancer, the Occupational Safety and Health Administration (OSHA) and Environmental Protection Agency (EPA) use a threshold of proof that is "reasonably lower than that appropriate in tort law, which 'traditionally make[s] more particularized inquiries into cause and effect'

---

1. ATSDR MRLs (June 2017), https://www.atsdr.cdc.gov/mrls/index.asp.
2. Molden v. Ga. Gulf. Corp., 465 F. Supp. 2d 606, 613 (M.D. La. 2006).

and requires a plaintiff to prove 'that it is more likely than not that another individual has caused him or her harm.'"[3]

The potential for toxicogenomics to play a growing role in the causation debate also bears mention. Toxicogenomics involves the analysis of how particular substances affect genetic material. While a detailed discussion of the subject is beyond the scope of this chapter, suffice it to say that proof of certain genetic markers (1) may indicate a plaintiff was predisposed to develop a particular disease without regard to exposure to the substance at issue, (2) could instead be characteristic of exposure, or (3) could indicate susceptibility to developing the disease from exposure. Juries could potentially be receptive to such individualized causation explanations, although this field is still developing and the corresponding analysis could be cost prohibitive in some cases.

With the understandable emphasis on causation, litigants must still be mindful not to lose sight of exactly what the plaintiffs contend the defendants did wrong, no matter what label is placed on the theory of recovery. In other words, in a chemical products liability case, is the claim that the product was unreasonably dangerous for lack of an adequate warning? If so, why was the warning insufficient? In cases involving claims that a product contained carcinogens, but was not so labeled (such as claims that products with hydrocarbon solvent ingredients may contain benzene as a contaminant), plaintiffs may attempt to demonstrate that the federal Hazardous Communication Standard required certain carcinogen warnings because the product contained more than 0.1 percent of the carcinogen at issue.[4] In that event, the parties may focus on company or raw material supplier records regarding product content and testing, as well as relevant literature on the typical composition of the substances at issue, such as the percentage of benzene potentially found in toluene during different time periods.

Plaintiffs who are able to prove exposure but not physical harm may pursue medical monitoring claims, arguing that even in the absence of any current manifestation of physical injury, they are entitled to compensation for future medical monitoring to make an early diagnosis of exposure-related disease. In *Meyer ex rel. Coplin v. Fluor Corp.*, the Missouri Supreme Court described a medical monitoring claim as seeking "to recover the costs of future reasonably necessary diagnostic testing to detect latent injuries or diseases that may develop as a result of exposure to toxic substances."[5] Whether such damages are recoverable without manifestation of physical injury varies from state to state. In *Meyer*, for example, the court found that such damages are recoverable under Missouri law, while noting that it was not creating a new tort. Rather, it was simply recognizing a compensable item

---

3. Allen v. Pa. Eng'g Corp., 102 F.3d 194, 199 (5th 1996) (quoting Wright v. Williamette Indus., Inc., 91 F.3d 1105, 1107 (8th Cir. 1996)); Milward v. Acuity Specialty Prod. Grp., Inc., 969 F. Supp. 2d 101, 110 (D. Mass. 2013), *aff'd sub nom.* Milward v. Rust-Oleum Corp., 820 F.3d 469 (1st Cir. 2016).

4. *See* Hazard Communication, 29 C.F.R. § 1910.1200.

5. Meyer *ex rel.* Coplin v. Fluor Corp., 220 S.W.3d 712, 716 (Mo. 2007); Elsea v. U.S. Eng'g Co., 463 S.W.3d 409, 416–17 (Mo. Ct. App. 2015) (citing *Meyer*, 220 S.W.3d at 712).

of damage. The court also rejected the argument that recovery for medical monitoring is contingent upon the existence of a present physical injury.[6] In contrast, the Mississippi Supreme Court has rejected a cause of action for medical monitoring without establishing a physical injury from exposure.[7]

One theory that has received recent attention in the courts is secondary or "take-home" exposure. Such cases normally involve allegations that a worker's spouse or other family member was exposed to contaminants away from the work site, such as by washing work clothes at home. Questions of duty and foreseeability become paramount, as courts look to factors such as whether and when the defendant knew or should have known of the risk of secondary exposure, and even the possible impact of having a laundry service available at work. For example, in *CSX Transportation, Inc. v. Williams*, a wrongful-death action based on the plaintiff's late wife's exposure at home to asbestos on clothes he wore at work, the Supreme Court of Georgia concluded that under Georgia negligence law "an employer does not owe a duty of care to a third-party, non-employee, who comes into contact with its employee's asbestos-tainted work clothing at locations away from the workplace."[8] The court declined to use a foreseeability theory to extend the employer's duty beyond the workplace to encompass all who might come in contact with an employee or his or her clothing.

In contrast, the New Jersey Supreme Court concluded in *Olivo v. Owens-Illinois, Inc.* that the defendant's fears of limitless exposure based on a theory of foreseeability were overstated.[9] The court found that to the extent the defendant owed a duty of care to workers on its premises for the foreseeable risk of exposure to friable asbestos and asbestos dust, it similarly owed a duty of care to spouses handling work clothing based on the foreseeable risk of exposure.[10] Other decisions also have yielded mixed results, with some courts extending a duty to cover secondary exposure in certain circumstances and others declining to do so.[11]

---

6. *Id.* at 717–18. *See also* Baker v. Deutschland GmbH, 240 F. Supp. 3d 341, 347 (M.D. Pa. 2016) ("Pennsylvania has recognized medical monitoring as a claim that is distinct from other tort claims involving actual physical injury.").

7. *See* Paz v. Brush Engineered Materials, Inc., 949 So. 2d 1 (Miss. 2007) (answering a certified question from the Fifth Circuit and referencing numerous cases from other jurisdictions on both sides of the issue); *see also* Sadler v. PacifiCare of Nev., 130 Nev. Adv. Op. 98, 340 P.3d 1264, 1270 (2014) ("[A] plaintiff may state a cause of action for negligence with medical monitoring as the remedy without asserting that he or she has suffered a present physical injury."). See Caronia v. Philip Morris USA, Inc., 715 F.3d 417, 443 (2d Cir. 2013) for a listing of cases that have permitted and precluded plaintiffs from recovering medical monitoring costs in the absence of a current physical injury.

8. CSX Transp., Inc. v. Williams, 608 S.E.2d 208, 210 (Ga. 2005); *see also* Union Carbide Corp. v. Fields, 726 S.E.2d 521, 525 (Ga. Ct. App. 2012).

9. Olivo v. Owens-Illinois Inc., 895 A.2d 1143 (N.J. 2006); *see also* Schwartz v. Accuratus Corp., 225 N.J. 517, 519, 139 A.3d 84, 86 (2016).

10. *Olivo*, 895 A.2d 1143, 1151 (N.J. 2006).

11. For examples of additional cases finding liability for secondary exposure, see Chaisson v. Avondale Indus., Inc., 947 So. 2d 171 (La. App. Dec. 12, 2006), *writ denied*, 954 So. 2d 145 (La. 2007); Kesner v. Superior Court, 1 Cal. 5th 1132, 210 Cal.Rptr.3d 283, 384 P.3d 283 (2016); Bobo v. Tenn. Valley Auth., 855 F.3d 1294, 1303 (11th Cir. 2017) (applying Alabama law). For examples of additional cases declining to find liability for secondary exposure, see Holdampf v. A.C. & S., Inc. (*In re* N.Y.C. Asbestos Litig.) 840 N.E.2d 115 (N.Y. 2005); Gillen v. Boeing Co., 40 F. Supp. 3d 534 (E.D. Pa. 2014) (applying Pennsylvania law); Quiroz v. ALCOA, Inc., 240 Ariz. 517, 382 P.3d 75 (Ariz. Ct. App. 2016).

In the property damage context, real estate appraisers may be retained as expert witnesses to testify to whether or the extent to which the presence of particular contaminants caused a diminution in property value. Any impact typically will depend in large measure on whether the property at issue has yet to be remediated, is undergoing remediation, or remediation is complete, with the last, of course, offering the least chance for any diminution in value or so-called stigma damages.

When dealing with potential property damage from contamination, a basic cause of action for trespass, including the subsurface or surface migration of contaminants, can be helpful to a plaintiff in combating a statute of limitations defense to the extent the trespass can be classified as continuing in nature. This typically involves demonstrating not only that the effects are continuing because the contaminants remain on the plaintiff's property despite the feasibility of remediation, but also that the tortious conduct is continuing. But there also may be room to argue that the defendant's failure to remedy the trespass, as opposed to simply continuing in the activities that caused it, is sufficient to keep the limitations period from beginning to run until the contaminants are removed.[12]

Fraudulent concealment or suppression allegations come into play in some cases. They are sometimes coupled with a conspiracy allegation and often run straight into the type of pleading difficulties addressed in the Supreme Court's *Bell Atlantic Corp. v. Twombly* decision.[13] Plaintiffs may, for example, allege that manufacturers of a particular chemical product conspired to conceal its dangers. The conspiracy allegation may help justify the joinder of numerous defendants, but it can be problematic, for many jurisdictions do not recognize a separate cause of action for conspiracy independent of an underlying tort.[14]

---

12. *Compare, e.g.*, Crump v. Sabine River Auth., 737 So. 2d 720, 728 (La. 1999) (stating "[a] continuing tort is occasioned by unlawful acts, not the continuation of the ill effects of an original, wrongful act"), *with* Estate of Patout v. City of New Iberia, 813 So. 2d 1248 (La. App. 2002), *writ denied*, 819 So. 2d 335, 1172 (La. 2002) (finding that a trespass was continuing by virtue of the defendant's failure to remove garbage from plaintiffs' land.).

13. Bell Atl. Corp. v. Twombly, 550 U.S. 544 (2007). The decision arguably altered the landscape surrounding federal notice pleading by requiring a plaintiff to demonstrate, through allegations in the complaint, more than the mere possibility of recovery and instead show the plausibility of recovery to meet federal pleading standards and survive a Rule 12(b)(6) motion to dismiss. In the authors' experience, however, the decision has not resulted in a sea change in terms of its practical impact.

14. *Compare* McClure v. Owens Corning Fiberglas Corp., 188 Ill. 2d 102, 133, 720 N.E.2d 242, 258 (1999) (In order to state a claim for civil conspiracy, a plaintiff must allege an agreement and a tortious act committed in furtherance of that agreement.), *and* Tanner v. Int'l Isocyanate Inst., Inc., No. CV 05-PWG-2341-E, 2008 WL 11374393, at *18 (N.D. Ala. June 9, 2008) ("While Alabama recognizes civil conspiracy, the conspiracy necessarily must be predicated upon an actionable tort."), *with In re* Ernie Haire Ford, Inc., 459 B.R. 824, 840 (Bankr. M.D. Fla. 2011) ("Normally, a claim for civil conspiracy requires the existence of an underlying tort. In the instant case, the most obvious claim would be conspiracy to commit a fraudulent transfer. However, Florida law does recognize civil conspiracy as an independent, stand-alone tort. In such cases, there must be a 'peculiar power of coercion' that is possessed and can be exercised by the conspirators, acting in concert, which would not otherwise exist by a single individual acting alone."), *and* Rickley v. Goodfriend, 212 Cal. App. 4th 1136, 1158, 151 Cal. Rptr. 3d 683, 703 (2013) ("Defendants seem to argue that an action for conspiracy must be based exclusively on tort principles, not on a statutory violation that provides civil penalties. No authority is cited for that proposition, and we cannot conceive of a basis for limiting conspiracy claims in that manner. It is sufficient that a conspiracy is based on an agreement to engage in unlawful conduct regardless of whether the conspiracy violates a duty imposed by tort law or a statute.").

When plaintiffs turn to theories of fraudulent concealment or suppression to furnish the underlying tort, pleading becomes all the more challenging. For example, in Maryland, the elements of fraudulent concealment are "1) that the defendant owed a duty to the plaintiff to disclose a material fact, 2) that the defendant failed to disclose that fact, 3) that the defendant intended to defraud or deceive the plaintiff, 4) that the plaintiff took action in justifiable reliance on the concealment, and 5) that the plaintiff suffered damages as a result of the defendant's concealment."[15] In *Hill v. Brush*, a case involving allegations of exposure to beryllium-containing dental alloys, the plaintiff's claim for conspiracy to commit fraudulent concealment did not survive a Rule 12(b)(6) motion to dismiss for failure to satisfy Rule 9(b)'s particularity requirement for pleading fraud.[16] This case was decided prior to *Bell Atlantic* and now would be even less likely to survive such a motion. Despite the potential difficulty with sufficiently pleading theories such as fraudulent concealment or conspiracy to commit fraudulent concealment, the prospect that they will result in the tolling of the applicable limitations period serves as a countervailing consideration. For example, pleading fraudulent concealment where the statute of limitations would have otherwise expired opens the door to arguing that the limitations period was tolled during the alleged concealment.[17]

III. DISCOVERY AND INVESTIGATION

Whether through the initial investigation or formal discovery, the need to gather key documents, identify witnesses, and assess information on the contaminant(s) involved quickly comes into play, particularly with one-time incidents of an emergency nature, such as an off-site chemical release. This section provides an overview of practical considerations.

A. Initial Investigation

In any toxic tort matter, it will always be important to pin down information on the characteristics of the contaminants involved. Helpful information can be found through safety data sheets (formerly known as material safety data sheets), as well as through publicly available toxicity profiles.[18] Even if the matter involves a sub-

---

15. Hill v. Brush Engineered Materials, Inc., 383 F. Supp. 2d 814, 820 (D. Md. 2005) (citations omitted); *see also* Todd v. XOOM Energy Md., LLC, No. GJH-15-0154, 2017 WL 667198, at *5 (D. Md. Feb. 16, 2017).

16. 383 F. Supp. 2d 814 (D. Md. 2005). The plaintiff was allowed an opportunity to amend the complaint, successfully stating a cause of action for civil conspiracy and fraudulent concealment. *See also* Boardley v. Household Fin. Corp. III, 39 F. Supp. 3d 689, 715–18 (D. Md. 2014) (failing to establish the duty element of a fraudulent concealment claim).

17. *See, e.g.*, Mest v. Cabot Corp., 449 F.3d 502 (3d Cir. 2006); *see also* Lomax v. Police Chief of Erie, 452 F. App'x 84 (3d Cir. 2011) ("the statute of limitations may be tolled by the discovery rule or the fraudulent concealment doctrine.").

18. For example, the Agency for Toxic Substances and Disease Registry (ATSDR), a federal public health agency of the Department of Health and Human Services, publishes toxicological profiles addressing the toxicological and adverse health effects of numerous hazardous substances. These

stance with which a practitioner is familiar from past litigation, conferring with a consulting expert regarding how the science may have evolved and the most recent authoritative literature is a step not to overlook.

When an incident occurs at a chemical manufacturing facility involving injuries from chemical exposure and possible off-site impact, defense counsel will need to balance numerous considerations, including scene preservation, ensuring that proper regulatory reporting takes place, and assisting the client in responding to investigations by regulatory agencies such as OSHA. Counsel for any injured parties may also want to seek, through cooperation with the site owner or court intervention, early site access for counsel and his or her experts to the extent that examining the scene in its "as is" condition may be helpful. With an industrial incident, early OSHA involvement may lead to a site preservation agreement among all interested parties (including OSHA) as to evidence collection, site access, and potentially a protocol for equipment testing depending upon the nature of the incident. Such agreements are often part and parcel of cooperating with a governmental investigation. They can also potentially preclude participating parties from later claiming that the scene or associated physical evidence was not properly preserved, or that destructive testing was improperly conducted.

Public records regarding reported releases should contain notes and reports from first responders in cases involving the release of contaminants. In some cases involving questions of long-term operations, historical aerial photographs of the site may be helpful in demonstrating the location of structures, the outline of former disposal pits, and the like. Such photographs often can be obtained from local vendors, with some photography availability on the Internet.

When current site conditions are at issue, the parties may wish to retain consultants early in the process to collect and analyze samples. Because this would involve issues such as landowner consent and potential spoliation of evidence, and could create conflicts with regulators already engaged in reviewing and approving work at the site, having the court approve an agreed-to protocol regarding sampling times, locations, split sampling, and related matters may be advisable.

An industrial site owner may decide to form an incident investigation team to better understand what happened and how to prevent reoccurrence, while also acting in anticipation of litigation. Of course, incident investigations and any resulting reports raise privilege questions should litigation indeed arise. A party undertaking such an investigation should consider at the outset what measures it can take to best position future privilege arguments. For example, any writings concerning the investigation team's creation should note that its work is in anticipation of litigation, provided that is indeed the case. Including outside counsel in the investigation, such as serving as one of the team members, may also help tip the scales in favor of the attorney-client privilege and work-product doctrine.

---

profiles and ATSDR reports are generally available on the agency's website at https://www.atsdr.cdc.gov/. (See the discussion in section II regarding the potential misuse of such information.)

Meanwhile, another litigant looking to obtain incident investigation materials may argue that the investigation was done primarily in the ordinary course of the company's business pursuant to company policy rather than in anticipation of litigation, and should therefore be produced. With more serious incidents, the investigating party may counter that the incident and the investigation were far beyond the routine type of workplace accidents envisioned by company policies on accident reporting and investigation. Treating such investigations as ordinary, nonprivileged business records could have a chilling effect on a company's willingness to undertake and memorialize the results of fulsome incident investigations, proponents of privilege can argue. There are cases that support either position as to privilege,[19] but suffice it to say the inquiry can be fact-specific as to how and why the incident investigation team was formed and counsel's role.

Other practical considerations can also come into play, such as how a site owner can share the root cause or other investigation results with affected employees (including those potentially at risk from similar incidents), without waiving privileges that might otherwise apply. Providing employees with key take-aways and safety points derived from the investigation without providing the full report counsel helped prepare is one potential approach.

In product exposure cases, the initial investigation (and expert witness work) could include inventory testing. For example, if the contention is that a product emits a certain contaminant under particular conditions, both sides may wish to test like products from the same manufacturing time frame, in addition to the actual product at issue. The testing of similar products could be informative regarding whether any product defect was limited to a particular lot or manufacturing range, which could be particularly relevant in putative class actions where defining the scope of the problem is a key point of contention.

As in other types of cases, timely litigation holds are necessary. Pertinent considerations include how wide to cast the net, both within and potentially outside the company. As to the latter, in product exposure cases, plaintiffs may argue that documents in the hands of a defendant's raw material supplier are within the defendant's "possession, custody or control" pursuant to Federal Rule of Civil Procedure 34 and state corollaries. In *Sergeeva v. Tripleton International Ltd.*, for example, the court explained that control is "the legal right to obtain the documents requested upon demand."[20] Accordingly, it may be necessary to resort to

---

19. *Compare* Transocean Deepwater, Inc. v. Ingersoll-Rand Co., 2010 WL 5374744 (E.D. La. Dec. 21, 2010), *with* Chevron Midstream Pipelines, LLC v. Settoon Towing, LLC, 2015 WL 65357 (E.D. La. Jan. 5, 2015). The nature of any incident investigation and related privilege arguments can be affected by whether the matter involved a process safety management (PSM)-covered incident pursuant to OSHA regulations. For such incidents, 29 C.F.R. § 1910.119(m) contains specific requirements regarding the investigation and corresponding report, including the requirement that a contract employee be on the investigation team if the incident involved a contractor's work, and that the investigation begin no later than 48 hours after the incident.

20. Sergeeva v. Tripleton Int'l Ltd., 834 F.3d 1194, 1201 (11th Cir. 2016) (citing SeaRock v. Stripling, 736 F.2d 650, 653–54 (11th Cir. 1984)).

the underlying contracts between the party responding to the discovery and the third party possessing responsive documents to the extent they may shed light on the degree of operative control. For example, there may be contractual provisions outlining the types of information that must be provided between the contracting parties upon request. To the extent a defendant believes it has the requisite control over information that lies with third parties, as a practical matter it may benefit from expanding the litigation hold circle to include such parties. Similar considerations are applicable to corporate parents, sister companies, and affiliates. In *Schultz v. Daimler Trucks North America, LLC*, for example, when determining that the defendant lacked the requisite control over sister companies, the court considered several factors, such as commonality of ownership; intermingling of directors, officers, or employees; and perhaps most importantly whether documents are exchanged between the companies in the regular course of business.[21]

In addition to documents, it is also critical for both sides to identify key employees with knowledge pertaining to current and historical operations. In cases where company actions spanning a long period of time are at issue, the most knowledgeable witnesses may turn out to be employees who have moved on or retired. If such a witness left on bad terms, it may be necessary to try and mend fences in the process. Accordingly, both sides may have an interest in reaching out to former employees. There is no per se bar to contacting former employees of an adverse party, at least pursuant to the ABA's Model Rules of Professional Conduct.[22]

B. Discovery

When formal discovery begins, its sequencing is an important consideration. Counsel will generally want to have the benefit of initial written discovery responses before taking depositions. That will arm deposing counsel with background information to make the most of any deposition, particularly given the likelihood counsel will not get a second bite at the apple with respect to a given deponent. Similarly, to the extent counsel properly requests the production of certain documents at the time of a corporate or individual deposition, it is typically more

---

21. Schultz v. Daimler Trucks N. Am., LLC, No. 2:12-CV-228-SWS, 2014 WL 11516082, at *12 (D. Wyo. Nov. 4, 2014).

22. ABA Model Rule of Professional Conduct 4.2 provides: "In representing a client, a lawyer shall not communicate about the subject of the representation with a person the lawyer knows to be represented by another lawyer in the matter, unless the lawyer has the consent of the other lawyer or is authorized to do so by law or a court order." Comment 7 to Rule 4.2 provides as to represented organizations: "[T]his Rule prohibits communications with a constituent of the organization who supervises, directs, or regularly consults with the organization's lawyer concerning the matter or has authority to obligate the organization with respect to the matter or whose act or omission in connection with the matter may be imputed to the organization for purposes of civil or criminal liability." Notably, Comment 7 also states: "Consent of the organization's lawyer is not required for communication with a former constituent." *See also* John P. Manard, Jr., Steven J. Levine & William H. Howard III, *Case Strategy and Trial Management Issues in Toxic Tort Cases, in* Toxic Tort Litigation 200–04 (D. Alan Rudlin ed., ABA 2007) [hereinafter Toxic Tort Litigation], for further discussion of communications with employees.

effective and efficient to stagger the timeline to ensure production occurs sufficiently in advance of the deposition for deposing counsel to digest the documents. Even when production is requested to occur at the time of the deposition, counsel defending the deposition should consider an earlier production on the theory that the deponent may also benefit from more orderly and efficient questioning than sometimes occurs when deposing counsel is simultaneously sifting through documents for the first time.

One of the more frequently used discovery tools is the corporate deposition pursuant to Federal Rule of Civil Procedure 30(b)(6) or state law equivalents. Plaintiffs' counsel often move toward corporate depositions early on in the discovery period in part as a short cut to potential serial depositions of fact witnesses identified in written discovery. This approach is understandable, particularly given the added benefit that the testimony is typically binding on the company. For that same reason and because the corporate designee(s) is often a higher-up who should and will want to feel that he or she has been more than sufficiently prepared by counsel, corporate depositions can become one of the most important pretrial steps in a case. Going hand in hand with that level of importance is the practical reality that selecting the right deponent(s) is also critical. In toxic tort cases that involve long-term product exposure, for example, it may be necessary for the deponent to become educated on matters that predate the deponent's employment with the company. This preparation could take the form of reviewing historical documents and interviewing current or former employees who possess relevant knowledge that cannot necessarily be gleaned from documents alone.

It is extremely important to give considerable thought to selecting the subjects for examination to be included in the corporate deposition notice. Failure to spell out a particular subject will result in not having the most knowledgeable witness present to address questions on that topic, and in a related objection that the notice did not cover the topic. Similarly, counsel defending the corporate deposition will want to take into account the possibility that the inclusion of multiple subject matters will require different witnesses for different categories, while also factoring in the natural desire to designate representatives who will handle themselves well in their roles. In certain cases, a former employee may be the most knowledgeable person and most logical choice to designate as a corporate representative for one or more topics.

Given all that goes into a corporate deposition from a defense standpoint, plaintiff's counsel can and do use the procedure to generate settlement leverage. A defendant that is seriously considering resolution may wish to further explore settlement prospects before producing a corporate witness. Meanwhile, counsel taking a corporate deposition will typically make a run at demonstrating the defendant has not produced a witness who is sufficiently knowledgeable about responsive information that is reasonably available to the company. Counsel may also use a corporate deposition as a vehicle for exploring record-keeping practices and procedures, including electronic databases and document-retention policies, sometimes through a limited records-focused corporate deposition early on in the case.

Because corporate designees must, pursuant to Rule 30(b)(6), "testify as to matters known or reasonably available to the organization," a cautionary word is in order. Even when there is no potential corporate designee with personal knowledge of the relevant subjects of examination (a realistic possibility in cases where the evidence spans decades of company operations), a corporate deponent nevertheless is obligated to make a good-faith effort to prepare or educate its designee. "If necessary, the deponent must use documents, past employees, and other resources in performing this required preparation."[23]

When there are a large number of defendants, plaintiff's counsel may prefer to select a few target defendants for initial corporate depositions. By the same token, defense counsel may prefer to see other defendants provide corporate depositions first to have an even better sense of what approach plaintiff's counsel will take during the examination.

Turning to plaintiff depositions, in toxic tort litigation involving a relatively small number of plaintiffs, it is safe to assume that each will be deposed. For larger numbers of plaintiffs, the parties may select just a sample of plaintiffs, such as bellwether plaintiffs who may be part of an agreed first wave of plaintiffs to proceed to trial. Nor is it uncommon to instead set up a streamlined procedure for deposing all plaintiffs despite their great number. The parties may opt to block out weeks at a time during which two or more plaintiffs may be simultaneously deposed, perhaps with a set of depositions going forward in the morning and a set in the afternoon. Sufficient attorney staffing will be an issue for both sides, not to mention costs. In these cases, the defendants typically will collaborate on an agreed-to deposition outline, rotating which attorneys for the various defendants will take the lead in the examination. Similarly, plaintiffs' counsel will develop their own game plan to defend the depositions. In the event that approximately eight to ten bellwether plaintiffs will be involved in the first trial, economies of scale often will militate against deposing all named plaintiffs and counsel rather will concentrate resources on this bellwether subset.

Another common discovery issue in toxic tort litigation is the deposition of regulators. A party may wish to depose state or federal agency employees involved in responding to the underlying incident, or perhaps the person who has been most involved historically with review and approval of site cleanup plans or permitting matters. Plaintiffs' counsel generally can expect that regulators will be inclined to defend the administrative record in such instances. However, counsel may seek, through the deposition, to present information and materials he or she contends the agency may not be aware of and inquire as to whether such information

---

23. Briddell v. Saint Gobain Abrasives, Inc., 233 F.R.D. 57, 60 (D. Mass. 2005) (citations omitted); Trs. of Bos. Univ. v. Everlight Elecs. Co., No. 12-CV-11935-PBS, 2014 WL 5786492, at *3 (D. Mass. Sept. 24, 2014); *see also In re* Vitamins Antitrust Litig., 216 F.R.D. 168 (D.D.C. 2003).

changes the landscape in any respect. The defendants, meanwhile, will be mindful of their continuing relationship with regulators and how that may be affected by litigation testimony and developments. Counsel for all parties should be cognizant of the reluctance regulators naturally have to becoming involved in private litigation that entails a different set of goals and standards than does the regulatory arena.[24]

In managing discovery, counsel also should be mindful of the possible need for independent medical examinations pursuant to Rule 35 of the Federal Rules of Civil Procedure or equivalent state rules, such as by an occupational medicine specialist or pulmonologist in cases involving claims of asthma-like symptoms.

IV. PARTIES AND FORUMS

Often, though not always, toxic tort cases involve multiple defendants. In chemical product exposure cases, for example, a plaintiff may name the product manufacturer, seller, and perhaps raw material suppliers. A plaintiff claiming benzene exposure may choose to name multiple chemical facilities where he or she worked as a contractor, or various vessel owners and product suppliers if maritime exposure is claimed. Part of the aim, of course, is to be sure to include parties who are capable of responding monetarily in a case that might involve large sums of money. Typical state court versus federal court considerations come into play, as well as issues concerning mass joinder versus class action. Meanwhile, personal jurisdiction has taken on increasing importance in light of recent U.S. Supreme Court decisions discussed in the following sections.

This section touches on some of the more common issues, procedures, and forums. Nonetheless, each case will generate its own unique set of circumstances that the parties and the court will struggle with to sort out an alignment of parties and a case management process that will allow the cases to be handled and brought to conclusion.

A. Personal Jurisdiction

While plaintiff and defense counsel at times take personal jurisdiction for granted except in the most obvious instances where it is lacking, recent U.S. Supreme Court cases have changed the landscape. In 2014, the Court in *Daimler AG v. Bauman*[25] made clear that a corporate defendant is subject to general jurisdiction only

---

24. Counsel should also be cognizant of *"Touhy regulations"* —i.e., federal agency regulations governing the release of information that a given agency may rely upon in determining how it responds to nonparty discovery. *See* Touhy v. Regan, 340 U.S. 462 (1951) (finding a contempt citation improper in light of the Department of Justice's reliance on agency regulations granting the attorney general the power to decide whether to comply with a subpoena). See also COMSAT Corp. v. National Science Foundation, 190 F.3d 269 (4th Cir. 1999), for discussion regarding balancing *Touhy* regulations with discovery rules.

25. Daimler AG v. Bauman, 134 S. Ct. 746 (2014).

where it is incorporated, where its principal place of business lies, or in another state in the "exceptional" case where its affiliations with that state are so constant and pervasive to otherwise render it "at home" there.[26] Post-*Daimler* jurisprudence suggests the exception will not swallow the rule. The U.S. Supreme Court in *BNSF Railway Co. v. Tyrrell*[27] concluded that BNSF's 2,000 miles of railroad track and employment of over 2,000 workers in Montana was not enough for general jurisdiction because it did not make BNSF at home there.[28] Accordingly, casting too wide a net for defendants without taking jurisdictional considerations into account could result in an early battle over jurisdiction before counsel can turn to the substance of the case. In that event, plaintiffs' counsel may wish to engage in jurisdictional discovery on matters such as sales data that defendants may prefer not to delve into, while defendants can argue that the jurisprudence suggests such discovery is not warranted.[29] For example, where general jurisdiction is at issue as to a manufacturer defendant that distributes products to numerous states (but is incorporated and has its principal place of business outside the forum state), should evidence of sales to the forum state be relevant in light of the Supreme Court's application of the "at home" test?

The jurisprudential trend as to specific jurisdiction is similar and could also have an impact on toxic tort litigation. In *Bristol-Myers Squibb Co. v. Superior Court of California*,[30] the U.S. Supreme Court explained that specific jurisdiction requires "an affiliation between the forum and the underlying controversy, principally, [an] activity or occurrence that takes place in the forum State and is therefore subject to the State's regulation."[31] The case involved the claims of resident and nonresident plaintiffs relating to the drug Plavix. General jurisdiction was not in dispute before the Supreme Court, as the focus was instead on specific jurisdiction. That Bristol-Myers Squibb conducted research in California on matters unrelated to Plavix was not sufficient or relevant for specific jurisdiction as to the nonresident plaintiffs, the Court determined.[32] Nor was contracting with a California company to distribute the drug nationally; the presence in California of 250 sales representatives, five research labs with 160 employees, and a government advocacy office; or the $900 million of Plavix sales within the state.[33] The resident California plain-

---

26. *Id.* at n.19.
27. 137 S. Ct. 1549 (2017).
28. *See also* Locke v. Ethicon Inc., 58 F. Supp. 3d 757 (S.D. Tex. 2014) (court determined that as to New Jersey corporate defendants principally located there, over $18 million in revenue from product sales in Texas (compared with less in New Jersey), the hiring and training of Texas-based sales personnel to market and sell products in Texas, and payment of a Texas-based consultant for training did not establish general jurisdiction in Texas).
29. *See generally In re* Crash of Aircraft N93PC on July 7, 2013, at Soldotna, Alaska, No. 3:15-CV-0112-HRH, 2018 WL 1613769 (D. Alaska Apr. 3, 2018) (discovery may be appropriately granted where pertinent facts bearing on the question of jurisdiction are controverted or where a more satisfactory showing of the facts is necessary.).
30. Bristol-Myers Squibb Co. v. Superior Court of Cal., S.F. Cnty., 137 S. Ct. 1773 (2017).
31. *Id.* at 1780 (quoting Goodyear Dunlop Tires Operations, S.A. v. Brown, 564 U.S. 915 (2011)).
32. *Bristol-Myers Squibb Co.*, 137 S. Ct. at 1781.
33. *Id.* at 1783.

tiffs would have received Plavix there and had it prescribed by their physicians there, which satisfied specific jurisdiction, but specific jurisdiction was lacking for the nonresident plaintiffs who did not allege they were injured by the drug in California or were treated for their injuries there.[34] The impact this and other such recent decisions may have on toxic tort litigation is still developing, but suffice it to say nonresident plaintiffs looking to join forces with other plaintiffs in a preferred forum may encounter difficulty with both general and specific jurisdiction, as more and more defendants seek to explore the new boundaries of personal jurisdiction.

B. Joinder of Plaintiffs

Apart from personal jurisdiction, joinder will be governed by either the Federal Rules of Civil Procedure or state procedural rules. Federal Rule of Civil Procedure 20 governs permissive joinder at the federal level, allowing such joinder where all the plaintiffs "assert any right to relief jointly, severally, or in the alternative in respect of or arising out of the same transaction, occurrence, or series of transactions or occurrences and if any question of law or fact common to all these persons will arise in the action." Often, state joinder rules share that theme.

Joinder, however, has its limitations in the toxic tort arena. Differences between the individual claims of particular plaintiffs can work against joinder, and it often is not possible to use joinder effectively with large numbers of plaintiffs' cases being tried simultaneously. This can become unmanageable and overwhelming for the courts, the jurors, and even the lawyers. Consequently, where one finds an aggregation of plaintiffs in a single action or an aggregation of actions through consolidation, the most common method of trial is by using bellwether plaintiffs (more on this in section VI, "Case Management," in this chapter).[35] Additionally, cases like *Bristol-Myers Squibb*, *supra*, may cut into plaintiff aggregation based on personal jurisdiction considerations.

C. Class Actions

Class actions, both state and federal, cover a great deal of ground—far more than can be covered comprehensively in this brief summary. Still, some of the basic concepts that a toxic tort litigator would want to focus on immediately are relatively straightforward. Perhaps the best place to start is with the big picture:

> The late 1980s and early 1990s were characterized by the development of the mass tort field, with class sizes and settlement values never seen before. The Supreme

---

34. *Id.* at 1782.

35. For additional information on this topic, see Richard L. Marcus, *Confronting the Consolidation Conundrum*, 1995 B.Y.U. L. Rev. 879 (1995); Charles Silver, *Comparing Class Actions and Consolidations*, 10 Rev. Litig. 495 (1991); Roger H. Trangsrud, *Joinder Alternatives on Mass Tort Litigation*, 70 Cornell L. Rev. 779 (1985); Thomas E. Willging, *Mass Tort Problems and Proposals: A Report to the Mass Tort Working Group*, 187 F.R.D. 328, 354 (1999).

Court's decisions in *Amchem* and *Ortiz* reined these in to some extent, while Congress, during the same period, attempted to slow the increase of securities class actions with its enactment of the Private Securities Litigation Reform Act of 1995 (PSLRA) and the Securities Litigation Uniform Standards Act of 1998 (SLUSA). Both sets of developments have had significant effects: Nationwide mass tort cases are far less prevalent than they were a decade ago, and securities class action filings are significantly down, even in an era marked by widespread securities fraud allegations.[36]

Indeed, toxic tort cases often involve numerous plaintiffs (with individual exposures and damages) and the potential for applying the laws of multiple states. Both factors have proved to be difficulties in connection with attempting to have those cases certified as class actions.

Some authorities cited for the proposition that class actions are not appropriate in mass tort cases include *The Manual for Complex Litigation, Fourth* (2005), at Section 22.72, which reads:

> Since *Amchem*, a number of the district courts have refused to certify dispersed personal injury or property damage mass tort class actions for the purpose of trial, or have decertified them, finding that varying state laws and individual issues of exposure, causation and damages defeat the predominance requirement of Rule 23(b)(3), making trial unmanageable. Another basis for rejecting certification is that such variations make class representatives inadequate or atypical of the interests of the absent class members.[37]

In some instances, claims with respect to medical monitoring have been tried as a means of justifying class treatment, though not with great success.

To better understand the issues courts balance in such situations, consider these three toxic tort cases. First, in 2002, in *In re Methyl Tertiary Butyl Ether Products Liability Litigation*, the owners of private wells in multiple states sued 20 oil companies alleging that their groundwater had been contaminated by virtue of MTBE, a gasoline additive.[38] The court was concerned about the injuries not being caused by a single event and that there were intervening parties that acted in each instance—not to mention the individuality of damages. The court held that "[p]redominance cannot be found because a different intermediate or third party

---

36. William B. Rubenstein, *Class Action Practice Today*, CLASS ACTIONS TODAY (ABA Section of Litig.) (2008) (internal citations omitted).

37. Cases often cited in opposing class certification include Barnes v. Am. Tobacco Co., 161 F.3d 127 (3d Cir. 1998); Walker v. Liggett Grp., 175 F.R.D. 226 (S.D.W. Va. 1997); Emig v. Am. Tobacco Co., 184 F.R.D. 379 (D. Kan. 1998); Rink v. Cheminova, 203 F.R.D. 648 (M.D. Fla. 2001); Benner v. Becton Dickinson & Co., 214 F.R.D. 157 (S.D.N.Y. 2003); In re Paxil Litig., 212 F.R.D. 539 (C.D. Cal. 2003); In re Baycol Prods. Litig., 218 F.R.D. 197 (D. Minn. 2003); Jones v. Allercare, Inc., 203 F.R.D. 290 (N.D. Ohio 2001); Mazzei v. Money Store, 829 F.3d 260 (2d Cir. 2016). *But see In re* Asbestos Litig., 134 F.3d 668 (5th Cir. 1998); *In re* Phenylproanolamine Prods. Liab. Litig., 227 F.R.D. 553 (W.D. Wash. 2004); *In re* Nat'l Football League Players' Concussion Injury Litig., 307 F.R.D. 351 (E.D. Pa. 2015).

38. *In re* Methyl Tertiary Butyl Ether Prods. Liab. Litig., 209 F.R.D. 323 (S.D.N.Y. 2002).

actor . . . has directly caused harm to each plaintiff by releasing gasoline in the vicinity."[39]

Then, in 2004, the Sixth Circuit decided *Olden v. Lafarge Corp.*[40] This involved the operation of a cement manufacturing plant in Michigan and principally involved property damage. The court certified the class, finding that common issues predominated. More particularly, the court concluded that the objective evidence was straightforward (cement dust falling on various properties), injunctive relief (the closing of the plant) was sought, and there was a single plant at issue.[41]

In contrast, the Sixth Circuit in 2004 also decided *Ball v. Union Carbide Corp.*,[42] affirming the district court's denial of a class certification motion. In *Ball*, the plaintiffs complained of personal injuries and property damage arising out of the government's nuclear facility at Oak Ridge, naming as defendants a variety of third-party contractors at the facility. While there were some plaintiffs who also alleged racial discrimination, the court concluded that the most fundamental claims were for personal injuries, environmental cleanup, and medical monitoring. The district court stated that mass tort cases generally are not appropriate for class treatment.[43] The Sixth Circuit went on to hold that "[e]ven though liability issues may have been common to the putative class, by seeking medical monitoring and environmental clean up of property, Plaintiffs have raised individualized issues. Each individual's claim was for that reason necessarily proportional to his or her exposure to toxic emissions or waste."[44]

The Sixth Circuit also distinguished *Sterling v. Velsicol Chemical Corp.*,[45] where the court had held that "[t]he mere fact that questions peculiar to each individual member of the class remain after the common questions of the defendant's liability have been resolved does not dictate the conclusion that the class action is impermissible."[46] In distinguishing that conclusion in *Sterling*, the Sixth Circuit in *Ball* highlighted the fact that the court in *Sterling* was dealing with a single defendant and a single incident. Moving from that premise, the court in *Ball* stated, "Here, however, there are multiple Defendants with presumably differing liability levels, if any. Accordingly, there is no 'single course of conduct.' Therefore, *Sterling* is distinguishable on its facts."[47]

There are two distinctions, at least, between *Olden* and *Ball*. First, *Olden* involved a single facility and a single defendant, while *Ball* involved multiple defendants over a protracted period of time. Second, *Ball* involved personal injuries and

---

39. *Id.* at 350.
40. 383 F.3d 495 (6th Cir. 2004).
41. *But see* Burkhead v. Louisville Gas & Elec. Co., 250 F.R.D. 287, 298 (W.D. Ky. 2008) (disapproving Olden v. LaFarge Corp., 383 F.3d 495, 510 (6th Cir. 2004)).
42. 385 F.3d 713 (6th Cir. 2004).
43. *Id.* at 726.
44. *Id.* at 728.
45. 855 F.2d 1188 (6th Cir. 1988).
46. *Id.* at 1197.
47. 385 F.3d at 728.

long-term exposure. *Olden*, in contrast, solely involved property damage. But do not be too quick to embrace that as a firm rule. Different facts could easily generate different results in any particular case.

A more recent example is *Modern Holdings, LLC v. Corning, Inc.*[48] The plaintiffs sought to certify subclasses of residents and property owners (from 1952 to 2013) within a five-mile radius of glass manufacturing plant they claimed released substances such as arsenic and trichloroethylene (TCE), allegedly contaminating the air, water, and soil. In denying plaintiffs' motion to certify a class, the court found there were "significant individual issues that outnumber common issues, precluding the use of 'common answers' to further the case at trial, and barring certification of the proposed class."[49] As an example, it commented that causation of one disease based on alleged lead contamination does not raise the same legal question as causation of a different disease claimed to have resulted from TCE contamination. With numerous substances and diseases at issue, the court determined that "Plaintiffs have failed to show their listed common questions will elicit *common answers* leading to *classwide* relief. This is especially so in the presence of named Plaintiffs with such disparate characteristics and alleged symptoms."[50]

With respect to the Rule 23 requirements for class certification, there is something of a debate and circuit split over whether Federal Rule of Civil Procedure 23 implicitly requires plaintiffs to prove that a class is ascertainable. Cases addressing this issue typically involve consumer claims, but the question can also arise in claims of exposure to substances that exist in a product at greater than advertised or regulated levels, for example. The Third Circuit has observed that "many courts and commentators have recognized that an essential prerequisite of a class action, at least with respect to actions under Rule 23(b)(3), is that the class must be currently and readily ascertainable."[51] Ascertainability entails having a reliable and administratively feasible mechanism for identifying class members without extensive and individualized fact-finding. According to the Third Circuit, a plaintiff need not identify all class members at the class certification stage, but need only show that class members *can* be identified.[52] Cases from the First Circuit have also endorsed the implied ascertainability requirement.[53]

In contrast, the Seventh Circuit has been critical of the Third Circuit for creating what the former describes as a new and heightened ascertainability requirement that furthers no interest of Rule 23 that is not already adequately protected

---

48. No. 5:13-CV-00405, 2018 WL 1546355 (E.D. Ky. Mar. 29, 2018).
49. *Id.* at 7 (citing Wal-Mart Stores v. Dukes, 564 U.S. 338, 349–50 (2011)).
50. *Id.* at 8.
51. Marcus v. BMW of N. Am., LLC, 687 F.3d 583, 593–94 (3d Cir. 2012).
52. See Byrd v. Aaron's Inc., 784 F.3d 154, 163 (3d Cir. 2015) for a review of Third Circuit jurisprudence on ascertainability.
53. *See In re* Nexium Antitrust Litig., 777 F.3d 9, 19 (1st Cir. 2015) ("At the class certification stage, the court must be satisfied that, prior to judgment, it will be possible to establish a mechanism for distinguishing the injured from the uninjured class members. The court may proceed with certification so long as this mechanism will be 'administratively feasible,' and protective of defendants' Seventh Amendment and due process rights.").

by its express requirements.[54] Similarly, the Ninth Circuit declined to follow what it described as the Third Circuit's "administrative feasibility requirement," concluding that "Rule 23's enumerated criteria already address the interests that motivated the Third Circuit and, therefore, that an independent administrative feasibility requirement is not necessary."[55] The existence and scope of such a requirement may remain an unresolved question unless and until the Supreme Court provides a definitive answer.

Finally, the Class Actions Fairness Act (CAFA) of 2005[56] drew many potential class actions into federal court and away from state courts, some of which were arguably more prone to certify a class. Nonetheless, state-based class actions are still a possibility, even under CAFA, and the laws of the state can vary considerably. A considerable body of law has developed around CAFA. It is a topic that goes well beyond the scope of this brief summary, but of which any practitioners seeking to certify a class action in state court should be familiar.

Interestingly, class actions can be good vehicles for settlements, even in cases where the defendants would not want the cases certified for any other purposes. Indeed, as a practical matter it is not uncommon for defendants that originally opposed certification of a litigation class to come back later—after having worked out a settlement—and join forces with the plaintiffs to support and propose certification of a settlement class. In so doing, defendants often expressly reserve their right to challenge a litigation class should the settlement not receive court approval or otherwise fall through. There is a substantial body of law on this topic, and it is something one should look into carefully, should those circumstances arise.[57] Also, an overview of settlement issues appears in section VIII, "Settlement," in this chapter.

D. Multidistrict Litigation

Aggregation of multiple claims is a common technique in toxic tort litigation. One aggregation mechanism is multidistrict litigation (MDL). In federal court, the process is established by statute with respect to civil actions "involving one or more common issues of fact" that are pending in different districts.[58] The MDL process involves transferring all the cases out of districts in which they originally were filed to a single judge in a single district for a proceeding that "will be for the convenience of parties and witnesses and will promote the just and efficient conduct of such actions."[59] Some states also have put an MDL process in place.[60]

---

54. *See* Mullins v. Direct Digital, LLC, 795 F.3d 654 (7th Cir. 2015).

55. Briseno v. ConAgra Foods, Inc., 844 F.3d 1121, 1127 (9th Cir. 2017).

56. 28 U.S.C. §§ 1332(1), 1453, and 1711–15 (2006).

57. For some interesting insights as to class-action settlements, see John B. Isbister, *Seven Steps to a Successful Class Action Settlement*, CLASS ACTIONS TODAY (ABA Section of Litig.) (2008).

58. 28 U.S.C. § 1407 (a).

59. 28 U.S.C. § 1407 (a).

60. *See* Alan D. Rudlin, *Case Management and Health Claims in Toxic Tort Litigation*, 8th Ann. Advanced ALI-ABA Course of Study (Jan. 22–23, 2004), SJ065 ALI-ABA 43, Sec. III(b); Paul D. Rheingold,

The MDL process at the federal level is handled by the Judicial Panel on Multidistrict Litigation (JPML).[61] The JPML consists of seven judges from separate circuits who are designated by the chief justice of the U.S. Supreme Court. The administrative offices are located in Washington, D.C., and are staffed by clerks, administrators, and lawyers. The JPML panel moves from coast to coast and north to south, as it rotates to various parts of the country. The JPML process begins with the filing of a motion by an interested party. The panel then will consider whether to allow an MDL and, if so, before what judge and in what location. It can appoint either a district judge or a circuit judge, and will take into consideration the convenience of the parties (including such things as availability of airlines, location of concentrations of witnesses, and other purely practical factors). The JPML breaks MDLs into ten separate categories: (1) air disasters, (2) antitrust, (3) contracts, (4) common disasters, (5) employment practices, (6) intellectual property, (7) product liability (where most toxic tort cases fall), (8) sales practices, (9) securities, and (10) miscellaneous.

Once the JPML decides that an MDL will be put in place, the district courts then need to go through their dockets to determine what cases should be transferred to it. The process before the JPML is governed by the Rules of Procedure of the Judicial Panel on Multidistrict Litigation.[62] Cases that are filed in the district courts after the MDL is established are treated as "tagalong" cases and get swept up into the MDL. These typically are identified by the party that provoked the MDL. Any appeals are made to the circuit court in the circuit in which the MDL court sits.[63]

There are some rules of thumb that one would want to consider when faced with a case that might end up as an MDL. First, if a large number of cases have not yet been filed, the filing of an MDL almost certainly will draw out a substantial number of additional filings. Depending upon how one is positioned in a particular case, that may be good or bad.

Second, some practitioners feel that important state law issues can get lost in this aggregation process, where cases are taken from districts in various states across the country. Indeed, there is some debate over which law would be applicable in certain circumstances.

Third, if the ultimate objective is to create a settlement, the MDL forum can, under some circumstances, prove to be a difficult vehicle to use. That is because

---

Symposium: MultiDistrict Litigation and Aggregation Alternatives, Prospect for Managing Mass Tort Litigation in the State Courts, 31 Seton Hall L. Rev. 910 (2001).

61. http://www.jpml.uscourts.gov.

62. 199 F.R.D. 425 (2001); *see also* Gayvont v. Davol, Inc., No. 07-1966ML, 2008 WL 2433258 (D.R.I. Feb. 26. 2008).

63. *See* Manual for Complex Litigation, Fourth § 20.13 (Fed. Judicial Ctr. 2004); Patricia D. Howard, *A Guide to Multi-District Litigation*, 124 F.R.D. 479 (1989); Earle F. Kyle IV, *The Mechanics of Motion Practice before the Judicial Panel on Multidistrict Litigation*, 175 F.R.D. 589 (1998); *Note, The Judicial Panel and the Conduct of Multi-District Litigation*, 87 Harv. L. Rev. 1001 (1974); Desmond T. Barry Jr., *A Practical Guide to the Ins and Outs of Multidistrict Litigation*, 64 Def. Counsel J. 58 (Jan. 1997).

the MDL can take the case only through pretrial discovery and pretrial motions, including *Daubert* hearings and rulings. At that point, cases are transferred back to their original districts for trial on remaining issues, such as specific causation and damages.[64] Obviously, in some circumstances, getting the *Daubert* ruling can be a strong driving force relative to settlement or dispositive as to whether the case is viable in the future or not. But there are other circumstances when the MDL has reduced effectiveness as to settlement because the cases must be transferred back to their original districts. Consequently, there is a balance to be struck with respect to whether an MDL is a good thing or a bad thing for any particular party.

Fourth, when it looks clear that an MDL is likely to occur, defendants opposing it may wish to consider, as a tactical matter, at least making suggestions about which district to recommend the case be transferred to so that they at least have a say on that issue.[65]

V. SCIENCE

The essential elements of every toxic tort case are causation and the reliability of the proof offered to support causation. Toxic tort cases can turn on a jury's finding as to a specific point of science, even when there is no unanimity in the relevant scientific community. Scientific inquiry, in and of itself, can extend indefinitely in time, as the search for scientific truth evolves. Meanwhile, lawsuits, by their nature, require a definitive answer regarding events at a precise moment in time. A lawsuit cannot be concluded unless someone—the jury, typically—comes to a conclusion. As the Supreme Court summarized:

> Scientific conclusions are subject to perpetual revision. Law, on the other hand, must resolve disputes finally and quickly. The scientific project is advanced by broad and wide-ranging consideration of a multitude of hypotheses, for those that are incorrect will eventually be shown to be so, and that in itself is an advance. Conjectures that are probably wrong are of little use, however, in the project of reaching a quick, final, and binding legal judgment—often of great consequence—about a particular set of events in the past. *We recognize that, in practice, a gate-keeping role for the judge, no matter how flexible, inevitably on occasion will prevent the jury from learning of authentic insights and innovations.* That, nevertheless, is the balance that is struck by Rules of Evidence designed not for the exhaustive search for cosmic understanding but for the particularized resolution of legal disputes.[66]

---

64. *See* Lexecon, Inc. v. Milberg Weiss Bershad Hynes & Lerach, 523 U.S. 26 (1998); *Case Comment, Lexecon, Inc. v. Milberg Weiss Bershad Hynes & Lerach, Respecting the Plaintiffs' Choice of Forum,* 74 Notre Dame L. Rev. 1337 (1999); *In re* Carbon Dioxide Indus. Anti-Trust Litig., 229 F.3d 1321 (11th Cir. 2000), *cert. denied,* 532 U.S. 920 (2001); *see also In re* Gerber Probiotic Prods. Mktg., 899 F. Supp. 2d 1378 (J.P.M.L. 2012) (stating that such transfers are not permanent and are limited to pretrial proceedings only).

65. Caryn M. Silverman, Lessons Learned from Recent Drug and Device Multi-District Litigation, 9 BNA Class. Lr. 79 (Jan. 25, 2008).

66. Daubert v. Merrell Dow Pharm., Inc., 509 U.S. 579, 596–97 (1993) (emphasis added).

Courts have faced the need to reach resolution in such cases with increasing frequency because the population has been exposed to an increasing number of possibly toxic substances over the past several decades and as the potential financial rewards in toxic tort litigation have grown. In response, lawyers, the experts with whom they work, and the courts have accommodated themselves to this new reality. The lawyers have learned science. The experts have found themselves engaged in advancing and defending against creative scientific theories and have learned to deal with the governing legal principles, while judges have become "gatekeepers" in a sophisticated debate over what constitutes "cutting-edge" science as opposed to "junk" science.

To succeed, indeed to survive, in that environment, the toxic tort lawyer must develop expertise in dealing with the legal principles, the scientific principles, and the relevant specific scientific evidence; in identifying, selecting, and presenting experts in multiple disciplines; in surviving challenges or challenging these experts; and in creating highly effective demonstrative trial exhibits in order to ultimately present all to a jury in a manner that the jurors can understand and will embrace.

In these few pages, we provide an overview on these topics and a sense of the skills necessary to prevail in a toxic tort case. Perhaps more importantly, we also will try to guide you toward some more detailed writings on each of these subjects.

A. Causation

The core issue in virtually all toxic tort cases—regardless of the toxic substance— is whether the plaintiffs can establish a causal connection between that substance to which plaintiffs claim exposure and plaintiffs' alleged injuries. Causation is the task of attributing cause and effect. It involves the process of weighing evidence and using judgment to conclude whether or not a result happened because of a stimulus.[67] As one court phrased it, "[W]as plaintiff exposed to the toxin, was plaintiff exposed to enough of the toxin to cause the alleged injury, and did the toxin in fact cause the injury?"[68]

The threshold question is whether the substance is capable of causing the injury. This is called general causation. General causation relates to whether the particular toxic substance can cause the general type of injury complained of by the plaintiffs in the general population. If general causation is established, the next question is whether this substance caused this particular plaintiff's condition.[69] This is called specific causation. Specific causation relates to whether that toxic

---

67. For a comprehensive discussion of the scientific and technological disciplines likely to be encountered in determining causation, see REFERENCE MANUAL ON SCIENTIFIC EVIDENCE (Fed. Judicial Ctr. & Nat'l Research Council of the Nat'l Acads., 3d ed. 2011).

68. McClain v. Metabolife Int'l, Inc., No. 03-12776, 2005 WL 477861, at *3 (11th Cir. Mar. 2, 2005).

69. Burst v. Shell Oil Co., 650 F. App'x 170, 174 (5th Cir. 2016), *cert. denied*, 137 S. Ct. 312 (2016).

substance, more likely than not, actually caused the complained-of damage to a specific individual plaintiff.[70]

Though a number of principles may be involved in the analysis, depending upon the case, the two most common issues are those of exposure and dose. The plaintiff must prove that he or she actually was exposed to the toxic substance. That is not always as easy as it sounds, particularly at the individual plaintiff level. Additionally, for virtually all toxic substances, the dose to which the individual plaintiff was exposed is critical to the analysis of whether the complained-of injuries could, in fact, have been caused by that particular substance. Most of the substances dealt with in toxic tort litigation are not harmful at a low-enough dose. Therefore, two questions often are presented: What was the dose for that particular plaintiff? How much is too much?

B. Samples and Testing

More often than not, toxic tort cases largely turn into a battle of the experts. That battle, in most cases, comes down to a fight over either or both of two things. First, the parties dispute the quality and reliability of specific evidence in the case, such as samples that have been taken and testing that has been conducted. Second, the parties fight vigorously with regard to what valid conclusions can be drawn from that evidence in this particular instance, based upon the state of scientific knowledge at that time.

An expert's analysis, when based on samples and testing, will be only as strong as the sampling, sample handling, and qualified testing that is conducted.[71]

If sampling is possible, then the first step is establishing rules controlling the gathering of samples in a scientifically correct and accepted fashion. The protocols and procedures that are utilized by the sampler, the transporter, and the laboratory performing the analysis need to be addressed. Things to consider include how it was determined that the sample was representative, were split samples collected and shared, testing methodology, the scientific reliability of test procedures, whether the actual testing in this case measured up to the requirements, how accurate the analysis seems to have been, and ruling out both contamination and tampering while imposing strict chain of custody documentation.

Generally, your own expert will guide you in examining the other side's evidence. But, as your experts undertake sampling and analysis, bear in mind that your opponent will be looking at these same factors, making it important for you to be alert to having testing correctly performed. Also, arrangements with opposing counsel for handling of any split samples must be established before collection begins.

---

70. For a particularly good explanation as to causation, the issues inherently involved in the proof, and good strategies to follow, see D. Alan Rudlin, *Causation and the Use of Experts in Toxic Tort Cases*, in Toxic Tort Litigation, *supra* note 22, 143–77.

71. For a through explanation on this topic and valuable citations, see William D. Dannelly, Rita A. Sheffey & Ashley Cummings, *Introduction to the Use of Scientific and Medical Evidence in Toxic Tort Litigation*, in Toxic Tort Litigation, *supra* note 22, 103–43.

Be sure to use a qualified laboratory that utilizes accepted procedures and methodologies to analyze your samples. EPA, for example, has extensive standards with regard to testing methodologies.[72] If you are working with your own experts to examine and, where possible, discredit your opponent's sample analysis, you will want to look carefully at the credentials and licensing qualifications of the laboratory and the methodology used in any specific tests, and also to determine whether any equipment used had been properly calibrated. It is common for opponents in litigation of this nature to engage in discovery on all three of those points, even before commencing expert discovery.

C. Experts

Experts come in all types and descriptions, depending upon the nature of the case. The focus of some is on "fate and transport" (these are the terms generally used to address what happens to toxic substances as they progress through the environment—how do they change—and the means by which they move through the environment). Experts on those topics include chemists, geochemists, hydrogeologists, hydrologists, environmental engineers, meteorologists, and dispersion modelers. Some experts deal with dose and the effects of particular doses on humans, such as epidemiologists, toxicologists, exposure scientists, and physicians who treat in specialized areas. Yet other experts deal with specific issues particular to a toxic substance. For the lawyer in a toxic tort case to be effective, he or she must become at least generally knowledgeable with regard to each area of science in which experts will be used.

Once the case evolves from "fate and transport" to what happens to exposed individuals, two particular fields of science tend to become the primary focus: epidemiology and toxicology.

"Epidemiology is the field of public health and medicine that studies the incidence, distribution, and possible causes of disease in humans."[73] Epidemiology tends to focus on general causation (how a particular substance can affect the general population). Epidemiology cannot prove causation, because causation is a judgment made by interpreting epidemiologic data. The significance of the data, however, is often the subject of much debate. For example, if there are studies reflecting an increased risk of developing a certain disease from exposure at a level matching plaintiff's alleged exposure, plaintiff will point to such studies as supportive of causation arguments. There may also be arguments among counsel and the experts over how much stock to place in studies that find such an association, but short of the 95 percent confidence interval required to achieve statistical significance, and in rarer diseases whether studies not finding an increased association are sufficiently powered in terms of case subjects.

---

72. 40 C.F.R. § 136 app. A.

73. *See generally* REFERENCE MANUAL ON SCIENTIFIC EVIDENCE THIRD EDITION, *supra* note 67, at 549–632 (Epidemiology).

Toxicology is "the study of the adverse effects of chemicals on living organisms."[74] Toxicology is relevant to both general and specific causation. More particularly, toxicology focuses on the dose: the route by which the substance gets into the body (respiration, ingestion, or absorption), the duration of the exposure, the frequency of the exposure, and how the body processes the substance and the temporal relationship between the alleged exposure and the symptoms if they are transitory. If there is a question about the exact dose, a qualitative or quantitative exposure assessment may be possible. This is a newly developing area called informally "exposure science."[75]

Another challenging aspect of these cases is the tendency of plaintiffs to use a smaller number of omnibus-type experts to cover various areas, while defendants often respond by using multiple experts, highly qualified in narrow disciplines. This implicates, through motion practice and trial presentation, the tension between the need for simplicity balanced against qualifications and the evolving jurisprudence concerning the qualifications of experts. Where you can find simplicity, you should focus on it, but not at the price of sacrificing quality.

That, of course, is not to ignore the role of treating and consulting physicians in any variety of specialty areas, depending upon the nature of the alleged toxic substance. Obviously, the areas of medical expertise germane to specific causation will vary depending upon the nature of the injuries claimed. As in any tort case, these are critical experts and that is critical evidence. Also, some states require that a medical doctor give a causation opinion.[76]

---

74. *Id.* at 633–84 (Toxicology).

75. *Id.* at 503–48, 505 n.5 (Exposure Science). This chapter focuses on measuring exposure to toxic substances as a specific developing area of scientific investigation.

76. *See* Cripe v. Henkel Corp., 318 F.R.D. 356, 359 (N.D. Ind.), *aff'd*, 858 F.3d 1110 (7th Cir. 2017) (holding expert as to disease causation was not qualified because expert was not a medical doctor, toxicologist, or epidemiologist); Zellers v. NexTech Ne., LLC, 533 F. App'x 192, 199 (4th Cir. 2013) (holding neuropsychologist and neurotoxicologist expert was not qualified to give causation opinion related to alleged poisoning with refrigerant gas containing fluorocarbons because expert was not a medical doctor); Leija v. Penn Mar., Inc., No. CIV.A. 06-10489, 2009 WL 211723, at *2 (E.D. La. Jan. 23, 2009) (holding expert "who is not a medical doctor, is not qualified to render a medical opinion as to whether workplace exposure to toxic substances more likely than not caused [plaintiff's] cancer"); Newton v. Roche Labs., Inc., 243 F. Supp. 2d 672, 677 (W.D. Tex. 2002) (holding nonmedical doctor was not qualified to render a general causation opinion); Plourde v. Gladstone, 190 F. Supp. 2d 708, 719 (D. Vt. 2002), *aff'd*, 69 F. App'x 485 (2d Cir. 2003) (holding toxicologist was not qualified to testify as to causation in herbicide-related toxic tort action because he was not a medical doctor); Ballinger v. Atkins, 947 F. Supp. 925, 927 (E.D. Va. 1996) (finding biochemist not qualified to testify as to causation of neurological injuries allegedly caused by chemicals in artificial sweeteners because he was not a medical doctor); Lee v. A.C. & S. Co., 542 A.2d 352, 355–56 (Del. Super. Ct. 1987) (holding that epidemiologist could not address specific causation as to cancer allegedly caused by asbestos exposure because a medical doctor must provide the causal link); 2 Toxic Torts Prac. Guide § 16:3, "Who can testify as an expert?" (2017) ("Until fairly recently in toxic tort cases, however, the general rule has been that experts testifying on causation had to at least be medical doctors. That rule is changing."); Henry F. Fradella et al., *The Impact of Daubert on Forensic Science*, 31 Pepp. L. Rev. 323, 340 (2004) ("In other toxic tort cases, courts have been much more hesitant to admit similar testimony by an expert who is not a medical doctor."); *but see* Cottle v. Superior Court, 3 Cal. App. 4th 1367, 1387, 5 Cal. Rptr. 2d 882, 893 (1992), *modified* (Mar. 20, 1992) ("Furthermore, some courts have suggested that in toxic tort cases, causation need not be established by a medical doctor and might in fact be established by a toxicologist."); Loudermill v. Dow Chem. Co., 863 F.2d 566, 569 (8th Cir. 1988) (permitting toxicologist to testify that exposure to

Once you have mastered each scientific discipline, identified the discipline needed to address the issues presented in your case and retained key experts, overseen their scientific inquiry and testing, and worked with them in connection with reports and depositions, you have only just begun. Now you must evaluate which of your opponents' experts and/or opinions to challenge and be prepared to defend your experts/opinions against your opponents' challenges.

D. The Law

While courts have always faced challenges in determining what science a jury might hear in the course of deciding a case, the issue saw a dramatic rise in prominence during the 1980s and early 1990s in environmental, product liability, and toxic tort litigation. The lack of a defined "gatekeeper" function for the trial judge and of rules for the judge to rely upon in separating good from inadequate science "led to the oddity of lay juries, on the basis of pioneering opinions by trial experts, making conclusory pronouncements about issues that were far from resolved in the real world of science, medicine and other technical areas."[77]

The U.S. Supreme Court addressed this issue in *Daubert v. Merrell Dow Pharmaceuticals, Inc.*[78] The Supreme Court built upon that decision in *General Electric Co. v. Joiner*[79] and *Kumho Tire v. Carmichael.*[80]

In 1993, faced with an ever-increasing dialogue over the growing use of experts in complicated cases turning on science, coupled with concerns about how fundamentally sound some of the science being presented to jurors was, the U.S. Supreme Court took up the question of whether the Federal Rules of Evidence (more particularly Rule 702) had changed the rule established in *Frye v. United States*, which required methodologies to be generally accepted in the scientific community before testimony based on them could be admissible.[81] In *Daubert*, the Supreme Court set up both a new test and a process for implementing that test. The Court made it clear that the trial judge would be the "gatekeeper" with regard to expert testimony, that he or she often should hold a pretrial hearing on admissibility of expert testimony, and that the inquiry would address two distinct aspects of the proffered evidence: reliability and relevance. As to reliability, the Court articulated a series of factors to consider, including whether the expert's technique or theory could be tested or replicated, whether it has been peer reviewed, the known or potential rate of error, the existence and maintenance of standards and controls, and whether the technique or theory has been generally accepted in the relevant scientific community. In the pretrial hearing, the proponent of the evidence carries the burden of proof and must

halogenated hydrocarbon was the cause of plaintiff's liver cirrhosis, despite the fact the witness was not a medical doctor).

77. Toxic Tort Litigation, *supra* note 22, at 160.
78. 509 U.S. 579 (1993).
79. 522 U.S. 136 (1997).
80. 526 U.S. 137 (1999).
81. 293 F. 1013 (D.C. Cir. 1923).

demonstrate reliability and relevance by a preponderance of the evidence.[82] Also note that the proponent need not prove that the proffered testimony is correct, but only that it is reliable and relevant.[83]

Subsequently, in 1997, the U.S. Supreme Court addressed this topic again in *Joiner* and clarified two points. First, the court clarified that the *Daubert* inquiry is intended to address both methodologies used by an expert and the conclusions of the proffered expert. There had been some debate with respect to whether *Daubert* was simply limited to the experts' methodologies, but *Joiner* clarified that the trial court can ensure that the expert's leap from facts and data to conclusions is similarly reliable. The Court explained that "conclusions and methodology are not entirely distinct from one another" and "nothing in either *Daubert* or the Federal Rules of Evidence requires a district court to admit opinion evidence that is connected to existing data only by the *ipse dixit* of the expert."[84] Thus, the Court found that expert testimony may be excluded when there is "too great an analytical gap between the data and the opinion proffered."[85] Accordingly, "trial judges may evaluate the data offered to support an expert's bottom-line opinions to determine if that data provides adequate support to mark the expert's testimony as reliable."[86] Second, in *Joiner* the court clarified that the trial judge has substantial discretion in connection with these admissibility rulings, holding that the abuse of discretion standard is applicable on appeal.[87]

In 1999, the U.S. Supreme Court again addressed this issue in *Kumho Tire*, where it clarified two further points.[88] First, it addressed whether the *Daubert* inquiry is limited to scientific knowledge.[89] Rule 702 states that it applies to "scientific, technical, or other specialized knowledge."[90] The court in *Kumho Tire* held that the *Daubert* analysis is applicable to "technical, or other specialized" knowledge, as well as "scientific" knowledge.[91] Second, the court in *Kumho Tire* clarified that the trial judge need not, in every case, consider all the *Daubert* factors.[92] Instead, the focus of the trial judge in conducting the *Daubert* analysis is to search

---

82. *See* Fed. R. Evid. 104(a) as to the preponderance of the evidence.

83. *In re* Paolie R.R. Yard, PCB Litig., 35 F.3d 717, 744 (3d Cir. 1994); *see also* Ellison v. United States, 753 F. Supp. 2d 468, 476 (E.D. Pa. 2010) ("The question is not whether the proponent of the expert has demonstrated that his or her opinion is correct . . . , but whether the opinion is based on reliable methodology and reliably flows from that methodology and the facts at hand.").

84. *Joiner*, 522 U.S. at 146.

85. *Id.*; Milward v. Acuity Specialty Prod. Grp., Inc., 639 F.3d 11, 15 (1st Cir. 2011).

86. *Milward*, 639 F.3d at 15 (quoting Ruiz–Troche v. Pepsi Cola of P.R. Bottling Co., 161 F.3d 77, 81 (1st Cir. 1998)). For example, in a recent decision by the Fifth Circuit, the court held that the trial court did not abuse its discretion in excluding expert testimony in a case based on exposure to the benzene in gasoline because the experts relied on general benzene studies that were not specific to gasoline exposure. Burst v. Shell Oil Co., 650 F. App'x 170, 174 (5th Cir. 2016) . The court found that the broader benzene studies were not sufficient to prove that the gasoline exposure caused plaintiff's acute myeloid leukemia under *Daubert*.

87. *Joiner*, 522 U.S. at 142–43.

88. Kumho Tire Co. v. Carmichael, 526 U.S. 137 (1999).

89. *Id.* at 147–49.

90. *Id.* at 147 (quoting Fed. R. Evid. 702).

91. *Id.* at 141, 149.

92. *Id.* at 141, 151–53.

for reliability, with the factors in *Daubert* simply being a listing of things that he or she should consider.[93]

Indeed, courts have explained that other factors, in certain cases, also should be considered, including whether the testimony grows out of research conducted for the litigation or independently of the litigation,[94] whether the expert has unjustifiably extrapolated from an accepted premise to an unfounded conclusion,[95] whether the expert adequately accounted for obvious alternative explanations,[96] whether the expert is being as careful as he or she would in his or her normal professional work,[97] and whether the field of expertise that the expert claims is one that is known to reach reliable results for that type of opinion.[98]

In 2000, Rule 702 was amended to follow *Daubert* and its progeny. However, Rule 702 was left relatively general, not including any specific listing of factors. The courts, over time, have continued to apply these general rules and to fine-tune them. For example, courts have developed a hierarchical system for scientific evidence with epidemiological studies being received very favorably by courts.[99] Conversely, toxicological and animal studies have not been received as favorably.[100] Additionally, while courts have determined that the *Daubert* standards must be met at bench trials, because the court's role as gatekeeper is less essential, some courts view *Daubert* less rigidly in the context of bench trials.[101] Regarding an

---

93. *Id.* at 151–53.

94. Daubert v. Merrell Dow Pharms., Inc., 43 F.3d 1311, 1317 (9th Cir. 1995); *see also* Johnson v. Manitowoc Boom Trucks, Inc., 484 F.3d 426, 434 (6th Cir. 2007) ("This Court has recognized for some time that expert testimony prepared solely for purposes of litigation, as opposed to testimony flowing naturally from an expert's line of scientific research or technical work, should be viewed with some caution."); Lewert v. Boiron, Inc., 212 F. Supp. 3d 917, 925 (C.D. Cal. 2016); Burst v. Shell Oil Co., 120 F. Supp. 3d 547, 551 (E.D. La. 2015).

95. Magbegor v. Triplette, 212 F. Supp. 3d 1317, 1325 (N.D. Ga. 2016) (citing advisory committee notes for Rule 702); Doe v. Ortho-Clinical Diagnostics, Inc., 440 F. Supp. 2d 465, 470 (M.D.N.C. 2006); Magistrini v. One Hour Martinizing Dry Cleaning, 180 F. Supp. 2d 584, 594 (D.N.J. 2002), *aff'd*, 68 F. App'x 356 (3d Cir. 2003).

96. Claar v. Burlington N. R.R., 29 F.3d 499 (9th Cir. 1994); *see also Burst*, 120 F. Supp. 3d at 551; *Magbegor*, 212 F. Supp. 3d at 1325; *Doe*, 440 F. Supp. 2d at 470; Ambrosini v. Labarraque, 101 F.3d 129 (D.C. Cir. 1996).

97. Sheehan v. Daily Racing Form, Inc., 104 F.3d 940 (7th Cir. 1997); *see also Magbegor*, 212 F. Supp. 3d at 1325; *Burst*, 120 F. Supp. 3d at 551; *Magistrini*, 180 F. Supp. 2d at 594.

98. *Kumho Tire*, 526 U.S. at 137; Moore v. Ashland Chem., Inc., 151 F.3d 269 (5th Cir. 1998); Sterling v. Velsicol Chem. Corp., 855 F.2d 1188 (6th Cir. 1988).

99. Jean Macchiaroli Eggen, *Toxic Torts and Causation: The Challenge of Daubert after the First Decade*, Nat. Res. & Env't, Spring 2003, at 213, 214–15; *see also* Brock v. Merrell Dow Pharm., Inc., 874 F.2d 307, 311 (5th Cir. 1989), *modified on reh'g*, 884 F.2d 166 (5th Cir. 1989) ("Undoubtedly, the most useful and conclusive type of evidence in a case such as this is epidemiological studies.").

100. Eggen, *supra* note 99, at 215 (citing Hollander v. Sandoz Pharms. Corp., 289 F.3d 1193 (10th Cir. 2002)).

101. *See* Seaboard Lumber Co. v. United States, 308 F.3d 1283, 1302 (Fed. Cir. 2002) ("While these concerns are of lesser import in a bench trial, where no screening of the factfinder can take place, the Daubert standards of relevance and reliability for scientific evidence must nevertheless be met."); Kenny A. v. Perdue, 356 F. Supp. 2d 1353 (N.D. Ga. 2005) ("As this case will be a bench trial, the court's 'role as a gatekeeper pursuant to Daubert is arguably less essential.'") (quoting *Magistrini*, 180 F. Supp. 2d at 596 n.10); Bristol-Myers Squibb Co. v. Andrx Pharms., Inc., 343 F. Supp. 2d 1124 (S.D. Fla. 2004) ("The court agrees that the question of reliability and relevance in this case is merely one of degree. . . . This is especially true since this is a bench trial, where the Court must evaluate the evidence regardless of whether it ultimately decides to exclude it.").

expert's qualifications, some courts have established that a medical doctorate is not sufficient and have insisted the doctor's specialty be a near-perfect fit with the subject in dispute. For example, in *Chikovsky v. Ortho Pharmaceutical Corp.*, the court held that an obstetrician/gynecologist was not qualified to give testimony that a mother's topical application of Retin-A during pregnancy could cause birth defects because the doctor had no specific expertise in embryology, teratology, or genetics.[102]

In considering the *Daubert* issues, you also should be cautious not to lose sight of other relevant evidentiary rules. For example, Rule 703 addresses one type of "fact and data" referenced in Rule 702, namely otherwise inadmissible facts or data upon which an expert may predicate all or part of his or her testimony. Where such inadmissible testimony is of a type reasonably relied upon by other experts in the field, it can be relied upon by the expert who is testifying.

It is also important to not lose sight of the fact that courts can fashion their own means of getting to this reliability and relevance inquiry, for example with the use of a group of experts impaneled by the court, as was done in the silicone breast implant litigation.[103] Similarly, today many judges are now holding "Science Days." On Science Days, state and federal judges permit the parties a chance to outline their positions/arguments regarding the technical or scientific issues presented in case at bar to the judge. There are no rules at either state or federal level regarding the procedures for science tutorials, but basically the three interested parties negotiate the plan.[104]

As another example, some courts employ the "weight of the evidence" methodology in determining the reliability of expert testimony. In 2011, in *Milward v. Acuity Specialty Products Group., Inc.*, the First Circuit reversed the district court and found that the expert testimony was reliable because although no particular body of evidence justified an inference of causation, each body of evidence "was treated as grounds for the subsidiary conclusion that it would, if combined with other evidence, support a causal inference."[105] The court found the expert's "inference of causation based on the totality of the evidence" was reliable and that it was error for the district court to "treat[] the separate evidentiary components of [the expert's] analysis atomistically, as though his ultimate opinion was independently supported by each."[106] However, it should be cautioned that in some instances, the "weight of the evidence" approach could run afoul of the Supreme

---

102. 832 F. Supp. 341, 344–46 (S.D. Fla. 1993).

103. *In re* Silicone Gel Breast Implant Litig., MDL No. 926 (N.D. Ala. Nov. 30, 1998), *reported in* 26 Prod. Liab. Rptr. 1194 (12/04/98).

104. For use of tutorials to assist the court in setting up a science tutorial, see Am. Bar Ass'n, Civil Trial Practice Standards, August 2007 and 2011 update.

105. 639 F.3d 11, 23 (1st Cir. 2011).

106. *Id.*

Court's directive in *Joiner* that expert testimony based solely on the expert's opinion and not linked to data should not be admitted.[107]

Additionally, your particular case may be governed by state evidentiary rules. While many states have adopted the *Daubert* approach, the earlier *Frye*[108] standard, or some version of it, may be applicable. Under the *Frye* rule, scientific expert testimony is admissible if the technique generally is accepted in the relevant scientific *Daubert* community. While that is part of the *Daubert* standard, it is only one of a number of factors.

E. Conclusion

In handling a toxic tort case, your legal team must be well versed in science, well versed in the relevant legal principles, and capable of distilling complex scientific concepts in a way that a jury can absorb and find persuasive. Because of the complexities involved, it is not uncommon for individual lawyers to develop niche expertise in connection with science and experts. Indeed, some law firms have a particular expertise in that subset of the overall toxic tort litigation field, which can be particularly valuable in very large cases involving extremely large exposure. Causation and how you prove or disprove it will be among the greatest challenges in your toxic tort case.

VI. CASE MANAGEMENT

Toxic tort cases often involve many plaintiffs and many defendants. For the parties and the court to manage them from beginning to end is a challenging process. Traditional scheduling orders have, over time, become case management orders (CMOs) that cover far more than simply scheduling. These vary from court to court, and you will need to know the practice in the court you are working with to determine what form this will take. When the parties prevail upon the court that its standard CMO is not suitable for the case at hand, judges will typically look to the litigants to submit an agreed CMO if possible. Negotiating how the deadlines are sequenced can be important to the strategy for prosecuting and defending the case, including with respect to the role of experts.

Key issues typically governed by such CMOs include (1) organizing the parties (lead counsel and committees in appropriate cases, fee and cost issues for plaintiffs' counsel, and mechanics of filing), (2) electronic discovery issues, (3) fact and expert discovery, (4) the sequencing of expert disclosures and reports, (5) motion practice, including the *Daubert* process, and (6) how the case will be handled at

---

107. David E. Bernstein & Eric G. Lasker, *Defending Daubert: It's Time to Amend Federal Rule of Evidence 702*, 57 Wm. & Mary L. Rev. 1, 41 (2015) ("The First Circuit's admission of this 'weight of the evidence' testimony [in *Milward*] blatantly disregarded *Daubert's* admonition that expert testimony must be derived by the scientific method, in other words, 'based on generating hypotheses and testing them to see if they can be falsified.'").

108. Frye v. United States, 293 F. 1013 (D.C. Cir. 1923).

trial (such things as bellwether trials, bifurcation, trifurcation, reverse bifurcation, and other techniques).[109]

In federal court, Federal Rule of Civil Procedure 16(c)(12) provides the court with authority to require "special procedures for managing potentially difficult or protracted actions that may involve complex issues, multiple parties, difficult legal questions or unusual proof problems."[110] Most states have similar provisions, including varying tracks for cases with different levels of complexity.

One particularly important aspect of case management and related discovery is e-discovery. The orders of the court that address electronic information can become critical to you and your case and deserve particular attention. It is an evolving area of law with enormous consequences for both client and attorney. One need read no further than *Qualcomm, Inc. v. Brodcom Corp.*[111] to see the consequences of a failure in the e-discovery realm. In this 2008 case, the court found that failures by counsel in the e-discovery area were sufficiently egregious that it awarded the other party defense costs plus postjudgment interest in an amount of $9,259,985. The point here, of course, is that you must understand the current jurisprudence with regard to e-discovery, and you must be very careful with regard to what is placed in orders of the court regarding e-discovery and electronic data, while also ensuring that a litigation hold is properly implemented in a fashion that preserves electronically stored information (ESI). In this regard, it is critical to work with the client's information technology department to make certain that the relevant players are on the same page as to what types of ESI are automatically preserved and for how long, and at the other end of the spectrum what measures should be put in place to suspend automatic ESI deletion policies that may otherwise go into effect after certain time periods.[112]

One particular type of provision that can be helpful to defendants in toxic tort litigation, particularly multiplaintiff mass tort litigation, is some form of a *Lone Pine* order.[113] In essence, a *Lone Pine* order requires that the plaintiff establish a prima facie case with regard to causation and damages before allowing the case to proceed forward. *Lone Pine* orders, whether standing alone or as part of a CMO, can come in all shapes and sizes. Courts react to them in different ways, often simply driven by the facts of that particular case. *Burns v. Universal Crop Protection Alliance* provides a good illustration.[114] That case involved crop contamination by virtue of alleged herbicide overspray from various fields to other fields in the

---

109. *See generally* MANUAL FOR COMPLEX LITIGATION, FOURTH (Fed. Judicial Ctr. 2004) for guidance on general principles and a good look at some forms that will illustrate these points.

110. *See also* FED. R. CIV. P. 16, 26, 37, 42, and 83.

111. No. 05-cv-1958-B (BLM), 2008 WL 66932 (S.D. Cal. Jan. 7, 2008), *vacated in part*, 2008 WL 638108 (S.D. Cal. Mar. 5, 2008); *see also* Klipsch Grp., Inc. v. ePRO E-Commerce Ltd., 880 F.3d 620, 633 (2d Cir. 2018) (discussing how monetary sanctions need not be tied to or restricted by the actual amount in controversy).

112. For a detailed discussion of the evolution and application of federal discovery rules to ESI, see Landry v. Swire Oilfield Servs., 323 F.R.D. 360 (D.N.M. 2018).

113. Lore v. Lone Pine, Inc., No. L-33606-85, 1986 WL 637507 (N.J. Super. Nov. 18, 1986).

114. No. 4:07CV00535 SWW, 2007 WL 2811533 (E.D. Ark. Sept. 25, 2007).

general area. In that case, the defendants sought to have the court require that the plaintiffs, by affidavit, demonstrate at the outset of the case (1) as to each defendant's herbicide, the date, amount, and location of use; (2) as to each plaintiff, the specific fields damaged; (3) as to each damaged field, the specific herbicide that carried over to it from the spraying in some other field; (4) the facts supporting those claims as to each specific defendant's herbicide; and (5) the facts and data relied upon by plaintiffs' experts. The court agreed to impose an order including such requirements.[115]

In contrast, some courts view *Lone Pine* orders as an unwarranted intrusion into the more conventional process of using discovery and motion practice to weed out claims that do not pass muster. In *Simeone v. Girard City Board of Education*, an Ohio appeals court reversed the trial court's enforcement of a *Lone Pine* order to dismiss with prejudice claims involving alleged health problems from school building defects.[116] In addition to questioning whether Ohio law allows for such an order in the first place, the appeals court viewed its entry before meaningful discovery as premature and tantamount to bypassing routine summary judgment procedure.[117]

The sequencing of expert disclosures can also play a key role in toxic tort cases. In some federal courts, providing staggered expert plaintiff and then defense identification and report deadlines is customary, sometimes with an additional deadline for rebuttal reports. This approach allows defendants to take into account which experts plaintiffs are using, their fields of expertise, and their opinions, before making final decisions on defense expert strategy. As a practical matter, when plaintiff and defense experts are not that far apart, such as 30 days, the practicalities of vetting and working with experts will not allow defendants the luxury of awaiting plaintiff expert materials before taking meaningful steps as to defense experts. Still, staggered deadlines can affect what topics defendants' experts cover and final decisions regarding which fields of expertise are indeed necessary. Meanwhile, in some courts plaintiffs' counsel may succeed in having the court require the simultaneous exchange of expert reports in states where full reports are utilized.

Similarly, in jurisdictions where expert depositions are permitted, those depositions could be staggered with plaintiff's experts deposed first, although even this structure sometimes gives way to practical scheduling considerations when dealing with multiple experts and parties in different geographic regions. A related consideration is whether fact discovery should conclude before expert reports and depositions to ensure that the experts are privy to all the pertinent facts and avoid

---

115. *Id.*; *see also* Trujillo v. Ametek, Inc., No. 3:15-CV-1394-GPC-BGS, 2016 WL 3552029 (S.D. Cal. June 28, 2016) (finding appropriate that before proceeding to class certification each named plaintiff be required to make a prima facie showing as to exposure, increased risk of specific injury, and causation).

116. 171 Ohio App. 3d 633, 872 N.E.2d 344. *See also In re* Digitek Prod. Liab. Litig., 264 F.R.D. 249 (S.D.W. Va. 2010) (finding a *Lone Pine* order was not presently warranted).

117. For a more detailed discussion of *Lone Pine* orders and corresponding jurisprudence, see David B. Weinstein & Christopher Torres, 14(1) ABA ENVTL. ENF'T & CRIMES COMM. NEWSL. 14 (Aug. 2013).

battles over whether supplemental opinions are warranted. In contrast, some litigants prefer a single cutoff for all discovery, in part to allow additional time for fact discovery if an expert opinion relied upon particular facts warranting further development.

Counsel should also be mindful of Federal Rule of Civil Procedure 26(a)(2)(C) regarding the content of expert disclosures for nonretained witnesses who are not required to provide reports, but may nevertheless provide expert testimony. Witnesses falling within this category can include a hybrid witness providing both fact and expert testimony, such as an employee of the defendant company whose job duties entail technical expertise, or a plaintiff's treating physician. When in doubt regarding whether the testimony of a particular hybrid witness could be considered expert testimony, the safer practice is to make a Rule 26(a)(2)(C) disclosure.

Provisions related to trial will be particularly important as well. Often these involve the order in which the trial will proceed (such as bifurcation, reverse bifurcation, or trifurcation, when dealing with the issues of liability, damages, and punitive damages) and the use of bellwether plaintiffs. These issues can be addressed in initial CMOs or, perhaps better in many cases, can be held off until later in the handling of the case, when more is known.

The use of bellwether plaintiffs has its own set of dynamics to which you should give careful consideration. Too many bellwethers and the jury will lose track of who is who. Too few bellwethers and neither side will learn much about the value of the case or the particular issue you are trying. Selecting the wrong bellwethers—that is, all the plaintiffs' best individuals or all the defendants' best individuals—will not tell anyone much about the case as a whole.[118]

CMOs may seem routine and mundane. But, as with many things, the devil is in the details, and these will be very important in a toxic tort case.

VII. TRIAL

Any trial involves a complex array of moving parts, requiring skill, knowledge, thoughtfulness, and planning. Add layers of complexity for the jury trial versus a bench trial, the complexities of science and the attendant experts, multiple defendants, multiple theories of liability, the challenges to the science concerning

---

118. *See also In re* Chevron USA, Inc., 109 F.3d 1016 (5th Cir. 1997); *In re* Medtronic, Inc. Implantable Defibrillator Prod. Liab. Litig., No. CIV 05MD1726 JMR/AJB, 2007 WL 846642 (D. Minn. Mar. 6, 2007); *In re* Guidant Corp. Implantable Defibrillators Prods. Liab. Litig., No. MDL 05-1708 DWFAJB, 2006 WL 409200 (D. Minn. Jan. 31, 2006); *In re* Neurontin Mktg., Sales Practices & Prods. Liab. Litig., 244 F.R.D 89 (D. Mass. 2007); *In re* Methyl Tertiary Butyl Ether (MTBE) Prods., No. 1:00-1898, MDL 1358(SAS), M21-88, 2007 WL 1791258 (S.D.N.Y. June 15, 2007); *In re* Welding Fume Prods. Liab. Litig., No. 1:03-CV-17000, MDL 1535, 2007 WL 1702953 (N.D. Ohio June 6, 2007); Ball v. Bayard Pump & Tank Co., 620 Pa. 289 (2013); Baker v. Chevron U.S.A. Inc., 533 F. App'x 509, 2013 WL 3968783 (6th Cir. 2013); Shanley v. Chalmette Ref., LLC, 2014 WL 6835771 (E.D. La. 12/3/14); Manual for Complex Litigation, Fourth § 22.315 (Fed. Judicial Ctr. 2004).

injury, and the challenges associated with having hundreds or even thousands of plaintiffs, and you have the components of a toxic tort trial.

In some respects, trials of toxic tort cases are like many others. A number of the general principles of the trial art are just as applicable there as they are in any type of case. All the same, the inevitable focus on science (sometimes stretching the bounds of established science), experts, and multiple plaintiffs generates some specialized requirements for toxic tort trials. More subjectively, emotions, including concerns about cancer and fears about unknown risks associated with chemicals, pharmaceuticals, and other products, may come into play with both juries and judges in the context of toxic tort trials.

Volumes have been written on those topics. In these few pages, we can provide only a glimpse of some key issues and, perhaps more importantly, steer you toward some interesting and useful authorities that will give you far more.

A common theme among trial lawyers and those who have written on the subject is the importance of "storytelling" in connection with developing the critical themes that one must have running through a trial presentation, particularly one to a jury. All agree that simplicity is the key, while still getting the necessary message across. It is also important not to get ahead of yourself in telling the story. The judge or jury may have preconceived notions, but they have not been living with the case like the litigants and will need the chance to catch up before they can potentially embrace one side's story.

For the advocate, the process of storytelling does not begin at trial or immediately before trial. Instead, it begins when you first get your case and even before you get heavily into discovery. Experienced trial lawyers will think through the broad themes, identifying key words that they will want to use at trial, right at the outset of the case (while remaining flexible to modify key themes when the case takes unexpected turns). That will allow them to take their discovery and marshal evidence with an eye to working those themes and key words in throughout, thus facilitating their ultimate goal—making the presentation at trial. Allan Kanner, an experienced trial lawyer, writes:

> Too often, lawyers shy away from toxic tort cases, fearing that they are too complicated to handle and try. But toxic tort cases, while fraught with highly technical issues, contain legal themes that are themselves simple and comprehensible. Good lawyers frame the debate in terms of these simple issues, and do not overwhelm the jury (or themselves) with complexities.[119]

In framing the story that will be told and in thinking through key words and phrases to use in that process, one obviously needs to be thoughtful with respect to the people who ultimately will judge the story and render the verdict. Another experienced trial lawyer, John C. Childs, wrote:

---

119. Allan Kanner, Environmental and Toxic Tort Trials (LexisNexis 2004), Section 1.00.

The civil jury trial is very much a people process. Therein lies the uncertainty. How individual jurors think, feel, act and make decisions is as important to the outcome as the rules of evidence and procedure. The attitudes, values and life experiences that a juror brings to a civil trial will play a greater role in how your client's case is perceived than your most compelling closing argument.[120]

What is the "story"? How does telling the story differ from mechanically laying out the facts, the science, the reasons why one witness is more persuasive than the other, and all the documents associated with that? Here is one answer:

Recognize the essential human quality of a trial; it is not a mechanical exercise. To be sure, there are of course essential elements of proof and a record to make for potential appeal, but at its core, the trial is indeed a people process.

The question for the advocate is how best to structure the case during opening and at trial, so as to link the underlying dispute to a morality play implicating core values and thereby uniting the very different members of the final jury to one's cause. Indeed, many commentators believe that the jury decision in toxic tort cases is more a "morality play" than a search for purely objective proof.[121]

Choosing key words to use during the course of the case—words that evoke images and emotions that are positive to your side of the case—will prove key to the persuasiveness of the story you ultimately tell. Working those words and themes into your case, even as early as discovery, will be important. Jurors do not come to trials as scientists or with legal analysis as the framework within which they normally think and operate. Instead, most experienced trial lawyers will tell you that jurors, in the end, tend to see things more in black and white, good and bad, and right and wrong. One summarized the result in these terms:

> Trials are not about truth. Trials are about justice. The jurors listen to the evidence and try to determine which side of the courtroom is good and which side is bad; which side is right and which side is wrong; which side is just and which side is unjust. That is about the best that they can do. It is not about truth. It is about justice.[122]

For a defendant, crafting the story requires placing yourself in the shoes of the listener. It is not uncommon for jurors to come to a toxic tort case with some predisposition, indeed a fear in some cases, with regard to chemicals and other toxic substances. Though your judge may give good jury instructions concerning who has the burden of proof, as a purely practical matter prudent defense counsel will approach both the story and the presentation of evidence with a presumption that some jurors are essentially predisposed to believe that the burden is really on

---

120. John C. Childs, *Cats, Dogs and Hammer Handles: The Predictive Value of Jury Research*, Litigation J. (ABA Section of Litig.) (Summer 2002).

121. Toxic Tort Litigation, *supra* note 22, at 242; *see also* Allan Kanner, Environmental and Toxic Tort Trials § 2.01, 2–3, 2–4 (LexisNexis 2004) (citing Richard L. Cupp, Jr., *A Morality Play's Third Act: Revisiting Addiction, Fraud and Consumer Choice in "Third Wave" Tobacco Litigation*, 46 U. Kan. L. Rev. 465, 471 (1998)).

122. Sidney K. Kanazawa, *Apologies and Lunch*, 46, 7 For the Defense 32 (July 2004).

the defendant to demonstrate that the toxic substance did not cause the plaintiff's illness. Whether or not that is precisely true as to your own jury, you generally are better off planning with that in mind.

How does one get to the good story and the best words? A couple of tips may be helpful. One is to test out your story, your theory, and your words on others. Do not just believe your own story and get carried away with it. You should test and retest your own story. Many toxic tort cases involve substantial financial rewards for the plaintiffs and substantial financial risks for the defendants. Consequently, using consultants, focus groups, mock trials, and jury research can and, where possible, should be brought into play. What is a brilliant story and powerful words to you may well leave blank stares on a focus group. Better to know this before you get to trial than to learn it from the jury after a verdict. Consultants in this field can be helpful for any number of reasons. For example, they have the professional background and training to assess what they are hearing from focus groups and learning from jury research. Furthermore, in this day of the "vanishing trial," few trial lawyers are regularly in court trying toxic tort cases, while top jury consultants have dealt with that exercise hundreds of times.

Technology and demonstrative evidence will be the next building blocks to contend with. Jury consultants will tell you of the substantial research that has been conducted on how different generations absorb and react to information and the manner in which it is presented. That influences how technology is used and the extent to which you wish to use it in a particular case. The layout of the courtroom, the nature of the case, and the amount of money involved also will have considerable impact on that. Where feasible, demonstratives that reduce complex matters to understandable visuals can be effective. Indeed, some use of technology and well-crafted exhibits often, if not always, is critical to bringing the story in a toxic tort case down to an understandable and persuasive simple story. Consistent with that thought is the concept that you need to know when enough is enough.[123]

VIII. SETTLEMENT

Conventional wisdom would dictate that once the parties agree to a settlement in principle, the hard part is over and only the details follow. That often is not so in toxic tort litigation.

Before touching on some of the pitfalls associated with perfecting a settlement, one initial issue with reaching a settlement in principle that includes a specific monetary sum is the allocation of funds among multiple plaintiffs. In the mass joinder context, defendants typically are looking to pay a set sum, leaving to plaintiffs' counsel or perhaps to a special master the work of allocating that sum on

---

123. There are many other writings on this subject, including Toxic Tort Litigation, *supra* note 22; Kanner, Environmental and Toxic Tort Trials, *supra* note 121; Lawrence G. Cetrulo, Toxic Torts Litigation Guide (Thomson West 2017–18 ed.); and Paul D. Rheingold, Litigating Mass Tort Cases (AAJ Press, Thomson West 2006).

an individual basis. In other instances, defendants may be involved in this allocation process. In either case, counsel should consult their respective state rules of professional conduct regarding allocation, including what information plaintiffs' counsel must provide to his or her clients when attempting to negotiate an aggregate settlement. For example, Model Rule of Professional Conduct 1.8(g) provides, "[a] lawyer who represents two or more clients shall not participate in making an aggregate settlement of the claims of or against the clients . . . unless each client gives informed consent, in a writing signed by the client."[124] The lawyer's disclosure shall include the existence and nature of all the claims or pleas involved and of the participation of each person in the settlement." Of course, in the class context, the claims resolution process often involves a court-appointed special master, typically called upon to handle the individual allocation of funds from the overall class settlement amount, with the allocation in some cases occurring on the back end of the process, after entry of a judgment releasing claims against the settling defendants in exchange for their lump-sum settlement contribution.

One issue that bears on the scope of any resolution is the treatment of future claims, including those involving injuries that have not yet manifested themselves. A related example is where the settlement involves a site from which substances may continue to migrate in the future, such as through groundwater. In that case, the parties will need to be clear on exactly what claims are being settled and to be conscious of the fact that jurisdictions differ on the extent to which future claims based on certain types of conduct can be released.

Another issue to consider is the appropriate procedure when funds are allocated to a minor plaintiff. For example, some jurisdictions will require that a parent accepting an award of a certain value on behalf of a minor child must take steps to obtain approval of the settlement or use of the funds, and not necessarily before the tribunal presiding over the underlying case.[125]

Some settlements may include a site cleanup component. There is an inherent difficulty with the defendant agreeing to take steps to clean up a particular site for the actions may or may not be consistent with the expectations of the agency with regulatory jurisdiction. For this reason, a defendant may take the position that it can agree only that it will address the site in conformity with a plan approved by the appropriate regulatory authority. Defendants may also wish to condition

---

124. ABA Formal Ethics Opinion 06-438 interprets Model Rule 1.8(g) as providing that "a lawyer must advise each client of the total amount or result of the settlement or agreement, the amount and nature of every client's participation in the settlement or agreement, the fees and costs to be paid to the lawyer from the proceeds or by an opposing party or parties, and the method by which the costs are to be apportioned to each client." Additionally, it broadly construes "aggregate settlement" to mean "when two or more clients who are represented by the same lawyer together resolve their claims or defenses or pleas." Further, it suggests that the "detailed disclosures must be made in the context of the specific offer or demand," and therefore "the informed consent required by the rule generally cannot be obtained in advance of the formulation of such an offer or demand."

125. *See, e.g.*, Alaska R. Civ. P. 90.2; Ind. Code § 29-3-9-7; La. Stat. § 9:196; Neb. Rev. Stat. § 30-2630.

final settlement on the appropriate agency approving their cleanup plan, lest the agency ultimately require more steps at a higher price tag than anticipated.

With respect to class-action toxic tort litigation, the associated procedures and strategies are beyond the scope of this chapter, so only a brief word follows. From a defense perspective, one of the most challenging components of a class settlement decision is balancing the desire to use the class vehicle to obtain maximum closure against the fear that publishing notice of a class-wide settlement could stir up claims that may have otherwise remained dormant. A settling defendant can try to manage risks by including in the class settlement agreement provisions allowing it to withdraw from the settlement based on the number of opt-outs. Class counsel may wish to have the same provisions for different reasons. No party can be certain as to how many people will opt out of a class settlement, nor whether such persons then will initiate separate litigation. So, the name of the game is to best manage the possibilities, while reluctantly recognizing that, at the end of the day, neither side can completely control all risk.

With any class settlement, counsel and the parties must be patient in allowing time for the process to work. Even after the portfolio of class settlement documents and pleadings are prepared and finalized (including a motion and order for preliminary approval, class notice, and class settlement agreement), it may be months before the entry of a final order and judgment and the expiration of the corresponding appeal period. Indeed, the CAFA provides that an order giving final approval of a proposed class settlement may not be entered until at least 90 days after the defendants serve the requisite statutory notice on the appropriate governmental officials.[126]

When embarking on a class settlement, one should take the time to become familiar early on with the CAFA. Even in a case in which jurisdiction is not based on the CAFA, it contains certain provisions that affect the mechanics of any class settlement. One of these is the previously mentioned requirement that appropriate governmental officials be served with notice of class settlements.[127] This can be more than just window dressing, as in certain circumstances a class member may refuse to be bound by the class settlement agreement if the notice is not appropriately provided.[128]

Defendants may also attempt to take the legs out from under a putative class action early on, before a class is certified, by settling with the named plaintiffs alone. After all, a proposed class representative may settle a putative class action or dismiss the class allegations under Rule 23 without court approval and notice to the putative class. Under Federal Rule of Civil Procedure 23 as clarified in 2003, the Rule 23(e) court approval and class notice requirements apply only to certified classes. Still, some courts have considered whether notice should be sent to

---

126. 28 U.S.C. § 1715(d) (2006); Class Action Fairness Act (CAFA) § 3(a).
127. 28 U.S.C. § 1715(a) (2006); CAFA § 3(a).
128. 28 U.S.C. § 1715(e) (2006); CAFA § 3(a).

the putative class even when voluntarily dismissing before class certification, to address potential prejudice to the class, such as in matters involving significant publicity that may have caused would-be class members to rely on the case to advance their cause.[129]

---

129. For further discussion of this issue and particular cases, see 2 McLaughlin on Class Actions § 6:1.

CHAPTER 7

Citizen Suits

Karl S. Coplan

I. HISTORY AND OVERVIEW

Congress enacted the first citizen-suit provision in the Clean Air Act Amendments of 1970.[1] The provision was included because of congressional frustration with the underenforcement of the prior Clean Air Act scheme.[2] Citizen-enforcement powers were seen both as a means of full enforcement as well as a goad to effective governmental enforcement of the regulatory scheme.[3] Each of the subsequent major federal environmental regulatory statutes similarly included a citizen-enforcement provision, with the exception of the Federal Insecticide, Fungicide, and Rodenticide Act (FIFRA).[4] Thus, citizens may enforce important parts of the federal environmental regulatory schemes governing air quality,[5] water quality,[6] solid and hazardous waste disposal,[7] contaminated-site cleanup,[8] drinking water,[9] community right to know,[10] toxic substances,[11] and the protection of endangered species.[12]

---

1. Pub. L. No. 91-604, § 12(a), 84 Stat. 1706 (1970) (codified as amended at 42 U.S.C. § 7604 (2012)).
2. S. Rep. No. 91-1196, at 35–36 (1970) ("Government initiative in seeking enforcement under the Clean Air Act has been restrained.").
3. *Id.* at 36.
4. Federal Insecticide, Fungicide, and Rodenticide Act (FIFRA), 7 U.S.C. §§ 136 *et seq.* (2012).
5. Clean Air Act § 304, 42 U.S.C. § 7604 (2012).
6. Clean Water Act § 505, 33 U.S.C. § 1365(b) (2012).
7. Resource Conservation and Recovery Act (RCRA) § 7002, 42 U.S.C. § 6972 (2012).
8. Comprehensive Environmental Response, Compensation, and Liability Act (CERCLA) § 310(a), 42 U.S.C. § 9659 (2012).
9. Safe Drinking Water Act § 1449(b), 42 U.S.C. § 300j-8 (2012).
10. Emergency Planning and Community Right-to-Know Act § 326, 42 U.S.C. § 11046 (2012).
11. Toxic Substances Control Act § 20, 15 U.S.C. § 2619 (2012).
12. Endangered Species Act § 11(g)(1), 16 U.S.C. § 1540(g) (2012).

A. Kinds of Statutory Citizen Suits

I. Citizen-Enforcement Suits

In general, citizen-suit provisions allow individual citizens and nongovernmental organizations (as well as governmental entities) to enforce compliance with regulatory standards in federal court, including requirements to obtain permits and to comply with permit provisions and administrative orders. Remedies include injunctive relief and, in most cases, assessment of civil penalties payable to the U.S. Treasury. They do not include damages payable to plaintiffs. Environmental citizen-suit provisions also generally provide for an award of attorneys' fees. Prior to commencing suit, citizen plaintiffs generally must provide advance notice of suit to the putative defendant, state environmental authorities, and the Environmental Protection Agency (EPA). A citizen may not bring suit if a government enforcement agency already has commenced and is diligently prosecuting its own enforcement action, or if the defendant has come into compliance prior to the citizen suit. Citizen plaintiffs must satisfy statutory and constitutional standing requirements as well.

In the 1980s and 1990s, citizen-enforcement cases primarily sought penalties and injunctive relief for Clean Water Act (CWA) permit violations. These cases were easy to investigate and bring based on discharge monitoring reports (DMRs) filed by the permittees. As a result, much of the leading case law governing citizen suits arose within the CWA permit-compliance context. More recently, as CWA-permitted dischargers have achieved better compliance rates, the focus of citizen-enforcement litigation has shifted to nonpermitted stormwater discharges under the CWA, waste site remediation under the Resource Conservation and Recovery Act (RCRA), and initiatives to enforce Clean Air Act (CAA) prevention of significant deterioration (PSD) preconstruction permit requirements against coal-fired power plants.[13]

2. Mandatory Regulatory Duties

Citizen-suit provisions also generally provide for actions against EPA to force the agency to perform mandatory statutory duties, such as to issue regulations setting standards by a statutory deadline. Much of the early citizen-suit litigation in

---

13. *See, e.g.*, Sierra Club, 2014 Annual Report: Sierra Club's Beyond Coal Campaign (2014), https://content.sierraclub.org/creative-archive/sites/content.sierraclub.org.creative-archive/files/pdfs/0921%20BC_annualreport2014_08_low.pdf; Riverkeeper, Inc. v. MLC Concrete Inc., 14-CV-3762, 2017 WL 3172897 (E.D.N.Y. June 26, 2017) (citizen suit for unpermitted discharges of stormwater); Conservation Law Found., Inc. v. Am. Recycled Materials, Inc., 16-12451-RGS, 2017 WL 2622737 (D. Mass. June 16, 2017) (citizen suit for unpermitted discharges of stormwater); Lajim, LLC v. Gen. Elec. Co., No. 13-CV-50348, 2015 WL 9259918 (N.D. Ill. Dec. 18, 2015) (citizen suit for remediation under RCRA); PennEnvironment v. PPG Indus., Inc., 127 F. Supp. 3d 336 (W.D. Penn. 2015) (citizen suit for remediation under RCRA); Sierra Club v. Talen Mont., No.: CV 13-32–BLG–DLC–JCL, 2017 WL 627384 (D. Mont. Jan. 30, 2017) (citizen suit against coal plant for attempting modifications without a PSD permit); Sierra Club v. Futuregen Indus. All., Inc., No. 13–CV–3408, 2014 WL 2581027 (C.D. Ill. June 9, 2014) (citizen suit against coal plant for attempting modifications without a PSD permit).

the 1970s was brought to compel EPA compliance with these regulatory deadlines. Courts have held that for a citizen to enforce a mandatory regulatory duty, there must be a "date certain" deadline for agency action.[14] Otherwise, the timing of the regulatory action is considered discretionary and beyond citizen enforcement. In response to these decisions, Congress amended Section 304 of the Clean Air Act to allow citizens to compel "agency action unreasonably delayed";[15] however, Congress has not similarly amended any other citizen-suit provisions.

3. Citizen Cleanup Remedies

RCRA Section 7002 provides for citizen-initiated cleanup remedies, even without regulatory violations.[16] Under this provision, a plaintiff may obtain a court-ordered cleanup of a site where the past or present storage, treatment, or disposal of solid or hazardous waste may present an imminent and substantial endangerment to human health or the environment.[17] This section provides a broad remedy. By its terms, it is retroactive—that is, it provides a remedy for environmental dumping that occurred before the enactment of RCRA. The threshold for obtaining relief is relatively low—the endangerment need not be certain. And RCRA's imminent and substantial endangerment remedy includes petroleum-contaminated sites that are excluded from coverage under the Comprehensive Environmental Response, Compensation, and Liability Act (CERCLA).[18] Citizens also may sue to enforce CERCLA remedial orders issued by EPA.[19]

B. Statutory Citizen-Suit Provisions

A number of federal environmental statutes provide for citizen enforcement.

Clean Air Act. CAA Section 304 provides for citizen enforcement of "emission standard(s) or limitation(s)" under the act, or any order issued by an administrator or state with respect to emission standards or limitations.[20] Emission standards and limitations include, among other things, PSD requirements and nonattainment zone permits issued under Title I of the Clean Air Act, implementation plan requirements relating to transportation control measures, permits issued under Clean Air Act Title V, and permits issued pursuant to state implementation plans.[21] Citizens also may enforce the mandatory duties of the EPA administrator under the CAA, as

---

14. Envtl. Def. Fund v. Thomas, 870 F.2d 892, 897 (2d Cir. 1989); Sierra Club v. Thomas, 828 F.2d 783, 791 (D.C. Cir. 1987).

15. 42 U.S.C. § 7604(a) (2012); Clean Air Act Amendments, Pub. L. No. 101-549 § 707(f), 104 Stat. 2399 (1990).

16. RCRA § 7002, 42 U.S.C. § 6972(a)(1)(B) (2012).

17. *Id.*

18. CERCLA § 101(14), 42 U.S.C. § 9601(14) (2012).

19. CERCLA Section 310(a)(1), 42 U.S.C. § 9659(a)(1) (2012), authorizes a citizen suit to enforce any "order which has become effective under this title," which would include a remedial order under CERCLA § 106, 42 U.S.C. § 9606 (2012).

20. Clean Air Act § 304(a)(1), 42 U.S.C. § 7604(a)(1) (2012).

21. *Id.* § 304(f), 42 U.S.C. § 7604(f).

well as the act's requirement that operators obtain a permit for any new or modified major emitting facility.[22] Citizens may obtain injunctive relief as well as awards of civil penalties to the U.S. Treasury.[23] In addition, the court may order that up to $100,000 of a civil penalty award go to environmental benefit projects in lieu of payment to the Treasury.[24]

Clean Water Act. Similar to the Clean Air Act, CWA Section 505 provides for citizen enforcement of an "effluent standard or limitation" set by the CWA, or an order issued with respect thereto.[25] An "effluent standard or limitation" is defined to include any violation of the general prohibition against nonpermitted discharges of pollutants into waters of CWA Section 301(a), violations of permits issued pursuant to CWA Section 402, and violations of state water-quality certifications issued pursuant to CWA Section 401.[26] Although the definition of an enforceable "effluent limitation" does not include violations of the terms of dredge-and-fill permits issued pursuant to CWA Section 404, dredge-and-fill discharge activities conducted in violation of such permits likely constitute violations of the general prohibitions of CWA Section 301.[27] Citizens also may enforce the mandatory duties of the EPA administrator to implement the CWA.[28] Citizens may obtain injunctive relief as well as civil penalties.[29]

Resource Conservation and Recovery Act. RCRA provides for citizen enforcement of the act's requirement that operators obtain a permit for hazardous waste treatment, storage, and disposal (TSD) facilities, as well as enforcement of RCRA's provisions of TSD facility permits and of the EPA administrator's mandatory implementation responsibilities.[30] In addition, RCRA provides citizen remedies against operation of an open dump of any solid waste in violation of RCRA Section 4005(a), and provides for an "imminent and substantial endangerment" cleanup remedy against any person responsible for the "handling, storage, transportation, treatment, or disposal of any solid or hazardous waste which may present an imminent and substantial endangerment to health or the environment."[31] Citizens may obtain injunctive relief, but civil penalties are available only for violations of RCRA Subchapter III regulations, permitting requirements, and permits governing generators, transporters, and TSD facilities.[32] Civil penalties are not available for open

---

22. *Id.* § 304(a)(2)–(3), 42 U.S.C. § 7604(a)(2)–(3).
23. *Id.* § 304(a), 42 U.S.C. § 7604(a).
24. *Id.* § 304(g), 42 U.S.C. § 7604(g).
25. Clean Water Act § 505(a)(1), 33 U.S.C. § 1365(a)(1) (2012).
26. *Id.* § 505(f), 33 U.S.C. § 1365(f).
27. *See* Phillip M. Bender, *Slowing the Net Loss of Wetlands: Citizen Suit Enforcement of Clean Water Act § 404 Permit Violations*, 27 Envtl. L. 245 (1997); Coeur d'Alene Lake v. Kiebert, 790 F. Supp. 998, 1013 (D. Idaho 1992); *but see* Atchafalaya Basinkeeper v. Thompson-Decoteau, 2011 WL 13186277 (W.D. La 2011) (holding that § 505(f)'s failure to include § 404 permit violations precludes citizen suit based on violation of § 301).
28. Clean Water Act § 505(a)(2), 33 U.S.C. § 1365(a)(2).
29. *Id.*
30. RCRA § 7002(a), 42 U.S.C. § 6972(a) (2012).
31. *Id.* § 7003, 42 U.S.C. § 6973.
32. *Id.* § 7002(a), 42 U.S.C. § 6972(a).

dumping violations or for imminent and substantial endangerment actions.[33] One court held that a citizen suit may not be brought to enforce provisions of a state hazardous waste permitting program that operates "in lieu of" the federal program under RCRA Section 3006.[34]

Comprehensive Environmental Response, Compensation, and Liability Act. CERCLA allows citizens to enforce "any standard, regulation, condition, requirement, or order which has become effective pursuant to this chapter," as well as the EPA administrator's mandatory regulatory duties.[35] Relief includes injunctions and civil penalties.[36] Because neither the CERCLA statute nor its implementing regulations impose any requirement to commence a site cleanup prior to issuance of a remedial order under CERCLA Section 106, CERCLA citizen-suit relief depends upon prior issuance of an enforceable remedial order by EPA. As a result, citizen remedies rarely are invoked, for EPA usually enforces its own orders.

Endangered Species Act. ESA Section 11(g) authorizes a citizen suit to enforce "any provision" of the act, as well as to require performance of mandatory duties by the secretaries of Commerce and the Interior.[37] Thus, citizens may enforce both the ESA Section 9 prohibition against the taking of endangered species and the ESA Section 7 consultation requirements for federal agency actions that impact endangered species. Only injunctive relief is available; ESA Section 11(g) does not provide for the award of civil penalties.

Safe Drinking Water Act. SDWA Section 1449(a) provides for citizen enforcement of "any requirement prescribed by or under this subchapter," as well as for enforcement of mandatory regulatory duties of the EPA administrator.[38] This section provides only for injunctive relief and does not provide for civil penalties.

Emergency Planning and Community Right-to-Know Act. EPCRA limits citizen suits to the enforcement of the act's specific information-filing requirements for facility operators. These include filing follow-up emergency notices, material safety data sheets, and toxic release inventory forms.[39] Suits to compel action by the EPA administrator likewise are limited to enforcing the administrator's listed duties. The district court is authorized to award civil penalties, as well as to order injunctive relief.[40]

Toxic Substances Control Act. Section 20 of TSCA authorizes a citizen to bring suit in response to "any violation of this chapter" as well as violations of rules

---

33. *Id.*

34. U.S. Tech. Corp. v. Johnson, No. 2:08-CV-82, 2009 WL 86745, at * 5 (S.D. Ohio Jan. 13, 2009); Covington v. Jefferson Cnty., 358 F.3d 626, 641–42 (9th Cir. 2004); *cf.* Ashoff v. City of Ukiah, 130 F.3d 409, 411–12 (9th Cir. 1997) (RCRA authorizes jurisdiction over citizen suits based on the federal minimum standards but it does not authorize suits brought to enforce state standards that exceed the federal minimums).

35. CERCLA § 310(a), 42 U.S.C. § 9659(a) (2012).

36. *Id.* § 310(a), 42 U.S.C. § 9659(c).

37. Endangered Species Act § 11(g), 16 U.S.C. § 1540(g) (2012).

38. Safe Drinking Water Act § 1449(a), 42 U.S.C. § 300j-8(a) (2012).

39. EPCRA § 326(a)(1), 42 U.S.C. § 11046(a)(1) (2012).

40. *Id.* § 326(c), 42 U.S.C. 11046(c).

or orders issued under the toxics control, asbestos exposure, and lead exposure titles of the TSCA.[41] Citizens also may compel performance of the EPA administrator's mandatory duties. TSCA Section 20 does not provide for civil penalty awards in a citizen suit.

II. CONDITIONS PRECEDENT TO SUIT

Although citizen-enforcement litigation for the most part follows the usual conventions of federal civil litigation, there are several statutory conditions precedent to commencing a suit that are unique to environmental citizen suits. These conditions precedent include the requirement of advance notice to the violator and the governmental enforcement agency, the requirement that there be no diligent agency enforcement activities at the time of the suit's commencement, and the requirement that a violation be continuing at the time of a suit.

A. Notice

Each of the environmental citizen-suit provisions requires that would-be plaintiffs give prior notice to the defendant, the state environmental agency, and EPA. Typical of these provisions is CWA Section 505(b), which provides:

> No action may be commenced . . . prior to 60 days after the plaintiff has given notice of the alleged violation (i) to the Administrator [of EPA], (ii) to the State in which the alleged violation occurs, and (iii) to any alleged violator of the standard, limitation, or order.[42]

The Supreme Court has posited that the purpose of the notice and waiting period is to permit the defendant to come into compliance, to allow for government agency enforcement that would eliminate the need for a citizen suit, and to allow for settlement discussions between the would-be plaintiff and the violator.[43]

I. Waiting Period

The waiting period between the time the notice is given and the time when the suit may be commenced generally is 60 days. The exception is RCRA, which provides for a 90-day waiting period in some cases.[44] The CAA and the CWA allow suit to be filed immediately in the case of violations of provisions relating to hazardous

---

41. Toxic Substances Control Act § 20(a), 15 U.S.C. § 2619(a) (2012).

42. Clean Water Act § 505(b)(1)(A), 33 U.S.C. § 1365(b)(1)(A) (2012).

43. *See* Hallstrom v. Tillamook Cnty., 493 U.S. 20, 29–31 (1989); *see also* Ctr. for Biological Diversity v. Marina Point Dev. Co., 566 F.3d 794, 800 (9th Cir. 2009); Jones Creek Inv'rs, LLC v. Columbia Cnty., No. CV 111-174, 2013 U.S. Dist. LEXIS 46149, at *27 (S.D. Ga. Mar. 28, 2013).

44. *See* Clean Air Act § 304(b), 42 U.S.C. § 7604(b) (2012) (60 days); Clean Water Act § 505(b), 33 U.S.C. § 1365(b) (60 days); RCRA § 7002(b)(1)–(2), 42 U.S.C. § 6972(b)(1)–(2) (2012) (90 days for imminent and substantial endangerment actions; 60 days for regulatory enforcement and suits to compel administrator action); CERCLA § 310(d)(1), 42 U.S.C. § 9659(d)(1) (2012) (60 days); Toxic Substances Control Act § 20(b)(1)(A), 15 U.S.C. § 2619(b)(1)(A) (60 days); Safe Drinking Water Act § 1449(b),

air pollutants and toxic water pollutants, respectively.[45] Similarly, RCRA allows for suit immediately after notice in the case of an alleged violation of RCRA's Subchapter III hazardous waste generator, transporter, and TSD facility regulations.[46] Some courts have held that where a citizen-suit complaint contains good-faith allegations of a violation that is immediately enforceable, combined with allegations subject to the waiting period, suit may be commenced immediately.[47] This is true even when allegations relating to the immediately enforceable violations are ultimately dismissed. According to EPA regulations, the waiting period commences upon the actual date of delivery by personal service.[48] If service is affected by mail, EPA regulations provide under some statutes that the notice period commences on the postmark date, and under other statutes that the notice period commences on the date of actual receipt.[49]

2. Means of Service

Depending on the statute, EPA regulations provide for service of notice by personal delivery, certified mail, or registered mail.

3. Contents of Notice

EPA regulations typically provide that notice shall include sufficient information to permit the recipient to identify the specific standard, limitation, or order that has allegedly been violated, the activity alleged to be in violation, the person or persons responsible for the alleged violation, the location of the alleged violation, the date or dates of such violation, and the full name and address of the person giving the notice.[50] Although EPA has not promulgated regulations governing citizen-suit

---

42 U.S.C. § 300j-8(b) (2012) (60 days); Endangered Species Act § 11(g)(2), 16 U.S.C. § 1540(g)(2) (2012) (60 days); EPCRA § 326(d), 42 U.S.C. § 11046(d) (2012) (60 days).

45. *See* Clean Air Act § 304(b)(2), 42 U.S.C. § 7604(b)(2) (2012); Clean Water Act § 505(b)(2), 33 U.S.C. § 1365(2) (2012).

46. RCRA § 7002(b), 42 U.S.C. § 6972(b) (2012).

47. Dague v. City of Burlington, 935 F.2d 1343, 1352 (2d Cir. 1991) (sustaining complaint that combined RCRA Subtitle III claims with Clean Water Act claims), *rev'd on other grounds*, 505 U.S. 557, 567 (1992); Schmucker v. Johnson Controls, Inc., 90 F. Supp. 3d 786, 795–96 (N.D. Ind. 2015); *see also* AM Intern, Inc. v. Datacard Corp., 106 F.3d 1342, 1351 (7th Cir. 1997) (finding waiting period inapplicable in hybrid complaint); Covington v. Jefferson Cnty., 358 F.3d 636, 636–37 (9th Cir. 2004); *see also* Nat'l Parks & Conservation Ass'n v. Tenn. Valley Auth., 502 F.3d 1316, 1329 (11th Cir. 2006) (reading hybrid cases to require notice but not compliance with the waiting period).

48. *See* 40 C.F.R. § 135.2(c) (2017) (service under the Clean Water Act); 40 C.F.R. § 54.2(d) (2017) (service under the Clean Air Act).

49. *Compare* 40 C.F.R. § 135.2(c) (2017) (Clean Water Act notice period commences on postmark date) *and* 40 C.F.R. § 54.2(d) (2017) (Clean Air Act notice period commences on postmark date) *with* 40 C.F.R. § 254.2(c) (2017) (RCRA notice period commences on date of actual receipt) *and* 40 C.F.R. § 374.2(c) (2017) (EPCRA notice period commences on date of actual receipt).

50. *See* 40 C.F.R. § 54.3(b) (2017) (describing the necessary contents of notice under the Clean Air Act); 40 C.F.R. § 135.3(a) (2017) (describing the contents of notice under the Clean Water Act); 40 C.F.R. § 135.12(a) (2017) (contents of notice under the Safe Drinking Water Act); 40 C.F.R. § 374.3(a) (2017) (contents of notice under EPCRA); 40 C.F.R. § 702.62(a) (2017) (contents of notice under the Toxic Substances Control Act).

notice under the ESA, the Ninth Circuit has applied this regulatory standard to ESA citizen suits.[51]

Courts have applied standards for notice content with varying degrees of strictness. Some courts have required the notice to specify each individual instance of violation alleged.[52] Other courts have allowed a citizen suit to proceed based on a less specific notice where the details of violation dates were available from the defendants' own records.[53] Cases also have been dismissed for failure to identify the plaintiff who actually commenced suit.[54] Other courts have allowed cases to proceed with plaintiffs who were not named in the notice letter.[55] Some cases also have been dismissed where the notice letter did not specify the precise legal theory upon which the plaintiffs were proceeding.[56] Courts have also reached differing conclusions about whether citizen plaintiffs can seek penalties for similar violations occurring after the date of notice and therefore not included in the notice letter.[57]

---

51. *See* Klamath-Siskiyou Wildlands Ctr. v. MacWhorter, 797 F.3d 645 (9th Cir. Aug. 10, 2015) (citing Sw. Ctr. for Biodiversity v. U.S. Bureau of Reclamation, 143 F.3d 515 (9th Cir. 1998)).

52. *See, e.g.*, Brod v. Omya, Inc., 653 F.3d 156, 166 (2d Cir. 2011) (finding RCRA notice inadequate); Karr v. Hefner, 475 F.3d 1192, 1201–06 (10th Cir. 2007); Stone v. High Mountain Mining Co., LLC, No. 17-cv-01295-RM-KMT, 2018 WL 1175039 (D. Colo. Mar. 5, 2018) (requiring strict approach to notice requirement); Ctr. for Biological Diversity v. Marina Point Dev. Co., 566 F.3d 794, 802–04 (9th Cir. 2009) (dismissing CWA claims because lack of specificity in notices as to dates and wetlands affected).

53. *See, e.g.*, Klamath-Siskiyou Wildlands Ctr. v. MacWhorter, 797 F.3d 645, 653 (9th Cir. 2015); Paolino v. JF Realty, LLC, 710 F.3d 31, 38–42 (1st Cir. 2013); Puget Soundkeeper All. v. Rainier Petroleum Corp., No. C14-0829JLR, 2015 WL 13655379 (W.D. Wash. Dec. 16, 2015) (citing WaterKeepers N. Cal. v. AG Indus. Mfg., 375 F.3d 913, 917–18 (9th Cir. 2004) (finding notice letter reliant on rain tables sufficient)); Cal. Cmty. against Toxics v. Weber Metals, Inc., No. CV 15-0148PA, 2015 WL 2084580, at *5–6 (C.D. Cal. May 4, 2015).

54. Wash. Trout v. Scab Rock Feeders, 823 F. Supp. 819, 820 (E.D. Wash. 1993); : Petrowsky v. NextEra Energy Res., LLC, No. 17-1043-EFM-KGG, 2017 WL 2666361, at *3 (D. Kan. June 21, 2017) (dismissing ESA claim because notice did not include plaintiff's name); Kern v. Wal-Mart Stores, Inc., 804 F. Supp. 2d 119, 133 (W.D.N.Y. 2011); Assateague Coastkeeper v. Alan & Kristin Hudson Farm, 727 F. Supp. 2d 433, 438 (D. Md. 2010); Affholter v. Franklin Cnty. Water Dist., No. 1:07-CV-0388 OWW DLB, 2008 WL 4911406, at * 6 (E.D. Cal. Nov. 13, 2008) (dismissing multiple plaintiffs not included in initial notice).

55. Hernandez v. Esso Standard Oil Co., 571 F. Supp. 2d 305, 315 n.8 (D.P.R. 2008) (declining to dismiss eight plaintiffs not included in notice letter that identified nearly 100); *see* Cal. Pub. Interest Research Grp. v. Shell Oil Corp., 38 Env't Rep. Cas. (BNA) 1950, at *8 (N.D. Cal. 1994); Klickitat Cnty. v. Columbia River Gorge Comm'n, 770 F. Supp. 1419, 1424 (E.D. Wash. 1991); Student Pub. Interest Research Grp. of N.J., Inc. v. AT&T Bell Labs., 617 F. Supp. 1190, 1194 (D.N.J. 1985).

56. *See* Nat'l Parks & Conservation Ass'n v. Tenn. Valley Auth., 502 F.3d 1316, 1329–30 (11th Cir. 2007) (affirming dismissal of Clean Air Act citizen suit where notice letter alleged general violations, but failed to specify violation of New Source Performance Standards); ONRC Action v. Columbia Plywood, Inc., 286 F.3d 1137, 1143–44 (9th Cir. 2002) (Clean Water Act notice letter alleging operation without required permit held insufficient to pursue theory that prior permit had expired); Fitzgibbons v. Cook, No. 1:08-CV-165, 2008 WL 5156629, at *7 (W.D. Mich. Dec. 8, 2008) (finding the plaintiffs' notice insufficient "because it notified Defendants of one violation (failure to apply for or obtain an NPDES permit), but Plaintiffs sued Defendants for another (violation of an existing NPDES permit)").

57. *Compare* Cmty. Ass'n for Restoration of the Env't v. Henry Bosma Dairy, 305 F.3d 943, 950–53 (9th Cir. 2002) (affirming assessment of civil penalties against the defendant for violations not appearing in notice), *and* Pub. Interest Grp. of N.J., Inc. v. Hercules, Inc., 50 F.3d 1239, 1250–52 (3d Cir. 1995) (concluding that the plaintiffs could proceed on violations occurring during or after the period covered by the notice letter), *and* Puget Soundkeeper All. v. Cruise Terminals of Am., LLC, 216 F. Supp. 3d 1198, 1214–15 (W.D. Wash. 2015) (allowing the plaintiffs to proceed on violations after notice letter was sent), *and* Friends of the Earth, Inc. v. Gaston Copper Recycling Corp., 629 F.3d 387, 400–02 (4th Cir. 2011)

EPA regulations also generally require that the notice letter identify counsel representing the proposed plaintiffs.

4. Persons to Be Served with Notice

In general, the environmental citizen-suit provisions require that notice of intent to sue be served upon (1) the EPA administrator (or other agency head in charge of the regulatory program), (2) the state in which the alleged violation occurs, and (3) the alleged violator. These regulations further specify that notice to the state should be served upon the head of the appropriate pollution-control agency, and that a copy of a notice of violations of the CWA and the CAA be served on the EPA administrator and regional administrator. Under the regulations, if the alleged violator is a corporation, notice must be served on both the plant manager of the facility where the violation occurs and the registered agent of the corporation.[58]

Plaintiff's counsel should take great care to determine and follow the service requirements set forth in both the statute and regulations, which vary by statute. For example, notice of intent to sue under the ESA must be served upon the Secretary of Commerce in the cases involving aquatic species, the Secretary of the Interior in cases involving terrestrial species, and the Secretary of Agriculture when the importation or exportation of plant species is at issue.[59] Cases have been dismissed for failure to serve the proper parties under the statute and regulations.[60]

(affirming assessment of penalties for violations occurring after notice), *with* Historic Green Springs, Inc. v. Louisa Cnty. Water Auth., 833 F. Supp. 2d 562, 567–68 (W.D. Va. 2011) (barring the plaintiffs from relief sought for violations not included in the notice letter), *and* Stephens v. Koch Foods, LLC, 667 F. Supp. 2d 768, 786–87 (E.D. Tenn. 2009) (refusing to consider effluent violations occurring after the notice letter), *and* Am. Canoe Ass'n, Inc. v. City of Louisa Water & Sewer Comm'n, 2009 WL 8520576 (E.D. Ky. 2009) (penalties not assessed for any violations occurring after date of notice letter).

58. *See* 40 C.F.R. § 54.2(c) (2017) (notice to the violator under the Clean Air Act); 40 C.F.R. § 135.2(a) (2017) (notice to the violator under the Clean Water Act); 40 C.F.R. § 135.11(a) (2017) (Safe Drinking Water Act notice requirements); 40 C.F.R. § 374.2(a) (2017) (notice to the violator under EPCRA); 40 C.F.R. § 254.3 (2017) (notice requirements under RCRA); 40 C.F.R. § 702.61(d)(1) (2017) (notice requirements under the Toxic Substances Control Act).

59. Endangered Species Act § 11(g)(2), 16 U.S.C. § 1540(g)(2) (2012). Section 3 of the Act defines "Secretary" to mean "the Secretary of Interior or the Secretary of Commerce as program responsibilities are vested pursuant to the provisions of Reorganization Plan Numbered 4 of 1970; except that with respect to the enforcement of the provisions of this Act and the Convention which pertain to the importation or exportation of terrestrial plants, the term also means the Secretary of Agriculture." *Id.* § 3(10), 16 U.S.C. § 1532(15).

60. *See* Hawksbill Sea Turtle v. Fed. Emergency Mgmt. Agency, 126 F.3d 461, 465 (3d Cir. 1997) (dismissing ESA claims relating to aquatic species because notice was served on the Secretary of Interior and not the Secretary of Commerce); Petrowsky v. NextEra Energy Res., LLC, No. 17-1043-EFM-KGG, 2017 WL 2666361, at *7 (D. Kan. June 21, 2017) (dismissing subsidiaries after concluding that notice to parent company did not constitute notice to subsidiaries); Darbouze v. Chevron Corp., No. 97-2970, 1998 U.S. Dist. LEXIS 81, at *7 (E.D. Pa. Jan. 9, 1998) (dismissing for identifying defendant as "Chevron, Inc." instead of "Chevron USA, Inc.," in notice letter and for failure to mail to registered agent). *But see* Long v. KZF Dev., 935 F. Supp. 3d 889, 892 (N.D. Ill. 2013) (notice to parent company that managed subsidiary, which owned the property, satisfied notice requirement as to both parent and subsidiary); Two Rivers Terminal, L.P. v. Chevron USA, Inc., 96 F. Supp. 2d 426, 432 (M.D. Pa. 2000) (notice to parent company in RCRA suit satisfied notice requirement as to subsidiary).

5. Importance of Careful Compliance with Notice Requirements

In *Hallstrom v. Tillamook County*, the Supreme Court declared that the notice requirements of the environmental citizen-suit provisions are mandatory conditions precedent to commencement of a citizen suit.[61] In *Hallstrom*, the Court specifically rejected the practical remedy, fashioned by the district court, of staying the citizen-suit litigation for 90 days while plaintiffs' counsel complied with the notice requirement. Although the *Hallstrom* decision stopped short of holding that notice was a jurisdictional requirement in the strictest sense, other decisions have treated the notice requirement as "jurisdictional" in nature.[62] Treatment of notice requirements as jurisdictional is significant for several reasons. First, it means that notice objections may be raised at any point in the litigation, including for the first time on appeal. In addition, if notice is considered jurisdictional, defective notice cannot be cured by serving a proper notice, waiting 60 or 90 days, and filing an amended complaint. Rather, the proper procedure for curing defective notice is to commence a second action after the waiting period, or, if not all claims from the first action are dismissed, filing a second action and moving to consolidate it with the first action.[63]

Because most courts treat notice as a jurisdictional requirement and the Supreme Court has strictly applied notice requirements, plaintiffs' counsel must take great pains to ensure that citizen-suit notice is complete in substance and that its service is formally proper. Because a 60-day or 90-day waiting period must elapse before suit can be recommenced after inadequate notice, and because it is impossible to cure notice violations by filing an amended complaint, it is more difficult to cure defective notice than it is to cure pleading defects in a complaint. Thus, plaintiffs' counsel should ensure that all potential violations are described in detail in the notice, and that all parties are properly named and served in the

---

61. 493 U.S. 20, 26 (1989).

62. *See* Klamath-Siskiyou Wildlands Ctr. v. MacWhorter, 797 F.3d 645, 647 (9th Cir. 2015) ("The sixty-day notice requirement [under the ESA] is jurisdictional."); Paolino v. JF Realty, LLC, 710 F.3d 31, 36 n.4 (1st Cir. 2013) (noting that most courts that have considered the issue have concluded that the CWA's notice requirement at least implicates subject-matter jurisdiction, but declining to decide the issue); Ecological Rights Found. v. Pac. Gas & Elec. Co., 713 F.3d 502, 506 (9th Cir. 2013) (noting that notice requirements in CWA and RCRA are jurisdictional). *But see* Adkins v. VIM Recycling, Inc., 644 F.3d 483, 492 n.3 (7th Cir. 2011) (explaining that RCRA's 60-day notice requirement is not jurisdictional); Am. Canoe Ass'n v. City of Attalla, 363 F.3d 1085, 1088 (11th Cir. 2004) (finding CWA's notice requirement more procedural than jurisdictional); Lockett v. EPA, 319 F.3d 678, 682–83 (5th Cir. 2003) (concluding that although the notice requirement is mandatory, it is not jurisdictional); Sierra Club v. Yeutter, 926 F.2d 429, 437 (5th Cir. 1991) (holding that ESA notice provisions are mandatory but not jurisdictional); Mich. Dep't of Envtl. Quality v. City of Flint, No. 17-2017, 2017 WL 4863316 (E.D. Mich. Oct. 27, 2017) (concluding that SDWA notice requirement is a claim processing rule that must be raised in a timely manner).

63. *See, e.g.*, *Hawksbill Sea Turtle*, 126 F.3d at 473; City of Newburgh v. Sarna, 690 F. Supp. 2d 136, 153 (S.D.N.Y. 2010) (noting plaintiffs must comply with 60-day requirement to bring claim against the defendant after dismissing entire claim), *aff'd in part, appeal dismissed in part*, 406 F. App'x 557 (2d Cir. 2011); Forest Guardians v. U.S. Bureau of Reclamation, 462 F. Supp. 2d 1177, 1184–86 (D.N.M. 2006) (holding that the plaintiff could not cure defective notice by sending notice, waiting 60 days, and filing supplemental complaint).

notice, including corporate registered agents and the proper agency heads. In addition, the notice letter must identify appropriate plaintiffs who will have standing to litigate the citizen suit, for it may be impossible to add substitute plaintiffs not named in the notice letter later on.

B. Diligent Prosecution

In addition to the notice requirement, each environmental citizen-suit provision precludes commencement of a citizen suit where either the state or federal government has already initiated and is "diligently prosecuting" an enforcement proceeding for the same violations. Typical of these provisions is CWA Section 505(b)(1)(B), which provides:

> No action may be commenced . . . if the Administrator or State has commenced and is diligently prosecuting a civil or criminal action in a court of the United States, or a State to require compliance with the standard, limitation, or order, but in any such action in a court of the United States any citizen may intervene as a matter of right.[64]

In considering diligent prosecution defenses, practitioners should note that there are two kinds of potential "diligent prosecution" preemption—those involving enforcement actions in court (as described in CWA Section 505 and similar citizen-suit provisions) and those involving administrative enforcement actions.

For a government enforcement action to preempt a citizen suit under the citizen-suit provisions such as CWA Section 505, courts have held that the government action must be commenced in court, rather than in an administrative proceeding.[65] In addition, to preempt the citizen suit, the government action must be filed first. Courts have held that a subsequently filed government action is not grounds for dismissal of an earlier filed citizen suit, even in a case where the government suit was filed mere minutes after the citizen suit.[66] Some courts, however, have applied principles of res judicata to dismiss a citizen suit based on a government settlement reached in an action filed after the citizen suit.[67]

---

64. Clean Water Act § 505(b)(1)(B), 33 U.S.C. § 1365(b)(1)(B) (2012).

65. *See, e.g.*, Cal. Sportfishing Prot. All. v. Chico Scrap Metal, Inc., 728 F.3d 868, 873 (9th Cir. 2013); Chico Serv. Station, Inc. v. Sol P.R. Ltd., 633 F.3d 20, 35 (1st Cir. 2011); Black Warrior Riverkeeper, Inc. v. Cherokee Mining, LLC 548 F.3d 986, 992 (11th Cir. 2008).

66. *See, e.g.*, Adkins v. VIM Recycling, Inc., 644 F.3d 483, 493 (7th Cir. 2011) (RCRA citizen suit not barred by subsequent state action); Friends of Milwaukee's Rivers v. Milwaukee Metro. Sewerage Dist., 382 F.3d 743, 754–55 (7th Cir. 2004) (finding state action filed hours after citizen suit did not bar citizen suit); Chesapeake Bay Found. v. Am. Recovery Co., 769 F.2d 207, 208–09 (4th Cir. 1985); Cape Fear River Watch, Inc. v. Duke Energy Progress, Inc., 25 F. Supp. 3d 798, 811 (E.D.N.C. 2014); Long Island Sound-keeper Fund v. City of New York, 27 F. Supp. 2d 380, 382–83 (E.D.N.Y. 1998) (allowing citizen suit filed minutes before state enforcement action to proceed).

67. Sierra Club v. Two Elk Generation Partners, Ltd., 646 F.3d 1258, 1263 (10th Cir. 2011) (collecting cases); Ellis v. Gallatin Steel Co., 390 F.3d 461, 473–74 (6th Cir. 2004); EPA v. City of Green Forest, 921 F.2d 1394, 1403–05 (8th Cir. 1990).

In addition to the diligent court prosecution defense, some citizen-suit statutes contemplate preemption by certain kinds of administrative proceedings. For example, CWA Section 309(g)(6)(a) provides for preemption of a "civil penalty action" under CWA Section 505 where EPA or a state agency has commenced and is diligently prosecuting an administrative enforcement proceeding under state law equivalents to the CWA, or has completed such a prosecution and collected a penalty. Some courts have held that this section preempts only a citizen suit seeking penalties and does not preempt a citizen suit seeking injunctive relief.[68] RCRA's citizen-suit section provides for preemption where the state or EPA has commenced its own imminent-hazard proceeding, is engaged in a removal action under CERCLA, or has incurred costs to initiate a remedial-action feasibility study under CERCLA.[69] Not all citizen-suit statutes provide for such administrative preemption, however.[70]

Courts generally apply a deferential standard when determining whether government enforcement is sufficiently diligent to preempt a citizen suit. The burden is on the citizen plaintiff to show that the government's enforcement action is inadequate.[71] Mere dissatisfaction with the amount of penalties sought or the speed of compliance efforts generally is insufficient to show lack of diligence.[72] However, citizens have been successful in showing lack of diligent prosecution in cases of collusion between the violator and the government enforcement agency.[73] Factors a court may consider in evaluating the diligence of governmental prosecution include: whether the government required or sought compliance with the specific standards at issue in the citizen suit, whether the government was monitoring the defendant's activities after settlement, the possibility that the citizen-alleged

---

68. Paper, Allied-Industrial, Chem. & Energy Workers Int'l Union v. Cont'l Carbon Co., 428 F.3d 1285, 1297 (10th Cir. 2005); Borough of Upper Saddle River v. Rockland Cnty. Sewer Dist. # 1, 16 F. Supp. 3d 294, 321 n.32 (S.D.N.Y. 2014) (noting that in the Second Circuit, plaintiffs may seek injunctive relief even if civil penalties are unavailable); Gulf Restoration Network v. Hancock Cnty. Dev., LLC, No. 1:08-cv186-LG-RHW, 2009 WL 3841728, at *3 (S.D. Miss. Nov. 16, 2009) (collecting cases). *But see* N. & S. Rivers Watershed Ass'n v. Town of Scituate, 949 F.2d 552, 555–56 (1st Cir. 1991) (citizen suit barred by state's diligent enforcement action, precluding both civil penalties and injunctive relief).

69. RCRA § 7002(b)(2), 42 U.S.C. § 6972(b)(2) (2012).

70. For other examples of administrative preemption, see EPCRA § 326(e), 42 U.S.C. § 11046(e) (2012) (providing for preemption by administrative enforcement); Safe Drinking Water Act § 300h-2(c)(5), 42 U.S.C. § 300h-2(c)(5) (2012); Marine Protection Research and Sanctuaries Act § 105(g)(2)(c), 33 U.S.C. § 1415(g)(2)(c) (2012).

71. *See, e.g.,* Piney Run Pres. Ass'n, 523 F.3d at 459; Karr v. Hefner, 475 F.3d 1192, 1198 (10th Cir. 2007); Friends of Milwaukee's Rivers v. Milwaukee Metro. Sewerage Dist., 382 F.3d 743, 760 (7th Cir. 2004); Yadkin Riverkeeper, Inc. v. Duke Energy Carolinas, LLC, 141 F. Supp. 3d 428, 441 (M.D.N.C. 2015); Ohio Valley Envtl. Coal., Inc. v. Maple Coal Co., 808 F. Supp. 2d 868, 883 (S.D.W. Va. 2011).

72. *See, e.g.,* Piney Run Pres. Ass'n v. Cnty. Comm'rs of Carroll Cnty., 523 F.3d 453, 459 (4th Cir. 2008) (noting that a citizen suit cannot "overcome the presumption of diligence merely by showing that the agency's prosecution strategy is less aggressive than he would like or that it did not produce a completely satisfactory result"); EPA v. Green Forest, 921 F.2d 1394, 1404 (8th Cir. 1990); Citizens for Clean Power v. Indian River Power, LLC, 636 F. Supp. 2d 351, 357–58 (D. Del. 2009); Envtl. Integrity Project v. Mirant Corp., No. JFM-06-2249, 2007 WL 62619 (D. Md. Jan. 3, 2007).

73. *See* Friends of the Earth, Inc. v. Laidlaw Envtl. Servs. (TOC), Inc. (Laidlaw I), 890 F. Supp. 470, 479 (D.S.C. 1995) (noting that the government's complaint in the enforcement proceeding and the consent decree settling the government's case were drafted and filed by attorneys for defendant).

violations will continue despite the defendant's settlement with the government, and how the amount of penalties compares to the economic benefits of not complying with the law.[74] A citizen suit may avoid dismissal for diligent prosecution where the citizen plaintiffs allege violations other than, or broader than, those being enforced by the government agency.[75]

C. Continuing Violation

Many of the citizen-suit statutes describe the violations that may be enforced in the present tense. For example, the CWA allows enforcement against a defendant who "is alleged to be in violation of an effluent standard or limitation."[76] In *Gwaltney of Smithfield, Ltd. v. Chesapeake Bay Foundation, Inc.*, the Supreme Court held that this language precluded citizen suits in which the plaintiff could not make a good-faith allegation that the violations were continuing at the time the complaint was filed.[77] The *Gwaltney* opinion posited that citizen suits were meant to supplement—not replace—governmental enforcement and compliance efforts, and that the notice and delay provisions of the citizen-suit statutes would not make sense unless a defendant could avoid suit by coming into compliance prior to expiration of the waiting period.

Although *Gwaltney* was by its terms a statutorily based decision, the Supreme Court subsequently constitutionalized the requirement of an ongoing violation in *Steel Company v. Citizens for a Better Environment.*[78] *Steel Company* involved a citizen suit brought in response to a defendant's failure to file the toxic release inventory reports required by EPCRA. After the citizens' group gave notice, but before it filed suit, the defendant filed the missing report. Despite this, the plaintiffs filed suit for the past violations in federal district court. The case made its way to the Supreme Court, which declined to reach the question of whether EPCRA, like the CWA, required an ongoing violation. Instead, the Court dismissed the case on the grounds that redressability, a necessary element of Article III standing (discussed next), was missing once the defendant came into compliance with the statute. According to the Court, because civil penalties are payable to the U.S. Treasury (not to plaintiffs), and because there no longer was a violation to enjoin, no judicial

---

74. *See* Grp. against Smog & Pollution v. Shenango, Inc., No. CIV.A. 14-595, 2015 WL 1405447, at *4 (W.D. Pa. Mar. 26, 2015); Jarrett v. Water Works & Sanitary Sewer Bd., No. 00-A-527-N, 2001 U.S. Dist. LEXIS 522, at *19–20 (D. Ala. Jan. 16, 2001).

75. Adkins v. VIM Recycling, Inc., 644 F.3d 483, 495 (7th Cir. 2011).

76. Clean Water Act § 505(a)(1), 33 U.S.C. § 1365(a)(1) (2012); *see also* RCRA § 7002(a)(1), 42 U.S.C. § 6972(a)(1)(A) (2012) (allowing enforcement against any person "who is alleged to be in violation of any permit, standard, regulation, condition, requirement, prohibition, or order"); *cf.* Clean Air Act § 304(a)(1), 42 U.S.C. § 7604(a)(1) (2012) (providing for enforcement against any person "who is alleged to have violated (if there is evidence that the alleged violation has been repeated) or to be in violation of").

77. 484 U.S. 49 (1987).

78. 523 U.S. 83 (1998).

relief was available to redress the plaintiffs' informational injuries. As a result, the plaintiffs no longer had a stake in a live Article III controversy.

The Supreme Court's holding in *Steel Company* means that the continuing-violation element of citizen suits applies to all citizen-suit statutes as a constitutional matter—at least in the absence of a specific judicial remedy that benefits plaintiffs particularly.[79] Where a defendant comes into compliance after the citizen suit is commenced, however, courts retain jurisdiction to assess penalties unless the defendant can meet the heavy burden of showing that the case is moot because further violations are impossible.[80] In addition, a citizen suit can be maintained as long as the plaintiff has a good-faith basis to allege that violations are continuing at the time of the complaint or are likely to recur even though the defendant might not be in violation at the time of the complaint.[81]

III. STANDING TO SUE AND MOOTNESS

In addition to the statutory preconditions to sue, citizen-enforcement suits must satisfy justiciability requirements of Article III of the U.S. Constitution. The Article III issues that most often prove controversial in citizen suits are the requirement that the plaintiff have standing to sue and the possibility of mootness by reason of postcomplaint compliance. Although plaintiffs must satisfy statutory standing requirements as well as constitutional standing requirements, the statutory standing requirements generally are considered commensurate with the constitutional limits on standing.[82]

---

79. Section 304(g)(2) of the Clean Air Act allows $100,000 of a penalty judgment to be applied to environmental benefit projects. As a result, a Clean Air Act citizen-suit plaintiff might be able to argue that the redressability element that was lacking in *Steel Company* is present in a Clean Air Act citizen suit. Note also that Clean Air Act § 304(a)(1), 42 U.S.C. § 7604(a)(1) (2012), specifically authorizes citizens to bring suit in response to repeated past violations.

80. Friends of the Earth v. Laidlaw Envtl. Servs. (TOC), Inc. (*Laidlaw II*), 528 U.S. 167, 189 (2000); Bldg. & Constr. Trades Council of Buffalo v. Downtown Dev., Inc., 448 F.3d 138, 152 (2d Cir. 2006); Tamaska v. City of Bluff City, 26 F. App'x 482, 484 (6th Cir. 2002); Puget Soundkeeper All. v. BNSF Ry. Co., No. C09-1087-JCC, 2010 WL 11565190, at * 4–6 (W.D. Wash. Aug. 10, 2010); Riverkeeper, Inc. v. Mirant Lovett, LLC, 675 F. Supp. 2d 337, 347 (S.D.N.Y. 2009).

81. Gwaltney of Smithfield, Ltd. v. Chesapeake Bay Found., 484 U.S. 49, 64 (1987) (holding that citizen suit may be maintained on good-faith allegation of continuous or intermittent violation); Am. Canoe Ass'n v. Murphy Farms, Inc., 326 F.3d 505, 521 (4th Cir. 2003); Ohio Valley Envtl. Coal., Inc. v. Alex Energy, Inc., 12 F. Supp. 3d 844, 864–65 (S.D.W. Va. 2014); Assateague Coastkeeper v. Alan & Kristin Hudson Farm, 727 F. Supp. 2d 433, 443 (D. Md. 2010) ("[A]t the motion to dismiss stage, plaintiffs need only make a good faith allegation of continuous or intermittent violation to satisfy the jurisdictional requirement of the statute.").

82. *See* Bennett v. Spear, 520 U.S. 154, 165 (1997); Save Our Cmty. v. EPA, 971 F.2d 1155, 1160 n.10 (5th Cir. 1992); Pub. Interest Research Grp. of N.J., Inc. v. Powell Duffryn Terminals, Inc., 913 F.2d 64, 70 n.3 (3d Cir. 1990); Davis v. Jackson, No. 8:09-CV-1070, 2010 U.S. Dist. LEXIS 72370, at *4 (M.D. Fla. July 19, 2010).

A. Individual Standing

To establish individual standing to sue in the federal courts, a citizen plaintiff must establish three elements: injury in fact, causation, and redressability.[83]

1. Injury in Fact

To establish injury in fact, the plaintiff must show that the defendant's violations have injured the plaintiff in some tangible way. In *Sierra Club v. Morton*, the Supreme Court's seminal case on environmental standing, the Court held that environmental injury in fact is not limited to injury to pecuniary or property interests.[84] Instead, injury in fact can include interference with recreational, environmental, and aesthetic interests. Under *Morton*, an interest in abstract values of environmental protection is insufficient; thus, the Sierra Club was held to lack standing. The plaintiff must show that he or she personally has suffered the injury, usually by reason of regular recreational use of the environmental resource in question. The Supreme Court has rejected standing claims made by persons who claimed recreational use of lands in the general vicinity of lands affected by challenged mineral leases where the plaintiffs could not show they used the specific lands in question.[85] In addition, the Supreme Court has rejected plaintiffs' claims that the loss of an opportunity to view endangered species constitutes an injury in fact in a case where plaintiffs could not show that they were likely to visit the endangered habitats in the future.[86]

Although an injury must be "concrete and particularized" to establish the requisite "injury in fact," and courts will not consider "generalized grievances,"[87] the Supreme Court explained in *Friends of the Earth v. Laidlaw Environmental Services (Laidlaw II)* that a plaintiff need not prove a measurable harm to the environment to establish standing.[88] The fact that harms are widely shared does not preclude standing for an individual. In so ruling, the Supreme Court upheld the plaintiff's standing in a CWA citizen suit despite the district court's finding that the defendant's mercury discharges caused no perceptible damage to the river in question. The Court based its opinion on affidavits alleging that the plaintiff had curtailed recreational use of the river because of concerns about environmental pollution. The Court found that these affidavits established standing because "[t]he relevant showing for purposes of Article III standing . . . is not injury to the environment but injury to the plaintiff."[89] Thus, "environmental plaintiffs adequately allege injury in fact when they aver that they use the affected area and are persons 'for whom the aesthetic and recreational values of the area will be lessened' by the challenged

---

83. *Laidlaw II*, 528 U.S. at 180–81.
84. 405 U.S. 727 (1972), *superseded by statute*, Clean Water Act § 505, 33 U.S.C. § 1365 (2012).
85. Lujan v. Nat'l Wildlife Fed'n, 497 U.S. 871 (1990).
86. Lujan v. Defenders of Wildlife, 504 U.S. 555 (1992).
87. *Id.* at 575.
88. 528 U.S. 167 (2000).
89. *Id.* at 181.

activity."[90] More recently, in *Massachusetts v. EPA*, the Court held that the plaintiff state had established injury in fact even though the global-warming harms of which it complained were widely shared.[91]

Citizen-suit plaintiffs usually will establish individual standing by showing individual use of the environmental resource in question, together with an identification of the impacts the challenged activity has had on their ability to enjoy the resources. Typical individual standing interests include hikers, boaters, bird-watchers, or fishermen whose recreational enjoyment of a resource has been diminished by the challenged conduct. These types of interests—as well as aesthetic concerns because of visible smokestack emissions and breathing and smelling polluted air—have been held sufficient to support standing in citizen suits involving Clean Air Act violations.[92]

2. Causation

To establish standing, a plaintiff also must establish that the injury he or she claims is causally related to the violation at issue. Courts have not required a strict, tort-like, "but-for" causation requirement in applying this test. Rather, a plaintiff may establish causation by showing that the kinds of pollution complained of, in general, cause the kinds of harms complained of. Thus, in the leading case on causation for standing purposes, the Third Circuit held that a plaintiff who suffered aesthetic injuries from seeing oil sheens on waters he hiked and jogged next to could sue to enforce oil and grease discharge limits of a CWA permit for a discharger on that water body, even without proof that the defendant caused the specific oil sheens observed.[93]

The Supreme Court lent its support to this relaxed approach to causation in *Massachusetts v. EPA* and *Laidlaw II*. In *Massachusetts v. EPA*, the Court found that the plaintiff had Article III standing to challenge EPA's failure to regulate certain greenhouse gas emissions from motor vehicles despite the incremental contribution of U.S. motor-vehicle emissions to the global problem of greenhouse gases.[94] In addition, in *Laidlaw II*, the Court acknowledged that a plaintiff may suffer environmental injury without proof of perceptible injury to the environment.[95] This holding likewise implies a relaxed standard of causal relationship to the specific environmental harms identified. The Ninth Circuit has suggested that *Massachusetts*

---

90. *Id.* at 183 (citing Sierra Club v. Morton, 405 U.S. 727, 735 (1972)).

91. 549 U.S. 497 (2007).

92. Sierra Club v. Tenn. Valley Auth., 430 F.3d 1337, 1344–45 (11th Cir. 2005); Texans United for a Safe Econ. Educ. Fund v. Crown Cent. Petrol. Corp., 207 F.3d 789, 792–93 (5th Cir. 2000); Friends of Mariposa Creek v. Mariposa Pub. Util. Dist., No. 1:15-cv-00583-EPG, 2016 WL 1587228, at *4–5 (E.D. Cal. Apr. 19, 2016) (finding plaintiff who used creek for recreational pursuits had standing); Sierra Club v. PacifiCorp, No. 07-CV-42-J, 2009 WL 10690777, at *7 (D. Wyo. Aug. 24, 2009) (aesthetic interests sufficient to establish standing to bring citizen suit against power plant).

93. Pub. Interest Research Grp. of N.J., Inc. v. Powell Duffryn Terminals, Inc., 913 F.2d 64 (3d Cir. 1990).

94. 549 U.S. 497 (2007).

95. 528 U.S. 167 (2000).

v. EPA's recognition of the causation element of standing for global-warming injuries may be based on a relaxation of standing requirements for governmental environmental plaintiffs that would not extend to nongovernmental litigants.[96]

3. Redressability

The plaintiff also must establish that the claimed injury in fact is subject to judicial redress. This element usually is not difficult to establish, for the potential availability of injunctive relief requiring compliance with the environmental standard in question usually suffices.[97] However, the Supreme Court has held that where the violations have ceased prior to commencement of the citizen suit, the redressability element is missing and the citizen plaintiff lacks standing—at least where the statute provides only for penalties payable to the U.S. Treasury.[98]

B. Organizational Standing

Most environmental citizen suits are prosecuted by organizational plaintiffs. The Supreme Court held in *Sierra Club v. Morton* that such plaintiffs may not rely on an organizational interest in environmental issues to establish standing. Instead, they must rely on the doctrine of representational standing, which recognizes that an organization has standing to advance the interests of its supporting members.[99]

To establish standing in a representational capacity, the organizational plaintiff must show (1) that it has at least one member who would have standing in his or her own right as an individual; (2) that the matter of litigation is germane to the organizational purposes of the plaintiff organization; and (3) that the litigation does not require the direct participation of the individual members to afford complete judicial relief.[100] In general, these requirements are not difficult for an organizational environmental plaintiff to meet. The plaintiff organization should be certain to identify individual members who will satisfy the individual standing requirement prior to commencing the litigation and ensure that these individuals will be willing to submit affidavits, submit to depositions, and testify at trial if necessary. Because standing is a jurisdictional requirement, members who join the

---

96. Wash. Envtl. Council v. Bellon, 732 F.3d 1131 (9th Cir. 2013) (rejecting standing of environmental groups asserting global-warming harms on grounds that global warming not sufficiently causally related to EPA's failure to establish greenhouse gas controls for stationary sources).

97. *See, e.g.*, Steel Co. v. Citizens for a Better Env't, 523 U.S. 83, 106–07 (1998); *Powell Duffryn*, 913 F.2d at 73; *Texans United*, 207 F.3d at 793–94; Clean Water Action v. Searless Auto Recycling Corp., 268 F. Supp. 3d 276, 281 (D. Mass. 2017); Domino v. Didion Ethanol, LLC, 670 F. Supp. 2d 901, 917 (W.D. Wis. 2009).

98. *Steel Co.*, 523 U.S. at 106–07. As noted previously, since Clean Air Act Section 304(g) allows penalty payments to be made to an environmental benefit project, a Clean Air Act plaintiff may be able to argue that redressability is present even for past violations.

99. Sierra Club v. Morton, 405 U.S. 727 (2007).

100. Friends of the Earth v. Laidlaw Envtl. Servs. (TOC), Inc. (*Laidlaw II*), 528 U.S. 167, 181 (2000)); Save Our Cmty. v. EPA, 971 F.2d 1155, 1160 (5th Cir. 1992).

organization after the complaint is filed will not satisfy standing requirements.[101] Some defendants have challenged the capacity of an organization to represent its supporters when the organization does not have a voting membership. Courts generally have rejected such challenges as long as the supporters bear sufficient "indicia of membership" in the organization.[102]

If there is any question about the ability of the organization to satisfy organizational standing requirements, plaintiff's counsel should seek to join individual plaintiffs who would have standing as co-plaintiffs. In such a case, the individual plaintiffs should be identified in the notice letter. Plaintiffs' counsel will have to address issues such as resolution of conflicts between the organizational plaintiff's goals and individuals' goals, as well as address potential individual liability for fees and costs.

C. Mootness

As noted, citizens generally may not commence suit if the violator has come into compliance prior to filing the complaint. At times, a violator will come into compliance after the complaint is filed and seek to dismiss the citizen suit as moot. The courts have held that postcomplaint compliance does not moot a claim for civil penalties.[103] This is so even in a case where the violator has obtained a necessary permit[104] and where the discharger has shut down the plant that was operating in violation of its permit.[105]

---

101. Friends of the Earth v. Crown Cent. Petrol. Corp., No. 6:94-CV-489, 1995 U.S. Dist. LEXIS 16338, at *15 (D. Tex. Sept. 22, 1995).

102. *See* Friends of the Earth v. Chevron Chem. Corp., 129 F.3d 826, 829 (5th Cir. 1997) (finding "indicia" of membership to be adequate even though organization had no formal members); Quad Cities Waterkeeper v. Ballegeer, 84 F. Supp. 3d 848, 859–60 (C.D. Ill. 2015) (finding organization had associational standing despite self-perpetuating board membership), *order clarified sub nom.* Quad Cities Waterkeeper Inc. v. Ballegeer, No. 4:12-CV-4075-SLD-JEH, 2015 WL 6541181 (C.D. Ill. Oct. 27, 2015); Citizens Coal Council v. Matt Canestrale Contracting, Inc., 40 F. Supp. 3d 632, 637–642 (W.D. Pa. 2014) (finding that organization had associational standing to pursue RCRA claim where individual members lacked voting rights at time suit filed); Concerned Citizens around Murphy v. Murphy Oil USA, Inc., 686 F. Supp. 2d 663, 678 (E.D. La. 2010) (finding "indicia of membership" adequate despite informal nature of organization); *cf.* Hunt v. Wash. Apple Advert. Comm'n, 432 U.S. 333 (1977) (state apple commission had standing based on "indicia" of membership even though it had no formal members). *But cf.* Basel Action Network v. Mar. Admin., 370 F. Supp. 2d 57, 68–70 (D.D.C. 2005) (finding that an organization did not meet the indicia of membership standard).

103. *See* Friends of the Earth v. Laidlaw Envtl. Servs. (TOC), Inc. (*Laidlaw II*), 528 U.S. 167, 190–93; Bldg. & Constr. Trades Council of Buffalo v. Downtown Dev., Inc., 448 F.3d 138, 151–52 (2d Cir. 2006); S.F. BayKeeper, Inc. v. Tosco Corp., 309 F.3d 1153, 1160 (9th Cir. 2002); Comfort Lake Ass'n v. Farmland Indus., Inc., 138 F.3d 351, 356 (8th Cir. 1998); Atl. States Legal Found, Inc. v. Stroh Die Casting Co., 116 F.3d 814, 820 (7th Cir. 1997), *cert denied*, 522 U.S. 981 (1997); Nat. Res. Def. Council, Inc. v. Texaco Ref. & Mktg., Inc., 2 F.3d 493, 503 (3d Cir. 1993); Rogue Advocates v. Mountain View Paving, Inc., No. 1:15-cv-01854-CL, 2016 WL 6775636 (D. Or. Nov. 15, 2016) (noting that the majority of circuits have found that postcomplaint compliance does not moot a claim for civil penalties).

104. Envtl. Prot. Info. Ctr. v. Pac. Lumber Co., 430 F. Supp. 2d 996, 1004 (N.D. Cal. 2006).

105. *See Laidlaw II*, 528 U.S. at 188–90.

IV. PLEADING ELEMENTS OF A CITIZEN SUIT

Citizen suits are subject to the usual notice pleading requirements of the Federal Rules of Civil Procedure. Under the Supreme Court's decisions in *Bell Atlantic Corp. v. Twombly*[106] and *Ashcroft v. Iqbal*,[107] plaintiffs may not rely on conclusory allegations, but must allege sufficient facts to establish a claim for relief that is plausible on its face. Because environmental citizen suits are also subject to certain statutory and constitutional conditions precedent to suit, plaintiffs should take care to plead satisfaction of these conditions precedent. These include standing, notice, continuing violation, and lack of diligent state enforcement. Failure to plead these elements can result in dismissal of a citizen suit. Although Rule 9(c) of the Federal Rules of Civil Procedure allows a general allegation of satisfaction of conditions precedent to suit, this rule generally has not been applied to the allegations supporting a citizen suit, and the practice is to plead satisfaction of the conditions precedent specifically.

A. Standing

The level of detail necessary to support standing at the pleading stage is less than the level required at the summary judgment or trial stage. In the most extreme case, the Supreme Court upheld standing based on allegations by members of a student group that increased rail freight rates would reduce the amount of recycling, leading to increased demand for raw materials and consequent destruction of forests used by the student group members for hiking and recreation.[108] Courts have reached different conclusions as to whether the *Twombly* and *Iqbal* pleading standards require plaintiff organizations to identify in the complaint the individual members who will be used to establish standing.[109] In addition, the complaint should plead that the affected members are regular users of the environmental resource at issue and intend to continue using the environmental resource (or would do so but for their concern about environmental contamination).[110]

---

106. 550 U.S. 544 (2007).

107. 556 U.S. 662 (2009).

108. United States v. Students Challenging Regulatory Agency Procedures, 412 U.S. 669, 687–90 (1973).

109. *Compare* W. Va. Highlands Conservancy, Inc. v. Fund 8 Domestic, LLC, No. 2:13–28801, 2014 WL 2740388 (S.D.W. Va. June 17, 2014) (holding that failure to identify individual members with standing requires dismissal of complaint), *with* Ohio Valley Envtl. Coal., Inc. v. Hernshaw Partners, LLC, 984 F. Supp. 2d 589 (S.D.W. Va. 2013) (finding sufficient allegation that "at least one member" of plaintiff organization lived and recreated in vicinity), *and* Ohio Valley Envtl. Coal., Inc. v. Patriot Coal Corp. No. 3:11–0115, 2011 WL 6101921 (S.D.W. Va. Dec. 7, 2011) (general allegations sufficient); *cf. also* Conservation Law Found., Inc. v. Plourde Sand & Gravel Co., No. 13–cv–214–SM, 2014 WL 5781457 (D.N.H. Nov. 6, 2014) (failure to name individual member probably defective, but cured by declaration of individual member establishing injury in fact).

110. *See* Pape v. Lake States Wood Preserving, 948 F. Supp. 697, 700 (D. Mich. 1995).

B. Notice

The complaint should plead compliance with notice requirements, including the date of notice and recipients of the notice letter. It may be advisable to include a copy of the notice letter as an exhibit to the complaint. Even if the notice letter is not attached, a court may deem the notice letter to be part of the complaint and test its sufficiency as part of a motion to dismiss for failure to state a claim under Rule 12(b)(6).

C. Continuing Violation

The complaint must include a good-faith allegation that the challenged violations are continuing or, if intermittent, are likely to recur.[111]

D. Lack of Diligent Prosecution

The complaint should include an allegation that neither EPA nor the state has commenced or diligently prosecuted its own enforcement action against the same violations. One court has held that a mere general allegation that a governmental enforcement proceeding was not diligent was not sufficient and dismissed a complaint for failure to establish specific factors that would rebut the presumption of government diligence.[112]

E. Substantive Elements

Of course, the plaintiff must allege facts sufficient to establish either the substantive violation sought to be remedied or the existence of an imminent and substantial endangerment subject to a remedial order. The exact elements will depend on the statute being enforced.

V. DISCOVERY AND PROOF

The scope and particulars of citizen-suit discovery will vary considerably according to the kind of citizen suit, the violations or conditions complained of, the remedies sought, and the resources available. Discovery efforts usually will focus on the evidence of the violations or conditions complained of (or the nature of the environmental endangerment), the environmental harms or risks caused by the defendants, the defendants' remedial and compliance efforts, the economic

---

111. The Clean Air Act (but not the Clean Water Act) was specifically amended in 1990 to allow suits for wholly past violations. *See* Clean Air Act of 1990, Pub. L. No. 101-549, 104 Stat. 2574, *as recognized in* Fried v. Sungard Recovery Serv.'s, Inc., 916 F. Supp. 465, 467 (E.D. Pa. 1996).

112. N. Cal. River Watch v. Humboldt Petrol., Inc., No C-00-1329 VRW, 2000 U.S. Dist. LEXIS 15939, at *6–7 (N.D. Cal. Oct. 31, 2000); *cf.* Osorio v. Municipality of Loiza, 39 F. Supp. 3d 159 (D.P.R. 2014) (denying motion to dismiss on diligent prosecution grounds based on "well pleaded allegations" of complaint inconsistent with diligent prosecution).

benefits of noncompliance to the defendants, the factors implicated by injunctive relief, and the plaintiffs' standing and capacity to sue. Evidentiary and proof issues in citizen-enforcement suits often focus on the admissibility and weight given to defendants' monitoring records as proof of violations, the sufficiency of plaintiffs' proof of individual injuries in support of standing, and the admissibility of expert testimony to establish environmental harm.

A. Violations

In the typical citizen-enforcement case under the CWA, the plaintiff will rely on publicly filed discharge monitoring reports (DMRs). However, plaintiffs usually will seek any additional evidence or sampling performed by the defendants, and the defendants usually will seek any independent sampling the plaintiffs are aware of. Plaintiffs also usually will seek discovery concerning procedures followed in generating DMRs. Plaintiffs use this information to assess the accuracy of the defendants' monitoring data and to investigate any methodological mistakes or possible falsification of sampling data. In response to this, defendants usually seek any independent sampling obtained by the plaintiffs.

National Pollutant Discharge Elimination Systems (NPDES) permit violations are simplest to prove where the permittee has submitted DMRs showing that it has exceeded permit limitations. Courts have recognized that DMRs submitted by an NPDES permittee constitute judicial admissions of violations.[113] As a result, these reports usually are sufficient to establish a defendant's liability at the summary judgment stage.[114] Plaintiffs also might seek to establish violations of permit standards by conducting their own sampling, but this may be problematic if plaintiffs do not have access to the discharge pipe, and defendants may challenge plaintiffs' sampling and analysis methodology. Some violations, such as violations of narrative water-quality standards that provide for no visible oil sheens or no substantial visible contrast to background conditions, may be subject to proof using lay witnesses and photographic evidence; however, other narrative standards violations, such as toxicity or excess algae growth, may require independent sampling and expert testimony.[115]

---

113. Nat. Res. Def. Council, Inc. v. Cnty. of L.A., 725 F.3d 1194, 1204 (9th Cir. 2013); United States v. Allegheny Ludlum Corp., 366 F.3d 164, 175–76 (3d Cir. 2004) (concluding that DMRs operate as admissions of violation, but leaving open the laboratory-error defense); PennEnvironment v. PPG Indus., Inc., 127 F. Supp. 3d 336, 374 (W.D. Pa. 2015) ("Submissions [of DMRs] to a state agency constitute admissions of liability."); Sierra Club v. Simkins Indus., Inc., 847 F.2d 1109, 1115 n.8 (4th Cir. 1988); United States v. Aluminum Co. of Am., 823 F. Supp. 640, 648 (E.D. Tex. 1993) ("Most courts which have addressed this issue have held that the DMRs filed by a permittee are 'virtually unassailable' as admissions that the violations reflected in the reports occurred.").

114. See Simkins Indus., Inc., 847 F.2d at 1115 n.8; PennEnvironment v. PPG Indus., Inc., 127 F. Supp. 3d 336 (W.D. Pa. 2015) (granting the plaintiff's motion for summary judgment on CWA claims based on the defendant's DMRs).

115. Cf. Nw. Envtl. Advocates v. City of Portland, 56 F.3d 979 (9th Cir 1996) (allowing citizen enforcement of narrative permit standards), Nat. Res. Def. Council v. Metro. Water Reclamation Dist., 175 F. Supp. 3d 1041 (N.D. Ill. 2016) (same).

Continuous air monitoring data compiled by stationary sources of air pollutants also may be admitted to prove a violation of applicable emissions limitations as "credible evidence" of a violation under Clean Air Act Section 113(e).[116] One court also has found that "unauthorized discharge emissions" reports submitted under CERCLA and the Clean Air Act are sufficient to establish a violation of a Clean Air Act Title V permit when they show emissions in excess of permit limitations.[117]

In contaminated-site cases where there may be no publicly filed testing reports, plaintiffs should seek documentation of and examine witnesses who can testify about historic waste generation, management, and disposal practices at the site. Examination of plant employees is often the best way to discover information about actual waste-disposal practices and sources of contamination. Plaintiffs also should seek any remedial investigation studies or environmental audit information generated by the defendant or by third parties.

Where an enforcement action involves conduct of an activity without a required permit, there usually will be no record of discharges generated by the defendant. As a result, plaintiffs must be prepared to prove the elements of the violation independently. For example, in a CWA suit for failure to obtain a permit, plaintiffs must be prepared to prove that the defendant discharged a pollutant from a point source to waters of the United States, and thus was subject to permitting requirements under CWA Sections 301 and 402. Similarly, in a Clean Air Act case brought for failure to obtain a permit, the plaintiffs must show that the defendant's facility is a "major source" subject to permitting requirements under that act.[118] Note that a state permitting agency's determination that a facility is not a major source does not necessarily preclude a citizen suit seeking to establish that the facility is, in fact, subject to permitting requirements.[119]

B. Proof of Imminent and Substantial Endangerment

Proof of an imminent and substantial endangerment subject to judicial remediation under RCRA Section 7002 is considerably more complex and expensive. Expert testimony often will be required. Plaintiffs must be prepared to prove a release of contaminants, exposure of pathways to human or environmental receptors, and risk to exposed people and wildlife. Although government investigations

---

116. Unitek Envtl. Servs., Inc. v. Hawaiian Cement, No. 95-00723 SPK, 1997 U.S. Dist. LEXIS 19261, at *16–17 (D. Haw. Aug. 7, 1997); Sierra Club v. Pub. Serv. Co. of Colo., Inc., 894 F. Supp. 1455, 1459–61 (D. Colo. 1995). *But see* Sierra Club v. Tenn. Valley Auth., 430 F.3d 1337, 1352–53 (11th Cir. 2005) (rejecting reliance on continuous emissions monitoring reports submitted prior to state's adoption of the "credible evidence" rule, which normally would allow the plaintiff to use "any credible evidence" (including required reports) to establish a violation of the statute at issue).

117. St. Bernard Citizens for Envtl. Quality, Inc. v. Chalmette Ref., LLC, 399 F. Supp. 2d 726, 734–36 (E.D. La. 2005).

118. Clean Air Act § 165, 42 U.S.C. § 7475(a)(1)–(2) (2012); Clean Air Act § 172, 42 U.S.C. § 7502(c)(5).

119. *See* Weiler v. Chatham Forest Prods., 370 F.3d 339, 346 (2d Cir. 2004); Citizens for Pa.'s Future v. Ultra Res., Inc., 898 F. Supp. 2d 741, 746 (M.D. Pa. 2012) (finding court had subject-matter jurisdiction to consider the state's failure to designate defendant's facility a major source).

and the defendant's own investigations and reports may be admissible to prove the release, plaintiffs often require their own experts to prove exposure and risk.

C. Proof of Environmental Harm

Although proof of environmental harm may not be required to demonstrate a violation of permitting standards or requirements, or to establish standing, it may be required to make a case for imposition of civil penalties. A showing of environmental harm helps to establish the "seriousness" of the violation—one of the statutory-based factors a judge considers in determining civil penalties.[120] To make such a showing, a plaintiff generally will need to present expert testimony. For example, in a CWA enforcement action, a plaintiff may present an aquatic biologist or fisheries expert to testify about harms to an aquatic ecosystem. In cases where a plaintiff seeks to prove that defendant's violations caused specific public-health harms, plaintiff's expert testimony under the *Daubert* test for admissibility may pose problems.[121] In some cases, plaintiffs may be able to rely on lay testimony to establish environmental harm where direct observation of the harm is possible, as where turbidity impacted a trout fishery.[122]

D. Compliance or Cleanup Efforts

Because compliance efforts may be considered in mitigation of penalties, citizen plaintiffs will be interested in learning about all compliance efforts made by defendants. Prior cleanup efforts by the defendants also may reveal information about the scope of environmental releases or contamination. Furthermore, an examination of plant employees may reveal that they made recommendations for process improvements that the defendant never implemented.

Plaintiffs can obtain this information through a variety of methods. First, communications between the defendants and government agencies often are important sources of information about the scope of environmental pollution and compliance efforts, as well as efforts by defendants to minimize the level of compliance or cleanup required. Such communications normally are available under freedom of information laws. In addition, the defendants' files may contain records of communications that are missing from the public agency's file. Finally, where the defendant claims that it was acting under a reasonable belief that it was in compliance

---

120. *See, e.g.*, Clean Air Act § 113(e), 42 U.S.C. § 7413(e) (2012).

121. *See, e.g.*, Lewis v. FMC Corp., 786 F. Supp. 2d 690, 700–707 (W.D.N.Y. 2011) (rejecting expert opinion that discharges of pesticides posed a risk to human health and environment for purposes of RCRA and CWA claims); Cameron v. Peach Cnty., No. 5:02-CV-41-1 (CAR), 2004 WL 5520003, at *5–6 (M.D. Ga. June 28, 2004) (excluding testimony regarding environmental harm stemming from RCRA violation); *but see* Idaho Rural Council v. Bosma, 143 F. Supp. 2d 1169, 1184–85 (D. Idaho June 2001) (allowing expert testimony over *Daubert* challenge).

122. Catskill Mountains Chapter of Trout Unlimited, Inc. v. City of New York, 244 F. Supp. 2d 41, 48–49 (N.D.N.Y. 2003) (lay testimony described interference with recreational trout fishing), *aff'd in part and remanded in part*, 451 F.3d 77 (2d Cir. 2006).

with environmental requirements, defendant waives its attorney-client privilege and plaintiffs may be able to obtain discovery about compliance advice given by defendant's counsel.[123]

E. Proof of Economic Benefit of Noncompliance

The economic benefit of noncompliance is also a factor considered in assessing penalties. Proof of economic benefits may take several different forms. For example, benefits can include the capital costs avoided or deferred by delaying construction of needed pollution-control facilities. They also can include the operation and maintenance costs of operating such facilities, or the incremental costs of operating such facilities at the level of effectiveness necessary to achieve compliance. In addition, economic benefits can take the form of profits earned by operating in violation of regulatory requirements. Proof of these economic benefits may require expert engineering testimony about the types and costs of effective treatment technologies.

Using capital costs avoided to determine economic benefit is complicated because, assuming the court orders eventual compliance, these costs ultimately are not avoided, but simply deferred. As a result, the true economic benefit to the defendant is the discount value of the use of funds during the delay. This calculation may be further complicated if construction costs increase during the delay. Because of this, plaintiffs usually require expert testimony to establish the defendant's net economic benefit from deferring capital costs.

F. Feasibility and Effectiveness of Compliance Measures

Where citizens seek injunctive relief, they will have to present testimony establishing the appropriate remedial measures. In cases of permit or regulatory violations, this may include expert testimony about appropriate treatment and disposal methods. In cases of contaminated-site remediation, experts may testify to the feasibility and effectiveness of cleanup measures.

G. Plaintiffs' Standing and Organizational Capacity

Defendants often will seek discovery concerning plaintiffs' standing to sue. Organizational plaintiffs may resist discovery into their membership lists on First Amendment privacy and associational grounds.[124] To avoid this conflict, plaintiffs can

---

123. *See* United States v. Bilzerian, 926 F.2d 1285 (2d Cir. 1991) (defendant who asserts defense of good-faith belief in legality of actions waives attorney-client privilege, even where defendant does not propose to testify about advice received from counsel); Catskill Mountains Chapter of Trout Unlimited v. City of New York, No. 00-CV-511 (N.D.N.Y. Sept. 2002) (ordering disclosure of communications with counsel by Clean Water Act defendant asserting good-faith belief in legality of discharges as factor in mitigation of penalties).

124. *See* NAACP v. Alabama *ex rel.* Patterson, 357 U.S. 449, 466 (1958); Sierra Club v. Union Elec. Co., No. 4:14-cv-00408-AGF, 2015 WL 9583394, at *3–5 (E.D. Mo. Dec. 31, 2015); Sierra Club v. Energy Future Holdings Corp., 5:10-cv-156, 2013 WL 21244352, at *3–4 (E.D. Tex. Dec. 30, 2013).

disclose the identities of those members who they intend to rely on as standing witnesses at trial. Defendants often will take the depositions of plaintiffs' standing witnesses to evaluate the genuineness of their claims that they are regular recreational users of the affected environmental resource. Plaintiffs' counsel should be certain to advise standing witnesses that their participation in the litigation may require their attendance at depositions or trial.

Defendants also may seek information about an organizational plaintiff's charter and membership structure to test whether the organization's representation is germane to its purposes. It also will want to determine whether the organization has sufficient membership participation for representational standing.

Plaintiffs must offer proof of standing at trial, even where they have already prevailed against a defendant's motion for summary judgment on standing grounds.[125] To do this, plaintiffs should call individual standing witnesses to testify about their use of the environmental resources at issue, as well as how the challenged activity has diminished or prevented their enjoyment of the resource. An officer of an organizational plaintiff should be prepared to testify about the organization's structure and purpose and to offer the organizational charter into evidence.

VI. DEFENSES

A variety of defenses are available to citizen-suit defendants, apart from contesting the substantive claim of violation. For example, defendants can claim that plaintiffs have failed to meet any of the statutory and constitutional preconditions to suit. They also can bring defenses based on standing, statute of limitations, res judicata, abstention, mootness, or governmental immunity.

A. Statutory Conditions to Suit

Defendants may seek dismissal based on plaintiffs' failure to observe the notice and delay requirements addressed previously. Defendants also can ask for dismissal where the government already is diligently prosecuting an enforcement action. The First Circuit has affirmed summary judgment in favor of citizen-suit

---

125. *See* Nat. Res. Def. Council, Inc. v. Texaco Ref. & Mktg., Inc., 2 F.3d 493, 504–05 (3d Cir. 1993). Prior to the Third Circuit's opinion in *Texaco*, plaintiffs won partial summary judgment on liability but failed to offer evidence of standing at trial. As a result, the district court reopened the trial record to allow plaintiffs to present proof of standing. In other cases where plaintiffs win partial summary judgment on liability, it might not be necessary to establish standing at trial if it is clear that the district court was finally determining the standing issue in plaintiffs' favor, not simply rejecting defendants' challenge to standing. *See also* Borough of Upper Saddle River, N.J. v. Rockland Cnty. Sewer Dist. #1, 16 F. Supp. 3d 294, 315 (S.D.N.Y. 2014) ("At summary judgment phase, the plaintiff must provide specific facts in support of its allegations, and then ultimately, it must prove them at trial."); Friends of the Earth, Inc. v. Gaston Copper Recycling Corp., 9 F. Supp. 2d 589, 600–01 (D.S.C. 1998) (dismissing action after concluding the plaintiffs failed to show standing during trial), *rev'd*, 204 F.3d 149, 155–56 (4th Cir. 2000) (reversing and remanding after concluding plaintiffs had standing).

defendants based on previously issued state administrative orders, even though no penalty was collected.[126] Other courts have found that such orders do not prevent a citizen suit that addresses continuing violations of the underlying permit.[127]

B. Standing

Defendants frequently challenge plaintiffs' standing to sue. In light of the liberalization of the constitutional standing doctrine by the Supreme Court in *Laidlaw*, challenges to standing in citizen actions that enforce regulatory standards generally have not been successful.[128] However, defendants have succeeded in having cases dismissed on standing grounds where plaintiffs cannot identify individual plaintiffs who use the specific environmental resource affected or where an organizational plaintiff lacks representative capacity.[129] Standing challenges also have been more successful in actions seeking review of EPA rulemaking activities.[130]

C. Statute of Limitations

The five-year limitations period of 28 U.S.C. § 2462 has been applied to citizen suits.[131] During the 60-day statutory notice period, the statute of limitations is tolled.[132] Most circuits to address the issue hold that a Clean Air Act suit challenging the failure of an existing source to undergo new source review (NSR) for major plant modifications becomes barred five years after the modifications, but

---

126. N. & S. Rivers Watershed Ass'n, Inc. v. Town of Scituate, 949 F.2d 552, 558 (1st Cir. 1991). *But see* Sierra Club v. Powellton Coal Co., LLC, 662 F. Supp. 2d 514, 523–530 (S.D.W. Va. 2009) (discussing approaches of different circuits before concluding that CWA did not preclude the plaintiffs' claims because the state's law was not comparable to CWA).

127. Cal. Sportfishing Prot. All. v. Chico Scrap Metal, Inc., 728 F.3d 868, 877 (9th Cir. 2013) (noting that only those state administrative compliance orders that impose penalties will bar citizen-enforcement suits); Citizens for a Better Env't v. Union Oil Co., 83 F.3d 1111, 1118 (9th Cir. 1996).

128. *See, e.g.*, Bldg. & Constr. Trades Council of Buffalo v. Downtown Dev., Inc., 448 F.3d 138 (2d Cir. 2006); Am. Canoe Ass'n v. City of Louisa Water & Sewer Comm'n, 389 F.3d 536 (6th Cir. 2004); Citizens Coal Council v. Matt Canestrale Contracting, Inc., 40 F. Supp. 3d 632, 643 (W.D. Pa. 2014); Borough of Upper Saddle River, N.J. v. Rockland Cnty. Sewer Dist. #1, 16 F. Supp. 3d 294, 315–321 (S.D.N.Y. 2014); Concerned Citizens around Murphy v. Murphy Oil USA, Inc., 686 F. Supp. 2d 663, 678 (E.D. La. 2010); Resurrection Bay Conserv. All. v. City of Seward, No. 3:06-CV-0224-RRb, 2008 WL 508499 (D. Alaska Feb. 21, 2008); Kersenbrock v. Stoneman Cattle Co., LCC, No. 07-1044-MLB, 2007 WL 2219288 (D. Kan. July 30, 2007).

129. *See* Basel Action Network v. Mar. Admin., 370 F. Supp. 2d 57, 68 (D.D.C. 2005).

130. *See* Wash. Envtl. Council v. Bellon, 732 F.3d 1131, 1141–44 (9th Cir. 2013) (finding environmental association lacked standing to challenge the agency's failure to regulate greenhouse gas emissions); Ass'n of Battery Recyclers, Inc. v. EPA, 716 F.3d 667, 671 (D.D.C. 2013) (finding industry groups lacked standing because they failed to show a substantial probability of injury); Defenders of Wildlife v. Perciasepe, 714 F.3d 1317, 1323 (D.D.C. 2013) (concluding utility association lacked standing to intervene in lawsuit alleging EPA failed to revise CWA effluent guidelines); Food & Water Watch v. EPA, 5 F. Supp. 3d 62, 74–80 (D.D.C. 2013).

131. Sierra Club v. Okla. Gas & Elec. Co., 816 F.3d 666, 671 (10th Cir. 2016); Sierra Club v. Otter Tail Power Co., 615 F.3d 1008, 1013–1019 (8th Cir. 2010); Nat'l Parks & Conservation Ass'n, Inc. v. Tenn. Valley Auth., 502 F.3d 1316, 1322–25 (11th Cir. 2007).

132. Pub. Interest Research Grp. of N.J., Inc. v. Powell Duffryn Terminals, Inc., 913 F.2d 64, 75 (3d Cir. 1990).

the Sixth Circuit has held that continued operation creates ongoing violations of NSR emissions standards that may be enforced.[133]

D. Res Judicata

Defendants sometimes will claim that a previously concluded government enforcement action precludes a citizen suit on the theory that citizens are deemed to be in privity with the government enforcement agency. Some courts have accepted this defense and dismissed citizen suits on res judicata grounds.[134] Other courts have declined to afford res judicata effect to a prior government action to which citizens were not a party.[135] Courts sometimes give res judicata effect to government enforcement actions commenced after the citizen suit, even though such actions would not invoke the diligent prosecution defense, which comes into play only where the government action is filed first.[136]

E. Abstention

Some courts have abstained from addressing citizen suits while state administrative proceedings addressing the same environmental problem are pending, relying on the doctrine of abstention as in *Burford v. Sun Oil Co.*[137] In that case, the

---

133. *Compare* Sierra Club v. Okla. Gas & Elec. Co., 816 F.3d 666, 673 (10th Cir. 2016), *and* United States v. EME Homer City Generation, L.P., 727 F.3d 274, 284 (3d Cir. 2013), *and* United States v. Midwest Generation, LLC, 720 F.3d 644, 647 (7th Cir. 2013) ("Nothing in the text of § 7475 even hints at the possibility that a fresh violation occurs every day until the end of the universe if an owner that lacks a construction permit operates a completed facility"), *and* Sierra Club v. Otter Tail Power Co., 615 F.3d 1008, 1014–17 (8th Cir. 2010), *and* Nat'l Parks & Conserv. Ass'n v. Tenn. Valley Auth., 502 F.3d 1316, 1326 (11th Cir. 2007) (enforcement of NSR requirements barred), *with* Nat'l Parks Conservation Ass'n, Inc. v. Tenn. Valley Auth., 480 F.3d 410, 418–19 (6th Cir. 2007) (finding that PSD regulations imposed ongoing duties and, therefore, ongoing violations).

134. EPA v. City of Green Forest, 921 F.2d 1394, 1404 (8th Cir. 1990) (consent decree reached as the result of subsequently filed government action barred pending citizen suit); St. Bernard Citizens for Envtl. Quality, Inc. v. Chalmette Ref. LLC, 500 F. Supp. 2d 592, 605–09 (E.D. La. 2007) (holding that government consent decree precludes citizen suit); Ellis v. Gallatin Steel Co., 390 F.3d 461, 473 (6th Cir. 2004) (expressly rejecting diligent prosecution requirement to establish privity).

135. United States v. Metro. Water Recl. Dist. of Chi., 792 F.3d 821 (7th Cir. 2015); Friends of Milwaukee's Rivers v. Milwaukee Metro. Sewerage Dist., 382 F.3d 743, 759 (7th Cir. 2004); Sierra Club v. City & Cnty. of Honolulu, No. CV-4-463, 2008 U.S. Dist. LEXIS 37896, at *6–7 (D. Haw. May 7, 2008); *St. Bernard Citizens for Envtl. Quality, Inc.*, 500 F. Supp. 2d at 604–06.

136. *See Friends of Milwaukee's Rivers*, 382 F.3d 743, 759 (quoting Comfort Lake Ass'n, Inc. v. Dresel Contracting, Inc., 138 F.3d 351, 356 (8th Cir. 1998) ("Even when an agency enforcement action is not commenced until after the citizen suit, final judgment in the agency's court action will be a res judicata or collateral estoppel bar to the earlier citizen suit."); *City of Green Forest*, 921 F.2d at 1404 (consent decree reached as the result of subsequently filed government enforcement action barred pending citizen suit).

137. 319 U.S. 315, 332 (1943); *see* Ellis v. Gallatin Steel Co., 390 F.3d 461, 480 (6th Cir. 2004) (affirming district court's application of *Burford* abstention where citizen suit claimed state misapplied the CAA); Coal. for Health Concern v. LWD, Inc., 60 F.3d 1188, 1193–95 (6th Cir.1995) (holding that district court should have dismissed RCRA claims under *Burford*); Palumbo v. Waste Tech. Indus., 989 F.2d 156, 159–60 (4th Cir. 1993) (same); Ohio Valley Envtl. Coal. v. River Cities Disposal, LLC, No. CV 15-47-DLB-EBA, 2016 WL 1255717, at *7 (E.D. Ky. Mar. 29, 2016). *But see* Weiler v. Chatham Forest Prods. Inc., 370 F.3d 339, 346 (2d Cir. 2004) (allowing citizen suit to proceed despite state agency determination that facility was not a "major source" subject to permitting).

Court declined to hear an appeal of a Texas state regulatory agency decision, holding that "these questions of regulation of the industry by the state administrative agency . . . so clearly involves [*sic*] basic problems of Texas policy that equitable discretion should be exercised to give the Texas courts the first opportunity to consider them."[138] However, some courts have declined to apply *Burford*'s abstention doctrine in environmental cases, reasoning that the federal statutory scheme preempts the state administrative scheme.[139] Courts have relied on this reasoning to reject arguments for abstention based on the asserted primary jurisdiction of state agencies as well.[140]

F. Mootness

As discussed previously, a court may dismiss a citizen suit as moot if violations have ceased and there is no possibility of recurrence. In one such case, the Second Circuit dismissed a citizen suit in which a subsequently filed administrative enforcement action resulted in a consent decree that the court found was certain to result in compliance.[141]

G. Governmental Immunity

The typical citizen-suit provision specifically contemplates citizen enforcement against governmental entities. For example, CWA Section 505 allows citizens to bring suit against "any person (including (i) the United States, and (ii) any other governmental instrumentality or agency to the extent permitted by the eleventh amendment to the Constitution)."[142] However, the Supreme Court has held that this provision does not subject U.S. government agencies to civil penalties.[143] In response to this and similar rulings, Congress amended one environmental citizen-suit provision—RCRA—to allow courts to levy civil penalties against federal facilities.[144] State facilities enjoy 11th Amendment immunity from citizen-penalty actions, but still are subject to injunctive relief under *Ex parte Young*.[145]

---

138. *Burford*, 319 U.S. at 332.

139. *See, e.g.*, Chico Serv. Station, Inc. v. Sol P.R. Ltd., 633 F.3d 20, 31–32 (1st Cir. 2011); Adkins v. VIM Recycling, Inc., 644 F.3d 483, 505–07 (7th Cir. 2011); Flint Riverkeeper, Inc. v. S. Mills, Inc., 276 F. Supp. 3d 1359 (M.D. Ga. 2017) (finding *Burford* abstention does not apply to citizen suits under the CWA and collecting cases).

140. *See, e.g.*, Nat. Res. Def. Council v. Metro. Water Rec. Dist., 175 F. Supp. 3d 1041, 1049 (N.D. Ill. 2016); Ass'n of Irritated Residents v. Fred Schakel Dairy, 2008 WL 850136, at *10–11 (E.D. Cal. 2008).

141. *See* Atl. States Legal Found., Inc. v. Eastman Kodak Co., 933 F.2d 124, 128 (2d Cir. 1991) (remanding to district court for a determination of whether consent decree rendered plaintiffs' claims moot).

142. 33 U.S.C. § 1365(a)(1) (2012).

143. U.S. Dep't of Energy v. Ohio, 503 U.S. 607 (1992), *superseded by statute*, Federal Facility Compliance Act of 1992, Pub. L. No. 102-386, 106 Stat. 1505 (codified as amended at 42 U.S.C. § 6961 (2012)).

144. RCRA § 6001; 42 U.S.C. § 6961(a) (2012).

145. 209 U.S. 123 (1908).

VII. REMEDIES

Remedies available in a citizen suit include injunctive relief and, where provided by statute, civil penalties. In addition, successful plaintiffs may be entitled to recover attorneys' fees and litigation costs.

A. Injunctive Relief

Generally, citizen-suit provisions authorize the district courts to "enforce" the environmental standard or order that the defendant is accused of violating.[146] In addition, the RCRA citizen-suit provision authorizes courts to "restrain" any person responsible for "an imminent and substantial endangerment" to the environment, and "to order such person to take such other action as may be necessary."[147] This relief does not include restitution for cleanup costs incurred by the plaintiff.[148]

In addition, the Supreme Court has held that ESA Section 7 requires courts to issue an injunction against a defendant charged with jeopardizing the existence of an endangered species.[149] However, a court will not automatically enjoin violations of other environmental statute requirements. Rather, the court will engage in a traditional balancing of the equities to determine the appropriate injunctive relief.[150] The objective of injunctive relief is to secure prompt compliance with statutory mandates.[151]

Injunctive relief may take the form of an injunction against the violative activity, where warranted,[152] or may take the form of an injunction requiring the defendant to take prompt action to obtain necessary permits.[153] In addition, in an RCRA

---

146. *See, e.g.*, Clean Water Act § 505(a), 33 U.S.C. § 1365(a) (2012).

147. RCRA § 7002(a), 42 U.S.C. § 6972(a).

148. Meghrig v. KFC W., Inc., 516 U.S. 479, 488 (1996).

149. Tenn. Valley Auth. v. Hill, 437 U.S. 153, 194–95 (1978); *see also* Hawksbill Sea Turtle v. Fed. Emergency Mgmt. Agency, 126 F.3d 461, 478 (3d Cir. 1997) (remanding to district court to determine whether ESA § 9 claim similarly requires courts to issue an injunction).

150. Weinberger v. Romero-Barcelo, 456 U.S. 305, 311 (1982) (an injunction is "not a remedy which issues as of course); Friends of the Earth, Inc., v. Laidlaw Envtl. Servs., Inc. (*Laidlaw II*), 528 U.S. 167, 192–93 (2000); Sierra Club v. Va. Elec. & Power Co., 247 F. Supp. 3d 753, 764–767 (E.D. Va. 2017) (denying the plaintiff's request for injunction requiring the defendant to move millions of tons of coal ash after balancing the equities); City of Newburgh v. Sarna, 690 F. Supp. 2d 136, 163–64 (S.D.N.Y. 2010) (denying injunctive relief in CWA citizen suit after finding no irreparable harm), *aff'd in part, appeal dismissed in part*, 406 F. App'x 557 (2d Cir. 2011).

151. *Laidlaw II*, 528 U.S. at 192.

152. Waste Action Project v. Astro Auto Wrecking, LLC, 274 F. Supp. 3d 1133, 1138 (W.D. Wash. 2017) (ordering stipulated injunctive relief); Idaho Conservation League v. Magar, 2015 WL 632367, at *8–10 (D. Idaho Feb. 13, 2015) (granting injunction in CWA claim requiring the defendant to take "immediate action to prevent illegal discharges in the short term").

153. *See, e.g.*, *Weinberger*, 456 U.S. at 320; Miccosukee Tribe of Indians v. S. Fla. Water Mgmt. Dist., 280 F.3d 1364, 1371 (11th Cir. 2002), *vacated on other grounds*, 541 U.S. 95 (2004); Waste Action Project v. Astro Auto Wrecking, LLC, 274 F. Supp. 3d 1133, 1138 (W.D. Wash. 2017) (ordering injunctive relief including requiring compliance with CWA and improvements of facility); Sierra Club v. Va. Elec. & Power Co., 247 F. Supp. 3d 753, 764–767 (E.D. Va. 2017) (requiring the defendant to conduct more extensive testing and reopen its solid waste permit application).

imminent and substantial endangerment case, the court may order site-remediation remedies, including excavation and disposal of contaminated soils.[154]

B. Civil Penalties

Most, but not all, of the environmental citizen-suit provisions authorize the district court to "apply any appropriate civil penalties."[155] Penalties assessed in citizen suits are payable to the U.S. Treasury, not to plaintiffs.[156]

Under the CWA, courts setting civil penalties should consider "the seriousness of the violation or violations, the economic benefit (if any) resulting from the violation, any history of such violations, any good-faith efforts to comply with the applicable requirements, the economic impact of the penalty on the violator, and such other matters as justice may require."[157] The Clean Air Act sets forth similar factors.[158] Courts also sometimes consider EPA penalty settlement policy guidelines in assessing penalties.[159] Courts have held that under the CWA, a penalty is mandatory once a violation has been established.[160] EPA periodically adjusts the maximum available amount of civil penalties to account for inflation.[161]

---

154. Voggenthaler v. Md. Square LLC, 724 F.3d 1050, 1056 (9th Cir. 2013) ("RCRA, in 42 U.S.C. § 6972, authorizes citizen suits for two types of injunctive relief—an injunction ordering the responsible parties to clean up the contamination and an injunction ordering them to stop any further violations."); Francisco Sanchez v. Esso Standard Oil Co., 572 F.3d 1, 20 (1st Cir. 2009) (finding the broad equitable power granted by RCRA means that a private citizen may seek an injunction that "orders a responsible party to 'take action' by attending to the cleanup or proper disposal of toxic wastes"); Interfaith Cmty. Org. v. Honeywell Int'l, Inc., 399 F.3d 248, 264–67 (3d Cir. 2005); LAJIM, LLC v. Gen. Elec. Co., No. 13-CV-50348, 2017 WL 3922139, at *2 (N.D. Ill. Sept. 7, 2017) ("Despite the awkward wording, courts have consistently found that all types of injunctive relief are available.").

155. Clean Water Act § 505(a), 33 U.S.C. § 1365(a) (2012).

156. *See* Middlesex Cnty. Sewerage Auth. v. Nat'l Sea Clammers Ass'n, 453 U.S. 1, 14 n.25 (1981) ("under the [Federal Water Pollution Control Act], civil penalties, payable to the Government, also may be ordered by the court").

157. Clean Water Act § 309(d), 33 U.S.C. § 1319(d) (2012).

158. Clean Air Act § 113(e)(1), 42 U.S.C. § 7413(e)(1) (2012).

159. U.S. Envtl. Prot. Agency, Office of Regulatory Enf't, Enforcement Response Policy for Sections 302, 311 and 312 of the Emergency Planning and Community Right-to-Know Act and Section 103 of the Comprehensive Environmental Response Compensation, and Liability Act (1999), https://www.epa .gov/sites/production/files/documents/epcra304.pdf; U.S. Envtl. Prot. Agency, RCRA Civil Penalty Policy (2003), https://www.epa.gov/sites/production/files/documents/rcpp2003-fnl.pdf; U.S. Envtl. Prot. Agency, Supplemental Guidance to the 1995 Interim Clean Water Act Settlement Penalty Policy for Violations of the Industrial Stormwater Requirements (2016), https://www.epa.gov/sites/production /files/2016-09/documents/industrialswpenaltyguidance.pdf; U.S. Envtl. Prot. Agency, Interim Clean Water Act Settlement Penalty Policy (1995); *see also* Atl. States Legal Found. v. Tyson Foods, 897 F.2d 1128, 1131 (11th Cir. 1990) (noting position taken by EPA in assessing certain penalties); Nat. Res. Def. Council v. Texaco Ref. & Mktg., Inc., 800 F. Supp. 1, 23 (D. Del. 1992) (citing EPA training manual), *aff'd in part, rev'd in part on other grounds*, 2 F.3d 493 (3d Cir. 1993); Atl. States Legal Found. v. Simco Leather Corp., 755 F. Supp. 59 (N.D. N.Y. 1991).

160. *See* United States v. Lexington-Fayette Urban Cnty. Gov't, 591 F.3d 484, 488 (6th Cir. 2010) (finding that "several courts of appeals have read [CWA] to require that a civil penalty must be imposed in every case in which a court has found a . . . violation"); *Tyson Foods, Inc.*, 897 F.2d 1128, 1140–41 (11th Cir. 1990) (awarding penalties under the Clean Water Act); Idaho Conservation League v. Atlanta Gold Corp., 879 F. Supp. 2d 1148, 1156 (D. Idaho 2012) ("[T]he Act mandates civil penalties if violations of the CWA are found.").

161. *See* 40 C.F.R. § 19.4 (2017).

C. Attorneys' Fees

Each of the statutory citizen-suit provisions allows for "costs of litigation (including reasonable attorney and expert witness fees)" where the court determines such fees to be "appropriate."[162] Most of the statutes limit the award of such fees to the "prevailing or substantially prevailing" party.[163] Courts have interpreted these fee-shifting provisions consistently with similar fee-shifting provisions of the civil-rights statutes, allowing successful plaintiffs to recover fees as a matter of course, but limiting fee awards to successful defendants in cases that were frivolous.[164] A fee award will be based upon the reasonable hours spent on the matter multiplied by an hourly rate appropriate to the location of the litigation. A court may not award a contingency enhancement to such an hourly rate–based fee award.[165]

VIII. SETTLEMENTS

Several factors promote the likelihood of settlements in an environmental citizen suit. Penalty awards are payable to the U.S. Treasury, not to the private plaintiffs, so plaintiffs lack a strong economic incentive to go to trial. In addition, defendants often would rather negotiate compliance and remediation plans than take their chances with having a federal district judge determine what the appropriate technology for compliance and remediation should be. Finally, both sides would prefer that money that might otherwise be paid in penalties be used for local environmental improvement and remediation projects (for which the defendant may claim some public relations benefit).

A typical settlement of an environmental citizen suit usually will provide a schedule for remediation and compliance measures, stipulated penalties for future violations of regulatory or permit standards, and an environmental benefit project to ameliorate environmental impacts of the violation. The court may maintain jurisdiction over the controversy for the purposes of enforcing the settlement terms.

---

162. Clean Air Act § 304(d), 42 U.S.C. § 7604(d) (2012); Clean Water Act § 505(d), 33 U.S.C. § 1365(d) (2012); RCRA § 7002(e), 42 U.S.C. § 6972(e) (2012); CERCLA § 310(f), 42 U.S.C. § 9659(f) (2012); Safe Drinking Water Act § 1449(d), 42 U.S.C. § 300j-8(d) (2012); Endangered Species Act § 11(g)(4), 16 U.S.C. § 1540(g)(4) (2012); EPCRA § 326(f), 42 U.S.C. § 11046(f) (2012); Toxic Substances Control Act § 20(c)(2), 15 U.S.C. § 2619(c)(2) (2012).

163. *But see* Endangered Species Act § 11(g)(4), 16 U.S.C. § 1540(g)(4) (2012); Toxic Substances Control Act § 20(c)(2), 15 U.S.C. § 2619(c)(2) (2012); Safe Drinking Water Act § 1449(d), 42 U.S.C. § 300j-8(d) (2012) (all omitting "prevailing party" language).

164. *See* Browder v. City of Moab, 427 F.3d 717, 723 (10th Cir. 2005); Sierra Club v. City of Little Rock, 351 F.3d 840, 846 (8th Cir. 2003); Morris-Smith v. Moulton Niguel Water Dist., 234 F.3d 1277 (9th Cir. 2000); Simsbury-Avon Pres. Soc'y, LLC v. Metacon Gun Club, Inc., No. CIV3:04CV803 JBA, 2010 WL 1286812, at *1 (D. Conn. Mar. 29, 2010) (collecting cases); *cf.* Hensley v. Eckerhart, 461 U.S. 424, 433 n.7 (1983) (standards for fee-shifting under Clean Air Act are the same as standards under the Civil Rights Act).

165. Dague v. City of Burlington, 505 U.S. 557 (1992); *see also* Loesel v. City of Frankenmuth, 743 F. Supp. 2d 619, 641 (E.D. Mich. 2010).

The CWA and CAA citizen-suit provisions require that the parties notify the Department of Justice (DOJ) and observe a 45-day waiting period prior to entry of any consent judgment.[166] EPA has published the regulations governing the procedure for notice at 40 C.F.R. § 135.5. Once notified, DOJ usually files a reservation of rights, stating that it is not bound by the provisions of the settlement and may object to the settlement. DOJ is most likely to object if it determines that the proposed settlement inappropriately fails to provide for a payment of penalties to the United States, though the objection may be overruled if the court decides a civil penalty is not mandatory.[167] DOJ also is likely to object to any consent judgment that provides for a payment to the citizen plaintiffs (other than payment of attorneys' fees and costs). DOJ also may consider EPA's supplemental environmental project policy in commenting on the proposed consent judgment.[168] Some citizen suits are settled with stipulations of dismissal combined with a separate settlement agreement rather than via a consent decree. Since these stipulations do not result in a consent judgment, they do not fall within the CWA and CAA requirement that notice be provided to the Department of Justice.

A settlement also may resolve plaintiffs' claim for attorneys' fees, but it need not. If the attorneys' fees claim is not resolved by the settlement, a court usually considers the plaintiffs to have prevailed as long as the settlement agreement grants the plaintiffs some form of substantive relief.[169]

---

166. Clean Water Act § 505(c)(3), 33 U.S.C. § 1365(c)(3) (2012); Clean Air Act § 304(c)(3), 42 U.S.C. § 7604(c)(3) (2012).

167. *See* Sierra Club v. Elec. Controls Designs, Inc., 909 F.2d 1350, 1352 (9th Cir. 1990); Friends of the Earth v. Archer Daniels Midland Co., 780 F. Supp. 95, 98 (N.D.N.Y. 1992). *Cf.* Haw.'s Thousand Friends, Life of Land, Inc. v. City & Cnty. of Honolulu, 149 F.R.D. 614, 617 (D. Haw. 1993) ("[C]ivil penalties, *if assessed*, must be paid to the United States Treasury . . . a consent *decree can be entered* even if it does not provide for a civil penalty to be paid to the United States Treasury.").

168. 63 Fed. Reg. 24,796–97 (May 5, 1998).

169. *See, e.g.*, Idaho Conserv. League, Inc. v. Russell, 946 F.2d 717, 719 (9th Cir. 1991)); Cmty. Ass'n for Restoration of the Env't v. Henra Bosma Dairy, No. CY-98-2011, 2001 U.S. Dist. LEXIS 3579, at *34 (E.D. Wash.); Pa. Envtl. Def. Found. v. Packaging Corp. of Am., No. 87-4739, 1989 U.S. Dist. LEXIS 380, at *8 (E.D. Pa. Jan. 18, 1989).

CHAPTER 8

Pesticide Litigation

Claudia O'Brien, Stacey VanBelleghem, Laura Glickman, and Stijn Van Osch

I. INTRODUCTION

The Environmental Protection Agency (EPA) comprehensively regulates pesticides under the Federal Insecticide, Fungicide, and Rodenticide Act (FIFRA), which requires registration of pesticides before they can be lawfully sold.[1] FIFRA establishes a risk-benefit standard that EPA implements for approval of registrations.[2] Pesticide residues in food are even more stringently regulated under the Federal Food, Drug, and Cosmetic Act (FFDCA), which imposes a health-only safety standard for approval.[3] Pesticide litigation often involves application and interpretation of FIFRA and FFDCA, but it takes many other forms as well. Some of these forms include EPA civil penalty actions for statutory violations; cases seeking to enforce regulatory duties under other environmental statutes, including the Endangered Species Act (ESA), the Clean Water Act (CWA), and the National Environmental Policy Act (NEPA); arbitrations seeking compensation for use of a registrant's proprietary data to obtain "follow-on" registrations; litigation addressing new regulatory questions relating to biotechnology; and tort cases implicating the preemption of certain common law claims by pesticide law. This chapter discusses these as well as other forms of pesticide litigation.

---

1. 7 U.S.C. § 136a(a) (2018).
2. 7 U.S.C. § 136(c)(5) (2018).
3. 21 U.S.C. §§ 301–399 (2018).

II. FIFRA LITIGATION

A. Registration and Labeling

Under FIFRA Section 3, all pesticides distributed or sold in the United States must be registered with EPA.[4] As a threshold matter, the term "pesticide" is defined in the statute,[5] and EPA generally regulates a substance as a pesticide if it is intended for a pesticidal purpose.[6] In determining such intent, EPA's regulations identify factors, including the claims or conduct of the seller, characteristics of the product, or the seller's knowledge of the pesticidal use of the product.[7]

When applying for a registration, the prospective registrant must submit to EPA a complete copy of the pesticide labeling, including a statement of all claims to be made for the pesticide and directions for use; the complete formula of the pesticide; and description of the tests, data, or public literature upon which the claims are based.[8] FIFRA expressly protects trade secrets or other confidential commercial or financial information with certain limitations.[9]

In order to register a pesticide under FIFRA, EPA must make certain findings, including that the product's "composition is such as to warrant the proposed claims for it," the proposed label complies with FIFRA, and the chemical "when used in accordance with widespread and commonly recognized practice . . . will not generally cause unreasonable adverse effects on the environment."[10] The statute defines "unreasonable adverse effects on the environment" to include "any unreasonable risk to man or the environment, taking into account the economic, social, and environmental costs and benefits of the use of any pesticide[]."[11] Thus, EPA's registration evaluation takes into account both risks and benefits.

Upon evaluating these factors, EPA can approve a registration, deny a registration, or conditionally approve a registration.[12] Conditional registrations under FIFRA may be granted in circumstances where there are missing data and the registration is conditioned upon submission of required data.[13] EPA may also impose conditions unrelated to data requirements when it conditionally registers

---

4. 7 U.S.C. § 136a(a).

5. 7 U.S.C. § 136(u) ("'pesticide' means (1) any substance or mixture of substances intended for preventing, destroying, repelling, or mitigating any pest, (2) any substance or mixture of substances intended for use as a plant regulator, defoliant, or desiccant").

6. 40 C.F.R. § 152.15 (2018) (explaining when "[a] substance is considered to be intended for a pesticidal purpose").

7. *See id.*

8. 7 U.S.C. § 136a(c)(1). *See also* 40 C.F.R. § 152.50 (describing application materials for new product registration, including data requirements). Under 7 U.S.C. § 136d(a)(2), "[i]f at any time after the registration of a pesticide the registrant has additional factual information regarding unreasonable adverse effects on the environment . . . the registrant shall submit such information to the Administrator."

9. 7 U.S.C. § 136h.

10. 7 U.S.C. § 136a(c)(5)(D).

11. 7 U.S.C. § 136(bb) (2018).

12. 7 U.S.C. § 136a(c)(5), (6), (7).

13. *Id.* § 136a(c)(7).

a pesticide.[14] In recent years, EPA has also utilized the conditional registration provision when an active ingredient is scheduled to undergo registration review and EPA anticipates that additional data submissions will be required through that process.

EPA issues a label for each registered pesticide, setting forth the manner in which it may be used; the statute makes it unlawful "to use any pesticide in a manner inconsistent with its labeling."[15]

Although there has long been litigation focused on EPA's implementation of FIFRA registration and labeling, the focus of litigation shifts with developments in pesticide law and policy. In recent years, EPA has focused on developing additional tools and guidance to evaluate potential effects of pesticide registration and reregistration on bees and other pollinators—an emerging issue in pesticide registration. As part of this effort, EPA has developed a number of guidance documents on assessing risks to pollinators as part of EPA's stringent risk assessment process.[16] EPA has relied upon these new policy and guidance documents in recent pesticide registrations under FIFRA, and EPA's application of these policies have been the subject of litigation in recent years. For example, in *Pollinator Stewardship Council v. EPA*, the Ninth Circuit vacated EPA's unconditional registration of an active ingredient, finding EPA's record lacked sufficient data regarding risk to bees and EPA did not follow its own risk assessment framework.[17] In *Ellis v. Housenger*, a district court deferred to EPA and dismissed a challenge to EPA's decision to deny an imminent-hazard petition and not to suspend its approval of an active ingredient in the face of allegations regarding harm to pollinators.[18]

Another recent issue in registration litigation is the consideration of synergistic effects of pesticides in registration analysis. Synergism, when used in this context, refers to additive effects of combining two or more chemicals. In *Natural Resources Defense Council v. EPA*, the agency abandoned its defense of its approval of certain uses involving two active ingredients in light of new information in a patent application that the agency had not considered—specifically claims involving synergistic effects of those ingredients that led to greater effects on target pest species.[19] The court granted EPA's motion for voluntary remand for consideration

---

14. *See* Woodstream Corp. v. Jackson, 845 F. Supp. 2d 174, 179–82 (D.D.C. 2012).

15. 7 U.S.C. § 136j(a)(2)(G) (2018).

16. *See, e.g.*, U.S. Envtl. Prot. Agency, Pollinator Risk Assessment Guidance, https://www.epa.gov/pollinator-protection/pollinator-risk-assessment-guidance (last visited on June 13, 2018); U.S. Envtl. Prot. Agency, How We Assess Risk to Pollinators, https://www.epa.gov/pollinator-protection/how-we-assess-risks-pollinators (last visited on June 13, 2018).

17. Pollinator Stewardship Council v. EPA, 806 F.3d 520, 529–30 (9th Cir. 2015).

18. Ellis v. Housenger, 252 F. Supp. 3d 800, 809–11 (N.D. Cal. 2017). Ultimately, the district court granted summary judgment to plaintiffs due to EPA's failure to consult with the U.S. Fish and Wildlife Service or National Marine Fisheries Service. *Id.* at 825–27.

19. EPA, Respondents' Motion for Voluntary Vacatur and Remand, Nat. Res. Def. Council v. EPA, No. 14-73353, Dkt. #121 (9th Cir. Nov. 24, 2015) ("[I]n light of the new information regarding the potential synergism of the two . . . ingredients, EPA seeks a voluntary remand with vacatur to reconsider the . . . registration.").

of this information.[20] On remand, EPA reviewed the potential for synergistic effects and reaffirmed the original approval of the new uses.[21]

Finally, it should be noted that FIFRA requires EPA to periodically review each registered active ingredient to determine whether it still satisfies the registration standard. The statute mandates that EPA complete this process, called registration review, for every active ingredient registered as of October 1, 2007, by October 1, 2022, and then periodically review registrations every 15 years after registration.[22] The statute gives EPA authority to seek data from registrants in support of this process[23] and EPA may impose requirements and restrictions in a registration review decision. Given the significant volume of decisions that EPA will make through this process, litigation is likely to follow.

B. Enforcement

Section 12(a) of FIFRA specifically lists all unlawful acts.[24] These acts include selling or distributing a pesticide that is not registered, contains different claims or has a different composition than registered, or is misbranded or adulterated.[25] It is also unlawful to, inter alia, alter required labeling in any way, fail to keep or submit records, improperly advertise or sell restricted pesticides, use a pesticide inconsistent with its labeling, or violate cancellation or suspension orders.[26]

Section 14 of FIFRA contains penalties for violations of the Act, and provides for both civil and criminal liability.[27] First, "[a]ny registrant, commercial applicator, wholesaler, dealer, retailer or other distributor" may be civilly liable up to $5,000 per offense under FIFRA for violating any provision of the statute.[28] The civil penalty as of 2018 has been raised to $19,446 to account for inflation under the Federal Civil Penalties Inflation Adjustment Act amendments of 2015.[29] Private

---

20. Nat. Res. Def. Council v. EPA, No. 14-73353, Dkt. #128 (9th Cir. Jan. 25, 2016).

21. U.S. Envtl. Prot. Agency, Final Registration Decision of Enlist Duo, EPA-HQ-OPP-2016-0594-0660 (Jan. 12, 2017), https://www.regulations.gov/docket?D=EPA-HQ-OPP-2016-0594.

22. 7 U.S.C. § 136a(g)(1)(A).

23. *Id.* § 136a(g)(2).

24. 7 U.S.C. § 136j(a).

25. *Id.*

26. *Id.*

27. *Id.* § 136*l*.

28. *Id.* § 136*l*(a)(1). EPA may also determine that a warning in lieu of a fine is appropriate, if the violator exercised due care or did not cause significant harm to health or the environment. *Id.* § 136*l*(a)(4). The term "offense" is not defined in the statute or any EPA regulations or guidance. Thus, EPA has significant discretion in deciding what counts as a single "offense" for purposes of enforcement. For example, EPA has a "graduated penalty" policy that adjusts the cumulative penalty for multiple unlawful sales or distributions downward. Within that context, EPA has "the discretion to group together similar product violations" for purposes of calculating the penalty, or on the opposite end of the severity scale, "assess penalties of up to the statutory maximum for each violation, when appropriate." U.S. Envtl. Prot. Agency, FIFRA Enforcement Response Policy 25–26 (2009), https://www.epa.gov/sites/production/files/documents/fifra-erp1209.pdf. Negotiating over what exactly constitutes a single "offense" may therefore be part of EPA's strategy in negotiating settlements. *Cf. id.* at 28 (noting that "EPA has broad discretion to settle cases with appropriate penalties").

29. Civil Monetary Penalty Inflation Adjustment Rule, 83 Fed. Reg. 1190, 1193 (Jan. 10, 2018); Memorandum from Susan Parker Bodine, Assistant Adm'r, U.S. Envtl. Prot. Agency, to EPA Staff, Transmittal

applicators are subject to lower fines, and can only be fined for violations after having received prior warnings or having previously been subject to a citation.[30] Penalties are assessed following a hearing, and in determining the penalty, EPA must take into account "the size of the business of the person charged, the effect on the person's ability to continue in business, and the gravity of the violation."[31]

Second, any registrant, registration applicant, or producer who "knowingly violates" any provision of FIFRA may be criminally liable up to $50,000 in total, or imprisoned for up to one year, or both.[32] Commercial applicators and private applicators are subject to lower maximum criminal penalties for knowing violations.[33] Successor liability may be levied by EPA for fines imposed under FIFRA, where doing so "will facilitate enforcement of the Act."[34]

Because penalties are assessed on a per-instance basis,[35] the total penalty arising out of an ongoing FIFRA violation can be much larger. For example, in 2014, after years of proceedings, a registrant paid a $738,000 civil penalty in response to allegations of multiple violations of advertising restrictions and making unrestricted claims about its restricted-use pesticide. EPA stated this was the largest penalty ever imposed by an administrative law judge for a FIFRA violation.[36]

States that have adopted pesticide-use laws and implemented proper enforcement procedures for such laws are primarily responsible for enforcing FIFRA.[37] EPA issued an interpretive rule in 1983 that sets forth when it will grant enforcement primacy to states.[38] EPA and at least one court has clarified, however, that Congress's vesting of primary enforcement responsibility in the states does not divest

---

of the 2018 Annual Civil Monetary Penalty Inflation Adjustment Rule (Jan. 11, 2018), https://www.epa .gov/sites/production/files/2018-01/documents/amendmentstotheepascivilpenaltypoliciestoaccountfo-rinflation011518.pdf.

30. 7 U.S.C. § 136*l*(a)(2).

31. *Id.* § 136*l*(a)(3)–(4).

32. *Id.* § 136*l*(b)(1)(A).

33. *Id.* § 136*l*(b)(1)(B) (commercial applicators liable for maximum of $25,000, one year imprisonment, or both); § 136*l*(b)(2) (private applicators can only be guilty of a misdemeanor and fined up to $1,000, 30 days imprisonment, or both).

34. Oner II, Inc. v. EPA, 597 F.2d 184, 186 (9th Cir. 1979); *accord* Washington v. United States, 930 F. Supp. 474, 481 (W.D. Wash. 1996). There has been some debate on whether state law or federal common law determines successor liability. *See In re* William E. Comley, Inc. & Bleach Tek, Inc., 11 E.A.D. 247, at n.11 (EPA, Jan. 14, 2004) (discussing split of authority with respect to CERCLA liability, but finding that successor liability may apply under both state and federal common law).

35. As noted *supra* note 28, the definition of a single "instance" or "offense" is subject to significant agency discretion.

36. Press Release, U.S. Envtl. Prot. Agency, EPA Ensures Company Discloses Pesticide Hazards (June 6, 2014), https://archive.epa.gov/epapages/newsroom_archive/newsreleases/15e500e1ffaf8ca 085257cef006a6026.html.

37. 7 U.S.C. § 136w-1(a).

38. Federal Insecticide, Fungicide, and Rodenticide Act, State Primary Enforcement Responsibilities, Final Interpretive Rule, 48 Fed. Reg. 404 (Jan. 5, 1983) (codified at 40 C.F.R. § 173).

the federal government of the power to criminally prosecute violators.[39] On the other hand, private citizens do not have a private right of action to enforce FIFRA.[40]

EPA's most recent FIFRA enforcement response policy was issued in December 2009, and provides guidance on what type of civil enforcement action—such as warnings, seizures, injunctions, or penalties—EPA will take under which circumstances.[41] It also provides guidance on the computation of civil penalties, taking into account the required statutory factors.[42]

C. Cancellation, Reclassification, and Suspension

If EPA later determines that a pesticide, pesticide label, or other related materials do not comply with the registration requirements of FIFRA or later determines that a pesticide "when used in accordance with widespread and commonly recognized practice, generally causes unreasonable adverse effects on the environment,"[43] FIFRA provides express processes that EPA must follow. EPA may (1) cancel the registration or change a pesticide's classification, (2) suspend the registration pending cancellation or reclassification, or (3) issue an emergency order immediately suspending a registration pending further proceedings.[44]

I. Cancellation and Reclassification

Upon a finding of noncompliance with FIFRA or that a pesticide "generally causes unreasonable adverse effects on the environment," EPA may either issue a notice of intent to cancel or reclassify a pesticide or may issue a notice of intent to hold

---

39. *Id.* at 406–07 ("If, after consultation with the State, EPA determines that the State's intended enforcement response to the violation is inappropriate . . . EPA may bring its own action after notice to the State."); U.S. Envtl. Prot. Agency, FIFRA Enforcement Response Policy 15 (2009), https://www.epa.gov/sites/production/files/documents/fifra-erp1209.pdf ("While Congress delegated to the states primary enforcement authority for pesticide use violations, FIFRA does not create exclusive enforcement jurisdictions in the states."); United States v. Orkin Exterminating Co., 688 F. Supp. 223, 227 (W.D. Va. 1988) ("Absent 'clear and unambiguous' language restricting the Attorney General's authority, it would be improper for this court to rule that the Attorney General does not have the authority to bring a criminal prosecution. After reviewing FIFRA, and its legislative history, this court holds that there is no such language in the Act diminishing the Attorney General's authority."); *cf.* Reckitt Benckiser Inc. v. EPA, 613 F.3d 1131, 1134–35 (D.C. Cir. 2010) ("EPA can pursue a criminal misbranding action, in which it bears the burden to prove a violation beyond a reasonable doubt.").

40. *See, e.g.*, Voss v. Saint Martin Co-op, 376 F. App'x 662, 663 (8th Cir. 2010) (citing Bates v. Dow AgroSciences, LLC, 544 U.S. 431, 448 (2005)) (affirming district court's holding that "FIFRA does not provide a private right of action to farmers and others injured as a result of a manufacturer's violation of FIFRA's labeling requirements"); No Spray Coal., Inc. v. City of New York, 252 F.3d 148, 150 (2d Cir. 2001) ("FIFRA is not enforceable by a private right of action."); Cottrell, Ltd. v. Biotrol Int'l, Inc., 191 F.3d 1248, 1255 (10th Cir. 1999) (holding that FIFRA does not explicitly or implicitly allow private enforcement); Almond Hill Sch. v. USDA, 768 F.2d 1030 (9th Cir. 1985) (holding that FIFRA does not allow private enforcement and the statute is not of the type for which Section 1983 enforcement claims are available); Fiedler v. Clark, 714 F.2d 77, 79 (9th Cir. 1983) (holding that neither FIFRA nor FFDCA allow private enforcement).

41. FIFRA Enforcement Response Policy, *supra* note 39, at 4–5.

42. *Id.* at 15–28.

43. 7 U.S.C. § 136d(b).

44. *Id.* § 136d(b), (c).

a hearing to determine whether or not a registration should be canceled or reclassified.[45] Courts have construed "generally causes unreasonable adverse effects" to mean that "the Administrator may cancel a registration if it appears to him that the pesticide commonly causes unreasonable risks. . . . [T]he Administrator need not find that use of a pesticide commonly causes undesirable consequences. . . ."[46]

FIFRA authorizes reclassification of a pesticide from general to restricted use if EPA determines "that the pesticide, when applied in accordance with its directions for use . . . or in accordance with a widespread and commonly recognized practice, may generally cause, without additional regulatory restrictions, unreasonable adverse effects on the environment, including injury to the applicator."[47] Before issuing a cancellation, reclassification, or hearing notice, FIFRA generally requires[48] EPA to provide the Department of Agriculture with notice and the opportunity to comment, consult with the Secretary of Health and Human Services "when a public health use is affected," and submit the issue to an independent Science Advisory Panel.[49]

Courts have given significant weight to FIFRA Section 6(b)'s procedural protections of notice and hearing prior to cancellation. For example, a 2011 decision in the U.S. District Court for the District of Columbia rejected EPA's attempt to enforce a misbranding action against a registrant who did not amend its registration to incorporate an EPA risk mitigation decision.[50] The court concluded that FIFRA unambiguously precluded EPA from bringing "a misbranding action in lieu of a cancellation proceeding against a product that . . . in EPA's view, no longer meets the Section 3(c)(5) criteria."[51] The court explained that FIFRA "establishes a detailed, multi-step process that EPA *must* follow when it wants to cancel or suspend a registration."[52]

FIFRA Section 6(e) provides a separate cancellation provision for pesticides that are conditionally registered by EPA.[53] For those conditionally registered pesticides, EPA may issue a notice of intent to cancel if EPA determines "that the registrant has failed to initiate and pursue appropriate action toward fulfilling a condition imposed" by EPA or if EPA determines at the end of the conditional

---

45. *Id.* § 136d(b). If EPA issues a notice of intent to cancel or reclassify, the registrant may request a hearing. *Id.*

46. Ciba-Geigy Corp. v. EPA, 874 F.2d 277, 279 (5th Cir. 1989); *see also* Reckitt Benckiser, Inc. v. Jackson, 762 F. Supp. 2d 34, 36 (D.D.C. 2011) (noting that an EPA administrator may commence cancellation proceedings of a pesticide product if such product causes "unreasonable adverse effects" on the environment).

47. 7 U.S.C. § 136a(d)(1)(C), (d)(2).

48. These requirements may be waived if EPA "determines that suspension of a pesticide registration is necessary to prevent an imminent hazard to human health." *Id.* § 136d(b)(2).

49. *Id.* § 136d(b); § 136w(d).

50. *Reckitt Benckiser, Inc.*, 762 F. Supp. at 49.

51. *Id.*

52. *Id.* at 42.

53. 7 U.S.C. § 136d(e). *See generally* Final Decision and Order, *In re* Bayer CropScience LP, No. FIFRA-HQ-2016-0001, 2016 WL 4125892 (EAB July 29, 2016).

registration period that the condition has not been met.[54] The cancellation becomes final 30 days after the registrant has received the notice of intent to cancel from EPA unless the registrant requests a hearing.[55]

2. Suspension

FIFRA authorizes EPA to suspend a pesticide's registration pending the outcome of the cancellation or reclassification proceedings if EPA determines that suspension is necessary to prevent an "imminent hazard."[56] FIFRA defines an imminent hazard as when "the continued use of a pesticide during the time required for cancellation proceeding would be likely to result in unreasonable adverse effects on the environment," including people, plants, or animals, including species protected under the Endangered Species Act.[57] A suspension order may only be issued if EPA (1) has notified registrants of the intention to cancel the registration and provides a basis for the imminent-hazard finding included in the notice; and (2) provides registrants an opportunity for an expedited hearing on whether an imminent hazard exists.[58] If the registrant does not request a hearing, the suspension goes into effect.[59] If the registrant does request a hearing to oppose suspension, EPA will have the burden of presenting an "affirmative case for the suspension."[60] However, the "ultimate burden of persuasion" for the registration in light of any proposed reclassification or cancellation will rest with the proponent of the registration.[61]

3. Emergency Suspension

Where EPA determines that an emergency exists, it may issue the suspension order "in advance of notification to the registrant."[62] EPA then must issue a notice of intent to cancel within 90 days of issuing an emergency suspension order or the suspension expires.[63] The registrant may request an expedited hearing, which is limited to participation of the registrant and EPA, with other persons adversely

---

54. 7 U.S.C. § 136d(e)(1).

55. *Id.* § 136d(e)(2). The hearing requested under this provision is limited to evaluating whether the registrant has initiated or pursued appropriate actions to comply with the conditions, whether the conditions were satisfied in the time provided, and whether any EPA decision regarding existing stocks is consistent with the statutory directive. *Id.*

56. *Id.* § 136d(c)(1).

57. *Id.* § 136(j), (*l*); *see* Wash. Toxics Coal. v. EPA, 413 F.3d 1024, 1033 (9th Cir. 2005) ("EPA retains discretion to alter the registration of pesticides for reasons that include environmental concerns."); *see also, e.g.*, Love v. Thomas, 858 F.2d 1347, 1350 (9th Cir. 1988) (explaining EPA's suspension of a pesticide on EPA's perception of "serious health risks"); Ellis v. Housenger, 252 F. Supp. 3d 800, 810 (N.D. Cal. 2017) (denying plaintiffs' request for an immediate suspension where the plaintiff failed to show "that the asserted harm outweighed the pesticide's benefits").

58. 7 U.S.C. § 136d(c)(1), (c)(2).

59. *Id.* § 136d(c)(1), (2).

60. 40 C.F.R. § 164.121(g).

61. *Id.*

62. 7 U.S.C. § 136d(c)(3).

63. *Id.*

affected only permitted to file briefs.[64] If EPA issues an emergency order, the suspension goes into effect immediately and remains in effect pending the result of the expedited hearing, unless EPA fails to issue a notice of intent to cancel.[65] EPA has exercised its imminent-hazard emergency suspension authority sparingly. A court reviewing an EPA emergency suspension order has considered FIFRA's use of the term "emergency" with "reference to the principles and rationale for the granting by a court of a temporary restraining order," which the court noted would be designed to "prevent unreasonable adverse effects on the environment during the time necessary to conduct a suspension hearing."[66] Reviewing courts have evaluated whether EPA properly considered both the potential risks of continued use of a pesticide and the economic disruption of suspension in evaluating emergency orders.[67] In evaluating this standard, the D.C. Circuit Court of Appeals explained, "[t]he extraordinary step of emergency suspension is available only if the requisite unreasonable harm would be likely to materialize during the pendency of ordinary suspension proceedings."[68] That is a high bar to meet. A recent district court decision upheld EPA's determination to deny a request for immediate suspension on an emergency basis, finding plaintiffs had the burden to show EPA's decision was improper and did not meet that burden.[69]

D. Judicial Review

FIFRA expressly authorizes two types of judicial review under the statute. Section 16(a) provides for district court review of "the refusal of the Administrator to cancel or suspend a registration or to change a classification *not following a hearing* and other final actions of the Administrator not committed to the discretion of the Administrator by law."[70] However, under Section 16(b), "controversy as to the validity of any order issued by the Administrator *following a public hearing*" (1) may only be brought by "any person who will be adversely affected by such order and who had been a party to the proceedings," (2) may only be heard in the U.S. Court of Appeals, and (3) must be within 60 days after the entry of the order.[71]

---

64. *Id.*

65. *Id.*

66. Dow Chem. Co. v. Blum, 469 F. Supp. 892, 901 (E.D. Mich. 1979); *see also* Nagel v. Thomas, 666 F. Supp. 1002, 1007 (W.D. Mich. 1987).

67. *See, e.g.*, *Love*, 858 F.2d at 1357 (noting that "the statute thus requires the EPA to consider the benefits as well as the risks of its use, including the economic consequences of suspension"); *Dow Chem. Co.*, 469 F. Supp. at 902 (listing the factors that courts examine when reviewing emergency suspensions as: "(1) [t]he seriousness of the threatened harm; (2) [t]he immediacy of the threatened harm; (3) [t]he probability that the threatened harm would result; (4) [b]enefits to the public of the continued use of the pesticides in question during the suspension process; and (5) [t]he nature and extent of the information before the Administrator at the time he made his decision").

68. Nat'l Coal. against Misuse of Pesticides v. EPA, 867 F.2d 636, 644 (D.C. Cir. 1989); *accord Ellis*, 252 F. Supp. 3d at 807.

69. *Ellis*, 252 F. Supp. 3d at 808–10.

70. 7 U.S.C. § 136n(a) (emphasis added).

71. *Id.* § 136n(b) (emphasis added).

Though the term public hearing is not defined in the statute, courts have consistently construed it to mean a formal or informal public proceeding, generally notice and comment, that produces an adequate record for review.[72] Where an EPA registration decision under FIFRA is challenged under another statutory scheme, such as an ESA citizen-suit claim, courts have found FIFRA's specific jurisdictional provision to govern.[73]

III. FIFRA DATA COMPENSATION

Under FIFRA, every applicant for registration of a pesticide must support his or her application with data that establish the safety of the product. Applicants may meet this requirement either by presenting their own data or by citing data previously submitted to EPA by other registrants.[74] Applicants relying on previously submitted data (commonly referred to as "me-too" or "follow-on" registrants) must offer to pay compensation to the data owner when making such citation, unless 15 years have passed since the original submission of the data.[75] If there is no agreement on the amount and terms of compensation within 90 days of the offer, either party may initiate binding arbitration to establish the appropriate level of compensation.[76]

The Supreme Court, in *Thomas v. Union Carbide Agricultural Products Co.*, recognized that FIFRA's data-compensation regime "does not impose an explicit standard" for determining compensation.[77] Rather, by assigning to private arbitrators the task of determining appropriate compensation, FIFRA adopts a "pragmatic solution to the difficult problem of spreading the costs of generating adequate information regarding the safety, health, and environmental impact of a potentially dangerous product."[78] FIFRA's compensation provisions often are characterized as

---

72. *See, e.g.*, Ctr. for Biological Diversity v. EPA, 861 F.3d 174, 187 (D.C. Cir. 2017) (hereinafter *Ctr. for Biological Diversity Cyantraniliprole*) (citing Envtl. Def. Fund, Inc. v. Costle, 631 F.2d 922, 932 (D.C. Cir. 1980)) (giving "broad interpretation" to the term "public hearing," including notice and comment); *accord* Humane Soc'y of U.S. v. EPA, 790 F.2d 106, 111 (D.C. Cir. 1986) (defining "public hearing" as a hearing with a "reviewable record"); *see also* Ctr. for Biological Diversity v. EPA, 847 F.3d 1075, 1089–90 (9th Cir. 2017) (explaining that a challenge to registration actions taken after public notice and comment is governed by FIFRA Section 16(b)); United Farm Workers of Am. v. EPA, 592 F.3d 1080, 1082–83 (9th Cir. 2010) (defining public hearing broadly, including "proceedings in which there is no presentation of public argument[,]" though requiring notice of a decision and presentation to anyone affected by the decision).

73. *Ctr. for Biological Diversity Cyantraniliprole*, 861 F.3d at 179 (FIFRA section 16(b) requires that an ESA citizen-suit challenge to FIFRA registration action taken after "public hearing" must be brought in a court of appeals and within 60 days of order); *Ctr. for Biological Diversity*, 847 F.3d at 1089 (same).

74. 7 U.S.C. § 136a(c)(1)(F).

75. 7 U.S.C. § 136a(c)(1)(F)(iii). During at least the first ten years after the first registration of a pesticide, a data owner has exclusive rights over the data used for its registration and may refuse to permit use of its data completely. 7 U.S.C. § 136a(c)(1)(F)(i). Under certain circumstances, the exclusive use period can be extended. *See* 7 U.S.C. § 136a(c)(1)(F)(ii).

76. 7 U.S.C. § 136a(c)(1)(F)(iii).

77. Thomas v. Union Carbide Agric. Prods. Co., 473 U.S. 568, 593 (1985).

78. *Id.* at 590 (discussing FIFRA data-compensation provisions generally).

intended to reconcile four goals: (1) preventing "free riding" by follow-on registrants, (2) avoiding the necessity of duplicative expenditures on testing, (3) providing incentives for pesticide research and testing, and (4) fostering competition.[79] The role of the arbitration panel is to find the pragmatic solution to a given dispute that best meets these goals. Because courts have limited power of review over arbitration awards, arbitration awards are normally enforced by the courts.[80]

The appropriate compensation in any case is a highly fact-specific matter. It is important to note from the outset that prior data-compensation decisions do not create binding precedent. Nonetheless, the consistency in reasoning among panels makes reference to the analysis of prior arbitration decisions useful. Parties who take reasonable, good-faith positions based on prior arbitration decisions will have more credibility with arbitration panels.[81]

Arbitration decisions have focused on the elements of compensation: defining the body of compensable studies, determining the study costs (both direct and indirect), deciding what adjustment should be made for inflation and interest, considering whether the risks incurred during testing should be reflected in the amount of the award, and determining the share of the costs that should be allocated to the follow-on firm. Panels also have considered whether compensation should be discounted for various reasons, such as reliance on estimated costs or the me-too registrant's lack of ownership rights in the data.

---

79. *See, e.g.*, S. Rep. No. 95-334 at 31 (1977) ("[FIFRA] recognize[s] the proprietary interest in health and safety data on the part of pesticide registrants who underwrite the expense of obtaining such data. It eliminates the 'free-rider' situation to which industry has objected, but keys the amount of payment by subsequent registrants to the costs of developing data necessary for government approval, not the costs of developing the pesticide."); 118 Cong. Rec. 32,258 (1972) ("As concerns use of such data in support of another application without permission of the originator of the test data, however, it is recognized that in certain circumstances it might be unfair or inequitable for government regulation to require a substantial testing expense to be borne by the first applicant, with subsequent applicants thereby gaining a free ride."); 123 Cong. Rec. 25,706 (1977) (statement of Sen. Leahy, chair of the Agriculture Committee, introducing bill and committee report prior to debate and passage) ("The intertwined issues of trade secrets and data compensation are very complex. There must be a balance between a data developer's right to recoup the costs of generating data . . . while simultaneously protecting a competitive situation among all pesticide producers."); S. Rep. No. 95-334 at 34, 35, 64 (1977) (citing the need to balance between allowing market entry and motivating both continued and new research); *see also Union Carbide*, 473 U.S. at 571 (purpose of data-sharing provision was "to streamline pesticide registration procedures, increase competition, and avoid unnecessary duplication of data-generation costs").

80. *See, e.g.*, Non-Dietary Exposure Task Force v. Tagros Chems. India, Ltd., 309 F.R.D. 66, 67–69 (D.D.C. 2015) (enforcing arbitration award and explaining that the court's review of arbitration awards under FIFRA, including settlements, was limited to review for "fraud, misrepresentation, or other misconduct by one of the parties.").

81. *See* Microgen, Inc. v. Lonza, Inc., No. 23-171-00003-96 (Am. Arbitrators Ass'n May 10, 2000) (stating that the panel might have reduced the interest paid by Lonza for delays caused by Microgen except that Lonza never offered compensation that even approached what the panel found to be reasonable under the circumstances).

IV. PREEMPTION

A. FIFRA Preemption

Although both federal and state governments may regulate pesticides, FIFRA creates a nationally uniform standard for pesticide labeling and packaging that the states are prohibited from interfering with their own laws. These laws may be expressly preempted under FIFRA Section 24 or impliedly preempted under the Supremacy Clause of the U.S. Constitution.[82] This section traces the evolution of express and implied preemption under FIFRA and underscores recent developments in these areas.

1. Express Preemption under FIFRA

Section 24(a) specifically permits states to "regulate the sale or use of any federally registered pesticide or device in the State, but only if and to the extent the regulation does not permit any sale or use prohibited by this subchapter."[83] Section 24(b), however, expressly preempts state actions that would "impose or continue in effect any requirements for labeling or packaging" in addition to EPA-approved packaging or labeling requirements.[84]

After the Supreme Court's 1992 decision in *Cipollone v. Liggett Group*, most lower federal courts applied Section 24(b) to preempt all state and common law claims against pesticide manufacturers for inadequate labeling.[85] *Cipollone* took a broad approach to express preemption, finding that the language of the Public Health Cigarette Smoking Act of 1969 expressly preempted state actions against cigarette companies.[86] In addition, *Cipollone* interpreted the term "requirements" to include not only state rules and regulations, but also common law rules.[87] Following *Cipollone*, many lower courts held that Section 24(b) preempted any rules for which a finding of liability might "induce" a company to alter its product label.[88]

---

82. FIFRA does not occupy the field of pesticide regulation. Wis. Pub. Intervenor v. Mortier, 501 U.S. 597, 611–12 (1991) ("FIFRA fails to provide any clear and manifest indication that Congress sought to supplant local authority over pesticide regulation impliedly."); *accord* United Auto., Aerospace & Agric. Workers of Am. Local 3047 v. Hardin Cnty., Ky., 842 F.3d 407, 414 (6th Cir. 2016) (noting that under *Mortier*, FIFRA does not preempt local authority).

83. 7 U.S.C. § 136v(a).

84. *Id.* § 136v(b).

85. Cipollone v. Liggett Grp., 505 U.S. 504 (1992).

86. 505 U.S. 504, 530 (1992) ("To summarize our holding: . . . the 1969 Act pre-empts petitioner's claims based on a failure to warn and the neutralization of federally mandated warnings to the extent that those claims rely on omissions or inclusions in respondents' advertising or promotions. . . ."); *accord* McCracken v. R.J. Reynolds Tobacco Co., No. 17-4495, 2018 U.S. Dist. LEXIS 84573, at *12 (E.D. Pa. May 21, 2018) (holding that the plaintiff's "failure to warn" claim against a cigarette company was preempted by the Public Health Smoking Act of 1969 under *Cipollone*).

87. *Cipollone*, 505 U.S. at 521; *accord* Bates v. Dow AgroSciences, LLC, 544 U.S. 431, 443 (2005) ("Our decision in *Cipollone* supports [the] conclusion[]" that "the term 'requirements' in § 136v(b) reaches beyond positive enactments, such as statutes and regulations, to embrace common-law duties."); *Carias v. Monsanto Co.*, No. 15-CV-3677 (JMA) (GRB), 2016 U.S. Dist. LEXIS 139883, at *9 (E.D.N.Y. Sept. 30, 2016) (noting that a common law claim constitutes a state law labeling "requirement" under *Bates*).

88. *See Bates*, 544 U.S. at 436.

In applying the *Cipollone* test, lower courts frequently found that various common law claims, including those for design defects, breach of warranty, and fraud, were preempted.[89]

The Supreme Court's decision in *Bates v. Dow AgroSciences LLC* in 2005 halted lower courts' expanded interpretation of Section 24(b) post-*Cipollone*. The plaintiffs in *Bates* were peanut farmers whose crops allegedly were damaged by the application of the defendant's pesticide, which was designed for soils with pH levels lower than those of the plaintiffs' soils.[90] Plaintiffs alleged a number of claims, including fraud, failure to warn, defective design, defective manufacture, negligent testing, and breach of express warranty.[91] The Supreme Court reversed the Fifth Circuit's finding that all but one of the claims was expressly preempted, holding that although common law rules themselves are "requirements" because they must be obeyed, Section 24(b) bars only those requirements "for labeling or packaging."[92] This category excludes rules that do not require manufacturers to label or package their products in any particular way.[93] As a result, plaintiffs' defective design, defective manufacture, negligent testing, and breach of express warranty claims were not preempted.[94] In addition, the Supreme Court emphatically rejected the inducement test, finding that Section 24(b) spoke only of "requirements."[95]

Unlike plaintiffs' other claims, their fraud and failure-to-warn claims were premised on rules that qualified as "requirements for labeling or packaging."[96] The Supreme Court reasoned that these rules set a standard for labeling that defendant's pesticide is alleged to have violated by containing false and inadequate warnings.[97] Nevertheless, "requirements for labeling or packaging" are not preempted unless they are in addition to the applicable labeling and packaging requirements under FIFRA.[98] Accordingly, the Supreme Court established a two-part test for determining whether a state law requirement is preempted. First, the requirement must be "for labeling," and second, the requirement must impose a labeling or packaging requirement that is "in addition to or different from those required under [FIFRA]."[99] The Supreme Court provided examples of certain judge-made rules not affected by Section 24(b): "Rules that require manufacturers to design reasonably safe products, to use due care in conducting appropriate testing of their products, to market products free of manufacturing defects, and to honor

---

89. *Id.*
90. *Id.* at 434.
91. *Id.* at 444.
92. *Id.* at 434–44.
93. *Id.* at 444.
94. *Id.*
95. *Id.* at 443.
96. *Id.* at 446.
97. *Id.*
98. *Id.* at 447.
99. *Id.* at 444.

their express warranties or other contractual commitments plainly do not qualify as requirements for 'labeling or packaging.'"[100]

Post-*Bates*, courts have applied preemption to state law claims far less frequently.[101] In *Indian Brand Farms, Inc. v. Novartis Crop Protection Inc.*, for example, plaintiff blueberry farmers alleged that a pesticide manufactured by the defendant had damaged their crops.[102] The court concluded that because plaintiffs' negligent misrepresentation/fraud and state consumer fraud protection act claims were based on alleged misrepresentations in defendant's marketing brochure—which did not qualify as "labeling"—those claims were not preempted.[103] In addition, because plaintiffs' failure-to-warn claim, if successful, would not have resulted in a labeling requirement in addition to or different from those required by FIFRA, that claim was not preempted.[104] The court came to a similar conclusion in *Gucciardi v. Bonide Products*, a case in which plaintiff homeowners brought negligence, warranty, and strict liability claims against defendant companies for alleged damages associated with in-home use of the pesticide product.[105] Invoking *Bates*, the court found that plaintiffs' claims were not preempted because they "[did] not implicate the Product's label," and because the claims did not "impose any obligations in addition to or greater than those required by FIFRA."[106] These cases illustrate that there may be tensions between allowing states to regulate pesticide use and FIFRA's prohibition on using any pesticide in a manner that is inconsistent with its labeling.

Outside of the state law claims context, courts have found that state and local government regulation of pesticide use is not preempted by FIFRA.[107] Relying upon the specific grant of authority in Section 24(a), the Supreme Court in *Wisconsin Public Intervenor v. Mortier* upheld a sweeping pesticide ordinance passed by a Wisconsin town.[108] The ordinance required a permit be issued by the town before any pesticides could be applied to public lands or to private lands subject to public

---

100. *Id.*

101. *See, e.g.*, Arlandson v. Hartz Mountain Corp., 792 F. Supp. 2d 691, 702 (D.N.J. 2011) (breach of implied warranty of merchantability, breach of express warranty, violation of state consumer fraud protection statute, and unjust enrichment claims not preempted); Wuebker v. Wilbur-Ellis Co., 418 F.3d 883 (8th Cir. 2005) (defective design, breach of implied warranty of fitness, breach of implied warranty of merchantability, and recklessness claims not preempted); Peterson v. BASF Corp., 711 N.W.2d 470 (Minn. 2006) (fraud, deception, and state consumer fraud protection statute claim not preempted); Gucciardi v. Bonide Prods., 28 F. Supp. 3d 383 (E.D. Pa. 2014) (negligence, warranty, and strict liability claims not preempted). *But see* DJ Coleman, Inc. v. Nufarm Arms., Inc., 693 F. Supp. 2d 1055 (D.N.D. 2010) (state consumer fraud protection statute claim preempted); Smith v. Hartz Mountain Corp., No. 3:12-cv-00662, 2012 U.S. Dist. LEXIS 159557 (N.D. Ohio Nov. 7, 2012) (inadequate warning claim preempted).

102. Indian Brand Farms, Inc. v. Novartis Crop Prot. Inc., 617 F.3d 207 (3d Cir. 2010).

103. *Id.* at 214–16.

104. *Id.* at 221–23.

105. 28 F. Supp. 3d 383 (E.D. Pa. 2014).

106. *Id.* at 391–92.

107. In addition to *Mortier* and *Schoenhofer*, discussed *infra*, see Chem. Mfr. Specialties Ass'n v. Allenby, 958 F.2d 941, 944 (9th Cir. 2000) (finding that FIFRA did not preempt California's Proposition 65 warning requirements).

108. 501 U.S. 597 (1991).

use, and to any aerial applications of pesticides—even if those applications were entirely to private lands.[109] A local landowner applied for a permit to aerially apply pesticides to his land, but the town refused to allow the aerial application, and, importantly, further limited the private lands on which he could ground-apply the pesticides.[110] The Supreme Court found that both localities and states possess the authority to regulate pesticides under FIFRA, and that the ordinance posed limitations on "sale or use" and thus was not preempted.[111]

More recently, in *Schoenhofer v. McClaskey*, pesticide applicators challenged a Kansas regulation that required both the horizontal and vertical application of termite pesticides in preconstruction areas, but the federally approved label contained no such requirements.[112] Here, the Tenth Circuit turned to the text of Section 24(b), finding that preemption did not apply because the regulation at issue governed *use*, not labeling. The Kansas regulation is "even further removed from the mandate of § 136v(b)" because it addresses pesticide applicators, not the manufacturers that package or label the pesticides.[113] The court also pointed to the rationale for national uniformity in labeling—to avoid forcing manufacturers to produce different labels for each state—and found that it was not implicated in this case, because applicators could adjust their operations.[114] Lastly, even though the regulation and label were "not congruent," it was possible for the applicator to comply with both.[115]

2. Conflict Preemption

Conflict preemption occurs when "compliance with both state and federal law is impossible" or when a state law "stands as an obstacle to the accomplishment and execution of the full purposes and objectives of Congress."[116] The authority for conflict preemption comes not from FIFRA, but from the Supremacy Clause of the Constitution, which invalidates "state laws that interfere with, or are contrary to the laws of congress, made in pursuance of the constitution."[117] Post-*Bates*, several

---

109. *Id.* at 602–03.
110. *Id.* at 603.
111. *Id.* at 607–08.
112. Schoenhofer v. McClaskey, 861 F.3d 1170, 1172–73 (10th Cir. 2017).
113. *Id.* at 1175.
114. *Id.*
115. *Id.* at 1176.
116. Oneok, Inc. v. Learjet, Inc., 135 S. Ct. 1591 (2015) (citing Cal. v. ARC Am. Corp., 490 U.S. 93, 100, 101 (1989)); *see also* Murphy v. NCAA, 138 S. Ct. 1461, 1480 (2018) (explaining that conflict preemption occurs where state law imposes a duty that is inconsistent with federal law).
117. *Mortier*, 501 U.S. at 604 (citing Gibbons v. Ogden, 22 U.S. 1, 9 (1824)); *accord* D & S Remodelers, Inc. v. Wright Nat'l Flood Ins. Servs., LLC, No. 17-5554, 2018 U.S. App. LEXIS 3382, at *9–10 (6th Cir. Feb. 14, 2018).

courts have rejected conflict preemption arguments made in relation to FIFRA.[118] In *Ansagay v. Dow AgroSciences LLC*, for example, the court found that the Supreme Court's reversal of the court of appeal's decision in *Bates* implicitly rejected Dow's conflict preemption arguments.[119]

B. State Law Preemption of Local Pesticide Laws

Separate from FIFRA, courts have found that state pesticide laws conflict with, or impliedly preempt, local pesticide laws. In *Syngenta Seeds, Inc. v. County of Kauai*, the Ninth Circuit found that Hawaii state law impliedly preempted an ordinance passed by Kauai County that required commercial farmers to (1) maintain buffer zones between crops to which pesticides are applied and surrounding properties; (2) provide notifications before and after applying pesticides; and (3) file annual reports disclosing the cultivation of genetically engineered crops.[120] The Hawaii Pesticides Law granted the Hawaii Department of Agriculture the authority to "establish limitations and conditions for the application of pesticides" by equipment and to "establish, as necessary, specific standards and guidelines which specify those conditions which constitute unreasonable adverse effects on the environment."[121] Pursuant to this authority, the Department of Agriculture enacted rules that addressed pesticide use and created notification and record-keeping requirements.[122] Additionally, it was clear that the Hawaii legislature intended for the state's regulation of pesticides to be uniform, comprehensive, and exclusive of additional, local rules.[123] Similarly, in separate decisions, the Ninth Circuit found that county ordinances banning the testing and cultivation of genetically engineered plants were impliedly preempted by Hawaii state law.[124]

---

118. *See, e.g.*, Indian Brand Farms, Inc. v. Novartis Crop Prot. Inc., 617 F.3d 207, 224 (3d Cir. 2010) ("*Bates* teaches that there is a strong presumption against preemption of state law. . . ."); Wuebker v. Wilbur-Ellis Co., 418 F.3d 883 (8th Cir. 2005); Blitz v. Monsanto Co., No. 17-cv-473-wmc, 2018 U.S. Dist. LEXIS 62747, at *8–10 (W.D. Wisc 2018) (holding that the plantiff's claims are not preempted because the requirements of the state law at issue are not inconsistent with those of FIFRA); Turner v. Chevron U.S.A. Inc., No. B173622, 2006 Cal. App. Unpub. LEXIS 4159 (Cal. Ct. App. May 15, 2006); Hardin v. BASF Corp., Nos. 4:00CV00500, 4:00CV00503, 2005 WL 6151334 (E.D. Ark. 2005).

119. 153 F. Supp. 3d 1270, 1282 (D. Haw. 2015).

120. 842 F.3d 669 (9th Cir. 2016).

121. *Id.* at 677 (citing Haw. Rev. Stat. § 149A-33 (2018)).

122. *Id.*

123. *Id.* at 678.

124. Atay v. Cnty. of Maui, 842 F.3d 688 (9th Cir. 2016); Haw. Papaya Indus. Ass'n v. Cnty. of Haw., No. 14-17538, 2016 WL 6819700 (9th Cir. Nov. 18, 2016).

V. FEDERAL FOOD, DRUG, AND COSMETIC ACT

FFDCA,[125] as amended by the Food Quality Protection Act (FQPA),[126] prohibits the adulteration of food,[127] which means, in part, that a food must not contain "a pesticide chemical residue that is unsafe."[128] A pesticide residue is considered "unsafe" unless either (1) EPA has established a tolerance for such residue and the amount of residue is within the tolerance or (2) the pesticide is exempted from the tolerance requirement.[129]

Upon receipt of a petition by any person or on its own initiative, EPA may establish, modify, or revoke a pesticide residue tolerance, but EPA must determine if a residue level is "safe" before establishing or leaving any tolerance in effect.[130] "Safe," within the FFDCA, means "there is a reasonable certainty that no harm will result from aggregate exposure to the pesticide chemical residue, including all anticipated dietary exposures."[131]

The FQPA required EPA to reassess the safety of all then-existing tolerances and "added to the FFDCA a range of detailed, scientific factors to be considered in the assessment of pesticide risks."[132] These factors, "among other relevant factors," include: the "validity, completeness, and reliability of the available data" concerning the pesticide; the "nature of any toxic effect" of the pesticide; available information about consumers' dietary consumption patterns; cumulative effects; aggregate exposures; variability of sensitivities among population subgroups; such information that EPA may require on "whether the pesticide chemical may have an effect in humans that is similar to an effect produced by a naturally occurring estrogen or other endocrine effect"; and safety factors experts generally use when dealing with animal experimentation data.[133] Although the statute does explicitly state that EPA may consider "other relevant factors," the D.C. Circuit has ruled that EPA principally must consider the statutorily listed factors, and any nonlisted factors considered by EPA must be "linked" to the listed factors.[134]

When EPA receives a petition to establish, modify, or revoke a pesticide tolerance, EPA must (1) issue a final regulation (whether or not in accord with the contents of the petition), (2) establish a proposed regulation subject to administrative notice-and-comment rules and then issue a final regulation, or (3) issue an order

---

125. 21 U.S.C. §§ 301–399 (2018).
126. Food Quality Protection Act of 1996, Pub. L. No. 104-170, 110 Stat. 1489 (1996).
127. 21 U.S.C. § 331.
128. *Id.* § 342(a)(2)(B).
129. *Id.* § 346a(a)(l).
130. *Id.* § 346a(b)(2)(A)(i).
131. *Id.* § 346a(b)(2)(A)(ii).
132. Nat. Res. Def. Council v. EPA, 461 F.3d 164, 168 (D.C. Cir. 2006) (citing 21 U.S.C. § 346a(b)(2) (C)–(D)).
133. 21 U.S.C. § 346a(b)(2)(D).
134. Nat'l Coal. against the Misuse of Pesticides v. EPA, 809 F.2d 875, 881–82 (D.C. Cir. 1987) (pre-FQPA case).

denying the petition.[135] The petitioner may file objections within 60 days after a petition is denied and also may request a public evidentiary hearing, after which EPA must issue a final order.[136] Appellate court review is available provided the petitioner or "any person who will be adversely affected by such order or regulation" first exhausted these administrative remedies.[137]

Aside from the regulatory requirements for establishment of tolerances, the FFDCA also establishes penalties for an individual or corporation who introduces adulterated food into interstate commerce. The Food and Drug Administration (FDA) may bring criminal charges, may seize the adulterated food, or may seek an injunction.[138] The standard of intent for establishing criminal violations is low. The Supreme Court has found that the "Government establishes a prima facie case when it introduces evidence sufficient to warrant a finding by the trier of the facts that the defendant had, by reason of his position in the corporation, responsibility and authority either to prevent in the first instance, or promptly to correct, the violation complained of, and that he failed to do so."[139] The FDA can also seek civil penalties against any person who introduces or delivers for introduction into interstate commerce any food adulterated by a pesticide chemical.[140]

VI. ENDANGERED SPECIES ACT

The ESA[141] protects endangered species—those identified as at risk of extinction—and threatened species—those identified as likely to become endangered within the foreseeable future.[142] The ESA is administered by the U.S. Fish and Wildlife Service (FWS), which has responsibility for terrestrial and freshwater organisms, and the National Marine Fisheries Service (NMFS; collectively, "the Services"), which has responsibility for marine organisms and anadromous fish species. ESA compliance as it relates to EPA's approval of pesticides under FIFRA has increasingly become the subject of litigation. This section discusses the relationship between obligations and prohibitions in the ESA and pesticide registration.

---

135. 21 U.S.C. § 346a(d)(4)(A); *see also* Nader v. EPA, 859 F.2d 747 (9th Cir. 1988), *cert. denied*, 490 U.S. 1034 (1989).
136. 21 U.S.C. § 346a(g)(2).
137. *Id.* § 346a(h)(l); *see also Nader*, 859 F.2d at 751.
138. 21 U.S.C. §§ 332–334.
139. United States v. Park, 421 U.S. 658, 673–74 (1975); *accord* United States v. Quality Egg, LLC, 99 F. Supp. 3d 920, 923 n.3 (N.D. Iowa 2015); Commissioner v. RLG, Inc., 755 N.E.2d 556, 559–60 (Ind. 2001) (citing the *Park* standard to explain how the government establishes a prima facie violation of the Food, Drug, and Cosmetic Act).
140. 21 U.S.C. § 333.
141. 16 U.S.C. §§ 1531 *et seq.*
142. 16 U.S.C. § 1532(6), (20).

A. Pesticides and Section 9 of the ESA

Section 9 of the ESA prohibits the "take" of any species listed as threatened or endangered under the ESA.[143] The ESA defines "take" as "to harass, harm, pursue, hunt, shoot, wound, kill, trap, capture, or collect, or to attempt to engage in any such conduct."[144] "Harm" is further defined by ESA implementing regulation as "an act which actually kills or injures wildlife" and may include "significant habitat modification or degradation where it actually kills or injures wildlife by significantly impairing essential behavioral patterns, including breeding, feeding or sheltering."[145] "Harass" is defined by regulation as "an intentional or negligent act or omission which creates the likelihood of injury to wildlife by annoying it to such an extent as to significantly disrupt normal behavioral patterns which include, but are not limited to, breeding, feeding, or sheltering."[146] Incidental take may be authorized by the Services in biological opinions (where there is consultation under Section 7 of the ESA), and in incidental take permits (where no federal nexus is available).[147] Both civil and criminal penalties may be imposed under the ESA, as well as injunctive relief via a citizen-suit provision.[148]

In *Defenders of Wildlife v. EPA*, the Eighth Circuit held that EPA's regulation of a pesticide under FIFRA does not bar a citizen suit under the ESA where pesticide use affects endangered species.[149] The Defenders of Wildlife plaintiffs, an environmental organization, brought suit against EPA under the ESA's citizen-suit provision.[150] They alleged, inter alia, that EPA's continued registration of challenged pesticides under FIFRA resulted in an unauthorized and, therefore, illegal "taking" under the ESA.[151] EPA argued that plaintiffs were prohibited from challenging a pesticide registration under the ESA and thus were limited to seeking a cancellation of the pesticide's registration under FIFRA.[152] The Eighth Circuit rejected EPA's argument, holding that because "Congress has made 'a conscious decision to give endangered species priority over the "primary missions" of federal agencies[,]' . . . FIFRA does not exempt the EPA from complying with ESA requirements when the EPA registers pesticides."[153] The court concluded that the ESA citizen-suit provision permitted the plaintiffs to sue EPA to enjoin the alleged violation of the ESA, and agreed with the district court that the pesticide registrations resulted in an unauthorized taking of protected species in violation of the ESA.[154] The court, however, did allow EPA to seek to have the injunction lifted by showing it had subsequently

---

143. 16 U.S.C. § 1538.
144. 16 U.S.C. § 1532(19).
145. 50 C.F.R. § 17.3.
146. *Id.*
147. 16 U.S.C. §§ 1536(b)(4); 1539(a).
148. 16 U.S.C. § 1540(g)(1).
149. Defenders of Wildlife v. EPA, 882 F.2d 1294, 1303 (8th Cir. 1989).
150. *Defenders of Wildlife*, 882 F.2d at 1298 (citing 16 U.S.C. § 1540(g)(1)).
151. *Id.*
152. *Id.*
153. *Id.* at 1299 (quoting Tenn. Valley Auth. v. Hill, 437 U.S. 153, 185 (1978)).
154. *Id.* at 1300.

complied with the incidental take provisions of the ESA.[155] As noted in the next section, the vast majority of ESA pesticide litigation that followed alleged violations of Section 7 rather than Section 9.

B. Pesticides and Section 7 of the ESA

Under Section 7 of the ESA,[156] federal agencies are required to consult with the Services to ensure that any action authorized, funded, or carried out by the agency is not likely to jeopardize the continued existence of any threatened or endangered species or result in the destruction or adverse modification of habitat designated as critical habitat for any such species.[157] Under the ESA implementing regulations, EPA, as action agency, must first determine whether its action may affect particular listed species.[158] If EPA identifies potential effects on particular species, the regulations then require that EPA engage in informal or formal consultation with the Services regarding those species or habitats for which it has made a "may affect" determination.[159] In contrast, if EPA determines that its actions will have "no effect" on listed species or critical habitat, it is under no duty to consult with the Services.[160]

A Ninth Circuit decision in *Washington Toxics Coalition v. EPA* (*Washington Toxics I*)[161] confirmed EPA's Section 7 consultation requirements when it registers pesticides pursuant to FIFRA. *Washington Toxics I* concerned an ESA citizen suit claiming that use of 54 pesticides endangered protected species of salmon throughout the Pacific Northwest, and that EPA had violated Section 7(a)(2) of the ESA by failing to consult with NMFS before approving the pesticides for use under FIFRA.[162] EPA agreed that the ESA requires consultation with NMFS for agency actions affecting the protected salmon, and admitted that it had not consulted with NMFS before authorizing the pesticides.[163] However, EPA argued that in registering a pesticide, it is bound to follow only the requirements of FIFRA, which include a provision dealing with endangered species. Therefore, EPA argued that because it had complied with the requirements of FIFRA, it did not have to meet the ESA's Section 7 consultation requirements.[164] The Ninth Circuit rejected EPA's arguments and held that compliance with FIFRA does not exempt EPA from compliance with the ESA when protected species are affected.[165] The court held that EPA "cannot

---

155. *Id.* at 1303.
156. 16 U.S.C. § 1536.
157. 16 U.S.C. § 1536(a)(2); 50 C.F.R. pt. 402 (Section 7 consultation regulations).
158. *See* 50 C.F.R. § 402.14(a).
159. *Id.*
160. Ctr. for Biological Diversity v. EPA, 279 F. Supp. 3d 121, 130–31 (D.D.C. 2017) (citing Nat'l Parks Conservation Ass'n v. Jewell, 62 F. Supp. 3d 7, 12 (D.D.C. 2014)).
161. 413 F.3d 1024 (9th Cir. 2005).
162. *Id.* at 1028.
163. *Id.*
164. *Id.* at 1031.
165. *Id.* at 1032.

escape its obligation to comply with the ESA merely because it is bound to comply with another statute that has consistent, complementary objectives."[166] In the years following *Washington Toxics I*, plaintiffs brought a number of ESA Section 7 challenges to EPA registration decisions.[167]

Two recent court of appeals decisions addressed EPA's obligations under ESA Section 7 and the circumstances under which plaintiffs may challenge EPA pesticide registration decisions for failure to consult under Section 7. In *Center for Biological Diversity v. EPA*, the Ninth Circuit considered a district court's dismissal of failure to consult claims related to 31 pesticide active ingredients.[168] The plaintiffs had alleged four different categories of claims related to those active ingredients, which the Ninth Circuit described as follows: "category 1" claims challenged the Registration Eligibility Determinations for each active ingredient; "category 2" claims alleged that EPA's "continued discretionary control" over each active ingredient was sufficient to trigger an obligation to consult under Section 7; "category 3" claims alleged that EPA's completion of pesticide product reregistration for a particular pesticide active ingredient was sufficient to trigger an obligation to consult under Section 7; and "category 4" claims challenged EPA's approval of pesticide products containing the active ingredients.[169]

With respect to "category 1" claims, the Ninth Circuit found that ESA citizen-suit challenges to "any order issued by the Administrator *following a public hearing*" is subject to FIFRA Section 16(b)'s specific jurisdictional mandate and must be heard in the courts of appeals within 60 days of entry of the order.[170] Thus, any active ingredient reregistration eligibility decision that had been subject to notice and comment could be challenged only in the court of appeals and only within that 60-day period,[171] and all other reregistration eligibility decisions that had not been subject to notice and comment were subject to the general six-year statute of limitations.[172] With respect to "category 2" claims, the Ninth Circuit agreed with the district court that, although EPA has an ongoing duty to comply with the ESA, Section 7 consultation must be triggered by an affirmative agency action and plaintiffs' reference to EPA's continued discretionary control over pesticides did not identify an affirmative agency action.[173] With respect to "category 3"

---

166. *Id.*

167. *See, e.g.,* Ctr. for Biological Diversity v. Whitman, Stipulated Injunction and Order, No. C-02-1580-JSW (N.D. Cal. Oct. 20, 2006) (case addressing the California red-legged frog); Ctr. for Biological Diversity v. EPA, Order Dismissing Case upon Settlement, Case No. 04-cv-0126 (D.D.C. Mar. 31, 2005) (case addressing the Barton Springs salamander); Ctr. for Biological Diversity v. EPA, Order Approving Stipulated Injunction, Case No. C07-02794 JCS (N.D. Cal. May 17, 2010) (case addressing 11 species); Ctr. for Biological Diversity v. Pirzadeh, Stipulation of Voluntary Dismissal, Case No. c-JCC (W.D. Wash. May 12, 2010) (case addressing the polar bear).

168. Ctr. for Biological Diversity v. EPA, 847 F.3d 1075 (9th Cir. 2017).

169. *Id.* at 1083.

170. *Id.* at 1089–90 (emphasis added).

171. *See supra* section II.D.

172. *Ctr. for Biological Diversity*, 847 F.3d at 1087 (citing 28 U.S.C. § 2401(a)).

173. *Id.* at 1091 (citing Karuk Tribe of Cal. v. U.S. Forest Serv., 681 F.3d 1006, 1021 (9th Cir. 2012) (en banc)).

claims, the Ninth Circuit agreed with the district court that completion of pesticide product reregistration "is simply a fact," and not an affirmative agency action that triggers Section 7 consultation.[174] However, the Ninth Circuit disagreed with the district court's dismissal of the "claim 4" challenges to products containing the challenged active ingredients as a "collateral attack" on the reregistration eligibility decisions.[175] Rather, the Ninth Circuit found "[t]he collateral attack doctrine is not at issue here; [plaintiff] does not seek to unravel a prior agency order."[176] Instead, the Ninth Circuit found that the "category 4" claims could survive a motion to dismiss because "a product reregistration incorporates data not available during the process for issuing a [reregistration eligibility decision], and necessarily involves a determination distinct from those made during the [reregistration eligibility decision] process because a pesticide active ingredient and a pesticide product are not the same."[177] Thus, the Ninth Circuit reversed the district court's dismissal of all "category 4" claims,[178] opening the door for litigation challenges to individual pesticide product formulation approvals rather than the broader challenges to active ingredient approvals.

In *Center for Biological Diversity v. EPA*, the D.C. Circuit considered an ESA citizen-suit challenge to EPA's registration of a pesticide active ingredient.[179] Plaintiffs in that case had filed challenges both in the district court and the court of appeals. The district court dismissed, finding that only the court of appeals had jurisdiction in light of FIFRA Section 16(b).[180] The D.C. Circuit affirmed the district court dismissal, finding "[b]ecause FIFRA's grant of exclusive jurisdiction to the court of appeals to review registration orders is more specific than the ESA's citizen-suit provision, ... we believe [plaintiffs] must bring their ESA section 7(a)(2) challenge to us if 7 U.S.C. § 136n(b) is satisfied."[181] And the D.C. Circuit found the elements of FIFRA Section 16(b) satisfied, since notice and comment was the equivalent of the "public hearing" referenced in the statute.[182] With respect to defendants' arguments that plaintiffs lacked standing to bring the ESA Section 7 claims, the D.C. Circuit evaluated the requirements to establish standing and found that plaintiffs' and their members established standing.[183] Since EPA conceded that it had not consulted under Section 7, the D.C. Circuit did not need to evaluate the

---

174. *Id.*
175. *Id.* at 1091–92.
176. *Id.* at 1093.
177. *Id.*
178. In a later district court decision, the court adopted the reasoning of the Ninth Circuit in *Center for Biological Diversity* and granted summary judgment to plaintiffs on 59 challenges to pesticide products where the active ingredient registrations were beyond the statute of limitations, but the individual product approvals were within the six-year statute of limitations and not subject to FIFRA section 16(b) because there was no notice and comment to constitute a "public hearing" on the product approvals. *Ellis v. Housenger*, 252 F. Supp. 3d 800, 825–27 (N.D. Cal. 2017).
179. *Ctr. for Biological Diversity Cyantraniliprole*, 861 F.3d at 174.
180. *Ctr. for Biological Diversity v. EPA*, 106 F. Supp. 3d 95 (D.D.C. 2015).
181. *Ctr. for Biological Diversity Cyantraniliprole*, 861 F.3d at 187.
182. *Id.*
183. *Id.* at 181–85.

merits of the claims and, instead, remanded the registration to EPA to make an effects determination.[184]

C. Judicial Review of Pesticide-Related Biological Opinions

Although there have been very few ESA consultations regarding pesticides, even those formal consultations have been subject to litigation. In *Dow AgroSciences LLC v. National Marine Fisheries Service*,[185] the Fourth Circuit evaluated several pesticide registrants' challenge to an NMFS biological opinion for registration of several insecticides. The court reviewed the biological opinion under the "arbitrary and capricious" standard of review in the Administrative Procedure Act[186] and found the opinion "was not the product of reasoned decisionmaking" because NMFS "failed to explain or support several assumptions critical to its opinion" that the registrations would jeopardize the continued existence of identified species.[187] As an initial matter, the Fourth Circuit reviewed the opinion on the administrative record before NMFS when it made its determination and specifically rejected extra-record justifications and postdecisional material the agency sought to introduce for the first time in the litigation proceedings.[188] The court then enumerated infirmities in the agency's opinion, including an unsupported exposure assumption,[189] reliance on outdated data without explanation despite the availability of newer data,[190] and failure to address a regulatory factor to support its determination.[191] Because the Fourth Circuit found the biological opinion "arbitrary and capricious," it vacated the opinion and the decisions made therein.[192]

VII. CLEAN WATER ACT

The CWA prohibits the "discharge of any pollutant,"[193] which means "addition of any pollutant to navigable waters from any point source,"[194] by any person unless in compliance with enumerated provisions. The Act defines "pollutant" to mean "dredged spoil, solid waste, incinerator residue, sewage, garbage, sewage sludge, munitions, chemical wastes, biological materials, radioactive materials, heat, wrecked or discarded equipment, rock, sand, cellar dirt and industrial, municipal, and agricultural waste discharged into water."[195] The CWA exempts "agricultural

---

184. *Id.* at 189 & n.13.
185. 707 F.3d 462 (4th Cir. 2013).
186. 5 U.S.C. § 706.
187. Dow AgroSciences LLC v. Nat'l Marine Fisheries Serv., 707 F.3d 462, 464 (4th Cir. 2013).
188. *Id.* at 467–69 (finding that the district court erred in relying upon a staff affidavit that provided justifications and facts not contained in the administrative record).
189. *Id.* at 472.
190. *Id.* at 472–73.
191. *Id.* at 473–75.
192. *Id.* at 475.
193. 33 U.S.C. § 1311(a).
194. 33 U.S.C. § 1362(12)(A).
195. 33 U.S.C. § 1362(6).

stormwater discharges or return flows from irrigated agriculture," which are excluded from the definition of "point source."[196] Therefore, for many years the CWA was not a focus of the pesticide regulatory framework.

Nonetheless, questions subsequently arose regarding treatment of pesticides within the CWA National Pollutant Discharge Elimination System (NPDES) permitting program, under which EPA (or a delegated state) may issue permits for certain pollutant discharges in accordance with specified terms and conditions.[197] The Act imposes significant civil (and potentially criminal) penalties for any unauthorized pollutant discharge or violation of permit conditions.[198]

The only CWA provision that specifically refers to pesticides is Section 104(l), which required EPA to develop information on the effects of pesticides in water and required the U.S. president to investigate methods to control releases of pesticides into the environment and to make "recommendations for any necessary legislation" to implement those methods.[199] Moreover, EPA has promulgated wastewater effluent guidelines and standards for the pesticide manufacturing industry, among other industries.[200]

Over many years, EPA took the position that pesticides applied for beneficial purpose were not subject to NPDES permitting under 40 C.F.R. part 122.[201] Nonetheless, a series of citizen suits alleging that pesticide application constitutes a discharge of a "pollutant" under the CWA resulted in disparate results.[202] The Ninth Circuit in *Headwaters, Inc. v. Talent Irrigation District* found that residuals that remained after application of a pesticide to an irrigation canal constituted a "chemical waste" and therefore a "pollutant" under the CWA.[203] Similarly, in *League of Wilderness Defenders/Blue Mountains Biodiversity Project v. Forsgren*, the Ninth Circuit found that aerial spraying of pesticide to a forest canopy directly over streams was a discharge of a "pollutant."[204] However, in *Fairhurst v. Hagener*, the Ninth Circuit found a pesticide application was not a "discharge of a pollutant" where it was applied in compliance with FIFRA, did not leave residue, and had no "unintended effects."[205] In *No Spray Coalition, Inc. v. City of New York*, the Second Circuit determined that pesticide use in substantial compliance with FIFRA did not

---

196. 33 U.S.C. § 1362(14).

197. 33 U.S.C. §§ 1311(a), 1342.

198. *See id.* § 1319(b), (c); 40 C.F.R. § 19.4.

199. 33 U.S.C. § 1254(l)(2).

200. *See* 40 C.F.R. pt. 455.

201. *See, e.g.,* Interpretive Statement on Applications of Pesticides to Waters of the United States in Compliance with FIFRA, 70 Fed. Reg. 5093, 5098 (Feb. 1, 2005).

202. *Compare* Nat'l Cotton Council of Am. v. EPA, 553 F.3d 927, 936 (6th Cir. 2009) (holding that the term "pollutant" in the CWA encompasses pesticides), *with* Peconic Baykeeper, Inc. v. Suffolk Cnty., 585 F. Supp. 2d 377, 415 (E.D.N.Y. 2008) (holding that the pesticides at issue, adulticides, are not pollutants within the meaning of the CWA).

203. Headwaters, Inc. v. Talent Irrigation Dist., 243 F.3d 526 (9th Cir. 2001).

204. League of Wilderness Defenders/Blue Mountains Biodiversity Project v. Forsgren, 309 F.3d 1181 (9th Cir. 2002).

205. Fairhurst v. Hagener, 422 F.3d 1146 (9th Cir. 2005).

in and of itself render the CWA citizen-suit provision inapplicable.[206] However, the court did not reach the question or whether pesticide application constitutes discharge of a pollutant in that case.

Against this backdrop, EPA issued a 2006 rule to clarify that certain pesticide applications made in compliance with relevant FIFRA requirements on, over, or near navigable waters were not a discharge of pollutants and not subject to NPDES permitting requirements.[207] However, this rule was immediately challenged in 11 courts of appeals, with litigation consolidated in *National Cotton Council v. EPA* in the Sixth Circuit.[208] The Sixth Circuit found that the "plain language" of the CWA mandates that there is a "discharge of a pollutant" subject to NPDES permitting whenever a pesticide residue makes its way to navigable waters.[209] The court reasoned "but for the application of the pesticide, the pesticide residue and excess pesticide would not be added to the water; therefore, the pesticide residue and excess pesticide are from a 'point source.'"[210] The court concluded that "dischargers of pesticide pollutants are subject to the NPDES permitting program," and that "the statutory text of the [CWA] forecloses the EPA's Final Rule."[211]

In response to the Sixth Circuit decision in *National Cotton Council*, EPA has since promulgated a NPDES Pesticide General Permit for Point Source Discharges to Waters of the United States from the Application of Pesticides.[212] Applicators wishing to proceed under the NPDES Pesticide General Permit must generally submit to the regulatory agency a notice of intent to be covered under the general permit, implement certain management measures to meet the technology-based effluent limitations that are based on integrated pest management principles, and comply with reporting requirements.[213]

VIII. PESTICIDES AND BIOTECHNOLOGY

The biotechnology sector has successfully leveraged cellular and biomolecular processes to develop cutting-edge genetically modified crops that incorporate herbicide tolerance, insect resistance, and drought-tolerant properties. The 2017

---

206. No Spray Coal., Inc. v. City of New York, 351 F.3d 602 (2d Cir. 2003).

207. U.S. Envtl. Prot. Agency, Application of Pesticides to Waters of the United States in Compliance with FIFRA, 71 Fed. Reg. 68,483 (Nov. 26, 2006).

208. 553 F.3d 927 (6th Cir. 2009), *cert. denied sub nom.* CropLife Am. v. Baykeeper, 130 S. Ct. 1505 (2010), and Am. Farm Bureau Fed'n v. Baykeeper, 130 S. Ct. 1505 (2010).

209. *Id.* at 936.

210. *Id.* at 940.

211. *Id.*

212. U.S. Envtl. Prot. Agency, Final National Pollutant Discharge Elimination System (NPDES) Pesticide General Permit for Point Source Discharges from the Application of Pesticides, 76 Fed. Reg. 68,750 (Nov. 7, 2011); U.S. Envtl. Prot. Agency, Final National Pollutant Discharge Elimination System (NPDES) Pesticide General Permit for Point Source Discharges from the Application of Pesticides; Reissuance, 81 Fed. Reg. 75,816 (Nov. 1, 2016). The general permit has not been challenged in litigation.

213. U.S. Envtl. Prot. Agency, Final National Pollutant Discharge Elimination System (NPDES) Pesticide General Permit (PGP) for Point Source Discharges to Waters of the United States from the Application of Pesticides, Fact Sheet, EPA-HQ-OW-2015-0499-0117.

Update to the Coordinated Framework for the Regulation of Biotechnology (the "Coordinated Framework")[214] is a formal policy document, initially adopted in 1986 and updated over time, that outlines the roles and responsibilities of each of the primary agencies within the Coordinated Framework to ensure the safety of biotechnology products, consistent with existing statute and regulation. EPA regulates pesticides under FIFRA, establishes tolerances under the FFDCA, and regulates under the Toxic Substances Control Act (TSCA) biotechnology products that are new organisms not specifically excluded by TSCA.[215] The U.S. Food and Drug Administration regulates human and animal foods (including dietary supplements), cosmetics, human and veterinary drugs, human biological products, and medical devices under the FFDCA and the Public Health Service Act.[216] Relevant to pesticides and biotechnology, the U.S. Department of Agriculture (USDA) regulates biotechnology through its Animal and Plant Health Inspection Service (APHIS) under the Plant Protection Act.[217] This regulatory framework includes permitting procedures and determinations of nonregulated status.[218]

Over the years, questions and challenges to this complicated framework have been addressed in litigation. In an important clarifying decision in *Center for Food Safety v. Vilsack*, the Ninth Circuit upheld USDA's interpretation regarding its regulatory authority over herbicide-tolerant genetically modified crops.[219] Specifically, the Ninth Circuit agreed that EPA properly regulates under FIFRA the effects of the herbicides to which the genetically modified crop is designed to resist, and that the herbicides themselves are not regulated by USDA under the Plant Protection Act.[220] In a separate suit, the Ninth Circuit found that the Plant Protection Act expressly preempts county ordinances that ban the testing and cultivation of genetically engineered plants to the extent those genetically engineered plants are regulated by APHIS as plant pests.[221]

IX. NATIONAL ENVIRONMENTAL POLICY ACT

NEPA establishes a procedure by which federal agencies must evaluate the environmental impact of all "major Federal actions significantly affecting the quality of the human environment" and assess potential alternatives.[222] NEPA implementing

---

214. U.S. Envtl. Prot. Agency, Modernizing the Regulatory System for Biotechnology Products (2017), https://www.epa.gov/sites/production/files/2017-01/documents/2017_coordinated_framework_update .pdf. This is a sequel to the 1986 Coordinated Framework for the Regulation of Biotechnology (the 1986 Coordinated Framework) and the 1992 Update to the Coordinated Framework.

215. *Id.* at 10–15.

216. *Id.* at 15–22.

217. *Id.* at 22–23.

218. *Id.* at 22–25.

219. Ctr. for Food Safety v. Vilsack, 718 F.3d 829 (9th Cir. 2013).

220. *Id.*

221. Atay v. Cnty. of Maui, 842 F.3d 688 (9th Cir. 2016); Haw. Papaya Indus. Ass'n v. Cnty. of Haw., No. 14-17538, 2016 WL 6819700, at *1 (9th Cir. Nov. 18, 2016).

222. 42 U.S.C. § 4332(2)(C); *see* 40 C.F.R. § 1500.1–.6.

regulations define "major federal action" to include "projects and programs entirely or partly financed, assisted, conducted, regulated, or approved by federal agencies."[223] The policy goals of NEPA are achieved through "'action-forcing' procedures requiring agencies to make a 'hard look' at the environmental consequences of proposed actions.'"[224] NEPA implementing regulations require that an environmental impact statement (EIS) "provide full and fair discussion of significant environmental impacts and shall inform decisionmakers and the public of the reasonable alternatives which would avoid or minimize adverse impacts or enhance the quality of the human environment."[225]

Numerous courts have evaluated whether NEPA's EIS requirement applies to various actions taken pursuant to the FIFRA regulatory scheme. Although various courts have adopted different rationales, courts have found EPA is not required to prepare an EIS before registering a pesticide,[226] or before canceling or suspending a registration,[227] for example. However, when evaluating other agencies' use of pesticides, a number of courts have required NEPA analysis, finding that EPA's compliance with FIFRA in registering a pesticide does not fulfill an action agency's obligations under NEPA.[228]

X. RESOURCE CONSERVATION AND RECOVERY ACT

The Resource Conservation and Recovery Act (RCRA) is a comprehensive "cradle to grave" law regulating the storage, transport, and disposal of solid and hazardous waste.[229] RCRA allows private citizens to sue for an injunction where "the past or present handling, storage, treatment, transportation, or disposal of any solid or hazardous waste . . . may present an imminent and substantial endangerment to health or the environment."[230] However, the Second Circuit has found that environmental plaintiffs may not use this provision to enjoin pesticide-spraying programs, because a material cannot be "discarded" and a "solid waste" subject to regulation

---

223. 40 C.F.R. § 1508.18(a).

224. W. Watersheds Project v. U.S. Forest Serv., 2017 U.S. Dist. LEXIS 193021, at *5 (D. Ohio Nov. 20, 2017) (citing Robertson v. Methow Valley Citizens Council, 490 U.S. 332, 348 (1989)). *See also* Nat'l Parks Conservation Ass'n v. Semonite, No. 17-CV-01361-RCL; 2018 U.S. Dist. LEXIS 97555, at *5 (D.D.C. May 23, 2018) (explaining that the goal of NEPA is to prohibit uninformed agency action, and ensure fully informed and well-considered decision making).

225. 40 C.F.R. § 1502.1.

226. Merrell v. Thomas, 807 F.2d 776 (9th Cir. 1986); *accord* San Luis & Delta-Mendota Water Auth. v. Jewell, 747 F.3d 581, 651 (9th Cir. 2014).

227. Wyo. v. Hathaway, 525 F.2d 66 (10th Cir. 1975).

228. *See, e.g.*, Or. Envtl. Council v. Kunzman, 714 F.2d 901, 905 (9th Cir. 1983) (noting that the "mere fact that a program involves use of substances registered under FIFRA does not exempt the program from the requirements of NEPA") (citation omitted); Save Our Ecosystems v. Clark, 747 F.2d 1240 (9th Cir. 1984).

229. 42 U.S.C. §§ 6901 *et seq.*

230. *Id.* § 6972(a).

under RCRA until "after it has served its intended purpose."[231] Thus, in *No Spray Coalition*, the Second Circuit found that the pesticide sprayed to kill mosquitoes under New York's West Nile virus eradication program were not "discarded," and thus not subject to regulation under RCRA.[232] Thus, analysis of whether or when a pesticide may be considered discarded under RCRA is necessarily focused on the intended purpose.[233]

XI. COMPREHENSIVE ENVIRONMENTAL RESPONSE, COMPENSATION, AND LIABILITY ACT

The Comprehensive Environmental Response, Compensation, and Liability Act (CERCLA)[234] provides, in part, that private plaintiffs who have incurred response and remediation costs because of the releases of hazardous substances to recover such costs from four broad statutory categories of "covered persons."[235] Nonetheless, CERCLA provides the following exception: "No person . . . may recover . . . for any response costs or damages resulting from the application of a pesticide product registered under the Federal Insecticide, Fungicide, and Rodenticide Act."[236] Several courts, however, have found that the pesticide exception applies only to "the typical pesticide user" who has simply "purchased and applied a pesticide in the customary manner."[237] Thus, this carve-out has been interpreted somewhat narrowly and manufacturers themselves may be subject to CERCLA liability in the normal course of their business.

In evaluating one of the categories of CERCLA liability—arranger liability—the Supreme Court in *Burlington Northern & Santa Fe Railway Co. v. United States* considered whether the unintentional spill of pesticides constitutes "arrang[ing] for disposal" of hazardous substances.[238] In *Burlington*, the Ninth Circuit had found Shell Oil Company liable under CERCLA for "arrang[ing] for disposal" of a hazardous substance, regardless of whether Shell intended to dispose of the substance,

---

231. No Spray Coal., Inc. v. City of New York, 252 F.3d 148 (2d Cir. 2001).

232. *Id.* at 150; *accord* Ecological Rights Found. v. Pac. Gas & Elec. Co., 713 F.3d 502, 516 (9th Cir. 2013) (noting that the court would not consider "airborne pesticide that drifts beyond its intended target" as having been "discarded") (dictum).

233. *See* Chart v. Town of Parma, 2014 U.S. Dist. LEXIS 140463 (W.D.N.Y. Sept. 30, 2014) (pesticide left to accumulate in the soil became a solid waste when soil was removed and sold, at which time the pesticide no longer served its intended purpose).

234. 42 U.S.C. §§ 9601 *et seq.*

235. *Id.* § 9607(a).

236. *Id.* § 9607(i).

237. Jordan v. So. Wood Piedmont Co., 805 F. Supp. 1575, 1581 (S.D. Ga. 1992); *see also* Cameron v. Navarre Farmers Union Coop. Ass'n, 76 F. Supp. 2d 1178, 1183 (D. Kan. 1999) (denying government's motion to dismiss under the pesticide exemption because "there is no proof that the fumigant was FIFRA-registered or that the government applied the fumigant in a customary manner"); United States v. Tropical Fruit, S.E., 96 F. Supp. 2d 71, 90 (D.P.R. 2000) (pesticide exemption does not shelter misapplication of pesticides that causes contamination on adjacent properties).

238. Burlington N. & Santa Fe Ry. Co. v. United States, 556 U.S. 599 (2009).

where Shell sold and delivered a pesticide to an agricultural chemical distribution company and some of the pesticide spilled during transfer.[239] The Supreme Court reversed the Ninth Circuit, holding that Shell Oil could not be held liable under CERCLA for "arrang[ing] for disposal" of a hazardous substance because Shell did not *intend* to dispose of the pesticide.[240] The Court looked to the "ordinary meaning" of the term "arrange for," and found that "under the plain language of the statute, an entity may qualify as an arranger. . . when it takes intentional steps to dispose of a hazardous substance."[241] Therefore, the Court concluded "knowledge [of spillage of the product] alone is insufficient to prove that an entity 'planned for' the disposal, particularly when the disposal occurs as a peripheral result of the legitimate sale of an unused, useful product."[242]

XII. CONCLUSION

As illustrated by the foregoing, there are areas of pesticide litigation that have remained constant over a number of years—for example, EPA's registration processes and standards. Yet there are a number of areas that continue to evolve rapidly. In particular, the intersection of pesticide registration and ESA review has been the source of much of the pesticide litigation in the past several years. Practitioners should follow developments in this area closely in the coming years.

---

239. *Id.* at 606–07.
240. *Id.* at 612–13.
241. *Id.* at 611.
242. *Id.* at 612.

Table of Cases

Index